THE HOLLYWOOD STUDIOS

THE HOLLYWOOD STUDIOS

Roy Pickard

FREDERICK MULLER LIMITED
LONDON

First published in Great Britain 1978
by Frederick Muller Limited, London, NW2 6LE

ISBN: 0 584 10445 6

British Library Cataloguing in Publication Data

Pickard, Roy
The Hollywood studios.
1. Moving-pictures — United States — History
2. Moving-picture — industry — California — Hollywood
I. Title
791.43'09794'94 PN1993.5.U65

ISBN 0—584—10445—6

Typeset by Texet, Leighton Buzzard, Bedfordshire.

Printed and Bound in Great Britain by
William Clowes & Son Ltd., Beccles, Suffolk.

Preface

This book concerns itself with the nine major studios which made the name of Hollywood famous throughout the world, the studios which during the golden days of the 30s, 40s and 50s, combined to make the movie capital seem like some far-off Eldorado, a town of searchlights in the sky, glittering premieres, larger-than-life personalities and escapist entertainment.

The book does not aim at being a critical history of the American cinema nor a critical appraisal of its films. Yet in its own way it is a kind of history concerned as much with razzamatazz, statistics, scandal and trivia as it is with fine movies and creative directors. In other words it is a pastiche just as Hollywood itself was a pastiche of the sublime and the ridiculous. It paints a portrait of Hollywood in the round — Hollywood with its shimmering facade, Hollywood grinding mercilessly away at work on the sound stages, Hollywood suddenly exposed through sensational headlines and grubby, back-street scandals.

The book's approach is unusual. Each chapter is divided into two parts. The first summarises briefly the atmosphere and style of the studio under discussion and provides pen portraits of the moguls and tycoons who controlled its destiny. The second, much larger section, presents a year-by-year chronology covering every aspect of the studio's development from its very beginning to the present day: the great (and not so great) films, the stars and directors, box-office winners, statistics, anecdotes, snappy lines of dialogue, bizarre events, crazy advertisement lines, in fact everything but the proverbial kitchen sink.

The Hollywood Studios is very much an Aladdin's cave although there's no need for an 'Open Sesame.' Just dip into any of the pages and something of interest, something to raise a smile, something that will bring back an affectionate memory, should emerge. The book is a diary of a world of magic and make-believe, a tribute to days gone by and to days that are still very much with us, albeit in a different form, in the 70s.

Hopefully, the book will find its way onto many reference shelves for no such other study of the major Hollywood Studios exists in one volume. Hopefully too it will reach its audience, i.e. the film enthusiast rather than the film specialist, for it tries for entertainment, not pretension, gaiety and not criticism.

Basically it is for all those people who have stood, over the years, in long queues down damp cinema alleys, waiting in the bitter cold for the chance to experience a two-hour journey into Technicolor escapism, a journey that whisked them away for a moment from the monotony of the week gone by. As one who has waited in those queues, complete with raindrops dripping down my neck, I submit this affectionate valentine to the Hollywood studios, each of which made escape possible.

Director Vincente Minnelli once put the aims of movie-making into one succinct sentence: "The main thing is to provide a little magic in our lives," he said. With luck this book will bring alive again some of that celluloid magic, the studios which manufactured it, and, at the same time, provide a little of its own.

Roy Pickard
October, 1978

* * *

For Joan, Claire, Doreen, Anne, Susan, Brenda. . . . .

UNIVERSAL

Universal

The crowd murmured impatiently as the band master waited, his baton raised in front of the smart brass band. Expectantly, he turned his head, waiting for the guest of honour to arrive. Those at the back of the 20,000 crowd strained their necks to get a better view. Feet stood on tiptoe and collapsed again. Backs were accidentally charged into and breathless apologies muttered.

Stars, directors, technicians, extras and the plain, ordinary man-in-the-street were all there. Some sensed that movie history was about to be made. Others thought of the event as nothing more than a good day out, a big gaudy show that would make the morning papers the next day and then quickly be forgotten.

They were right. It *was* a big show and it *did* make the papers the next day. But it was not forgotten.

As the band struck up at last and 'The Star Spangled Banner' blasted across the clear California air, the stars and stripes unfurled from a flag pole and a small, diminutive man, no more than five ft three ins tall, stepped forward to receive 'the freedom of the city' from actress Laura Oakley.

The man's name was Carl Laemmle. The date, March 15, 1915. The city — Universal City on the 230 acre Taylor ranch some five miles north of Hollywood. As the studio gates opened, a stream of cowboys and Indians thundered through into the lot, and Universal was in business.

It is still in business today. After surviving more rough patches than perhaps any other studio in Hollywood, except the ill-fated RKO, it is now the dominant American studio, streamlined, geared to Television and making some of the biggest and most successful movies in the world — the *Airport* films, the multi-Oscar winner, *The Sting, American Graffiti*, the record-breaking *Jaws*.

Luck, it seems, has always been on Universal's side. For twenty five years it had its guardian angel 'Uncle Carl Laemmle' to care for its well being. After that it had a succession of stars who, at most other studios, would not have rated a second glance but who, at Universal were not only money-makers but life-savers: singing teenager Deanna Durbin in the late 30s, Abbott and Costello in the 40s, The Kettles and Francis The Talking Mule in the 50s.

Plenty there for the discerning critic to look down his nose at; enough for him to wave his hand and dismiss the studio as one belonging strictly to the Hollywood minor league. But in doing so he would be overlooking other stars: Lon Chaney, Boris Karloff, Colin Clive, Claude Rains, Basil Rathbone, W. C. Fields, James Stewart, Cary Grant, Rock Hudson and Doris Day, and films of the quality of *All Quiet On The Western Front, Frankenstein, Magnificent Obsession, Imitation Of Life, Destry Rides Again, Show Boat, Scarlet Street, The Killers, Winchester 73, Pillow Talk* and *Duel.*

And he would be overlooking the courage of a studio that dared to concentrate, often admittedly through necessity, on film forms that other studios were loathe to tackle.

The double feature programme was for years the staple diet of Universal. So too were cheap quickies set in the West or the city streets. So were the soap operas dabbled at by several studios (especially RKO) in the 30s but not in the 50s and 60s when Universal, with all the lavish production values that producer Ross Hunter could muster, brought back the *genre* for post-war audiences.

And so, most of all, were the horror movies, despised, derided, frequently ignored, but films which continually provided Universal with both a reputation and a lucrative source of revenue.

For a studio to be linked so closely with one particular *genre* was and still is a rarity, but Universal and horror have gone hand in hand since the 1920's when Lon Chaney appeared as *The Hunchback Of Notre Dame* and *The Phantom Of The Opera.* It is perhaps no accident that the studio's biggest-ever financial hit, *Jaws,* can be referred to in the same breath as both a horror movie and an adventure thriller.

The Universal story began three years before Carl Laemmle opened those sound stages in Hollywood in 1915. The studio was formed on June 8, 1912 when Laemmle amalgamated his own Independent Motion Picture Company Of America (Imp) with Pat Powers Picture Plays and Adam Kessel and Charles Bauman's Bison Life Motion Pictures (both founded in 1909).

There were no long discussions about selecting a name for the new company. It happened by accident. During a board meeting Laemmle happened to glance out of the window and saw a van, labelled Universal Pipe Fittings, passing by in the street.

From such poetic beginnings do great studios grow.

The first release of the studio was *The Dawn Of Netta*, directed by Tom Ricketts. In the same year Juliet Shelby (later to become Mary Miles Minter) appeared in the one-reeler, *The Nurse*, and Laemmle moved his cameras to California.

Universal had been in operation for about a year when it discovered it had a sensation on its hands. By accident as much as design it stumbled onto the delightful equation: sex equals box-office.

The film was *Traffic In Souls*, a white slavery story that revolved round the secretary of a businessman who recognises a voice on the dictaphone as that belonging to the man who had lured her younger sister to a brothel. Quick as a flash, she contacts her handy policeman boy friend who apprehends the criminal before any more harm can be done.

In 1913 the subject was dynamite. Laemmle, who in his Imp days had concocted plenty of publicity stunts for stars Florence Lawrence and King Baggot, knew just how to handle it.

Said the advertisements: "The sensational motion picture dramatization based on the Rockefeller White Slavery Report and the investigation of the Vice Trust by District Attorney Whitman — a 200,000 dollar spectacle in 700 scenes with 800 players, showing the traps cunningly laid for young girls by vice agents — Don't miss the most thrilling scenes ever staged, the smashing of the Vice Trust."

There were industry rumours that the movie had cost no more than 50,000 dollars and been shot in four weeks which was probably nearer the truth. Notwithstanding *Traffic In Souls* grossed well over 500,000 dollars and played to 30,000 spectators in its first week alone. Laemmle, for all his vague, quixotic ways, knew how to handle a movie.

A former book-keeper in a Wisconsin clothing store, he was, like so many of the movie pioneers, from European stock, very humble German stock in fact, the tenth of a poor Jewish estate agent's thirteen children.

He broke into the movie business in 1906, but, unlike his fellow Europeans, Goldwyn, Zukor and Mayer, he was not a ruthless man. Tenacious and shrewd, yes, but ruthless, no. Hence his liking to be called 'Uncle Carl' not only by his family, but by his employees.

Laemmle's family became something of a standing joke in Hollywood. If he had a relation who might fit into an executive capacity at Universal that relation was *in*, no matter whether he could do the job or not.

One who could was nephew William Wyler who Laemmle

brought over from Germany and who went on to become one of the greatest of all Hollywood directors.

One who couldn't was another nephew (unnamed) who was employed by Uncle Carl as a casting director. ''Crosseyed'' was his verdict on Bette Davis; ''consumptive'' his opinion of Katharine Hepburn. He was also reputed to have turned down Rudolph Valentino because he was ''a wop'' and refused to cast Boris Karloff on the grounds that he was a Russian. It was only when it was mentioned that Karloff was English that he was allowed to stay.

At Universal in the twenties it was not unusual to see a picture beginning with the credits:

Carl Laemmle Presents
A Carl Laemmle Jr. Production
Produced by Carl Laemmle Jr.
Directed by Edward Laemmle

Ogden Nash conjured up the apposite phrase: ''Uncle Carl has a very large faemmle.''

Laemmle, however, had other qualities besides giving jobs to his relations. During the formative years of the studio he built slowly, concentrating on the classics — *Uncle Tom's Cabin, Ivanhoe, Dr. Jekyll And Mr. Hyde* — and joining in on the serial boom with films like *Lucille Love* with Grace Cunard and Francis Ford and *The Trey O'Hearts* with Cleo Madison and George Larkin.

He quickly built up a nucleus of stars that included Florence Lawrence, King Baggot, Wallace Reid, Ethel Grandin, Herbert Rawlinson and Pauline Bush and in the first year of production at Universal City was responsible for no fewer than 250 movies.

At the height of all this feverish activity he kept at the studio a veritable zoo — thirty lions, ten leopards, several elephants, scores of monkeys and hundreds of horses and more domesticated animals. Included among all the livestock were some chickens which had already been in occupation when Laemmle had purchased the acreage and which he kept on as a small business venture.

As if this wasn't enough, he even opened up the studio for public inspection, partly as a publicity gimmick to create more interest in films and partly because it too brought in a small revenue as eager sightseers paid twenty-five cents a time to sit in the specially constructed spectators' gallery and watch the various antics of cast and crew.

Only when the talkies began to take over in the late twenties was the practise discontinued.

More importantly, Laemmle was responsible for launching

three of the greatest talents in the history of Hollywood, directors John Ford and Erich von Stroheim, and boy wonder producer Irving G. Thalberg.

John Ford's elder brother, actor Francis Ford, was already working in Universal serials when John took his first hesitant steps into the film business as a prop boy.

It was as a prop boy, which meant doing just about every odd job on the lot, that the young beginner came face to face with Wyatt Earp.

''In the very early silent days,'' said Ford later, ''he would come up to visit pals, cowboys he knew in Tombstone; a lot of them were in my company. He'd come up a couple of times a year. I used to give him a chair and a cup of coffee and he told me about the fight at the O.K. Corral.''

John Ford was a stunt man in several of Universal's two-reel westerns. He did anything that was asked of him. He engaged in fist fights, caught speeding trains on horseback, jumped horses off cliffs. He did most of his brother's stunts for they were built alike and looked alike. For risking his neck every other day of his young life, he got fifteen dollars a week.

Like Wyler, he owed his start as a director to Laemmle — and fate. His first job as a director happened by accident. The film was a western. There had been a studio party the night before and nobody was around on the set, just prop boy Ford who was doubling as a bartender and a few cowboy extras.

News arrived that Laemmle was on his way to see how work was progressing. The general manager went into a blind panic. He looked desperately at Ford. ''The boss is coming, we've got to do something.''

Ford politely asked the manager what he would have him do. ''*Anything*,'' gasped the distraught man.

As Laemmle appeared, Ford told the cowboys to canter to the end of the street and then ride back towards the camera fast, yelling like hell. Laemmle seemed to like it. Encouraged by his ploy Ford had the cowboys ride back again, this time ordering that several of them fall to the ground.

Laemmle, still impressed, asked for another scene. Ford, whose day of inspiration it must have been, then burned the street down.

''Give Jack Ford a job as a director,'' said Laemmle. ''He yells the best.''

So began the greatest directorial career Hollywood has ever known.

Erich von Stroheim could also count himself to be a little lucky to have achieved the breakthrough to director status. During the war years in Hollywood he worked as an extra and technical adviser to D. W. Griffith and also made a name for himself playing unpleasant Prussian officers. So well did he play them that he became known as "The Man You Love To Hate".

With the ending of the war, however, his career looked finished. Prussian officers were no longer fashionable villains.

Seduction, sin and debauchery though were *not* out of fashion and von Stroheim was quick to seize on the mood of the time. He allegedly sold Laemmle on the idea of his first film, *Blind Husbands*, by showing him an outline on a single sheet of paper. It smacked of audacity and it smacked of confidence too.

The story presented to Laemmle was a triangular sex melodrama about a neglected American wife who is seduced by an unscrupulous military officer while holidaying with her surgeon husband in the Austrian Tyrol.

Laemmle liked it. He liked it even more as von Stroheim went into lengthy detail about the film and how it would develop. The only thing he didn't like was the title. Von Stroheim wanted to call it *The Pinnacle*. "What means the pinnacle," said Laemmle. "People won't know what it's about. They'll confuse it with pinochle. There are more blind husbands than there are pinnacles so we'll call it *Blind Husbands*."

The picture, filmed quickly, was a big success. Shooting took under three months and the editing was done efficiently and without incident. Admittedly no expense was spared — an entire Alpine village was built on the Universal lot — but that didn't bother Laemmle, at least not at the time. The total cost was 100,000 dollars.

The critics voted the movie, which starred Francilla Billington, Sam de Grasse and von Stroheim himself as the seducer, as one of the best three films of the year. It shared top honours with D. W. Griffith's *Broken Blossoms* and James Cruze's *The Miracle Man*.

Laemmle felt more than satisfied. He had discovered a new and formidable talent and the prospects for the studio looked healthy. He immediately gave von Stroheim permission to go ahead with his next production, *The Devil's Passkey*.

Sophisticated sex, seduction and intrigue in a continental setting again made up the formula with director von Stroheim and actor Clyde Fillmore seducing another American wife, played this time by Una Trevelyan.

Somewhat lighter in tone than *Blind Husbands* the film was equally well received by the critics and once again everything went smoothly during its production: four months' shooting, little extravagence, no murmurs from the director as the film was firmly edited down to a tight eight reels.

Von Stroheim was suddenly the man of the moment. A director of high quality films which made money. Several studios made overtures, trying to persuade him to leave Universal and work for them.

Laemmle answered them quickly in the Motion Picture News: "When Mr. von Stroheim was unknown and untried as a director, why didn't you gamble on him as Universal did? Failing to do this, why do you hang over him like vultures, seeking to grab him by hook or by crook, with the accent on crook? Unfortunately for you, von Stroheim comes from good old stock, and your money and your wiles cannot tempt him from the path of honour."

Shortly afterwards, Laemmle signed von Stroheim to a five year contract and agreed to his next film, *Foolish Wives*. It was then the trouble started. It was almost as if von Stroheim had been waiting for the moment, taken 'Uncle Carl' for a ride, and was now going to make the film he really wanted, regardless of time or expense.

For *Foolish Wives*, a story of a bogus Russian nobleman who earns his living by seducing and then blackmailing rich women living on the Riviera, he built a full-scale replica of the central plaza of Monte Carlo with its Casino, the Hotel De Paris and the huge cafe. He also protected himself from any protests from the studio by shooting all the important scenes in which *he* appeared, first. If there was any trouble it would mean reshooting the entire picture.

Shooting took almost a year. Costs rose to nearly a million dollars. Thirty-two reels were filmed. Extravagance ran riot. Real food and real liquor were used on the set even when no-one ate or drank. If the scene had to be filmed several times then the food and liquor were replaced lest they should appear cold and flat. Expensive excursions were made for important coastal scenes.

The rumours about von Stroheim began to grow. Studio heads who had begged his favours began to feel pleased they had been turned down. As for Laemmle, he too was getting worried about the director's seemingly inexhaustible appetite for perfection, but he finally threw up his hands and advertised the fact that *Foolish Wives was* going to be expensive. "The first million dollar picture," he claimed more in desperation than with pride.

But another man was watching the von Stroheim circus on *Foolish Wives*. He was small, slim and only twenty-one and was already production head of Universal. Since Laemmle had brought him from the New York office a couple of years earlier, he had learned quickly about movies. His name was Irving Thalberg and although he admired artistry and talent, he loathed waste and extravagance. Several times he clashed with von Stroheim as *Foolish Wives* drew to a close.

Satisfied at last with his thirty-two reels von Stroheim announced that the film would run for six hours and be shown in two parts. He reckoned without Laemmle and Thalberg. They suggested that he cut the film. He refused. They suggested it again. Still, no.

Drastic measures were needed and drastic measures were taken. They took the film, locked von Stroheim out of the cutting rooms, and themselves reduced the film to a manageable fourteen reels.

Von Stroheim raged and ranted at what was being done to his work, but there was little he could do. He had no control over the picture. Universal had that. The picture belonged to them. It was a case of the artist versus the businessman. And the businessman won.

Nevertheless Laemmle did allow von Stroheim one last throw. There wasn't much in the way of quality at the studio and whatever his faults, von Stroheim certainly brought class to everything he touched.

Merry-Go-Round was to be von Stroheim's fourth Universal picture. The central plot was about the impossibility of marriage between an aristocrat and a girl of the people. It was also to prove to be a case of an impossible marriage between artist and studio.

Von Stroheim ran riot. After five weeks he had spent nearly a quarter-of-a-million dollars and had very little film to show for it. Stories about his extravagance again spread round Hollywood.

At one point he ordered that all the stars be fitted with silk underwear so that they would feel properly aristocratic in their roles as royalty. It didn't matter that the blue-blooded underwear would never be seen on the screen.

He also spent three days teaching Hollywood extras to salute correctly in their roles of Imperial Guardsmen, even though they would be seen for only a few seconds. Hours and hours were also spent teaching them the goose-step. Every scene went to fifteen takes or more.

After five weeks the bubble burst. Von Stroheim was shooting a key sequence a few minutes after midnight. The night air was getting cold when the director received a message to report to Thalberg in his office. The reception inside was even colder.

"You're fired Erich," said Thalberg. "You're off the picture." From all accounts von Stroheim neither ranted nor raved. He simply turned in contempt and left the office and the studio. Rupert Julian was called in to finish the picture.

The businessman had won again and this time von Stroheim had nothing to fall back on. Rather foolishly he had not cast himself in the picture so he was expendable. He made his way to Metro where, ironically, Thalberg was to follow him just six months later as vice-president of the Mayer company at 600 dollars a week.

The departure of both Stroheim and Thalberg left a great hole in the Universal production scene. With John Ford moving over to Fox there was nothing left but the routine for Laemmle to promote. Except, that is, two films by horror king Lon Chaney, *The Hunchback Of Notre Dame* and *The Phantom Of The Opera.*

That he made them at Universal didn't count for very much. Chaney had been a bit player and minor actor at the studio for years without ever having been recognised as star potential. He made nearly a hundred films for them in eight years and was one of those attending the celebrations at Universal City in 1915. But he was no more than an onlooker. It wasn't until 1919 when he appeared as the phoney cripple *The Miracle Man* that he got his first break — away from Universal.

When he returned, the 'Man Of A Thousand Faces' as he had become known, made sure the studio paid him what he was worth.

There was a hint of bitterness in his salary demands. Maintaining that he had been 'shorted' eight dollars a week by Universal in his early cheques he insisted, before signing, that his contract read 2,008 and not 2,000 dollars a week.

Off screen, Chaney, the son of deaf and dumb parents was poker-faced, almost a male Garbo. He was called 'the star who lives like a clerk' and 'the worst dressed man in pictures'. He customarily wore a dark blue suit, red tie and a cap pulled low over his right eye. He shunned parties and premieres — even gala showings of his own films. But he was recognised as one of the industry's perfectionists. He took three to four hours daily to make up for the contortionist Hunchback and Phantom roles, often experiencing severe pain to achieve his gruesome effects.

Chaney too went to Metro in the twenties. What was left at Universal was very little. The studio struggled. Big pictures were a rarity. For a time the famous trademark of a silent globe spinning in darkened space came to represent mediocrity.

But Chaney's brief return had, at least, kindled one spark. It had opened the studio's eyes to the potential of the horror film. Later in the decade German director Paul Leni reflected the mood in films like *The Man Who Laughs* and *The Cat And The*

Canary. In the thirties, after looking with compassion at the real horrors of modern warfare in the Academy Award-winning *All Quiet On The Western Front*, the studio turned to horror in earnest.

Its stars were Boris Karloff and Bela Lugosi.

Had it not been for the untimely death of Chaney neither actor might have made it to stardom, for at the time of his death Chaney was being considered for the role of Dracula by director Tod Browning. Plans were already being discussed when the great actor died in August 1930 at the age of forty-seven.

It was ironic that Chaney should pass from the scene just as Universal's golden age of horror got under way for the studio had on its payroll a young director whose sophistication, humour and imaginative approach to the horror *genre* would have appealed greatly to Chaney. His name was James Whale and although it was Tod Browning who made the studio's first big hit, *Dracula*, it was Whale who proved to be the most consistent Universal director, producing four classics of the macabre in as many years.

He directed both *Frankenstein* and its satirical sequel *Bride Of Frankenstein*, had enormous fun in *The Old Dark House* and enjoyed himself even more with the menace and visual trickery of *The Invisible Man*. Today, his films still impress. Although they appear more as thrillers than horror pictures, the passage of time has done little to diminish their quality.

Yet both Whale and his legendary 'monster' Boris Karloff were lucky to become associated with *Frankenstein* at all. The picture had originally been assigned to director Robert Florey and actor Bela Lugosi who had just created a sensation as *Dracula* and who was still basking in the 'reflected' glory he was receiving from his performance as the vampire count.

But he baulked at the idea of appearing as the monster. All that make-up would render him unrecognizable. At the very moment that his sharp, cold, unusual features had become well-known to screen audiences. Universal wanted to cover them up again. The answer was a very firm, 'no'.

Not wishing to upset their new horror star, Universal quickly shifted both Lugosi and Florey to another horror project, *Murders In The Rue Morgue*, and assigned James Whale, who had recently directed the weepie *Waterloo Bridge*, to *Frankenstein.*

When asked later why he had agreed to direct the Frankenstein story Whale replied, "Of thirty available stories it was the strongest meat and gave me a chance to dabble in the macabre. I thought it would be amusing to try and make what everybody knows is a physical impossibility seem believable for sixty minutes. Also it offered fine pictorial chances, had two grand characterizations and had a subject matter that might go anywhere.''

The biggest problem, of course, was finding a suitable actor to play the monster. Colin Clive was quickly signed for the role of the obsessed Dr. Frankenstein. But what of his creation?

Numerous actors were tested. None of them seemed appropriate, except one, Boris Karloff, a British actor whose real name was William Pratt. He had been around for many years playing character parts and, at that particular moment in time, was almost certainly resigned to playing them for the rest of his acting career.

Whale, however, saw something in Karloff's test, something he hadn't seen in those of the other actors. ''Karloff's face fascinated me,'' he said. ''I made drawings of his head, added sharp bony ridges where I imagined the skull might have joined. His physique was weaker than I would have wished, but that queer, penetrating personality of his, I felt, was more important than his shape, which could easily be altered.''

When he showed the test to Laemmle, the studio head agreed. It was Karloff's eyes that impressed him. ''They mirrored the suffering of the poor dumb creature, in contrast to his frightful appearance and hideous strength.''

Karloff himself was naturally delighted. It meant the big break at last but it is doubtful whether he could possibly have envisaged what lay in store for him in the years ahead. That he, not Lugosi, who would soon begin the downward slide, would become the king of horror and remain so for a quarter-of-a-century.

''It was a fascinating job,'' said Karloff. ''The creature had no speech and hardly any intelligence, yet you had to convey a sense of the tragic. Half-a-dozen actors tested for the part, but I was the lucky one. I say 'lucky' because any one of them probably would have played the part as well as I did — and would also have reaped the benefits that came to me.

''But despite the fact that the picture made me, it was a rather horrible experience. The make-up was quite an ordeal. I had to arrive at the studio every morning at 5.30 and spend three-and-a-half-hours in the make-up chair getting ready for the day's work. The make-up itself was quite painful, particularly the putty used on my eyes. There were many days when I thought I would never be able to hold out until the end of the day, but somehow or other I always did.''

Frankenstein went on to gross twelve million dollars from its original 250,000 dollar investment.

Karloff, like Whale, remained an integral part of Universal's horror line-up of the early and mid-thirties. He appears as *The Mummy* in which he participated in one genuinely frightening sequence – snapping the bonds that have held him captive for nearly four thousand years and slowly, so slowly, opening his eyes – and teamed with Lugosi in several lesser vehicles, *The Black Cat, The Raven, The Invisible Ray*. He returned to the studio in the forties when Universal reintroduced the horror film into their famous double bills.

The horror film and just about every other kind of movie that Universal had been producing in the first part of the decade came to an end when Carl Laemmle was ousted from the company in 1936. There were no more soap operas of the kind that John Stahl had been directing so expertly, pictures like *Back Street, Imitation Of Life, Magnificent Obsession*, no William Wyler pictures, nothing that could remotely be called ambitious.

The new regime opted for the inexpensive and the unambitious. Of the major directors only Whale remained at the studio and he stayed only briefly. What Laemmle himself thought of the situation is not on record. He had been a parent to the company for nearly twenty-five years and by 1936 was in his seventies and too old to care.

He lived but three years after his retirement and according to legend spent those last three years entertaining friends to dinner and making jokes about his large collection of ill-fitting dentures. ''Just listen to them, how these teeth rattle,'' he would gurgle. It was like a scene from one of his horror films and a bizarre end for a famous movie pioneer.

Luck was with the new regime. They discovered Deanna Durbin, a young fifteen year old singing star who was an immediate favourite with American audiences. She first appeared in a movie in 1936 in *Three Smart Girls*.

Universal combined her charming singing voice and bubbling personality with stories that cast her as a matchmaker, or a teenager constantly meddling in adult affairs. A favourite device was to pair her off with a much older man – Herbert Marshall, Melvyn Douglas, Walter Pidgeon, Franchot Tone – thus setting off her youthful exhuberance against their quiet sophistication. Later she was teamed romantically with stars of her own age, but as far as Universal was concerned it was her early years at the studio that mattered most.

Deanna Durbin didn't fail them. Films like *One Hundred Men And A Girl, Mad About Music, That Certain Age, Three Smart Girls Grow Up*, were all substantial box-office hits. Had they not been so successful Universal might well have been in serious financial trouble.

During the forties, when she grew into an attractive young woman, Universal tried to mould her into the conventional Hollywood glamour star. At Metro or Paramount it might have worked. Not at Universal. They had neither the resources nor the vehicles. Durbin's pictures became more and more routine until in 1948 she decided that enough was enough and retired from the screen, aged twenty-seven. She invested her money wisely and retired a rich woman.

"Just as a Hollywood pin-up represented sex to dissatisfied erotics," she said after her retirement, "so I represented the ideal daughter millions of fathers and mothers wished they had."

Shortly after the success of the early Durbin vehicles Universal (Universal-International when it merged for a time with International films in 1946) assumed a new identity, an identity born of financial necessity and one that was to remain with the studio for more than two decades. Horror, both in the traditional *Frankenstein-Dracula* sense and in the *sub-genre* of science-fiction, was incorporated into the new look, but it was a very different scene from the Universal of the Laemmle regime.

The two words that came to sum up Universal were 'double-feature'.

In the 40s and 50s no studio was more expert at producing double-feature programmers than Universal. Cheap and cheerful, the films rarely rated a mention in the critics' columns and when they were noticed their prize was not a 'best of the week' plaudit, but a snide remark about mindless entertainment.

Universal were not in the least worried about the critics. They were far more concerned with keeping solvent. Not a studio of big stars or top directors, they quickly learned how to cut their cloth and aimed at inexpensive features ranging from seventy to eighty minutes in length.

Their target was a mass audience that didn't want to think too hard about what it was seeing up on the screen. It was an audience that was quite happy to pay its one-and-nine for a good belly laugh at Abbott and Costello, or a tantalising glimpse of Yvonne De Carlo's bosom. If, during the course of events, Jon Hall or Tony Curtis ran a villain through with a rapier, so much the better.

While the great films were being produced at Metro, Warners and Paramount, the little movies were pouring out of Universal. Alongside the railway hoardings advertising *Citizen Kane* or *The Treasure Of The Sierra Madre* were companion posters that were split down the middle with *House Of Dracula* and a host of horror stars on one side and a Donald O'Connor teenage musical on the other.

Another combination might have been Abbott and Costello plus Tony Curtis swashbuckling in Old Arabia; another, Francis The Talking Mule and an Audie Murphy western; yet another might have had Ma and Pa Kettle sharing the honours with Jeff Chandler in a drama of the US Cavalry or a giant spider in a science-fiction thriller.

The permutations were endless. Yet, more than anything else, these double bills were responsible for making Universal what it is today.

The few grade 'A' movies produced by the studio during the period – Hitchcock's *Shadow Of A Doubt*, the W. C. Fields comedies, Lang's *Scarlet Street*, Siodmak's *The Killers* and *Criss Cross* – were of undoubted quality, but had little to do with the studio's development. It was the seemingly never-ending stream of 'mindless entertainments' that kept Universal alive.

Abbott and Costello, Ma and Pa Kettle, even Francis The Talking Mule, were all rumoured to have 'saved' the studio at various times. Saved is perhaps a bit of an exaggeration, but there can be little doubt that these cheaply-made comedies, some of them shot in just twenty days, did much to help the studio keep its head above water.

Abbott and Costello began their long Universal career in 1940. Derided, often ignored by the critics, their humour was simple, but expertly timed. A typical example:

Abbott: "Lou, suppose you were forty and you were engaged to a girl who was ten." Costello: "Oh, boy, this is gonna be a pip!" Abbott: "Never mind. Now, you're four times older than that little girl. So you wait twenty more years. The little girl is thirty and you're sixty. Now you're only twice as old as that girl. The question is, how long do you have to wait before you and the little girl are of the same age?"

Confusing? Ridiculous? Yes, but also very funny when delivered at a crackerjack pace by Abbott and Costello.

Ma and Pa Kettle's hillbilly humour was even more down-to-earth. Pa (Percy Kilbride) whose main aim in life was to do as little as possible would sidle into the kitchen and drawl, "Anythin' you want. .doin'. .Ma?" "There's the roof needs mendin'" would come the raucous retort from Ma (Marjorie Main) as she whipped up eggs in a bowl with the strength of an all-in wrestler. "O.K. Ma," Kilbride would drawl and then wander off and do precisely nothing.

Lunchtime in the Kettle household was chaotic. "Come and get it!" roared the magnificent Miss Main and suddenly hordes of kids, fifteen of them, would stream into the room clambering for places at the wooden table. Never one for the soft touch, Ma would clip the nearest head in sight with the end of her ladle and bellow, ''Mind your manners Danny.'' ''I'm Willie ma,'' would come the hurt reply. ''Uh. .oh, well mind 'em anyway.''

The colourful Eastern sagas begun by Maria Montez in the forties cost, inevitably, rather more than the comedies, but they were still cheap movies compared to the product of other studios.

Known around the lot as 'tits and sand' pictures (Universal provided the latter, Yvonne De Carlo, Maureen O'Hara and co. the former), they were launching pads for a group of young actors whom Universal were grooming for stardom. Rock Hudson, Jeff Chandler, Tony Curtis, all got their start in Easterns. Then they went into westerns, then into urban dramas, then into comedies. . .

In the 50s Universal began to get among the top moneymakers again with films like *Winchester 73* and *The Glenn Miller Story*. The studio, and producer Ross Hunter, thought it time to gamble and preceeded to bring back soap opera on a lavish scale with Technicolor remakes of the studio's pre-war hits *Magnificent Obsession, Imitation Of Life, Back Street*. Other studios thought Universal mad. The *genre* was surely long since dead.

They were proved wrong. Universal discovered that people liked to cry just as much after the war as they had done before. More so, in fact, Jane Wyman, Susan Hayward, June Allyson and Lana Turner went through agonies on behalf of suffering womanhood in a whole series of weepies and the Universal tills clinked with gold coin.

Then the studio gambled again, this time on comedy. In 1959 when big pictures like *Ben-Hur* were 'in', they teamed Rock Hudson with Doris Day in a glossy little comedy called *Pillow Talk*. It was harmless enough, touched upon sex without ever being sexy and, more important, was actually funny — all the way through. The picture, quite simply, took off. It even earned Miss Day an Oscar nomination.

Again the studio weren't slow to see the possibilities. Comedy, like soap opera, was meant to be dead. *Pillow Talk* proved that it wasn't. Out came the glossy sets and costumes once more and another popular series was born. It lasted well into the mid-sixties.

The writing in all the films was sharp, crisp, witty; the playing of stars like Cary Grant, Rock Hudson, Doris Day, James Garner, polished and sophisticated; the backup of Gig Young, Thelma Ritter and Tony Randall impeccable.

Universal kept its glossy image right up until 1968. That was when Doris Day had her first studio flop in a film called *The*

Ballad Of Josie. Apart from Disney, Universal had maintained its Hollywood type character longer than any other studio. The cadillacs were always long, sleek and brightly coloured; Cary Grant's suits immaculate; the dresses and hair styles of Doris Day and Lana Turner always 'just right'; the settings, both interiors and exteriors, always lavish. But in 1967 Universal decided it was time to join the other studios. The party was over. No more series, no more gloss. From now on in it would be 'one-off' pictures. Universal was at last without a style.

So what of Universal today? Where does it stand? What is its future? Its big movies of the seventies — *The Sting, American Graffiti, The Day Of The Jackal, Duel, Jaws* — are the equal to those of any produced at other studios. Indeed it is hard to reconcile the fact that they come from the same stable that produced those cheap little double features of twenty years ago.

Many would say Universal's future lies in television because once again the studio has adapted to the times and entered TV in a big way with series like *Kojak, McLeod, MacMillan And Wife, Madigan.*

As always they have not been afraid to gamble. Their resources are now huge. Universal City today covers four hundred and twenty acres. It boasts thirty-six sound stages and is the biggest of all Hollywood studios with a backlot complete with waterfalls, lakes, city streets and towns.

The famous 'globe' trademark still precedes each film, still twirling but less realistic and dignified than it was in the days of Universal-International. Less garish too than the luminescnt sphere surrounded by glittering letters and the famous globe around which a tiny plane circled in the thirties.

But for all Universal's present eminence one is still somehow drawn back to the years of 1949 and 1950. It was then that Rock Hudson, Tony Curtis, Jeff Chandler and others went 'to school' at the studio. It caused some amusement around Hollywood at the time for the school not only taught acting lessons, but stunt work, fencing and horseriding, plus a few other things.

As wooden-faced heroes spoke wooden-sounding lines to stoney-faced villains there must have been many a method actor who literally cringed in his seat. *This* was acting!

But in view of the way things have turned out and judging how many of those wooden-faced heroes made it to the top — and stayed there — there must be a few of those method actors who might now be thinking that just possibly they may have gone to the wrong school after all!

Universal begins operations in 1915.

Lon Chaney, unmasked, as *The Phantom Of The Opera*.

Widow murderer 'Uncle Charlie' (Joseph Cotten) loose among his unsuspecting family in Hitchcock's '43 thriller *Shadow Of A Doubt*.

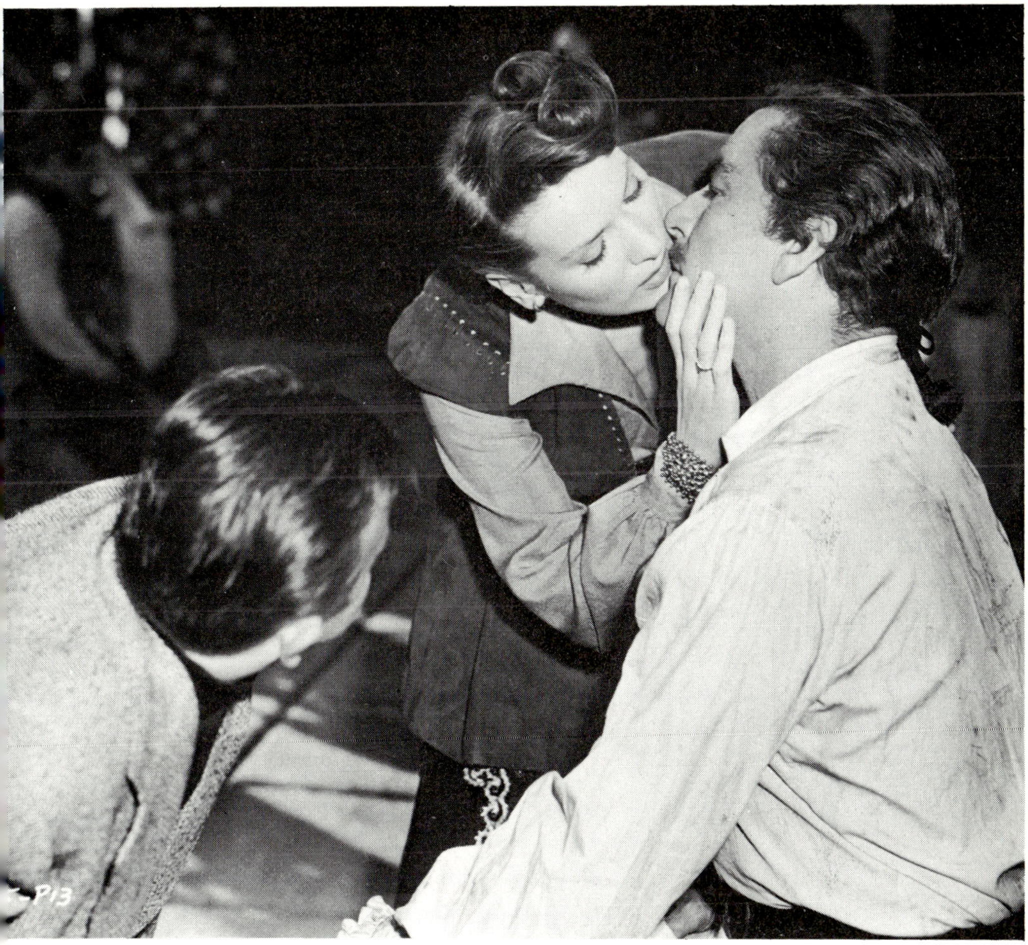

How to kiss Errol Flynn. Maureen O'Hara demonstrates for director George Sherman during filming of the swashbuckler *Against All Flags*.

Universal's hit comedy team of the 40s and 50s, Abbott and Costello, about to embark on interplanetary space travel in *Abbott And Costello Go To Mars*.

Alfred Hitchcock celebrating the completion of his 53rd movie, *Family Plot*.

Potential *Jaws* victims, Robert Shaw, Lorraine Gary, Roy Scheider and Richard Dreyfuss; potential killer, Bruce the shark.

Chronology

1912 The Universal Film Manufacturing Company is formed on June 8 when Carl Laemmle amalgamates his own Independent Motion Picture Company of America (Imp) – the company which had promoted the first major woman star, 'Queen Of The Screen' Florence Lawrence at a salary of 1,000 dollars a week – with Pat Powers Picture Plays, Adam Kessel and Charles Bauman's Bison Life Motion Pictures, and the Nestor, Champion, Eclair, Yankee companies.

The company's head offices are based in Union Square, New York. Its first release is *The Dawn Of Netta*, directed by Tom Ricketts.

By the end of the year it is operating two studios in Hollywood, the Nestor studio and another at Edendale, a suburb of Los Angeles.

1913 *Traffic In Souls* is the company's first big success. A 6 reel production concerned with white slavery, it stars Jane Gail, Matt Moore and Ethel Grandin and grosses half-a-million dollars. In New York it is so popular it is given 4 shows daily at an increased price of 25 cents.

The classics also feature prominently among the studio's product. There are versions of *Ivanhoe* and *Dr. Jekyll And Mr. Hyde* (both with King Baggot), *Robinson Crusoe* and *Uncle Tom's Cabin*. The latter stars: Harry Pollard (Uncle Tom), Ivy Shepherd (Tessie), Gertrude Short (Little Eva) and Margarita Fischer (Topsy).

1914 The 7 reel *Neptune's Daughter* with international swimming star Annette Kellermann as a mermaid able to turn into a human being is the studio's big movie. Made by Herbert Brenon over a period of three months in Bermuda, it costs 50,000 dollars.

J. Warren Kerrigan fights with a lion in *Samson*; Grace

Cunard and Francis Ford star in the company's first serial, *Lucille Love, The Girl Of Mystery*; Ethel Grandin and Irving Cummings (Rochester) appear in *Jane Eyre*.

Shakespeare is also put before the cameras as Phillips Smalley stars as Shylock in *The Merchant Of Venice*.

Top Universal stars include Florence Lawrence, King Baggot, Edwin August, Pauline Bush, Frank Lloyd, Wallace Reid, Irving Cummings and Robert Leonard.

1915 Universal City opens on March 15 in the 230-acre Taylor estate in the San Fernando Valley. The site was purchased by Laemmle the previous year for 165,000 dollars. Just two sound stages are open on inauguration day, each 300 ft long. Thomas A. Edison and Henry Ford dedicate the first artificially lighted stage. Buffalo Bill Cody and opera star Madame Schumann-Heink are among the personalities attending.

The first full year sees 250 pictures produced at Universal City. Among the most popular: *Damon And Pythias*, an historical spactacular with Herbert Rawlinson, William Worthington and Anna Little (and a wild chariot race); the serials *The Black Box, The Master Key* and *The Broken Coin*, the latter with Grace Cunard and Francis Ford in search of two halves of a coin which together make up the map to a priceless treasure; and *The Corsican Brothers* with King Baggot in the dual role.

1916 Lois Weber becomes the first important woman producer-director in movies. One of her first productions, starring Tyrone Power Sr., is *Where Are My Children* about 'the evil practices in marriage and the wrecking of health and happiness.' Another is *The Dumb Girl Of Portici* with Anna Pavlova.

Grace Cunard and Francis Ford are together again in another serial *Peg O' The Ring* about a circus girl subject to strange spells because her mother has been clawed by a lion; J. Warren Kerrigan and Lois Wilson are teamed in *A Silent Conquest*, a moral piece about the evils of alcohol; Rupert Julian features in *The Bugler Of Algiers*; and there's a version of Jules Verne's *20,000 Leagues Under The Sea* with Alan Holubar as Captain Nemo.

1917 The top Universal stars include Dorothy Phillips, Harry Carey, Ella Hall and Jack Mulhall.

The Grace Cunard/Francis Ford serial is *The Purple*

Mask; John Ford directs his first film, a two reel western called *The Tornado* ("Nothing but a bunch of stunts" he says later); he also films several Harry Carey westerns, among them *The Soul Herder, Cheyenne's Pal* and *Straight Shooting*.

Carmel Myers is in *Sirens Of The Sea*; Dorothy Phillips, Alfred Allen and Lon Chaney in *Hell Morgan's Girl*; Ruth Clifford and Rupert Julian in *A Kentucky Cinderella*.

1918 Carmel Myers stars in *All Night* (with Rudolph Valentino in a brief role) and *City Of Tears* with Edwin August; Rupert Julian is *The Kaiser, The Beast Of Berlin*. John Ford directs seven movies, most of them westerns and all with Harry Carey; Dorothy Phillips features in *The Heart Of Humanity*; Marie Walcamp and Eddie Polo are a popular serial team.

In the East, Irving G. Thalberg begins his career in the movie business. Aged 19 he works in Universal's New York offices at 35 dollars a week. Later in the year he rises to become Carl Laemmle's private secretary.

1919 Von Stroheim's first film for Universal, *Blind Husbands*, premieres in December and is voted one of the best pictures of the year. A story of ruthless wife seduction in post-war Europe it stars von Stroheim, Gibson Gowland, Sam de Grasse and Francilla Billington.

John Ford is still out West with some *fifteen* westerns, the most ambitious being the 6 reel version of Bret Harte's *The Outcasts Of Poker Flat* with Harry Carey and Cullen Landis; Lon Chaney is in love with jewel thief Priscilla Dean in *The Wicked Darling*; he also appears with Miss Dean and Dorothy Phillips in the Klondike thriller *Paid In Advance*.

Universal feature boxers James J. Corbett and Jess Willard in top movie roles. Corbett stars in *The Midnight Man,* Willard in *The Challenge Of Chance* and *The Heart Punch*. Say the ads for the latter: "A financial knockout for exhibitors. Jess Willard, heavyweight champion of the world in the thrilling photo drama *The Heart Punch*. Wire your bookings now to your nearest Universal exchange."

Irving Thalberg, having served his apprenticeship in New York, arrives in Hollywood and becomes studio manager in charge of day-to-day operations. Later in the year he is made general manager in charge of all studio productions and becomes the youngest studio head in the history of Hollywood. Such is his power, he is answerable only to Laemmle.

1920 Erich von Stroheim's second movie as director, *The Devil's Passkey* is nearly as big a hit as his first. Advertised 'Paris The Wicked, Paris The Wonderful' it is based on the story 'Clothes And Treachery' by Baroness de Meyer and once again centres round a dissatisfied wife flattered by the attentions of an army officer. Sam de Grasse, Una Trevelyan, Mae Busch and Clyde Fillmore co-star.

Priscilla Dean and Wheeler Oakman are in *The Virgin Of Stamboul*; Dorothy Phillips in *Once To Every Woman*; Gladys Walton in *Pink Tights*; and John Ford directs James J. Corbett in *The Prince Of Avenue A*.

1921 Lon Chaney is in a dual role, a gangster and a chinaman in Tod Browning's *Outside The Law*; society girl Priscilla Dean dynamites a dam in *The Conflict*; Leo McCarey directs Eva Novak in *Society Secrets*; and Harry Carey is out West as Ol' Santa Fe in *The Fox* and 'Ohio, the stranger' in *The Freeze Out*.

Busiest stars of the year: Gladys Walton, who chalks up half-a-dozen movies, Carmel Myers and Herbert Rawlinson.

1922 Von Stroheim's million dollar extravaganza, *Foolish Wives*, is released. The story of a bogus nobleman who earns his living by seduction and blackmail on the Riviera, it is trimmed from 32 reels to 14 and is the last complete film made by von Stroheim on the Universal lot. The director's original 32 reel version would have run to some six hours and been released in two parts if things had gone according to plan.

Tod Browning films Ouida's Foreign Legion story *Under Two Flags* with Priscilla Dean as the French-Arab girl 'Cigarette' – the daughter of the regiment; Marie Prevost is busy as a society girl in *The Dangerous Little Demon*, a chorus girl in *Don't Get Personal* and a New York model in *Her Night Of Nights*; Lon Chaney is a French Canadian trapper in *The Trap*.

Harry Carey and Hoot Gibson take care of the western scene; Reginald Denny is mixed up in *The Kentucky Derby*; Herbert Rawlinson is the busiest male star.

1923 Lon Chaney appears in one of his most famous roles, *The Hunchback Of Notre Dame*. He spares no time or effort to make the role the most convincing he's ever played.

His make-up: A thirty pound breastplate is attached in

front to shoulder pads of the kind American footballers use. A hump moulded from forty pounds of rubber is joined to the false front by a leather harness. Once in the rig Chaney can no longer stand upright. Over the whole contraption he wears a tight, pink, hairy skin, also made of rubber. On his head is a matted wig; on his face lumps of putty; in his mouth fanged false teeth.

Chaney is also an underworld cripple in *The Shock*; Wallace Beery a vengeful Russian revolutionary in *Bavu*; Priscilla Dean an opium smuggler in China in Tod Browning's *Drifting*; Gladys Walton a runaway circus performer in Jack Conway's *Sawdust*.

Norman Kerry and Mary Philbin star in a romance of pre-war Vienna, *Merry-Go-Round*, the film that was begun by von Stroheim (he was fired after five weeks) and completed by Rupert Julian.

Thalberg, aged 23, leaves Universal to assume the post of vice-president of Metro at a salary of 600 dollars a week.

1924 Laura La Plante, Priscilla Dean and Herbert Rawlinson are among the top Universal stars; King Baggott and Clarence Brown the leading directors.

The latter directs Virginia Valli and Wallace Beery in *The Signal Tower* and La Plante and Ruth Clifford in the romantic drama *Butterfly*.

Jazz gal Clara Bow is mixed up with bootlegging in *Wine*; Mary Philbin is a French orphan girl in *The Rose Of Paris*; Virginia Valli buries Earle Foxe in the cellar in *A Lady Of Quality*; Creighton Hale is a compulsive gambler in *Riders Up*; Pat O'Malley rescues Mary Astor from revolutionists in China in *The Fighting American*.

1925 Chaney returns to the studio for *The Phantom Of The Opera*. It's one of his greatest triumphs and he endures considerable pain to achieve his hideous facial make-up.

As the disfigured musician who haunts the Paris Opera House, he wears false teeth, pushes wires into his nose and eye sockets and foxes adhesive tape that drags back his nose, exposing the nostrils. He also has wire prongs attached to his teeth (so that they can draw back the corners of his mouth) and celluloid discs inside the mouth to distort the cheek bones!

House Peters is the aristocratic jewel thief *Raffles, The Amateur Cracksman* (directed by King Baggot); Pauline Frederick, Laura La Plante and Malcolm McGregor star in Clarence Brown's love triangle, *Smouldering Fires*; Brown is also responsible for *The Goose Woman*, about a former opera star-turned-drunkard who inadvertently involves her son in murder; and William Wyler directs his first movie, a western called *Crook Buster*.

Laura La Plante, Virginia Valli and comedy star Reginald Denny are all busy; so too are western heroes Hoot Gibson and Jack Hoxie.

1926 Not the most distinguished of years. No Chaney, nothing from Clarence Brown who has moved to Metro. William Wyler, however, now given his head, makes half-a-dozen two-reel westerns including *The Gunless Bad Man, Ridin' For Love* and *Don't Shoot*.

Laura La Plante is a regular comedy star in *The Beautiful Cheat, Butterflies In The Rain* and *Her Big Night*; Francis X. Bushman and Billie Dove team in the theatrical romance *The Marriage Clause*; Norman Kerry and Greta Nissen enjoy a Ruritanian love affair in *The Love Thief*; Marian Nixon is a circus bare-back rider in *Spangles*.

Reginald Denny continually provides the comedy and Hoot Gibson the western action. *The Cohens And Kellys*, a store owner (George Sidney) and an Irish cop (Charlie Murray) who go into business together, make the first of several appearances.

1927 Universal film the first version of *The Cat And The Canary*, the famous thriller about the reading of the will of an eccentric recluse — in a mansion twenty years after his death! German Paul Leni directs, Laura La Plante, Creighton Hale and Tully Marshall are among the stars.

Leni also directs the macabre *The Man Who Laughs* with Conrad Veidt as a famous clown whose features have been distorted into a permanent grin by order of James II.

Veidt is a magician who murders for the love of Mary Philbin in *The Last Performance*; Anna Q. Nilsson and Francis X. Bushman star in the murder drama *The Thirteenth Juror*; Reginald Denny clowns his way through *The Cheerful Fraud, Fast And Furious* and *On Your Toes*; Wyler's westerns include *Tenderfoot Courage, Galloping Justice, The Lone Star* and *The Home Trail*.

A new version of *Uncle Tom's Cabin* stars James Lowe as Uncle Tom, Virginia Grey as Little Eva and George Siegmann as Simon Legree.

1928 *Melody Of Love*, a romantic triangular drama in 9 reels, featuring Walter Pidgeon, Mildred Harris and Jane Winton, is the first all-talkie produced by Universal. It is released on December 2.

As sound takes over, Universal paint signs, each in 50 ft letters, on the roofs of their three stages: 'Universal Pictures — Quiet!'

Other movies: William Wyler's *Anybody Here Seen Kelly?* with Bessie Love; *The Count Of Ten* with Charles Ray as a prizefighter; *Alias The Deacon* in which Jean Hersholt stars as a professional cardsharp and gambler; *Thanks For The Buggy Ride* with Laura La Plante.

1929 With the coming of sound, musicals are 'in'. Universal's biggest is *Show Boat* with Laura La Plante as Magnolia, Joseph Schildkraut as Gaylord Ravenal and Alma Rubens as Julie. *Broadway* with Evelyn Brent (and two-colour Technicolor sequences) and *Melody Lane* are others in the *genre*.

William Wyler directs James Murray in the oilfield drama *The Shakedown*; Paul Leni delivers *The Last Warning* with Laura La Plante, Montague Love and John Boles all involved in murder and nasty goings-on inside a theatre; Wesley Ruggles directs Miss La Plante (as a socialite) in the three way romance *Scandal*.

Also prominent during the year: Joseph Schildkraut who works the riverboats in *Mississippi Gambler*; Gladys Brockwell who is accused of murder in *The Drake Case*; Hoot Gibson and Ken Maynard, both of whom are out West; and Reginald Denny who provides the humour in *His Lucky Day*.

As the studio prepares for the thirties Carl Laemmle Jr. is appointed general manager in charge of production.

1930 The year of *All Quiet On The Western Front*, Lewis Milestone's movie about a group of German youths who volunteer to serve the fatherland during the Great War and are gradually disillusioned by the endless death and misery surrounding them in the trenches. A classic movie, it is taken from the novel by Erich Maria Remarque and becomes Universal's first best picture Academy Award winner. Director Milestone also wins an Oscar.

The King Of Jazz, a series of musical sketches in two-colour Technicolor is another big trailblazer, with Paul

Whiteman and his orchestra, George Gershwin (directing 'Rhapsody In Blue') and The Rhythm Boys (with Bing Crosby) among the star turns. The spooky *The Cat Creeps*, with Helen Twelvetrees, is another version of *The Cat And The Canary*; comely Lupe Velez is 'bought' by Chop Suey King, Edward G. Robinson in *East Is West*; Edward G. getting into practice for his Warner career, is also gang leader Cobra Collins in Tod Browning's *Outside The Law*.

The death of horror king and make-up master Lon Chaney (aged 47) from bronchial cancer comes as a great shock to everyone around the world. Although he made the majority of his films at Metro during the 20s, Chaney spent his early years at Universal appearing in nearly 100 films between 1913 and 1922. His two most famous roles, *The Hunchback Of Notre Dame* and *The Phantom Of The Opera* were also filmed at the studio. At the time of his death he was considering yet another return to the Universal lot as Bram Stoker's *Dracula*.

1931 The actor eventually chosen to play the vampire count is Hungarian-born Bela Lugosi who recreates the role he first played on stage in 1927. The action is transferred from Transylvania to London, where Dracula intends making his new home but it matters little; the shudders induced by the quiet-voiced, malevolent nobleman are the same whatever the setting. "I never drink. . .wine," he says softly.

Advertised as 'The story of the strangest passion the world has ever known', *Dracula* immediately makes Lugosi a star. At the height of his fame in the 30s, this unusual actor receives as many fan letters as the romantic screen idols. 97 per-cent of them come from women.

Six months after Dracula's appearance another Universal monster makes his debut. In *Frankenstein* Boris Karloff lands the part of the creature assembled from the organs of dead bodies. Make-up man Jack Pierce has the job of turning him into that creature — in just three-and-a-half hours — every morning.

Pierce breaks down his make-up into the following categories:

Head: Square and flat like a box and made of rubber. A scar across the forehead indicates where the head has been opened and the brain popped inside. Two metal clamps hold the head together.

Face: Coated with blue-green grease-paint which photographs grey.

Eyes: Lizard-like and made of rubber.

Neck: Accentuated by two metal studs, one on each side, which are inlets for electricity plugs.

Arms: Normal size but made to look longer by shortening the sleeves of the jacket.

Fingernails: Blackened with shoe polish.

Legs: Stiffened by steel struts and two pairs of trousers.

Feet: Made to appear large by the wearing of boots warn by asphalt spreaders.

During shooting, Karloff, a six-footer, becomes 18 inches taller and 60 pounds heavier. He also *loses* 20 pounds in weight!

A performer who doesn't get a part in *Frankenstein* is Bette Davis. Producer Carl Laemmle Jr. decrees that she isn't the right type of actress for horror films and replaces her with Mae Clarke. Bette does get to make her screen debut, however, (as the sister of Sidney Fox) in *Bad Sister*, a version of Booth Tarkington's 'The Flirt.'

Frankenstein director James Whale also films Robert Sherwood's classic tearjerker *Waterloo Bridge* with Mae Clarke turning to prostitution when she believes fiancée Kent Douglas (later Douglass Montgomery) to have been killed in the war; Jean Harlow is teamed with Lew Ayres in Tod Browning's boxing drama *Iron Man*. Ayres is also a reporter in *Up For Murder* and involved in American football in *The Spirit Of Notre Dame*; Ricardo Cortez and Mae Clarke run a speakeasy in *Reckless Living*; Charles Bickford and Rose Hobart find themselves deep in the jungle, *East Of Borneo*, where one of the customs is throwing natives to the alligators.

On a somewhat higher plane, John Boles and Lupe Velez star in Tolstoy's *Resurrection*.

1932 The horror cycle gathers momentum as Karloff and Lugosi follow-up their triumphs of a year before.

In *The Mummy* (directed by German cameraman Karl Freund) Karloff is the 3,700 year-old mummified Egyptian priest Imhotep who is accidentally brought back to life by an English archaeologist. "He went. . .for a little walk" blabbers the archaeologist insanely as he points to the empty space in the tomb wall.

Lugosi is particularly unpleasant in Robert Florey's *Murders In The Rue Morgue*. He features as Dr. Mirakle.

His speciality? Injecting gorilla blood into beautiful women in order to prove they are derived from — gorillas!

James Whale's contribution is *The Old Dark House*, a version of J. B. Priestley's 'Benighted' in which a group of travellers are forced to take shelter in a Welsh mansion on a stormy night. This film features Charles Laughton, Melvyn Douglas and Lilian Bond as the luckless visitors — wet but sane. Boris Karloff is a dumb, murderous waiter, Brember Wills, a pyromaniac dwarf, Ernest Thesiger and Eva Moore, an insane brother and sister, and John Dudgeon, a 100-year-old baronet, are the hosts — dry but nuts!

Universal also show the first signs of taking serious interest in the soap opera as they film Fannie Hurst's *Back Street* (directed by John Stahl) and borrow tear-jerking queen Irene Dunne from RKO to play the woman whose love and devotion to a married man (John Boles) results in her staying permanently in the 'back streets' of his life.

Elsewhere, Walter Huston and Harry Carey are Wyatt Earp and Doc Holliday (with fictional names) in *Law And Order*; Wyler directs *A House Divided* in which widowed fisherman Huston takes a wife (Helen Chandler) young enough to be his daughter with inevitable tragic results; Tom Mix appears in the first version of Max Brand's *Destry Rides Again*; Jack Oakie, Sidney Fox and Aline MacMahon star in the Moss Hart/George Kaufman Hollywood comedy *Once In A Lifetime*; John Ford makes sure a group of courageous pilots get the mail through in *Airmail*; and Charles Bickford, Rose Hobart and Pat O'Brien are together in the newspaper story *Scandal For Sale*.

1933 James Whale switches from Shelley and Priestley to H. G. Wells and casts British actor Claude Rains (debut) in one of the most unusual film roles of all time — *The Invisible Man*. Heard but not seen until the final reel, the scientist thoroughly enjoys his power of invisibility. He also gets an acute case of megalomania. "We'll start with a few murders," says he. "Big men. Little men. Just to show we make no distinction."

John Stahl, having achieved some success with Irene Dunne in *Back Street*, now puts Margaret Sullavan through the treadmill in *Only Yesterday*. Miss Sullavan is an unwed mother seduced and then forgotten after a one-night affair in the war. The cad and the guy with the bad memory? None other than Miss Dunne's former heart-throb, John Boles.

Lew Ayres and Ginger Rogers get together in the race-track comedy *Don't Bet On Love*; Chester Morris and Helen Twelvetrees star in a boxing drama spiced with murder, *King For A Night*; George Stevens (soon to be a top director at RKO) films *The Cohens And Kellys In Trouble*; and William Wyler directs John Barrymore, a self-made lawyer with a past, in Elmer Rice's *Counsellor-At-Law*.

1934 The two Universal horror kings, Karloff and Lugosi, get together for the first time in *The Black Cat*. Lugosi is an eccentric scientist who revenges himself on architect Karloff, a devil worshipper who has stolen his wife and daughter and uses human life for sacrifice. Sample grisly dialogue: Lugosi to Karloff, "I'm going to tear the skin from your body — bit by bit!"

John Stahl repeats the soap opera dose for the third year running with a version of another Fannie Hurst novel, *Imitation Of Life*, a story of a white women who finds success in the business world through the help of a coloured woman. A beautifully mounted film, it centres on the racial theme and the relationship between the two adults and their children. Claudette Colbert is the third Stahl actress to endure the agonies inflicted on her by the Universal scriptwriters.

Frank Borzage's *Little Man, What Now?* with Margaret Sullavan and Douglass Montgomery as a young German couple struggling to make a living during the post-war Depression is another successful drama but the studio's attempt at Dickens, via *Great Expectations*, is a near disaster. Henry Hull's Magwitch is one of the film's redeeming features.

Wyler's contribution is *Glamour* in which married chorus girl Constance Cummings falls for composer Paul Lukas; Fay Wray is a phoney countess in *The Countess Of Monte Cristo* and a Russian agent who spies on her German husband in *Madame Spy*; and John Boles stars in the musical *Beloved*.

1935 James Whale brings humour as well as horror to the satirical *Bride Of Frankenstein*, one of the few sequels to surpass its predecessor. Colin Clive (Frankenstein) and necromancer Ernest Thesiger join forces to produce a she-mate for the Karloff monster as it begins to learn its first words: ''Alone bad, friend good.'' Admirable sentiments, but unfortunately not appropriate. When his mate is eventually produced — a shrieking Elsa Lanchester — the two don't hit it off at all!

Lugosi and Karloff, together again in *The Raven*, find themselves saddled with some unintentionally humorous dialogue. Says plastic surgeon Lugosi: ''What about the time when you tortured a man you held captive by shoving a blow torch in his face?'' Answer: ''Sometimes, you can't help things like that.''

Werewolves also enter the horror scene. *The Werewolf Of London* has Henry Hull as a London botanist who is bitten by a werewolf while on an expedition to Tibet. On returning to London he periodically changes into a werewolf and goes on the rampage in the dark city streets. The tender white skin of lovely Valerie Hobson compensates somewhat for all the hair around.

John Stahl, obviously enjoying himself (with considerable skill) in the soap opera *genre*, recalls Irene Dunne for *Magnificent Obsession*, a Lloyd C. Douglas tale about a wealthy playboy (Robert Taylor) who falls in love with the woman he accidentally causes to go blind. Filled with remorse he becomes a surgeon and eventually restores the woman's sight. Trite in theme but on screen a ten handkerchief experience.

The studio again tackle Dickens, this time with more success as Claude Rains excels as John Jaspar in *The Mystery Of Edwin Drood*; William Wyler films a Preston Sturges script, *The Good Fairy*, with Margaret Sullavan as an innocent named Luisa Ginglebusher; Edward Arnold is Diamond Jim Brady and Binnie Barnes Lillian Russell in *Diamond Jim*; Edmund Lowe and Jean Dixon are involved in a casino murder in *Mr. Dynamite*; and Charles Bickford, stranded *East Of Borneo* four years earlier, now finds himself in a similar situation, shipwrecked with his cargo of lions and tigers on a lonely island *East Of Java*.

1936 The year when Carl Laemmle (aged 69) relinquishes control of Universal after nearly a quarter-of-a-century at its helm.

The new, somewhat faceless regime, headed by new president Charles Cochrane, decides to cut back on cost and aim for smaller pictures. The big ones of 1936 therefore are the last produced during the Laemmle era — the lovely *Show Boat* (directed by James Whale) with Irene

Dunne as Magnolia, Allan Jones as Gaylord Ravenal, Helen Morgan as the tragic Julie and Paul Robeson ('Ole Man River') memorable as Joe; *Sutter's Gold*, a James Cruze western about the discovery of gold in '49; and *The Invisible Ray* with Karloff and Lugosi reunited once more, the former turning into a killer after getting a dose of 'Radium X' in Africa!

Gloria Holden is *Dracula's Daughter* (Countess Marya Zaleska); Buster Crabbe the new serial king *Flash Gordon*; and John Wayne a coastguard in *The Sea Spoilers*.

Carole Lombard has the most fun, though. In La Cava's delightful *My Man Godfrey* she's a socialite who picks up a bum (William Powell) in the city dump and takes him home to be her family's butler; and in *Love Before Breakfast* she has both Preston Foster and Cesar Romero as would-be suitors.

The big surprise is the sudden emergence of 15-year-old Deanna Durbin. Co-starring with Binnie Barnes, Alice Brady and Charles Winninger in Henry Koster's *Three Smart Girls*, she appears as one of three girls determined to reunite their parents by breaking up their divorced father's plans to marry a gold digger.

For the moment, at least, horror is out and charm (coupled with innocence and song) is in!

1937 Durbin's 1937 contribution is *One Hundred Men And A Girl* in which she spends most of her time persuading an unwilling Leopold Stokowski to conduct an orchestra of Depression-hit musicians, among them her unemployed dad Adolphe Menjou.

It works like a charm at the box-office. Universal quickly revise the young singer's contract, doubling it to 3,000 dollars a week and adding a bonus of 10,000 dollars a film.

Joe Pasternak, producer of many Deanna Durbin films, says: "Durbin is one of those personalities whom the world will insist on regarding as its personal property." And he is right!

Durbin apart, however, the cupboard looks bare. The only major film is *The Road Back*, a James Whale misfire about a group of German soldiers trying to find their way back to normal life after four years of hell in World War I. Starring John King, Richard Cromwell and 'Slim' Summerville and based on a novel by Erich Maria Remarque, it is intended to be a signficant successor to *All Quiet On The Western Front*. It isn't.

George Murphy and Doris Nolan star in the Manhattan musical *Top Of The Town*; Virginia Bruce makes it to Broadway in another musical *When Love Is Young*; Alice Faye helps save a show in *You're A Sweetheart*; Ray Milland, Wendy Barrie and William Gargan are romantically involved in *Wings Over Honolulu*; and Edward Everett Horton is a hypochondriac in *Oh, Doctor*.

However, it's all pretty inconsequential stuff and the 60 minute dramas with stars like John Howard, Robert Wilcox, Noah Beery Jr., James Dunn and William Gargan predominate.

1938 It's no surprise that Deanna Durbin has two movies on parade. In *Mad About Music* she sings 'I Love To Whistle' and brings romance (in the form of Herbert Marshall) to her Hollywood mom, Gail Patrick; and in *That Certain Age* she imagines herself in love with handsome war correspondent Melvyn Douglas.

Buster Crabbe is off into the galaxy again in *Flash Gordon's Trip To Mars*; Constance Bennett stars in the comedy *Service De Luxe*; Parisian singer Danielle Darrieux tries to snare a wealthy husband but succumbs to true love in *The Rage Of Paris*; and ex-vaudeville team Alice Brady and Charles Winninger buy a broken-down hotel in *Goodbye, Broadway*.

It's not one of Universal's most auspicious years especially when, once again, names like Kent Taylor, Preston Foster and Noah Beery Jr. are made to seem all-important in such mundane films as *The Lady In The Morgue, The Last Warning, Midnight Intruder* and *Prison Break*.

1939 Deanna Durbin, now at her peak, stars in *Three Smart Girls Grow Up*, is awarded an honorary Oscar and receives her first screen kiss — from Robert Stack — in *First Love*.

But a new regime sees to it that she no longer has to carry the studio on her slim shoulders.

Reinforcements arrive in the form of W. C. Fields (hired at 125,000 dollars a picture plus 25,000 dollars for his story outline), more Stahl soap opera, a revival of the Frankenstein monster and a smash-hit comedy western.

Fields' '39 offering is *You Can't Cheat An Honest Man* (story by Charles Bogle) in which he features as circus owner Larson E. Whipsnade. His co-stars are Edgar Bergen and Constance Moore but the movie is best remembered for lines like "Me dishonest! Meishack, Shadrack and Abednego!" and, "Somebody left the cork out of my lunch!"

John Stahl directs Irene Dunne in *When Tomorrow Comes*, about a waitress who falls heavily for a concert pianist (Charles Boyer) saddled with a marriage to a mentally ill wife; Rowland V. Lee takes over from James Whale as the Frankenstein director by guiding Karloff through *Son Of Frankenstein*. It is Karloff's third and last appearance as the monster.

"The monster was the best friend I ever had," says Karloff later.

Son Of Frankenstein is intended to be Universal's first production in three-colour Technicolor but after shooting begins it is discovered that Karloff's make-up doesn't photograph convincingly and the film reverts to black-and-white. Gilbert and Sullivan's *The Mikado*, filmed in England, is Universal's first three-colour release although audiences have to wait another three years for the studio's first three-colour American movie.

The comedy western is *Destry Rides Again*. Peace-loving sheriff James Stewart cleans up a rough-tough town without using any guns and Marlene Dietrich (as fabulous saloon entertainer Frenchy) proves again that her legs are among the best in the business as she sings 'See What The Boys In The Back Room Will Have.'

Bela Lugosi, on the slide, is reduced to appearing in the serial *The Phantom Creeps*, and Douglas Fairbanks Jr., Lionel Atwill and Basil Rathbone find adventure in Africa where *The Sun Never Sets*. Rathbone also portrays the scheming Richard III in *Tower Of London*; and singing cabbie Bing Crosby skips over from Paramount to be with Joan Blondell on the *East Side Of Heaven*.

1940 W. C. Fields appears twice — in *The Bank Dick* as Egbert Souse, a lazy bum who accidentally traps a bank robber, and *My Little Chickadee* in which he teams with Mae West.

"Ah! What symmetrical digits. Soft as the fuzz on a baby's arm" he cries in the latter movie, pressing his lips against Miss West's hand. Says he in the former, "The jockey was a very insulting fella. He referred to my proboscis as an adsatious exrescious."

One of Universal's most popular comedy duos, Abbott and Costello, make their debut in *One Night In The Tropics*.

They support Allan Jones and Robert Cummings. Within a year they are stars in their own right.

Another comedy character, the animated Woody Woodpecker, appears for the first time on screen in the cartoon short *Knock Knock*. Early the following year he receives star billing in *Woody Woodpecker*. Grace Stafford, wife of the cartoon's producer Walter Lantz, is the voice of WW.

The Invisible Man Returns (wich Cedric Hardwicke) and *The Mummy's Hand* (with Tom Tyler) continue the resurgence of the horror film; Dietrich stays at the studio after her success in *Destry*. Her 1940 offering? *Seven Sinners* in which she stars as honky tonk singer Bijou Blanche. Attracted to her this time? John Wayne.

Flash Gordon makes his final appearance in the serial *Flash Gordon Conquers The Universe*; George Sanders is the evil Jaffray Pynchon in Nathaniel Hawthorne's classic *The House Of Seven Gables*; Douglas Fairbanks Jr., Joan Bennett and Sanders share expedition adventure in *Green Hell*; Rosalind Russell and Brian Aherne star in the comedy *Hired Wife*.

The studio also take the plunge with a large-scale musical, *The Boys From Syracuse*, a version of the 1938 Rodgers and Hart Broadway hit. Allan Jones and Martha Raye star. Among the songs: 'Falling In Love With You' and 'This Can't Be Love'.

1941 Lionel Atwill, a key player in Universal's horror revival of the forties, becomes the subject of a sleazy trial in Los Angeles early in the year. Two women, a Cuban dress designer and a sixteen year old unwed mother, give evidence in a rape trial.

Part of their testimony tells of a 1940 Christmas orgy which they attended at the home of a famous Hollywood actor. After showing obscene movies, he led his guests in stripping and re-enacting the pornography on a tigerskin rug while Viennese waltzes were played on the piano. Atwill's name slips out during the trial and despite issuing two denials he eventually admits the truth and pleads guilty to the offence, and also (in 1942) to perjury.

Most studio's shun Atwill but Universal show no vindictiveness and hire him regularly until his death in 1946. "But for the courage and magnaminity of one particular studio, I guess I should be a dead egg now," he says gratefully.

Nothing Universal can produce on screen can quite match the flamboyance of Mr. Atwill's private activities but it's not a bad year all the same.

Olsen and Johnson star with Martha Raye in that craziest of all crazy comedies *Hellzapoppin'*; La Cava's *Unfinished Business* has small-town girl Irene Dunne finding romance and adventure with Robert Montgomery and Preston Foster; Marlene Dietrich is *The Flame Of New Orleans*; Margaret Sullavan is the new sufferer (over Charles Boyer) in the remake of *Back Street*; Lon Chaney is turned into an electric monster (by Lionel Atwill!) in *Man-Made Monster*; and Abbott and Costello have The Andrews Sisters for company in hit films like *Buck Privates, In The Navy* and *Hold That Ghost!*

A newcomer to the studio's horror ranks is *The Wolf Man* with Lon Chaney Jr. as the unfortunate guy who turns into a murdering beast whenever there's a full moon.

Says Maria Ouspenskaya with menace:

"Even the man who is pure in heart
And says his prayers by night
May become a wolf when the wolf bane blooms
And the moon is pure and bright."

Deanna Durbin has no such problems in *It Started With Eve* in which she poses as the fiancée of Robert Cummings for the benefit of ailing millionaire Charles Laughton. Nor does W. C. Fields, who is still causing comedy havoc in *Never Give A Sucker An Even Break*. "Somebody put too many olives in my martini last night," he growls during the course of the film.

1942 Abbott and Costello (by this time the top moneymaking stars in America) also enjoy some fine moments of dialogue. In *Who Done It?* in which they appear as two soda jerks who write radio mysteries on the side, Bud tries to explain to Lou about volts and watts.

Abbott: "You know what volts are?"
Costello: "They're what?"
Abbott: "That's right, volts are watts."
Costello: "Well, go ahead and tell me."
Abbott: "You just said it."
Costello: "I'm asking you — what's volts?"
Abbott: "That's right — watts are volts."
Costello: "What are you askin' *me* for?"

Bud and Lou also star as peanut vendors mistaken for

cowboys in *Ride 'Em Cowboy* and two bus drivers in *Pardon My Sarong*.

Marlene Dietrich, still very much at home at Universal, teams with John Wayne and Randolph Scott in *Pittsburgh* then has them fight over her yet again in a new version of Rex Beach's *The Spoilers*, Basil Rathbone and Nigel Bruce, who two years earlier had been successful as Sherlock Holmes and Dr. Watson at Fox, reappear as the characters in the first of what turns out to be a long series — *Sherlock Holmes And The Voice Of Terror* (loosely based on Doyle's 'His Last Bow') and *Sherlock Holmes And The Secret Weapon* (with Lionel Atwill as Moriarty).

George Raft recalls his life during Prohibition in *Broadway*; Robert Stack joins the RAF in *Eagle Squadron*; Constance Bennett is suspected of being a Nazi agent in *Madame Spy*; Irene Dunne is an heiress out West looking for gold in La Cava's *Lady In A Jam*; and Lon Chaney Jr. (as Kharis) is among those keeping the horror scene alive in *The Mummy's Tomb*.

Alfred Hitchcock provides the year's most terrifying death, Maria Montez the most exotic glamour.

In *Saboteur*, Hitchcock has his villain hanging by a thread from the torch of the Statue Of Liberty. Stitch by stitch the jacket arm comes apart and poor Norman Lloyd has no option but to plunge to his death hundreds of feet below.

In *Arabian Nights*, the first piece of Maria Montez-Jon Hall hokum (and the first American Universal film in Technicolor) Montez plays the beautiful Princess Scheherazade of Arabia. When she sees her performance for the first time she is quoted as saying, "When I look at myself on the screen I am so beautiful I scream with joy."

1943 The class picture of the year is Hitchcock's *Shadow Of A Doubt* with Joseph Cotten as a psychotic widow murderer hiding out with his unsuspecting family in a quiet American town. Composer Dimitri Tiomkin uses Lehar's 'The Merry Widow' as his musical theme; Hitchcock does away with his villain by throwing him in front of a train.

The Phantom Of The Opera with Claude Rains (complete with sombrero, red-tipped cloak and blue mask) in Chaney's old role is the only colour Universal horror film of the 30s and 40s. It duly wins Academy Awards for its camerawork and design.

White Savage is another Technicolor vehicle. Montez is once more a princess, Hall a shark hunter. Villain Thomas

Gomez wants both Montez *and* her jewel-studded swimming pool. Hall only wants her but gets both!

Deanna Durbin is concerned over nine orphans in *The Amazing Mrs. Holliday*, starts a musical career in New York in *His Butler's Sister* and falls in love with handsome bomber pilot Joseph Cotten in *Hers To Hold*.

Rathbone and Bruce star in *Sherlock Holmes Faces Death* and *Sherlock Holmes In Washington* in which they investigate the disappearance of a secret service agent; Lon Chaney Jr. visits the USA in *Son Of Dracula*; Randolph Scott is at war in *Corvette K-225* and in the marines in *Gung Ho!*; *Frankenstein Meets The Wolf Man*, inevitably; and Abbott and Costello team in *It Ain't Hay* and *Hit The Ice*.

An intriguing and unusual picture is the three-story *Flesh And Fantasy*, directed by Julien Duvivier. Edward G. Robinson dominates as a man told by a fortune teller that his palm says 'murder!'

1944 Robert Siodmak emerges as Universal's top thriller director when Hitchcock, after a brief stay at the studio, moves on to work with Selznick.

Siodmak provides two thrillers, each of completely different character. The urban *Phantom Lady* has Alan Curtis as a man framed for the murder of his wife, desperately seeking the woman who can give him an alibi. *The Suspect* features Charles Laughton as an elderly Crippen-like character who murders his shrewish wife for the love of a young girl.

The rest of the lineup is very much in the Universal double feature tradition of the 40s. Rathbone and Bruce investigate three cases; *The Spider Woman, The Scarlet Claw* and *The Pearl Of Death*; Lon Chaney Jr. appears twice as Kharis, in *The Mummy's Curse* and *The Mummy's Ghost*; Karloff is the mad murderer of an opera singer whose body he keeps embalmed in his attic in *The Climax*.

Maria Montez is 'up for grabs' three times. In *Gypsy Wildcat* she's a dancing girl who's really a countess; in *Ali Baba And The Forty Thieves* she longs for Jon Hall and loathes villain Kurt Katch ("Rubies. . .blood red. . .for the people of Baghdad who stood in my way," murmurs the latter as he lays a necklace around her neck); in *Cobra Woman* she plays two sisters, one good, one bad, who rule over a remote Pacific island where natives worship snakes and are sacrificed into volcanoes. 'Pagan Witch. . .No

Man Could Resist, Or Subdue' trumpet the ads. In 1944 no-one really wants to.

1945 Miss Montez appears again with Jon Hall in *Sudan* but it's the last of their six films together and a new beauty, Yvonne De Carlo, now rivals her for the top female spot at the studio.

Billed as 'The Most Beautiful Girl In The World' she measures 36-24-32 and in *Salome, Where She Danced* zooms to stardom after twenty innocuous movies at other studios. Like Montez, she never remotely suggests any great acting ability, but her physique is more than enough to carry her through several years at Universal.

In *Salome,* De Carlo plays a Viennese ballerina who lands up in Arizona. In another movie, *Frontier Gal,* she's a French dance hall hostess.

Deanna Durbin has nothing to sing about in *Lady On A Train* (she witnesses a murder from her compartment window) but is more at home in *Because Of Him* as the musical protégée of Charles Laughton; Universal's horror series ends with *House Of Dracula,* starring Chaney and John Carradine; Rathbone and Bruce have another three crimes to solve in *The House Of Fear, The Woman In Green* and *Pursuit To Algiers*; soap opera is represented by Merle Oberon and Claude Rains in *This Love Of Ours*; and George Sanders plans murder in Siodmak's *The Strange Affair Of Uncle Harry.*

Abbott and Costello continue on their merry way in *Here Come The Co-Eds* and *The Naughty Nineties.*

1946 Universal lose two of their key stars of the 40s, W. C. Fields and Lionel Atwill. Fields (67) who spent his last half-dozen years at Universal after a successful career at Paramount, dies of dropsy and other ailments, Atwill (61) a horror specialist, of pneumonia.

Fields, who dies on Christmas Eve, leaves a typically bizarre will. He leaves an estate of some 800,000 dollars, most of it to go to the 'W. C. Fields College For Orphaned White Boys And Girls' where no religion of any sort is to be preached. His wife and son successfully contest the will, however, and the orphanage is never established.

Variety's list of top box-office hits of the year reveals that the studio doesn't have a hit in the top forty money-makers. Siodmak's psychological thriller *The Dark Mirror* with Olivia de Havilland as twin sisters, one good, one evil, comes out the best with a take of two and three quarter million dollars.

Another Siodmak movie, *The Killers*, a cleverly expanded version of Hemingway's short story, is next with two and a half million. *The Killers* introduces Burt Lancaster to the screen as the victim of small-talk assassins William Conrad and Charles McGraw. Slinky Ava Gardner introduces seduction and double cross.

Murder seems to be the key to several of Universal's movies. Respectable store cashier Edward G. Robinson becomes infatuated with and eventually murders whore Joan Bennett in Fritz Lang's *Scarlet Street*, allowing her pimp boy friend (Dan Duryea) to be executed for the crime; Duryea is also in trouble in *Black Angel* as a songwriter who murders his ex-wife in an alcoholic blackout; and elegant Merle Oberon poisons with style in Egypt at the beginning of the century in *Temptation*. "The men in her life sometimes lived to regret it" lament the ads.

Rathbone and Bruce make their final bow as Holmes and Watson in *Terror By Night* and *Dressed To Kill*; Ginger Rogers is Dolly Madison in *The Magnificent Doll*; Abbott and Costello enjoy *The Time Of Their Lives* in the days of the American Revolution; and the big western is Jacques Tourneur's *Canyon Passage* with Dana Andrews, Susan Hayward and Brian Donlevy. The film becomes famous not for its gunplay but for a song, 'Ole Buttermilk Sky' composed by Hoagy Carmichael and nominated for an Academy Award.

1947 The studio gets among the big money (five and a half million) with a delightful version of Betty MacDonald's *The Egg And I* about a couple of city slickers who venture into the country, buy a farm and attempt to raise chickens. Fred MacMurray and Claudette Colbert star as the two innocents, but it is the supporting players, Marjorie Main and Percy Kilbride as the poverty-stricken hillbillies Ma and Pa Kettle who capture the notices. Ma (described as "a hard-boiled egg who hasn't cracked yet") and Pa, plus their fifteen kids, are to have a series of their own within a couple of years and prove life-savers for the studio.

Ronald Colman wins an Oscar for his performance as a schizophrenic actor in *A Double Life* (the studio's first major award since *All Quiet On The Western Front*); Joan Fontaine takes over as chief poisoner in Sam Wood's

Ivy; Agnes Moorehead is made up to be a hundred years old in *The Lost Moment*; and Robert Montgomery and Thomas Gomez star in the sleeper of the year, the New Mexico thriller *Ride The Pink Horse*.

Maria Montez, now near the end of her flamboyant career is in Spanish California (without Jon Hall) in *Pirates Of Monterey*; Deanna Durbin, also nearing the end of her twelve years of stardom, is a female disc jockey in *Something In The Wind*; Yvonne De Carlo, at her peak, brings some oomph into the life of Rimsky-Korsakov in *Song Of Scheherazade*.

Abbott and Costello, teamed with Marjorie Main, amuse as always in *The Wistful Widow Of Wagon Gap*; Hume Cronyn, as a sadistic guard who tortures his victims to the strains of Tannhauser on the gramophone, repels in Jules Dassin's stark prison drama *Brute Force*.

1948 The murder of a blonde and the tracking down of her killer provides the theme for Universal's big hit of the year, *The Naked City*. Not a particularly original storyline perhaps but Dassin's realistic handling — the film is shot in New York in a heat wave and uses 107 different locations — makes it appear fresh and exciting.

Barry Fitzgerald leads the homicide squad investigations, killer Ted De Corsia finishes up trapped on the dizzy heights of the Brooklyn Bridge and cameraman William Daniels wins an Oscar for photographing it all.

Deanna Durbin, now at the end of her career, is *Up In Central Park* with Dick Haymes and mixed up in Washington politics in her very last film of all, *For The Love Of Mary*. In the latter movie she sings 'Let Me Call You Sweetheart' and 'On Moonlight Bay' and suddenly it's all over. Universal's songstress quits at the age of twenty-seven.

Yvonne De Carlo brings her glamour to three movies: *Casbah* (a remake of *Algiers*) in which she teams with Tony Martin, *River Lady* and *Black Bart* in which she features as the infamous Lola Montez.

The most financially successful film of the year is the Civil War story *Tap Roots* with Van Heflin and Susan Hayward; the most delicate Max Ophuls' *Letter From An Unknown Woman*, a sad, reflective tale about the brief romance between a young girl (Joan Fontaine) and a philandering concert pianist (Louis Jourdan) in turn-of-the-century Vienna; the screwiest, *Abbott And Costello Meet Frankenstein*.

Says Lon Chaney in the latter film:

"You don't understand. . .every night when the moon is full, I turn into a wolf.

Costello replies:

"You and fifty million other guys!"

1949 Marjorie Main and Percy Kilbride become stars in their own right in *Ma And Pa Kettle*, a 75 minute picture made for just 200,000 dollars. It becomes the biggest Universal hit of the year with a gross of more than two and a quarter million.

New faces begin to appear on the Universal lot. Rock Hudson debuts as a plain clothes cop (one scene, five lines) in *Undertow*; Tony Curtis (unbilled) dances with Yvonne De Carlo in Siodmak's caper thriller *Criss Cross*; Jeff Chandler, after appearing in a bit role in Columbia's *Johnny O'Clock* two years before, is signed to a seven-year-contract after his performance as a rebel Israeli leader in *Sword In The Desert*.

Most of the output is strictly double-feature formula stuff, the bread and butter of Universal for many years and for many years in the future.

Abbott And Costello Meet The Killer, Boris Karloff; Yvonne De Carlo and Howard Duff are *Calamity Jane And Sam Bass*; Miss De Carlo is also *The Gal Who Took The West*; Maureen O'Hara, encroaching now on De Carlo territory, is a tribal princess in *Baghdad* and receives an epithet from the New York Times for all her trouble. "Framed in Technicolor," says the critic, "Miss O'Hara somehow seems more significant than a setting sun."

1950 James Stewart makes movie history by becoming the first actor since the silent days to obtain a percentage of the profits from his films as well as a top salary. His first two pictures under contract to Universal – *Harvey*, in which he repeats his stage role of the eccentric Elwood P. Down whose best friend is a 6 ft invisible rabbit and the western *Winchester 73* – are the only two 'A' pictures produced on the lot during the year.

A newcomer to the scene, *Francis*, a talking mule with G.I. Donald O'Connor as his less-than-bright master is the studio's biggest hit. Number 13 on the top money-makers list he grosses three million dollars.

Marjorie Main and Percy Kilbride, loose in Manhattan with gangsters in *Ma And Pa Kettle Go To Town*, and

Abbott And Costello In The Foreign Legion are other useful money-makers.

Maureen O'Hara of the flaming red hair moves out West in *Comanche Territory* as the owner of The Crooked Tongue Saloon (''If you call me lady once more, I'll fill you full of lead,'' she snarls at Macdonald Carey). New star Audie Murphy is also out West in *The Kid From Texas* (as Billy The Kid) and *Kansas Raiders* (as Jesse James); so too are Joel McCrea, in charge of four orphans in *Saddle Tramp*; the elegant Alexis Smith in *Wyoming Mail*; Shelley Winters in *Frenchie*, a loose remake of *Destry Rides Again*; and Donald O'Connor who finds the place more amusing in *Curtain Call At Cactus Creek*.

Yvonne De Carlo reverts to historical times in *The Desert Hawk* and *Buccaneer's Girl*; and unexpected charm is provided by *Louisa* when fifty-seven year old Spring Byington is courted by seventy-five year old Edmund Gwenn and seventy-three year old Charles Coburn. In real life Coburn lived until he was eighty-four. He believed that ''sex appeal, like brandy, improved with age.''

1951 The major feature of the year is Mark Robson's *Lights Out*, a tender and moving story of an army veteran, blinded in North Africa in World War II, attempting to readjust to life back home. A little behind the times with its theme, the film is nonetheless one of the most sensative of its kind yet made and earns Arthur Kennedy a best actor Oscar nomination.

Financially, it seems that Universal are kept solvent by a pair of hillbillies and a talking mule. *Ma And Pa Kettle Back On The Farm* and *Francis Goes To The Races* take more money than any other studio offering of the year!

The new stars of the studio are beginning to make their presence felt, however. Jeff Chandler searches for sunken treasure in *Smuggler's Island*; stars in the boxing drama *Iron Man* with Rock Hudson as one of his opponents; and rides the desert for the hand of Princess Maureen O'Hara in *Flame Of Araby*.

Audie Murphy is settling into his double-feature western mould with *The Cimarron Kid* and Tony Curtis gives his all for Piper Laurie (another Universal starlet) in *The Prince Who Was A Thief*.

Curtis' curly haircut is becoming famous. 10,000 letters arrive weekly at the studio asking for any cut-off locks. There's a contest 'Win Tony Curtis For A Week' and, as a consolation prize, 'Talk To A Movie Star.' 245 girls speak to the actor on the phone during a single hour!

Boris Karloff, sympathetic for once, serves evil master Charles Laughton in *The Strange Door*, in which the latter imprisons his brother in order to marry his own niece. It does him no good. His head and shoulders are mashed in a water mill as he suffers a nasty come-uppance.

Abbott and Costello continue to do their stuff in *Comin' Round The Mountain* and *Abbott And Costello Meet The Invisible Man*. One regular who will no longer appear is Maria Montez. She dies in her bath from either heart failure or drowning on September 7. A popular Universal star of the 40s she was just thirty-three. Her real name was Maria de Santo Silas.

1952 The big pictures are gradually coming back to the studio. Universal's biggest box-office hits are *Where The River Bends* and *The World In His Arms*, the former a western with James Stewart leading a wagon train of farmers to Oregon, the second a Raoul Walsh sea adventure with tough nineteenth century skipper Gregory Peck enamoured with the charms of beautiful Russian countess Ann Blyth.

But for the moment the double-feature still reigns supreme with Chandler, Hudson and Curtis all doing their stuff in a wide variety of actioners.

Chandler is extra busy in *Yankee Buccaneer, Red Ball Express* and as Cochise in *The Battle Of Apache Pass*. It's Loretta Young who gives him most trouble, however. In *Because Of You* she's a reformed gun moll. Say the ads: 'Even in the first wild joy of her arms, he realised that she would be. . .an unfit mother!'

Rock Hudson gets star billing, fourth behind Stewart, Arthur Kennedy and Julia Adams in *Where The River Bends*; romances Piper Laurie in Sirk's charming *Has Anybody Seen My Gal?*; fights in the Civil War in *Horizons West*; and sweeps dance hall girl Yvonne De Carlo off her feet in *Scarlet Angel*.

Curtis is a deaf-mute boxer in *Flesh And Fury*; Irene Dunne (her last movie) finds she can grow five and ten dollar bills on her trees in the aptly titled *It Grows On Trees*; Ann Sheridan, Howard Duff and John Lund provide hot stuff, in more ways than one, in *Steel Town*; Maureen O'Hara is 'Spitfire Stevens' in the Errol Flynn swashbuckler *Against All Flags*; Abbott and Costello are *Lost In Alaska*;

Francis Goes To West Point; and Marjorie Main and Percy Kilbride star in *Ma And Pa Kettle At The Fair.*

1953 Universal joins the short-lived 3-D hysteria by filming the science-fiction thriller *It Came From Outer Space* in the process. The movie, does not rate colour but the studio does its best to convince the public otherwise. ''Filmed in scientifically perfected eye-resting full sepia mono colour!'' persuade the ingenious ads. But the public are disappointed. The film *is* in black and white.

The film itself — about some mysterious aliens who land in the Arizona desert — is a miniature classic. Directed by Jack Arnold and starring Richard Carlson, it begins a series of quality science-fiction dramas from the Universal studio.

Tyrone Power, on brief loan from Fox, ensures that the studio have at least one hit in the top twenty as the *Mississippi Gambler*; James Stewart and director Anthony Mann exchange the Old West for the oil rigs of modern-day Louisiana in *Thunder Bay*; and Alan Ladd has not only sand to contend with but also the beautiful Arlene Dahl in *Desert Legion.*

Beautiful women abound: Piper Laurie is won by Rock Hudson with 'The Magic Sword Of Damascus' in *The Golden Blade*;Maureen O'Hara is a cavalry widow in *War Arrow* with Jeff Chandler and John McIntyre; and Julia Adams is down Mexico way with van Heflin in *Wings Of The Hawk.*

The men too do their rugged stuff, month in month out. Rock Hudson journeys to Canada in *Back To God's Country*; is up against Indians in *Seminole*; and stars as real-life western outlaw John Wesley Hardin in the above-average *The Lawless Breed.*

Jeff Chandler is another who's got his troubles. He's involved with *The Great Sioux Uprising*, a mining engineer in *East Of Sumatra* and drafted into the cavalry in *War Arrow.*

Tony Curtis plays football in *All-American*; Audie Murphy rides and shoots his way through three films, *Column South, Gunsmoke* and *Tumbleweed*; *Francis Covers The Big Town*; The Kettles are in Paris in *Ma And Pa Kettle On Vacation*; Abbott and Costello, having been just about everywhere else, opt for outer space in *Abbott And Costello Go To Mars.*

Nigel Bruce, the stalwart Dr. Watson of the Sherlock

Holmes adventures, dies from a heart attack, aged fifty-eight. He appeared as the bluff doctor on fourteen occasions, twelve of them at Universal between 1942 and 1946.

1954 Universal, after threatening to make a comeback into the big league, at last hit the jackpot with two movies in the box-office top ten.

The Glenn Miller Story with James Stewart as the famous trombonist bandleader grosses seven-and-a-half million dollars and becomes the studio's biggest financial success to date; *Magnificent Obsession* with Jane Wyman and Rock Hudson in the original Irene Dunne and Robert Taylor roles earns five-and-a-quarter million.

Sirk's Technicolor film, glossy and lavishly mounted, is the first in a series of large-scale soap operas the studio are to make in the 50s.

Creature From The Black Lagoon — a 3,000 year old Gill Man found among the upper reaches of the Amazon — ensures that the science-fiction boom continues to prosper; Audie Murphy earns his salary with *Drums Across The River* and *Ride Clear Of Diablo*; Rock Hudson earns his as *Taza, Son Of Cochise*; and Alan Ladd appears as a mountie in *Saskatchewan.*

Tony Curtis, after appearing in the musical *So This Is Paris?* and as racing car driver *Johnny Dark* has the privilege of starring in the studio's first CinemaScope film, *The Black Shield Of Falworth*, a costume spectacular about knighthood in medieval England. Unfortunately, one of his lines comes out not quite as intended: "Yonda lies the castle of my fodda!"

Sign Of The Pagan, starring Jeff Chandler and Jack Palance, about Attila The Hun's invasion of Rome in 450 AD, is the studio's second movie in the wide-screen process.

1955 Rich widow Joan Crawford suspects Jeff Chandler is trying to kill her in *Female On The Beach* but, as the ads put it, 'She was too hungry for love. . .to care where she found it.' On the other hand, as Miss Crawford herself says to a poker-faced Chandler: "I wouldn't take you if you were covered in diamonds — upside down!"

Science-fiction really catches hold with *Tarantula, This Island Earth* and *Revenge Of The Creature*; and the old West is well represented by *Chief Crazy Horse* with Victor Mature as the chief of the Sioux Indians; *Man Without A*

Star in which Kirk Douglas is mixed up in a bitter range war; and *Destry*, a remake of the pre-war classic with Audie Murphy and Mari Blanchard in the Stewart/Dietrich roles.

Another remake is *The Spoilers* with Jeff Chandler and Rory Calhoun slugging it out in the bar-room over Anne Baxter.

James Stewart and director Anthony Mann return to the wide open spaces in *The Far Country* with Stewart and grizzled side-kick Walter Brennan on a cattle drive to Alaska; Tony Curtis is a boxer in *The Square Jungle* and a 19th century French nobleman in *The Purple Mask*; Maureen O'Hara *Lady Godiva Of Coventry*; and Rock Hudson a 19th century Irish 'Robin Hood', *Captain Lightfoot*.

Sirk reunites Wyman and Hudson in a big weepie *All That Heaven Allows* — about the scandal caused when a lonely widow falls for a much younger man; *The Benny Goodman Story* is a hopeful follow up to *Glenn Miller* but the same appeal is missing; not so with Audie Murphy's *To Hell And Back*, a true story of the actor's wartime experiences when he became the most decorated soldier in the American army. It's the studio's biggest grosser of the year with six million dollars.

Marjorie Main and Percy Kilbride finally split up as a team in *Ma And Pa Kettle At Waikiki*. Marjorie carries on for another couple of films, but without Percy the series is all but dead.

Abbott And Costello Meet The Mummy is the last film the famous comedy duo make at Universal. Since their debut in 1940 they have appeared in 36 movies, 28 of them at Universal. They make their last film of all, *Dance With Me Henry*, at United Artists in 1956.

1956 The death of Hungarian-born Bela Lugosi (aged 73) overshadows all else on the Universal scene even though he has not worked at the studio for many years.

The most famous Dracula of them all, he was unable, like Karloff, to maintain his position in the horror field and by the late thirties was already appearing in B movies. During his career he made half-a-million dollars playing horror roles but spent it all, much of it on drugs which he had been taking for twenty years.

His death is due to a heart attack. His last instructions are that he be buried with his Dracula cape!

Horror has changed since Lugosi's day. In 1956 it is *The Creature Walks Among Us* and *The Mole People* which are responsible for the audience's frightmares.

The studio's big four, Hudson, Chandler, Curtis and Murphy swap roles as if participating in a studio game of musical chairs. Westerns one year, Easterns the next, boxing and war movies the next!

Chandler is out West with Dorothy Malone in *Pillars Of The Sky*; he's also adopted as the perfect father in the comedy *Toy Tiger*; boxer Audie Murphy has the *World In My Corner* and God on his side as he tries to bring peace between Apaches and the white man in *Walk The Proud Land*; Tony Curtis is a riverboat gambler of the 1870's in *The Rawhide Years*; Hudson is in soap opera in *Never Say Goodbye* and the Korean War in *Battle Hymn*.

The big ones are *Away All Boats* (Jeff Chandler, Lex Barker, George Nader), a kind of American *The Cruel Sea* about a ship and the men who serve her; and *Written On The Wind*, a Texas melodrama which earns Dorothy Malone a supporting actress Oscar for her nymphomaniac sister of multi-millionaire Robert Stack. Rock Hudson and Lauren Bacall are also along for the ride.

Esther Williams, free from her contract at MGM, ventures into straight drama in *The Unguarded Moment*. She plays a high school teacher who is almost raped by one of her students. The moral seems to be: 'Stay at MGM. . . and stay wet!'

1957 Another Universal 'horror-king', James Whale, who retired from film-making in the late thirties, leaves the scene. The director of such classics as *Frankenstein, The Old Dark House, The Invisible Man* and *Bride Of Frankenstein*, he is found drowned in the swimming pool of his Hollywood home. Some mystery surrounds his death. He was seventy.

Lon Chaney, an actor Whale never had the opportunity to direct, is admirably recreated by James Cagney in the stolid biography *Man Of A Thousand Faces*.

The best Universal film of the year is Jack Arnold's *The Incredible Shrinking Man*, an 'effects of radiation' piece of science-fiction about a young man who is infected by a radioactive cloud and diminishes at the rate of an inch a week until he is no larger than an atom. The highlights: when the miniature hero has to escape from a giant sized cat and fights to the death with a huge spider.

James Stewart and Audie Murphy are unlikely *brothers*

in *Night Passage*; spunky Debbie Reynolds appears in *Tammy And The Bachelor*; Errol Flynn is in *Istanbul*; Tony Curtis rises from slum boy to big-time gambler in *Mister Cory*; and Parker Fenelly is the new Pa Kettle in *The Kettles On Old MacDonald's Farm*, but the film is the last in the series.

Rock Hudson is voted number one moneymaking male star in the Motion Picture Herald's annual poll. His 1957 con-tribution: *The Tarnished Angels*, Douglas Sirk's version of William Faulkner's novel 'Pylon'.

Sirk also remakes *When Tomorrow Comes* as *Interlude* with librarian June Allyson falling for married concert pianist Rossano Brazzi. June Allyson stars too in another remake, *My Man Godfrey*. David Niven replaces William Powell which is plausible. Allyson replaces Carole Lombard which is not. The best thing about the movie is its advertising tag line: 'She wanted her breakfast in bed — but not alone!'

1958 "Darling you're a mess. You should lay off the candy bars," says Marlene Dietrich to a grossly overweight Orson Welles in *Touch Of Evil*. Overweight or not, the actor-director produces his best movie since *The Magnificent Ambersons*; a bizarre thriller with Charlton Heston and Janet Leigh as victims of corruption and intrigue in a small Mexican border town.

Sirk films the story of a romance amid the death and destruction of World War II in Erich Maria Remarque's *A Time To Love And A Time To Die*. Despite its expensive budget, the movie fails to do for World War II what *All Quiet On The Western Front* (by the same author) did for World War I.

Skipper Rock Hudson is saddled with a boat-load of awkward passengers in Ernest Gann's *Twilight For The Gods*; Hedy Lamarr is, appropriately enough, a beautiful movie star in *The Female Animal*; Audie Murphy is still on the track of the baddies in *Ride A Crooked Trail*; Debbie Reynolds features in the Blake Edwards comedy *This Happy Feeling*; Lana Turner takes pilot Jeff Chandler in *The Lady Takes A Flyer*.

The science-fiction/monster cycle comes to a suitably grisly end with *Monster On The Campus* in which a college professor has the blood of an ancient fish injected into his bloodstream. The result? A rampaging monster, naturally.

1959 As MCA buy Universal for 11,250,000 dollars, Blake

Edwards' *Operation Petticoat*, a World War II submarine comedy with Cary Grant and Tony Curtis becomes the studio's top financial hit of all time with a take of nine-and-a-half million dollars.

Pillow Talk, another comedy, with Rock Hudson and Doris Day, is also a smash with seven-and-a-half million. The story of a playboy songwriter who shares the same telephone line with an attractive interior decorator, it is the first in a long series of glossy comedies that Universal are to produce in the next five or six years. Doris Day is nominated for an Oscar; so too is Thelma Ritter for her inebriated maid.

Douglas Sirk, who has done for Universal in the 50s what John Stahl did for the studio in the 30s, makes his last film, *Imitation Of Life*, a remake of Stahl's 1934 movie with Claudette Colbert. Lana Turner is emotional in the Colbert role, the racial element is played down, the Technicolor production values played up!

Rock Hudson is again voted number one moneymaking star and features in Henry King's *This Earth Is Mine*, a family soap opera set in the California vineyards of the 30s. Jean Simmons, Claude Rains and Dorothy McGuire co-star; Audie Murphy finds there's *No Name On The Bullet*; James Cagney is a waterfront union racketeer in *Never Steal Anything Small*.

Another Universal favourite passes on. Lou Costello, the chubby half of the famous comedy team, dies of a heart attack in Los Angeles, aged fifty-two.

1960 *Operation Petticoat's* box-office record is soon swept away by the studio's new all-time champ, the three-and-a-quarter hour spectacular *Spartacus*. The gross: fourteen-and-a-half million dollars. With a twelve million dollar budget, it is the most expensive film ever made by Universal. The story of a slave who forms his own army and challenges the might of the Roman Empire, it stars Kirk Douglas, Jean Simmons, Laurence Olivier, Tony Curtis, Charles Laughton and Peter Ustinov and is directed by Stanley Kubrick.

It gets among the Oscars at Academy Award time, winning four, including a supporting actor award to Peter Ustinov and a cinematography Oscar to long-serving Universal cameraman Russell Metty.

Doris Day, after being eventually seduced via the telephone the previous year, is now sent almost mad as whining threats of murder start coming over the line in Ross Hunter's elegant thriller *Midnight Lace*. The setting: a fog-infested London. The culprit: Miss Day's business tycoon husband Rex Harrison. The hero: John Gavin, who stoically provides the sanity that Doris is quickly losing.

Portrait In Black is another Ross Hunter production. As the title suggests, it's glossy but grim. Scheming Lana Turner murders not once but three times. Wealthy husband Lloyd Nolan, suspicious lawyer Richard Basehart and lover Anthony Quinn all perish at her lovely hands.

Hudson retains his position as number one moneymaker but it's Cary Grant, Bob Mitchum, Jean Simmons and Deborah Kerr who provide the year's most amusing moments in Stanley Donen's elegant drawing room comedy *The Grass Is Greener*.

1961 Rock Hudson makes it a hat-trick as the world's most popular movie star and proves his worth by appearing in two of the most engaging comedies of the year: *Come September* with Gina Lollobrigida and *Lover Come Back* in which he's reunited with pert Doris Day. He's a smug advertising tycoon with all the contacts, she's a competitor. Confusion, not helped by a meddling Tony Randall, inevitably follows.

Ross Hunter revives yet another soap opera, *Back Street*, which Universal films on this occasion for the third time, with Susan Hayward; Audie Murphy is in a minor western, *Posse From Hell*; Rock Hudson and Kirk Douglas are in a major one, *The Last Sunset*; Richard Widmark is behind the Iron Curtain in *The Secret Ways*; and in *The Outsider* Tony Curtis is the Pima Indian Ira Hamilton Hayes, who was a hero at Iwo Jima.

Sandra Dee takes over from Debbie Reynolds in *Tammy Tell Me True* but the happiest gal around is Nancy Kwan who sings 'I Enjoy Being A Girl' in Ross Hunter's lavish screen version of the Rodgers and Hammerstein musical *Flower Drum Song*.

Jeff Chandler, popular Universal star for several years, dies of blood poisoning contracted in hospital after spinal surgery. He was 42. The silver-haired star appeared in more than twenty-five movies, both as the good guy and the bad guy. Among his pictures: *The Battle Of Apache Pass* (as Cochise), *Sign Of The Pagan, Foxfire, Female On The Beach, The Spoilers* and *Away All Boats*.

1962 Gregory Peck wins a long-deserved Oscar for his portrait of Atticus Finch, a lawyer and widower bringing up two children in the Depression South of the 30s. The film is *To Kill A Mockingbird*, the director Robert Mulligan, the author of the original novel Harper Lee. Rarely has a time and sense of period been so sensitively caught.

Peck is also a lawyer in *Cape Fear* but this time he has much more than the Depression to deal with. Wandering lazily into town is sexual psychopath Robert Mitchum. On his mind just one thing. Revenge on the man (Peck) who has sent him to jail eight years earlier. A nasty study in sadism, in many ways akin to a modern dress *High Noon*.

The modern West, in fact, is represented by *Lonely Are The Brave* with Kirk Douglas as the last of the cowboys trying and failing to come to terms with the modern way of life; the old West is portrayed in *Six Black Horses* with Audie Murphy and Dan Duryea; and although it sounds like a western, *Forty Pounds Of Trouble* turns out to be a comedy with gambling casino manager Tony Curtis being forced to take care of a little girl.

Doris Day, after rejecting and then accepting the advances of Rock Hudson in two movies, does the same to Cary Grant in *That Touch Of Mink* but keeps coming out in spots before she finally succumbs. Grant is a handsome tycoon who takes his lady victims to Bermuda, Miss Day an honest working girl and Gig Young, Grant's associate who keeps getting slaps instead of snacks from the automat lunchbar.

The year's most intense performance? Montgomery Clift as *Freud*, the Viennese doctor who founded psychoanalysis.

1963 It's the year of Alfred Hitchcock's return to the studio. '*The Bird's* Is Coming' say the ads. It sounds wrong. But there's nothing wrong with the movie, as thousands of birds invade the community of a small Californian coastal town. Rod Taylor and Tippi Hedren star. Or do they? The birds themselves have the best parts. Says the studio publicity: "There are 3,200 of them, all especially trained by Hitchcock for the picture!"

Doris Day and James Garner star in *The Thrill Of It All*. He's a genial gynaecologist. She's his wife who becomes the rage of the country after appearing in a series of TV commercials for 'Happy Soap.' Perhaps it's best identified as being the movie in which Garner drives his car into a garden swimming pool which wasn't there when he left for the office in the morning.

Very Hitchcockian in theme and the biggest hit of the year is Donen's *Charade*, a light-hearted thriller set in Paris with Audrey Hepburn as the wide-eyed bewildered heroine, Walter Matthau as the heavy (he 'gets his' by plunging to his death through a stage trapdoor) and Cary Grant as the mysterious hero. 'Cary Grant as Alexander Dyle or Peter Joshua or Adam Canfield or Bryan Cruickshank' say the credits. It doesn't really matter. Hepburn gets him in the end.

Kirk Douglas almost murders his way to a family fortune, via a variety of different disguises, in *The List Of Adrian Messenger*; Rock Hudson and Rod Taylor are in the Strategic Air Command in *A Gathering Of Eagles*; Gregory Peck is at work on neuro-psychiatry in *Captain Newman, M.D*; Brando is an ambassador to Asia in *The Ugly American.*

The Audie Murphy western is *Showdown*; Sandra Dee pops up pertily again with Peter Fonda in *Tammy And The Doctor.*

1964 Comedy dominates especially when Rock Hudson's around. In *Strange Bedfellows* he has a constant battle with highly strung Italian wife Gina Lollobrigida; in Howard Hawks' *Man's Favourite Sport?* he's a bogus fishing expert forced to enter a major fishing competition; and in *Send Me No Flowers*, the best of the three, he's teamed again with his most perfect co-star Doris Day. He's a hypochondriac husband who believes he is dying, she's his exasperated wife for whom he's anxious to find a new husband and Tony Randall is the fussy neighbour next door who compiles, in advance, Hudson's eulogy.

Cary Grant in *Father Goose*, is a beachcomber whose idyllic life on a South Seas island in World War II is shattered by the arrival of French girl Leslie Caron and seven children. Also contributing to the comedy are competing gigolos Marlon Brando and David Niven in *Bedtime Story.*

Hitchcock's movie is *Marnie*, the one for which he wanted Grace Kelly to come out of retirement. Instead Tippi Hedren stars as a kleptomaniac terrified of the colour red. Marriage to Sean Connery doesn't help.

Universal organise for the first time the famous public tours around the studio but a link with the old is severed with the death of Percy Kilbride who starred as Pa Kettle in eight movies with Marjorie Main. He dies of a brain injury sustained through a car accident. He was seventy-six.

1965 The big commercial hit is *Shenandoah* with widowed farmer James Stewart trying desperately to keep his family out of the Civil War. A moving story, directed by Andrew V. McLaglen, it is reminiscent of John Ford at his best. It earns Universal 8 million dollars.

Gregory Peck stars in Dmytryk's expert 40s-type urban thriller, *Mirage*, as a man who suspects he has amnesia and finds himself involved in murder; Charlton Heston is back in 11th century France in Schaffner's *The War Lord*; and Ann-Margret is one of the main reasons *Bus Riley's Back In Town*.

Comedy is taken care of by James Garner and Dick Van Dyke in *The Art Of Love* (the latter faking suicide so that his paintings sell well); Sandra Dee, Bobby Darin and Donald O'Connor in *That Funny Feeling*; and Rock Hudson who is paid by Charles Boyer to pursue his spinster daughter, psychologist Leslie Caron, in *A Very Special Favour*.

1966 Alfred Hitchcock is below form in his cold war story thriller *Torn Curtain*. It's the movie which has Julie Andrews in bed with Paul Newman (no fireworks) and one of the director's most grisly sequences, the prolonged murder — butcher's knife, shovel, oven gas — of an East German agent in a remote farm house.

Arabesque with Gregory Peck showing bewilderment, Sophia Loren beauty and Alan Badel acid treachery is a more likeable and fast-moving thriller; so too is *Gambit* with inadequate crook Michael Caine and Eurasian Shirley MacLaine set on stealing a valuable art treasure.

Director François Truffaut burns books in a version of Bradbury's futuristic tale *Fahrenheit 451*; Brando makes a rare venture West as he chases a stolen horse into Mexico in *The Appaloosa*; Audie Murphy, needless to say, is still in God's own country in *Gunpoint*; so too are James Stewart and Maureen O'Hara in *The Rare Breed* and Dean Martin and Alain Delon in *Texas Across The River*.

Lana Turner is the latest *Madame X* in yet another lavish Ross Hunter production. It's the Alexandre Brisson story of a lawyer who defends a woman of murder unaware that she's his long believed dead mother. Keir Dullea does his best for his mom, Turner suffers terribly.

1967 The Ross Hunter/George Roy Hill musical *Thoroughly Modern Millie* is the new box-office champ. The madcap 20s musical grosses 16 million dollars, more than any Universal film to date. Julie Andrews is a gold-digging secretary in love with her boss; Mary Tyler Moore her innocent 'pal'; Beatrice Lillie a white slave trader and Carol Channing ('Jazz Baby') a socialite. It's screwy but fun.

Chaplin directs his last film, *A Countess From Hong Kong* with Brando as an American diplomat and Sophia Loren a beautiful stowaway together on board an ocean liner. The film is a flop, the theme song 'This Is My Song' a smash.

Rosalind Russell is *Rosie*, an eccentric widow whose daughters are trying to get their hands on her fortune by having her declared insane; Debbie Watson is the new Tammy in *Tammy And The Millionaire*; Simone Signoret, James Caan and Katharine Ross play a deadly round of murderous *Games*; and *The War Wagon* with John Wayne and Kirk Douglas and *Rough Night In Jericho* with Dean Martin, George Peppard and Jean Simmons are the top westerns.

The most famous Sherlock Holmes of them all, Basil Rathbone, dies from a heart attack in New York on July 21. He was seventy-five and played the great detective on fourteen occasions.

1968 Director Don Siegel provides two class urban thrillers, *Madigan* and *Coogan's Bluff*.

Both deal with tough cops, the former with a dedicated but ruthless policeman (Richard Widmark) whose daily life, all 24 hours of it, is devoted to cleaning up New York; the latter with a modern Arizona lawman (Clint Eastwood) who uses any methods to capture a prisoner he has let escape into the city streets. Lee J. Cobb watches his unconventional antics with weary resignation: "Yeah, I know, a man's gotta do what a man's gotta do," he comments from time to time.

Doris Day, her popularity at last on the wane, is a Wyoming widow in *The Ballad Of Josie*; Vanessa Redgrave is the famous dancer Isadora Duncan in *Isadora*; Paul Newman goes for laughs with only partial success in the POW comedy *The Secret War Of Harry Frigg*; Taylor and Burton are together in *Boom!*, a version of Tennessee Williams' story 'Man, Bring This Up Road' and his play 'The Milk Train Doesn't Stop Here Anymore.'

Death claims famous Universal make-up man Jack Pierce (aged seventy-nine) and character actor Dan Duryea, a Universal regular for more than twenty years. Duryea made 24 films for Universal, among them *Lady On A Train, Scarlet Street, Criss Cross, Winchester 73* and *Thunder Bay*. He dies of cancer in Los Angeles, aged sixty-one.

1969 Boris Karloff dies in England, aged eighty-one. Since his memorable performance as the Frankenstein monster in 1931 he made more than eighty movies, twenty of them at Universal. Among his Universal roles: *The Old Dark House, The Mummy, The Black Cat, The Raven, The Invisible Ray, Bride Of Frankenstein, House Of Frankenstein, Son Of Frankenstein* and *The Strange Door*. One of the most modest of men, he was quoted as saying, "You could heave a brick out of the window and hit ten actors who could play my parts. I just happened to be on the right corner at the right time."

Hitchcock films Leon Uris' complex novel *Topaz* about Russian agents infiltrating high government positions in France; John Wayne is a Texas oilfighter in *Hellfighters*; Sidney Poitier a hunted criminal in *The Lost Man*, an updated version of Carol Reed's classic *Odd Man Out*; Robert Redford a sheriff hunting down a young Paiute Indian in Polonsky's *Tell Them Willie Boy Is Here*; and Elvis Presley, making the trip to Universal from Paramount and Metro, is a doctor involved with three nuns in *Change Of Habit!*

Paul Newman and Robert Wagner hit the motor racing circuit in *Winning*, the studio's biggest financial hit; *Anne Of The Thousand Days* with Richard Burton as Henry VIII and Genevieve Bujold as Anne Boleyn is the most lavish Universal film of the year; Bob Fosse's *Sweet Charity*, with Shirley MacLaine as the ever hopeful taxi dancer, the most vigorous.

1970 Forty-five-and-a-half million dollars! That's the staggering box-office take of *Airport* which financially far outstrips any other movie in Universal's history.

Airport boss Burt Lancaster battles against a blizzard to keep his runways open, cigar-chomping George Kennedy tries to clear a blocked plane, married pilot Dean Martin loves air hostess Jacqueline Bisset, Helen Hayes stows away — and wins an Oscar — and mad bomber Van Heflin tries to blow everyone to smithereens.

Western drifter Clint Eastwood joins up with liquor drinking 'nun' Shirley MacLaine in Mexico in *Two Mules For Sister Sara*; Burt Reynolds is on a New Guinea safari in *Skullduggery*; a mighty computer designed to serve mankind finishes up dominating the world in *The Forbin Project*; and bored New York housewife-mother Carrie Snodgrass finds a much needed release through an affair in *Diary Of A Mad Housewife*.

1971 Audie Murphy, Universal's most reliable cowboy star of the post-war period, dies in a plane crash on May 21. He was forty-six. A Texas farm boy who became the most decorated American soldier of World War II, he won every US medal there was to win during his two years in combat, 24 all told including the Congressional Medal Of Honour. He was said to have killed, wounded or captured 240 Germans and survived wounds incurred by a mortar shell bursting beneath his feet, a series of perforations from an artillery shell and a sniper's bullet in the hip.

When he became a movie star in 1948 he found life in Hollywood much less exciting. He once said, "I made the same western about thirty times. Only the horses were changed."

Universal films of the year: *The Andromeda Strain* (the top moneymaker) about a satellite that returns to Earth and releases a deadly microbe that threatens the safety of the world; *Mary, Queen Of Scots* in which Vanessa Redgrave fights Glenda Jackson's Elizabeth for the throne of England; *The Hired Hand* with Peter Fonda; *Duel* with car driver Dennis Weaver involved in a fight to the death with a huge truck that pursues him along the highways; and *The Beguiled* with Clint Eastwood as a wounded Union soldier seeking peaceful refuge in a Louisiana girls' school and getting more than he bargained for.

Eastwood also makes his debut as a director with *Play Misty For Me*. He features as a disc jockey who whispers seductive nothings over the air only to find his act rebounding on him when a homicidal listener begins to threaten his very existence. Jessica Walter is the *femme fatale*, director Don Siegel has a guest part as a barman.

1972 Hitchcock returns to England for *Frenzy* and weaves an intriguing net around the activities of 'Necktie Murderer' Barry Foster; Eastwood is in turn-of-the-century New Mexico in *Joe Kidd*; Indian scout Burt Lancaster and the cavalry are up against the Apaches in *Ulzana's Raid*; and Cliff Robertson and Robert Duvall are involved in *The Great Northfield Minnesota Raid*, one of the West's most famous bank robberies and the one that spelt the beginning of the end for the James gang. Cliff Robertson is Cole Younger, Duvall is Jesse James.

Science-fiction is represented by *Silent Running* and *Slaughterhouse-Five*; Walter Matthau and Carol Burnett make *Pete 'n' Tillie* the top box-office attraction.

1973 *The Sting* becomes the first Universal film to win the Best Picture Academy Award since *All Quiet On The Western Front* forty-three years earlier. The story of two con men, Paul Newman and Robert Redford, who set out to swindle mobster Robert Shaw, it wins seven Oscars in all. It chalks up two studio records — the most Oscars for a single film — and the most money, 72 million dollars.

Director George Lucas recaptures the American teenage scene of the early 60s in *American Graffiti*; Edward Fox is the would-be assassin of General De Gaulle in Zinnemann's *The Day Of The Jackal*; Ted Neely is *Jesus Christ, Superstar*; and Clint Eastwood is the *High Plains Drifter*.

Eastwood directs his second feature, *Breezy*, a tender romance between a middle-aged man (William Holden) and a young girl (Kay Lenz); in *Charley Varrick* Walter Matthau pulls a bank heist only to find the loot belongs to the Mafia; and in *SSSSSSSSS* Strother Martin turns men into snakes.

In the old days Martin's part is the kind that would have been played by Lon Chaney Jr. who passes away on July 12, aged sixty-three. Never the star his father was, he nonetheless featured regularly in the horror *genre* and of his 160-plus films nearly forty were made at Universal. His most famous role was probably Kharis, The Mummy which he played on several occasions. Like his father he dies from cancer of the throat.

1974 Sensurround, a process in which cinema seats rattle and sound bursts the eardrums, is introduced in Mark Robson's *Earthquake*, an all-star movie about a huge tremor which strikes the city of Los Angeles. Charlton Heston, Ava Gardner, Lorne Greene, George Kennedy and Genevieve Bujold do their best to survive.

A 747 jet liner collides with a private plane in *Airport 75*. Ever-handy Charlton Heston saves the day; Michael Caine is mixed up in espionage in *The Black Windmill*; and escaped prisoners Goldie Hawn and William Atherton try to regain custody of their adopted baby in Steven Spielberg's *Sugarland Express*.

Bud Abbott, the other half of the Abbott and Costello team, dies aged seventy-nine; Billy Wilder films one of the best remakes of recent times, *The Front Page*, with Walter Matthau and Jack Lemmon.

Wilder favours the material of the past. He comments on modern audiences: "They don't want to see a picture unless Peter Fonda is running over a dozen people or unless Clint Eastwood has got a machine gun bigger than 140 penises."

1975 *Jaws*, the story of a monster shark which creates a reign of terror along the beaches of a Long Island holiday resort, becomes the biggest moneymaker of all time, taking over from *The Godfather* which has held the record for three years. *Jaws* becomes the all-time champion on September 5.

During the making of the movie, director Steven Spielberg uses three mechanical sharks, all nicknamed 'Bruce.' One is entirely open on the left side for right hand camera shots, one on the right side for left hand shots and one is solid and complete. The latter model weighs 2000 lbs.

Universal also film *The Great Waldo Pepper* with Robert Redford as a World War I flying ace who becomes a barnstorming 20s stunt flyer; *The Eiger Sanction* with Clint Eastwood involved with spies and mountain climbing in Switzerland, and *Rooster Coburn* in which John Wayne repeats his famous Oscar winning role and teams with preacher's daughter Katharine Hepburn.

Another big one: *The Hindenburg*, an account of the events leading up to the crash of the famous German dirigible at Lakehurst, New Jersey, on May 6, 1937. The dirigible burned itself out in just 34 seconds when it crashed. In Hollywood's version the destruction takes ten minutes!

Marjorie Main (Ma Kettle in ten movies, eight of them with Percy Kilbride) dies aged eighty-five. Miss Main who mothered fifteen children in the Kettle films but in real life was childless, often recalled the character with affection: "I loved that role," she used to say. "I always thought of Ma Kettle as a real person. Someone to drive out into the country to see. Ma Kettle was a grand woman.''

1976 *Midway*, the story of the famous 1942 air and sea battle between the Americans and the Japanese off Midway Island in the Pacific, is the financial hit of the year. Charlton Heston is there again to help out when things get rough.

Hitchcock's *Family Plot* is one of his best. Medium Barbara Harris and cab driver boyfriend Bruce Dern search for the missing heir to a fortune; Rod Steiger is impressive as W. C. Fields in Arthur Hiller's otherwise inadequate bio-pic *W. C. Fields And Me*; James Brolin and Jill Clayburgh are unimpressive in the equally inadequate *Gable And Lombard*.

Swashbuckling gets a brief fling in *The Scarlet Buccaneer*; Heston and Cassavettes prise out a killer hidden in a packed football stadium in the gripping *Two Minute Warning*.

1977 Airport time again, this time *Airport 77* and a sunken airliner to deal with. Jack Lemmon skippers both in the air and underwater.

Gregory Peck is *MacArthur*; Paul Newman a fading ice hockey star in the foul-mouthed *Slap Shot*; and Michael Winner turns away from the urban violence that has preoccupied him for so long to dwell on horror of the supernatural kind. His movie is *The Sentinel*. His stars: Chris Sarandon, Cristina Raines, Martin Balsam, John Carradine, Ava Gardner.

Smokey And The Bandit with Burt Reynolds is the year's biggest hit; *The Seven-Per-Cent Solution* with Nicol Williamson as Sherlock Holmes and Robert Duvall as Dr. Watson the biggest disappointment.

1978 The Broadway hit *The Wiz*, a musical version of *The Wizard Of Oz* with Diana Ross as Dorothy is filmed by Sidney Lumet; less musical but still in the swim of things is another great ocean shark in *Jaws II*; Charlton Heston is also underwater as the commander of a nuclear submarine trapped 1500 ft below the surface in *Gray Lady Down*.

America's new young stars figure prominently in the studio line-up: Sylvester Stallone directs and stars in *Paradise Alley*, a drama of Hell's kitchen (where Stallone was raised) the most depressed area of New York in the late 40s; Henry Winkler is a disturbed war veteran in

Heroes; Oscar winner Richard Dreyfuss an unsuccessful private-eye in the mystery-comedy *The Big Fix*.

David Carradine and Brenda Vaccaro feature in *Moonbeam Rider*, the story of a motorcycle race from St. Louis to San Francisco just after World War I; Alan Alda and Ellen Burstyn in one of Broadway's comedy hits *Same Time Next Year*; and Anthony Quinn and Jacqueline Bisset in *The Greek Tycoon*.

PARAMOUNT

Paramount

It was a clear, sunny day when five men clambered eagerly off the train at Flagstaff, Arizona. The year was 1913, the month December, the expectations of the quintet high.

Anyone who might possibly have been waiting on the station on that particular day would have stared in amazement at the bewildered expressions that crossed the mens' faces as they looked slowly about them. Bewilderment gave way to disbelief. *This* was Arizona?

The five men were film makers. They had come to make their first movie, a western set in Wyoming. There was only one snag and they had just discovered it. Arizona didn't look anything like Wyoming.

If Cecil B. DeMille and his co-director Oscar Apfel had taken time to glance out of the window of their speeding train they would have realised it much sooner. As it was, they were much too occupied scribbling in pencil the first draft of their screenplay for *The Squaw Man*. Finding a fast typist in Flagstaff who could type out their 'script' was uppermost in their minds, not the possibility that the terrain might prove unsuitable.

As the train steamed motionless in the station their hearts sank. It looked like the end of the line before they had even got started. Already, the Jesse Lasky Feature Play Company looked a non-starter. Money was tight. The four partners of the company — Lasky, DeMille, Sam Goldfish (later Goldwyn) and Arthur Friend — had but 20,000 dollars on which to operate. They couldn't afford to waste one cent. It looked like a return trip to New York.

It didn't occur to them to stay where they were and change the locale of the story to Arizona. The thought never crossed their minds. They were in a complete state of shock.

It was DeMille who snapped out of it. As the whistle blew and the conductor cried ''all aboard'', he urged the other artists, Apfel, actor Dustin Farnum, his dresser Fred Kley and cameraman Alfred Gandolfi — back onto the train and settled them down in their seats. They looked at him, aghast. They were now heading even further away from New York. It seemed like more money down the drain.

But DeMille had remembered that Los Angeles, resting snugly in the hills amid orange groves, lay at the end of the line and people had been making the odd film there for some years. Rather than give up and return to New York he was determined to gamble on the right facilities being found in Los Angeles.

That split-second decision 'made' the Lasky company. Within days of arriving in Hollywood DeMille cabled, "We have rented a barn for two hundred dollars a month. . ." They were in business after all.

The barn, an old L-shaped construction off Selmar and Vine Streets, was their first studio. It was where DeMille cried "action" for the first time and where he shot and cut *The Squaw Man* in eighteen days. He brought the film in for 15,000 dollars. By the time it had finished its release it had grossed nearly a quarter of a million.

Earlier that same year another key event in the history of Paramount studios took place. Only this time there was no panic, excitement or improvisation attached to the making of a first movie. Instead, a methodical and civilised conversation in a New York restaurant.

The place was Delmonico's. It was lunchtime and the restaurant was packed to capacity, bustling with waiters and buzzing with small talk. At a corner table sat a pretty young woman with an innocent face and large blue eyes, her fair hair done up in braids about her head. Her name was Mary Pickford. Sitting closely alongside her was her mother.

They were talking in earnest to a small, quiet forty year old film executive, Adolph Zukor. Within a few minutes they would make a deal. Mary, barely twenty, would sign a contract worth 500 dollars a week and take the first steps to becoming the most successful woman star in the history of silent pictures. She would appear for Zukor in films made by his recently formed Famous Players Company which had begun filming 'Famous Players In Famous Plays', but which was now branching out into new territory.

Hungarian-born Zukor, a former furrier, had his eyes set on the big time. Shrewd, unobtrusive and more astute about money than any other Hollywood mogul, he sensed that the little girl star Mary Pickford, already successful, would become an even greater star. He was right. Shortly after that historic day at Delmonico's, Mary was already at work for Zukor and on her way to achieving not only the title 'the world's most famous actress', but also the affectionate label 'everybody's sweetheart'.

The filming in the barn on Selmar Avenue and the high finance of Delmonico's had no connection in 1913. Both the Lasky and Zukor companies were separate units. Neither had any link with the other. But just a year later they were unexpectedly brought together by a man named W. W. Hodkinson who had formed a new nation-wide distributing organization called Paramount Pictures Corporation.

Hodkinson wanted product. He put forward the suggestion that Zukor, with fifty films, and Lasky with thirty, provide him with the bulk of the 104 pictures he needed per year. Zukor jumped at the idea. He had a major star under contract and a well-oiled company to provide the product. The Lasky Company was a little taken aback. It was just a few months since that first hesitant train ride and already they were being asked to more than double their yearly output and really get down to work. They didn't have a Pickford but if things went according to plan it wouldn't be long before stars of their own would begin to emerge. It was too good an opportunity to miss. They too agreed.

Hodkinson wasn't a major figure in the silent cinema, but he was responsible for giving Paramount both its name and its trademark.

The name came about when, during the setting up of his distributing organization, he passed, on the way to a New York conference, a building called the Paramount apartments. The symbol emerged during that same conference when he doodled on his desk blotter and let his mind wander for a moment back to the Wasatch Range, one of the scenic glories of Utah and the place where he had got his start. The doodle grew more recognizable until it appeared sharp and crystal clear, a tall, towering snow-capped mountain.

Perhaps Hodkinson day-dreamed too much. In any case he didn't last long. In 1916, with both Famous Players and the Jesse Lasky Company flourishing under the distribution deal, the two organizations decided they would be in an even stronger position if they merged. The new company, Famous Players-Lasky was formed on July 19. Zukor was made president, Lasky vice president, Goldwyn chairman and DeMille director general.

Zukor, with his eyes on overall control, also began buying Paramount stock, so that one day, when Hodkinson called to order a routine stockholders' meeting, he found himself being promptly voted out of office and a Zukor nominee voted in.

Paramount — Zukor expressed a liking for the name — had been born.

There was no discernible style to the early Paramount Films. Like all pioneer companies the studio tried its hand at anything that might make money — westerns, comedies, epics, classics, outdoor adventures, lacing its films whenever possible with such sexual trimmings as the censorship code would allow.

The big difference between Paramount and the other studios of the period, including Fox, was that it had size and panache. It operated in a big way. It drew big stars and name directors and it made money. The mountain peak, an ideal trademark as it turned out, came to represent 'peak achievement'.

Paramount was lucky in having Mary Pickford as its insurance against failure of other product. Everything she did made money. She couldn't put a dainty foot or an innocent smile wrong. And Zukor knew just how to keep her — by giving her more money. That meeting in Delmonico's when he and Mary vied over the pros and cons of her 500 dollar-a-week contract was the first of many. Mary was never satisfied. She was an actress first, a businesswoman a close second. She knew her worth. When she demanded an increase Zukor, after a bit of lighthearted stonewalling, gave way. They played the game regularly.

Zukor put her through half-a-dozen films a year. So popular were her pictures that he was able to blackmail exhibitors into booking his more expensive productions, thus giving a blanket coverage to all his films. More than any other pictures, the Pickford movies made Zukor — and Paramount — all powerful in Hollywood. The actress's reward was a salary that grew larger every year — 500 dollars a week in 1913, 1000 in 1914, 2000 in 1915. . .

Six years after that meeting at Delmonico's Zukor and Pickford negotiated for the last time. Again the discussion was about money, but this time the figure was 750,000 dollars, the amount First National had just offered Pickford for a three picture deal. They had also offered total artistic control, something Mary had had long been striving for.

Mary had banked once more on Zukor giving way, but this time the stonewalling was for real. Zukor wouldn't up the figure and Mary Pickford's days at Paramount were over.

There were two main reasons for Zukor's refusal. One was that the industry, worried that stars' salaries were getting out of control, was determined to cut back and prove that the studios, and not the stars, were running the business. The other was that, since Famous Players and Lasky had combined three years earlier, new stars had emerged to rival Pickford — handsome young Wallace Reid, opera star Geraldine Farrar and, most important of all, Gloria Swanson who in 1919 was already soaring to superstardom.

By 1920 Zukor was in complete command at Paramount. At the beginning of the merger it was one for all and all for one.

The one, it soon became apparent, was Zukor. The weaker Lasky was soon under his control. DeMille, a film-maker first, a company man second, managed to keep out of his way, at least for a time. Goldwyn who, in 1917 was chairman of the board of directors, found Zukor insufferable.

Zukor was cool, calm, calculating, Goldwyn exactly the opposite. A salesman by nature – he had worked himself into the ground selling Lasky movies when the company was first formed in 1913 – he liked to operate in a continual state of frenzy, his brash breezy methods disturbing the methodical caution of Zukor who liked to work to a more detailed plan.

The two of them rowed continually, so much so that it was obvious to all concerned that it was only a matter of time before something, or rather someone, had to give. Zukor mulled over the problem for some time. Long nocturnal walks through New York helped him reach his decision. In the end he told vice president Lasky, "I'm sorry to have to tell you but Famous Players-Lasky is not large enough to hold Mr. Goldwyn and myself. You brought him into the company and I don't want to ask him to leave. But you'll have to choose between Mr. Goldwyn and me. I'm going to the country for the weekend and I'll await your decision there."

To no-one's surprise it was Goldwyn who went.

What might have happened if Goldwyn had been allowed to stay and have a hand in running Paramount is as intriguing a question as what might have happened had he gained control of United Artists in the late 30s. But Goldwyn and major studios were never to see eye-to-eye. Goldwyn was basically an independent. He was his own man and he remained so until his retirement from the business (at the age of seventy-seven) in 1959.

Meanwhile, DeMille continued 'in the field'. There were other directors working at Paramount at the time, many of whom were to become famous; men like Sam Wood, James Cruze, Maurice Tourneur. It was DeMille, however, who was responsible for just about every major film Paramount produced in those early years, quite an accomplishment considering that, before embarking on that train ride to Hollywood, he had literally no experience of directing a motion picture.

His entire knowledge of making a film had been gained through one day's visit to the old Edison studio in the Bronx. Goldwyn had arranged the visit. DeMille watched as the director and cameraman set up the camera and pointed it at the scene, enacted by the players in silent pantomime. Then he listened as the director cried, "Cut!" DeMille went back to Jesse and Sam and reported,

"If that's pictures, we can make the best pictures ever made."

In Hollywood, DeMille immediately attracted attention by his garb – a flannel shirt, well-tailored riding breeches and puttees, and high leather boots which later became a fashion of directors. This was inspired by his fear of snakes which still crawled in the gardens of his Hollywood home and by the need to support his weak heels. He also carried a revolver.

He pushed himself and his crew to the limits, learning all there was to learn about the technique of film-making. His subjects were many and varied. Between 1913 and 1920 he delivered thirty-eight movies to Paramount studios, among them westerns, melodramas, historical dramas, sex comedies. Yet even in those early days his love of the spectacular was becoming apparent. *Joan The Woman* with Geraldine Farrar as Joan of Arc had a cast of a thousand and *Male And Female*, a version of James Barrie's 'The Admirable Crichton' had, of all unlikely things, a flashback to ancient Babylon.

In the latter sequence Gloria Swanson (a DeMille favourite) played a stubborn Christian slave who refuses to give herself willingly to the Babylonian king. As a consequence she is thrown into a den of lions.

The scene demanded that a ferocious looking, but extremely well fed lion sneak up behind her bejewelled figure, crouch over her and, without warning, put a paw on her bare shoulder. The scene could not be faked or doubled. It had to be done by Miss Swanson. She uttered not a word of complaint and went ahead with the scene unaware that DeMille had a sharpshooter standing by with a gun off camera – just in case. "That's what's so wonderful about Gloria," said DeMille later, "She never even asked."

After it was all over Swanson came into his office shaking with a kind of delayed hysteria and saying she didn't think she could work the following day. DeMille opened a locked drawer and brought forth a box of jewellery on consignment from Los Angeles' best jeweller. He suggested she selected something to soothe her nerves. "I picked out a gold-mesh evening bag with an emerald clasp and immediately felt much better," she said. "I acquired my expensive tastes from Mr. DeMille."

If DeMille quickly showed a penchant for the spectacular, he was also not slow in bringing to the fore the other ingredient so vital to his movies – sex. Later in his career the formula 'spectacle plus sex plus religion' would become one of the surest ways of making money in Hollywood, especially with the name of DeMille attached. But in 1919 the sex part of the formula was only just beginning.

DeMille's silent sex comedies and melodramas were considered by many to be hypocritical. They allowed actors (and audiences) to indulge in the delights of marital disharmony, infidelity and seduction, often against the most opulent surroundings, then brought them up sharply in the final reel with a severe 'Thou shalt not' message. The fact that 'They had' in the previous seven or eight reels was irrelevant. As long as the sanctity of marriage was seen to triumph all was forgiven.

Gloria Swanson was a vital part of DeMille's 'sin and forget' confections. She appeared in six of his films, her elegant body clothed in the most extraordinary costume creations. With Gloria, glamour and seduction went hand in hand, the very costumes she wore suggesting intrigue and sophistication. "Make it sleeveless, backless, skirtless — in short go to the limit. I won't be dressed like anyone's aunt," she cries to a costumier in *Why Change Your Wife*?

Usually a wronged socialite she was a woman who vamped, but was not a vamp; a living demonstration that riches don't always bring happiness. DeMille used her sex appeal brilliantly, showing her in various stages of undress, deliberately calculated to excite an audience, and even on one occasion presenting her completely unclothed, discreetly of course, as she dipped into an ornate bath, a gimmick that was to become a DeMille trademark in the years ahead.

DeMille helped Swanson to stardom. She, in turn, allowed him to promote his 'wages of sex' themes to the full. Together they made a small fortune for the studio.

DeMille, like other big-name directors, had one major fault — extravagance. Although his name was synonymous with success it also gave the New York front office more than a few qualms on occasion. They weren't too happy, for instance, with his annoying habit of frequently raising the cost of his pictures by including scenes of ancient times when the story he had to tell was a contemporary one with contemporary values. Ostensibly DeMille's idea was to parallel the events of the day with those of historical times. If truth be known, it allowed him to indulge his taste for the lavish and exotic.

After *Male And Female* he did the same again with *Manslaughter*, a modern drama about a wealthy society girl on trial for a killing which included a flashback to decadent Roman times. When he came to *The Ten Commandments* in 1923, the spectacle 'took over' for the first time. The story was part modern, part biblical. The biblical section which included the parting of the Red Sea and the Exodus from Egypt cost a fortune.

During the filming of *The Ten Commandments* DeMille had

his first clash with Zukor. DeMille's respect for the little man was evident in that he always referred to him as 'Mr. Zukor', but the respect didn't last. The two clashed violently.

The first argument was over money. Worried by the continuing rise in *The Ten Commandments'* cost, Zukor wired DeMille from New York that he was concerned about the budget which at that time stood at over 700,000 dollars. He was having difficulty persuading the bankers that the expense was worthwhile. DeMille managed to placate him for a while, but the cost continued to rise, eventually hitting one million.

The final straw was a bill for 2,500 dollars which the director had paid for two superb black horses to pull Pharaoh's chariot. The New York office exploded. Horses could be bought for as little as 200 dollars in Hollywood. This was unnecessary extravagance.

Zukor threw in his hand. He wanted nothing more to do with the picture. The bankers were on his back and he was convinced *The Ten Commandments* would be a disaster. DeMille, furious, asked him if he would sell him the picture for a million dollars. Zukor agreed. But such was the speed with which DeMille raised his million that the New York bankers began to think again.

Zukor would have gone through with the sale had not one of the company's executives advised him not to sell what he hadn't seen. He viewed the picture and it remained at Paramount. The final production cost was one-and-a-half million, but the final gross, as audiences gasped at the magnificence of the parting of the Red Sea, more than four million.

DeMille had got his way and the picture was a hit, but it wasn't long before the two men were at loggerheads once more, again over production costs, and this time it was Zukor who triumphed with the result that DeMille, like Goldwyn before him, left the company.

DeMille's departure was only temporary, however, and in the thirties he would return to play an important role in the fortunes of the studio.

Meanwhile, in the twenties, Paramount boomed. Gloria Swanson, Rudolph Valentino, and Wallace Reid became the industry's top stars. Pictures like the epic western *The Covered Wagon, The Sheik, Blood And Sand, Beau Geste, Wings*, added enormously to the company's profits. Even with the emergence of the super studio, MGM, the studio held its own for a while.

Of the stars, Gloria Swanson in particular believed in and became part of the Hollywood everyone expected to read and hear about. In New York she leased an apartment on top of the

Park Chambers Hotel and bought a twelve-room house on a twenty-five acre estate. In Hollywood she splurged again and bought one of the six great houses of Hollywood, a twenty-four room mansion built by the razor magnate King Gillette.

The New York apartment was described by Hollywood publicists as a 100,000 dollar penthouse with a perfumed private elevator. In reality it was nothing of the kind. The penthouse was no more than servants' quarters remodelled by an architect friend and the private lift was the freight elevator at the rear of the hotel.

Swanson later talked fondly of all the razzamatazz. "The public didn't want the truth and I shouldn't have bothered giving it to them," she said. "In those days they wanted us to live like kings and queens. So we did — and why not? We were in love with life. We were making more money than we ever dreamed existed, and there was no reason to believe that it would ever stop."

Swanson made a fortune and spent it just as quickly. She was not a businesswoman like Pickford. She thought money was to be enjoyed. Her parties at her luxury Hollywood house were literally 'fabulous'.

"It would be impossible nowadays, but then I had eleven servants. You had to have that many to keep up such a place — a governess for my children, gardeners, cooks, butlers, upstairs maids and downstairs maids. The butlers were a problem. You'd have one for a year and then he would quit. Then you'd go to Rudolph Valentino's house and your former butler would open the door and say, 'Good Evening Miss Swanson.' The butlers moved from house to house, improving their salaries as they went.

"The parties we used to have. It was not uncommon to have seventy-five or a hundred people for a formal, sit-down dinner. But they weren't stuffy. We all knew each other, and we had fun. I once had a ju-jitsu exhibition after dinner and Ronald Colman and Dick Barthelmess insisted on trying it and they threw each other all around the living room. Mary Pickford and Doug Fairbanks gave smaller parties at 'Pickfair' and they were more formal."

But if the twenties were successful for Paramount they were also at times a little turgid. In three successive years the studio was affected by sensational headlines that had people debating the morals and wisdom of Hollywood and the people who lived there.

In 1921 Roscoe 'Fatty' Arbuckle, who had joined Paramount from Sennett, attended a party in a San Francisco hotel. It was a long party that went on for several days. A young starlet named Virginia Rappe was one of those attending. During the festivities she suddenly tore off all her clothes and collapsed. She was carried into the next door bedroom. The 266lb Arbuckle followed.

What happened next was never adequately proved. Some say that several women from the party accompanied Arbuckle and tried to revive the girl. Others say that he went in alone and began to indulge in sexual excesses of the most unsavoury kind. A soft drink bottle and a piece of jagged ice were both mentioned during the subsequent trials. Whatever happened, the girl finished up dead.

Certainly the public wanted Arbuckle guilty. An obese man in a hotel room with a naked starlet. The mind ran riot. The lips of an expectant public smacked with self-righteous anticipation.

Arbuckle had three trials with two hung juries. After the third he was acquitted. His wife stood by him through all three trials. But although the jury eventually found him innocent of all charges and came to the verdict that the young girl had died of peritonitis, Arbuckle's career was finished. The mud stuck. Zukor refused to finish negotiating the three million dollar contract he had been discussing when the scandal broke. Arbuckle himself was bankrupt, all his savings gone on the defence proceedings which had cost him 750,000 dollars. Only his old friend Buster Keaton gave him a job — as a director of small-scale comedies. Arbuckle used the pseudonym Will B. Good, but even that was discovered. Arbuckle declined into alcoholic obscurity and an early death, aged forty-six in 1933.

A year later the careers of two actresses were also ruined when Paramount director William Desmond Taylor was found shot dead in his Hollywood home. The actresses, Mary Miles Minter and Mabel Normand, had both been having affairs with Taylor, a strange mysterious man with a somewhat shadowy past. Minter was hoping shortly to announce her engagement to him and Normand had actually visited him the night before his death. Neither actress was accused of being involved in the murder, but suspicion inevitably lingered.

All kinds of theories were propounded, even the possibility that Taylor was mixed up in drug trafficking, but there were few clues to the murder and the Los Angeles police simply found themselves clutching at straws. The investigations slowly fizzled out and no-one ever discovered the truth about the murder of William Desmond Taylor whose death remains one of the greatest of all Hollywood mysteries.

If Zukor felt that the Arbuckle and Taylor cases were more than enough for any one studio to bear he was sadly mistaken.

In 1923 more headlines blazed across the Hollywood tabloids, this time about Paramount's top male star of the period, Wallace Reid. On this occasion it was not a scandal that made the news, but a tragedy.

Unknown to the general public Reid had been injured four years earlier when travelling on a specially chartered train to the High Sierras for the film *The Valley Of The Giants*. The train, packed with film people, came off the rails and Reid was struck on the head by falling debris as he struggled to free the women from the wreckage. He was one of the last to receive medical attention. A gash on the head quickly healed, but just a few days later he found himself troubled by blinding headaches that kept re-occuring. Equally painful was a sciatic nerve impingement at the base of his spine which had also been damaged.

On returning from location he spent three months in bed recuperating. To ease the pain and to enable him to continue acting the doctor gave him morphine. But when the time came for the morphine to be slowly withdrawn, the injections were carried on with the result that Reid became an addict.

When he tried to kick the habit he found it was too late. He drank heavily so that his colleagues would believe that alcoholism, and not addiction, was his problem. Somehow, despite the intense pain and personal anguish, he managed to keep on acting. For four years he remained Paramount's top male star, still handsome, still a fine actor, still at the top of his profession.

But his last four pictures made in 1922 revealed just how much the drugs and alcohol had taken toll of his system. In all the films he looked thin, tired, strained and in his last movie, *Thirty Days*, grostesquely ill.

Determined to cure himself once and for all he went into a sanitorium. Just before he was admitted he told Cecil B. DeMille, "I'll either come out cured or I won't come out at all." The latter proved sadly to be the case. The total withdrawal from morphine he experienced in the sanitorium completely changed his metabolism. On top of which he suffered a severe case of influenza. On January 18 he died, aged just thirty-one.

This time the public did not say with relish, "I told you so." They mourned.

By the time Paramount's golden aged arrived in the thirties the tragedies of Arbuckle, Taylor and Reid, and the movie hits of Swanson and Valentino already seemed to belong to the distant past. Suddenly, a studio that had always been a fore-runner in the business but never one to boast a particular style, blossomed into one of glittering sophistication, wit and elegance. It scurried away from the effects of the Depression and threw light where there was darkness, gaiety where there was despair.

Warners, as will later be seen, reflected the Depression and sought, through its gangster films and social dramas, to bring home the misery caused by economic chaos. Paramount deliberately distorted it. The cameras of Charles Lang and Victor Milner turned life into something that was exotic, erotic and full of luxury and fun. Escape was the key word. At Paramount in the thirties there were only a few wet streets and turned-up raincoats. Instead, there was sleekness, ultra-modern apartments, shimmering costumes, champagne permanently on ice, witty dialogue to accompany the cocktails and supreme elegance.

More often than not that elegance and sophistication would be found in films based in Paris, on the Riviera or in Spain. An imaginative sleight of hand by production designer Hans Dreier would turn the Paramount backlot into any clandestine corner of Europe or seamy back street in Shanghai, China or Morocco.

When asked whether he had been to Europe lately, ace Paramount director Ernst Lubitsch nodded, then added as an afterthought, "But you know, I think I prefer Paris, Paramount to Paris, France."

So did millions of others. They shut off the real world and ventured into the magical 'Cabinet Of Dr. Adolph Zukor' where a team of conjurers and illusionists, led by directors Lubitsch, Mamoulian, von Sternberg, Borzage and Leisen and writers Billy Wilder, Charles Brackett, Preston Sturges, operated with taste, skill and imagination.

Teamwork was the major factor in the success of Paramount in the thirties. Lubitsch imparted his deft sophisticated touches to the musical Ruritanian romances of Chevalier and MacDonald; Wilder, Brackett and Sturges wrote regularly for Leisen; Dietrich sulked mysteriously for von Sternberg; Gary Cooper found ideal directors in Hathaway and DeMille.

But of all the partnerships, the Marlene Dietrich/Josef von Sternberg combination was the most newsworthy.

Sternberg first directed Dietrich in Germany in 1930 in *The Blue Angel*. The story of an elderly college professor (Emil Jannings) who is entranced then completely destroyed by a heartless cabaret artist, it was a bitter, sad, finally tragic movie. It demanded a special kind of actress for the role of the cabaret singer, Lola Lola, and von Sternberg was positive he had found her with the then unknown Dietrich. Jannings was unhappy with his choice and argued against her for the part, but von Sternberg insisted. In retrospect it is not difficult to understand Jannings' reluctance to appear with the glamorous newcomer. From the moment she first appeared on screen, she completely dominated the film.

Reclining on a barrel, a silk top hat perched nonchalantly on her head, her right leg pulled up seductively towards her breasts by two sensuous arms, she looked out at the audience and sang the now famous melancholy refrain: "Falling in love again; never wanted to; what I am to do; I can't help it."

Suspendered stockings, a flash of white thigh and high heels added to an effect of almost overwhelming sensuality. Not only did Jannings' professor fall for her charms but most of the movie-going public.

The Lola Lola performance was Dietrich's passport to America where she carried on her partnership with von Sternberg. The partnership became one of the most talked about in Hollywood. He was described as her Svengali. She refused to make films for any other director. Inevitably, there were rumours that the alliance was not just professional, that each of them, although married, was enjoying eroticism not only on screen, but off screen as well.

The gossip mongers crashed away at their typewriters and so intense did the rumours become that von Sternberg's wife actually took action against Dietrich. Marlene, protesting her innocence, took up arms, fought and won. The rumours, fabrications of a publicity man, proved groundless.

Von Sternberg's wife (later Mrs. Riza Royce) recalled her husband's period with Dietrich with some bitterness: "Before he worked with her his films were presented with the legend 'A Josef von Sternberg Production'. After he was in Marlene's hooks his films advertised Marlene Dietrich in big letters and his name was small and insignificant underneath.

"Before Marlene he was known as a director who could turn out a film in twenty-four days. He never shot a scene more than twice. But when he started to work with Marlene he would shoot a scene twenty or sixty times. That's why his films cost a fortune."

There was a great deal of truth in what she said. Whereas before *The Blue Angel* von Sternberg had been a fast-rising Paramount director with films like *Underworld, The Docks Of New York* and *The Last Command,* after his period with Dietrich he found his career nearly in ruins. He never again reached the heights. In 1936, at the age of forty-two, he was, to all intents and purposes, washed up. The films he made at other studios — *The King Steps Out, Sergeant Madden, The Shanghai Gesture* —

were few and undistinguished. Rarely had a talent been so quickly extinguished. In many ways it seemed that instead of being Svengali he was more akin to the college professor of Emil Jannings.

Together, director and star made six films for Paramount starting with *Morocco* in 1930 and ending with *The Devil Is A Woman* in 1935. Von Sternberg cultivated his star as if he was Leonardo da Vinci painting the 'Mona Lisa'. Dietrich was not just photographed. She was cossetted, feathered, furred and glamourised to such an extent that on screen her swept back hair, heavy lidded eyes and mannish face were hypnotic.

Audiences couldn't keep their eyes off her. Broody, sultry, with a hint of mystery and cynicism, she was Paramount's answer to Garbo at MGM. Indeed, two of her films, *Dishonoured* and *The Scarlet Empress*, were direct competitors to *Mata Hari* and *Queen Christina*.

Von Sternberg's recipe for movie glamour was very carefully calculated. In his own words it was "the result of the dark-light in colours, the play of the lights on the landscape of the face, the use of the background through the composition, through the aura of the hair, and by casting mysterious shadows into the eyes".

With a plan such as that and a director of von Sternberg's status, it seemed that no actress could go wrong. Yet after a short while Dietrich's career faltered. She received an Oscar nomination for her first American role, cabaret singer Amy Jolly in *Morocco* and achieved a huge financial success with her second film, *Shanghai Express*. After that things began to slide. The reasons remain obscure. It may have been that one mystery woman, i.e. Garbo, was enough for any one decade. More probably it was because of the arrival at the studio of bawdy, flamboyant Mae West who flaunted her appeal in such an obvious All-American way that it left no room for mystery or subtlety in relation to sexual matters.

Whatever the reason, the decline set in. Von Sternberg was largely at fault. Instead of allowing her personality to emerge and develop into new directions he over-dressed and over-glamourised her. Every detail of lighting and costume design was calculated to the last degree. Furs, sequins, veils became more prominent with each succeeding film. He created a mystery of light and shadow, so much so that it seemed at times there was no actress beneath all the careful shading, just a beautiful talking doll.

Eventually, after a succession of box-office failures, von Sternberg and Dietrich split up. Although he found it difficult to function without her, she continued to work at the studio where she filmed in lighter vein for Borzage (*Desire*) and Lubitsch (*Angel*). But when, in 1937, Paramount discovered she rated number 126 at the box-office it quickly bought up her contract and she moved to other studios.

Paramount moved from the 30s into the early 40s with consummate ease. There was no marked loss of style, just a slight change of emphasis, a quick change of gears. Sophisticated comedy and romance, previously handled with such skill by Lubitsch, was put into the hands of Mitchell Leisen; wisecracking humour, so long the province of Mae West and W. C. Fields, was delivered by the slicker more topical Bob Hope; eccentricity as personified by the early films of The Marx Brothers (*Animal Crackers, Monkey Business, Duck Soup*) disappeared and was replaced by satire of the most brilliant kind from former Paramount writer Preston Sturges who aimed his sights at such targets as hero worship (*Hail The Conquering Hero*), crooked politics (*The Great McGinty*) and Hollywood (*Sullivan's Travels*), scoring a bulls-eye every time. Simpler, less ambitious entertainments such as the musical comedies of Bing Crosby (*Holiday Inn, Going My Way, Blue Skies, Welcome Stranger*) proved to be the box-office hits, the master crooner figuring as the top box-office star for five consecutive years during the mid-40s.

It was when Billy Wilder became a director that things first began to change. Although his first film, *The Major And The Minor*, was a comedy, Wilder quickly showed a penchant for exploring the darker regions of life. His films disturbed. They had an acidity and realism. *Double Indemnity* probed into murder, double-cross and the motivations of a *femme fatale*, the award-winning *The Lost Weekend* into the horrors of alcoholism. Later, in the 50s, the brilliant *Sunset Boulevard* looked ruthlessly at the inner-workings of Hollywood and *Ace In The Hole* at gutter journalism.

On a more mundane level, Alan Ladd who became 'a star overnight' (in reality after twenty movies) as the professional killer Raven in *This Gun For Hire* brought the same kind of matter-of-fact toughness to the studio, even down to the essential prop of a turned-up raincoat, which Bogart had brought to Warners a decade earlier.

Suddenly it was a whole new ball game. Comedy still played an important part in the studio line-up and there was still the chance for escape, but now it was escape into the more frightening worlds of the supernatural (*The Uninvited*), the underworld (*The Blue Dahlia*), terror (*Sorry, Wrong Number*), repression (*The Heiress*) and madness (*Sunset Boulevard*).

Cities such as Paris, London, Calcutta and Saigon were no longer filled with gaiety and laughter, but suspicion and murder.

Only one man remained unaffected by the changing scene around him. Cecil B. DeMille. He and his films remained unaltered throughout the Depression 30s, the war period and the 50s that followed when the class films of the studio were being produced by George Stevens (*A Place In The Sun, Shane*), William Wyler (*The Heiress, Detective Story, Roman Holiday*) and the ever reliable Billy Wilder.

DeMille knew the secret of success. People referred to him as a hypocrite because he mixed religion with sex, bathtubs and spectacle. But his formula worked. Even when he returned to Paramount after an indifferent six years as an independent and at MGM, he was still revered and respected as a showman and an air of expectancy hung around the studio as he passed through the Paramount gates in 1932.

Zukor had been reluctant to have him back. Only *The King Of Kings* had been a success in DeMille's period away from the studio. Zukor labelled him box-office poison, restricted the budget of his first film, the Roman epic *The Sign Of The Cross*, to just 650,000 dollars and insisted that he draw no more than 450 dollars a week salary.

It was humiliating, undignified, like having to start from the bottom again at the age of fifty. But DeMille badly wanted to make *The Sign Of The Cross*. He swallowed his pride, accepted the conditions and determined to bring in the movie on time and within the budget, which is exactly what he did. The film was an enormous success and within a few years DeMille was able to write his own meal-ticket at the studio. It remained that way until his death. Zukor acknowledged his value and DeMille never again left Paramount.

Performers would do anything to get into one of his pictures even though he was known to be one of the toughest of taskmasters. They would write him letters, they would beg, they would cajole, they would openly call him the greatest in the business — all to get a role in one of his spectaculars.

Claudette Colbert was one who didn't have to beg. She was asked. DeMille stopped her on the Paramount lot one day and suddenly remarked, "How would you like to be the wickedest woman in history?"

"I'd love it," came Claudette's reply, her beautiful big eyes opening wide with surprise.

Her test was for the role of Poppaea, wife of Nero, in *The Sign Of The Cross*. It still ranks as one of the shortest on record. Five words!

Claudette's partner was Fredric March, the star of the film. Said March, "You harlot!" Said Colbert, "I love you." Said DeMille, "That's enough, you've got the part."

Just as he had with Gloria Swanson twelve years earlier, DeMille revealed that Claudette had a more than shapely anatomy by having her bathe in a sunken pool of asses' milk, something Miss Colbert found luxurious at first, but which quickly turned into something of an ordeal as the milk hardened into foul-smelling cheese after just two days' shooting.

DeMille again chose Colbert when he came to film *Cleopatra* two years later. Once more star and director got along famously until DeMille came to the scene when the Egyptian queen commits suicide by clasping an asp to her breast. DeMille, never a man to fake a scene when it could be done for real, as Miss Swanson had found out to her cost, tentatively suggested to Claudette that she should handle a real snake for the scene.

Miss Colbert shuddered. "Oh, Mr. DeMille, I couldn't touch a snake," she said in horror. She insisted that the hand of a stand-in be shown dipping into the snake basket. DeMille gently persisted. The answer was still a very firm 'no'. Snakes as far as Claudette Colbert was concerned, were definitely out!

The next day DeMille appeared on set with a huge snake coiled round him, a boa constrictor eight feet long; its head lying on the palm of his outstretched hand. Colbert shrieked in horror and backed away up the marble steps of the set, imploring DeMille to take it away.

DeMille smiled and brought out from behind his back a tiny snake which was exactly like an Egyptian asp. "Oh, *that* little thing! Give it to me," said Claudette eagerly and played the scene without a murmur.

DeMille delighted in testing the courage of his players. If they failed his tests they usually earned his undying scorn. Paulette Goddard, for instance, a regular DeMille player of the 40s, refused to do a dangerous fire sequence in his colonial epic *Unconquered* and never appeared for him again. DeMille didn't forget her refusal. When she wrote to him asking for a part in *The Greatest Show On Earth* he wrote back with a polite but definite 'no'.

Victor Mature and Cornel Wilde also didn't endear themselves to him, Mature for refusing to wrestle with a real lion in *Samson And Delilah*, even though it was well fed and well trained, Wilde for freezing in the trapeze scenes in *The Greatest Show On Earth* when he realised for the first time in his life that he suffered from vertigo.

But although he could be contemptuous of players who opted

out of the dangerous stuff DeMille was also quick to praise when the occasion arose. Betty Hutton earned his undying admiration for doing her own trapeze stunts in *The Greatest Show On Earth*, so did Gloria Grahame who in the same film risked death by letting an elephant's foot dangle close above her genuinely frightened face. So too did a young boy extra who played a bit part of a drummer in *Unconquered*.

The boy's bravery came as a complete surprise. The scene was the Indian attack on Fort Pitt at the climax of the picture. DeMille had the drummer boy strategically placed in the stockade beating out an alarm call.

The sequence, full of action, fire, smoke and noise, just wouldn't go right. Take followed take. Indians rushed again and again. By the twenty-first take tempers had become frayed. It was a complex scene with a great deal of carefully constructed detail. Somewhat wearily DeMille called "action" for the twenty-first time and once again the Indians charged. This time a burning arrow was misdirected and plunged straight into the boy's drumhead.

DeMille closed his eyes, uttered a short prayer, and prepared to shout "cut" yet again. Only the scene didn't stop. The Indians went on charging, the redcoats went on defending and in the middle of it all the boy kept on drumming, the flames now scorching up the drumsticks and onto his gloved hands. He uttered not a word. The scene went through without a hitch then the boy rushed across the stage and plunged his fists into a pail of water. Luckily the burns were not serious. DeMille awarded him one of his famous Commemorative silver fifty cent pieces 'for courage above and beyond the call of duty'.

Courageous the boy undoubtedly was. On the other hand, like others in the cast and crew, he might simply have been fed up with the scene and wanted to get home on time!

DeMille was not above showing a bit of bravery himself when the occasion arose. During the filming of *Samson And Delilah* Victor Mature, who had a most harrowing film, expressed doubts about being whipped round the waist from twenty yards by a 6 ft 5 in. eighteen stone wrestler named "Wee Willie" Davis. Mature's confidence in Willie's talents was not overwhelming. He made a tentative suggestion to DeMille that the scene might be filmed in some other way.

Angrily, DeMille strode out onto the set and stood defiantly some twenty yards from the bearded giant. "Okay Willie, let me have it," he commanded the wrestler. Willie took a long backhand swing then cracked the bullwhip forward slashing it across DeMille's chest which was protected only by his shirt.

It left a welt on his body as thick as a pencil, but no-one was allowed to know of the injury. DeMille walked loftily back to his high chair and suggested that they get on with the picture.

The high chair was just one of the features of a DeMille set. He was followed on all occasions by three assistants. Number one was the chairboy who never saw his master face to face but was ready in the rear with a chair for the great man to sit down in. Number two was the mikeboy who trailed a microphone around so that DeMille could seize it when necessary and pass on his orders. Number three was the waterboy. He stood ready with a tray of iced water maintained at exactly the right temperature.

No-one ever called DeMille 'Cecil'. Only a few close friends, among them top cameramen and writers, were allowed to call him 'CB'.

Ray Milland who worked on what many regard as DeMille's best picture *Reap The Wild Wind* and had to grapple with a giant squid when suffering a hangover from the night before, bears out the fact that no-one ever walked in front of DeMille on a set.

''He'd never walk anywhere on the lot unless he had three or four people behind him all the time. People *always* walked behind him, never in front. All the production assistants and Anne Bauchens who I think was his editor for thirty years.

''DeMille was very much a gentleman,'' recalls Milland. ''His manners were impeccable and, of course, he dressed the part. Dark rust coloured tweed breeches. Specially made knee length field boots. And he changed his jewellery every day to fit the clothing he wore.

''If he dressed in dark rust, which he did very often, he'd change his ring to a black iron ring with a garnet in it. A beautiful thing. Or if he dressed in beige he'd have a gold ring. Everything was in keeping.

''He had everything planned out in advance. Just like a field general.''

Even so, despite years of experience, things didn't always go to plan.

''That famous line 'Ready when you are, C.B.' was actually spoken on *Reap The Wild Wind*,'' says Milland. ''We were shooting in the Paramount tank which was the biggest tank in Hollywood. A huge thing, about the size of two Olympic pools. We had a storm at sea rigged up in this tank and at the top of the stage, which was about eighty feet high, were arranged six other tanks, each of which held about ten thousand gallons of water. They had special doors, operated hydraulically, which were to flip up and release all these gallons of water down onto the sailing ships which had been built on the set.

"All around the tank we had aeroplane engines with big wooden propellors to create the hurricanes. And in the water were great wave machines. They rehearsed it all and had four cameras set up for the shot, two close-up cameras, one for medium shots and a master camera up high between the six tanks shooting the whole thing.

"Then came the take. 'All ready,' said DeMille. 'Rolle 'em'. All hell broke loose. Wave machines, aeroplane engines going, wind howling. At a given moment the sluices opened and the water rushed out. A giant wall of water smashed into the boats.

"You've never seen such a mess. When it was all over DeMille looked over at the medium shot cameraman and said 'You alright?' The cameraman nodded, 'Yes C.B.' Then to the men on the two close-up cameras. 'You alright?' Both nodded. Then he shouted to the master camera 80 ft up. 'Are you alright up there?' 'Ready when you are C.B.' came the reply."

Says Milland. "It took them two days to fill those tanks again."

Cary Grant once called DeMille "the man who puts stardust on the stars". It was a neat and apt description. DeMille had the magic. He was make-believe at its very best. When he died three years after completing his last film, a triumphant remake of *The Ten Commandments* which remained Paramount's biggest moneymaker for sixteen years, a link snapped. Something went out of pictures, and out of Paramount.

Zukor remained and would live on until 1976 to the remarkable age of one hundred and three. Of the Paramount pioneers he was the only one to live to see, through ageing eyes, the studio's enormous hits of the 60s and 70s, the two *Godfather* films, *Love Story, Paper Moon*, the Neil Simon comedies *Barefoot In The Park, The Odd Couple*, John Wayne's Oscar winner *True Grit*.

"If I had known I would live this long I would have taken better care of myself," he quipped just before he died.

But Zukor, as always, had just been a figurehead. DeMille had been the film-*maker*, a man who combined brilliance with vulgarity, epic vision with pure corn. No-one before or after his death could quite capture that special DeMille touch. The producer-director who made seventy films in over forty years of film-making and was as famous in the silent period as he was in the contemporary cinema, took his special kind of talent with him to the grave.

When Paramount celebrated its twenty-fifth anniversary an office boy at the studio suggested that the mountain trademark which had always been surrounded by a half circle of twenty-four stars might now be ringed by twenty-five. The boy was hailed as a genius, but when the studio came to reckon up the cost of changing the trademark, the emblems, the stationery office forms etc, the idea suddenly seemed less than bright.

If that twenty-fifth star *had* been added it shouldn't have been for the contributions of Swanson or Dietrich or Mae West or even Lubitsch. That twenty-fifth star should have been for DeMille. Although even that would have been inappropriate. DeMille was the mountain!

Gary Cooper sacrificing himself during the Spanish Civil War in Paramount's version of Hemingway's *For Whom The Bell Tolls*.

Bob Hope near peak form as Damon Runyon's *The Lemon Drop Kid*. Pointing the accusing finger: character actor Fred Clark.

James Stewart and Kim Novak in *Vertigo*, one of Hitchcock's key films of the 50s.

Mary Pickford at the height of her Paramount fame as *Rebecca Of Sunnybrook Farm*.

Fred Astaire sits it out for a change, entranced by Audrey Hepburn in Donen's Parisian musical *Funny Face*.

Cecil B. DeMille on location in Egypt directing Charlton Heston on Mount Sinai in *The Ten Commandments* (56).

Two of Hollywood's greats, Mae West and 102 year old Adolph Zukor, at a party to celebrate the production of *Won Ton Ton, The Dog That Saved Hollywood*.

Alan Ladd in his first starring role with Veronica Lake in *This Gun For Hire*.

Chronology

1913 The Jesse Lasky Feature Plays Company is born — on the back of a menu in a New York restaurant!

Jesse L. Lasky, his brother-in-law, former glove salesman Samuel Goldfish (later Goldwyn), actor Cecil B. DeMille and lawyer Arthur Friend form the company with a capital of just 20,000 dollars.

They decide on *The Squaw Man*, a western starring Dustin Farnum as their first production. DeMille and co-director Oscar Apfel shoot the picture (filming begins on December 29) in just eighteen days.

Earlier in the year when the Lasky company was still no more than a dream, Adolph Zukor's Famous Players Company (formed in 1912) was gathering momentum with movies devoted to 'Famous Players In Famous Plays' for the screen. *The Prisoner Of Zenda, The Count Of Monte Cristo, Tess Of The D'Urbevilles* and *A Lady Of Quality* are among the company's releases; James O'Neill, Mrs. Fiske, Lily Langtry, Carlotta Nillson among its stars.

Zukor's most profitable acquisition however is twenty-year-old Mary Pickford whom he signs for 500 dollars a week. Her first two releases: *In The Bishop's Carriage* and *Caprice*.

1914 *The Squaw Man* is released on February 15 and the Jesse Lasky company is in business. The picture costs 15,000 dollars. It grosses 244,700.

DeMille's studio for *The Squaw Man* is an old L-shaped barn situated at the corner of Selma Avenue and Vine Street in Hollywood, a few miles west of Los Angeles. It belongs to a man called Jacob Stern who uses it primarily for tethering his horses and parking his carriage. Its address: 6284 Selma Avenue.

During the year W. W. Hodkinson arranges with both the Famous Players and Lasky companies to provide him with product for his newly formed, nationwide releasing organisation Paramount Pictures. The first link between Zukor and Lasky/Goldwyn/DeMille is formed.

John Barrymore, Marguerite Clark, Carlyle Blackwell, H. B. Warner are among those who star for Zukor. None measure up to the popularity of little Mary Pickford who appears in seven films including *Tess Of The Storm Country, Cinderella, Hearts Adrift* and the Southern mountain romance *The Eagle's Mate*.

The Lasky company continues with such films as *Brewster's Millions, The Call Of The North, The Virginian, What's His Name, Rose Of The Rancho.*

1915 The two companies, still separate organizations, continue to release through Hodkinson's Paramount Pictures. Both continue to thrive.

Mary Pickford, now called 'America's Sweetheart' is the biggest moneymaking star in the industry and ups her total to eight pictures a year. In *A Girl Of Yesterday* she becomes 'the first girl to fly in the movies'. Only Marguerite Clark, also busy with seven films, threatens her supremacy.

Pauline Frederick, who appears in *Bella Donna* and *The Eternal City* (an eight-reeler filmed in Rome), Marie Doro who debuts in *The Morals Of Marcus,* and John Barrymore are other Zukor stars.

Lasky is beginning to find stars of his own. On June 26 he signs Wallace Reid to a long-term contract and also scoops the industry by signing opera star Geraldine Farrar to a three-picture deal. For this privilege he pays 20,000 dollars and throws in a furnished house, servants, a motor car, groceries during the star's stay in Hollywood, plus a private railroad car for her transportation to and from New York.

Miss Farrar's first release, *Carmen,* with Wallace Reid as her Don José and DeMille as her director, is a smash.

Japanese actor Sessue Hayakawa brings about female fainting fits in another DeMille movie, *The Cheat*. Key fainting scene: When Fannie Ward, struggling with Hayakawa, has the dress torn from her shoulders and is branded with a Japanese symbol saying she's his property!

1916 The two companies merge on June 28 to become the Famous Players-Lasky Corporation. It is the beginning of Paramount Studios. Zukor absorbs Hodkinson's distributing company shortly after the formation and adopts the Paramount name. Zukor is president, Lasky vice-president, Goldwyn chairman and DeMille director-general.

The company which absorbs Morosco, Pallas, Bosworth and others, forges ahead as one of the most important in the industry. Wallace Reid is quickly getting a fan-following; Marguerite Clark, Pauline Frederick, Hazel Dawn and John Barrymore are all top stars; so too are Blanche Sweet, Fannie Ward and Marie Doro who plays the lead in *Oliver Twist*.

DeMille offers five movies including two with Geraldine Farrar, *Temptation* and *Maria Rosa*, and the famous story of a mountain feud, *The Trail Of The Lonesome Pine* starring Thomas Meighan. Pickford, as popular as ever signs for Zukor for two more years.

Sam Goldwyn, after bitter clashes with Zukor, leaves the company and together with Edgar Archibald Selwyn, Margaret Mayo and Arthur Hopkins, forms the Goldwyn Pictures Corporation. The company is not a success. Within five years it founders and merges with the mighty Metro unit. Goldwyn is forced out and restarts with his newly formed independent company, Samuel Goldwyn Productions, Inc.

1917 DeMille reveals his penchant for the spectacular as he directs Geraldine Farrar, Wallace Reid and a thousand extras in *Joan The Woman*. He also directs the studio's top box-office star Mary Pickford in *Romance Of The Redwoods* and *The Little American*. DeMille and Miss Farrar hit it off famously. The DeMille-Pickford combination is somewhat less ecstatic. Says Pickford, "I was absolutely terrified of him. It was like being in an iron cage."

Mary also appears as *Rebecca Of Sunnybrook Farm*; Jack Pickford, Mary's brother, as *Tom Sawyer*; and Marguerite Clark as *Snow White*.

The star roster is impressive to say the least. Wallace Reid, Pauline Frederick, Thomas Meighan, Marie Doro, William S. Hart, Sessue Hayakawa, Billie Burke and Douglas Fairbanks are just some of those operating on the lot. Directing them: DeMille, his brother William C. DeMille, Maurice Tourneur, William Desmond Taylor, Marshall Neilan, Robert Z. Leonard.

A new acquisition is Roscoe 'Fatty' Arbuckle who leaves Sennett to make his comedies at Paramount.

1918 Zukor receives two setbacks. At the year's end Mary Pickford signs with First National for 750,000 dollars a year, fifty per cent of the gross and complete artistic control. Zukor can't or won't match it. Also his gamble of trying to make opera singer Enrico Caruso into a screen star collapses when the first film, *My Cousin*, is a flop and the second, *The Splendid Romance*, so bad it has to be shelved.

Before she finally leaves the lot for good, Mary Pickford contributes *M'Liss* with Thomas Meighan, *Stella Maris* in which she plays two parts for the first time and *Captain Kidd Junior,* her final movie for the studio, released early in 1919.

"She taught me a great deal," says Zukor later. "I was only an apprentice when we started. She was an expert workman."

Arbuckle is still playing the fool in his slapstick comedies; Marguerite Clark also has a dual role as Topsy and Little Eva in *Uncle Tom's Cabin*; Wallace Reid, now the most popular male Paramount star has Ann Little as his leading lady in *seven* movies.

DeMille offers bizarre melodrama *The Whispering Chorus* with Raymond Hatton, wartime spying *Till I Come Back To You* with Florence Vidor and a remake of *The Squaw Man* with Ellitt Dexter in the Farnum role.

In a William Hart western, *Riddle Gawne*, an actor who has been hanging around at Universal for years waiting for a break, gets it — at Paramount. He plays a villainous gunfighter called Hame Bozzam. His name? Lon Chaney.

1919 Paramount are now the *creme-de-la-creme* of Hollywood. Wallace Reid retains his popularity but the big newcomer is Gloria Swanson.

It's Swanson who takes over the mantle from Pickford, but whereas Pickford had brought innocence and little girl sweetness to her Paramount films, Swanson brings a new kind of woman, sumptuously gowned and jewelled, the modern girl (usually a victim) indulging in *avant garde* morality. She starts with three DeMille films in one year — *Don't Change Your Husband* and *For Better, For Worse*, both with Elliott Dexter, and *Male And Female* with Thomas Meighan.

Says she: "I have gone through a long apprenticeship. I have gone through enough of being nobody. I have decided that when I am a star, I will be every inch and every moment the star! Everybody from the studio gateman to the highest executive will know it!"

Lon Chaney is making it to stardom with slightly less noise as the phoney legless cripple in *The Miracle Man*;

Wallace Reid begins his popular series of motor racing films by winning the 400 mile Santa Monica Road Race in James Cruze's *The Roaring Road.*

Jesse Lasky comments: "The audiences couldn't get enough of him behind a steering wheel. We virtually turned those road racing items out on an assembly line and every one was a moneymaker. But that didn't type Wally. He was believable in almost any role we gave him!"

1920 Gloria Swanson appears twice more for DeMille in *Why Change Your Wife?* and *Something To Think About* and becomes indisputedly Paramount's top star. She lives up her prophecy of a year before. She buys a twenty-four room house, employs eleven servants and becomes known as 'the second woman in Hollywood to make a million and the first to spend it'.

The classics figure very much on the studio's schedule. John Barrymore plays both *Dr. Jekyll And Mr. Hyde* *without* the aid of make-up; Lon Chaney features in a double role (as Blind Pew and pirate George Merry) in Maurice Tourneur's *Treasure Island*; and Lewis Sargent is *Huckleberry Finn.*

Wallace Reid (six movies), Thomas Meighan, Mae Murray, Lois Wilson, Alma Rubens, Agnes Ayres, Betty Compson and Ann Little are among the top Paramount stars. Heading the directing team: DeMille, James Cruze, Sam Wood, George Fitzmaurice.

1921 Rudolph Valentino, after creating a sensation in *The Four Horsemen Of The Apocalypse* at Metro and as Armand opposite Nazimova's *Camille* arrives at Paramount to set more feminine hearts beating.

In *The Sheik* he's a smouldering Arab lover who humbles proud aristocratic Agnes Ayres in his desert tent. A phallic symbol (his cigarette holder!) ends up on the lady's dressing table the morning after the night before; the lady herself eventually sums up most women's opinions, "I am not afraid with your arms around me, Ahmed, my desert love, MY SHEIK."

Studio boss Zukor is not over-impressed with his new star: "His acting is largely confined to potruding his large, almost occult, eyes until the vast areas of white are visible, drawing back the lips of his wide sensuous mouth to bare his gleaming teeth and flaring his nostrils."

DeMille bets fifty dollars *The Sheik* will be a flop. He

loses. Paramount beats the drum loudly: 'Shriek For The Sheik Will Seek You TOO!'

'Shriek' is what young actress Virginia Rappe unfortunately does at an infamous party at the St. Francis Hotel in San Francisco. The party goes on for days. Miss Rappe finishes up nude and dead. Fatty Arbuckle is accused of her rape and murder. After three trials (two hung juries) he is acquitted but the publicity has put his career in ruins and made him bankrupt. His Paramount days and to all intents and purposes, his film days are over.

Despite all the Valentino-Arbuckle hysteria Paramount release a hundred pictures, Swanson still reigns as queen of the lot and Wallace Reid as king. They co-star in DeMille's *The Affairs Of Anatol.*

1922 Nita Naldi takes on Valentino in the bullfighting drama *Blood And Sand.* She fares no better than Miss Ayres and duly succumbs. "Someday you will beat me with these strong hands," she says. "I would like to know what it feels like." So would millions of women throughout the world.

Valentino plus Swanson in *Beyond The Rocks* seems an explosive combination. He's a handsome nobleman, she's an English aristocrat with an elderly husband but the film fizzles instead of sizzles. Nonetheless, Valentino and Swanson, plus Wallace Reid and Thomas Meighan, remain Paramount's top stars.

Meighan appears for DeMille as a district attorney in *Manslaughter*; Reid stars in *nine* movies including *Forever* in which he plays his best-ever role as George du Maurier's Peter Ibbetson; Mary Miles Minter is in Fiji as a native sacrifice in *South Of Suva* and accused of murdering her husband in *The Cowboy And The Lady.*

Miss Minter gains more publicity through her connection with the real-life murder of director William Desmond Taylor, who, on February 1, is shot in his Hollywood bungalow by an assailant whose identity is never discovered. Both she and Mabel Normand are romantically involved with Taylor, Normand having visited him the night before his death, Minter being about to announce their engagement that very week. Both actresses have their careers ruined even though they are cleared of any suspicion.

Despite exhaustive investigations and scores of rumours

the Los Angeles police never come close to an arrest. More than fifty years later the case remains unsolved.

1923 After ten years in the business DeMille shows what he's all about. In a word it's 'spectacle'. In his thirteen-reel *The Ten Commandments* he combines the events that led to Moses receiving the commandments on Mount Sinai with a triangular story showing the importance of the commandments in modern life. The Exodus and Parting Of The Red Sea (filmed in two-color Technicolor) swamp the valiant attempts of Theodore Roberts as Moses and Charles de Roche as Rameses.

James Cruze is another director concerned with the epic. In *The Covered Wagon* he tells a pioneer tale of the 1849 trek to California and Oregon and elevates the western into a major *genre*. As in the DeMille picture the actors are runners-up to the spectacle. J. Warren Kerrigan, Lois Wilson and Alan Hale compete with the action and scenery and lose; Ernest Torrence and Tully Marshall, as a couple of drunken old frontier scouts, compete and earn a draw.

The studio bring the first European import to Hollywood — Polish actress Pola Negri. She starts as an adventuress in *Bella Donna* and is also seen in *The Cheat* and *The Spanish Dancer*. 'She has eyes like dark lagoons' say the publicists. For a short time she becomes Swanson's only rival on the lot.

Swanson herself is the Parisian music hall soubrette *Zaza* and a French nobleman's daughter married to seven times divorced Huntley Gordon in *Bluebeard's Eighth Wife*; British valet Edward Everett Horton is won in a poker game and taken to the Old West in *Ruggles Of Red Gap*; and the studio remake one of their favourite outdoor tales *The Trail Of The Lonesome Pine*.

A tragic loss is that of Wallace Reid who dies from the effects of morphine addiction and alcoholism on January 18. He was only thirty-one and a Paramount star for eight years during which time he made more than fifty films for the studio.

1924 Photoplay Magazine holds a popularity contest among its readers asking them to name their top ten stars. Paramount takes four of the top places with Swanson, Valentino, Negri and Meighan. DeMille is voted top director.

Valentino is Booth Tarkington's *Monsieur Beaucaire* but the 'great lover' spark temporarily disappears beneath

18th century foppishness and swordplay. Swanson and Negri, however, feverishly battle it out for the queen of the lot spot, the former with five movies, the latter with four. Swanson still comes out ahead despite Miss Negri's efforts as queen of the Apaches in *Shadows Of Paris* and Catherine The Great of Russia in *Forbidden Paradise* – Lubitsch's first film for Paramount.

Herbert Brenon puts Betty Bronson through her delightful paces as J. M. Barrie's immortal *Peter Pan*; DeMille returns to more run-of-the-mill productions, *Triumph* and *Feet Of Clay*, after indulging his spectacular whims the year before; Allan Dwan, Sidney Olcott and William C. DeMille are other top directors; Lois Wilson, Nita Naldi, Richard Dix, Rod LaRocque, Betty Compson and Bebe Daniels among the leading stars.

1925 Paramount lose their ace director. Cecil B. DeMille resigns early in the year after a series of bitter quarrels with Zukor who insists on trimming the budgets of DeMille's pictures an refuses him permission to film Marie Corelli's novel *The Sorrows Of Satan*. DeMille goes independent and decides to release his pictures through the Producers Distribution Corporation. His last picture for Paramount, until his return in the 30s, is *The Golden Bed* with Lillian Rich and Henry B. Walthall.

DeMille's departure is a body blow, but the industry is in the doldrums and the studio finds it hard to sustain his extravagance.

Swanson delivers a trio – *The Coast Of Folly, Stage Struck* and *Madame Sans-Gêne* in which she plays the French laundress of Napoleon; Miss Negri goes one better with a quartet including Raoul Walsh's version of Somerset Maugham's play *East Of Suez*.

Victor Fleming, a major Paramount director of the future, casts Percy Marmont as Joseph Conrad's *Lord Jim*; James Cruze goes West again with Betty Compson, Ricardo Cortez, Ernest Torrence and Wallace Beery for *The Pony Express*; so does director George B. Seitz who, with *The Vanishing American*, produces the first movie to look sympathetically at the plight of the American Indian.

Another farewell is made – by Valentino. His last picture for the studio is *Cobra*. He stars as an impoverished young Italian count.

1926 Now it's Swanson's turn to go. United Artists lure her

to their independent company with a lucrative offer she finds too good to refuse. Her last two pictures for Paramount are a Fannie Hurst story *The Untamed Lady* and *Fine Manners*. Zukor, desperate to hold her, offers her a sensational 18,000 dollars a week, then an even million a year. But nothing will change her mind. She's on her way out of the studio gates for pastures new. She will return to the same sound stages just one more time, in sensational fashion nearly a quarter of a century later.

Paramount turn to major novels for their big movies of the year – P. C. Wren's *Beau Geste* with Ronald Colman, Neil Hamilton and Ralph Forbes as brothers Beau, Digby and John and Noah Beery as sadistic legionnaire Sergeant Lejaune; J. M. Barrie's *A Kiss For Cinderella* with Betty Bronson; and Scott Fitzgerald's *The Great Gatsby* with Warner Baxter as the tragic millionaire bootlegger, Jay Gatsby and Lois Wilson his lost love, Daisy. Herbert Brenon directs all three.

With Swanson leaving the scene Pola Negri battles for better roles, but doesn't get them. In *The Crown Of Lies* she's a queen of a mythical kingdom, in *Good And Naughty* she's an ugly duckling.

The studio are more interested in sexy, twenty-one year old flapper Clara Bow whom they cast in four movies including Victor Fleming's *Mantrap* in which the vivacious Miss Bow is caught between elderly Ernest Torrence and young city lawyer Percy Marmont.

W. C. Fields signs a long-term contract and starts off with *That Royle Girl, It's The Old Army Game* and *So's Your Old Man*; Harold Lloyd agrees to distribute his comedies through the studio; Gilda Gray is the beautiful island dancer *Aloma Of The South Seas*; Ricardo Cortez stars with Adolphe Menjou in the movie DeMille wanted so badly to direct, *The Sorrows Of Satan*.

1927 The Paramount scene begins to change. The first indications of the 'style' that will emerge in the 30s are becoming apparent. W. C. Fields has a trio of comedies on view; director Josef von Sternberg, the man who will 'discover' Dietrich, joins the studio and makes the first major gangster film *Underworld* with George Bancroft; and lanky newcomer Gary Cooper is signed for 150 dollars a week.

Cooper features in several minor westerns and also has a small part in William Wellman's spectacular aviation film *Wings*, a World War I story of two American pilots (Richard Arlen and Charles 'Buddy' Rogers) who find themselves rivals for the affections of small-town girl Clara Bow.

Coop's also in the movie specially built for the red-headed Miss Bow, Elinor Glyn's *It*. The film makes Clara famous the world over as The 'It' Girl and countless girls adopt her hair and make-up styles.

What is 'It?' Says Elinor Glyn: "To have 'It', the fortunate possessor must have that strange magnetism which attracts both sexes. 'It' is a purely virile quality, belonging to a strong character. He or she must be entirely unselfconscious and full of self-confidence, indifferent to the effect he or she is producing, and uninfluenced by others. There must be phyisical attraction, but beauty is unnecessary. Conceit or self-concsiousness destroys 'It' immediately."

Whichever way you look at things Clara distributes plenty of 'It' around during the year with Antonio Moreno (*It*), Reed Howes (*Rough House Rosie*), Clive Brook (*Hula*) and Charles 'Buddy' Rogers (*Get Your Man*).

Doubtless she would also lead Emil Jannings astray, but that task is left to Phyllis Haver who brings about Jannings' degradation and downfall in the noted German actor's first American film *The Way Of All Flesh*, directed by Victor Fleming.

1928 Von Sternberg quickly establishes himself with three realistic Paramount movies: *The Dragnet*, another gangster film with George Bancroft as 'Two-Gun' Nolan and Evelyn Brent as 'The Magpie', *The Docks Of New York*, the story of a coal stoker (Bancroft) and the waterfront tramp (Betty Compson) he saves from suicide, and *The Last Command* with Jannings as a commander in the Russian army who flees the Revolution and ends up a Hollywood extra.

Things in fact 'is tough all over'. Cop Thomas Meighan hunts down killer Louis Wolheim in Milestone's *The Racket*; Jannings comes to an untimely end as Russia's Czar Paul in *The Patriot*; Pola Negri ends her Paramount career ignominiously with a succession of drab flops; and Louise Brooks murders her father and tastes the lower forms of existence in Wellman's *Beggars Of Life*.

The silver lining includes *Speedy* with Harold Lloyd in pursuit of a gang of car thieves, and Anita Loos' *Gentlemen Prefer Blondes* with Ruth Taylor as blonde gold-digger

Lorelei Lee, Alice White, Ford Sterling and Holmes Herbert.

The most miserable event of the year is the release of the mutilated version of von Stroheim's *The Wedding March*, a massive two-part tale of a royal officer who is torn between the love for a cripple (Fay Wray) and the girl he is forced by parental decree to marry (Zazu Pitts). Paramount follow the example of other studios in dealing with the extravagant von Stroheim and take part two away from him while he is still shooting. The film is released cut as *The Wedding March*. Part two, mutilated, is shown as *The Honeymoon*, but only in Europe.

1929 A year of consolidation. Also of change and uncertainty. *Interference*, a ten-reel society melodrama with William Powell, Evelyn Brent and Clive Brook is the studio's first all-talkie, released on January 5; Clara Bow, soon to become a casualty of sound, reveals a voice that is flat and uninteresting; von Sternberg's first talkie is *Thunderbolt*, a third gangster movie with George Bancroft; and Gary Cooper's is *The Virginian*, a remake of Owen Wister's western classic. Says he to a menacing Walter Huston (Trampas), "If you want to call me that, smile!"

The first Oscars are announced on May 16 and Paramount nabs the best picture award with *Wings*, Wellman's aviation movie first released in 27. At the same ceremony Emil Jannings (for his performances in *The Way Of All Flesh* and *The Last Command*) wins the first best actor Oscar and Ben Hecht the first writing award for *Underworld*.

Maurice Chevalier signs for Paramount and hits the mark almost immediately with *The Love Parade*, a Lubitsch musical with Jeanette MacDonald as his co-star and music and lyrics by Victor Schertzinger and Clifford Grey; Claudette Colbert is another who signs with the studio; Rouben Mamoulian experiments with sound and realistically evokes the seedy atmosphere of New York's twice nightly burlesque theatres in *Applause*; Jeanne Eagels is Somerset Maugham's bitchy murderess Leslie Crosbie in *The Letter*; Richard Arlen prowls stealthily among the fuzzy-wuzzies of the Sudan to return *The Four Feathers*.

William Powell debuts as detective Philo Vance in *The Canary Murder Case* and *The Greene Murder Case*; The Marx Brothers also hit the screen for the first time in *The Cocoanuts*. Groucho immediately seizes the chance to grapple with the formidable Margaret Dumont.

"Just think, tonight, tonight. When the moon is sneaking around the clouds, I'll be sneaking around you. I'll meet you tonight under the moon. Oh, I can see you now. You and the moon. . . You wear a necktie so I'll know you."

1930 A seductive German actress in a sleazy cabaret leans back, flaunts her magnificent stockinged legs and sings 'Falling In Love Again'. A flash of thigh and a touch of melancholy means the arrival of Marlene Dietrich. She destroys aged college professor Emil Jannings in the German-made *The Blue Angel* and triumphantly arrives in Hollywood in April with her mentor — some say her Svengali — Josef von Sternberg.

Her salary at Paramount is 125,000 dollars per picture. Her first American film is *Morocco* in which she's a sultry cabaret singer in love with legionnaire Gary Cooper. In the last scene she removes her three inch high heels and pads after him barefoot in the desert in search of love and an Oscar. No Academy Award, only a nomination. As for love, one can only guess.

New York stage director George Cukor makes his movie bow with *Grumpy, The Virtuous Sin* and *The Royal Family Of Broadway* in which Fredric March delightfully impersonates John Barrymore; Jackie Coogan 'Talks For The First Time' as *Tom Sawyer*; William Powell as Philo Vance solves *The Benson Murder Case*; and in *Animal Crackers* Groucho Marx is the memorable Captain Spaulding ("One morning I shot an elephant in my pajamas. How he got in my pajamas I'll never know!").

Otherwise the scene is mainly musical. *Paramount On Parade* (with scenes in two-colour Technicolor) is the studio's answer to Warners' *Show Of Shows* and MGM's *Hollywood Revue*; Dennis King and Jeanette MacDonald sing Rudolf Friml ('Only A Rose', 'Love Me Tonight', 'Song Of The Vagabonds') in *The Vagabond King*; and MacDonald also sings in her other, more famous movie, *Monte Carlo*. She's a penniless countess and sings 'Beyond The Blue Horizon', one of the most inventive cinematic renderings of a major song, sung on a speeding train to the accompaniment of flying rails and whirring train wheels. She co-stars with Jack Buchanan and is directed by Lubitsch.

1931 Ernst Lubitsch, now firmly ensconced at Paramount,

indulges in romance and intrigue in period Vienna in *The Smiling Lieutenant*. Chevalier and Claudette Colbert perfectly translate his lightweight wit and sophistication.

Tallulah Bankhead and Clive Brook do the same for George Cukor in *Tarnished Lady*, a satire by Donald Ogden Stewart on loose living in Manhattan high society; The Marx Brothers appear in their third film for the studio, *Monkey Business* with Groucho, as usual excelling in insults. Says he to Margaret Dumont: ''I know, I know. You're a woman who's been getting nothing but dirty breaks. Well, we can clean and tighten your brakes, but you'll have to stay in the garage all night.''

Claudette Colbert, Miriam Hopkins, Kay Francis, George Bancroft, Sylvia Sidney and William Powell all star for Paramount, Powell appearing twice with Carole Lombard in *Ladies' Man* and *Man Of The World.*

Rouben Mamoulian and Josef von Sternberg look at the seamier side of life, Mamoulian with the Gary Cooper/Sylvia Sidney gangster film *City Streets*, von Sternberg with a version of Theodore Dreiser's classic novel about American class structure, *An American Tragedy*.

Von Sternberg also directs Dietrich for the third time in *Dishonoured* with the moody German actress cast this time as a World War I streetwalker who becomes notorious spy X27. It's also the film in which Gustave von Seyffertitz, having been picked up by Marlene and brought to her rooms, stands his wet umbrella in the bowl of her bidet!

1932 Jeanette MacDonald: ''Don't you think of anything but men dear?''
Myrna Loy: ''Oh, yes.''
Jeanette MacDonald: ''Oh, of what?''
Myrna Loy: ''Of schoolboys.''

It sounds like Lubitsch but, in fact, it's Ruritanian Mamoulian in the Chevalier/MacDonald musical *Love Me Tonight*. One of the Paramount hits of the year, the movie has a Rodgers and Hart score that includes 'Lover' and 'Isn't It Romantic?'

Lubitsch, however, is very much at his peak with *One Hour With You*, again with Chevalier and MacDonald, a stylish remake of his silent *The Marriage Circle*; and *Trouble In Paradise*, a masterpiece about two charming society crooks, Herbert Marshall and Miriam Hopkins, who meet up in Venice and plan to rob rich widow Kay Francis of her jewellery. Paramount's copywriters almost drown in their own invective: 'They made their Garden Of Eden. . .until the snake shook them a Paradise Cocktail and their 'Angel' took a run-out powder. . .He handed both his Eves a Big Red Apple. . .but one was wormy!'

Lubitsch also has a hand in *If I Had A Million,* a portmanteau picture about eight assorted people who suddenly find themselves worth a million dollars. His sequence? The one in which downtrodden clerk Charles Laughton hands in his notice — and a raspberry — to his employers.

Lasky is ousted from the company, but DeMille returns with the 'first real spectacle of talking films', *The Sign Of The Cross.* A tale of ancient Rome it stars Fredric March, Elissa Landi, Claudette Colbert and Charles Laughton (Nero) — plus 7500 others! "Delicious debauchery," mutters Laughton as another bunch of Christians head for the arena of lions.

Dialogue crackles throughout the year. Says a hatcheck girl to Mae West in her film debut in *Night After Night,* "Goodness, what lovely diamonds." Replies Mae, "Goodness had nothing to do with it, dearie."; grumbles W. C. Fields in *Million Dollar Legs,* "I've been drinking too much orange juice."; and in *Shanghai Express* Marlene Dietrich issues the firm statement, "It took more than one man to change my name to Shanghai Lily."

Marlene — a notorious prostitute who saves a former lover from Chinese revolutionaries — is at the peak of her popularity. Von Sternberg's film makes a three million dollar profit.

Marlene also pops up in a monkey costume musical number in *Blonde Venus*; nurse Helen Hayes gives herself to ambulance officer Gary Cooper in Hemingway's *A Farewell To Arms*; and in *Devil And The Deep* Tallulah Bankhead finds herself trapped in a submarine with Cooper which isn't so bad, but also with paranoiac sub-commander/ husband Charles Laughton which is grim.

Two key events: radio crooner Bing Crosby signs a Paramount contract for 300,000 dollars for five pictures in three years (his debut is in *The Big Broadcast*) and Fredric March becomes the first Paramount actor to win an Oscar for his performance in Mamoulian's *Dr. Jekyll And Mr. Hyde.*

1933 Very much the mixture as before although this time DeMille goes modern with *This Day And Age* (Charles Bickford, Richard Cromwell) and Dietrich has a temporary break from von Sternberg's influence by appearing for Rouben Mamoulian as a sculptor's model in *Song Of Songs*. The Dietrich/Mamoulian combination is not a success.

The comediennes — and comedians — continue to sparkle. Mae West, in *She Done Him Wrong* (a screen version of her stage success 'Diamond Lil') issues her famous invitation "come up and see me some time" to Cary Grant, and in *I'm No Angel* replies to Kent Taylor's imploring "When may I see you — breakfast, lunch, dinner?" with, "Well — I always breakfast in bed — so that's out!"

Tillie And Gus (the famous movie during the making of which W. C. Fields spikes the orange juice of child star Baby LeRoy with gin) has Fields babbling "There comes a time in the affairs of man when he must take the bull by the tail and face the situation."; and in *Duck Soup*, the last Marx Brothers film for Paramount, Groucho comments about the formidable Dumont, "Remember men, we're fighting for this woman's honour which is probably more than she ever did."

An all-star version of *Alice In Wonderland* includes W. C. Fields as Humpty Dumpty, Cary Grant as The Mock Turtle, Edna May Oliver as The Red Queen, Gary Cooper as The White Knight, Richard Arlen as the Cheshire Cat and May Robson as the Queen of Hearts. Lombard is stuck again with Laughton in an Eastern backwater ('The last outpost of hell') in *White Woman* and also goes through it in *Supernatural* as a girl possessed by the spirit of a dead murderess.

Bing appears in two (*College Humour, Too Much Harmony*); former DeMille art director Mitchell Leisen directs for the first time with *Cradle Song*; Lubitsch, as always, provides the ultimate in sophistication with a version of the 'scandalous' Noel Coward play *Design For Living* about a girl loving two men equally at the same time. Miriam Hopkins is the girl, Fredric March and Gary Cooper the men she shares.

1934 Mae West suffers attacks from the Legion Of Decency in *Belle Of The Nineties*, a story of a saloon entertainer in love with two men. It worries her not a jot. Says she in the movie: "A man in the house is worth two in the street." Says she about women, "There's no good girls gone wrong, there are just bad girls found out."

Lubitsch, on temporary loan to MGM has nothing to

offer. W. C. Fields has four, including *The Old-Fashioned Way* in which he gets to kick Baby LeRoy in the rear and *Six Of A Kind*, a richly comic tale about three couples — and a dog — driving west. "I feel as though the Russian army has been walking over my tongue in their stocking feet," grunts Fields at one point.

DeMille has Claudette Colbert, Herbert Marshall, Mary Boland and William Gargan fleeing from cholera through a Malaysian jungle in *Four Frightened People*; he also directs the tempting Miss Colbert in *Cleopatra*. Supporting the Siren Of The Nile: A cast of 8000, 75 tons of armour worn by 5000 men, an exotic love boat 500 ft long and massive sets that cover 400,000 square feet. Henry Wilcoxon and Warren William are also around.

Dietrich (Catherine The Great) and von Sternberg opt for spectacle of the more exotic kind in the remarkable *The Scarlet Empress*; Adolphe Menjou and Shirley Temple star in a version of Damon Runyon's *Little Miss Marker*; Leisen combines backstage murder with large-scale musical numbers in *Murder At The Vanities*; singing deck-hand Bing Crosby wins Carole Lombard in *We're Not Dressing*; and George Raft reveals his talents as a dancer in *Bolero*. Lombard again tags along. Ray Milland, in a small part, lands a long-term contract.

1935 Indian villain Douglas Dumbrille actually says, 'We have ways of making men talk'' in Henry Hathaway's thrill-a-minute adventure *The Lives Of A Bengal Lancer*. He has too. By lighting the ends of bamboo shoots slotted under the fingernails. Gary Cooper and Franchot Tone hang on. Richard Cromwell gives way.

Von Sternberg and Dietrich, after seven films together, call it a day with *The Devil Is A Woman* ("Come share my lips and I'll break your heart"); DeMille, despite a cast of 10,000, comes a cropper with *The Crusades*, the least successful of his epics; so does King Vidor with *So Red The Rose*, the story of the fate of an old Southern family at the hands of the North in the Civil War.

On the credit side: Charles Laughton as a gentleman's gentleman out West in Leo McCarey's remake *Ruggles Of Red Gap*; Gary Cooper as *Peter Ibbetson*; Edward Arnold and George Raft in *The Glass Key*, a Dashiell Hammett thriller of murder and crooked politics; Raft again, dancing the *Rumba*; and Carole Lombard who gets material much more worthy of her in *Hands Across The Table*. She's a gold-digging manicurist. Fred MacMurray the millionaire she's out to snare.

W. C. Fields (teamed with Crosby) runs a showboat and does his cardsharp act in *Mississippi*; he's also a bank clerk immersed in domestic tyranny in *The Man On The Flying Trapeze*.

Question: "It must be hard to lose your mother-in-law?"

Fields: "Yes it is. . .almost impossible."

1936 Paramount release their first Technicolor feature and the first to be shot outdoors — a remake of their old favourite *The Trail Of The Lonesome Pine*, the story of a Kentucky mountain feud between two rival clans. At odds with each other this time: Henry Fonda, Fred MacMurray and Sylvia Sidney.

Several of Paramount's top hits are set in the wide open spaces. DeMille goes West for *The Plainsman* and proves he's even more at home with American history than ancient times. Jean Arthur is Calamity Jane, Gary Cooper Wild Bill Hickok, Porter Hall the timid assassin who shoots him in the back. King Vidor casts Fred MacMurray, Jack Oakie and Lloyd Nolan in *The Texas Rangers*, and sarong girl Dorothy Lamour makes her debut as *The Jungle Princess*, a Malayan girl brought up in a cave with a tiger and a chimp! Ray Milland co-stars and manages to survive lines like, "You savage, untamed she-devil, I adore you."

Lewis Milestone brings a touch of von Sternberg to the Gary Cooper-Madeleine Carroll vehicle *The General Died At Dawn*, a stylish political thriller of modern China dominated by Akim Tamiroff as the corrupt General Yang; Crosby stars in *Anything Goes* and sings 'I'm an old cowhand' in *Rhythm On The Range*; and the extraordinary combination of producer Lubitsch and director Frank Borzage guides Marlene Dietrich and Gary Cooper through the deft comedy *Desire*. Dietrich is a jewel thief who steals a pearl necklace and flees across the border to Spain, Coop' is the innocent American she employs as her partner in crime.

The comedy regulars, Mae West and W. C. Fields, are now nearing the end of their Paramount careers. Mae is *Klondike Annie* of the Barbary Coast ("some men are alright in their place — if they only knew the right places!") and a film star stranded on a cross country journey in *Go West, Young Man* ("a thrill a day keeps the chill away").

Fields stars in a remake of *Poppy*. He's a carnival bum

who tries to pass off his daughter as a missing heiress. A typically Fieldsian piece of nonsense rounds off the year: "I will now render the allegro movement from the Duggi Jig Schreckensnack opera of Gilka Kimmel, an opus Piptitone."

1937 Bob Hope arrives in Hollywood in September. "At last Paramount could no longer ignore the inevitable and I was brought to Hollywood with great fanfare. A man with a red cap met me at the station and showed me the nearest streetcar."

His buddy, Bing Crosby, goes from strength to strength and in *Waikiki Wedding* renders the year's Oscar winning song 'Sweet Leilani'; director Mitchell Leisen and screenwriter Preston Sturges combine wit, slapstick and farce with Jean Arthur, Ray Milland and Edward Arnold in *Easy Living*; Lubitsch directs Dietrich in *Angel*, a suave romantic comedy of Paris with Herbert Marshall and Melvyn Douglas.

Slave ships (*Souls At Sea*), the pioneer West (*Wells Fargo*) and the Spanish Civil War (*The Last Train From Madrid*) provide backgrounds for three Paramount adventures. The unexpected quality hits: *Ebb Tide*, with Ray Milland, a version of Robert Louis Stevenson's savage story about three beachcombers who steal a cargo ship, and *Maid Of Salem*, with Claudette Colbert and Fred MacMurray caught up in puritanical bigotry and Massachussetts witchcraft.

The most tender film of '37? Leo McCarey's *Make Way For Tomorrow* about an elderly couple who, for the first time in fifty years of marriage, find they are unable to support themselves and have to take up residence with their offsprings hundreds of miles apart. Victor Moore and Beulah Bondi steal the film — and the year!

1938 The scene begins to change once more. *The Big Broadcast Of 1938* marks the debut of Bob Hope (as a radio M.C. with three wives seeking alimony) but is also the last Paramount movie of long serving W. C. Fields.

Lubitsch and Mae West are others who make their Paramount swan songs. Lubitsch, plus a Wilder-Brackett screenplay, turns *Bluebeard's Eighth Wife* into a minor comedy gem. Gary Cooper is the much-married modern 'Bluebeard', Claudette Colbert his latest spouse, a young lady with a surefire cure for chronic insomnia — spelling Czechoslovakia backwards.

West goes out as Peaches O'Day in *Every Day's A Holiday*. Says she as she leaves: "The only picture to make money recently was *Snow White And The Seven Dwarfs* and that would have made twice as much if they had let me play Snow White."

In general, the year is mediocre. Fredric March is Jean Lafitte in DeMille's pirate adventure *The Buccaneer*; Fonda-Raft-Lamour team in *Spawn Of The North* a story of rival fishermen; native goddess Dorothy Lamour, Ray Milland and Technicolor make up another piece of foliage nonsense *Her Jungle Love*; Ronald Colman is roguish poet Francois Villon in *If I Were King*; MacMurray and Milland air pioneers in *Men With Wings*.

The song 'Thanks For The Memory' (from *The Big Broadcast Of 1938*) marks Paramount's historical moment of the year. It wins the Academy Award as best song and remains Hope's theme tune for the rest of his career.

1939 Something of an improvement. With Lubitsch gone, Mitchell Leisen comes into his own as the studio's master of sophistication. *Midnight*, scripted by Billy Wilder and Charles Brackett, allows Claudette Colbert to play at peak comedy form as a penniless American girl in Paris who masquerades as a Hungarian countess. Don Ameche, John Barrymore and bitchy Mary Astor add to the fun.

Bob Hope and Paulette Goddard, in a new version of the haunted house tale *The Cat And The Canary*, provide goose-pimpling wisecracks of a different kind; so does Jack Benny, who imagines himself a great lover in *Man About Town*.

Otherwise, it's mainly adventure that's stock-in-trade. Chief Thundercloud, twelfth on the cast list, is *Geronimo*; Douglas Fairbanks Jr. is in action in the days of the great sailing ships in *Rulers Of The Sea*; and DeMille brings together the building of a railroad, an Indian attack, sabotage, a train crash, a trouble-shooter (Joel McCrea) and an Irish postmistress (Barbara Stanwyck) in his best-ever western *Union Pacific*.

Wellman tops him however with two: Kipling's *The Light That Failed* with Ronald Colman superb as an artist losing his sight, and a remake of *Beau Geste*. As always the opening scene at the desert outpost, manned only by rows of dead men, the bodies of hero Gary Cooper and scarred villain Brian Donlevy lying close by, brings an immediate thrill of expectancy. How did they get there? How did it happen? Wellman tells all.

1940 Hemingway's Spanish Civil War novel *For Whom The Bell Tolls* is purchased by Paramount for a record fee of 150,000 dollars. The property is bought specifically for DeMille, but for one reason or another the epic master never gets round to making it.

What he does offer in 1940 is his first movie in Technicolor, *North West Mounted Police*, a story of the Riel Rebellion in Canada in 1885. Superb scenery, Canadian mounties (Preston Foster, Robert Preston), a Texas Ranger (Gary Cooper) and a half-breed schemer (Paulette Goddard) go to make up top-class action entertainment.

Crosby and Hope get together for the first of their famous 'Road' movies, *Road To Singapore*. On a South Seas island they come across native girl Dorothy Lamour and that's the trio set up for a whole series of zany adventures of the future.

All three stars are also in action singly for the studio. The Sarong Girl is again in the South Seas, this time with Robert Preston and a mighty wind in *Typhoon*; Bing croons and spoons with Mary Martin in *Rhythm On The River*; Hope is teamed once more with Paulette Goddard in another creepy comedy *The Ghost Breakers*.

With *Dr. Cyclops* Paramount venture into almost unknown territory, the horror film. Albert Dekker is the villain of the piece, a bio-physicist who reduces men to the size of mice in a radio-active chamber; Fredric March features in John Cromwell's version of Conrad's *Victory*; Mitchell Leisen serves up his usual Preston Sturges-scripted cocktail, *Remember The Night* with assistant D.A. Fred MacMurray falling for the lovely jewel thief he is prosecuting, Barbara Stanwyck.

Sturges himself at last breaks through as a director with *The Great McGinty*, a brilliant satire on American politics about a dumb palooka (Brian Donlevy) who gains the favour of crooked political boss Akim Tamiroff by voting thirty-seven times in one day. He rises quickly to become Governor of the State and in true Sturges fashion only falls from power when he attempts to go straight. A writing Oscar for Sturges and a deserved one!

1941 Sturges carries on from where he left off the year before, bringing both wit and mischief to *The Lady Eve*, a comedy about a cardsharp adventuress (Barbara Stanwyck) who sets out to con accident-prone brewery heir Henry Fonda. A crooked 'father' (Charles Coburn), a millionaire (Eugene

Pallette) and a fake lord (Eric Blore) combine to make the movie one of the funniest of the decade.

In *Hold Back The Dawn,* Paramount's other comedy master Mitchell Leisen opts this time for high-grade melodrama as he follows the experiences of a European gigolo (Charles Boyer) who finds himself stranded in a Mexican border town and decides to marry a naive school-teacher (Olivia de Havilland) in order to gain admittance to the States. Novelettish, but the sheer expertise of the acting, literacy of the Wilder-Brackett screenplay and professionalism of the direction, raise it to a level far above that of the basic material.

Otherwise it's that trio, Crosby-Hope-Lamour, together again in *Road To Zanzibar,* who rule the Paramount lot.

Bing is with Mary Martin in *Birth Of The Blues,* a tribute to the original Dixieland Jazz Band; Lamour brings out the sarong once more, this time for Jon Hall, as they prepare for the eruption of the 'Sacred Fire God' in *Aloma Of The South Seas;* as for Hope, he's in his usual mess, tasting army life in *Caught In The Draft* and betting 10,000 dollars of Paulette Goddard's cash that he can go twenty-four hours without telling a lie in *Nothing But The Truth.*

1942 Alan Ladd arrives on the scene, tough as nails and 5 ft 6 ins of expressionless dynamite. He's already appeared in twenty movies at other studios, but *This Gun For Hire* rockets him into the big time. He's an unsmiling killer involved with blonde cabaret girl, Veronica Lake, and fifth columnists selling a poison gas formula to the Japanese. Asked, during the film, how he feels when he kills, he replies, "I feel fine." A star is born! For the next ten years he features in some of the studio's toughest melodramas.

Ladd and Lake are together again in Stuart Heisler's remake of *The Glass Key;* Billy Wilder debuts as a director with a bright Ray Milland-Ginger Rogers comedy *The Major And The Minor;* Brian Donlevy, Preston Foster and William Bendix recreate for John Farrow's cameras the courage of the marines who held *Wake Island* for two terrible weeks after Pearl Harbour.

Preston Sturges is still on song with *The Palm Beach Story,* starring Joel McCrea and Claudette Colbert, and *Sullivan's Travels* in which he takes a swipe at the hand that feeds him — Hollywood. McCrea stars as a top comedy director ('Ants In Your Pants Of 1939') who yearns to go serious and make a more meaningful film called 'Oh Brother, Where Art Thou?' Disguised as a tramp he sets out to find what life's all about. Not everything he finds is to his liking.

DeMille delivers sea storms, shipwrecks, gang fights and a giant squid in what is probably his finest film *Reap The Wild Wind*, a story of America's southern coast during the 1840s. Ray Milland, Paulette Goddard and John Wayne are his stars, the latter as "a man who can ride out a sou'wester and clew up a topsail".

Hope the dope is involved with Madeleine Carroll and secret spy activities in *My Favourite Blonde*. "I'm a British agent," she reveals at last. "Too late sister, I've already got an agent," replies the dim-witted hero.

Bing sings another Oscar-winning song, Irving Berlin's 'White Christmas' in the Crosby-Astaire musical *Holiday Inn*; he also goes on the road again with Bob and Dottie, this time to *Morocco*. The song 'Moonlight Becomes You' catches the ear, a camel turning to the camera and commenting, "This is the screwiest picture I was ever in," makes one blink in disbelief!

1943 Claudette Colbert, Paulette Goddard and Veronica Lake do their bit for the war effort as army nurses on Bataan in *So Proudly We Hail*.

Miss Lake is now known as 'The Peek-A-Boo Girl' because of her gimmicky hair style. The slinky look in which Veronica's hair (17 inches long) hangs down loosely over one eye, came about by accident when she was making one of her early screen tests. As she prepared for the scene her elbow slipped off a table and sent a cascade of hair down over one eye. The producer liked it that way and that was that!

The top Paramount box-office hit is *For Whom The Bell Tolls* which at last gets filmed by Sam Wood. Gary Cooper is the American dynamiter Robert Jordan, Ingrid Bergman the orphaned Spanish girl, Maria. "Where do the noses go?" she asks as she kisses Coop for the first time.

Von Stroheim makes Rommel an ogre with a tasselled fly-swatter in Billy Wilder's desert adventure *Five Graves To Cairo*; Crosby is Virginia minstrel man Dan Emmett in the Technicolored *Dixie*; Bob Hope teams with Betty Hutton in *Let's Face It*; Ladd is in *China* with Loretta Young.

1944 *The* Paramount year of the 40s.

Leo McCarey's *Going My Way* wins both the box-office and Oscar honours by grossing more than six million dollars and becoming the first Paramount best picture winner since *Wings* seventeen years earlier. Crosby's singing priest wins him the nod for best actor, irascible Barry Fitzgerald the supporting award. "Rich, warm and human" is the unanimous cry of the critics, which is just about right.

Preston Sturges' fantastic burst of film-making comes to an end with not one, not two, but three movies.

The audacious *The Miracle Of Morgan's Creek* hits out at motherhood by allowing Betty Hutton's Trudy Kockenlocker to fall pregnant after an all night 'Kiss the boys goodbye party'; *Hail The Conquering Hero* knocks hero worship by having Eddie Bracken — discharged from the marines because of hay fever — unwittingly welcomed in raptures by his townsfolk; *The Great Moment*, in more serious vein, looks at how a Boston dentist (Joel McCrea) successfully demonstrated ether as an anaesthetic during the 1850s.

Mitchell Leisen demonstrates what Technicolor is all about with the extravagant Ginger Rogers musical *Lady In The Dark* and the Daphne du Maurier costume romance *Frenchman's Creek*; DeMille pays tribute to an American naval hero in Java in 1942 with *The Story Of Dr. Wassell*; *The Uninvited* is 'the first intelligent ghost story'; Robert Watson (Hitler), Martin Kosleck (Goebbels), Victor Varconi (Hess) and Luis Van Rooten (Himmler) are *The Hitler Gang*.

The year's most malevolent couple: Fred MacMurray and Barbara Stanwyck in Billy Wilder's brilliant *Double Indemnity*. They bump off the latter's elderly husband for the insurance money. MacMurray's on the make from the off.

Stanwyck: "There's a speed limit in this State, Mr. Neff. 45 miles an hour."

MacMurray: "How fast was I going officer?"

Stanwyck: "I'd say around 90."

MacMurray: "Suppose you get down off your motor-cycle and give me a ticket."

Stanwyck: "Suppose I let you off with a warning this time."

MacMurray: "Suppose it doesn't take."

Stanwyck: "Suppose I have to wack you over the knuckles."

MacMurray: "Suppose I burst out crying and put my head on your shoulder."

Stanwyck: "Suppose you try putting it on my husband's shoulder."
MacMurray: "That tears it."

1945 Three agonizing days in the life of a dipsomaniac novelist (Ray Milland) who pours out his shattered dreams to a New York bartender and drinks himself into a horrifying bout of the D.T.'s. It's *The Lost Weekend* and the stuff the modern cinema is made of for it's the first movie to look seriously at the problems of alcoholism. The picture, another best film Oscar winner, proves Milland an actor to be reckoned with as he goes through 99 minutes of torment. The film's writer/director, Billy Wilder, is now the major figure at the studio.

Crosby, Hope and Lamour are off again, this time on the *Road To Utopia*; Betty Hutton is gutsy night club queen Texas Guinan in *Incendiary Blonde*; Jennifer Jones suffers from amnesia in a broody romance with Joseph Cotten in *Love Letters*; Mitchell Leisen opts for eighteenth century elegance with *Kitty*, the story of guttersnipe Paulette Goddard who becomes a duchess through the caddish scheming of Ray Milland.

Milland, in fact, is a busy man. In the sinister *The Ministry Of Fear* he's immersed in espionage in wartime London. The director is Fritz Lang. The author is Graham Greene. The end result: Nazi conspiracy, stolen microfilm, fake seances, murder!

1946 All the big stars are in action.

Alan Ladd, especially, has his hands full coping with slinky Veronica Lake and tracking down the killer of his faithless wife in *The Blue Dahlia*; being parachuted into occupied France in *O.S.S.*; and suffering aboard a square rigger in 'the days of wooden ships and iron men' in *Two Years Before The Mast*.

Bob Hope, Louis XV's timid barber, is whisked off to Spain to masquerade as a dashing court dandy in *Monsieur Beaucaire*; Joel McCrea and Brian Donlevy (Trampas) star in a remake of *The Virginian*; Bing Crosby and Fred Astaire reunite in *Blue Skies*. Highlights: The Astaire solo 'Puttin' On The Ritz' and the Crosby-Astaire duet 'A Couple Of Song And Dance Men'.

Milland's reward for winning an Oscar is to lead a wagon train to *California*. Barbara Stanwyck, in her first film in colour, offers cynical compensations which is more than she does in *The Strange Love Of Martha Ivers*. As a wealthy murderess she polishes off Judith Anderson and sends an innocent man to the gallows. Kirk Douglas and Van Heflin totter uneasily on the dark fringes of her life.

Olivia de Havilland provides a two hour cry in *To Each His Own*, the old, old story of an unwed mother who, rather than cause a scandal, watches her son grow up from afar. Old it may be, but it brings de Havilland a surprise best actress Oscar, the first time the studio has won the award after twenty years of trying.

1947 The death of Ernst Lubitsch, aged fifty-five, from a heart attack brings to an end one of the most remarkable of Hollywood careers. Lubitsch made his great films at Paramount in the 30s. The 40s were less attractive to him even though 'the style' was frequently in evidence at other studios.

At the funeral Charles Brackett delivers the eulogy, Jeanette MacDonald sings Lubitsch's favourite songs and Walter Reisch, Mervyn LeRoy and Billy Wilder are among the pallbearers. Says Billy Wilder to William Wyler: "No more Lubitsch." Replies the latter, "Worse than that, no more Lubitsch films."

Lubitsch's Paramount pictures: *Forbidden Paradise, The Patriot, The Love Parade, Paramount On Parade, Monte Carlo, The Smiling Lieutenant, The Man I Killed, One Hour With You* (co-directed with Cukor), *Trouble In Paradise, If I Had A Million, Design For Living, Desire* (producer), *Angel, Bluebeard's Eighth Wife*.

By coincidence, Marlene Dietrich, who starred in Lubitsch's later Paramount films, reappears on the Paramount lot in *Golden Earrings*. Her co-star Ray Milland gets no chance to glimpse those beautiful legs. They're hidden beneath greasy rags for the entire film. She's a German gypsy girl, Mr. Milland a British spy.

DeMille's first post-war film is *Unconquered*, a colonial adventure of the 1760s. Two of DeMille's favourite stars, Gary Cooper and Paulette Goddard, whom campy Indian Chief Boris Karloff nearly burns at the stake, see him through — just!

The biggest commercial hit: *Welcome Stranger*, which reunites the *Going My Way* team of Crosby and Fitzgerald, this time as doctors, and grosses six million.

1948 Billy Wilder, perhaps with the death of Lubitsch in mind, tries to recapture some of the master's elegance with *The Emperor Waltz*, a Bing Crosby-Joan Fontaine romance set in turn-of-the-century Vienna. It's his first in Technicolor and his first flop.

He's more successful among the ruins of post-war Berlin where he finds surprising humour in a tale of a staid congresswoman (Jean Arthur) who is sent to Germany to investigate the morale of American troops. The film is *A Foreign Affair*. Co-star Dietrich, as the ex-girl friend of a top Nazi, shows the glamour is still there.

Alan Ladd, teamed with Lake for the fourth time, 'socks 'em' and 'busts 'em' in *Saigon*; the ever-hopeful trio, Crosby, Hope and Lamour, embark on the *Road To Rio*; and in *The Paleface*, Hope as dentist Painless Peter Potter goes West to meet the sexiest Calamity Jane of them all – Jane Russell. 'Buttons And Bows' is the hit song of the year and both *Paleface* and *Rio* Paramount's top grossers. Bob Hope is at his peak.

Barbara Stanwyck, after proving in *Double Indemnity* and *Martha Ivers* that she's the most dangerous dame in the business, gets her come-uppance in *Sorry, Wrong Number*. As a bed-ridden hypochondriac heiress she accidentally overhears a crossed line telephone conversation planning her murder. She waits in terror for eighty-nine minutes. Then dies.

Ray Milland in *The Big Clock* is more mobile, but in equally bad a fix. He's a crime magazine editor who finds himself framed and on the run for a murder committed by his tycoon boss Charles Laughton. A 17-jewel entertainment, the movie keeps perfect time right to the finish when Laughton plunges down a lift shaft to his death.

1949 Wyler's impeccable *The Heiress* is the studio's class film of the year, a handsomely mounted version of Henry James' 'Washington Square'. Olivia de Havilland earns her second Oscar for her repressed, young 'old maid'; Ralph Richardson as her arrogant, taunting father and Montgomery Clift her fortune-hunting suitor co-star.

Bob Hope, teamed with Lucille Ball, is at his best as the Damon Runyon bookie *Sorrowful Jones*. Otherwise things are routine rather than inspired.

Alan Ladd, ambitiously cast in the studio's second version of *The Great Gatsby*, goes West for the first time as the soft-spoken railroad detective *Whispering Smith*; Crosby, William Bendix and Cedric Hardwicke sing the hit number 'Busily Doin' Nothing' in *A Connecticut Yankee In King Arthur's Court*; Dean Martin and Jerry Lewis debut in *My Friend Irma*.

The desert, sadism, diamonds and double-cross go to make up Dieterle's savage *Rope Of Sand*. Corinne Calvert flaunts her sexuality; Burt Lancaster, Paul Henreid, Claude Rains and Peter Lorre ineffectively try to hide their greed and lust.

1950 Gloria Swanson makes a triumphant return to the studio she left in 1926 as the faded movie queen Norma Desmond. The film: Billy Wilder's ruthless 'Hollywood looks at Hollywood' picture *Sunset Boulevard*. "I'm ready for my close-up now Mr. DeMille," says Gloria in the final scene as she walks half-crazed down the staircase of her decaying mansion, into the camera and into movie history.

The house used by Wilder in the film is situated not on Sunset but Wilshire Boulevard and belongs to the Paul Getty family. Built in 1908 by a Mexican millionaire, it is a castle of French-Italian design and contains twenty-five rooms. The swimming pool in which gigolo William Holden meets his death is built by Paramount as payment for using the premises. The house is eventually demolished in 1960.

DeMille, who has a guest part as himself in Wilder's movie, makes his first biblical spectacular since the 30s, *Samson And Delilah*, described by one critic as "the most expensive haircut in history". It's the studio's biggest-ever moneymaker grossing over eleven million dollars. Victor Mature provides strength and Christianity, Hedy Lamarr sex and temptation, DeMille himself the spectacle as he destroys the Philistine Temple of Dagon in the closing scenes of the film. The set takes the epic master five months to build and eight days to destroy. Another publicity gem: 2,000 peacock feathers plucked from birds on DeMille's own ranch go to make up one of Miss Lamarr's exotic dresses!

Hedy also journeys West with Ray Milland in John Farrow's *Copper Canyon*; so does Alan Ladd, posing as the long-lost son of a rich cattleman in *Branded*, Barbara Stanwyck who hurls a pair of scissors into the face of Judith Anderson in Anthony Mann's broody *The Furies*, and Bob Hope who in *Fancy Pants*, a loose remake of *Ruggles Of Red Gap*, finds himself in the New Mexico cow town of Lucille Ball. No scissor throwing here.

Just neat comedy and a bright song, 'Home Cooking'.

The studio, which makes a habit of winning best song Oscars, win another for 'Mona Lisa' from *Captain Carey U.S.A.*; Dean Martin and Jerry Lewis are given starring roles in *At War With The Army*; Charlton Heston debuts as a crooked gambler in *Dark City*; Crosby stars for Capra in *Riding High*, a remake of the director's 1934 Columbia success *Broadway Bill*.

1951 Jan Sterling has the best line of the year. In Billy Wilder's vitriolic newspaper story *Ace In The Hole*, she says to Kirk Douglas, "I've met some hard boiled eggs in my time but you're at least twenty minutes!"

She has good reason. He's an on-the-skids reporter who discovers a man trapped in a remote desert cave and delays the rescue operations so that he can exploit the situation in the national headlines. The guy's also Sterling's husband. Not that she cares. She's leaving him anyway. For good measure she also disposes of Mr. Douglas by planting a pair of scissors in his crutch. Nasty, but brilliant.

Brilliant too is George Stevens' *A Place In The Sun*, an updated version of 'An American Tragedy' with Montgomery Clift as a poor factory worker and Shelley Winters the plain working girl and Elizabeth Taylor the spoilt society belle he becomes tragically involved with. Chaplin calls it, "One of the greatest films ever to come out of Hollywood". It wins six Oscars, but not, surprisingly, for best film.

Kirk Douglas is again in top form as a rough tough cop (once more he doesn't make it past the final reel) in Wyler's *Detective Story*; producer George Pal joins the studio for the first of his science-fiction dramas *When Worlds Collide*; Bob Hope remains on form, flirting with Hedy Lamarr in Tangier in *My Favourite Spy* and starring as Damon Runyon's racetrack tout *The Lemon Drop Kid*; his competitors in the comedy field, Dean Martin and Jerry Lewis, are in the navy in *Sailor Beware* and at college in *That's My Boy*.

Bill Holden, Rhonda Fleming, John Lund, Corinne Calvert, Joseph Cotten and Joan Fontaine, who endure a melancholy romance in *September Affair*, are all on the Paramount roster. So is a cat called *Rhubarb*. So still is Crosby who wins yet another best song Academy Award for the studio with 'In The Cool, Cool, Cool Of The Evening' from Capra's *Here Comes The Groom*.

1952 Bob Hope gets to sleep with Trigger, but not Jane Russell in *Son Of Paleface* and goes globe-trotting once more with Crosby and Lamour in *Road To Bali*. It's the trio's first in colour, but their last at the studio, the final film in the series, *Road To Hong Kong* being released by United Artists in 1962.

Shirley Booth is the year's best actress for her slovenly housewife in *Come Back, Little Sheba*; William Wyler tackles Dreiser with *Carrie* (Laurence Olivier, Jennifer Jones), a drama with strong echoes of *The Blue Angel* in its theme of decline and degradation; Martin and Lewis are parachutists (*Jumping Jacks*) and in vaudeville (*The Stooge*); Charlton Heston is *The Savage*, a white man raised by the Sioux.

Heston's big break comes when he's cast as the tough circus manager in DeMille's *The Greatest Show On Earth*, the year's top moneymaker. Its gross of fourteen million dollars surpasses the record set by *Samson And Delilah* three years earlier.

Betty Hutton does her own trapeze stunts; James Stewart hides behind a clown's make-up for the entire picture; Gloria Grahame risks being squashed to a pulp as an elephant's foot dangles dangerously close to her face; DeMille tops it all with a spectacular train crash and wins an Oscar as producer of the best film of the year.

DeMille is among the 100 film personalities chosen to select the ten best films ever made at the Brussels World Fair. He lists four of his own films – *The Ten Commandments, King Of Kings, The Sign Of The Cross* and *Samson And Delilah* – among his selections!

1953 Paramount follow other studios into the short-lived 3-D craze. Their first film in the process is *Sangaree*, a costume adventure with Fernando Lamas and Arlene Dahl. Routine in the extreme, it is dressed up to sound like an Oscar winner – 'Stars That Are Big, Action That Thrills, Adventure That Excites, Sex That Allures, Sets And Exteriors That Amaze, Technicolor That Beautifies It All!'

Audrey Hepburn *does* win an Oscar for her runaway princess in *Roman Holiday*; so does William Holden for his hardbitten POW in Wilder's *Stalag 17*; George Pal shifts *The War Of The Worlds* a little to the left, from Woking, Surrey to Los Angeles, USA; Jerry Lewis goofs around and Dean Martin sings 'That's Amore' in *The Caddy*;

Tony Curtis temporarily bounds free from the flashing blades at Universal to play master-escapist *Houdini*.

Bob Hope (*Off Limits*) and Bing Crosby (*Little Boy Lost*) are still active but '53 is the year of that other Paramount stalwart Alan Ladd. He gets keelhauled by sadistic skipper James Mason in *Botany Bay*, but soon gets his moment of triumph as one of the most heroic westerners of all time, *Shane*, a mysterious stranger who rides into a Wyoming Valley to help the homesteaders in their fight against the cattlemen.

Director George Stevens aims for perfection in every scene, even capturing on film a distant thunderstorm. The distant rumbling and storm clouds that accompany Jack Palance's murder of Elisha Cook outside Grafton's saloon are caught on celluloid because Stevens carefully checked the weather report before each day's shooting. A 4.30 a.m. phone call to the nearest weather station at Pocatello, Idaho, determined exactly what scenes he would shoot.

Shane, filmed at Jackson Hole, Wyoming and Paramount Studios, grosses nine million dollars.

1954 Paramount films Clifford Odets' *The Country Girl*, the story of an alcoholic actor on the skids (Bing Crosby), his shrewish wife (Grace Kelly) and the playwright (William Holden) who tries to help him make a comeback. Says Holden about wives, "They all start out Juliets and wind up as Lady Macbeths." For her "Lady Macbeth" Kelly wins an Oscar as best actress of the year.

The cool, blonde beauty also appears for Hitchcock in *Rear Window*, the first of six films the director is to make for the studio in the next six years. "Preview of forthcoming attractions" she smiles at James Stewart as she holds up a slinky nightgown. He can't do much about it though. His leg's in plaster because of an accident. But he sees a murder from his apartment window which is almost, if not quite as exciting.

Billy Wilder's Paramount swan song, *Sabrina* (he's been a director at the studio for twelve years) with Audrey Hepburn, is close to Lubitsch in tone; *Living It Up*, a Martin and Lewis vehicle, is a reworking of *Nothing Sacred*; and in *The Naked Jungle* an army of soldier ants eating its way towards Charlton Heston's plantation proves almost as deadly as Pal's Martians of the year before.

Bing Crosby's musical *White Christmas*, co-starring

Danny Kaye, Vera-Ellen and Rosemary Clooney is Paramount's box-office champ with twelve million. It's also the studio's first movie in Vista Vision, a deep focus process retaining the old 4 × 3 ratio.

Paramount, by using VistaVision, are the only major studio not to convert to the revolutionary CinemaScope process.

1955 Miss Kelly is up to her tricks again. This time it's Cary Grant on the receiving end in another Hitchcock picture *To Catch A Thief.*

"Do you want a leg or a breast?" she asks as they picnic in a car overlooking the Riviera. "You make the choice," says a wary Mr. Grant. For once the publicity boys get it right. Say the adds: 'Cary Grant as the jewel thief they called 'The Cat', Grace Kelly as a jewel anxious to be stolen!'

Bill Holden and Mickey Rooney are in Korea destroying *The Bridges At Toko-Ri.* Miss Kelly, with less to say for herself in this one, waits and suffers — not for Rooney, but for Holden; Anna Magnani, Burt Lancaster and Jo Van Fleet star in Daniel Mann's *The Rose Tattoo*, sleazy, steamy Tennessee Williams stuff down 'The Gulf Of Mexico' way.

Bogart appears twice as an escaped con — bad in Wyler's *The Desperate Hours* (death by shooting), good in Curtiz's *We're No Angels* (returns to jail); the popular James Stewart and June Allyson combination brings in the most dollars with the somewhat less than romantic *Strategic Air Command.*

Highspot of the year: Hope as vaudevillian Eddie Foy and Cagney (guesting as George M. Cohan) doing a soft shoe shuffle to the tune of 'Mary' in *The Seven Little Foys.*

1956 DeMille makes his last movie, a remake of his '23 hit *The Ten Commandments*, only this time it's all in the past, a 3 hour 41 minute account of Moses leading the Israelites from bondage in Egypt and into the promised land.

The studio vies with United Artists (*Around The World in 80 Days*) over the most important set of statistics:

THE GREATEST MOTION PICTURE IN HISTORY!

Ten years in the making. . .

Three years of research. . .

100,000 props. . .

25,000 extras. . .

950 books consulted. . .
984 periodicals. . .
1,286 clippings. . .
2,964 photographs. . .
Three months location shooting in Egypt, on the shores of the Red Sea, in the Sinai desert and on the slopes of Mount Sinai. . .
120 days on the Paramount lot. . .
Total cost, 13,500,000 dollars including one million for the parting of the Red Sea. . .

Moses did it all for less, but didn't make as much — forty-three million dollars!

Hitch, now without a retired Grace Kelly, turns to pert blonde Doris Day in his remake of his own *The Man Who Knew Too Much*. No coolness here. Instead anguish as her son is kidnapped by spies. But time for a quick song 'Whatever Will Be Will Be', before son is returned and a murder prevented at the Albert Hall. James Stewart performs nobly all along the way.

Hitchcock also has a little black comedy on view, *The Trouble With Harry* about a body which keeps being dug up, buried and dug up again *ad infinitum*. One of those involved in all the digging — Shirley MacLaine (debut).

Audrey Hepburn, Henry Fonda and Mel Ferrer are Natasha, Pierre and Andrei in King Vidor's multi-million *War And Peace*; Spencer Tracy and Robert Wagner are *brothers* in *The Mountain*; Martin and Lewis split up and go their separate ways after the appropriately titled *Hollywood Or Bust*; and Bing Crosby makes his last Paramount movie, *Anything Goes*.

Bing has made nearly fifty Paramount films since debuting in *The Big Broadcast*. He was top money-making star for five years running between 1944 and 1948 although his greatest box-office triumph, *White Christmas*, occurred in the 50s.

Victor Young, a prolific Paramount composer for nearly twenty years, dies aged fifty-six. Among his scores: *Reap The Wild Wind, For Whom The Bell Tolls, The Uninvited, Frenchman's Creek, Kitty, Love Letters, The Blue Dahlia, Unconquered, Golden Earrings, Samson And Delilah, September Affair, The Greatest Show On Earth, Shane.*

1957 It's now Bob Hope's turn to leave Paramount. *Beau James*, a sentimental, almost straight account of the career of

New York mayor Jimmy Walker is his last film on the lot. During his twenty years with the studio Hope has appeared in thirty-seven movies and figured thirteen times in the top ten moneymakers list between 1941 and 1953. His top commercial hit: *The Paleface*.

The box-office winner for '57 is a western, *Gunfight At The O.K. Corral* with a smiling Burt Lancaster (Wyatt Earp) and tubercular Kirk Douglas (Doc Holliday) cleaning up the Clantons with nonchalant ease. Frankie Laine sings a ballad of death behind the titles.

Sinatra has the year's Oscar song 'All The Way' in *The Joker Is Wild*; Astaire and Hepburn are loose in a musical Paris in *Funny Face*; Jerry Lewis goes it alone as a janitor who yearns to be a cop in *The Delicate Delinquent*; and rock singer Elvis Presley moves over from Fox for *Loving You*.

Newcomer Anthony Perkins, superb as baseball star Jimmy Piersall in *Fear Strikes Out*, also ventures West as a rookie sheriff in *The Tin Star*. Wily bounty hunter Henry Fonda teaches him all he needs to know!

1958 In *Vertigo* Hitchcock careers off into new and unnerving territory — sexual obsession — with ex-cop James Stewart trying desperately to recreate the image of a woman he has lost in death by reclothing and restyling the hair of a woman who closely resembles her. Kim Novak is both girls. There's murder too. Complex and frightening; a movie many regard as the director's masterpiece.

Several degrees down the scale: Anthony Quinn's remake (under DeMille's guidance) of *The Buccaneer*; Elvis Presley in *King Creole*; Jerry Lewis as a misfit G.I. in *The Sad Sack*; and a disappointing Cary Grant/Sophia Loren comedy *Houseboat*.

Much more zippy, Fay and Michael Kanin's *Teacher's Pet* with Gable as a hard-boiled city editor going to night school to study journalism from Doris Day. Gig Young as a tipsy playboy is another plus.

Jesse Lasky, one of the founding fathers of Paramount, dies aged seventy-eight. Vice president of the studio between 1916 and 1932, he later worked as a producer at Fox, Warner and RKO.

1959 The greatest Paramount pioneer, master-showman Cecil B. DeMille, dies from a heart attack on January 21, aged seventy-seven. More than any other film-maker his name has come to be synonymous with Paramount and success.

Derided by the critics, he knew what the public wanted and gave it to them in a big way. At the time of his death three of his pictures — *The Ten Commandments, The Greatest Show On Earth* and *Samson And Delilah* — rank among the top four Paramount moneymakers of all time.

The funeral is held on January 23. Both Adolph Zukor and Sam Goldwyn are among the pallbearers.

A New York editorial reads: "Mr. DeMille combined the flair for showmanship of a Barnum with the cinematic inventiveness of a Griffith. . .His mere name symbolized the raw energy, unlimited abundance and florid romance of a make-believe world that multitudes of many tongues thirsted for."

DeMille's most famous films: *The Ten Commandments* (23), *King Of Kings* (made independently), *The Sign Of The Cross, Cleopatra, The Plainsman, Union Pacific, Reap The Wild Wind, Unconquered, Samson And Delilah, The Greatest Show On Earth, The Ten Commandments* (56).

Later in the year, on August 6, the death also occurs of satirist Preston Sturges who, in a dazzling five year period (1940-44), hit out at everything from American politics and Hollywood to hero worship, mother love and the idle rich. He dies of a heart attack, aged sixty. Paramount films as writer/director: *The Great McGinty, Christmas In July, The Lady Eve, Sullivan's Travels, The Palm Beach Story, The Miracle Of Morgan's Creek, Hail The Conquering Hero, The Great Moment.*

Jerry Lewis loses a destroyer and becomes the studio's top moneymaker in *Don't Give Up The Ship*; Danny Kaye is jazzman Red Nichols in *The Five Pennies*; theatrical producer Clark Gable is chased by secretary Carroll Baker in *But Not For Me*; and Al Capp's famous cartoon-strip characters of Dogpatch are brought to cinematic life by Mel Frank in *L'il Abner*. Peter Palmer is the muscle-bound hero, Leslie Parrish Daisy Mae, Stubby Kaye Marryin' Sam.

1960 In his last Paramount movie, *Psycho*, Hitchcock scares everyone half to death with a tongue-in-cheek nightmare of a homidical psychopath (Anthony Perkins) who runs a lonely Arizona motel and lives with his unseen 'mother' in an adjoining Victorian mansion.

Lovely, on-the-run thief Janet Leigh seeks solace there. Alas, all she gets is knifed to death in her shower. Janet's famous murder takes seven days to shoot. There are 70 camera angles for just 45 seconds of footage. A plastic torso which spurted blood when slashed with a knife was devised by the special effects men, but Hitch didn't use it. Instead, he used a naked model, Janet Leigh's hands, shoulders and head — and the editing machine.

People the world over queue hour after hour to be frightened and pay eleven million dollars for the privilege.

American painter William Holden falls in love with prostitute Nancy Kwan in *The World Of Suzie Wong*; star Sophia Loren and manager Anthony Quinn run a hard-luck theatrical troupe in the Old West in *Heller In Pink Tights*; saxophonist Tony Curtis and defeated taxi-dancer Debbie Reynolds grapple with *The Rat Race* in New York City; Elvis, still a big draw, leaves the army and knocks 'em dead with *G.I. Blues*.

1961 Marlon Brando turns director. At a cost! He stars in and takes over the revenge western *One-Eyed Jacks* from Stanley Kubrick (who works just a few weeks on the project) and exposes more than a million feet of film during the six months' shooting schedule. 250,000 ft of this is printed resulting in a running time of over 4 hours. This is finally cut to 2 hours 21 minutes. The original budget was 1,800,000, the final cost nearly 6 million. Shades of von Stroheim!

Elivs Presley's *Blue Hawaii* is a top Paramount money-maker. So too is *Breakfast At Tiffany's* with Audrey Hepburn as Truman Capote's notorious super-tramp Holly Golightly, forever calling people 'quelle rat' and suffering from the 'mean reds'. George Peppard and 'Cat' share her highs and her lows.

On May 13 Gary Cooper dies of cancer, aged sixty. A top box-office star for more than three decades, he appeared in over ninety films during his thirty-four year career, forty-eight of them at Paramount. A favourite performer of Hathaway and DeMille, he starred in such Paramount productions as *City Streets, A Farewell To Arms, Design For Living, The Lives Of A Bengal Lancer, Desire, The General Died At Dawn, The Plainsman, Bluebeard's Eighth Wife, Beau Geste, For Whom The Bell Tolls, Unconquered.*

He is buried at Holy Cross Cemetery. His pallbearers include James Stewart, William Goetz, Jack Benny and Sam Goldwyn.

Just a month before his death he is awarded an honorary Oscar for 'his many memorable screen performances and the international recognition he, as an individual, has gained for the industry.' James Stewart, near to tears when accepting the award on behalf of a mortally ill Cooper says to the TV cameras, "We're all very proud of you Coop. All of us are extremely proud."

1962 Berlin and Sweden (*The Counterfeit Traitor*), Tokyo (*My Geisha, A Girl Named Tamiko*), Paris (*Too Late Blues*), even Africa provide the backgrounds to some of Paramount's '62 movies. Helping make the real-life backdrops interesting as well as beautiful: William Holden, Laurence Harvey, Shirley MacLaine, Paul Newman, Sidney Poitier, Joanne Woodward, John Wayne.

Hatari, Howard Hawks' piece about the tough guys who round up African wild animals and ship them to zoos around the world is top moneymaker with seven million, but it's the good old Wild West which produces the best movie, *The Man Who Shot Liberty Valance*, the story of a greenhorn lawyer (James Stewart) who wins fame and fortune for killing the notorious Liberty Valance (Lee Marvin), an outlaw who actually meets his death at the hands of sharp-shooting rancher John Wayne.

Not only is it one of John Ford's finest films but it also boasts one of the most famous sayings in movie westerns. Says newspaper editor Carleton Young to James Stewart: "This is the West sir. When the legend becomes fact, print the legend."

1963 Paramount take a liking to the plays of Neil Simon and film his Broadway success *Come Blow Your Horn*, which becomes the studio's film success of '63. Sinatra tops the cast as a Manhattan ladykiller initiating younger brother Tony Bill into the pleasures of 'The Sweet Life'.

Martin Ritt's *Hud* reflects the changing face of the American West, contrasting the pioneer values of ageing cattleman Melvyn Douglas with those of his arrogant cadillac-owning son Paul Newman; *Love With The Proper Stranger* on the other hand concentrates on the urban scene with jazz musician Steve McQueen being pursued by Macy's salesgirl Natalie Wood whom he has made pregnant during a one night stand. A humorous, likeable, often uncomfortably realistic movie especially during one horrific scene of a clinical, matter-of-fact back street abortion.

Elvis is still around, with Ursula Andress, having *Fun In*

Acapulco; so is Jerry Lewis who really excels as*The Nutty Professor*, a comic updating of *Dr. Jekyll And Mr. Hyde*; Dorothy Lamour, though, makes her farewell. Billed sixth as a Hawaiian saloon entertainer in John Ford's romp *Donovan's Reef*, she says goodbye to the studio where she has made nearly forty films.

'Call Me Irresponsible' is the Oscar-winning song but it's not new. The Sammy Cahn/Jimmy Van Heusen number was composed ten years before it was selected for *Papa's Delicate Condition*. It was originally scheduled for a Bing Crosby musical, but dropped because it wasn't considered suitable.

1964 Paramount casts its net wide.

Astronaut Paul Mantee finds himself stranded with only a monkey for company in *Robinson Crusoe On Mars*; Richard Burton's *Becket* is murdered in Canterbury Cathedral by order of Peter O'Toole's Henry II; General Burt Lancaster tries for a military coup of the USA in Frankenheimer's *Seven Days In May*; and half-naked Carroll Baker swings on a chandelier in the year's biggest financial hit, *The Carpetbaggers*, a version of Harold Robbins' phenomenally successful best-seller.

The film is Alan Ladd's last. He is found dead in his Palm Springs home on January 29. The cause of death is 'the effects of sedatives on top of a high level of alcohol'. Ladd was just fifty. The personification of the soft-spoken tough guy and the western hero, especially *Shane*, he made thirty of his films at Paramount. Among his best: *This Gun For Hire, The Glass Key, The Blue Dahlia, Two Years Before The Mast, Whispering Smith, Branded, Shane*. His last role was that of the half-breed western film actor Nevada Smith.

He once said: "I have the face of an ageing choirboy and the build of an undernourished featherweight. If you can figure out my success in this business you are a better man than I."

Later in the year, William Bendix, gruff, genial character actor who was Ladd's buddy in several movies — *The Glass Key, China, The Blue Dahlia, Two Years Before The Mast, Calcutta* — dies from pneumonia, aged fifty-eight.

1965 Henry Hathaway, who worked regularly with Gary Cooper at the studio in the 30s, returns for a large-scale John Wayne western, *The Sons Of Katie Elder*. Dean Martin

Earl Holliman and Michael Anderson Jr. co-star as the remaining sons who turn up at their ma's funeral to defend their family name.

Howard Hawks indulges once more in one of his favourite pastimes, motor racing, in *Red Line 7000*; Otto Preminger goes to war *circa* Pearl Harbour time in *In Harm's Way*; Martin Ritt provides more food for thought with a close look at modern espionage, double-cross and disillusionment in Le Carré's *The Spy Who Came In From The Cold.* Richard Burton is a washed-up British intelligence officer passing himself off as a defector in East Germany.

Harlow, despite the valiant efforts of Carroll Baker, manages to make one of the screen's most exciting women seem dull and *unexciting*; Jerry Lewis, after nearly twenty years at the studio, says farewell with *The Family Jewels* and *Boeing, Boeing.*

1966 Michael Caine's *Alfie* uses his cockney accent and seduction techniques to his own and Paramount's advantage. ''What's it all about, Alfie?'' sings Cher on the soundtrack. Roughly eight and a half million dollars is the answer.

Steve McQueen plays a young *Nevada Smith*, the half-breed character portrayed in middle age by Alan Ladd in *The Carpetbaggers*. A brutal Hathaway western of revenge it has McQueen seeking out the three men who murdered his father and raped and killed his Indian mother. The luckless trio: Karl Malden, Arthur Kennedy and Martin Landau.

Enjoying the best and worst of all possible worlds – Rock Hudson who in John Frankenheimer's *Seconds* grows tired of his tedious middle age and begins to long for his youth. A mysterious, Kafka-like rejuvenation organization provides the answer – at a price. But there's no way back as the luckless Mr. Hudson finds to his cost as he is carried screaming back to the operating theatre and certain death.

Science-fiction at its most chilling!

In October Paramount merges with Gulf & Western Industries, with Paramount as a subsidiary with its own management.

1967 It's Howard Hawks' turn for the studio's big western *El Dorado*, virtually a remake of his Warners' success of '59, *Rio Bravo*. John Wayne is in the John Wayne role, drunken sheriff Robert Mitchum in the drunken sheriff

Dean Martin role and riverboat gambler James Caan in the Ricky Nelson role. The only difference is that James Caan doesn't sing.

Stewart Granger is a professional hunter in search of a rogue elephant in Henry Hathaway's *The Last Safari*; Michael Caine exchanges accents – cockney for Deep South in Preminger's racial melodrama *Hurry Sundown*; detective David Janssen tries to clear himself of murder in *Warning Shot*. A massive all-star cast – Eleanor Parker, George Sanders, Joan Collins, Walter Pidgeon, Lillian Gish, Stephanie Powers etc, help and hinder his efforts.

Neil Simon again proves to be a good commercial bet. *Barefoot In The Park* takes nine million dollars as newly weds, Jane Fonda and Robert Redford, arrive at their fifth floor walk-up apartment with relative ease and everyone else, particularly Jane's tottery ma Mildred Natwick, in a state of physical collapse. Bohemian lodger Charles Boyer brings suave romance to the out-of-breath visitors.

1968 Neil Simon again, with a bigger hit than ever as ill-matched room-mates, neatness fanatic Jack Lemmon and slob Walter Matthau, team in a version of the Broadway play *The Odd Couple*. The film's take – twenty million dollars – makes it the biggest Paramount success of the 60s.

The supporting line-up is a strong one. Jane Fonda is *Barbarella*, the sexiest astronaut in the universe; Leonard Whiting and Olivia Hussey are Zeffirelli's *Romeo And Juliet*; Tommy Steele H. G. Wells' draper's assistant Kipps in the musical *Half A Sixpence*; and Yul Brynner the Mexican rebel leader Pancho Villa in *Villa Rides!*

No-one wants to know about the Mafia in Martin Ritt's *The Brotherhood* (things change a bit four years later), nor very much about Charlton Heston's loneliness and hardships in the Old West in *Will Penny*.

Everybody wants to know about *Rosemary's Baby*, Roman Polanski's superior chiller about a happily married young couple involved in witchcraft and satanism in an old New York apartment building. An evil smelling tannis root charm, disturbing next door neighbours, a nightmare rape by the Devil, even innocent puffs of cigar smoke wafting up from behind two occupied armchairs bring menace and terror.

1969 "Fill your hand, you sonavubitch," cries one-eyed marshall John Wayne to Robert Duvall in *True Grit*. Astride a horse, reins between his teeth, a pistol in one hand, a twirling rifle in the other, he charges across a meadow to an Oscar. Director Henry Hathaway pays homage to the great western star in the final scene, freezing the frame as Wayne, arms outstretched, waves his hat and leaps his horse over a four ft fence.

True Grit and the Alan Jay Lerner musical western *Paint Your Wagon* with Clint Eastwood, Jean Seberg and Lee Marvin ('Wanderin Star') top the commercial hits; Ali MacGraw and Richard Benjamin star in *Goodbye, Columbus*; arrogant Robert Redford goes in for Olympic skiing in *Downhill Racer.*

Three Paramount stalwarts of the 30s and 40s pass from the scene: producer-writer Charles Brackett (76) long-time partner of Billy Wilder; director Leo McCarey (71) who filmed the Marx Brothers (*Duck Soup*), W.C.Fields (*Six Of A Kind*), Mae West (*Belle Of The Nineties*) and Charles Laughton (*Ruggles Of Red Gap*); and Josef von Sternberg (75) a key figure on the Paramount scene in the late 20s and early 30s.

Von Sternberg's Paramount films: *Underworld, The Last Command, The Dragnet, The Docks Of New York, The Case Of Lena Smith, Thunderbolt, The Blue Angel, Morocco, Dishonoured, An American Tragedy, Shanghai Express, Blonde Venus, The Scarlet Empress, The Devil Is A Woman.*

1970 A young Harvard student (Ryan O'Neal) falling in love with a young Radcliffe student (Ali MacGraw) dying of leukaemia brings the tearjerker back into fashion. The revival is short-lived! Even so, *Love Story* becomes Paramount's biggest-ever box-office hit with a fantastic fifty million dollar gross. The favourite — and wettest quote of the year comes from the movie, "Love means never having to say you're sorry."

Mainly, though, it's a year of expensive failures. The Julie Andrews World War I 'spy musical' *Darling Lili* and the Barbra Streisand 'reincarnation musical' *On A Clear Day You Can See Forever* cost a lot, but make little. So does Mike Nichols' film of Joseph Heller's black war comedy *Catch-22.*

In *The Out-Of-Towners* Neil Simon puts every conceivable hazard in the way of ulcer-prone executive Jack Lemmon travelling, with wife Sandy Dennis, from Iowa to New York for an important business interview. The catalogue of disasters includes the twosome being fogbound, mugged, kidnapped, beaten and attacked by demonstrators. It's a comedy!

Paramount's most interesting movie: *The Molly Maguires*, Martin Ritt's penetrating look at betrayal and political upheaval in the Pennsylvania coalfields of the 1870s. Sean Connery and Richard Harris add superb performances to the uncompromising reality of the surroundings.

1971 Walter Matthau time at the studio. He stars in their two big hits, *A New Leaf* and *Plaza Suite*.

In the first he's a once wealthy, now bankrupt middle-aged playboy who sets out to find a rich wife in six weeks. Somehow, he settles for the clumsiest woman in the world, botanist Elaine May. "All I am or was is rich and that's all I ever wanted to be," bemoans Matthau as he becomes more and more entwined with Miss May.

In *Plaza Suite*, Neil Simon's Broadway play about three couples who stay at Suite 719 at the New York Plaza Hotel, he has three bites at the cherry. He's a businessman 'back on honeymoon' after twenty years, a Hollywood producer and a father of the bride — and superb as all three.

Black comedy is represented by *Such Good Friends*, Otto Preminger's darkly humorous joke at the expense of the medical profession and Hal Ashby's *Harold And Maude* in which twenty year old Bud Cort and eighty year old Ruth Gordon find they are both preoccupied with death.

Somewhat lighter fare is provided by *Willy Wonka And The Chocolate Factory* with Gene Wilder as a world-famous candy maker who offers a tour of his magical factory to five lucky kids. The song 'The Candy Man' features in the Newley/Bricusse score.

1972 The gangster slays the nun. After seven years *The Sound Of Music* is toppled from its perch as the top moneymaker of all time. The new champ is Paramount's *The Godfather*.

"I'm gonna make him an offer he can't refuse," mutters Mafia chief Brando and suddenly a new standard is reached in gangster films. Francis Ford Coppola's Mafia home movie, about the struggles of Brando's Corleone family to keep its ascendancy over rival New York factions, hits the mark critically (it's the best film of the year at Oscar time) as well as commercially.

The head of a prize racehorse left in the bed of a Hollywood producer; a strangulation from behind, the victim's hand pinned to a bar top by a dagger; a *Bonnie And Clyde* death at a tollgate; and a monstrous bloodbath finale are what pull in the crowds, not the expertise of Coppola's direction or the performances of the cast — Brando, Al Pacino, Robert Duvall, James Caan — all of which are close to brilliant.

The Godfather (take eighty-five million) remains box-office champ for five years until its record is gobbled up by *Jaws*.

Diana Ross is Billie Holliday in *Lady Sings The Blues*; Woody Allen a film buff haunted by Bogart in *Play It Again, Sam*; Robert Preston is Satan disguised as a schoolmaster in Lumet's *Child's Play*, a chilling story of the sinister goings-on at a Catholic boarding school for boys.

Mitchell Leisen, to whom most films of the year would appear entirely foreign, dies on October 28, aged seventy-four. A former set designer for DeMille, he turned to directing in the 30s and filmed several of the studio's most polished productions: *Murder At The Vanities, Easy Living, Midnight, Remember The Night, Hold Back The Dawn, Lady In The Dark, Frenchman's Creek, Kitty, To Each His Own, Golden Earrings*.

1973 Al Pacino graduates to stardom as Frank *Serpico*, a real-life cop who exposes corruption in the New York police force; Robert Duvall is also a cop, up against New York hoods in *Badge 373*; Robert Mitchum lingers among dark alleys and streets as an ageing small-time mobster turned police informer in *The Friends Of Eddie Coyle*.

Veronica Lake, who shared so many of those same dark alleys with Alan Ladd in the 40s, dies suddenly of hepatitis on July 7, aged fifty-three.

Peter Bogdanovich's *Paper Moon* with con man Ryan O'Neal working the American midwest in the Depression and selling bibles to newly widowed women is the surprise hit of the year. Ryan's daughter, Tatum O'Neal, steals the movie from under her dad's nose as his junior partner in crime and nabs a supporting Oscar at the grand old age of nine.

The major acting Oscar goes to Jack Lemmon, superb in *Save The Tiger* as a frustrated middle-aged businessman on the verge of a breakdown because his garment business is disintegrating. Lemmon becomes the first performer to win both a best actor and best supporting actor Academy Award, having won earlier for *Mister Roberts* in 1955.

1974 Paramount film Scott Fitzgerald's *The Great Gatsby* for the third time with Robert Redford and Mia Farrow as Jay and Daisy. The evocation of period by Jack Clayton is perfect, but despite a huge budget and calculated publicity build-up, the film is a disaster. It's a classic case of a pre-sold movie that doesn't sell!

It's a fine Paramount year though.

Polanski investigates the criminal regions of prewar Los Angeles in the Jack Nicholson/Faye Dunaway private-eye thriller *Chinatown*; Bogdanovich films Henry James' *Daisy Miller*; Pakula probes into the nightmare world of political conspiracy in *The Parallax View*; and Coppola achieves the unique feat of turning *The Godfather Part II* into an even more superior film than its predecessor.

Robert DeNiro plays Brando's Corleone as a young man arriving in the States from Sicily, Al Pacino rises to become the undisputed Mafia king of the United States.

In *The Conversation* Coppola also looks into the unsavoury aspects of modern wire-tapping and bugging. The setting is San Francisco. The star is Gene Hackman, a master electronics spy and "The best bugger on the West Coast".

1975 Sydney Pollack's *Three Days Of The Condor* brings in most coin at the box-office — nearly twenty million dollars. Robert Redford is the drawing card, a small-time CIA worker caught up in a political conspiracy within his own organization.

Robert Altman parodies the music metropolis of *Nashville*; Donald Sutherland is torn to pieces by a frenzied mob in Schlesinger's ambitious, but ultimately disappointing version of Nathaniel West's ruthless Hollywood story *The Day Of The Locust*.

Fashion model Diana Ross sings 'Do You Know Where You're Going To?' in *Mahogany*; black slave Ken Norton has no doubts. In *Mandingo*, a story of Deep South atrocities during the 1840s, Southern belle Susan George invites him for intercourse. He accepts.

Also on show: Jacqueline Susann's *Once Is Not Enough*. It is.

William Wellman, a director of several major Paramount movies, dies aged seventy-nine. Among his films: *Beggars*

Of Life, Wings (the studio's first Oscar winner), *Men With Wings, Beau Geste, The Light That Failed, The Great Man's Lady*.

1976 Tatum O'Neal, now aged eleven, receives the highest salary ever paid to a child star when she films *The Bad News Bears* with Walter Matthau. She receives 350,000 dollars plus eight per cent of the net profits. Her contract also states that she is to get an additional one per cent of the gross after the break-even point up to a total of 13,000,000 dollars!

It's a long way from the Mary Pickford days which Adolph Zukor must wistfully recall just prior to his death at the remarkable age of one hundred and three.

King Kong is a stinkeroo remake of the Schoedsack classic, but the great ape's box-office strength is still there — nearly thirty-six million dollars. Not so that of *Won Ton Ton, The Dog That Saved Hollywood*, a Michael Winner send up of the Rin Tin Tin days with fifty old stars and a big fat zero at the box-office.

The studio burn their fingers on Scott Fitzgerald yet again by tackling his last, unfinished novel *The Last Tycoon*. Robert DeNiro is Monroe Stahr, Elia Kazan the director, the result another dud.

John Wayne, an ageing gunfighter dying of cancer in Don Siegel's chamber western *The Shootist* goes out in the correct manner, in a bar-room shootout; Laurence Olivier, effectively cast against type as a Nazi War Criminal in Schlesinger's bloody *Marathon Man*, proves he can be as ruthless as the best of them. A knife blade attached to his wrist disposes of Roy Scheider, his skill at concentration camp dentistry results in him drilling holes through the front of Dustin Hoffman's teeth!

1977 Two great singers pass from the scene within just a few weeks of each other. Elvis Presley dies in August, aged forty-two, Bing Crosby in October, aged seventy-six.

Presley made most of his early rock 'n roll hits at Paramount before moving on to MGM later in his career. Paramount movies: *Loving You, King Creole, G.I. Blues, Blue Hawaii, Girls! Girls! Girls!, Fun In Acapulco*.

Bing appeared in nearly fifty films for the studio, won a best actor Oscar for *Going My Way* and sang four Academy Award winning songs. His most popular pictures — *Holiday Inn, Going My Way, Blue Skies, Welcome*

Stranger, White Christmas – and all the Road movies.

On the Paramount big screen in '77: schoolteacher Diane Keaton looking for kicks, and getting them, in singles bars in *Looking For Mr. Goodbar*; George C. Scott as, to all intents and purposes, Ernest Hemingway in *Islands In The Stream*; Israeli commando Robert Shaw trying to prevent mass murder in an American football stadium in *Black Sunday*; and John Travolta, sensational new dancing star in *Saturday Night Fever*.

1978 John Travolta carries on from where he left off in *Saturday Night Fever* by starring with Olivia Newton John in *Grease*, a high school musical about the the heyday of 'rock 'n roll.' Hit songs: 'You're The One I Want,' 'Grease Lightning', 'Rock 'n Roll Is Here To Stay.'

Sergeant Pepper's Lonely Hearts Club Band with the music of Lennon and McCartney plus an all-star cast and *American Hot Wax* carry on the musical revival; Ryan O'Neal and Ray Milland return to the studio for the *Love Story* sequel *Oliver's Story*; and in *Pretty Baby* director Louis Malle shocks everyone by casting eleven year old Brooke Shields as a girl living in the red light district of New Orleans in 1917.

Goldie Hawn discovers a plot to assassinate Pope Pius XIII in *Foul Play*; ace footballer Warren Beatty discovers himself in heaven fifty years too early in *Heaven Can Wait*, an updated remake of the 1941 Columbia hit *Here Comes Mr. Jordan*. Replacing guardian angel Claude Rains, the equally suave James Mason.

UNITED ARTISTS

United Artists

The story of United Artists can, in many ways, be likened to one of those superior double bills one used to see so often in the movies. It's a story in two parts, each as interesting as the other and each full of experiment, courage and imagination.

And just as it was difficult to select which was the better of two excellent films on a double-feature programme so it is difficult to assess which was the key phase in the development of Hollywood's most famous independent studio.

Many would select the opening years when the studio was first formed and a group of courageous film-makers took their lives — and fortunes — in their hands and decided to go it alone and break free from the shackles of the big studios. Others would choose the post-war period when the old guard of Pickford, Fairbanks and Chaplin had disappeared from the scene and a new brand of independence had begun to establish itself.

But, whichever way one looks at the development of United Artists, one thing clearly emerges. Without its revolutionary founders and their fight for individual freedom the dominance of the big studios would have lasted for a longer period and the independent producers and actors of today would have found it harder to gain a foothold in an industry traditionally run by moguls and studio power.

It all began in 1919 when Mary Pickford, Douglas Fairbanks, Charles Chaplin and D. W. Griffith decided to form a company that they hoped would become known as the 'Tiffany's of the Industry'. *They* would put the money into the studio; *they* would choose the pictures and *they* would make the profits which, all being well, would be ploughed back into the company.

It was a gamble. Even Mary Pickford, the toughest member of the quartet and the lady credited for thinking up the idea of the independent studio, must have had a few qualms as the four of them laid their money and reputations on the line. They were the wealthy elite of Hollywood, millionaires who had made their fortunes by driving hard bargains with the major studios and becoming the first superstars (in Griffith's case, the first super-director) of the early Hollywood.

Should United Artists fail, however, they could quickly become the unemployed poor and find themselves crawling back on their hands and knees to the very studios at whom they had cocked a defiant snoop.

When Richard Rowland, the president of Metro, heard that the four rebels had started their own company he wisecracked, "So the lunatics have taken charge of the asylum."

It was an amusing remark, but a long way from the truth. The quartet not only proved themselves artists of outstanding ability, but also highly astute at business. Pickford's business acumen was well known through her long battles with Zukor at Paramount. Producer Joe Schenck, who was to join the company in 1924, said of Fairbanks, "Don't go up against Doug in a business deal. He's poison even to California real estate men and they *are* tough birds."

As for Chaplin, he was reputed to keep half a million at all times in cash in a safe deposit vault. According to his fellow comic Chester Conklin, "Charlie always declined anything that threatened to cost money."

So with one eye on the screen and the other on the cash register and both hands firmly on their cheque books the 'United Artists' plunged into competition against the major studios.

The original idea was for each of the partners to produce three pictures a year, thus allowing the company to release a film a month. It sounded fine on paper. In practice it soon proved unworkable. Both Pickford and Chaplin had movies to finish for First National and only Fairbanks and Griffith were immediately free to work for the new company.

So from the very start, the company limped rather than sprang into action. In fact, for four years it operated on only three cylinders, Chaplin being tied up with First National until 1923. The problem that was to beset them throughout the first decade of their existence became immediately apparent — shortage of product. Without additional films the company would not survive. A revised estimate suggested two films a year from each partner, but, with Chaplin out of action, that too proved impracticable.

Other, second rate product was put alongside the pictures of Griffith, Pickford and Fairbanks and top class productions like *Broken Blossoms, Pollyanna* and *The Mark Of Zorro* were accompanied by such 'also rans' as *The Iron Trail* and Sennett's *Down On The Farm*. The studio struggled. The partners cast around desperately for suitable quality films to go alongside their own. None were available. All were being produced by the majors. Within two years of United Artists' formation rumours began to circulate about its future.

The industry with a smug "I told you so" attitude looked on with tolerant amusement and gave the 'rebellious four' little more than a year to survive.

During those first years the industry was very nearly right. On several occasions the company looked like foundering and always on the same rock, shortage of quality product.

So sure had the partners been that they could carry the studio between them in its formative years that they were not a little dismayed when they found themselves having to lower their standards in order to survive. Outside pictures such as *Fair Lady, A Woman's Woman, The Shriek Of Araby* and *Garrison's Finish* did little to help the reputation of a company whose grandiose 'Tiffany's' sub-title was beginning to look a little pretentious to say the least.

Mary Pickford, twenty-seven year old of the golden curls, dimples and winning smile, continued on her same sweet way, just as she had done at Paramount, in child roles in *Little Lord Fauntleroy* and *Tess Of The Storm Country*; Fairbanks, after a hesitant start, suddenly found his true metier in costume spectaculars and for a decade became the hero of millions of boys all over the world; Chaplin, when he did eventually arrive at United Artists, increased the range of his comic genius with films like *The Gold Rush* and *The Circus*.

Only Griffith found it difficult to function effectively. Although no-one knew it at the time, his great days were already behind him. He would never again reach the heights of *Birth Of A Nation* and *Intolerance*. UA for him was a mistake. His pictures slowly lost their epic quality and declined into indifferent melodramas that almost any competent director could have handled. He, and only he, would have fared better had he remained under the studio system.

The most interesting aspect of United Artists in the early days was that they were able to function at all. All of the partners were, by their very nature, supreme egotists. That was why they had wanted their freedom in the first place, to operate their way and suffer no outside interference. But, just as they had often clashed with their respective studios earlier in their careers, they now found themselves clashing with each other.

Mary Pickford has said of those early times, "We maniacs had fun and made good pictures and a lot of money. In the early days United Artists was a private golf club for the four of us."

Nonetheless, the partners still had their differences. Chaplin, for instance, found Griffith aloof and remote, too immersed in his epics and frail heroines to have any understanding of comedy. Griffith for his part had no idea what made Chaplin tick, and no time for the little man's special, subtle kind of humour. As for Fairbanks, Griffith commented, "Fairbanks thinks that acting is leaping from one place to another."

Two who did get on were Pickford and Fairbanks. Less than a year after the formation of the company they were married. The wedding made headlines all over the world. The pair were hailed as 'The King and Queen of America' and their magnificent Beverly Hills mansion nicknamed 'Pickfair'.

Every word they uttered made news, no matter how trivial. They were the personification of luxury and style. When they built their studio on Santa Monica Boulevard in 1922 Mary had a six room bungalow included on the lot and Doug a dressing room, gymnasium, pool and steam bath added to his office.

Fairbanks was a physical fitness fanatic. He had to be. When he made his first swashbuckler, *The Mark Of Zorro*, in 1920, he was thirty-seven years of age. He would continue to run, jump, leap and somersault until he was forty-seven. And that meant keeping in shape. Any let up in his rigorous keep-fit schedule would have immediately shown on the screen. Fairbanks enjoyed his training and exercise. A likeable show-off he was never happier than when performing his daily physical fitness routines.

"Douglas Fairbanks was a dynamic person who lived for good health," said Lillian Gish. "He drank about two glasses of champagne a year. He and Chaplin trained themselves to be fit. In those early days we were really all health minded."

Fairbanks never thought of himself as a great actor. As long as he was the hero and could play the dashing cavalier he was happy. Veteran director Allan Dwan who guided him through two of his biggests hits, *Robin Hood* and *The Iron Mask*, said of him, "Douglas worked with speed and basically with grace. Stunts per se were of no interest to him or me. The only thing that could possibly interest either one of us was a swift, graceful movement — the thing a kid visualised in his hero.

"But everything was gauged for him. We never made him strain. If he had to leap on a table to fight a duel we'd cut the legs off that table so it would be just the leap he ought to make. He never had to reach an extra inch for anything. Otherwise it wouldn't be graceful — it wouldn't be for him and it wouldn't be right. Stunt men have tried to imitate him and it always looked like a stunt when they did it. With him it always looked natural."

During the twenties, when United Artists was heaving about

like a small ship in a rough sea, it was Fairbanks who was the mainstay of the studio. His importance has sometimes been underestimated. But after *Zorro* he didn't have a flop for ten years. *The Three Musketeers, Robin Hood, The Thief Of Baghdad, Don Q, Son Of Zorro, The Black Pirate, The Gaucho, The Iron Mask* followed one another like clockwork. All made money, all combined a surefire box-office formula of action, spectacle and romance. Without him it is possibly true to say that United Artists would not have survived.

The others did have their flops however. Mary Pickford who by this time could play little girl roles in her sleep ("I hadn't any method of acting. It was easy for me to act the part of a child because I adored children, I forgot I was grown up.") made a disastrous attempt at an adult part in *Rosita*; Chaplin left his little tramp behind for the first time in *A Woman Of Paris* then hurriedly brought him back for *The Gold Rush*; and Griffith, after two typical pictures, *Broken Blossoms* and *Way Down East*, fell away altogether, his talent evaporating so quickly that Hollywood stood back amazed at his rapid decline.

By 1924, United Artists, although able to boast a succession of fine films, was still struggling. The old problem — too few films — that had been with the studio since the very beginning raised its head yet again, this time more forcibly. Fairbanks and Pickford tried to bring in new talent, but with inauspicious results, Chaplin was busy at work on his next picture, Griffith had left the company.

The time to bring in new blood had arrived. The man who joined them as a partner was producer Joseph Schenck, a man who knew just about everything there was to know about the movie business. He was just the right person to inject life into the flagging company. He also brought the promise of new product through films from his actress wife Norma Talmadge, famous glamour star Gloria Swanson whom he lured across from Paramount and, most important of all, producer Sam Goldwyn who had an independent company of some substance and whose pictures were to sustain United Artists throughout the hard days of the thirties.

None of the partners wanted Goldwyn. They opposed the move. Goldwyn meant trouble. They knew his reputation. Ever since his Paramount days he had caused friction and dissent. If anything he was even more egotistical than they were. But economic necessity carried the day. Goldwyn was brought in and stayed in. He brought with him stars Ronald Colman and Vilma Banky, directors Henry King and George Fitzmaurice, and contributed a regular three pictures a year. Those three pictures, many of them top class productions, made all the difference.

Before long, however, the sniping and wrangling the partners had been afraid of began to occur. It was always Goldwyn versus the rest. Chaplin especially found it difficult to get along with him. Goldwyn, who had great respect for Chaplin as a comedian, but none whatsoever for him as a businessman, commented wryly after one particularly stormy meeting, "The only thing Charlie knows about business is that he can't afford to take less."

Chaplin, in fact, had his hands more than full at the time of Goldwyn's arrival. *The Gold Rush*, hailed by many as his masterpiece, had reinforced his position as the cinema's greatest comedian and *The Circus* had been another success, albeit a minor one. On the debit side he had to contend with a loveless marriage to a young starlet, Lita Grey, who had more or less blackmailed him into marriage and then, in 1927, threatened to reveal some sordid personal scandal if Chaplin didn't agree to a handsome divorce settlement.

Chaplin was always the most complex of the United Artists personalities. As early as 1915 he had feared for the loss of his fame. He suffered moments of deep depression and would often say to himself, "I must get back to work — but I don't feel like it. I don't *feel* funny. What will happen if I can never be funny again?"

Convincing himself of his certain failure he would say, "You're through. You've lost your creative streak for good."

A couple of days in bed thinking about his problems would usually put matters to rights. Complete solitude and rest was his formula for recharging the batteries. During those periods he refused to see anybody. Two days later he would emerge refreshed, brimming with ideas, ready to go.

He spared no expense during the shooting of a film. Money was no object, neither was time. If it needed fifty or a hundred takes to get things right, then that's what it took. Anything between twelve and twenty months was the average shooting time for a Chaplin film. One and a half million dollars was the average cost.

When sound came in Chaplin stopped filming *City Lights* and closed production. He considered all the possibilities carefully. Should he, like all the others, go for sound pictures? He was in no doubt that talkies were here to stay. It was just that he was afraid his kind of pantomime might appear less effective with dialogue. On the other hand he had a good voice and stage experience and was admirably qualified for the sound medium. In the end he opted to remain silent and reopened the set.

City Lights was a harrowing experience for some. Chaplin

shot thousands of feet of film, improvising and retaking constantly. If things didn't go right he fired people. One such unlucky individual was actor Henry Clive who had been cast as a millionaire in the picture and acquitted himself very well, at least up until the drowning scene in the river — Chaplin's pool in the studio.

Protesting that he had a heavy cold, Clive refused to do the scene until the water had been warmed by the sun. It was a valid point. He did have a heavy cold and didn't want to make it worse. Chaplin, who had been working all night with the crew, was near exhaustion. He insisted Clive went through with the scene. Clive refused point blank. Chaplin, in a furious rage, left the set and immediately fired the actor. It was of no consequence that Clive had already completed most of the role. That was immaterial. But the fact is that it took Chaplin fully six months to again reach the drowning scene in the river.

On one occasion Chaplin, something of a practical joker, had his own 'pool experience'. He was sitting around the pool at Pickfair with Doug and Mary when he suddenly plunged, fully clothed, into the water. "I am an atheist," he gurgled. "If there is a God let him save me."

Gasping, bubbling and choking, he was just about going down for the third time when Fairbanks, also completely dressed, jumped in and rescued him. Mary, the world's sweetheart, was meanwhile racing round the pool, screaming, "Let the heathen drown, let the heathen drown."

The marriage of Pickford and Fairbanks lasted until 1935, but their careers began to falter several years earlier, with the coming of sound. Age was creeping up on them and both were only too well aware of it.

In order that she might play more dramatic adult roles Mary had her famous curls cut from her head, but in doing so she removed the one thing that made her unique, so different from all the other Hollywood actresses of the time. After winning an Oscar for *Coquette* she became just another star, no different, no better than all the rest.

Fairbanks was even more aware of the passing of time. In 1929 when he repeated his role of D'Artagnan in *The Iron Mask*, he was forty-seven. He was still blessed with a slim, trim body, but the face was strained, the eyes restless and worried, the hair line receding. He knew that without the athletics and derring-do he was nothing. What stretched before him was too hideous to contemplate.

His temper became short and he had sullen moods of indifference. Mary tried to raise his spirits by suggesting they co-star in a version of Shakespeare's *The Taming Of The Shrew*. Reluctantly he agreed.

It was Fairbanks' first sound picture and filming was horrendous. The great swashbuckler was completely disinterested. The make-up call was 9 a.m., but Fairbanks deliberately dawdled over his daily exercises and morning sunbath and frequently arrived on the set two and a half hours late. As well as stretching everyone's nerves to breaking point he was costing, according to Mary's financial mind, United Artists thirty dollars a minute.

Worse, Fairbanks often didn't know his lines which had to be written on large blackboards. If Mary was dissatisfied with a scene and wanted a retake Fairbanks would snap at her in front of the entire crew and refuse to do it, "The making of that film was my finish," said Mary. "My confidence was completely shattered and I was never again at ease before the camera or microphone. All the assurance of *Coquette* was gone."

So too in many ways was the assurance and bubbling enthusiasm with which she, Fairbanks, Chaplin and Griffith had begun United Artists just a decade before. Griffiths' career was finished, both she and Fairbanks would soon be names of the past, only Chaplin would continue. The 'Tiffany's of the Industry' hadn't exactly lived up to its name. To be sure there had been several glittering gems, but there was plenty of dross too. If there was a feeling among the partners, at the time, it would almost certainly have been 'dreams and potential unfulfilled'.

Yet UA was still in business after many had predicted it would fall. Chaplin was active and Goldwyn was going strong with three, sometimes four films a year, keeping the company on an even keel. He remained at United Artists for fourteen years right through until 1940. During those years other producers, Korda, Selznick and Wanger among them, were all brought in to bolster up the company's product, but it was Goldwyn who was the mainstay.

The initial Goldwyn period was dominated by the films of Ronald Colman, handsome, debonair and with a rich speaking voice simply made for the talkies; the middle period was basically one of musicals, the Goldwyn Girls and Eddie Cantor; the final and best period belonged to the films made by William Wyler.

"I am a rebel," Goldwyn would say. "I make a picture to please me. If it pleases me I feel there is a good chance it will please others. But it has to please me first."

Nine times out of ten he was right. Goldwyn, like others, had that uncanny instinct. A quick glance at some of the films he made for United Artists proves the point: *Stella Dallas,*

Raffles, Whoopee, Arrowsmith, Kid Millions, Dodsworth, The Hurricane, Dead End, Wuthering Heights, The Westerner. Yet he could still make mistakes and when he did they were usually lulus.

In 1926 he made *The Winning Of Barbara Worth*, one of his first films for United Artists. It starred Ronald Colman and Vilma Banky and also introduced to the screen Gary Cooper, a tall, lanky shit-kicking young man who really came from the West and had actually been a cowboy.

Goldwyn hired him for fifty dollars a week, featured him in the film then let him go. He was convinced that it would be much too difficult to find parts for him in the future. He paid dearly for his mistake. Paramount immediately signed Cooper to a long term contract at one hundred and fifty dollars a week and built him into a superstar. When Goldwyn wanted to use him again ten years later he had to pay three thousand dollars a week for his services.

An even bigger mistake was the signing of Anna Sten, a Russian-born actress whom Goldwyn thought would become an even bigger attraction than Dietrich or Garbo. She had a gorgeous body, a seductive face and a beguiling smile. Goldwyn was taken in by all three. In 1932 he brought her to the States and signed her to a five year contract at three thousand dollars a week.

A larger error of judgment has seldom been made. For despite her undoubted physical charms, Miss Sten had a voice as thick as a Russian general. She was also prone to over-eating. As a frantic Goldwyn provided daily elocution lessons to improve the voice, he watched in dismay as the figure he had found so attractive begin to gain in proportions. He put Miss Sten on a crash diet and waited patiently for her voice to improve. Unfortunately, for the producer, most of the Hollywood press was also waiting and continually asking when Mr. Goldwyn's new discovery was going to make her screen bow.

When Goldwyn at last realised that Miss Sten's voice was not going to improve to any great extent he decided to take the plunge by casting her as Zola's *Nana*. The director was George Fitzmaurice, the filming fraught with tension. "Speak more naturally, darling," Fitzmaurice kept repeating as take followed take and things still didn't come right. Some scenes went to 25, 30, 35 takes. Miss Sten, near to exhaustion, kept collapsing. Tempers frayed. Fitzmaurice grew more and more frustrated.

Goldwyn let things continue until he had spent some 400,000 dollars. By then he knew he had a disaster on his hands. Enough was enough. He called a halt and scrapped the picture and began again with a different director, Dorothy Arzner.

It was a brave thing to do. The money that went down the drain was his money. He was taking the loss. *Nana*, to no-one's surprise, was a flop. Anna Sten instead of rocketing to stardom spluttered out like a damp squib. She made three films for Goldwyn, but was then dropped.

Goldwyn, however, was not a man of failures. He was a man of success. He really was a maker of stars and he generally drove everyone who worked for him crazy, maintaining that "usually when people are happy making a picture, it's a flop".

He also knew the value of publicity: "People say that whenever I have a picture coming out I always start a controversy about something that gets into the papers. Well, in all sincerity, I want to assure you that as a general proposition – there's not a single word of untruth in that."

His famous Goldwynisms – phrases which murdered the English language – belong to Hollywood folklore even if most of them can be credited not to him personally, but to his team of publicity writers.

"In two words, im-possible," was one of his best-known remarks. "Start with an earthquake and work up to a climax" was another. Others included: "Anyone who visits a psychiatrist needs his head examined," "Tell me, how did you love the picture?" "We've all passed a lot of water since then," "I'll give you a definite maybe," and "Write music like Wagner, only louder."

The part mixed metaphor – part illiteracy was also applied to directors. "The trouble with directors is that they're always biting the hand that lays the golden egg," he grumbled. He was particularly sensitive about directors. When a reporter once mentioned, "William Wyler's *Wuthering Heights*" he snapped back, "*I* made *Wuthering Heights*, Wyler only directed it."

A more amusing story concerns Billy Wilder, who once tried to persuade Goldwyn to let him make a picture about the life of the great Russian ballet dancer Nijinsky, a man who spent the last years of his life in an asylum convinced he was a horse. "Now listen Billy," argued Goldwyn. "If you think I'm going to invest three million dollars in a picture about a man who thinks he's a horse, you're even crazier than he is."

"But Sam, we can give the story a happy ending," urged Wilder. "We can have him win the Kentucky Derby."

Many people admired Goldwyn, few really liked him. When Scott Fitzgerald was working on a rewrite of *Raffles* he commented, "I like Sam Goldwyn. You always know where you stand with him – nowhere."

By the end of the 30s Goldwyn had established himself as the key figure at United Artists. Selznick had been responsible for some fine movies – *Nothing Sacred, The Prisoner Of Zenda, A Star Is Born* – but Goldwyn was the regular supplier of quality.

With Chaplin now faltering — his satirical *Modern Times*, released in '36, had made only a small profit — Goldwyn sensed that studio power was within his grasp. He badly wanted control of the company and felt that he had a legitimate right to it. His pictures were the *key* pictures at United Artists. Without them, he maintained, the studio would fall apart. He offered to buy out Pickford, Fairbanks and Chaplin for half a million dollars each. They retaliated by saying that if he could raise the offer to two million each he had a deal.

The offer was there. All that was needed was to raise the money. He approached Korda who said he was interested. Together they made overtures to everyone who might be willing to contribute finance to the company. All they could raise was four million. The deal was off.

Goldwyn had been within an ace of gaining control. He was bitterly disappointed. He had been with the company for more than twelve years and set his sights on ownership since the early 30s. With his chance gone he realised that his future lay elsewhere. He still rowed incessantly with Pickford, Fairbanks and Chaplin. Now, even more, they opposed his every move. After much legal wrangling over his contract he left the studio for RKO. His last film for United Artists was *The Westerner* starring Gary Cooper.

How UA would have developed if Goldwyn had taken control remains one of the great imponderables of Hollywood. Certainly it would have developed into a very different kind of studio. Almost equally certainly it would have remained a successful studio with Goldwyn as an all-powerful mogul to rival Mayer, Zanuck and Cohn. Whether independence would have been an integral part of a Goldwyn set-up is another matter. But the fact that Goldwyn's RKO hits — *The Little Foxes, Ball Of Fire, Pride Of The Yankees, The Best Years Of Our Lives* and the films of comedian Danny Kaye — would have gone to UA indicates the level on which the studio could have operated if Goldwyn had been able to raise the extra capital.

As it was the studio declined rapidly. Without Goldwyn, the old problem of product shortage returned, worse than ever before. During the 40s United Artists became the studio of the mediocre. Wanger left, then Korda. Selznick remained for a time, producing two of the studio's few commercial hits, the tear-jerker *Since You Went Away* and the Hitchcock thriller *Spellbound*, then he left too when the company refused to distribute his massive sex western *Duel In The Sun*, a movie which grossed nine million dollars within just a few months of its release.

Chaplin, plagued with income tax difficulties, a paternity suit and political troubles, contributed *The Great Dictator* and the disastrous *Monsieur Verdoux* which failed to muster even a half-million gross. Both he and Pickford (Fairbanks had died in 1939) lost interest in the company which sank lower and lower until, by the end of the decade, it was producing minor thrillers and comedies and facing bankruptcy.

Such a decline had been forecast by the pundits when the company had entered its first decade in the 20s. Then it survived because of the courage and artistry of its founders. In the late 40s there was no-one to rescue the company from what seemed like almost certain disaster. The pictures were second rate, the stars such as they were, had no drawing power, the directors no style. As 1949 became 1950 it looked like the end of the road.

Two people however did think United Artists could be saved — Arthur B. Krim and Robert S. Benjamin. Both were partners in a thriving law firm in the film industry. Well versed in all aspects of the movie business they were brought in as a managerial team to change the company's image.

They approached Chaplin and Pickford with the suggestion that they be made trustees for 100 per cent of United Artists stock which would, in effect, give them operating control of the company for ten years. Chaplin and Pickford (both of whom sold their interests in the mid-50s) agreed. The new United Artists, saved in the nick of time, was under way. The second half of the 'double-feature' programme had begun. It is still continuing to this day.

Since 1950 United Artists has prospered. It would not be stretching a point to say that it has prospered more than any other company. The reason isn't hard to find. It lies in one word. And it's the same word that first fired Pickford, Chaplin and co. in 1919. Independence. Only this time it was independence of a different kind. The studio was no longer a company run by four powerful partners. It was a studio to which independent producers, directors and actors could bring their properties and stand a good chance of having them financed.

United Artists moved with the times. It was not afraid of controversy as can be seen from films like *The Man With The Golden Arm, Paths Of Glory* and *I Want To Live*. Nor was it afraid to spend money in a big way if it felt the subject warranted it, hence blockbusters like *Around The World In Eighty Days, Exodus, The Alamo, West Side Story*.

It is no accident that the studio boasts more best picture Oscar winners than any other company during the 60s and 70s. It is also no accident that nearly all the top directors in the industry chose to work there during the post-war period, hence pictures like Wilder's *Some Like It Hot* and *The Apartment*,

Kramer's *Judgment at Nuremberg*, Frankenheimer's *The Manchurian Candidate*, Schlesinger's *Midnight Cowboy*, Foreman's *One Flew Over The Cuckoo's Nest*, Lumet's *Network*, Woody Allen's *Annie Hall*.

It was Otto Preminger who perhaps best described the UA set-up. "Only United Artists has a system of true independent production," he said. "They recognise that the independent has his own personality. After they agree on the basic property and are consulted on the cast, they leave everything to the producer's discrimination."

The remark was made some years ago, but it is equally relevant today for that system has continued throughout the 60s and into the 70s with ever-increasing success.

Nevertheless United Artists owes it all to those four courageous pioneers who first went ahead with their revolutionary plans in 1919. Without their courage UA would not be what it is today and true independence, the kind enjoyed by nearly all producers in modern Hollywood, would have been much, much longer in arriving on the scene.

The four never really fulfilled their dreams. They made their share of mistakes, letting Goldwyn and Selznick go being their two biggest errors. Their pictures were often disappointments and yet a few, *The Three Musketeers, Robin Hood, The Gold Rush, City Lights*, stand the test of time well and remain classics. Their individual mistakes, jealousies, ambitions and human failings frequently got in the way of their initial ambition, to make United Artists the 'Tiffany's Of The Industry'.

How ironic that today, sixty years later, the studio can justly boast of such a title!

Fairbanks' final swashbuckler and his last appearance as Dumas' D'Artagnan.

Douglas Fairbanks and Mary Pickford in their only movie together, Shakespeare's *The Taming Of The Shrew*.

Charlie Chaplin in *Modern Times*.

The famous boots that together with bowler, cane and baggy pants, turned Chaplin into the greatest screen comic the world has ever known.

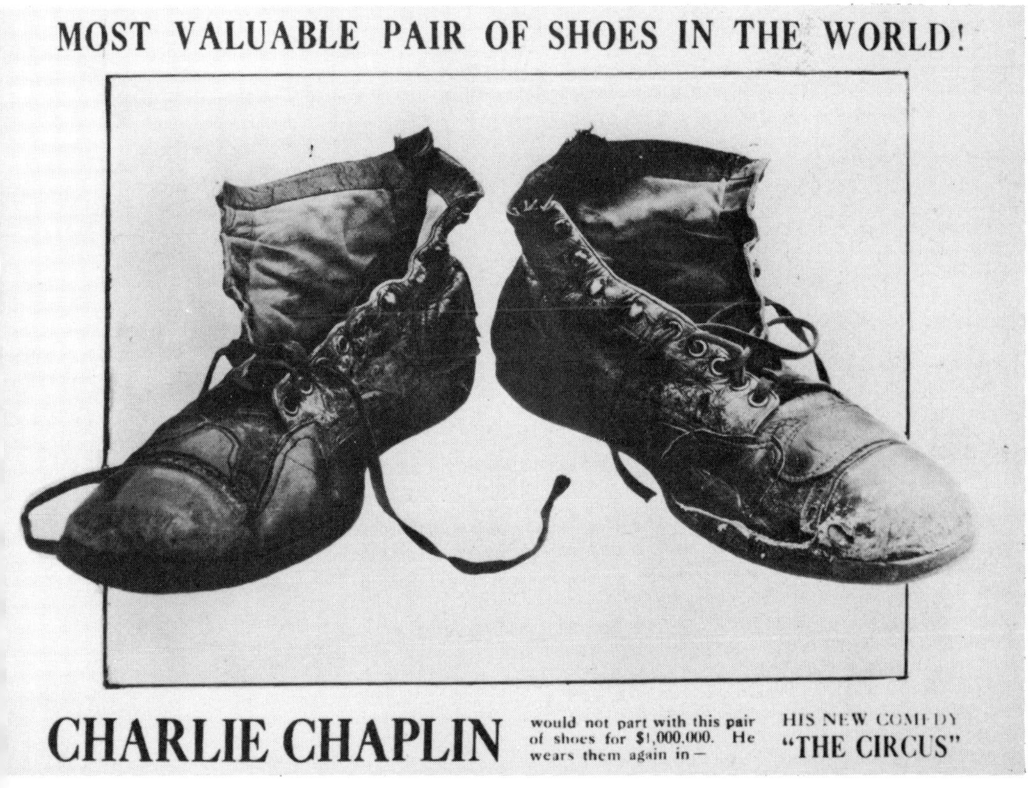

The man whose movies 'saved' United Artists during the 30s, controversial producer Sam Goldwyn.

David Niven (right) on his trip *Around The World In 80 Days*. Temporary obstacles: bouncer George Raft and saloon entertainer Marlene Dietrich.

Marilyn Monroe's 'Running Wild' number from Wilder's classic drag comedy *Some Like It Hot*. Among those accompanying her, Tony Curtis on sax (far left) and Jack Lemmon on bass.

The most dynamic movie debut in post-war cinema. Marlon Brando as the rebellious paraplegic in Zinnemann's *The Men*.

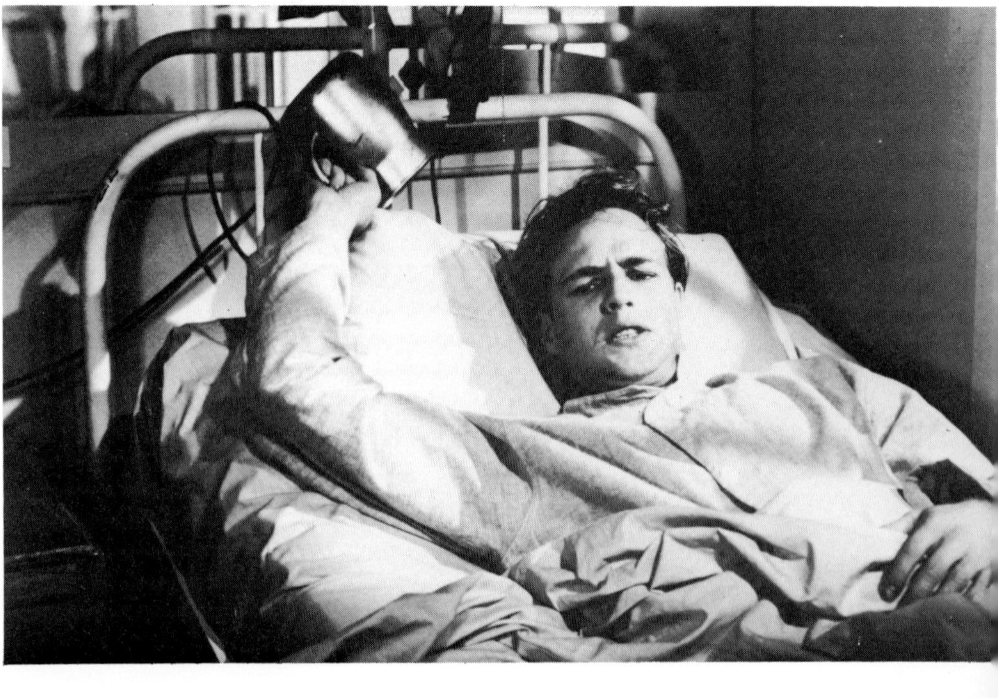

Director Billy Wilder (far left) and producer Arthur Hornblow off set with Charles Laughton and Marlene Dietrich during the filming of *Witness For The Prosecution.*

pany by an astute Zukor for 250,000, and *When The Clouds Roll By*, a Fairbanks action romance directed by Victor Fleming.

1920 *Pollyanna*, Mary Pickford's first United Artists picture, is released in January. She plays a ten-year-old orphan who goes to live with her aunt in a small American town. Her co-stars: George Berrell, William Courtleigh and Helen Jerome Eddy.

Just two months later, On March 28, she marries Douglas Fairbanks at his Beverly Hills home, a converted hunting lodge with extra rooms and a swimming pool. The house is nicknamed 'Pickfair' by the press.

It is the second marriage for each of them and is labelled by Photoplay magazine as 'One of the great love stories of all time'. By the public it is looked upon as the perfect marriage – she the image of American girlhood, he the athletic hero of small boys all over the world. Mary and Doug become known as 'The King and Queen of America' and in June sail for Europe for a six-week delayed honeymoon.

All the publicity is good for the studio, but inevitably the romance and honeymoon delay the production schedule just when it should be shifting into top gear. A more realistic assessment of the studio's output is now eight films a year, two from each partner. But with Chaplin still tied to First National other product has to be found.

Consequently the company distribute Mack Sennett's *Down On The Farm* and finance the Broadway hit *Romance* starring Doris Keane. Griffith hires his studio rent free for the latter movie which is directed by Chet Withey.

Pickford's other 1920 offering is *Suds* in which she plays a laundry girl and co-stars with a horse called Lavender. Fairbanks features in two films, the romantic comedy *The Mollycoddle* and the swashbuckler *The Mark Of Zorro*, a fast-moving adventure of Old California. It's the picture in which he finds his true metier, the costume spectacular, an entertainment form which allows him to display his magnificent athletic prowess to the full. He stars in a dual role, as the dashing masked avenger Senor Zorro and the foppish Don Diego Vega.

1921 The cost of United Artists pictures begins to rise and, although the company finds itself with three big hits on its hands, it is still in the red at the year's end. The key factor is that Chaplin, perhaps the most important figure in the UA setup, has still not produced a movie and won't be free until 1923 when his contract with First National comes to an end.

Mary Pickford as *Little Lord Fauntleroy* and Griffith with his classic Lillian Gish melodrama *Way Down East* are responsible for two of the hits. The third is provided by Douglas Fairbanks in *The Three Musketeers.*

Now well and truly into his swing Fairbanks looks as though he enjoys every minute of his role as D'Artagnan. And he does. The character has been a favourite of his since boyhood.

He puts himself through a punishing training schedule prior to shooting, spending more than a month on the parallel bars, adding to his already numerous tricks on horseback and practising what is probably the most difficult single feat he ever attempts for the cameras — a left-handed handspin, balanced on a short dagger.

Writes Robert E. Sherwood in 'Life' magazine: "When Alexandre Dumas sat down at his desk, smoothed his hair back, chewed the end of his quill pen and said to himself, 'Well, I guess I might as well write a book called 'The Three Musketeers,' he doubtless had but one object in view — to provide a suitable story for Douglas Fairbanks to act in the movies."

Fairbanks co-stars: Leon Barry (Athos), George Siegmann (Porthos), Eugene Pallette (Aramis).

United Artists release eleven movies, four of them outside productions including *Disraeli* with George Arliss.

Mary Pickford is seen twice more — as an Italian lighthouse keeper betrayed by a German spy in *The Love Light,* a film directed by Frances Marion (the only time Miss Pickford was directed by a woman) and as a Belgian refugee maid in *Through The Back Door.*

1922 The studio's output is again eleven pictures but only four come from the original partners. The rest, which include two with George Arliss, *The Man Who Played God* and *The Ruling Passion* and one with Nazimova, *A Doll's House*, are not exactly of the high quality envisaged by Pickford and co. when forming UA just a few years before.

The big one, *Robin Hood,* comes from Fairbanks at the enormous cost of one and a half million dollars. A quality picture directed by Allan Dwan, it boasts the biggest set ever constructed for a Hollywood movie.

The gigantic medieval Nottingham castle is built regardless of cost. Its interiors are vast — 450 ft from one end of the hall to the other. During filming five thousand extras crowd into the hall and then file up to the ramparts, 90 ft up, to line the castle walls. Fairbanks becomes so enthusiastic that he arranges for stands to be erected so that the public can watch the shooting!

Mary Pickford is still on top form in a remake of *Tess Of The Storm Country*, a tale she first made for Zukor in 1914; Griffith too is near his best with *Orphans Of The Storm*, a story of the French Revolution starring the two Gish sisters Dorothy and Lillian. His other picture however, *One Exciting Night*, is just a routine melodrama and gives the first indications that the great director may be on the downward slide.

Pickford and Fairbanks show their confidence in the future by building the Pickford-Fairbanks studio on Santa Monica Boulevard. In addition to the shooting stages and offices they erect a luxurious six-room bungalow which Mary furnishes with three cages full of canaries, and a dressing room, pool, gymnasium and steam bath which Doug adds to his offices. A permanent masseur is also in residence.

1923 But the confidence begins to look as though it is misplaced. 1923 is a bad year, as bad as you can get if you're a member of a struggling independent company. The studio's deficit rises to 300,000 dollars, and for the first time the future looks in doubt.

Realising the gravity of the situation, Pickford and Fairbanks set about finding ways to bring additional product to the 'Tiffany's of the Industry'. They hire three well-known writers, Frank Woods, Elmer Harris and Thompson Buchanan, form them into Associated Authors Inc. and gamble on them writing some quality hits. The plan misfires. *Loving Lies, No More Women* and *Richard The Lionhearted* released in '23 and early '24 are all failures.

Worse, even the established stars are off form. Mary Pickford plays a guitar strumming Spanish street singer *Rosita*. Her director is German Ernst Lubitsch. They row all the way through the movie. Says Mary: "It's the worst picture, bar none, that I have ever made."

Griffith's decline is further emphasised by *The White Rose* with Ivor Novello as a fallen minister and Mae Marsh the reason for his fall; Fairbanks is preparing his next spectacular *The Thief Of Baghdad*; and Charlie Chaplin, at last free to contribute to the company he helped form four years earlier, briefly discards his famous tramp to direct *A Woman Of Paris*, a sophisticated intimate drama starring Edna Purviance and Adolphe Menjou.

Chaplin himself appears only briefly as a porter.

The making of the film indicates just how long the little clown will take to shoot his pictures in the future. Many scenes are shot fifty times, one difficult scene goes to 200 takes. The picture opens on October 23 at the Lyric, New York. Its box-office returns are no more than adequate.

The other UA releases of the year include a re-issue of *Birth Of A Nation* and *Salome* with Nazimova.

1924 Griffith, in deep financial trouble through the commercial failure of his recent films, concludes a deal with Adolph Zukor at Paramount to produce three pictures for 250,000 dollars. He leaves United Artists without consulting his partners who insist on releasing the first of his three Paramount films because of his breach of contract.

It is the beginning of the end for Griffith whose great days are now well and truly over. His two UA pictures of '24, *America*, a story of the American Revolution, and *Isn't Life Wonderful* about the lives of Polish refugees struggling against poverty in Germany, are both financial failures.

Hollywood pundits see Griffith's departure as the beginning of the end for United Artists and predict that Paramount will also soon swallow up Fairbanks, Pickford and Chaplin.

But the tenacious trio are not yet ready to throw in the sponge. In November they bring in producer/entrepreneur Joseph Schenck to run the business side of the studio. He is made a partner and chairman of the board. Schenck's shrewd business know-how is just what the faltering company needs. He also brings with him the promise of extra product — six pictures starring his wife Norma Talmadge.

Mary Pickford, now thirty-one, attempts to discard her adolescent image by appearing in *Dorothy Vernon Of Haddon Hall*, but meets with box-office disaster. Her adoring public simply refuse to accept her in adult roles.

Fairbanks has no such trouble. His epic, 140-minute *The Thief Of Baghdad*, is one of his most successful pictures. A lavish Arabian Nights fantasy, it is directed by Raoul Walsh and co-stars Julanne Johnston and Anna May Wong.

Chaplin makes news by marrying sixteen year old Lita Grey who becomes Mrs. Chaplin on November 24. It is the actor's second marriage. Miss Grey was to have played the female lead in Chaplin's forthcoming movie *The Gold Rush*, but when her parents demand an immediate marriage and threaten Chaplin with legal action unless he agrees, Chaplin has no option but to comply. The marriage is loveless and a living hell for the famous star. Lita Grey has no feeling for Chaplin and admits, on one occasion, that she was only attracted to him because of his name.

Seven months after their marriage, a son, Charles Spencer Chaplin Jr., is born.

1925 Schenck's arrival brings an upsurge in UA's fortunes. To safeguard the future he signs independent producer Sam Goldwyn to a five year distribution contract, a move that is to ensure the studio's continuing success throughout the thirties. At the same time he brings in some top Hollywood glamour in the seductive shape of Gloria Swanson. She joins United Artists in a six-picture deal and is backed mainly by Joseph C. Kennedy. Her salary is 20,000 dollars a week. She works out her Paramount contract until 1926.

Schenck is also responsible for bringing Valentino out of a short-lived retirement in *The Eagle*; releasing the William Hart western *Tumbleweeds*; and allowing Josef von Sternberg to have his first crack at directing with *The Salvation Hunters*, a story of three derelicts living on a steam dredge.

The studio's remaining big three also do themselves more than justice. Mary Pickford, somewhat in desperation, but definitely for the last time, returns to adolescence, as a twelve-year-old motherless slum child, *Little Annie Rooney*; Fairbanks features in a sequel to his 1920 success, *Don Q Son Of Zorro*; and best of all Chaplin revives his tramp in *The Gold Rush*, a comedy of the Klondike Gold Rush of 1898 with Charlie as a hard-up amateur prospector.

The long wait for a Chaplin success has been worth it. Within a few years *The Gold Rush* becomes one of the biggest successes of the twenties. It grosses four million throughout the world.

In production for fourteen months, it premieres on August 16 at the Strand Theatre, New York. Says Chaplin later, "It is the picture I would most like to be remembered by."

Goldwyn starts off in great style for the studio with the classic tearjerker *Stella Dallas* in which Belle Bennett, a young girl from the wrong side of the tracks, marries above her position and then sacrifices her happiness for that of her daughter.

Belle's great moment: the climactic scene when Stella, old and forgotten and unable to reveal herself, peers through the window at her daughter's wedding and is told to 'move on' by a city cop.

1926 Goldwyn contributes two more, *Partners Again*, a Potash and Perlmutter comedy, and *The Winning Of Barbara Worth*, a drama of the modern West with Ronald Colman, Vilma Banky and, in his screen debut, lanky Gary Cooper; Mary Pickford stars in *Sparrows* in which she fights for the rights of unwanted children 'cared for' by the owners of a Southern farm. An alligator swamp and quicksands are among the hazards. The movie is advertised: 'Mary Pickford's Christmas gift to everyone whose heart is young'.

Fairbanks, still at his athletic best, appears in two-colour Technicolor in *The Black Pirate*. Duelling with wild abandon, he runs through the whole gamut of swashbuckling activity — swimming underwater, climbing cliffs and, most famous of all, sliding down a ship's sails with his weight on a dagger, held at a 45 degree angle to the canvas, slitting it as he goes.

Earlier in the year UA release Rudolph Valentino's *The Son Of The Sheik*. After *The Eagle* the great lover is back to the peak of his popularity. Women still worship the very ground on which he treads.

On August 15, however, he is struck down after attending a New York party and rushed to hospital with a perforated ulcer and ruptured appendix. The world is stunned. Women wait in queues for the hospital bulletins. The real-life drama drags on for a week, but peritonitis gives way to pleurisy, the infection spreads and on August 23 Valentino, aged just thirty-one, dies.

The hysteria that follows Valentino's death is one of the greatest spectacles of his career. Before the funeral, his body — his face made up as carefully as it had been for the cameras — lies in state in New York, beseiged by more than 100,000 fans who file past his coffin and gaze their last on his remains. Police and a squad of private detectives protect the bier, supplemented by a guard of honour sent at the request of Benito Mussolini by the Fascist League Of America, complete with black shirts and salutes.

Valentino made over thirty films, fourteen of them as a star. He worked for numerous studios, among them Metro, Paramount and United Artists. His major pictures: *The Four Horsemen Of The Apocalypse, Camille, The Sheik, Blood And Sand, Monsieur Beaucaire, The Son Of The Sheik.*

1927 Gloria Swanson opens her United Artists account with *The Love Of Sunya*, a story of reincarnation and romance. John Boles is her co-star.

The movie is privileged to open on March 11, at the new Roxy theatre, in New York, now the world's largest movie palace. Built at a cost of ten million dollars the cinema receives better reviews than the film which barely breaks even. For Miss Swanson it is not an auspicious start.

Douglas Fairbanks, now forty-three, continues his adventuring down South America way in *The Gaucho*; for her role in *My Best Girl* Mary Pickford sets her famous curls on the top of her head and plays a twenty year old million dollar baby working as a clerk in a five and ten cent store. It's the film in which she kisses her leading man for the first time. The recipient? Buddy Rogers.

The other partner, Charlie Chaplin, has more personal things to occupy him. Whilst endeavouring to shoot his next film, *The Circus*, his wife (the former Lita Grey) files suit for divorce.

The forty-two page complaint includes sensational charges — infidelity, threats upon her life, lack of affection for the children, a variety of inhuman and indecent acts. In June she threatens to name five famous actresses with whom Chaplin had supposedly been intimate during their married life.

Chaplin gives in to save the actresses' reputations and the allegations are withdrawn. Lita Grey receives a 600,000 dollar settlement. The divorce is granted on August 22.

Sam Goldwyn, whose '27 offerings include two Ronald Colman/Vilma Banky pictures — the Spanish romance *The Night Of Love* and the circus film *The Magic Flame* — is made a UA partner in October; Joe Schenck signs comic genius Buster Keaton to a three picture distribution contract. Two of the three, *The General* in which railway engineer Buster is caught up in the Civil War and *College* in which he blunders his way to becoming the perfect athlete, are among the studio's '27 releases.

1928 One of United Artists best years to date.

Chaplin's little tramp becomes a clown and in one superb scene a stand-in tight rope walker in *The Circus* (the film costs 900,000 and grosses three times that amount); Gloria Swanson is Somerset Maugham's famous prostitute, *Sadie Thompson*. The film makes amends for her poor showing in *The Love Of Sunya*. It takes nearly a million and Miss Swanson gives her best ever screen performance.

She's less fortunate when she agrees to be directed by the volatile Erich von Stroheim in *Queen Kelly*. Four months into production and with the film only two thirds complete she wonders what she's got herself into,for she's playing not only an innocent young convent girl seduced by a Ruritanian prince, but also the madam of an East African brothel. Mad Queen Seena Owen adds to the highly erotic content of the movie by slinking naked round a vast, extravagantly decorated palace. Von Stroheim is fired, the unfinished film too salacious to release.

Goldwyn's favourite romantic team Ronald Colman and Vilma Banky are together again in the historical *Two Lovers*; Banky is also a peasant girl in another Goldwyn production, *The Awakening*; Norma Talmadge is the dance hall girl, *The Dove* and *The Woman Disputed*; Buster Keaton, *Steamboat Bill Jr.*; and Dolores Del Rio the half-breed girl, *Ramona*.

D. W. Griffith returns to the studio, not as a partner, but as an employee. Schenck hires him to direct five pictures costing a maximum of 400,000 dollars. It's the director's last chance, but both of his '28 releases – *Drums Of Love* and *The Battle Of The Sexes* are failures. "All he did was lose money for us," says Schenck later.

The studio dabble in sound for the first time with *Tempest*, the first United Artists release with a synchronised musical accompaniment and sound effects. The movie is a Russian romance with John Barrymore and Camilla Horn.

The biggest publicity event of the year occurs on June 21. Mary Pickford, in an effort to liberate herself from having to play any more juvenile roles, cuts off the most famous head of hair in movies. Press photographers are on hand to record the first momentous snip in the hairdressing salon of Charles Bock. Six of the famous curls still survive, two in a museum case at Pickfair and two each at museums in San Diego and Los Angeles.

1929 The haircut seems to work. Miss Pickford has the honour of appearing in UA's first all-talkie, *Coquette*, a nine reel melodrama directed by Sam Taylor. She's a heartless Southern belle, Johnny Mack Brown and Matt Moore are her co-stars. Mary wins an Oscar as best actress of the year and achieves a unique first – she becomes the first actress to weep at the awards ceremony!

An equally famous Pickford vehicle (critically it's a flop, commercially it's a smash) is *The Taming Of The Shrew*. She appears for the first and only time with husband Douglas Fairbanks, but although the Bard is by no means beyond Mary's capabilities he's certainly beyond those of Fairbanks. He's ill-at-ease throughout shooting and it shows in the movie which becomes famous, not for its acting, but for its famous credit line: 'By William Shakespeare, with additional dialogue by Samuel Taylor'.

Fairbanks is much more at home in *The Iron Mask* in which he once again plays his beloved D'Artagnan, but the film is to be his last in the *genre*. Swashbuckling is a young man's game and Fairbanks is now forty-six. The end of his dashing career is in sight.

So too is that of Gloria Swanson. Her film *The Trespasser*, about a girl who suffers in poverty after setting her sights on high society, proves to be her last hit for United Artists. From now on it's all downhill.

Griffiths' *Lady Of The Pavements* (with singing and talking sequences) is no better than his efforts of the previous year. Goldwyn, however, is beginning to emerge more and more as the dominant force in the company. He ups his three films a year to four and, as always, has his finger on the public pulse.

Ronald Colman stars in three of his films; as Joseph Conrad's Captain Lingard in *The Rescue*, as a debonair young thief in *Condemned*, and as Sapper's famous amateur detective, ex-army officer, *Bulldog Drummond*. Vilma Banky features in the fourth, a romantic comedy, *This Is Heaven*.

1930 Howard Hughes' *Hell's Angels* is the big picture of the year.

A spectacular air drama of World War I it finishes up costing nearly four million dollars. The main reasons:

Hughes takes two years over shooting, using forty World World War I aircraft, seventy-eight pilots and thirty cameramen. He also reshoots the picture as a sound movie after originally filming it as a silent. Ben Lyon, James Hall and Jean Harlow star, the latter replacing Greta Nissen when the picture becomes a talkie. Four of the barnstorming pilots are killed during production, two in an aerial crash over San Francisco during the filming of a dog fight.

The film takes big money, but, because of its enormous cost, takes several years to make a profit. Which doesn't exactly help United Artists. Chaplin, Pickford and Fair-Banks have nothing on view; Griffith makes one last despairing attempt at an epic, *Abraham Lincoln*, without success; and Gloria Swanson seeks romantic adventure in Paris in the inept *What A Widow!*

Goldwyn provides the most profitable picture of the year, an Eddie Cantor musical *Whoopee*. It is the first film of dance director Busby Berkeley and the first of six Goldwyn/Cantor musicals. It grosses one and a half million dollars. Another Goldwyn hit is *Raffles* with Ronald Colman ideally cast as the gentleman amateur cracksman. Kay Francis is his co-star.

1931 A sadness now surrounds the screen appearances of Mary Pickford and Douglas Fairbanks. To all intents and purposes their careers are are finished.

Mary stars in *Kiki* and finds herself out of place in a musical comedy chorus. Mary calls it "a misadventure". It is the first Pickford movie to lose money since the company was formed.

Fairbanks stars in *Reaching For The Moon,* his last film of any note. For the first time in ten years he's seen in contemporary clothes as a woman-shy millionaire travelling on board a modern ocean liner. Gloria Swanson continues to misfire in the comedies *Indiscreet* and *Tonight Or Never*.

Howard Hughes, however, has a critical success with *The Front Page*, Lewis Milestone's version of the Ben Hecht/Charles MacArthur play about a group of newsmen waiting in the reporters' room of a prison to cover an execution. Pat O'Brien stars as the reporter who shields the criminal when he breaks from jail, Adolphe Menjou as his thick-skinned managing editor.

Goldwyn releases five, including John Ford's *Arrowsmith*, King Vidor's *Street Scene*, and *Palmy Days*, another

Eddie Cantor musical with sixteen year old Betty Grable and Lucille Ball among the famous Goldwyn Girls.

But it is Chaplin who helps save the company's rocky financial position with a *silent movie, City Lights.* Subtitled 'a comedy romance in pantomime' it emerges as a melancholy little piece about the efforts of the tramp to restore the sight of a pretty young flower seller. At once excruciatingly funny and terribly sad, it is close to being a masterpiece.

An expensive movie to make – a million and a half dollars were spent during the two years of production and 800,000 ft of film exposed – it is nonetheless a financial smash and confirms that its maker will be the longest survivor of the four original UA partners.

1932 Just as it was in the twenties, the prime objective of United Artists is to find additional product. Chaplin's films are always resounding hits, but they appear only every five years or so.

The studio expect much from Howard Hughes who has proved his class with *Hell's Angels* and *The Front Page.* Now he is expected to make regular money. Alas, he tires quickly of the movie business. In 1932 he produces one success, *Scarface,* with Paul Muni as prohibition racketeer, Al Capone and two stinkeroos, *Cock Of The Air* and *Sky Devils.* It's the end of his involvement with movies, at least until the forties.

Director Howard Hawks has most fun out of *Scarface.* During filming Capone extends an invitation to Hawks to discuss the picture with him in Chicago. Hawks is met at the station by half-a-dozen of Capone's men who apologize for their lateness, but explain there has been a killing the night before and they have been to a funeral.

Hawks has 'tea' with Capone and discusses the film for some two or three hours. When the movie is released Capone sees it half-a-dozen times and purchases a print for his own private showing.

The studio take over the distribtion of the Disney cartoons from Columbia. Eddie Cantor in *The Kid From Spain* and romantic London barrister Ronald Colman in *Cynara* represent Goldwyn; the comedy romance *Mr. Robinson Crusoe* is Fairbanks' last feature for UA; Joan Crawford is the new Sadie Thompson in Lewis Milestone's *Rain.*

An unrecorded event is that Chaplin, recuperating after *City Lights,* meets the young Paulette Goddard on

Schenck's personal yacht and is immediately attracted to her. She becomes his personal and professional protégée and he lines her up for a leading part in his next film.

D. W. Griffith makes *The Struggle*, a story about the menace of drink. The film is a flop and the title only too aposite. Since the early twenties Griffith's career has always been a struggle, a struggle to keep from going downhill. Whereas UA did much for Pickford, Fairbanks and Chaplin it did little or nothing for Griffith. With a final ironic quote, "*The Struggle* was superlatively bad", the man who made the greatest of all silent American pictures, *The Birth Of A Nation*, disappears forever from the scene.

1933 Just a year after Griffith's departure into obscurity Gloria Swanson follows the same path — broke. In 1926 she joined United Artists a wealthy woman. Just seven years later, aged thirty-five, she is finished. Her last film, the doleful *Perfect Understanding*.

Secrets marks Mary Pickford's final appearance on the screen, although she is to remain a strong personality on the UA board for years to come. Goldwyn serves up his usual Cantor musical *Roman Scandals* and makes his final film with Ronald Colman, *The Masquerader*.

Joe Schenck, understandably anxious now that three of the four partners have left the screen, makes two astute moves. He joins with ex-Warner production chief Darryl F. Zanuck in forming Twentieth Century, a company that releases its product through UA; and he signs Alexander Korda and his British production company, London Films, to a lucrative distribution deal.

The Bowery, a rugged tale of the gay '90s with Wallace Beery and George Raft, is one of Twentieth Century's first successes; *The Private Life Of Henry VIII*, premiered at Radio City on October 12, the big Korda hit. For his intolerant monarch Charles Laughton wins an Oscar. "Six wives," he sighs, "and the worst of them was the best of them."

1934 The Twentieth Century and Korda deals increase the UA output although real quality is absent.

Twenty movies are released, among them *Bulldog Drummond Strikes Back* (with Ronald Colman), *The Mighty Barnum* and *The House Of Rothschild* from Twentieth Century, and *Catherine The Great* and *The*

Private Life Of Don Juan from Korda.

The ever-faithful Eddie Cantor inherits a fortune in the Goldwyn musical *Kid Millions*, but the producer's new 'star', Russian-born Anna Sten proves nowhere near as reliable. Imported by Goldwyn to America in 1932 she's a major disaster.

Goldwyn wants his own Dietrich, his own Garbo. All he gets is a beautiful woman with a gutteral voice and little acting ability. In '34, after being 'prepared' for two years she at last makes her appearance on American screens. She appears in two movies — as Zola's *Nana* and in the Russian costume romance *We Live Again* in which she's teamed with Fredric March.

Says the advertising slogan for the latter, 'The directorial genius of Mamoulian and the producing genius of Goldwyn have been combined to make the world's greatest entertainment.' Goldwyn's reaction? 'That's the kind of ad I like. Facts. No exaggeration.'

One of UA's most successful pictures is the little acclaimed *Our Daily Bread*. Directed by King Vidor it has no stars, but brings home the effects of the Depression with some force. It tells of a jobless city couple who, together with an out-of-work farmer, take over and make a success of a derelict farm and establish a self supporting community.

1935 A year of great activity. The King and Queen of Hollywood, Mary Pickford and Douglas Fairbanks, are divorced on February 13 after fifteen years of marriage. Mary announces her official retirement from the screen just a month after the divorce. The reasons for the break-up are never widely publicized.

Joe Schenck, the man who has continually pulled United Artists round since the mid-twenties, goes too after innumerable quarrels with his partners. Worse, he takes Twentieth Century with him when he links up with Fox.

In an attempt to bridge 'the product gap' Korda is made a full partner and David Selznick signed to an eight picture contract. Selznick's independent company has been formed after his brief, but successful stints at RKO and Metro.

The United Artists releases are a mixed bunch. Goldwyn films the soap opera *The Dark Angel* with Fredric March, Merle Oberon and Herbert Marshall, and tries once more to make a star out of Miss Sten. He sets her against the best, Gary Cooper, in *The Wedding Night*. But to no avail. Miss Sten is a millstone round his neck. He quickly drops her.

Clive Of India with Ronald Colman, *Cardinal Richelieu* with George Arliss and *Les Miserables* with Fredric March and Charles Laughton are among the final Twentieth Century releases; Leslie Howard is Baroness Orczy's dashing aristocrat *The Scarlet Pimpernel*; and Paul Robeson sings:

"Sandy The Strong, Sandy The Wise,
Righter of Wrongs, Hater of Lies"

in Korda's imperialistic *Sanders Of The River*. When he sees the picture in London, Robeson walks out of the premiere in disgust!

1936 Chaplin makes his last appearance in his famous tramp costume in *Modern Times*. The little fellow, who has appeared in more than seventy comedies in the previous two decades, walks off into the sunset arm-in-arm with Paulette Goddard and a movie era comes to an end.

Like all Chaplin movies it's expensive — one and a half million dollars — and is far from being one of Chaplin's biggest financial hits.

However, with Goldwyn and Selznick now operating at the studio, the company has every reason to expect quality — the quality its films have been lacking (Chaplin apart) during the thirties.

Selznick is still in the teething stages regarding his choice of subjects. His first UA picture, *Little Lord Fauntleroy*, is a remake of an earlier Pickford vehicle; his second, *The Garden Of Allah*, has Dietrich and Boyer in Technicolor in the Algerian desert. It is Marlene's first appearance in colour. Even so, one critic still refers to her as "just a monosyllabic clothes horse".

Goldwyn is now in full flow especially as his new director, William Wyler, immediately shows his potential with versions of Lillian Hellman's *These Three* about two young women teachers, Miriam Hopkins and Merle Oberon, ruined by the malicious gossip of a lying girl student, and Sinclair Lewis' *Dodsworth* about a middle-aged industrialist, Walter Huston, who finds a new set of values on a vacation to Europe.

Goldwyn's regular money-making star of the thirties, Eddie Cantor, is mixed up with Ethel Merman and gangsters in *Strike Me Pink*. It's his last film for the producer.

Korda's London Films contribute *Things To Come*, *Rembrandt* and *The Ghost Goes West*; Walter Wanger joins the company with his independent set up and for the first time in several years things are looking healthy.

1937 In many ways a key year in the history of UA. In the board-room a battle for power commences with Pickford, Fairbanks and Chaplin up against Goldwyn for control of the company. Goldwyn insists, rightly, that Pickford and co. are not putting any creative effort into the studio. He claims that *his* pictures have been sustaining the studio during the thirties.

Goldwyn offers each of the partners half a million dollars for their interest in the company. They refuse, but inform him that they would be prepared to listen to an offer of two million each. Goldwyn confers with Korda who's interested, but all they can raise between them is four million. The deadline of December 21 passes and the company remains in the hands of Pickford, Fairbanks and Chaplin.

Meanwhile, on the sound stages, John Ford, William Wyler, William Wellman, John Cromwell, King Vidor, Fritz Lang and Frank Borzage are all at work. And on the screen the dialogue just crackles with wit and imagination.

Selznick's *Nothing Sacred* is a screwball comedy about a supposedly dying small town girl (Carole Lombard) who is given the time of her life by a New York newspaper which hopes to gain publicity by following the last weeks of her life. Newsman Fredric March enjoys one of the best written comedy lines of the 30s when he says to dyspeptic editor Walter Connolly: "The hand of God reaching down into the mire couldn't elevate you to the depths of degradation."

Witty repartee also accompanies the clash of steel in the same producer's magnificent *The Prisoner Of Zenda*. And as if these two films aren't enough Selznick throws in a third trump movie. *A Star Is Born*. It's one of the best 'Hollywood looks at Hollywood' films with Fredric March as a movie actor on the way down because of drink, and Janet Gaynor as the young girl he discovers and turns into a star.

Even Goldwyn can't quite match Selznick's burst of brilliance despite the fact that he has on offer King Vidor's remake of *Stella Dallas*, John Ford's spectacular *The Hurricane* and Wyler's version of *Dead End*, Sidney Kingsley's play about the youngsters who, during the 1930s, fought for survival in the slums of New York's Lower East Side.

The only serious miscalculation is allowing Walt Disney to find a new distributor, RKO.

1938 Selznick's brilliance of a year before gives way to a quieter mood as he films a delightful *The Adventures Of Tom Sawyer* with Tommy Kelly and *The Young In Heart*, a comedy about a family of con-artists which is reformed by the kindness of a sweet old lady.

Not surprisingly his mind is on other things. *Gone With The Wind*. UA are disappointed they don't get the distribution rights when the film is released in 1939. The main reason is Gable. Selznick must have him for Rhett Butler. And MGM won't give Gable without receiving distribution in return.

Ancient China (*The Adventures Of Marco Polo*), the French Revolution (*The Return Of The Scarlet Pimpernel*) and adventure in British-occupied India (*The Drum*) are all considered suitable subjects by producers Goldwyn and Korda, but the results at the box-office don't bear them out.

Walter Wanger has two of the more interesting UA movies – *Blockade*, a drama of the Spanish Civil War with Henry Fonda and *Algiers*, a remake of *Pepe-Le-Moko* in which Charles Boyer is supposed to say, "Come With Me To The Casbah" but doesn't. Beautiful Hedy Lamarr lures him to his doom.

1939 Douglas Fairbanks, the most handsome and athletic swashbuckler of them all, dies in his sleep of a heart attack on December 11. He was fifty-six.

In the 'New York Times' Frank Nugent writes in his obituary: "Douglas Fairbanks was make-believe at its best, a game we youngsters never tired of playing. . . There wasn't a small boy in the neighbourhood who did not, in a Fairbanks picture, see himself triumphing over the local bully, winning the soft-eyed adoration of whatever ten-year-old blonde he had been courting and wreaking vengeance on the teacher who had made him stand in the corner."

The entire world mourns his passing.

Fairbanks' greatest successes: *The Mark Of Zorro, The Three Musketeers, Robin Hood, The Thief Of Baghdad, Don Q, Son Of Zorro, The Black Pirate, The Iron Mask.*

It is ironic that in the year of his death an inferior remake of one of his favourite tales, *The Man In The Iron Mask* with Louis Hayward, should be on the list of UA releases.

Wanger hires John Ford to direct a simple-sounding

western called *Stagecoach*, a classic movie that sends Ford scuttling to Monument Valley for the first time, taking with him lanky youngster John Wayne, who shoots his way to stardom, and character actor Thomas Mitchell, who drinks his way to a supporting Oscar as the alcoholic Doc Boone.

Milestone films Steinbeck's *Of Mice And Men* with Lon Chaney Jr. superb as the feeble minded Lenny; Goldwyn makes his favourite of all his own pictures, *Wuthering Heights* with Laurence Olivier as Heathcliff and Merle Oberon as Cathy. William Wyler directs, Gregg Toland's superb lensing brings him an Academy Award.

Korda's main contribution is *The Four Feathers*, the best-ever version of the A. E. W. Mason tale about a British officer who is branded a coward by his fiancée and fellow officers and sets out for Egypt to perform fantastic feats of endurance. John Clements is responsible for the heroics, Ralph Richardson goes blind in the desert sun, June Duprez wisely stays at home.

Selznick's big one is *Intermezzo*, the story of the love affair between a renowned but married violinist (Leslie Howard) and his young protégée (Ingrid Bergman).

1940 United Artists (Disney and Fox apart) become the last major studio to win a best picture Academy Award. They receive the honour for Selznick's version of *Rebecca*, Daphne Du Maurier's story of a timid young girl (Joan Fontaine) who finds wedded life to her moody aristocratic husband (Laurence Olivier) more than she bargained for. The movie opens with nine of the most famous words in contemporary fiction: "Last night I dreamed I went to Manderley again. . ." It also starts British director Alfred Hitchcock on his distinguished Hollywood career.

Words of a different kind — those uttered by Charlie Chaplin in *The Great Dictator* — create something of a sensation. The little man, having discarded his tramp in *Modern Times*,now disowns the silent medium. Thirteen years after the first talkie he speaks. His first words? A mumbled "Yes, sir," as, in the role of an army private, he obeys the order to fire in the opening war sequences of the film.

The picture, which takes 127 days to shoot, is a satire on the evils of fascism. It has Chaplin in a dual role, that of a Hitler-like dictator and a little Jewish barber; Paulette Goddard as an impoverished girl of the ghetto; and Jack Oakie as a Mussolini-style tyrant called Napaloni.

The opening title reads: 'This is a story of the period between two World Wars – an interim in which Insanity cut loose, Liberty took a nose dive and Humanity was kicked around somewhat.'

Hitchcock works equally well for Wanger with his second film, *Foreign Correspondent*, the story of an American journalist involved with fifth columnists and spies in Europe just prior to the outbreak of war. John Ford also does a stint for Wanger. His *The Long Voyage Home* is based on four one act plays by Eugene O'Neill and is heavy drama dealing with the lives of the crew of a British tramp steamer carrying munitions across the Atlantic in wartime.

Korda offers escapism with Sabu and *The Thief Of Baghdad*; Victor Mature has prehistoric monsters for company in *One Million B.C.*; Jon Hall is *Kit Carson*; Laurel and Hardy star for Roach in *A Chump At Oxford* and *Saps At Sea*.

Only Goldwyn seems unhappy. Still smarting at the failure of his takeover attempt in '37 he now wants to leave the company and take his product elsewhere. Legal difficulties over his contract hamper his attempts. He releases just two movies, a new *Raffles* with David Niven and *The Westerner*. Directed by William Wyler and starring Gary Cooper and Walter Brennan, it turns out to be Sam's last picture for United Artists.

1941 After nearly two years of legal wrangling Goldwyn obtains a release from his contract. It costs him 300,000 dollars.

But it becomes immediately apparent that UA's loss is the greater. The producer had indeed carried the main share of the burden during the thirties. Only when he has gone do the company come to realise it. Craftily, Goldwyn has held up production of his latest property, *The Little Foxes*, for one and a half years, so that UA will be unable to release it. He and *The Little Foxes* go to RKO.

With Goldwyn gone, Selznick is made a full partner in his place. But the producer has been unable to keep up the brilliance he sustained in the late thirties and does not, surprisingly, prove an adequate substitute for Goldwyn who, in his fourteen years with the company, delivered *fifty* films – thirteen more than Pickford, Fairbanks and Chaplin put together!

With the Walter Wanger unit also closing down (notable films like *Foreign Correspondent* and *The Long Voyage Home* played off too slowly) the lack of product is immediately apparent. Any vague aspirations to quality are carried by Korda with *Lady Hamilton* (Vivien Leigh is Emma, Olivier Lord Nelson) and the haunting *Lydia* in which an aged Merle Oberon recalls her courtship by former beaux.

Douglas Fairbanks Jr. swashbuckles in Dumas' *The Corsican Brothers*; Merle Oberon and Melvyn Douglas add elegance to Lubitsch sophistication in *That Uncertain Feeling*; *Topper Returns* with Joan Blondell and Roland Young; Gene Tierney, caught up in an Oriental gambling den in *The Shanghai Gesture*, is also a jungle gal who helps the allies against the Nazis in *Sundown*.

But the writing is on the wall. Without Goldwyn, the forties are to be a long hard struggle.

1942 Chaplin, in income tax difficulties during the early forties, reissues *The Gold Rush* and divorces Paulette Goddard. The two events aren't related, but Miss Goddard reputedly receives a million dollar settlement, allegedly in jewels which she is said to carry about in a cigar box!

Chaplin has no new movie to offer, but his off-screen antics are as entertaining as if he had. In July he enters the political arena with a speech that demands a second front in the war. "On the battlefields of Russia democracy will live or die," he says and demands England and the U.S. attack from the West while Russia has her back to the wall.

On screen UA's jaded lineup is illuminated by an occasional gem. Lubitsch pokes fun at the Nazis in *To Be Or Not To Be* with Jack Benny and Carole Lombard (her last film before her death in an air crash) as members of a Polish theatrical troupe; Sabu is raised by wolves in Korda's *The Jungle Book*; Rene Clair has some lighthearted fun at the expense of witches and politicians in *I Married A Witch* (Fredric March, Veronica Lake); and George Sanders impresses as the Gauguin-like artist in Maugham's *The Moon And Sixpence*.

1943 Chaplin makes news and again not through a movie. A young Brooklyn girl, Joan Barry, whom Chaplin had met in '41, files a paternity suit claiming that Chaplin is the father of the child she expects in three months time. Chaplin denies the charge.

Miss Barry claims that in 1941 Chaplin gave her a contract of seventy-five dollars a week and during the early months of their relationship "became interested in her as a woman". She underwent two illegal operations while preparing for her promised screen debut. The debut never came and, in October '42, Chaplin tired of her and cut her salary to twenty-five dollars a week. At Christmas she bought a pistol in a pawnship, broke into Chaplin's house, threatened to shoot him and then end her own life. Chaplin, amused, rather than scared, wooed her all over again.

Chaplin agrees to pay the costs of the confinement and submit to a blood test which proves that he is not the father of the child.

On June 16, the fifty-four year old actor-director marries for a fourth time to Oona O'Neill, the eighteen year old daughter of playwright Eugene O'Neill. Joan Barry gives birth to a daughter in October.

The films of United Artists are nowhere near as entertaining. Titles like *Prairie Chickens, Fall In, Yanks Ahoy, The Kansan, Bar 20, Border Patrol*, seem endless. Korda has gone and Selznick has produced nothing since *Rebecca*, selling those properties he had bought for UA — *Keys Of The Kingdom, Claudia, Jane Eyre* — to Fox. Chaplin, in particular, complains bitterly about his inactivity.

Frank Borzage delivers *Stage Door Canteen*, a romance between a soldier and a canteen hostess; James Cagney, who has joined as an independent in March, is a newspaperman in *Johnny Come Lately*.

Fritz Lang produces the one quality film of the year, *Hangmen Also Die*, an account of the assassination of Reichsprotektor Heydrich (Hitler's hangman) in Prague in 1942. A disturbing portrait of a Nazi-occupied country it has brilliant cameos from Gene Lockhart as a Nazi informer and Alexander Granach as a Gestapo inspector.

1944 Chaplin is indicted by a Federal Grand Jury on four separate counts including violation of the Mann Act and conspiring to deny Joan Barry her civil rights. He stands trial early in '44 and is photographed being fingerprinted. After seven hours the jury acquits him absolutely on all counts. His new wife Oona, four months pregnant, collapses when she hears the news.

Selznick at last stirs himself into activity by producing two movies, *I'll Be Seeing You*, a schmaltzy romance between paroled jailbird Ginger Rogers and mentally disturbed soldier Joseph Cotten, and *Since You Went Away*, the biggest UA grosser for many years.

Very similar to *Mrs. Miniver*, but looking this time at a middle-class American family when the men are away at war, it is produced at just the right moment and with just the right amount of tearful skill. Mother Claudette Colbert, daughters Jennifer Jones and Shirley Temple, and maid Hattie MacDaniel suffer, sacrifice and weep to keep the American flag flying.

Selznick apart, however, the line-up is distinctly routine. Again, many titles mean nothing — *Mystery Man, Texas Masquerade, Knickerbocker Holiday, Lumberjack*; William Bendix makes a good job of the ship's stoker in Eugene O'Neill's *The Hairy Ape*; Linda Darnell finds her charms are fatal to men and herself in *Summer Storm*; Merle Oberon and Franchot Tone are involved in a thriller in a Southern mansion in *Dark Waters*.

1945 Selznick once again hits the top box-office spot with the Hitchcock thriller *Spellbound*. The Ingrid Bergman/Gregory Peck combination makes it a big winner — five million dollar gross.

One of the first pictures about psychoanalysis, it has Peck as an amnesiac who subconsciously believes himself to be a murderer and Ingrid Bergman as the psychiatrist who cures him. Salvador Dali contributes a dream sequence, Miklos Rozsa a memorable music score and Hitch a moment of genuine shock as villain Leo G. Carroll kills himself in the subjective by firing a gun straight into the camera.

The writers also contribute a moment of unintentional humour. When informed that a patient has tried to kill a staff member and then cut his own throat, Bergman enquires, "Is it bad?"

Cagney is a newsman in Japan in *Blood On The Sun*; Greg McClure the famous boxer *The Great John L.* (Sullivan); Charles Laughton pirate *Captain Kidd*; and Claudette Colbert a *Guest Wife* in a frothy little comedy by Sam Wood.

Two admirable, though uncommercial works, raise the standard of the studio's output. Jean Renoir makes his best American picture, *The Southerner*, a realistic portrait of a young farmer and his family and their struggle to make a living from growing cotton on a derelict Texas farm; and William Wellman films *The Story Of G.I. Joe*, an account of the experiences of a small group of World War II infantrymen from the days of their first action in Tunisia to the fall of Cassino and the march on Rome. Burgess Meredith is Pulitzer Prize-winning war correspondent Ernie Pyle, Robert Mitchum, in an early role, a war weary sergeant.

1946 Another inferior year. United Artists are looking more and more second rate as the decade progresses. Very soon they will become the 'also ran' of the Hollywood Studios.

The worst blow is the loss of Selznick. Just as he is regaining something of his old form he leaves after a bitter row with the partners over the financing and distribution of his huge sex western *Duel In The Sun*.

Selznick releases the famous Gregory Peck-Jennifer Jones 'Lust In The Dust' movie via his own organization and daringly shows the picture simultaneously in big cities throughout America in order to show a fast return. It works. In six months, box-office receipts amount to nine million dollars, two million more than the cost of the film's production. The profits could have gone to UA. As it is, they go to Selznick.

The studio has nothing that is remotely commercial on its schedule. All of its pictures are small-scale. The Marx Brothers spend *A Night In Casablanca*; George Raft is *Mr. Ace* and a playboy caught up with Ava Gardner in *Whistle Stop*; Hedy Lamarr a man killer in *Strange Woman*; Robert Cummings, Michele Morgan and Peter Lorre down Cuba way in *The Chase*.

Renoir provides most interest with his half comic, half tragic story of a young chambermaid's experiences in a wealthy provincial household in 19th century France. The film is *The Diary Of A Chambermaid*, the star Paulette Goddard.

Chaplin provides more sensation during the final part of the Joan Barry saga. The paternity case is reopened. The evidence of the blood tests is ignored and after one hung jury Chaplin is forced to support the child.

1947 To add to his worries, Chaplin's first picture in seven years, *Monsieur Verdoux*, is a commercial disaster. Shot in a record time for Chaplin of just twelve weeks, it is eventually withdrawn from release after two years. An unusual and complex film about a modern Bluebeard who murders rich women in order to provide a comfortable life for his invalid wife and children, it plays in only 2075 theatres and grosses a mere 325,000 dollars.

From being the most popular entertainer of the twentieth

century the little clown has become one of the most disliked figures in America. In the States his political views and moral standards are widely criticised. He is called before the House of Un-American activities ("I am a citizen of the world. I am not a communist. I am a peacemonger.") and has a hate campaign of frightening proportions led against him, principally by the Catholic War Veterans and the American Legion.

A member of Congress actually calls for his deportation so that "he can be kept off the American screens and his *loathsome pictures* kept from the eyes of American youth".

It is one of the most unsavoury periods in movie history, a personal witch-hunt that leaves Chaplin embittered and near breaking point.

Nothing from UA gets anywhere near the four million dollar mark. Director Zoltan Korda films Hemingway's *The Macomber Affair* starring Greg Peck as a white hunter on safari with Joan Bennett the vicious wife of inferior husband, Robert Preston; Robert Rossen makes the best boxing film to date, *Body And Soul* with John Garfield as a Jewish boy from New York's Lower East Side being corrupted on his way to the middleweight championship of the world.

Edward G. Robinson (*The Red House*); George Sanders (*The Private Affairs Of Bel Ami*); Hedy Lamarr (*Dis-Honoured Lady*); and George Raft (*Intrigue*) are among the other stars on view.

1948 The death of two former studio artists creates more news than any great turn-around in the company's fortunes which are beginning to look dire, so ineffectual is the product.

On July 22 in the Hollywood Knickerbocker Hotel, D. W. Griffith suffers a massive cerebral haemorrhage and dies the next day, aged seventy-three. Since his last film, *The Struggle*, in 1932, he has been all but forgotten, attempting to write plays and making futile plans for further films. He supposedly worked in a supervisory capacity on Hal Roach's *One Million B.C.*, but for the man who gave America some of its greatest silent pictures – *Birth Of A Nation, Intolerance, Broken Blossoms* – it is a sad end.

Donald Crisp and Charles Brackett deliver eulogies at the funeral. Says Crisp: "I cannot help feeling that there should always have been a place for him and his talent in the motion picture field. It is hard to believe that the industry could not have found a use for his great gift.''

Griffiths' most famous United Artists films: *Broken Blossoms, Way Down East, Orphans Of The Storm, America, Isn't Life Wonderful, Abraham Lincoln.*

The other loss is of cameraman Gregg Toland who dies prematurely on September 28, aged forty-four. A former assistant to Arthur Edeson and George Barnes, he worked on most of Sam Goldwyn's United Artists movies and came to be regarded as the greatest American cameraman of the thirties and forties.

His major UA films, many with Wyler: *Les Miserables, These Three, Dead End, Intermezzo, Wuthering Heights, Raffles, The Westerner, The Long Voyage Home*. Toland also worked with Ford at Fox (*The Grapes Of Wrath*) and Welles (*Citizen Kane*) and Wyler (*The Little Foxes, The Best Years Of Our Lives*) at RKO.

Red River, Howard Hawks' epic tale of a cattle trek over the Chisholm Trail from Texas to Kansas is the life saver for the studio. John Wayne, newcomer Montgomery Clift and a few hundred head of cattle bring in four and three quarter million dollars.

Arch Of Triumph; Pitfall; The Time Of Your Life; and *So This Is New York*, an original little comedy and the first film of independent young producer Stanley Kramer, are the best of the rest.

1949 Kramer proves he's a force to be reckoned with by producing two controversial pictures. Neither are big moneymakers, but both draw attention to the studio and point the way for the future.

The two movies are *Champion*, a boxing tale about an arrogant young middleweight who fights his way up from poverty, and *Home Of The Brave*, a story of racial antagonism among G.I.'s in wartime. Lloyd Bridges and Frank Lovejoy appear in the latter; Kirk Douglas and his dimple become stars in the former.

The old style, run-of-the-mill UA forties pictures are represented by *The Big Wheel* with Mickey Rooney as a racing car driver; *Outpost In Morocco* with George Raft in action in the desert; and *Mrs. Mike* in which Evelyn Keyes marries mountie Dick Powell. Abbott and Costello, on leave from Universal, also make a brief showing in *Africa Screams.*

1950 The United Artists company is failing fast and by the end of the year losing in the region of 100,000 dollars a week. Once again, no big moneymaker is on the books to pull the company out of the red. Bankruptcy looms.

To give the company a completely new look, Arthur B. Krim and Robert S. Benjamin, both partners in one of the ablest law firms in the industry, are brought to the studio. There is little they do not know about movies and movie law and they quickly set about putting the company on its feet.

The 1950 product does not yet reflect the new regime but nonetheless some interesting little movies emerge: *The Underworld Story* with reporter Dan Duryea uncovering corruption in a small American town; *Champagne For Caesar* in which unemployed genius Ronald Colman becomes a national celebrity on a TV Quiz Show; and *Three Husbands*, a neat little comedy about a recently deceased playboy who leaves a note saying he had been intimate with one of three wives.

Kramer shows his bravery by filming *Cyrano de Bergerac*. As a film it doesn't work but it still wins Jose Ferrer an Oscar for his long nosed swordsman-poet.

Kramer's other picture of the year is the one that really makes an impact. It's called *The Men*. Much of its success stems from the performance of dynamic newcomer Marlon Brando, most of its tenderness and dignity comes from the guiding hand of director Fred Zinnemann who treats a difficult subject — the terrible emotional problems of paraplegics, men whose war injuries have left them paralysed from the waist down — with great skill and understanding.

Only the advertising people mess it up. It's not the easiest subject to sell by any means, but UA seem a little off target with their slogan: 'A completely new experience between men and women.'

1951 The new managerial team approach stubborn owners Chaplin and Pickford with an offer they can't refuse. And they don't. The deal is that Krim and Benjamin be made trustees for 100 per cent of UA stock which will give them operating control for ten years. By the end of the year the company is already out of the red.

Helping considerably in the financial turnaround is John Huston's *The African Queen*, a British-made Romulus production which United Artists release. The movie is a smash, grossing over four million. It's the first time in three years that a UA release has figured among the top moneymakers.

A C. S. Forester story, it follows the adventures of captain Charlie Allnut and missionary Rose Sayer when they take an old tugboat down an uncharted African river and blow a World War I German gunboat to smithereens. Bogie wins an Oscar for his grizzled skipper, Kate Hepburn a nomination for her prim accompaniment.

The other United Artists product of the year leans heavily towards the realistic: Joseph Losey's ice cold *The Prowler* has patrol cop Van Heflin committing murder for Evelyn Keyes; in *He Ran All The Way* John Garfield holds an innocent family hostage before finishing up dead in the gutter; and in the semi-documentary *The Well* directors Leo Popkin and Russell Rouse look at the reactions of a small town population when a negro child becomes lodged in a deep well.

The science-fiction quickie *The Man From Planet X* lightens the mood a shade.

1952 September, a fateful month for Charlie Chaplin. It's the month when he sails with his wife and four children from New York to England on 'The Queen Elizabeth'. His purpose? To promote his new film *Limelight*.

In mid-Atlantic he receives a cable telling him his re-entry visa has been revoked. If he wishes to continue to work in Hollywood he has first to satisfy an immigration board of his moral fitness to live in the U.S.

On arrival in England his bitterness overflows. "I have no further use for America. I wouldn't go back there if Jesus Christ was president." Shortly after the premiere of *Limelight* he and his family make their way to Switzerland and a new life.

Limelight is a return to form, a tender, nostalgic story of an elderly music hall comedian who saves a young dancer from suicide, nurses her back to health and later helps her become a successful ballerina. Claire Bloom becomes a star through the picture. The picture itself reaches the heights in the last fifteen minutes when Chaplin and Keaton (together for the only time in their long careers) combine in a brilliant knockabout duet.

Back in the States Krim and Benjamin now own half the company.

Stanley Kramer, who has signed a multi-picture deal

with Columbia, still owes UA one film. By coincidence it's the one which makes money. The 'talkie western' *High Noon* which Columbia don't want on their schedule, but which director Fred Zinnemann turns into a tension classic as retiring Marshal Gary Cooper, abandoned by the townspeople he has defended for so long, is left alone at noon to face a vengeful killer and his gang of outlaws.

The picture puts UA among the major Oscars. Cooper wins best actor; composer Dimitri Tiomkin two music awards, one for his score, the other for the famous song 'Do Not Forsake Me, Oh My Darlin''.

Glenn Ford returns to France for wartime gems in *The Green Glove*; Renoir makes a visually stunning movie out of Rumer Godden's *The River*, an enchanting tale of three teenage girls growing up by the River Ganges in India; and in *The Thief* Ray Milland wins the prize for the year's most unusual performance.

It's unusual because Milland doesn't speak a word. Nor do any of the cast. The film is silent, other than street noises, cars, elevators, etc.

UA's biggest commercial hit: *Moulin Rouge*, another John Huston production about the tragic life of Montmartre painter Toulouse-Lautrec. It grosses four and a quarter million. *High Noon* is close behind with three and a half.

1953 United Artists win the race to produce the first film in the 3-D process. The movie, *Bwana Devil*, opens at Loews State in New York on February 18.

A routine but nonetheless historic production, it stars Robert Stack and Nigel Bruce and tells how a British railway engineer tracks two man-eating lions after they have disrupted the construction of the first railroad in East Africa. It is advertised with the slogan 'A Lion In Your Lap'.

Otto Preminger's *The Moon Is Blue* is the top box-office hit however, an adaptation of a lightweight Broadway success about a young American girl (Maggie McNamara) and her experiences with a couple of New York wolves (William Holden, David Niven). A pleasant but strictly minor vehicle, it creates something of a sensation in using for the first time on screen such words as 'virgin', 'seduction' and 'mistress'.

Gary Cooper, still at the studio after displaying his courage in *High Noon*, opts this time for a South Seas romance in *Return To Paradise*; Biff Elliott is Mike Hammer in *I,The Jury*; child actor Richard Andrusco gives the year's most delightful performance in *The Little Fugitive* as a boy who spends his day wandering wide-eyed around Coney Island amusement park.

1954 John Huston directs Bogart in *Beat The Devil*, the actor's most complex thriller since he made *The Big Sleep* at Warners. Bogie's co-stars are Jennifer Jones, Gina Lolobrigida, Peter Lorre and Robert Morley.

Independent directors are now beginning to flock to UA to get financing for their product. In '54 Robert Aldrich, Joe Mankiewicz and Anatole Litvak are all at work at the studio.

Aldrich directs two westerns, one serious, *Apache*, one lightweight, *Vera Cruz*. In the former Burt Lancaster stars as an Apache warrior who carries on his own personal fight against the whites after the surrender of Geronimo; in the latter he features as an American outlaw involved with fellow adventurer Gary Cooper down Mexico way.

Mankiewicz turns his gaze on the film world in the witty *The Barefoot Contessa*, the story of the checkered career of a Spanish slum girl (Ava Gardner) from her days as a flamenco dancer to the time she becomes a leading Hollywood film star. Bogart co-stars as a cynical broken-down film director, Edmond O'Brien cops the supporting actor Oscar with his portrait of a sweating, fast-talking publicity man.

Litvak's *Act Of Love* has Kirk Douglas involved in a tragic love affair with a French girl in World War II Paris; Anthony Quinn is an amnesiac victim accused of murder in the Mickey Spillane thriller *The Long Wait*; Sinatra, elated at winning his Oscar in Columbia's *From Here To Eternity*, sets his sights on big time assassination — the murder of the President — in *Suddenly*. He fails.

1955 More independents move across to United Artists which is now fastly earning a reputation for quality and the courage to put into production controversial subjects often refused by other studios. At UA producers and directors find they have complete autonomy in the making of their pictures once story, cast, director and budget have been agreed with the company.

A key picture of the year is Preminger's *The Man With The Golden Arm* with Sinatra as a dope-addicted poker dealer struggling to kick 'the monkey on his back'. It's a brave subject to tackle, full of drunks, cardsharps and dope peddlars and set in the seamy Chicago slums.

The independent Hecht-Hill-Lancaster company find UA ideal distributors. They also bring the studio unexpected glory when their small-budget version of Paddy Chayefsky's TV play *Marty* wins not only the Grand Prize at Cannes, but also the studio's first best picture Oscar in fifteen years. Ernest Borgnine as an unattractive New York butcher who falls for a shy schoolteacher (Betsy Blair) at a Saturday evening dance, wins the Academy Award for best actor.

Producer Stanley Kramer, back with UA after his spell at Columbia, directs for the first time with *Not As A Stranger*. Nearly all the cast — Robert Mitchum, Frank Sinatra, Olivia de Havilland, Charles Bickford — are either doctors or nurses. Mitchum goes through medical school and barks out the necessary commands, "Scalpel. . . forceps. . .swab!" Result. The studio's biggest box-office hit of the year. A six million plus gross.

Burt Lancaster also makes his directorial debut with the pioneer story *The Kentuckian* and Charles Laughton is another who opts for a place behind the cameras as he guides Robert Mitchum through *The Night Of The Hunter*, a terrifying tale of a backwoods preacher and his relentless pursuit of two children who can tell him the whereabouts of their dead father's money.

David Lean and actress Katharine Hepburn reflect the loneliness of middle-aged spinsterhood in *Summertime*; Robert Aldrich casts a jaundiced eye at Hollywood via Clifford Odets' savage play *The Big Knife*. Jack Palance is a disillusioned film star, Rod Steiger a ruthless studio boss.

Another break with the past occurs when Chaplin, now permanently domiciled in Switzerland, sells his UA stock for a fraction over a million dollars.

1956 *Around The World In Eighty Days* is *the* big one. Producer Mike Todd decides to release his massive three-hour version of Jules Verne's famous story through United Artists with the result that the studio wins another best picture Oscar and earns its highest ever gross — twenty-three million dollars.

David Niven stars as around the world traveller Phineas Fogg, Shirley MacLaine the Indian damsel he picks up along the way and Robert Newton is the blundering detective Mr. Fix. But the really breathtaking aspect of the film is its statistics. In addition to having the longest credits of any movie (six minutes) the film boasts:

4,000,000	air passenger miles flown to make the film
680,000	feet of colour film exposed
100,000	hot meals served to cast and crew during shooting
74,685	costumes
68,894	people photographed in thirteen different countries
26,391	location lunches
8,972	bottles of wine drunk
7,959	animals used including thirty-four different species
4,220	pots of tea brewed for extras in London
3,660	doughnuts dunked in 2,869 gallons of coffee
2,000	different camera set ups
140	different locations plus the stages of six major Hollywood studios as well as studios in England, Hong Kong and Japan
70	make-up artists glued beards on 15,612 chins
33	assistant directors
13	cameras worth more than 600,000 dollars

and last, but not least, fifty top stars in cameo roles!

The rest of UA's '56 product does its best to compete. Richard Burton is *Alexander The Great*; Van Heflin is involved in the politics of big business in *Patterns*; Trevor Howard is a Nazi Zaroff in *Run For The Sun*, an updated remake of *The Most Dangerous Game* as those fleeing for their lives with Richard Widmark and Jane Greer; Carol Reed is under a Parisian big top in *Trapeze*; Robert Aldrich deep in officer corruption and cowardice in World War II in *Attack!*

The 'Sleeper' of the year is *The Killing*, a cheaply made crime movie in which a shabby gang of tired thugs, led by ex-con Sterling Hayden, clean out a racetrack of some two million dollars. A mini *The Asphalt Jungle* it is handled with great flair by a young twenty-seven year old whose name is to come to mean much in the world of the post-war cinema, Stanley Kubrick.

Alexander Korda, whose London Films productions were distributed by United Artists in the 30s and 40s, dies aged sixty-three. His major productions released by the company: *The Private Life Of Henry VIII, The Scarlet Pimpernel, Sanders Of The River, The Ghost Goes West, Things To Come, Rembrandt, Elephant Boy, The Four*

Feathers, The Thief Of Baghdad, Lady Hamilton, The Jungle Book.

The final break with the United Artists of old comes when Mary Pickford follows Chaplin's example and agrees to sell her stock. Her price is three million. She gets it. Krim and Benjamin now own the company outright. UA's worldwide gross is sixty-four million dollars, an increase of 45 million over that of 1950.

1957 Fifty independents are now working at United Artists. Actor-producers John Wayne, Frank Sinatra, Gregory Peck, Bob Hope and Robert Mitchum; producer-directors William Wyler, Joe Mankiewicz, Stanley Kramer and Otto Preminger; and production units such as The Mirisch Corporation and the Hecht-Hill-Lancaster group are all operating through the company which, early in the year, goes public.

Two classics emerge from all the activity, Kubrick's anti-war *Paths Of Glory*, a World War I movie which condemns the corruption of the French High Command and traces the court martial and execution of three soldiers chosen as scapegoats for the failure of a suicidal infantry attack; and Sidney Lumet's *Twelve Angry Men*, a version of Reginald Rose's TV play about juror (Henry Fonda) who pleads, argues and eventually convinces the other eleven members of the jury that the eighteen year old youth whose trial they have just presided over may, after all, be innocent of murder.

Another vivid piece is *Sweet Smell Of Success*, an acid look at the power of the press and the way it is corrupted when an all-powerful New York columnist (Burt Lancaster) and his press agent (Tony Curtis) dig among the gossip empires of Broadway for 'smear material'. British director Alexander Mackendrick emerges with laurels for his observations of the New York scene.

Mickey Rooney is in excellent form as *Baby Face Nelson* and Delbert Mann turns Chayefsky's *The Bachelor Party* into an effective piece of urban realism. But not everything is a success. *Saint Joan* with an inexperienced Jean Seberg in the title role is an Otto Preminger miscalculation and *The Pride And The Passion*, a version of C. S. Forester's Napoleonic adventure 'The Gun' with Cary Grant, Sophia Loren and Frank Sinatra is a Kramer 'misfire'.

1958 Producer Walter Wanger and director Robert Wise

investigate the horrors of capital punishment in *I Want To Live*.

The factual movie looks at the life, times and death of bad girl Barbara Graham who was executed in the gas chamber at San Quentin for a murder the film strongly implies she did not commit. No attempt is made to whitewash, Bloody Babs, as she became known during her trial. Instead, the film presents her as an habitual criminal who is both immoral and irresponsible. Where the film scores is in its strong indictment of capital punishment and in its harrowing clinical presentation of the prelude to an execution.

No actress could play Barbara Graham and not be in the reckoning at Oscar time. So it proves. Susan Hayward, after many years of trying, is at last named best actress at Oscar time, and deservedly so.

David Niven, best actor for his bogus English colonel in Terence Rattigan's *Separate Tables* is the male Oscar winner; Tony Curtis and Sidney Poitier, as two escaped convicts chained by the wrists, are nominees for *The Defiant Ones*.

Kirk Douglas and Tony Curtis are cast as Nordic adventurers in *The Vikings*. The former loses an eye to a falcon, the latter has his arm chopped at the wrist. Ernest Borgnine makes it even jollier by jumping into a pit of wolves. The box-office rings however to a take of six million dollars, the biggest UA gross of the year.

Wyler is out West with Gregory Peck, Jean Simmons and Charlton Heston in *The Big Country*; Joe Mankiewicz in Saigon in a watered down version of Graham Greene's angry novel *The Quiet American*; Bob Hope in France with Anita Ekberg in *Paris Holiday*; and Billy Wilder in London for an engaging version of the Agatha Christie stage hit *Witness For The Prosecution*. Tyrone Power and Marlene Dietrich star, but Charles Laughton as an ailing lawyer takes the honours. Says he to bossy nurse Elsa Lanchester, "Miss Plimsoll, if you were a woman I'd strike you!"

Ronald Colman dies in Santa Barbara, California, aged sixty-seven. A regular Goldwyn — and United Artists star during the twenties and thirties — he appeared twice as amateur sleuth Hugh Drummond (*Bulldog Drummond* and *Bulldog Drummond Strikes Back*), as the amateur thief *Raffles*, and as an amateur stand-in king in *The Prisoner Of Zenda*. But as an actor he was the complete polished professional. Other top UA films: *The Winning Of Barbara Worth, Stella Dallas, Arrowsmith.*

1959 Billy Wilder is on top form with the drag comedy *Some Like It Hot*, a prohibition tale of two jazz musicians (Tony Curtis, Jack Lemmon) who witness the St. Valentine's Day massacre and are forced to masquerade as members of an all-girl dance band in order to escape the attentions of mobster George Raft. Marilyn Monroe co-stars as the band's lead singer, but during filming is not at her most co-operative. Says Wilder, "I will *never* use Marilyn in a film again, unless of course, I *need* her."

Some Like It Hot is UA's commercial and critical success of the year. It takes nearly eight million dollars and is Marilyn's biggest-ever moneymaking hit.

Stanley Kramer, after investigating racial problems in *The Defiant Ones*, looks at the biggest problem of all, nuclear warfare. His version of Nevil Shute's *On The Beach* has Greg Peck, Ava Gardner and Fred Astaire stranded in Australia, the only country not yet affected by a nuclear conflict that has destroyed the rest of the world. It is only a matter of time before the radiation reaches them. A grim warning. The final scenes of desolation are shattering.

John Ford refights part of the Civil War with John Wayne and William Holden in *The Horse Soldiers*; Gregory Peck is in Korea in *Pork Chop Hill*; Robert Ryan, Harry Belafonte and Shelley Winters try for a caper that will put them on easy street in *Odds Against Tomorrow*.

Frank Capra makes his first movie in eight years, *A Hole In The Head*, a lightweight comedy about a small time operator, Frank Sinatra, who runs a fleabag hotel on Miami Beach. Sinatra sings the year's Oscar winning song 'High Hopes'.

1960 Wilder's *The Apartment* is the year's Oscar winner. Jack Lemmon stars as a frustrated office clerk who finds that the quickest way to career advancement is to hire out his apartment to executives for their extra-marital activities. A basically sordid movie, made palatable by a crackling screenplay, it co-stars Shirley MacLaine as one of the executives' victims'.

Richard Brooks' *Elmer Gantry* is another Oscar winner. Burt Lancaster, long a UA star, is named best actor for his performance in the title role, a whoring, whisky drinking salesman who tags on to a tent pitching revivalist group in the Midwest and turns it into big business.

The two big movies of the year are Preminger's 213 minute *Exodus* and John Wayne's 192 minute *The Alamo*. The former deals with the founding of the state of Israel and the subsequent conflict between Jew and Arab; the latter with how a handful of Americans defended a broken-down mission against the full might of the Mexican army. Both are top UA box-office hits.

Kramer again brings controversy with *Inherit The Wind*, a condemnation of bigotry and intolerance, based on the famous Tennessee monkey trial of the 20s when a young teacher was put on trial for teaching the Darwin theory of evolution in a Southern school. Spencer Tracy appears for the defence, Fredric March for the prosecution.

Bob Hope and Lucille Ball team again in the marital comedy *The Facts Of Life*; Yul Brynner and Steve McQueen ride into Western folklore in *The Magnificent Seven*.

Happiest gal of the year. Melina Mercouri (*Never On Sunday*), the most popular prostitute on the waterfront in the port of Athens!

1961 Wyler, Wilder, Huston, Kramer and Capra are all in action for the studio, but it's an unusual combination of *two* directors – Robert Wise and Jerome Robbins – which brings most success. The pair are responsible for transferring Leonard Bernstein's *West Side Story* to the screen. The result is a musical triumph which cops eleven Oscars and takes nearly twenty million.

Richard Beymer and Natalie Wood are the New York Romeo and Juliet; Russ Tamblyn and George Chakiris lead the rival street gangs, The Jets and The Sharks; Rita Moreno sets it all alight with a sizzling rooftop rendering of 'America'.

Wyler remakes his Goldwyn 30s hit, *These Three*, as *The Children's Hour* with Audrey Hepburn and Shirley MacLaine in the Oberon/Hopkins roles; Capra also turns to old material with *Pocketful Of Miracles*, a reworking of his old Columbia success, *Lady For A Day*. Bette Davis is the new Apple Annie.

Wilder and Kramer go to Germany, the former for *One, Two, Three*, a zippy, fast-moving East-West comedy with James Cagney as a Coca-cola executive; the latter for *Judgment At Nuremberg*, a three hour courtroom drama starring Spencer Tracy as an elderly small-town judge presiding over the trial of four former Hitler judges and attempting to appraise the guilt and responsibility of the German people for Hitler's Third Reich. Maximilian Schell is an Oscar winner for his fiercely nationalistic German defence lawyer.

The Huston picture, *The Misfits*, is tinged with sadness. It is the last film for Clark Gable who dies of a heart attack shortly after its completion and also for Marilyn Monroe who is desperately ill during most of the shooting. Gable features as the leader of a trio of cowboys unable to come to terms with the modern way of life, Marilyn as a disillusioned divorcee.

1962 The most famous secret agent in movie history makes his bow — James Bond, alias 007. Personified by Sean Connery he comes up against sinister Chinese master mind *Dr. No* in the shimmering heat of the West Indies. In the same film he also comes up against Ursula Andress who rises from the ocean clad only in a white bikini and a knife holster! Spy films will never be the same again. *Dr. No* makes 6.3 million, more than any other UA release of the year.

John Frankenheimer proves to be the studio's most versatile director. His unusual *Birdman Of Alcatraz* allows Burt Lancaster to give one of his most offbeat performances as Robert Stroud, who, during a lifetime in jail, became a world renowned bird authority; his political thriller *The Manchurian Candidate* has Laurence Harvey as a brainwashed Korean war veteran 'programmed' to assassinate a presidential candidate. Says the film's scriptwriter George Axelrod: "It went from failure to classic without ever passing through success."

The studio is once more among the Oscars. Anne Bancroft (as Annie Sullivan) and Patty Duke (as Helen Keller) both win for *The Miracle Worker*.

There is also spectacle with *Taras Bulba*; romance between disillusioned lawyer Bob Mitchum and New York beatnik Shirley MacLaine in *Two For The Seesaw*; music with Elvis Presley in a remake of the prewar boxing drama *Kid Galahad*; and comedy as Bob Hope and Bing Crosby appear in the last of the 'Road' films, *The Road To Hong Kong*. Joan Collins is their co-star, but Dottie Lamour inevitably makes a token appearance.

1963 James Bond continues on his nonchalant, sadistic way

in *From Russia With Love*. Assigned to steal a cipher machine from the Russians in Istanbul, he encounters not only the high kicking Rosa Klebb but also muscular killer Robert Shaw who does his best to rid him of his windpipe on board the Orient Express.

Stanley Kramer keeps Tracy on the right side of the law in *It's A Mad, Mad, Mad, Mad World*. He's a hard working cop eagerly awaiting his pension. Not for long though. Before the movie's run its course greed has taken over and he's joined the rest of the cast — Mickey Rooney, Ethel Merman, Terry-Thomas, Phil Silvers — in their wild chase across the States for 350,000 dollars worth of buried loot. A small amount compared with the film's box-office take, twenty million.

A superb Sidney Poitier as a roving handyman who builds a chapel in Arizona for three nuns in *Lilies Of The Field* is the year's best actor Oscar winner; Tony Richardson's *Tom Jones*, a colourful version of Henry Fielding's bawdy eighteenth century tale is the best film.

The Great Escape takes 168 minutes — McQueen jumps his motor bike, Bernstein contributes a rousing score, the scriptwriters a bitter finale; John Wayne is cattle baron *McLintock!* who has more trouble from one rebellious wife (Maureen O'Hara) than his entire stock of cows; Shirley MacLaine is the sweet-hearted Parisian tart *Irma La Douce*; Bob Hope a bogus big-game hunter/author drafted into secret service work in Africa in *Call Me Bwana*. Sharing things with him on safari: his Parisian companion Anita Ekberg.

1964 James Bond, now really in the big league financially, — *Goldfinger*, the third 007 movie grosses over twenty-two million dollars — acquires the most famous car in the history of the cinema, Aston Martin JB 007. As well as being able to travel at 150 m.p.h. it also boasts rotating scythes in the wheelhubs, a knife and hand grenade compartment, a radar scanner, a homing device, an ejector seat, revolving number plates, retractable machine guns, and an oil spiller.

Top villain in the movie, the gold-crazy Auric Goldfinger, is played by Gert Frobe, sexy Honor Blackman judos in the hay as Pussy Galore, Shirley Eaton, alas, lasts but a reel and finishes up very dead, covered from head to toe in gold paint.

Considerably less adept at his job than 007, but very

nearly as popular is the accident-prone Inspector Clouseau (Peter Sellers) who proves such a hit in *The Pink Panther* that he is immediately assigned to another case in *A Shot In The Dark*. Both movies are big grossers. Capucine, Claudia Cardinale and Elke Sommer help add to Clouseau's permanent confusion.

Sellers also appears as an egotistical concert pianist in *The World Of Henry Orient*; George Chakiris and Cliff Robertson (*633 Squadron*), Henry Fonda (*The Best Man*) and Yul Brynner (*Invitation To A Gunfighter*) are other top UA stars.

Melina Mercouri, Maximilian Schell, Robert Morley and Peter Ustinov enjoy themselves most of all in *Topkapi* when they try to rob the Topkapi museum in Istanbul of a priceless jewel-encrusted dagger. They fail, but none of them really seems to mind, not even Oscar winner Ustinov, employed for his brawn rather than his brain.

Eddie Cantor, star of several Goldwyn musicals of the early thirties, dies of a heart attack, aged seventy-two. Among his UA movies: *Whoopee, Palmy Days, Roman Scandals, Kid Millions, Strike Me Pink.*

1965 It's still 007 that dominates the United Artists scene. In *Thunderball* he's now at the height of his popularity as he pops over to Nassau to recover two stolen atomic bombs from SPECTRE. The spectacular jaunts add twenty-eight million dollars to the till, the biggest ever take of a Bond movie, a record that still stands.

Comedy is also big. In *What's New Pussycat?* sex-starved psychiatrist Peter Sellers is sent bananas by patient Peter O'Toole who just can't keep the women away; in *A Thousand Clowns* Jason Robards is at his best as a non-conformist writer; in *How To Murder Your Wife* newspaper cartoonist Jack Lemmon tries to dispose of his beautiful but unwanted spouse, Virna Lisi in the 'globadda, globadda machine'. Terry-Thomas assists.

John Frankenheimer engineers the most spectacular train crash since DeMille's *The Greatest Show On Earth* in *The Train*; George Stevens makes the year's most serious and expensive miscalculation with his 221 minute life of Christ, *The Greatest Story Ever Told.*

Producer David O. Selznick dies, aged sixty-three. One of the key figures in the studio's development, he worked at the company for ten years between 1936 and 1946 producing, among others: *Nothing Sacred, The Prisoner Of*

Zenda, A Star Is Born, The Adventures Of Tom Sawyer, Intermezzo, Rebecca, Since You Went Away, Spellbound.

1966 After four straight years of spying for M, 007 takes a year off to enjoy his dry martinis 'shaken, not stirred'.

Billy Wilder zooms in with one of his sharpest comedies, *The Fortune Cookie*, the story of a TV cameraman (Jack Lemmon) who is mildly concussed at a football game and then told to fake his injuries by lawyer brother-in-law Walter Matthau. Their aim? To sue for a million dollars. Matthau nabs a supporting Oscar for his shyster lawyer.

Humour is also provided by *The Russians Are Coming, The Russians Are Coming* and *A Funny Thing Happened On The Way To The Forum*; Yul Brynner is back out West leading another band of outlaws in *The Return Of The Seven*; Charlton Heston is General Gordon in *Khartoum.*

Sidney Lumet provides the most thought-provoking UA movie – *The Group*, a version of Mary McCarthy's best-selling novel about the hopes, loves and disappointments of eight young Vassar College girls as they experience the harsh realities of life in America during the Depression years. Candice Bergen as the lesbian Lakey, Shirley Knight as a young hospital worker and Joanna Pettet as a girl hopelessly caught up in a tragic marriage, head a superb cast.

1967 007 comes back as strong as ever in *You Only Live Twice.* The setting for the new movie is Japan; cat-stroking Donald Pleasence is Ernst Blofeld and feeds unhappy victims to piranha fish. It's Connery's fifth outing as Bond and he's now talking seriously about giving up the character. The take is still healthy enough to make him 'think twice' however, more than nineteen million dollars.

In The Heat Of The Night is the surprise Oscar winner of the year. A racial thriller of the Deep South it beats such hotly fancied contenders as *The Graduate* and *Bonnie And Clyde* to the best picture award. White police chief Rod Steiger and black homicide expert Sidney Poitier search for a killer in a small backwater town in Mississippi. Steiger is named best actor.

James Garner is Wyatt Earp and Jason Robards Doc Holliday in *Hour Of The Gun*; Kirk Douglas, Robert Mitchum and Richard Widmark feature in the all-star 'trek western' *The Way West*; in much more sophisticated vein Joe Mankiewicz updates Ben Jonson's 'Volpone' as *The Honey Pot.* Rex Harrison stars as a twentieth century millionaire who tricks three former mistresses — Susan Hayward, Capucine and Edie Adams — into sharing his 'last days'.

1968 *Yours, Mine, And Ours*, a wholesome family movie, is the surprise hit of the year. An old fashioned entertainment it takes more than eleven million dollars. Lucille Ball is a widow with eight kids, Henry Fonda a widower with ten. The twenty of them get together and contribute a delightful comedy.

Dick Van Dyke builds the flying car *Chitty Chitty Bang Bang*; director William Friedkin engagingly recalls old time burlesque in *The Night They Raided Minsky's*; and Steve McQueen, bored and a millionaire, plans an ingenious bank robbery in *The Thomas Crown Affair*. Among his rewards: a tantalising game of sex chess with sensual insurance investigator Faye Dunaway.

Tony Richardson's grimly realistic *The Charge Of The Light Brigade* leaves nothing to the imagination; The Beatles enter cartoonland in *Yellow Submarine*; and Clint Eastwood proves he really *is* indestructible by surviving his own hanging in *Hang 'Em High*.

1969 Jon Voight and Dustin Hoffman take the year's acting honours in Schlesinger's *Midnight Cowboy*. They're a couple of young drifters, one a stud hustler, the other a tubercular down-and-out, struggling to exist in a cold and unfriendly New York. A touching portrait of loneliness, it wins the studio its second best picture Oscar in three years.

Connery temporarily abandons 007. George Lazenby takes over in *On Her Majesty's Secret Service* and sets off for Switzerland where Blofeld is now domiciled. Telly Savalas (in his pre-*Kojak* days) is now the arch villain; Diana Rigg, Bond's trend setting but short lived wife.

Laurence Olivier, Michael Caine, Christopher Plummer and an all-star cast fight again in *Battle Of Britain*; British POW Oliver Reed escapes with an elephant across the Alps in *Hannibal Brooks*; Arthur Penn films *Alice's Restaurant*, a version of Arlo Guthrie's best-selling l.p.

James Garner, as he has done so often before, provides western amusement in *Support Your Local Sheriff!* He's an unwilling lawman in charge of a rowdy, gold-mad town.

Up against him Walter Brennan and his gang. By his side, drunken Jack Elam. The odds seem about right.

1970 Not the best of years. Mick Jagger is Australian outlaw *Ned Kelly*; Charlton Heston a plantation owner in *Master Of The Islands*, a sequel to the 60s hit, *Hawaii*; and in *They Call Me MISTER Tibbs* Sidney Poitier stars again as the homicide expert he first created in *In The Heat Of The Night*.

Black farce is provided by *Where's Poppa?* with George Segal trying to rid himself of his widowed mom Ruth Gordon, a sweet little old lady who's forever messing up his love life.

Real quality emerges in just two films, *The Private Life Of Sherlock Holmes* Billy Wilder's loving homage to a great detective, and Ken Russell's brilliant version of D.H. Lawrence's novel *Women In Love* in which love, passion and bitterness all overflow into tragedy in an English colliery town in the mid-20s. Oscar winner Glenda Jackson, Oliver Reed and Alan Bates star.

Top box-office hits: *Cotton Comes To Harlem* and *What Do You Say To A Naked Lady?*

1971 Topol looks up to heaven and sings 'If I Were A Rich Man'. If he looks once he seems to look a hundred times. Even so *Fiddler On The Roof* emerges as one of the best of filmed stage musicals, a movie that manages to fuse a serious theme with an imaginative and tuneful score. The setting is a small, pre-revolutionary village in the Ukraine; Topol is the honest milkman whose main aim in life is to find satisfactory husbands for his five daughters.

Connery returns as Bond, for the last time, in *Diamonds Are Forever*, one of the best in the series. For many he's still the only 007. This time he's in Las Vegas and narrowly avoids premature cremation. Charles Gray is Blofeld, Jill St. John Tiffany Case the least intelligent, but one of the most appealing of Bond's girl friends.

Woody Allen (*Bananas*), Dick Van Dyke (*Cold Turkey*), Burt Lancaster (*Lawman*) all appear for the studio; demented Shelley Winters and Debbie Reynolds commit murder in Hollywood in the 30s in *What's The Matter With Helen?*; George C. Scott, supposedly saner but near to breaking point, is a doctor with a mad killer roving his wards in *The Hospital*.

1972 Woody Allen provides the most laughs and brings in the

most dollars with his outrageous *Everything You Always Wanted To Know About Sex But Were Afraid To Ask*. A multi-story film it has every conceivable sex joke one can imagine including doctor Gene Wilder in love with a sheep named Daisy and Woody as a sperm, apprehensive of his destination just prior to orgasm. Tasteless, vulgar, splendidly funny.

Says Woody: "This picture contains every funny idea I've ever had about sex including several that led to my own divorce."

Otherwise the scene is violent. Bill Crosby and Robert Culp are down-and-out private eyes in *Hickey And Boggs*; Charles Bronson a professional assassin and Jan Michael Vincent his protégée in *The Mechanic*; and Burt Reynolds and Raquel Welch a unique and somewhat lighter team in *Fuzz*.

The Peter O'Toole-Sophia Loren musical *Man Of La Mancha* is off-key; *Avanti* with Jack Lemmon and Juliet Mills is Billy Wilder off form.

1973 Marlon Brando — Maria Schneider — Bertolucci — a moody love affair — and the notorious butter — make *Last Tango In Paris* the year's sensation and a box-office smash.

Equally successful, but on a very different level is *Live And Let Die*, the first Bond movie to star Roger Moore. Heroin smuggling — swamps — alligators — speed boat chases are somewhat different ingredients to those in Bertolucci's film, but the box-office take is the same. 15.8 million for each film.

Woody Allen, frozen during an operation and brought back to life 200 years later to find himself in a police state, again provides the year's funniest movie, *Sleeper*; Elliott Gould is an offbeat Philip Marlowe in *The Long Goodbye*; James Coburn an ace pickpocket in *Harry In Your Pocket*; Robert Blake a highway cop in *Electra Glide In Blue*; Paul Scofield a Russian agent in the cat and mouse spy thriller *Scorpio*.

Thirty-five years after Selznick filmed *The Adventures Of Tom Sawyer,* United Artists release another version of the story, this time a musical version entitled simply *Tom Sawyer*. Celeste Holm is Aunt Polly, Warren Oates Muff Potter. Johnnie Whitaker (Tom), Jodie Foster (Becky Thatcher) and Jeff East (Huck Finn) are the kids.

1974 Sam Goldwyn, who contributed fifty UA movies during his fourteen year association with the company, dies, aged ninety-one. He had been inactive since producing *Porgy And Bess* for Columbia in 1959. His United Artists movies include some of the finest ever produced by the studio: *Stella Dallas, Bulldog Drummond, Raffles, Street Scene, Arrowsmith, These Three, Dodsworth, The Hurricane, Dead End, Wuthering Heights, The Westerner.*

But times have changed somewhat since Goldwyn's day. The top movie of the year, critically and commercially, is *Lenny*, the harrowing story of controversial drug-addicted comedian Lenny Bruce (Dustin Hoffman).

Lenny apart, UA can offer little of substance. Robert Altman remakes *They Live By Night* as *Thieves Like Us* with Keith Carradine and Shelley Duvall as the doomed lovers; Clint Eastwood is a Vietnam veteran hoping to pull off a big heist in *Thunderbolt And Lightfoot*; Sam Peckinpah investigates man's greed in *Bring Me The Head Of Alfredo Garcia*; Robert Shaw holds a New York subway train to ransom for a million dollars in *The Taking Of Pelham One, Two, Three.*

Even the second Roger Moore Bond movie is lack-lustre. *The Man With The Golden Gun* has 007 in Hong Kong after a solar energy capsule. Apart from a pint-sized killer called Nick Nack, a flying car stunt and arch villain Scaramanga (Christopher Lee) boasting three nipples, little else is new.

1975 *One Flew Over The Cuckoo's Nest*, half funny, half sad, ultimately frightening, wins the five major Oscar awards — best picture, director, actor, actress and screenplay — the first picture to do so for forty-one years. Basically a movie about mental illness it is also about bucking the system. Patient Jack Nicholson represents rebellion, unemotional nurse Louise Fletcher authority and discipline. It's when Fletcher emerges victorious that the movie becomes frightening.

Woody Allen is back in Russia fighting against Napoleon in *Love And Death*. Diane Keaton's there too as his fickle fiancée; Jeff Bridges becomes a Gower Gulch extra in *Hearts Of The West*, a movie about the early days of Hollywood; Peckinpah offers confused violence in *The Killer Elite*; Norman Jewison calculated sadism in *Rollerball*, a game of the 21st century in which competitors are maimed and killed for spectator amusement.

Peter Sellers takes up where he left off ten years

before as Inspector Clouseau in *Return Of The Pink Panther*.

1976 Sylvester Stallone hits stardom as an 'Italian Stumbler' who gets a shot at the heavyweight championship of the world in *Rocky*. The movie's a 'sleeper' which surprises everybody. Part *On The Waterfront*, part *Marty*, it wins the best picture Oscar for the studio.

The acting awards go to *Network*. Peter Finch wins posthumously for his washed up TV newsman who threatens suicide over the air; Faye Dunaway is named best actress for her ruthless programme executive who exploits Finch's sudden news value.

Paul Newman is William Cody in *Buffalo Bill And The Indians*; David Carradine is Woody Guthrie in *Bound For Glory*; Sellers is back with more of the same in *The Pink Panther Strikes Again*.

Sissy Spacek takes up telekinesis in Brian De Palma's *Carrie*, creates horrific carnage at the local hop, crucifies her mom with flying kitchen knives then goes on to 'Burn In Hell'.

Even more chilling is a moment in *The Missouri Breaks*, an Arthur Penn western with Marlon Brando and Jack Nicholson, "You know what woke you up?" comes Nicholson's voice from behind a close-up of Brando whose eyes suddenly blink open and whose lips start trickling blood. "Well, you've just had your throat cut."

1977 *Annie Hall*, a Woody Allen 'home-movie' about the on-off love affair between a nightclub comedian and an aspiring singer (Diane Keaton) carries off another best picture Academy Award, making it three best films in a row for United Artists, a feat accomplished by no other studio.

It's a popular winner in a year of big movies – Richard Attenborough's all-star story of Arnhem, *A Bridge Too Far*; Scorsese's big band musical of the 40s, *New York, New York*; Ken Russell's flamboyant *Valentino*.

Richard Burton is near to his best as the psychiatrist in *Equus*; James Bond, however, sinks to the level of 'Carry On' farce in *The Spy Who Loved Me*. "Tell Bond To Pull Out," commands M to the accompaniment of Roger Moore in coitus with an attractive young damsel in a Swiss chalet. A long, long way from *Dr. No* and *Goldfinger*!

Charlie Chaplin dies on Christmas Day, aged 88. For

many, the greatest movie comedian of them all, his films remain the genuine classics of the early days of United Artists: *The Gold Rush, The Circus, City Lights, Modern Times, The Great Dictator, Monsieur Verdoux, Limelight.*

1978 Peter Sellers and Blake Edwards just can't let Inspector Clouseau go. He's back yet again in *Revenge Of The Pink Panther*. So too is the demented Inspector Dreyfus of Herbert Lom.

Otherwise things are deadly serious. Sylvester Stallone (actor-writer) and director Norman Jewison boldly investigate union formation and corruption in *F.I.S.T.*; Hal Ashby focuses on Vietnam war veterans in *Coming Home* with Jane Fonda, Jon Voight and Bruce Dern; even Woody Allen gets a touch of the Ingmar Bergman's in *Interiors*, a very straight drama about death, art and the human condition. Diane Keaton is a suffering poet, Richard Jordan her novelist husband.

WARNER BROTHERS

Warner Brothers

They used to say at Warner Bros. that whenever one of their thrillers faltered or came to a sticky patch (usually through too much talk) the answer was to stage a fight.

In the 30s, a quick sock on the jaw would cure most things at Warners. Within seconds there would be the inevitable return punch and then a huge *mêlée* with everybody on the set swinging away in all directions. Chairs were broken, tables overturned, glasses smashed.

Three minutes later everything would be calm again and the story would continue.

It didn't matter whether it was Cagney, Edward G. or Humphrey Bogart who had the boring lines. Great actors that they were, they were still interrupted if the story sagged, if not by fistfights then by gunplay and long moaning deaths in the gutter where it inevitably rained or snowed. No-one was ever allowed to die in a dry gutter at Warners. A wet, soggy one, with a copy of yesterday's newspaper draped loosely around a damp trouser leg, was the ultimate punishment.

In the 30s, when Warner Bros. first became a studio to be reckoned with, action was the name of the game. Cagney, Robinson, Bogart — and Flynn who provided action of a different kind with his romantic swashbuckling — reigned supreme. Admittedly Olivia de Havilland was invariably on hand to provide sweetness and light, Bette Davis the tartare sauce and Busby Berkeley the musical spectacle with what seemed like hundreds of dancing girls, all swinging their erotic white legs into positions that, even today, would do any sex manual proud.

But the tough stuff was the studio's real bread and butter. It was what Warners were all about. And it made their name. Everything, from top James Cagney vehicles to second feature programmers, had the same formula — action, fast dialogue and stories pared right to the bone.

It didn't matter either whether the stories had any particular originality. Warners were masters at disguising an already filmed tale and serving it up to an unsuspecting audience in a new form.

Producer Bryan Foy, known as the 'Keeper Of The Bs' at the studio in that he aspired to little else but routine programmers, once boasted, not without a certain amount of pride, that he made the same film eleven times.

It started off as *Tiger Shark*, a fishing story in which Edward G. Robinson lost an arm. Foy subsequently followed the same script, scene for scene, only this time he gave the movie a lumberjack setting and the leading character lost not an arm, but a leg. The third time round, the hero was a lion tamer and once more lost an arm. When the scriptwriters, aghast at this loss of originality, protested that he had already lost an arm in the first version of the story, Foy commented wryly, "He's got two arms hasn't he?"

Later, they did *Tiger Shark* over again in Africa with the leading man as a big-game hunter. Exactly what the luckless hero had lost by the time they arrived at remake number eleven doesn't bear thinking about.

But the story illustrates that Warners were willing to film just about any kind of action entertainment and not worry about originality. The prime requirements were that a film should entertain and thrill the audience. That the studio should provide such a tough, no-nonsence image isn't too surprising when one considers the personality of the man who ran the studio, Jack L. Warner.

Outwardly genial but inwardly as ruthless as any of the studio bosses, Warner had come up the hard way. With his three brothers he had stared bankruptcy in the face several times in the twenties before he struck lucky with sound and *The Jazz Singer*.

He knew how to fight and keep alive in the movie jungle. Like the other studio moguls he had that sixth sense of what the movie public wanted. And that sixth sense told him that, from Warners at least, they wanted movies straight from the shoulder – hard-hitting and snatched from newspaper stories of the day.

Occasionally, almost reluctantly, he would make concessions to art and quality, but always in the back of his mind was the experience of the mid-twenties when Warners had just two main stars, John Barrymore and Rin Tin Tin. The experience he remembered was that it was the dog who made the money.

His main concessions were the famous Paul Muni biographies directed by William Dieterle, films like *The Story Of Louis Pasteur, The Life Of Emile Zola, Juarez*. Although not exactly runaway box-office successes, they did ease Warners into a more serious groove of film-making and earned them several Academy Awards; something which, for all their slick expertise, the Cagney-Robinson entertainments had failed to do.

Warner, however, still continued to grumble. Once, when the

studio make-up men had done a particularly brilliant job of transforming Muni into the Mexican leader, Juarez, he exclaimed, "You mean we're paying Muni all this dough and we can't even recognise him!"

Producer Hal Wallis shared similar views. "Every time Paul Muni parts his beard and looks down a telescope this company loses two million dollars."

The man who really moulded Warner Bros. together was not Jack Warner. He was just the figurehead. The real driving force was a young whizz-kid called Darryl F. Zanuck or, as he was known on various Warner writing credits — Melville Crossman, Gregory Rogers, Mark Canfield.

It was Zanuck who gave the Warner studio its hard-grained, realistic style. He was the trail blazer, Jack Warner's first lieutenant. Without him it is difficult to see how the studio, even allowing for the advent of sound, could have functioned for very long.

Before he became head of production in 1929, Zanuck worked as a writer on scores of pictures and was so prolific he could knock out a scenario over a weekend. In one year he wrote nineteen features and the shareholders began to be a little worried that he was writing just about every picture on their books; which wasn't all that far from the truth.

Hence his three pseudonyms. Crossman he used for the class pictures, Gregory Rogers for the comedies and Mark Canfield for the melodramas, which included some of the famous Rin Tin Tin pictures.

Although it is rightly assumed that the Warners' gamble on sound saved them from ruin and allowed them to compete with the bigger studios, it is also true that if it hadn't been for Rin Tin Tin — and Zanuck — there would never have been enough money in the till for Sam Warner to finance the experiments with the Bell Telephone Company, experiments which lasted for two years and culminated with Al Jolson saying the historic words, "You ain't heard nothing yet!"

With Rin Tin it wasn't a case of, "You ain't heard nothing yet" but "You ain't *seen* anything yet!" The handsome German shepherd dog went through every conceivable cinematic adventure — rescuing children, chasing villains, fighting deadly animals, participating in just about any situation a writer could devise.

The public loved it. One title of a Rin Tin Tin picture read, 'Wolf heart or human heart, they are just the same wherever love sets.' With titles like that and a dog who could droop his ears, moisten his eyes and look completely forlorn, who needed talkies?

Rin Tin Tin earned Warners and his owner Leland Duncan, a soldier who had found the dog as a puppy on a French battlefield in World War I, a fortune. He was also lucky for Zanuck and allowed him the chance to make a name for himself. When Jack Warner first suggested making a star of the dog, director Mal St. Clair and Zanuck acted out a doggy story in Warner's office. Which of the two was the dog has never been verified, but their antics and the look on Warner's face must rank as one of the most bizarre moments in Hollywood history.

Zanuck's limitless energy and enthusiasm obviously paid dividends. He was just twenty-seven when Warner made him head of production, a fact that must have slightly worried the studio chief. ''Well, you're in,'' he said to Zanuck, ''but even if you don't need glasses, get some window panes and grow a moustache. It'll give you a little age.''

Zanuck stayed at Warners for four more years and it was during this period (1929-33) that the Warner style really evolved. Cagney and Robinson made their first gangster movies, Mervyn LeRoy and William Wellman tackled the first social protest films, Busby Berkeley resurrected the musical when everyone thought the *genre* was dead. It was an exciting time and Zanuck was the driving force.

The directors who made his pictures were professionals, men who knew how to make a movie quickly, without fuss and at a minimum cost. Men like Howard Hawks, Lloyd Bacon, Mervyn LeRoy, William Wellman, Archie Mayo and, later in the decade, William Keighley and Raoul Walsh.

The directing team also included two men, Michael Curtiz and William Dieterle, who had joined Warners in the 20s from Europe and who were to prove two of the most imaginative signings Jack Warner ever made, especially Curtiz who could literally direct anything, usually brilliantly, at a rapid pace at any time.

But, talented as they were, both men had their idiosyncrasies. Dieterle, the man responsible for the Muni biographies, was very much guided by his horoscope when making a movie. In 1938, when he was about to embark on one of his most ambitious productions, *Juarez*, he put in a call to his cameraman Tony Gaudio telling him that he wanted everybody connected with the picture on set at 8 o'clock the next morning. The picture wasn't due to begin that day. In fact, it wasn't due to begin shooting for another two weeks but the superstitious director wanted to make sure that the first scene he filmed coincided with his good astrological aspects.

Curtiz was even more eccentric. A manic depressive who used to miss lunch because it wasted time, he used to say he 'lived to work' and poured scorn on those who 'worked to live' even though so many were unable to do so because of the Depression. He was also a master of verbal garbage. Just how he managed to make so many films so quickly and with such flair remains a mystery if only because it was a miracle anyone could ever understand him.

Author of the now famous phrase "Bring on the empty horses" he also came out with such gems as "boy cows" instead of "cowboys", "This next scene will make your blood curl" and (to a young starlet) "It is morning and a haystack and lots of sunlight — turn over on your stomach and look sex."

On top of the world one day, right down in the dumps the next, Curtiz would dress according to his moods. Either he would be splendidly attired with breeches, riding boots, scarf and jewellery or he would be exactly the opposite, unkempt and sullen.

One of his most famous sayings was, "The next time I send a dumb sonofabitch to do something, I go myself!"

Combine that kind of language with that spoken by S. Z. 'Cuddles' Sakall, a Hungarian character actor whose prime claim to acting was to wobble his heavy jowls and go "phheeww. . ." and you really had a situation. For Sakall's command of the English language was, if anything, worse than Curtiz's. He used to drive Alan Hale, another famous Warner character actor, crazy with rage.

Once, when the burly Hale told Sakall that it was about time he could speak proper English the Hungarian replied: "And for vy Il should spik Englich better, ven mitt dis Englich I em makin more vit is you."

And to think, Michael Curtiz directed Cuddles in several Warner movies!

If Dieterle was superstitious, Curtiz a depressive, then Busby Berkeley was a worrier. The man who created the long series of fantastic dance sequences was always worrying what to do next to top his previous accomplishments. How could he top geometric shots of girls shaped like a violin glowing in the dark? Or one hundred and fifty extras marching on a half wheel to the tragic 'My Forgotten Man' number? Or girls plunging into beautiful patterns by a waterfall or a dance sequence of mirror reflections making a hundred dancers look like a thousand?

Berkeley suffered from exhaustion, strain and stress. When, accidentally, he killed three people when driving back from a Hollywood party and went through the agony of three trials before being found innocent, he still had to carry on and work at the studio.

"My musical routines for Warners used to average 100,000 dollars," he said shortly before his death. "That's 10,000 dollars per minute of screen time.'' Nicknamed 'The Million Dollar Dance Director', Berkeley would have been just that if he had operated in today's inflated industry.

But if Dieterle and Curtiz and Berkeley took their work a shade too seriously, there were others on the Warner lot who brought humour with them to the set every morning. Raoul Walsh and John Huston were two who fitted well into this category. Both were practical jokers and both couldn't resist playing a gag on someone if they saw a chance. The guy they both picked on, accidentally, was Humphrey Bogart.

On *High Sierra,* Walsh, who was in the act of making Bogie into a star, decided that as it was the first time Bogie had been on location he would make sure that the actor would get the full benefit of the beauty of it all. And it was some location — the massive, 11,000 ft Mount Whitney. They were filming the last scene in the picture and Bogart was high up in the mountains, hiding behind some rocks on a mountain flank.

As the morning's shooting drew to a close and the crew began thinking of the lunch break Walsh, out of sight of Bogart, ordered the property boy to hide the lunch wagon. He also told cameraman Tony Gaudio to 'roll 'em' again as soon as everyone had eaten.

Everyone tucked in, everyone that is except Bogie who was still sitting high up on the mountain ledge, sweating it out in the heat and waiting for his lunch.

Eventually, after a long wait, Walsh made the haul up to Bogart's ledge, the actor's lunch box behind his back.

When he approached the frustrated star, the property boy, as ordered, hollered, ''They forgot to send the lunches Mr Walsh.'' Bogart paled visibly behind all that running sweat when he heard the words then let off a tirade about the picture business that must have echoed round and round those beautiful, usually quiet mountains — Jack Warner eating in his private dining room at the studio, all the comfort of the lot, and where was he, out on . . . location!

Walsh, with a grin, at last produced the lunch box and Bogart, trouper that he was, saw the joke only to get a double dose when he saw what his lunch consisted of. At the studio lunch was lunch. What he got that day was a banana, a sandwich, a pichele, an olive and a doughnut.

''You don't like the great outdoors Bogie?'' asked Walsh. ''Screw the great outdoors,'' bellowed Bogart, ''and this lousy business.''

It wasn't too lousy for him that year, however. *High Sierra* in which he played Roy Earle, the last of the Dillinger gang, did make him a star and just a few months later Huston's *The Maltese Falcon* made sure he stayed one.

Huston was also responsible for Bogart's next big movie, *Across The Pacific* which he made the following year with Mary Astor and Sydney Greenstreet. During shooting Huston had his doubts as to whether he would be able to finish it. America was then in the war and he'd been expecting his call-up papers ever since they'd started filming.

Sure enough, when eventually the papers did come he still hadn't finished the picture. There wasn't that much left to shoot — just the ending. However, as there was no way of stalling the army, Huston knew he had to hand over the pictue to someone else. The unlucky guy was Vincent Sherman and Huston made sure that it wasn't going to be easy for him.

Even today, Huston relishes the situation: "I sat right down and altered the script and set up a wild scene with Bogie trapped in Panama. Made him a prisoner of the Japanese who were out to bomb the Canal. I fixed it so his hands were tied behind him and packed the room with Japanese soldiers armed with machine guns. Outside, more armed soldiers surrounded the house.

"That night we shot it right up to the part where Bogie is hopelessly trapped. I knew there was no way in God's green world he could logically have escaped. I also knew Warners would never reshoot the original ending. I had them. So I waved goodbye to Bogie and was in Washington next morning."

Poor Sherman had to call off shooting for two days while he tried to figure it out. Writers were also called in to solve the dilemma. Bogart finally *did* get out, but only because a Japanese soldier suddenly goes mad and begins shooting up the room. Bogart eventually came out of the *mêlée*, a machine gun in his hands, and calming Mary Astor with the words, "It's O.K. Angel."

The 30s and 40s were the peak years at Warners. The misery of the Depression suited them admirably. They fed on it. While other studios did their best to keep the misery away, Warners pressed it home. Not that they deliberately made capital out of people's wretchedness — instead, they reflected it. People associated with and liked the Warner style. When the country's misery was up there on the screen there was always the hope that something might be done to put things right.

During those twenty years the studio was run with clockwork precision, budgets adhered to and filming kept strictly on schedule.

So tight was the rein that in the 30s anybody visiting the studio would have noticed in offices all over the lot signs reading: "When not in use, turn off the juice.'' Jack Warner never wasted his company's money. He was as shrewd a businessman as any to be found in Wall Street.

Jack Warner had no pretentions about himself. When it came to saving a dollar he was a genius, but when it came to artistic decisions he was frequently in no-man's land. Jack Benny said of him: ''This is a man who would rather tell a bad joke than make a good movie — and he has proved it time and again.''

He never hid the fact that he hated reading a book. ''I would rather take a fifty mile hike than crawl through a book,'' he once said. ''I prefer to skip the long ones and get a synopsis from the story department.'' For instance, when one of his top directors, Mervyn LeRoy, cabled him suggesting that he read Hervey Allan's romantic best-seller *Anthony Adverse*, he replied. ''Read it? I can't even lift it!''

His rows with his performers were legion. He once boasted openly, and proudly, that he had twenty-five stars on suspension. ''I have ducked many a verbal rotten egg,'' he said, ''and I suspect that I have been hanged in effigy by more than one critic, agent or disgruntled actor.''

But he didn't care. Stars repeatedly indicated that although he could be a bastard to work for, outside the studio he was the best of company. ''I took about ten or twelve suspensions at Warners,'' said Bogart, ''but if I met Jack out some place we were the best of friends. I kind of miss the arguments I had with Warner. I used to love those feuds. It's like when you've fought with your wife and gotten a divorce, you kind of miss the fighting.''

Even Errol Flynn, who never liked letting Warner get the better of him, was often disarmed when he went into Warner's office prepared for a fight. ''Have a drink. . .heard this story. . .sit down, Baron,'' Warner would greet him as he entered through the door. Within minutes Errol Flynn's anger would have subsided.

When it came to awards Warner couldn't get his hands on them quick enough. When *Casablanca* was awarded the best picture Oscar of 1943 Hal Wallis, who was the executive producer of the film, and Warner who was the head of the studio, both rushed hell-for-leather down the aisle to see who could get to the rostrum first. Wallis won, but it was a sour victory. The next day he was on his way out of the studio, all his personal belongings having been removed from his private bungalow and placed on the lawn.

The story might be apocryphal, but it proved that no-one, not even a man of Wallis' stature, could stand in Warner's way — charm or no charm. Producers and directors just as much as stars got 'the treatment' when the needs arose.

Warner made his share of mistakes. In 1943, he was offered the chance to make a movie version of the life of Al Jolson. He declined. ''We had Jolson when he was hot,'' he said. ''That was at the time of *The Jazz Singer*. No-one wants him now. Today, he doesn't mean a thing.'' Three years later *The Jolson Story* starring Larry Parks was produced at Columbia and made the studio a fortune.

Similarly, he could have had Gable on his books to go alongside Cagney and Bogart, but he didn't listen to director Mervyn LeRoy who wanted the actor for a role in *Little Caesar*. ''You've just thrown away five hundred bucks on a screen test,'' LeRoy was told. ''Didn't you see the size of that guy's ears?''

When John Huston returned to the Warner studio just after World War II he chose for his first film *The Treasure Of The Sierra Madre*, a story of three prospectors searching desperately for gold in Mexico. So slow was he in filming certain scenes that Warner was not too far away from cancelling the picture. One scene in particular, when a crazed Humphrey Bogart is searching for water, took days to film. ''If that son-of-a-bitch doesn't find water soon I'll go broke,'' muttered Warner as he gazed trance-like at the rushes from Mexico. Luckily, on this occasion his good sense prevailed and the movie became one of the studio's most acclaimed pictures of the 40s.

In fairness to Jack Warner he almost certainly had the most temperamental set of stars on any Hollywood lot. His two biggest *prima donnas* were Bette Davis and Errol Flynn. Davis cared desperately about her career and actually took Warner all the way to court in England because he was giving her such lousy roles. Flynn didn't give a hoot and from being one of the most handsome men ever to grace a Hollywood sound stage, gradually drank and drugged himself to death.

Bette Davis, in fact, was the first rebel. For someone so tiny she was dynamite. She gave Jack Warner a series of headaches that must have caused even him quite a few sleepless nights. She threatened his whole authority — the entire idea of running a studio with an iron fist and treating actors like so many cattle.

In September 1936, after refusing to play in a movie called *God's Country And The Woman*, she took off for England. She was determined to test the contract to which, according to the studio, she was legally bound.

In the English courts she maintained that she was not receiving roles worthy of her capabilities as an actress and was therefore entitled to look for them elsewhere; something she had been doing, having been offered *I'll Take The Low Road* with Douglass

Montgomery and Nigel Bruce in Italy and an untitled film with Maurice Chevalier in France.

Warner, seeing that the gloves were off and that there was no way of avoiding bad publicity for the studio, hired Sir Patrick Hastings, one of the best legal brains in England, to fight his case. He knew that under no circumstances could he let Bette Davis get away with it. "If Bette were to win," he said, "all the studio owners and executives in Hollywood would get trampled in the stampede."

Hastings, famous enough for his legal powers, proved also that he was not without a sense of humour, and began his prosecution, "I cannot help but feel M'Lord that this is the action of a very naughty young lady."

The court thought so too. They found for the studio and Bette had no option but to return to Hollywood and work on whatever pictures Warners chose to give her. She has said that she trembled when she drove back through those studio gates. She had a good idea about what kind of reception awaited her.

But she couldn't have been more wrong. Warners had paid all the legal costs of the case and she found, on arrival in Jack Warner's office, that he was standing there, hand outstretched, and saying, "Let's forget all about it Bette. We've got work to do."

So although Bette Davis had lost, she had also won. She had earned the respect of the industry and, indirectly, she had won for herself better roles. It is doubtful whether her change of fortunes after the trial could be put down to coincidence. It was more likely that Warner instructed his team of screenwriters to come up with scripts that had real meat in them and the right amount of depth for an actress who, when given the right material, could act just about everyone off the screen.

Errol Flynn was even more trouble — and lasting trouble. From the moment he arrived at Warners he and Jack Warner were at it daggers drawn. The feud never let up. It went on until Flynn left the studio in 1952 and even then he left in a blazing row.

The amorous Flynn was his own worst enemy. Fun loving, a hard drinker, a womaniser, he wanted everything that life could offer. Acting was just a means to an end. He never once considered himself to be a performer of any quality and frequently turned up at the studio with a heavy hangover.

Even in the mid-thirties when he took over the starring role of *Captain Blood* from Robert Donat, he was living life about three times faster than anyone else, drinking heavily, keeping late hours and smoking some hundred cigarettes a day.

Jack Warner knew he had something special in Flynn. He knew

that he meant money. He also knew that he meant trouble. He often turned a blind eye to Flynn's philanderings, but he was shrewd enough to know what was going on — not just when Flynn set foot outside the studio gates, but also when he put two distinctly shaky feet inside them for make-up call early in the morning.

The normal call in those early days was 6.30 a.m. That was the time Flynn was supposed to be in the make-up chair of Warners famous make-up artist Perc Westmore. What Westmore saw staring up at him were not the handsome features that were to become so well-known on the screen, but the somewhat haggard face of a bleary-eyed individual who was still trying to come to terms with what he had been up to the night before.

His usual solution was to take a hair of the dog that bit him. A brilliant schemer, he used to make a big show of ordering 'malted milks', especially prepared to erase the signs of the night before. In reality they weren't malted milks at all, but Ramos gin fizzes, i.e. nine parts of gin and one part beaten egg white. He got away with it for a while then Westmore rumbled him and he had to think again.

Ingeniously, he devised other means to ensure that he got his quick nip during the day. Gin, vodka, scotch and bourbon were frequently put in bottles in his make-up case with disguise labels such as skin cleanser and hair preparation.

When that didn't work he began eating oranges. For a time he had everyone fooled. It really looked as though he had turned over a new leaf. All that Vitamin C! But as shooting progressed during the day so Flynn's acting became a little less steady, less assured — almost wobbly. Far from becoming health conscious he was getting more drunk than ever. Westmore eventually discovered that Flynn had been syringing his oranges with vodka before the morning shooting and smuggling them on to the sound stages.

But for all the trouble he caused, Flynn was still one of Jack Warner's most valuable properties. Even though they hated each other on sight Warner wasn't fool enough to let him go. Flynn's headline-making escapades were worth putting up with as long as the box-office kept turning over.

On one occasion, in a moment of sheer genius, Warner cast him as Essex opposite Bette Davis in *The Private Lives Of Elizabeth And Essex*. That juicy piece of casting meant news. So did the actual shooting of the picture.

In the female lead was an actress of skill, courage and power, a woman who had agreed to have her eyebrows shaved and hair cut back to the middle of her head to give the correct impression of a balding Elizabeth. Opposite her was a man who considered his role to be a bit of fun and nothing more.

With 'verbal garbage' Michael Curtiz directing, sparks were bound to fly. And they did. Fierce arguments blew up over the title. First of all the picture was called *The Knight And The Lady* which almost gave Bette Davis a seizure. It inferred that Essex was more important than Elizabeth and that she was less important than Flynn, even though he was on a slightly higher salary at the time.

Essex And Elizabeth was no better. In fact it was worse. ''You cannot give second billing to the Queen of England,'' hissed Bette at Jack Warner. ''Or to me. Change the goddam title or I'm walking out.'' And she did. On that particular day shooting on the *Elizabeth And Essex* lot finished very abruptly.

Bette Davis' anger was not difficult to understand. She had given up a lot for the role and wanted desperately to play it. Totally dedicated actress that she was, she had to wear wigs and false eyebrows for six months until her own grew back to normal.

Eventually, despite Flynn's higher salary, Bette got her way and the film became *The Private Lives Of Elizabeth And Essex.*

In his autobiography 'My Wicked, Wicked Ways', Flynn tells how Bette landed him one smack on the ear in the first scene of the movie when the script required her to give him a hearty slap. With heavy jewellery adorning her fingers, the slap became something more akin to one of those Warner sock-on-the-jaws mentioned earlier. According to Flynn it rocked him right back on his heels.

He also mentions that later in the shooting he had the chance to get his own back by whacking his hand right down on Bette's Elizabethan finery and onto ''Her Academy Award winning behind!'' Flynn swears that Miss Davis went at least two inches off the ground. Bette herself has since denied everything about Flynn's description of the making of the film.

''Everything that Mr. Errol Flynn said in his book about working with me is a total and complete lie,'' she said at a recent press conference. ''From scratching his face with my rings to. . . well, everything he said. But before I ever read the book there was no way I could discuss it with him because, unfortunately, he was gone.''

Gone he was, exhausted, worn out, eaten away. When doctors examined him after his death in 1959 they were amazed he was still in one piece. His liver had gone, his lungs were in shreds. They couldn't believe a man could have lived so long in such a condition. They had warned him twelve years earlier when they told him that if he didn't slow down and stop his drinking he wouldn't last another year.

That shook even Errol Flynn.

Shattered, he told his old friend, director Raoul Walsh, "I'm sick, uncle. My lungs have had it and the quacks say my liver is shot to hell. So what does it matter where I die. My last year will be a merry one."

That last year stretched into twelve. His parts went from bad to worse, his looks went, his face became flabby and he himself became a joke. Yet he always remained the friend of 'the little man.' The cameraman, the technicians on the studio floor. They were his real buddies. He also continued to fight authority whenever he could. If there was a way in which he could get back at Jack Warner he would take it.

Once, when he was suffering literally from a pain in the ass, he was told by a doctor that he should have a haemorrhoidectomy. But as he was between pictures he decided to wait and have the operation in Jack Warner's time, going through weeks of pain so that he could have the operation after he had started work on a new movie. Happy in the knowledge that his pain in the ass was costing Warners a fortune, he finally agreed to the operation.

But as the forties dwindled to a close at the Burbank Studios, the jokes, the feuds, the good times, all began to go sour. Suddenly, things were no longer the same. Television was threatening and the studio began to realise that they could no longer afford to hang on to the stars that had made them great. They were either too expensive or they didn't have box-office appeal anymore. In the end, it was not 'The Long Goodbye', but the quick one.

Davis went in 1949, Bogart in fifty-one, Flynn in fifty-four. Cagney too was nearing the end of his reign. Exactly how Jack Warner must have felt when he saw the stars who had made fortunes for his studio leave the lot for good is difficult to imagine.

Ruthless as he was — he asked both Bogart and Flynn to pay *him* 100,000 dollars so that they could break their contracts — there must still have been a tinge of sadness inside him as he watched his stars ride out of the studio gates forever.

Bette Davis maintains to this day that her pictures alone built Warners seven sound stages. Flynn, Cagney, Busby Berkeley and the rest undoubtedly built a few more.

But times *had* changed. The posters claimed defiantly 'Movies Are Better Than Ever' which, sadly, was just another way of saying 'Theatres Are Emptier Than Ever!' No longer did the Warner studio possess the character it had retained for so long. The musicals, the gangster films and the westerns were still there but instead of Dick Powell and Ruby Keeler, Cagney and Flynn, there were stars of a different calibre — Doris Day, Steve Cochran, Randolph Scott. Not by any means ideal replacements when times were getting bad and new battles had to be fought.

The studio, like others at the time, began floundering, trying to find the magical combination that would bring back the lost TV millions.

They had some lucky breaks. The young James Dean, the phenomenon of the 50s, made his three starring films (*East Of Eden, Rebel Without A Cause* and *Giant*) for Warners and brought the studio both financial and critical success; Judy Garland made her comeback in the ill-fated but brilliant *A Star Is Born*; John Ford filmed his classic western *The Searchers*; Huston made an ambitious attempt at Melville's *Moby Dick*; Kazan brought stark drama and Oscars with films like *A Streetcar Named Desire* and *Baby Doll*; and on a more mundane level John Wayne helped provide action and the traditional sock-on-the-jaw in films like *Hondo, The Sea Chase* and *Blood Alley*.

The top films, however, were already becoming isolated from the crowd. It became easier and easier to spot the quality pictures as soon as they were before the cameras, just as it was to spot the ever-increasing run-of-the-mill productions.

Things began to improve by the 60s and 70s which brought Warners greater success than any other period in their history. The musicals *My Fair Lady* and *Camelot*, Arthur Penn's gangster film, *Bonnie And Clyde*, John Boorman's *Deliverance* and their biggest hit of all time, the horror blockbuster *The Exorcist*, have enabled them to continue to flourish and remain one of Hollywood's major studios.

The definitive Warner movie, however, has completely disappeared. The style, the atmosphere, the familiar content have all gone. *The Exorcist* might just as easily have been financed by Paramount and *Bonnie And Clyde* by United Artists, so impersonal were the productions.

No longer is there a Greenstreet or Lorre to play cat and mouse with the thriller *genre*; no longer a George Brent or Claude Rains or Paul Henreid to help fight or save Bette Davis. No Flynn to fight for the Allies against the Nazis or run through a lurching Spaniard; no Cagney to snarl and stand in readiness, legs apart, hands outstretched. No leer from Bogart; no unquestioning adoration from Olivia de Havilland. . .The fun went out of Warners when Davis, Flynn and the rest went out of the studio gates. Things were never quite the same again.

The famous shield (formed back in the 20s) and accompanying fanfare has now, like so many Hollywood logos, been distilled into a single W, like a sign for a bank or an insurance company. You can see its like in any main town or city.

One is reminded of a scene in *Its A Mad, Mad, Mad, Mad World* (not a Warner movie) when Jimmy Durante, just literally before kicking the bucket, says, "The treasure is buried under a big doubleyer."

Today, the Warner treasure, the scratched celluloid of yesteryear, seems light years away, buried with the famous Warner shield, but still miraculously reactivated from time to time on television screens when Davis, Bogart and Cagney suffer and triumph once more to the accompaniment of the orchestra strings of Korngold and Max Steiner.

There used to be a sign on the Warner Burbank lot, a huge billboard with the words: 'Combining Good Picture Making With Good Citizenship.' It seemed a bit pretentious at the time, but, in retrospect, it may not have been so far from the truth. Warners were, in many ways, a studio of the people. They showed reality. They moralised a bit, but within the limitations of the censorship code of the time they aimed for a certain kind of truth.

Today, many of the gangster films (especially *The Roaring Twenties*) impress as social documents. Even the musicals, all minus Technicolor, are not over-romanticised. Powell, Keeler, Blondell and company were always on the outside looking in, fighting against an environment that was choking both the country and the world as a whole.

Warners was at its best in the 30s and 40s. There was Ingrid Bergman saying, "Play it Sam, play 'As Time Goes By' "; there was Bette Davis soothing Paul Henreid with, "Why wish for the moon Jerry? We have the stars"; and there was Flynn laughing at a scowling Rathbone and mocking, "You've come to Nottingham once too often Gisbourne."

The 30s and 40s were *the* time for the studio. The small guys were trying to make it then, sometimes honestly, usually dishonestly. Warners showed them all. It was the studio of the little guy!

A call girl on the line. Oscar-winning Jane Fonda in Alan Pakula's black thriller *Klute*.

Sydney Greenstreet, arch Warner villain of the 40s, frequently teamed with fellow conspirator Peter Lorre.

Paul Newman as *Cool Hand Luke*, boss-baiter of a Southern chain gang.

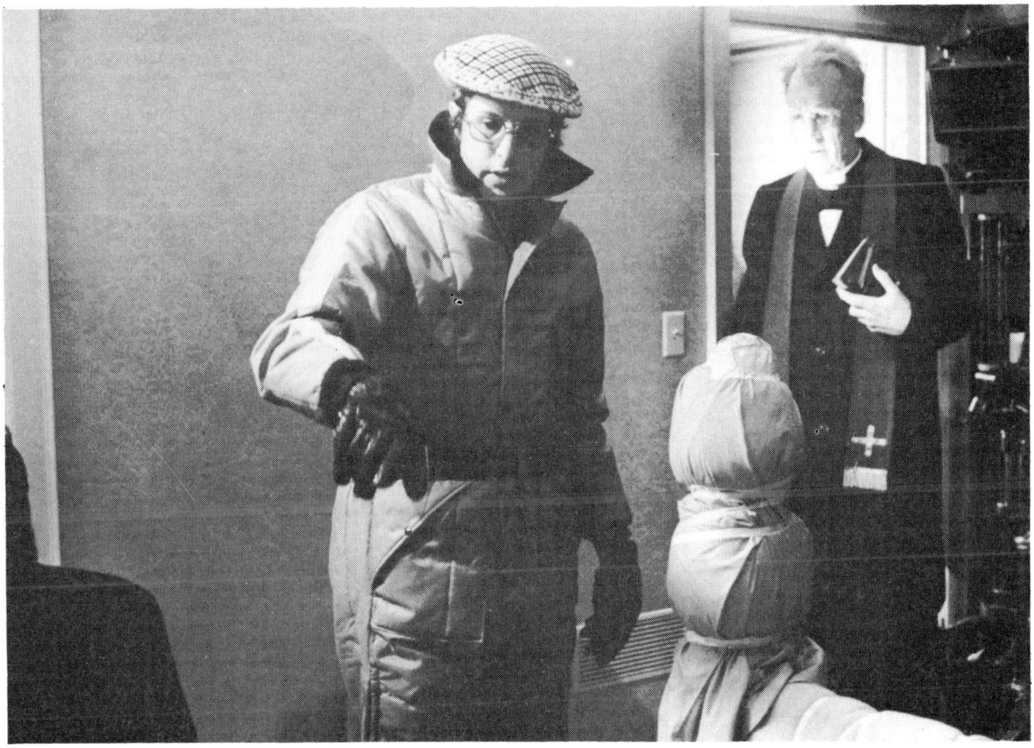

Director William Friedkin filming the studio's biggest-ever money-maker, *The Exorcist*.

Bank robbers Warren Beatty and Faye Dunaway in Arthur Penn's classic gangster movie, *Bonnie And Clyde*.

The most famous goodbye in movies. Bogart and Bergman. ''Here's Looking At You Kid.''

Doris Day, top Warner musical star of the 50s, in *April In Paris*. Her shipboard dancing partner: Ray Bolger.

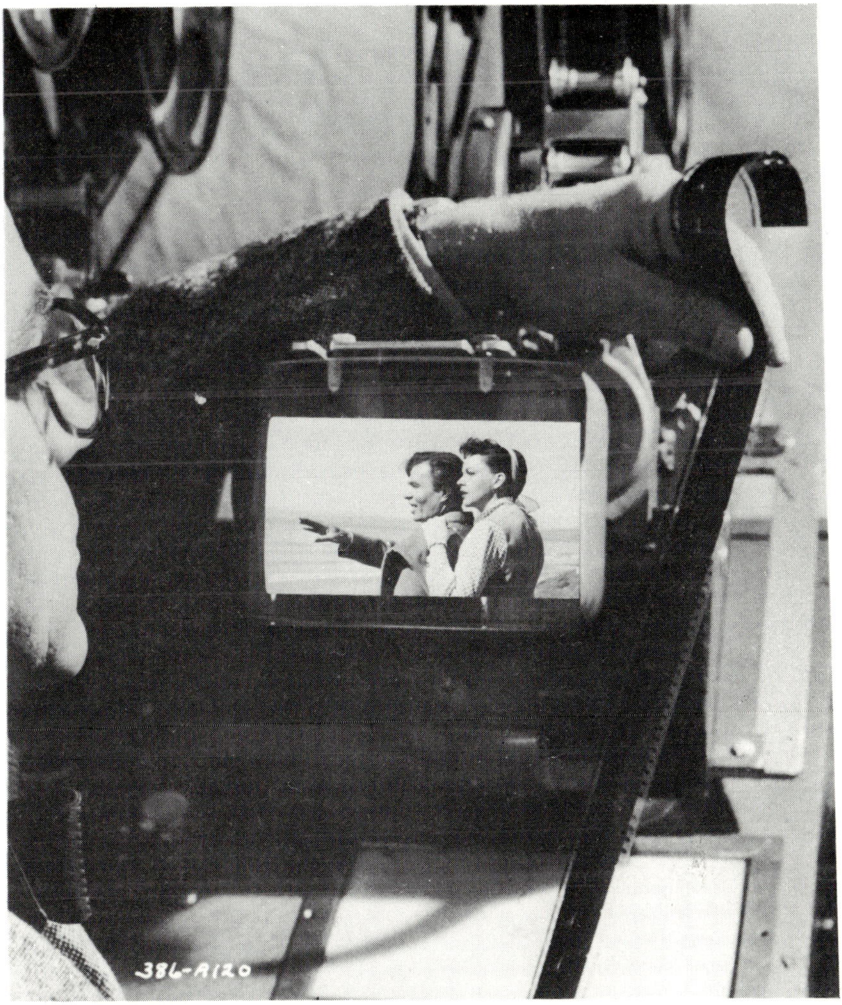

Cukor's *A Star Is Born*, with Judy Garland and James Mason, being edited by Folmar Blangsted in the Warner cutting rooms.

James Dean, young cult hero of the 50s, as the young Jett Rink — and the same character aged fifty — in George Stevens' Texas epic *Giant*.

Chronology

1923 The Warner Bros. Company (under the name of Warner Bros. Incorporated) is formed by the four Warner brothers on April 4. Harry and Albert, as president and treasurer respectively, operate from the company's New York headquarters; Jack and Sam manage the Hollywood studio.

It's the realisation of a twenty-year dream. In 1903 the brothers (all sons of a Polish emigré) opened their first movie show and criss-crossed Ohio and Pennsylvania exhibiting a used print of *The Great Train Robbery*.

Enthusiasm, but above all resilience and determination ensure their arrival as a new if minor force on the Hollywood scene. By the time of their official formation they are no strangers to movie production having filmed several shorts, a full-length feature – *My Four Years In Germany* (the story of James Gerard's four years as U.S. ambassador in Germany) – and a couple of serials, *The Lost City* and *Miracles Of The Jungle*.

But 1923 is when the adventure really begins and already Warners have their first star, a German shepherd dog found in the trenches of France, who goes by the name of Rin Tin Tin. His first Warner movie: *Where The North Begins*.

1924 The company's first full hesitant year of production. German director Ernst Lubitsch contributes a sexual comedy of manners, *The Marriage Circle* starring Florence Vidor, Monte Blue, Marie Provost and Adolphe Menjou; Milton Sills demonstrates the studio's early interest in swashbuckling by parrying with cloak and sword in Sabatini's *The Sea Hawk*; and John Barrymore is the elegant 19th century dandy *Beau Brummell*.

But when it comes right down to it, it's still the brilliant alsatian that brings home the bacon. His 1924 contribution: *Find Your Man*, a melodrama of rescue and murder in an American lumber camp. The young Darryl F. Zanuck is responsible for the story, adaptation and scenario.

Say Hollywood scribes: "Warners is kept afloat by two profiles, Rin Tin Tin and John Barrymore." If Barrymore lives in luxury so does the dog who earns as much as 2000 dollars a week and relaxes in a five-room kennel on his master's Beverly Hills estate.

1925 Despite Rin Tin Tin's success, the four Warner brothers know they must expand if they are to survive and challenge such major studios as Metro and Paramount. They absorb the ailing Vitagraph studio but their biggest moment of the year, although they are not fully aware of it at the time, takes place in the New York offices of Bell Laboratories where Sam and Harry hear sound combined with film for the first time.

In June, Warners reach an agreement with Western Electric, the parent company of Bell Laboratories, granting them exclusive rights in the new process.

As experiments with sound go ahead in New York, Warners struggle on with Rin Tin Tin who pads his way through four movies (one for each Warner brother); *The Dark Angel* with Ronald Colman as a British soldier blinded in World War I and Vilma Banky as his love; *Kiss Me Again*, a domestic comedy by Lubitsch starring Marie Prevost and Monte Blue; and a version of Conan Doyle's *The Lost World* with Wallace Beery as Professor Challenger after prehistoric beasts in the South American jungle.

Cries Beery in a moment of panic, "My brontosaurus has escaped! Keep off the streets until I recapture it!"

1926 The long days and nights of sound experimentation in a New York studio and the Manhattan Opera House finally bear fruit with the premiere, on August 6 in New York, of *Don Juan*, a costume spectacular starring John Barrymore. The star in this instance, however, is almost irrelevant for the picture has a synchronized music track as well as sounds of clashing swords and chiming bells. The audience is astounded.

Accompanying the film are eight Vitaphone shorts including the New York Philharmonic Orchestra playing the overture to Wagner's *Tannhauser*; violinist Mischa Elman playing Dvorak's *Humoresque*; opera star Giovanni Martinelli singing an aria from *I Pagliacci*; and, on a different level, 'Wizard Of The Strings' Roy Smeck doing a banjo solo.

During the programme Will H. Hays, head of the Motion

Picture Producers and Distribution Association of America becomes the first man to speak on film as he congratulates the Warner brothers and Western Electric for their pioneering efforts.

Meanwhile, not entirely convinced that sound is anything but a passing phase, Hollywood allows the silent cinema to continue in full flow.

At Warners, John Barrymore plays not only *Don Juan* but Melville's obsessed Captain Ahab in *The Sea Beast*; Harry Langdon gives notice that he is one of the funniest men around in *Tramp, Tramp, Tramp* as a hobo who enters a transcontinental walking contest and *The Strong Man* in which he proves too much for a gang of small town bootleggers; Monte Blue and Patsy Ruth Miller star for Lubitsch in the domestic comedy *So This Is Paris.*

1927 Warners make history for the second year running and this time really hit the jackpot. On October 6, *The Jazz Singer* becomes the first part-talking feature to be shown anywhere in the world.

Starring Al Jolson who speaks a few lines and sings 'Mammy', 'Toot, Toot, Tootsie' and 'Kol Nidre', the film was originally meant to contain only music; the dialogue such as it was coming only as an afterthought when Sam Warner heard Jolson cry out, "You ain't heard nothing yet folks! Listen to this!"

A schmaltzy tale about a cantor's son who decides on a Broadway career rather than sing in his father's synagogue, it is the beginning of the end for silent pictures. It is also, sadly, the end of Sam Warner the major driving force behind the coming of sound, who collapses and dies from exhaustion just twenty-four hours before the premiere. *The Jazz Singer* naturally dominates everything else around, and the year for Warners is a good one: *Long Pants* has Harry Langdon at the mercy of vamp Alma Bennett, but saved by small-town girl Priscilla Bonner; Norma Talmadge is the dying *Camille*; *Old San Francisco* (story by Darryl F. Zanuck) becomes the first motion picture with dramatic sound effects and includes an earthquake sequence in which men shout and women scream as walls collapse. *That* dog is still doing his best as well, appearing in another four movies during the year.

1928 Jolson again in *The Singing Fool* and Fannie Brice in *My Man*, but an elated Warners go on claiming new firsts.

Tenderloin, directed by Michael Curtiz, is announced as 'the first talking picture in which the characters speak their film roles'. The story, about a dancer (Dolores Costello) suspected of stealing 50,000 dollars and being plagued by both the law and the underworld, boasts a few dialogue sequences that make up some fifteen minutes of the film's eighty-five minute length — at the time of its release (March) — a new record.

The record is quickly broken, however, with the first all-talking picture *Lights Of New York*, a fifty-seven minute crime melodrama directed by Bryan Foy and starring Helene Costello, Cullen Landis and Gladys Brockwell. It is premiered at the Mark Strand Theatre in New York on July 7.

In a trade advertisement Warners announce that *Lights* will 'Revolutionize The Industry' and go on to try and convince cinema managers with: 'No Titles. No Subtitles. 100 per-cent Vitaphone all the way through. You see and you hear every character in the picture. A spine-tingling melodrama so good that previews in California convince showmen it's the year's clean-up picture. YOU CAN HAVE IT NOW!'

Trade paper *Variety* is not so sure: "This 100 per-cent talking picture is 100 per-cent crude."

The public has no doubts. The picture earns more than a million dollars after costing less than 75,000 to produce.

It is less than a month before Warners are trying to top even *Lights Of New York*. How can you top an all-talking movie? By having the credits 'talk' as well. In *The Terror*, a little-known thriller about a maniacal killer who terrorises the inhabitants of an old English inn, actor Conrad Nagel does just that — clad in sporting tails, opera cape and domino mask!

1929 There's no stopping Warners. They absorb the once powerful First National Studio and record a gross profit of 19,700,000 dollars over the 3,360,000 of the previous year. Says *Variety*: "It represents the highest increase ever reported for a picture company or any other concern for that matter."

With sound now being used by all the big studios, musicals are in! *On With The Show* with Sally O'Neil and Joe E. Brown is the first all-colour (i.e. two-colour) musical and John Boles is the screen's first Red Shadow in *The Desert Song*.

In historical vein George Arliss wins an Oscar for *Disraeli*, and Corinne Griffith and Victor Varconi are Emma Hamilton and Lord Nelson in *The Divine Lady*; in doggy vein, Rin Tin Tin, now nearing the end of his career, still finds time for his usual cluster of movies: *The Million Dollar Collar, Frozen River* and *Tiger Rose*.

1930 Edward G. Robinson becomes a household name in *Little Caesar*. As gang leader Rico Bandello, he is riddled with bullets and utters a last, disbelieving gasp, "Mother of God, is this the end of Rico?" It is but just the beginning of Warners famous gangster cycle of the 30s.

James Cagney also appears on the scene for the first time in *Sinner's Holiday*. Already cast to type, he features as a young guy mixed up in a rum-running racket.

Richard Barthelmess and Douglas Fairbanks Jr. take to the air over the German lines in France in *The Dawn Patrol*; John Barrymore repeats his role of Ahab in *Moby Dick*, this time with sound; Al Jolson is a singing hobo in *Mammy*; and Bernice Claire stars in the studio's part-colour version of the 1925 Broadway hit *No, No Nanette*.

1931 Cagney makes the same mistake as Edward G. and finishes up just as dead in his first major gangster film, *Public Enemy*. The movie is the one in which Cagney shoves a grapefruit into the face of luckless Mae Clarke, a scene based on a real-life incident in which a gangster named Hymie Weiss hit his girlfriend in the face with an omelette. Edward G. Robinson edits a scandal sheet in *Five Star Final* (Boris Karloff as a defrocked minister named T. Vernon Isopod is one of his chief reporters); Ricardo Cortez and Bebe Daniels star in the first of the three versions of *The Maltese Falcon*; and in *Svengali*, obsessed artist John Barrymore hypnotizes Marian Marsh into becoming a great singing star.

1932 Cagney says his famous "You dirty rat" in Roy Del Ruth's film *Taxi*. Bette Davis, not to be outdone, also comes out with one of her most famous lines in *Cabin In The Cotton*; "Ah'd love t' kiss yo, but ah jes washed mah hayuh."

Rin Tin Tin, Warners' life-saver of the 20s, dies aged sixteen years. The famous alsatian appeared in more than twenty films for the studio between 1923 and 1930 earning more than five million dollars for its owner, Leland Duncan.

Paul Muni suffers the horrors of a Southern chain gang in

the first of Warners social protest films of the 30s, *I Am A Fugitive From A Chain Gang*; Humphrey Bogart makes his studio debut — 10th on the cast list — in *Big City Blues*; Cagney and director Howard Hawks get together in the motor racing drama *The Crowd Roars*; and in *Dr. X* Preston Foster gets his kicks by strangling people at the full moon and, for dessert, devouring part of his victims' brains.

1933 "She only said 'no' once and then she didn't hear the question." The lady? Chorus girl Anytime Annie, played by Ginger Rogers in Warners' trend-setting musical *42nd Street*.

The studio's social conscience gathers force with William Wellman's *Wild Boys Of The Road*, a story of America's jobless hobo youth of the Depression; the Depression also features in Busby Berkeley's remarkable 'My Forgotten Man' number in *Golddiggers Of 1933*; Cagney goes musical in another Berkeley movie *Footlight Parade* ('Shanghai Lil' and 'By A Waterfall'); and on the more grisly side sculptor Lionel Atwill, disfigured by fire in his prized museum, finds new hope in life by murdering young girls and coating their naked corpses with boiling wax. The movie? Michael Curtiz's classic *Mystery Of The Wax Museum*. Atwill's co-star? Fay Wray, the best screamer in the business.

1934 Dick Powell, Ruby Keeler and Joan Blondell enliven a poor Warner year with the backstage musical *Dames* as, inevitably, does Busby Berkeley with his vivid dance sequences; *Wonder Bar* sees Al Jolson in a Paris nightclub with music — and murder! And Frank Borzage contributes another engaging piece of Powell-Keeler fluff, *Flirtation Walk*, about an army private in love with his commanding officer's daughter.

1935 The Academy Award voters begin to look at the Warner product more seriously and name Bette Davis best actress for her fallen stage star in *Dangerous*.

Less fortunate is Busby Berkeley who, after attending a party, crashes into oncoming traffic when the left front wheel of his roadster bursts. The accident occurs at night on the twisting Pacific Coast Highway and three people are killed. Berkeley himself is lucky to be alive and is dragged from his burning car. Tried three times on the charge of manslaughter (two of the trials result in hung juries) he is eventually acquitted.

The studio takes to swashbuckling as a dashing Errol Flynn disposes of Basil Rathbone in Sabatini's *Captain Blood*; Cagney, on the right side of the law for a change, hunts down Barton MacLane and assorted hoods in *G Men*; he also dons Shakespearean costume for his role of Bottom in *A Midsummer Night's Dream*, a lavish Max Reinhardt production which also sees Dick Powell as Lysander, Joe E. Brown as Flute and Mickey Rooney as Puck. Paul Muni is involved with social unrest in America's coal fields in *Black Fury* and with crazed murderess Bette Davis in *Bordertown*; and in *Golddiggers Of 1935* Berkeley, still managing to work despite the pressures of his trials, stages the tragic yet breathtaking 'Lullaby Of Broadway' number with hundreds of tapping, restless feet.

1936 Warners produce their first feature in the new three-colour Technicolor process – *God's Country And The Woman*, an outdoor story of rival lumber companies starring George Brent and Beverly Roberts. The film also has another claim to fame. It is the one at which Bette Davis finally baulks, says a publicity sized 'no' and then flees to England to fight her famous court case (see page 201).

The studio's Oscar year at last. They win eight of the sixteen awards, three going to *The Story Of Louis Pasteur* (including a best actor Oscar to Paul Muni) and four of them to *Anthony Adverse*.

Errol Flynn, still performing heroically in *The Charge Of The Light Brigade*, leads the 600 into the Valley Of Death at a cost of 1,200,000 dollars; Cagney, as a madcap pilot, and director Howard Hawks get together again in *Ceiling Zero*; Busby Berkeley's sexy dancing squad are on full view in *Stage Struck* and *Golddiggers Of 1937*; and Bette Davis, Warren William and Marie Wilson star in the second version of *The Maltese Falcon* – *Satan Met A Lady*.

1937 Lana Turner makes her screen debut in Mervyn LeRoy's film about lynch law, *They Won't Forget*. According to the publicity machine she receives more than one thousand proposals of marriage in the following twelve months. The next year she joins MGM for a long career. Warners aren't impressed with their own statistics.

Also appearing on the screen for the first time is Bugs Bunny in the cartoon short *Porky's Hare Hunt*. This famous cartoon rabbit ("What's Up Doc?") subsequently stars in

Warners 'Merry Melodies' series and is voiced over the years by Mel Blanc.

Warners win their first best picture Oscar after ten years of trying. The award goes to Dieterle's biography *The Life Of Emile Zola* starring Paul Muni. Joseph Schildkraut also wins best supporting actor for his wrongly accused Captain Dreyfus.

Flynn continues to swash and buckle in *The Prince And The Pauper*; Bette Davis is a night-club hostess involved in murder in *Marked Woman*; but the busiest Warner star of the year is Humphrey Bogart who prosecutes Miss Davis in *Woman*, falls foul of the Ku Klux Klan in *Black Legion*, is mixed up with the boxing racket and Edward G. Robinson in *Kid Galahad* and tastes a bit of prison life in *San Quentin*.

1938 Another good year for Warners at the Oscar ceremonies. Bette Davis wins her second for her spoiled Southern belle in Wyler's *Jezebel* while Fay Bainter wins the supporting award for her performance as Miss Davis' sympathetic aunt in the same film. The classic Flynn swashbuckler *The Adventures Of Robin Hood* also wins a cluster of Oscars, one for Erich Wolfgang Korngold's rousing music.

Flynn disposes of Rathbone yet again after leaping all over Nottingham Castle in *Robin Hood*; he features too with David Niven in a remake of *The Dawn Patrol*; James Cagney appears in one of his best-ever movies *Angels With Dirty Faces*, the story of two slum kids one of whom grows up good (priest Pat O'Brien), the other bad (gangster Cagney); Edward G. Robinson however goes for laughs as a bootlegger trying to go straight. The film? *A Slight Case Of Murder*. The author? Damon Runyon.

1939 Red-headed Ann Sheridan, often cast as the gal with the smart remark, is publicised by Warners as 'The Oomph Girl.' The word 'oomph', according to the lady herself is the sound a fat man makes when he bends over to tie his laces in a phone booth. On one occasion she writes an autograph for someone she dislikes with, "I'm The Oomph Girl — Oomph You!"

Flynn, having disposed of master-swordsman Basil Rathbone twice in three years finds he is no match for Bette Davis in *The Private Lives Of Elizabeth And Essex* and loses his head to the axeman. After that he goes West in *Dodge City* and survives. So too does James Cagney, teamed with Bogart in one of the silliest westerns ever made, *The Oklahoma Kid*; Edward G. Robinson exposes the Nazi underground operating in the U.S. in *Confessions Of A Nazi Spy*; and Bette Davis finally pays for getting rid of Mr. Flynn by dying more slowly — and tragically — in the tearjerker *Dark Victory*.

1940 Flynn, now at the peak of his fame, goes West again in *Virginia City* (with Miriam Hopkins) and *Santa Fé Trail* (with Olivia de Havilland). He also returns to Elizabethan times in Michael Curtiz's *The Sea Hawk* in which he finds a much more receptive and admiring Elizabeth (Flora Robson) and is allowed to keep his head.

Bored plantation wife Bette Davis shoots her lover and nearly gets away with it in *The Letter*; she also tearjerks for two-and-a-half hours with Charles Boyer in *All This And Heaven Too*; Edward G. takes over from Muni in the biography *genre*, appearing as Julius Reuter, the man who invented the world-wide news service in *A Dispatch From Reuters* and Dr. Paul Ehrlich, the German doctor who found the cure for syphillis in *Dr. Ehrlich's Magic Bullet*.

1941 Humphrey Bogart, who on occasions has been known to complain: "I've always been the guy behind the guy behind the gun" is elevated to star status as Roy Earle, the last of the Dillinger gang in *High Sierra*. Says the film's director Raoul Walsh, "George Raft was the studio's original choice for the role but he refused to die on screen so we got Bogie. He didn't mind getting shot by the cops."

Later in the year Bogart consolidates his new status as private-eye Sam Spade in *The Maltese Falcon*, a film which introduces the 280lb Sydney Greenstreet (then sixty-one) to the screen. During the actor's ten year screen career studio publicists make much of the fact that he can recite more than 12,000 lines of Shakespeare from memory; once became lodged in a telephone booth on the Warner lot and had to remain there while carpenters dismantled it; and in New York was hit by a runaway horse and cart with Greenstreet uninjured and the horse fatally hurt.

Sergeant York, the story of America's World War I pacifist hero wins Gary Cooper the first of his two Oscars and makes more money than any other Warner film of the year. Says Coop on winning the award, "Shucks. . .I've been in this business sixteen years and sometimes dreamed I might get one of these things. That's all I can say. Funny, when I was dreaming, I always made a good speech."

Among *York's* competitors: *High Sierra* and *The Maltese Falcon*; Frank Capra's *Meet John Doe*; *They Died With Their Boots On* (with Errol Flynn as Custer); *The Sea Wolf* with Edward G. Robinson as Jack London's blind skipper Wolf Larsen; and *Dive Bomber* in which Flynn, in the Naval Air Corps, 'goes to war' for the first time.

1942 In *Now Voyager*, soulful Paul Henreid saves Bette Davis the trouble of searching for her lighter by lighting two cigarettes in his mouth at the same time. Less romantically, in *The Man Who Came To Dinner*, Monty Woolley says to nurse Mary Wickes, "You have the touch of a sex starved cobra. . .I had an aunt who ate a box of chocolates every day of her life. She lived to be a hundred and two and when she had been dead three days, she looked healthier than you do now!"

Cagney nabs the best actor Oscar for his song-and-dance man George M. Cahn in *Yankee Doodle Dandy*, the studio's most successful commercial hit of the year.

Flynn is still at war in *Desperate Journey* but this time in trouble as an RAF bomber pilot trapped in Germany. Undeterred, he jibes at the film's climax: "Now for Australia and a crack at the Japs." Less fortunate is small town boy Ronald Reagan who in *King's Row* stares down at himself and asks pitifully, "Where's the rest of me?" after sadistic surgeon Charles Coburn has unnecessarily amputated both his legs.

1943 In February Errol Flynn is acquitted of the charge of raping seventeen year old Betty Hansen. The crime is alleged to have taken place in a Mediterranean-style mansion in Bel Air where such activities as swimming and tennis are enjoyed in its grounds and a few others, of a more intimate variety, inside its doors. Despite his acquittal Flynn finds it difficult to shake off the mud and 'In Like Flynn' becomes one of the best-known phrases of the war years.

This Is The Army, the film version of Irving Berlin's musical stage hit, is easily the studio's biggest money-maker, but it is *Casablanca* with Bogart, Bergman, Henreid, Rains, Greenstreet and company which makes history by snatching the best film Oscar from the hotly fancied *The Song Of Bernadette*. Michael Curtiz (best director) and writers Julius J. Epstein, Philip G. Epstein and Howard Koch also win, not least for writing lines like "Play it Sam, play 'As Time Goes By'."

Bette Davis sings 'They're Either Too Young Or Too Old' in the all-star cavalcade *Thank Your Lucky Stars*; Flynn is a mountie after a Nazi pilot in *Northern Pursuit* and a fisherman helping Norwegian rebels against German domination in *Edge Of Darkness*; Bogart too is occupied with the War, joining the Merchant Marines in *Action In The North Atlantic*; Dennis Morgan keeps the musical flag flying as the Red Shadow in a new version of *The Desert Song*.

1944 Sydney Greenstreet and Peter Lorre, the Laurel and Hardy of Warner crime, come together in one of their best movies, *The Mask Of Dimitrios*, an Eric Ambler thriller about a timid writer of detective stories (Lorre) who works his way across Europe tracing the career of master criminal Zachary Scott. The bowler-hatted Greenstreet forever gets in his way. Between 1941 and 46 the two actors make eight movies together: *The Maltese Falcon* (41), *Casablanca* (43), *Background To Danger* (43), *Passage To Marseilles* (44), *The Mask Of Dimitrios* (44), *The Conspirators* (44), *Three Strangers* (46), *The Verdict* (46).

Hollywood Canteen, another collection of variety sketches, is the biggest Warner grosser of the year; *The Adventures Of Mark Twain* stars Fredric March as the great American humourist; *Arsenic And Old Lace* has Cary Grant at his wits end trying to cover up the activities of his lovable old aunts, Josephine Hull and Jean Adair, two ladies whose greatest fun in life is murdering all their gentlemen callers; and in *Mr. Skeffington* Claude Rains provides formidable opposition for Bette Davis as a Jewish financier who loses his sight in a concentration camp.

1945 Lauren Bacall slinks into screen history in *To Have And Have Not* with the sultry invitation, "You know you don't have to act with me Steve. You don't have to say anything and you don't have to do anything. Oh, maybe. . .just whistle. You know how to whistle, don't you? You just put your lips together and blow."

Howard Hawks who directed her called her, "A warmer version of Marlene Dietrich." Humphrey Bogart (Steve) didn't say much. He married her.

Bette Davis' run of great parts is almost at an end as she plays a devoted middle-aged schoolteacher in a Welsh mining town in *The Corn Is Green*; Joan Crawford's best years at Warners are just beginning however. She starts off in great style by winning an Oscar for her long-suffering mother *Mildred Pierce*; Errol Flynn says farewell to World War II by helping paratroopers invade Asia in *Objective Burma* then returns to familiar western territory in *San Antonio*.

1946 Bogart and Bacall appear in their second film together, *The Big Sleep*, Howard Hawks' version of Raymond Chandler's private-eye novel.

Says Bacall to Bogie:
"You go too far Marlowe."
Says Bogie to Bacall:
"Those are hard words to throw at a man, especially when he's walking out of your bedroom."

Bogart also wins other verbal encounters, e.g. with gang boss John Ridgely.

Ridgely to Bogie:
"Is that any of your business?"
Bogie to Ridgely:
"I could *make* it my business!"
Ridgely to Bogie:
"And I could make *your* business *my* business."
Bogie to Ridgely:
"You wouldn't want to. There's no money in it."

The Big Sleep is not the biggest Warner money-maker of the year however. *Saratoga Trunk* with Gary Cooper and Ingrid Bergman and *Night And Day* with Cary Grant as Cole Porter top the box-office stakes.

Bette Davis shoots her composer-benefactor Claude Rains in *Deception*; Peter Lorre has trouble too in *The Beast With Five Fingers* when a severed hand crawls all over his house and eventually strangles him; and Eleanor Parker plays Davis' old role — the sluttish waitress Mildred — in a new version of Maugham's *Of Human Bondage*.

1947 Warners still can't get the Depression out of their system. Says Oscar Levant in the Joan Crawford melodrama *Humoresque*, "They've got new signs in the park now. Instead of saying 'Please keep off the grass' they say 'Please don't eat the grass'."

Bette Davis, with a salary of 328,000 dollars is ranked

the highest paid female in the USA. Bogart is the highest paid male with nearly 470,000. *Life With Father* with William Powell in irascible mood is Warners biggest moneymaker.

Otherwise crime runs rampant. On-the-run prisoner Humphrey Bogart has a face lift and is cared for by Lauren Bacall in *Dark Passage*; a paranoiac Joan Crawford shoots faithless lover Van Heflin in *Possessed*; and in *The Unsuspected* Claude Rains, a silken voiced broadcaster who tells murder stories over the radio at night, finds himself enjoying the thrill of the real thing when he's off the air.

1948 Bette Davis, now nearing the end of her Warner reign, seems to have her mind on other things. Even the dialogue in her movies — now second rate — seems to reflect her mood. Says Robert Montgomery in *June Bride*, "Even when I was making love to you I felt you were wondering what time it was."

If Bette Davis is out, Jane Wyman is in. Her portrayal of the deaf-mute *Johnny Belinda* wins her a best actress Oscar and helps make the film Warners biggest commercial success of the year. The studio, in fact, can't go wrong at Oscar time. John Huston wins two (for writing and direction) and his father Walter, one (supporting actor) for *The Treasure Of The Sierra Madre* and another Huston film, *Key Largo*, earns Claire Trevor a supporting actress award for her portrayal of a faded floozie.

Doris Day bounces into sight for the first time in *It's Magic*; over in England Hitchcock uses his famous 'ten-minute take' in *Rope* — with disastrous results; and Bogart and Bacall, together again for the fourth and last time, are trapped by Edward G. Robinson on the windswept Florida Keys in *Key Largo*.

Flynn makes a now tired stab at swashbuckling in *The Adventures Of Don Juan*.

1949 Bette Davis stars in *Beyond The Forest*, one of the worst films of her career. It's the one in which she walks into a room with Joseph Cotten and snarls, "What a Dump!" Billed as 'A Twelve O'Clock Girl In A Nine O'Clock Town' she decides to quit and leave the studio after 18 years. The last words she records in the movie are, "I can't stand it here any more."

Cagney, atop a huge gasometer at the climax of *White Heat*, blasts off bullet after bullet and with the words, "Top Of The World Ma, Top Of The World" blows himself to smithereens. It's a question of top that! Nobody can for nearly twenty years until Faye Dunaway and Warren Beatty get together as *Bonnie And Clyde*.

Joan Crawford is another who's still trigger happy. This time her target is small town sheriff Sydney Greenstreet who just has time to utter, "I should have spit you out the first time you got between my teeth" before hitting the deck. The film? *Flamingo Road*. Gary Cooper is Ayn Rand's architect Howard Roark in *The Fountainhead*; and in England Ingrid Bergman reunites with Hitchcock and Joseph Cotten in *Under Capricorn*.

1950 Michael Curtiz makes arguably the best Hemingway movie ever made, *The Breaking Point*, a version of 'To Have And Have Not' with John Garfield as Harry Morgan; Doris Day sings *Tea For Two*; Cagney shows his dancing feet are still nimble in *The West Point Story* and makes his last Warner gangster movie, *Kiss Tomorrow Goodbye*.

The studio's top acting honours go to Eleanor Parker, Oscar nominated for her role as a first offender in a women's prison in *Caged*, and Gertrude Lawrence, Kirk Douglas and Jane Wyman who feature in *The Glass Menagerie*, the first of Tennesse Williams' plays to go before the cameras.

1951 Warners go for Williams again, this time with even more success as they cast Vivien Leigh (as Blanche DuBois) and Marlon Brando (as Stanley Kowalski) in *A Streetcar Named Desire*. The movie wins three acting Oscars and takes five million dollars at the box-office.

Doris Day does her best to keep things merry and bright with *The Lullaby Of Broadway* and *On Moonlight Bay*, but otherwise many of Warners films have a distinct 30s flavour. Ginger Rogers and Miss Day (in a straight role) find themselves caught up with the Ku Klux Klan in *Storm Warning*; D.A. Humphrey Bogart investigates the professional killer organization *Murder Inc*; and former alcoholic James Cagney is a newspaper man in *Come Fill The Cup*. Even swashbuckling, with Gregory Peck as *Captain Horatio Hornblower*, is temporarily back in fashion.

1952 Biography time in a lean year. Danny Thomas is songwriter Gus Kahn in *I'll See You In My Dreams*; Will Rogers Jr. plays his famous father in *The Story Of Will Rogers*; and

Alan Ladd is Western knife fighter Jim Bowie in *The Iron Mistress.*

In lighter vein, Ray Bolger takes to drag for the musical version of *Charley's Aunt — Where's Charley?*

1953 Alfred Hitchcock directs one of his most sombre thrillers, *I Confess*, the story of a young priest (Montgomery Clift) who hears a murderer's confession but cannot, because of his vows, reveal the man's identity to the police. Warners somehow miss the point of the movie, advertising it: "Crushed Lips Don't Talk!"

Warners biggest box-office hit is *House Of Wax*, a remake of their 30s thriller, *Mystery Of The Wax Museum*. Say their advertisements: "The richest beauty of sound comes to you in the screen's first complete electronic merger of dimension camera and dimension microphone in their most fully dreamed of relations." Which, put more simply, means it was filmed in 3-D!

The film stars Vincent Price as the mad sculptor. Price later comments with some relish, "The film was remarkable in that it was directed by Andre de Toth who had only one eye and could not see the 3-D effect."

Doris Day, it seems, is permanently on view, but at least manages to shuffle her leading men: Ray Bolger takes her on in *April in Paris*, Gordon Macrae in *By The Light Of The Silvery Moon*, and Howard Keel (as Wild Bill Hickok) in *Calamity Jane*, the film in which she sings the year's Oscar-winning song, 'Secret Love'. Also on a musical note Macrae is the new Red Shadow in Warners third version of *The Desert Song* and Danny Thomas stars in a remake of *The Jazz Singer.*

The Beast From 20,000 Fathoms, a prehistoric rhedosaurus which is thawed out by an atomic test in the Arctic, offers compensations.

1954 Judy Garland in her comeback role in *A Star Is Born* and John Wayne, manoeuvring a plane-load of passengers to safety in *The High And The Mighty*, pull in the most paying customers. Warners also release their first film in CinemaScope, *The Command*, a Guy Madison western about a trek through the Indian infested territory of Old Wyoming.

Them, the story of giant ants made huge by atomic testing is the best horror film of the year; Ray Milland attempts, but fails to have Grace Kelly strangled in Hitchcock's *Dial M For Murder*; Wayne is out West in

Hondo; so is Alan Ladd in *Drum Beat*, a movie which has Charles Bronson in a supporting role as Captain Jack, leader of the Modoc Indians; and Jack Webb brings his popular TV cop Joe Friday to the big screen in *Dragnet*.

'The Fat Man', Sydney Greenstreet, dies on January 19, aged seventy-four. During the last years of his life he had suffered from Bright's disease and diabetes. In a busy ten year screen career he made twenty-four films, twenty of them at Warners.

1955 James Dean is killed in the late afternoon of September 30 on Route 466 (now 46) near Cholame, California. Driving his $6,900 Porsche Spyder at an estimated eighty-six miles per hour, he hits an oncoming black-and-white Ford sedan, the driver of which escapes with minor injuries. Dean is just twenty-four years old and the star of three movies (all made for Warners) only one of which – *East Of Eden* – had been released at the time of his death. His unreleased films, *Rebel Without A Cause* and *Giant*, follow in late '55 and '56 respectively.

As one young star disappears from the scene, another, Paul Newman, makes his screen debut, a somewhat undistinguished one (as a Greek sculptor called Basil!) in *The Silver Chalice*. Box-office wise Warners do better with World War II than ancient times; Leon Uris' tough marine saga *Battle Cry* and the smash Broadway hit *Mister Roberts*, a comedy-drama about a World War II cargo ship, coming out as the biggest moneymakers of the year. Both top the eight million dollar mark.

Mister Roberts is the last film Cagney makes for Warners. Since his debut at the studio in 1930 he has appeared in fifty-three films, forty-four of them for Warners.

1956 The James Dean myth still lingers. *Giant* becomes Warners biggest moneymaker of the decade and 'Dean fever' continues to sweep the country months after the young actor's death. Will he or won't he win a posthumous Academy Award is the big question of the day. Both he and his *Giant* co-star Rock Hudson are up for the Oscar. The answer is 'no'. The best actor award goes to Yul Brynner in *The King And I.* Only George Stevens (best director) wins for *Giant*.

John Huston is another Warner director among the honours. He wins the New York Critics Award for his ambitious *Moby Dick*, the third time Warners has filmed the Melville whaling story.

John Ford returns to Monument Valley for one of his most beautiful films, *The Searchers*; Carroll Baker creates a sensation by sucking her thumb and rolling about seductively in a shortie nightie in *Baby Doll*; but a ten year old Patty McCormack does most damage. In *The Bad Seed* she goes round killing off nearly everyone in sight, including luckless gardener Henry Jones who just happens to be locked in the garden shed when it burns down!

1957 Warners film the life of 20s torch singer Helen Morgan (Ann Blyth) who gained both fame and notoriety because of her talent and alcoholism. No Hollywood studio worth its salt misses an advertising opportunity like that and Warners duly oblige. Say the billboards for *The Helen Morgan Story*: "She Sat On A Piano, And No Star Ever Climbed Higher. She Fell In Love, And No Woman Ever Fell Lower."

The studio lose two of their stalwarts of the 30s and 40s. Erich Wolfgang Korngold, Czech-born composer of such scores as *Captain Blood, The Adventures Of Robin Hood, Juarez, The Sea Hawk* and *King's Row*, dies of a heart attack and Humphrey Bogart, one of Warners' greatest stars, succumbs to throat cancer before the year is a month old.

Bogart made his first Warner film in 1932, his last for the studio, *The Enforcer*, in 1951. His final movie was the boxing drama *The Harder They Fall*, released by Columbia in 1956. Of his seventy-eight films almost fifty were made at Warner Bros.

Says John Huston, long-time friend and director of Bogie: "He was endowed with the greatest gift a man can have — talent. The whole world came to recognize it. . . His life, though not a long one measured in years, was a rich, full life. . . We have no reason to feel any sorrow for him — only for ourselves for having lost him. He is quite irreplaceable. There will never be another like him."

Humphrey Bogart was fifty-six.

Sayonara with Marlon Brando is Warners' biggest moneymaker; *The Wrong Man* sees Hitchcock in one of his most downbeat moods as he casts Henry Fonda as a jazz musician arrested for armed robbery through a case of mistaken identity; Director Elia Kazan and writer Budd Schulberg attack the insidious influence of American TV in *A Face In The Crowd*; James Stewart is Colonel Lindbergh in *The Spirit Of St. Louis*; Doris Day and John Raitt bring cheer in the musical *The Pajama Game*.

The studio's most ghoulish release: the documentary *The James Dean Story* with a cast of 'People Who Knew, Knew Of Or Were Related To James Dean.'

1958 Errol Flynn returns briefly to the Warner lot for a role for which, sadly, he is only too qualified, the late alcoholic John Barrymore in *Too Much, Too Soon*. Dorothy Malone features as Diana Barrymore.

Rosalind Russell's eccentric *Auntie Mame* is more profitable, however, and finishes up the top financial hit of the year; Paul Newman portrays Billy The Kid as a homosexual in Arthur Penn's *The Left Handed Gun*, but the end result is just the same — a bullet in the back from the gun of Pat Garrett; Gwen Verdon sings 'Whatever Lola Wants' in *Damn Yankees*; Cary Grant does a Scottish reel in *Indiscreet*; and Spencer Tracy goes fishing with deep and profound results in Hemingway's *The Old Man And The Sea*.

Harry Warner, first president of the Company, dies on July 25.

1959 Another great Warner star goes. Errol Flynn collapses from a heart attack at Vancouver airport at the age of fifty and a legend comes to a close. Into his fifty years he has probably crammed one hundred years of living. Just prior to his death he says to former wife Nora Eddington, aghast at his appearance, "Don't be unhappy; you know I've lived twice and I've had a marvellous life."

Jack Warner delivers the eulogy at the surprisingly restrained Hollywood funeral. Jack Oakie, Mickey Rooney, Raoul Walsh, Guinn (Big Boy) Williams, restaurateur Mike Romanoff and Flynn's attorney Justin Golenbock are the pallbearers.

Errol Flynn made fifty-four feature films, forty of them at Warners.

John Wayne, at his most callous, clubs a man round the face with a rifle butt in *Rio Bravo*, but is slower off the mark as far as women are concerned. He can't make up his mind about long-legged Angie Dickinson until the last scene. Just about everybody connected with *The Nun's Story* is up for an Oscar but no-one wins; Paul Newman studies law in *The Young Philadelphians*; James Stewart enforces it in *The FBI Story*; and composer Max Steiner makes all seem sweetness and light with his score for *A Summer Place*.

1960 Not the best Warner year. Frank Sinatra, Dean Martin, Sammy Davis Jr. and co. rob five Las Vegas casinos of five million dollars in *Ocean's Eleven*; Ray Danton rises and inevitably falls as gangster *Legs Diamond*; Richard Burton goes to Alaska for Edna Ferber's *Ice Palace*; Robert Mitchum and Deborah Kerr to Australia for *The Sundowners*.

The debut of Jane Fonda as a college gal in *Tall Story* is one of the year's brighter spots. So too is Ralph Bellamy's portrayal of Franklin Roosevelt in *Sunrise At Campobello.*

1961 Elia Kazan, who helped make Brando a star with *A Streetcar Named Desire*, introduces another promising youngster, Warren Beatty, in *Splendour In The Grass*. A William Inge original, it tells of frustrated love in puritanical small-town America in the late 20s. Beatty's co-star is Natalie Wood.

Later the same year Beatty appears as Vivien Leigh's Italian gigolo in the screen version of Tennessee Williams' *The Roman Spring Of Mrs. Stone*.

Joshua Logan's film of *Fanny* with Leslie Caron, Maurice Chevalier and Horst Buchholz tops the studio's list of box-office hits.

1962 Jack Warner pays a world record price in order to film Lerner and Loewe's stage musical *My Fair Lady*. The fee? Five-and-a-half million dollars.

Meanwhile, the studio are more than happy with Robert Preston singing '76 trombones' in *The Music Man*, their biggest-financial success of the year, and a delicious Natalie Wood requesting 'Let Me Entertain You' as Gypsy Rose Lee in the musical *Gypsy*. Not to be outdone, Natalie's raucous screen mom Rosalind Russell has an equally big moment with 'Everthing's Coming Up Roses'.

The time of the filmed stage musical, begun a year earlier with United Artists' *West Side Story*, has started in earnest.

At the other end of the scale Bette Davis returns to the studio in a grisly piece of Grand Guignol, *Whatever Happened To Baby Jane?* Her co-star is Joan Crawford. Davis' portrayal of a faded child star earns her yet another Oscar nomination. She hopes to become the first actress in history to win three times. She fails and the award goes to Anne Bancroft for *The Miracle Worker*. Katharine Hepburn achieves the triple feat later in the decade. *Days Of Wine And Roses* with Jack Lemmon and Lee Remick struggling desperately against alcoholism, is the studio's critical success. For his famous song in the latter movie Henry Mancini does win an Oscar.

Michael Curtiz, Hungarian-born director who joined Warners in the mid-20s dies on April 11, aged seventy-four. Between 1926 and 1954 he directed eighty-six movies for the studio, an average of three pictures a year. Swashbucklers, westerns, melodramas, musicals – nothing was beyond him. Among his best: *The Adventures Of Robin Hood, Angels With Dirty Faces, The Sea Hawk, Yankee Doodle Dandy, Casablanca, Mildred Pierce, The Unsuspected, The Breaking Point.*

1963 *Spencer's Mountain* with Henry Fonda and Maureen O'Hara heading a poor family living in the Virginia mountains is the studio's biggest commercial hit.

Bob Hope and Lucille Ball team up again for *Critic's Choice*; Cliff Robertson is the young wartime President Kennedy in *P.T.109*; Sinatra, Dean Martin, Anita Ekberg and Ursula Andress are *Four For Texas*; and Kazan films a semi-biographical tribute to his Greek immigrant uncle in *America, America*.

1964 Jack Warner's five-and-a-half million dollar investment in *My Fair Lady* comes to fruition with a domestic take of twelve million dollars and eight Academy Awards. The big surprise is that Audrey Hepburn, Jack Warner's Eliza Dolittle, fails to get among the acting nominees. The best actress award, ironically, goes to Julie Andrews (the stage Eliza but passed over for the film) who wins for Disney's *Mary Poppins*.

Bette Davis (in a dual role) and under the direction of her former co-star Paul Henreid features in *Dead Ringer*; Frank Sinatra sings 'My Kind Of Town' in *Robin And The Seven Hoods*; Raoul Walsh makes his final movie, a cavalry western *A Distant Trumpet* and retires from the movie scene, aged seventy-seven. He worked regularly at Warners since 1939 making more than twenty-five films for the studio. His most famous accomplishment: Cagney's *White Heat*.

John Ford returns to Monument Valley for the last time for *Cheyenne Autumn*, the story of the flight of some 300 Cheyenne Indians from a barren Oklahoma reservation to their native Yellowstone country nearly 2000 miles away.

Says Ford philosophically, "I've killed more Indians than Custer, Beecher and Chivington put together. . . I wanted to show their point of view for a change. Let's face it, we've treated them very badly — it's a blot on our shield; we've cheated and robbed, killed, murdered, massacred and everything else, but they kill one white man and, God, out come the troops."

1965 Tony Curtis (the good guy), Natalie Wood (the heroine) and Jack Lemmon (the bad guy) participate in an auto race from New York to Paris — via Siberia — at the turn-of-the-century and earn Warners eleven million dollars. The film: *The Great Race*.

Natalie Wood is also a washed-up child star in *Inside Daisy Clover*; and Henry Fonda, Robert Shaw and Robert Ryan are among those grimly fighting at Bastogne in *The Battle Of The Bulge*.

1966 In *Who's Afraid Of Virginia Woolf?* Elizabeth Taylor and Richard Burton invite George Segal and Sandy Dennis to an 'evening of fun and games' the like of which has never been seen on screen before. Everyone's up for an award on Oscar night; only the women make it.

Neatest Warner movie of the year is *A Big Hand For The Little Lady* with Hank Fonda in carefree mood as a con artist hovering around a poker game in the Old West.

1967 Warners hit the jackpot with a movie that practically every other studio turned down, *Bonnie And Clyde*, an account of the activities of gangsters Bonnie Parker and Clyde Barrow in the American midwest during the 30s. The studio's biggest financial hit of the decade, it stars Faye Dunaway and Warren Beatty and is advertised with typical modern charm: "They're Young. . .They're In Love. . . And They Kill People." A hot favourite on Oscar night, it is defeated by United Artists' *In The Heat Of The Night*.

Liz Taylor is also in a violent mood, horsewhipping a homosexual Marlon Brando in *Reflections In A Golden Eye*; Alan Arkin and assorted hoods plague a blind Audrey Hepburn in *Wait Until Dark*; and Paul Newman and George

Kennedy defy the horrors of a modern chain gang in *Cool Hand Luke*.

On the lighter side Richard Harris and Vanessa Redgrave contribute 'How To Handle A Woman', 'If Ever I Would Leave You' and other songs in the film version of Lerner and Loewe's *Camelot*, and Francis Ford Coppola (of *The Godfather* fame) makes his directorial debut with *You're A Big Boy Now*.

On July 14, Jack Warner sells his shares in Warner Bros. to Seven Arts and ends his forty-four year association with the company. Albert Warner, former treasurer of Warner Bros., dies aged eighty-three.

1968 John Wayne defiantly puts forward his pro-Vietnam War case in *The Green Berets*. Say the ads: "Their badge of honour was a green beret and it said they had lived it all. . . the night jumps, the ambushes, the hand-to-hand combat, the operation they called Sky Hook. . .and the long nights of terror they filled with courage."

The movie is timed exactly right and takes nearly ten million dollars.

Coppola's *Finian's Rainbow* stars Astaire and Tommy Steele (as a leprechaun) and has Petula Clarke singing 'How Are Things In Glocca Morra?'; *Rachel, Rachel* marks Paul Newman's directorial debut, a distinguished one as he guides wife Joanne Woodward to a New York Critics Award; *The Heart Is A Lonely Hunter* stars Alan Arkin, brilliant as a deaf mute; and *Petulia* has Julie Christie as a beautiful kook.

But most people remember '68 for Steve McQueen and screeching cars hurtling up and down the streets of San Francisco. The film: *Bullitt*. McQueen's co-stars: Jacqueline Bisset and smooth-talking politician, Robert Vaughn.

1969 Maverick director Sam Peckinpah creates a sensation with *The Wild Bunch* and shows the Old West as it's never been shown before — really wild! The movie recounts the last months of a gang of outlaws who, by the turn-of-the-century, have outlived their time and make their way across the Mexican border to die as violently as they have lived.

Says slow-motion master Peckinpah, "At a preview of the film somebody rushed up to me and said 'I'm a pacifist. You ought to be shot for this picture. You ought to be killed'."

Comments veteran Howard Hawks: "I think I'm a better

director. I can kill three people and get them off to the morgue before he gets one down to the ground.''

The studio also go in for science-fiction (*The Illustrated Man*); fantasy (*The Valley Of Gwangi*) and, rather more ambitiously, filmed Giradoux (*The Madwoman Of Chaillot*). Elia Kazan films his own novel *The Arrangement* with Kirk Douglas as the advertising executive who suddenly opts out of the Madison Avenue rat race.

1970 The West again dominates. Wayne rides the range as cattle king *Chisum*; Peckinpah is in more frivolous mood with *The Ballad Of Cable Hogue*, the story of a prospector who stakes his claim in the middle of nowhere; even that master of urban wit, Joseph L. Mankiewicz, pays the great outdoors a visit in *There Was A Crooked Man*, a cynical tale based in a territorial prison of the 1880s. Kirk Douglas and Hank Fonda star.

1971 Clint Eastwood, the star of whom it was once said, ''he learned to act at the Mount Rushmore Academy Of Dramatic Art'' proves them all wrong with his performance as the tough cop *Dirty Harry* — and has been doing so ever since.

It's a good year all round for the studio. Nostalgia and remembrance of things past are beautifully recalled in *Summer Of '42*; sci-fi is represented by George Lucas' *THX II38* and Boris Sagal's *The Omega Man*; Warren Beatty and Julie Christie are *McCabe And Mrs. Miller*; *Billy Jack* earns a staggering thirty-two million dollars; and Stanley Kubrick creates a furore with his vision of a not-too-distant future in *A Clockwork Orange*.

Happiest girl on the lot is Jane Fonda who wins the best actress Oscar for her call girl in Alan Pakula's terrifying black thriller *Klute*.

Saddest news is the death of Max Steiner who dies on December 28, aged ninety-three. Steiner scored some one hundred and fifty movies for Warners winning an Oscar for *Now Voyager*. Notable scores: *Jezebel, The Letter, Casablanca, The Big Sleep, The Treasure Of The Sierra Madre, The Searchers, A Summer Place*.

1972 Peter Bogdanovich resurrects zany comedy with Barbra Streisand and Ryan O'Neal in *What's Up, Doc?*, a modern reworking of Hawks' pre-war *Bringing Up Baby*. Not all critics think it works. Too derivative, say they. Not so, say the public to the tune of a cool twenty-eight million.

Wayne is still out West in one of his finest westerns, *The Cowboys*, the story of a rancher who has no option but to take a group of boys with him on a cattle drive. Unusual to say the least. More unusual is that he dies along the way. Shot in the back of course. The killer: Bruce Dern.

John Boorman's *Deliverance* with Burt Reynolds and Jon Voight is the 'sleeper' of the year; Robert Redford makes his mark twice — as a contemporary politician in *The Candidate* and as a bewhiskered mountain man struggling against the elements and wild animals in *Jeremiah Johnson.*

William Dieterle, the German director who brought that touch of class to Warners in the 30s with his famous series of biographies, dies aged seventy-nine. His Warner bio-pics: *The Story Of Louis Pasteur, The Life Of Emile Zola, Juarez, A Despatch From Reuters, Dr. Ehrlich's Magic Bullet.*

1973 Suddenly it's horror time and if *Bonnie And Clyde* created a sensation in 1967 it's nothing compared with what director William Friedkin stirs up with *The Exorcist,* the story of a young girl possessed by the Devil who mouths obscenities masturbates with a crucifix, vomits green bile and twists her head round with a maniacal cackle.

'Ugh!' mutter the critics. 'No!' cries the church. 'Yes!' says the public. It's Warners biggest-ever box-office hit — eighty-two million dollars in America and Canada alone.

But it catches a backlash on Oscar night. Up for ten Academy Awards it wins only two, losing to the much more wholesome Newman-Redford starrer, *The Sting.*

John Wayne as *Cahill, U.S. Marshal,* Ryan O'Neal as *The Thief Who Came To Dinner*, Clint Eastwood (as Dirty Harry) in *Magnum Force* and Paul Newman in *The Mackintosh Man* all try hard but come across like flat beer in comparison.

1974 Warners go into co-production with Twentieth Century-Fox and produce the massive disaster movie *The Towering Inferno*, the story of what happens when fire breaks out in a 138-storey skyscraper. Heroic efforts by fireman Steve McQueen and architect Paul Newman help put out the fire but Richard Chamberlain, Robert Wagner, Robert Vaughn and Jennifer Jones are among those who don't make it.

Ellen Burstyn's struggling widow in *Alice Doesn't Live Here Anymore* is a surprise best actress Oscar winner; John Wayne exchanges his horse for a limousine in *McQ*; Lucille Ball is a box-office disaster as *Mame*; James Caan and Alan Arkin are more successful as a couple of zany cops in *Freebie And The Bean*.

Surprise hit of the year is Mel Brooks' spoof western *Blazing Saddles*, which has Gene Wilder as The Waco Kid who is more whacko on the booze than with the bullets, a character called Hedley Lamarr and also a Dietrich-type saloon singer Lili Von Shtupp (Madeleine Kahn) who rasps out to a spectator between song verses, "Is that a ten-gallon hat or are you just enjoying the show?"

1975 The most outlandish bank robbery in the history of movies occurs in *Dog Day Afternoon* when Al Pacino and pals hold up a New York bank in order to collect enough money to finance a sex change operation.

And it's based on truth. Such a robbery occurred in 1972 in a Chase Manhattan Bank, Flatbush, Brooklyn when a gay bank robber held out during a day-long siege.

Paul Newman tries again as private-eye Lew Harper in *The Drowning Pool* but despite all the water around proves he is not as successful in detective work as putting out skyscraper fires; Stanley Kubrick heads not for 2001 but Ireland in the 18th century in his three-hour version of Thackeray's *Barry Lyndon*. Beautiful to look at, the movie splits the critics, but is generally considered one of the major disappointments of recent years.

1976 Warners have the prestige movie of the year, *All The President's Men*, Alan Pakula's almost documentary account of how Washington Post reporters Carl Bernstein (Dustin Hoffman) and Bob Woodward (Robert Redford) gradually unravel the Watergate conspiracy. Hotly fancied for the major Oscar Award, it loses out to the smaller-scale boxing drama *Rocky*. Jason Robards, however, as Washington Post editor Ben Bradlee, is named supporting actor of the year.

Barbra Streisand wins her second Oscar, not for acting but for part-composing the song 'Evergreen' for the contemporary rock version of *A Star Is Born*. Kris Kristofferson is Streisand's co-star.

Clint Eastwood can do no wrong as Dirty Harry in *The Enforcer* nor as *The Outlaw Josey Wales*; Charles Bronson is the ex-newspaperman turned private-eye *St. Ives*; Robby Benson features in a tender movie version of the Bobbie Gentry song Ode To Billy Joe.

Busby Berkeley, arguably the greatest dance director who ever worked in a movie studio, dies at his Palm Springs home, aged eighty. He worked at Warners for just seven years between 1933 and 1939 but created some of the most spectacular dance sequences of all time. Among his films: *42nd Street, Gold Diggers Of 1933, Footlight Parade, Dames, Gold Diggers Of 1935, Stage Struck, Hollywood Hotel.* He was married six times.

1977 Clint Eastwood continues to prove that he's Warners' steadiest moneymaker of the 70s. In *The Gauntlet* he's as tough as ever as a second rate cop violently involved with an equally tough hooker, Sondra Locke.

Otherwise the year is mainly routine: Peter Fonda in *Outlaw Blues*; Evel Knievel as himself in *Viva Knievel!*; Richard Burton as a bewildered priest in John Boorman's *Exorcist* sequel *Exorcist II: The Heretic.*

Comedy provides the brightest moments: Oscar-winner Richard Dreyfuss in *The Goodbye Girl* and veteran George Burns as The Almighty in *Oh, God!*

Howard Hawks dies on December 26, aged eighty-one. A master director of many studios, he did much of his finest work on the Warner lot: *The Dawn Patrol, Sergeant York, To Have And Have Not, Rio Bravo* and the best private-eye movie ever made, *The Big Sleep.*

1978 Warners cash in on the new science-fiction craze and refuse to let the disaster movie go.

Marlon Brando and Gene Hackman head the cast of the star-studded *Superman* with 24 year old Christopher Reeve as the 'man of steel' super-hero; director Ronald Neame deals with a world crisis in *Meteor* when two planets collide in space and send massive fragments towards Earth. Sean Connery, Natalie Wood and Henry Fonda do what they can; in *The Swarm* producer Irwin Allen (*The Towering Inferno*) sends billions of South American killer bees to the U.S. and to hell with the consequences! Michael Caine, Katharine Ross, Richard Widmark, Richard Chamberlain and Olivia de Havilland are those up against it this time.

More down-to-earth are Dustin Hoffman, an ex-con on the loose in Los Angeles in *Straight Time* and Clint Eastwood, back once more with his *Gauntlet* co-star Sondra Locke in *Every Which Way But Loose*.

WALT DISNEY

Walt Disney

For many people the Walt Disney story is the rags to riches story come true, the personification of the American dream. From the ordinary beginnings as an artist in Kansas to the creation of Mickey Mouse, from the feature cartoon *Snow White And The Seven Dwarfs* to the wonders of the Disneyland Amusement Park, his career seems like a continually rising graph that starts at bottom left and heads in a perfectly straight line for top right, carrying on ever upwards into a disappearing spiral of millions and millions of dollars.

Nothing could be further from the truth. The success story is there all right. But that line on the graph was never straight. It shot up occasionally, frequently plummeted to danger level and then, by some miracle, limped up again. As late as 1951, twenty-three years after he had created Mickey Mouse, Walt Disney was heard to sigh, "Someday, I would like to reach the position where this company doesn't have to live from one picture to the next."

So much for the simple success story. Disney fought hard for his rewards. Ambition and success were the two words that fired him most and once he had become established in his small Hyperion studio in Hollywood in the mid-twenties, they motivated him even more and continued to do so right up until his death in 1966.

Any lesser man would have quit and thrown in his hand when the cartoon character he had made famous — Oswald The Lucky Rabbit — was 'stolen' by a New York distributor. Despite being 'ripped off' — the distributor had made sure that *he* and not Disney owned Oswald — and losing half his staff into the bargain, Disney was almost buoyant when he left New York by train for Los Angeles. There was a new challenge to meet. A new character to be found — and he had to be found quickly.

It was a situation Disney relished. By the time his train was nearing Los Angeles that character — a mouse called Mickey — had already been invented and the first scenario prepared. When Disney alighted in Hollywood he went into action immediately.

Roughs were drawn up, sketches made. Within days, 'the squeak that was to be heard around the world' was taking shape.

Mickey Mouse made his debut in 1928 in *Steamboat Willie*. He made Disney's name but not his fortune, for linked with Disney's ambition and dreams of success was another quality, a constant search for perfection. Nothing was spared in Disney's drive to improve his art. All profits from his Mickey Mouse shorts were ploughed back into the company to improve the next batch.

The Silly Symphonies, first introduced in 1929, marked an important step forward, for they adapted animation to musical themes. *Flowers And Trees* used Technicolor for the first time in 1932. But, despite the fact that Disney's name was becoming a household word, his studio was barely breaking even. Often it was running at a loss. *Three Little Pigs*, his greatest success of the early thirties grossed a remarkable 64,000 dollars, but cost 60,000.

Mickey Mouse was also a frequent embarrassment to him. "Mickey's our problem child," he used to say. "He's so much of an institution that we're limited in what we can do with him. If we have Mickey kicking someone in the pants we get a million letters from mothers telling us we're giving their kids wrong ideas. Mickey must be sweet, always lovable. What can you do with such a leading man?

"He's a pretty nice fellow who never does anybody any harm, who gets into scraps through no fault of his own, but always manages to come up grinning."

A large part of Disney's income came from merchandising. Even in those early days kids were being told to eat sweets because Mickey ate them, or use soap because Mickey did so. Any straying from the straight and narrow would have been disastrous.

Disney kept Mickey alive and fresh by changing his environment as often as possible with the consequence that the little mouse was frequently venturing to the South Seas, the Alps or the deserts of Africa. He was also cast in a variety of different roles: a gaucho, football player, circus performer, magician, hunter, detective, trapper, carpenter.

But in order to allow more mischief and dirty tricks in his cartoon stories Disney invented other characters — Pluto, Goofy and the irascible Donald Duck. Between them they got into more trouble than Mickey ever did, adding considerably to their creator's reputation and, at the same time, bolstering up his annual revenue.

Disney knew, however, that to succeed as he *meant* to succeed he had to break into the feature market as soon as possible. His studio had made a name for itself around the world, but it would soon become a name of the past if he didn't do something about feature-length animation.

When Disney announced to his wife Lillian and his elder brother Roy that he was going to risk 500,000 dollars on one movie, they thought he had gone mad. An ordinary movie might have been a different matter — a routine western or gangster film with one fairly well-known star would have got its money back and even showed a small profit. Disney, however, wasn't in that kind of movie business, not yet anyway. His market was the family. His art was animation. But there was no guarantee that the public would buy a cartoon feature. After all, it had never been tried before. Nevertheless, in 1934, Disney let it be known that the first feature from the studio would be *Snow White And The Seven Dwarfs*, and that planning would begin immediately.

Inevitably, there were those who thought he was crazy. There were even more who actually said he was. Who would sit through an hour and twenty minutes of cartoon? Surely audiences would get bored. A seven-minute Mickey Mouse or Donald Duck was all they needed. *Snow White* became known as 'Disney's Folly'.

There must have been times too when even Disney thought the risk too great, when he tossed and turned in his sleep at night and worried about the future and if there was to be a future. It was go for broke, literally. If *Snow White* failed then the studio would collapse. That was the only certainty.

The one major drawback to Disney's ambitious plans was time. Production of a feature-length cartoon was a long job. Three years at least from start to finish. The studio had to survive until such time when *Snow White* was ready for release.

Mickey Mouse, Donald Duck and the rest performed admirably at the box-office as work on *Snow White* commenced. So did The Silly Symphonies. But money was always tight. It was a hand to mouth existence, week by week, month by month, eventually year by year.

Somehow Disney managed to inspire his artists with his own burning enthusiasm and energy. Long hours were spent in overtime to keep the movie on schedule. No extra money was asked for. The animators did it for love. They felt they belonged to a cause.

There were vague promises of overtime bonuses if everything turned out well, but there was nothing definite. The animators realised, as did everyone in the studio on Hyperion Avenue, that they were involved in a race against time. They had to get the film finished before the money ran out. It was as simple as that.

They drew till their fingers ached. And till their jaws ached for that matter for, when trying to capture certain expressions, they would sit in front of mirrors, pull a face and then rush their pencils down to their drawing boards in an attempt to recapture what they had just seen reflected in the glass.

During the long hectic days of 1935, '36 and '37 Disney carried nearly all the production worries on his own shoulders. When he thought it necessary he could be a hard taskmaster. If things weren't up to the required standard then his artists and directors knew all about it.

In December, 1935, after viewing a Silly Symphony entitled *Cock Of The Walk*, he addressed the following memo to the film's director Ben Sharpsteen:

"The direction is fine from a technical standpoint. Some of the technical scenes and set-ups were well planned but the direction of the action is very poor from a personality and interest building angle. The main fault with the story lies with the director and the story men. Without a doubt the animators would have gotten a better result if the story had been properly worked out and if the director had taken the story and treated it from a fantastic comical angle. . .instead of having so many scenes that paralleled human actions."

Memos such as that would have angered many people. Disney animators just took them in their stride and vowed to do better. If they suspected just a hint of ruthlessness in their boss they overlooked it.

There were moments when it looked as though *Snow White* would never be finished. As filming passed the halfway mark, Disney simply ran out of money. Not only had he spent 500,000 dollars, he had also spent another million on top and still needed another quarter-of-a-million to complete. He didn't have it. The bank was the only answer.

The bank, however, wasn't handing over anything until it knew what *Snow White* was all about. It wanted to see what Disney had filmed. It wanted collateral.

Disney was adamant with a firm, "No." Roy, the level-headed business partner, pleaded, "Walt, you've got to show them what you've done on the picture so far. If you don't we won't get the loan."

"I can't do that," said Disney. "All I've got is bits and pieces. You know I never like to show anybody an uncompleted picture."

In the end financial necessity won out over human obstinacy. Disney brought together the completed sections of the feature, linked them with pencil sketches and a rough layout and presented a makeshift 'premiere' to banker Joe Rosenburg in the Hyperion studio on a quiet Saturday afternoon.

It was a strange scene. Just two men in an empty studio, one an artist, the other a businessman, bartering for an expensive deal over nothing more than a strip of celluloid.

When the 'preview' was over the banker put on his hat and coat and prepared to leave.

Disney recalled the incident many times. "He showed not the slightest reaction to what he had viewed. After the lights came on, he walked out of the projection room, remarked that it was a nice day — and yawned! Then he turned to me and said, 'Walt, that picture will make a pot full of money'."

From then on it was a straight, if hectic, run in on the home-stretch. To meet the December '37 release date artists worked Saturdays and Sundays and late in the week. Most of the work on *Snow White* was crammed into the last months of '36 and the first half of'37.

The premiere was fixed for December 21 at the Carthay Circle Theatre in Hollywood. Disney had always longed for a premiere of his own, a really big affair with all the stops pulled out. Up until now he hadn't had the opportunity. Now he had a full-length feature to promote.

"It went back to when I first came out here," he said. "I went to my first premiere and saw all those Hollywood celebrities coming in and I just had a funny feeling. I just hoped that some day they'd be going in to a premiere of a cartoon. Because people would deprecate the cartoon. You know, they would kind of look down."

Well they didn't that night. A star-studded audience thrilled to the experience of witnessing for the first time something completely new, something they had never seen before. The reviews were ecstatic. The public flocked in and with them came the much needed money. *Snow White's* enormous cost of one and three quarter million dollars seemed like chicken feed as the grosses began to mount up in 1938, one million, two, three, four million. . .

Little wonder there was a heady feeling about the Disney studio. All the hard work had been worthwhile. They'd made it. *Snow White* was a critical and commercial success. They'd 'done the double'. The film's statistics were released with pride.

As many as seven hundred and thirty artists worked on the picture between 1934 and 1937 including thirty-two animators, one hundred and two assistants, one hundred and sixty-seven in-betweeners (the artists who filled in the bits of action between the animators' drawings), twenty layout men, twenty-five back-ground artists, sixty-five special effects animators who drew smoke, water, clouds and other effects, and one hundred and fifty-eight young women skilled at inking and painting the cartoon figures on transparent celluloid sheets for reproduction in colour by Disney's multiplane camera. At least one million drawings went into the eighty-three minutes of film!

One animator who worked hard on the *Snow White* drawings was Ward Kimball, but for him, at least, the film was a personal disappointment.

''*Snow White* was one of the early tragedies of my life,'' he said. ''I was made a fully fledged animator and they decided that I might make a good job of the dwarfs' eating sequence. I would do the soup scene because I did the funny stuff.

''I animated the whole sequence and it got big laughs in the sweatbox (Walt's projection room) but when Walt started seeing the whole picture he thought that it was one of the places where we ought to get on with the story, go right from making them wash up to the next sequence. So as much as he hated to do it — he even called me on the phone to apologise — he took it out of the picture.

''So then I went on a bed-building sequence; they had a big ornate bed that the dwarfs were building as a present to Snow White. This was also taken out after I'd animated it, once again because it didn't help the story along.''

If *Snow White* was 'just one of those things' for Ward Kimball, it contained the seeds of nightmare for sensitive children who were unaware of just how horrific Disney had made the evil witch. A more unpleasant crone had rarely been seen on the screen.

Disney's artists followed his instructions to the letter: ''The Queen/Witch should be a mixture of Lady Macbeth and the Big Bad Wolf. Her beauty is sinister, mature, plenty of curves. She becomes ugly and menacing when scheming and mixing her poisons. Magic fluids transform her into an old witchlike hag.''

In some countries *Snow White* suffered a partial ban. In England the censor ruled that children under sixteen would not be allowed to see the film unless accompanied by adults.

Dr. Benjamin Spock liked to recall the story of Nelson Rockefeller telling his wife that the seats in the Radio City Music Hall had to be reupholstered because they were wet so often by frightened children.

The story is almost certainly apocryphal, but Disney would have ignored it even it it had been true. Sensing that children enjoyed being frightened, he continued to scare them half to death for years to come. Stromboli and The Coachman plus the whale in *Pinocchio* are enough to make even the most hardened adult want to head for the exit sign, and the yellow-eyed demon in the 'Night On A Bare Mountain' sequence from *Fantasia* is as terrifying as anything 'thrown up' by William Friedkin in *The Exorcist* more than thirty years later.

As well as being a triumph *Snow White* also proved to be a worry to Disney. A similar problem faced Orson Welles a few years later when he made *Citizen Kane*. How to top it? *Snow White* had faults, certainly. Technical imperfections had to be ironed out, character movements improved. But just how far could Disney go with feature-length animation? Were there any limits?

True to form Disney didn't puzzle the questions for very long. He plunged ahead with new projects. *Pinocchio*, the story of a wooden puppet which is turned into a real boy, and *Bambi*, Felix Salten's story of a forest deer, were first on the story boards. They were closely followed by the most ambitious of all Disney's cartoons, the two-hour *Fantasia*, a compromise of eight pieces of classical music, each animated in a different style and form.

The programme was ambitious. It was based on the principle that nothing succeeds like success. As Roy Disney commented at the time. "Success is hard to take. We thought we could do two animation films a year."

Disney had no doubts that his animators would produce class films. And in that respect he was right. *Pinocchio, Bambi* and *Fantasia* all contained draftsmanship of the highest order, particularly the former which to this day ranks as Disney's supreme accomplishment.

Where he went wrong was in gauging how much each would cost to produce and how much each would make in return. He had only *Snow White* as a yardstick. That had cost a lot, but it had made a lot too. He had every reason to expect that the next three features, with the possible exception of the experimental *Fantasia*, would perform in similar fashion.

He was wrong on both counts. By the time *Pinocchio* and *Fantasia* were ready for release in 1940 he was in debt to the bank to the tune of four and a half million dollars. *Pinocchio* had cost over two and a half million, *Fantasia* more than two and a quarter million. *Bambi* had run into animation problems. All its characters were animals which was causing delay after delay. It wouldn't be ready for another two years.

The hope lay in the box-office performances of *Pinocchio* and *Fantasia*. Both films were dismal financial flops. Despite critical acclaim neither earned a profit and Disney was in the deepest trouble.

The whole scene had suddenly turned sour. The war in Europe had deprived him of 45 per cent of his market. The word 'genius' was still used in connection with his name, but there was a distinct possibility that 'bankrupt genius' might be applied in the near future.

In 1940 the bank shut down his credit and he was forced, much against his will, to sell stock in the company; something he had never wanted to do.

Worse, for the first time in his career, he had trouble with his staff, many of whom had lost their jobs because he had been forced to cut back and keep only a relatively small nucleus working on *Bambi* and the new makeshift feature *The Reluctant Dragon.*

The new Burbank studio, built by Disney in 1939, didn't please everybody. The homely atmosphere of the old Hyperion Studio was missing. Somehow, in the thirties, it had all seemed different. Then, working conditions and salaries were never questioned. Now they were. The wages were poor. The vague bonus promises made during the filming of *Snow White* never materialized. Unrest grew and Disney was faced with a bitter confrontation.

Had he gone to his artists and explained his financial position there would certainly have been some give and take. Most of his staff still held him in great respect and would have appreciated the tremendous strain he was under to keep the studio afloat. But he didn't. He showed a stubborn streak and dug in his heels. He didn't believe the strike would last, but he was wrong. It lasted for nine weeks and, in the end, after much bad feeling, most of the staff demands were met. The studio began to function again, but it had been a chastening experience for Disney. Never before had he been faced with labour unrest. He didn't like the feeling. He had always been a father figure. Family pictures were his business. The strike had made him feel like a tycoon.

By a strange quirk of fate, the war which had so drastically reduced the returns of *Pinocchio* and *Fantasia,* came to Disney's financial rescue.

The rescue came in the shape of a long-term contract to produce information films for the armed forces.It was a life saver. When *Bambi* was eventually released in 1942, after five years in production, it too proved a financial disaster. Only *Dumbo,* a quickly made sixty-four minute cartoon about a baby circus elephant, was a success.

The army and navy contract meant steady work. Inevitably it meant that Disney lost his stride. His ambitious animation plans were temporarily shelved for the more urgent requirements of the moment — educational films directed at pilots, navigators, nurses and technicians, and his own part-animated, part-live action feature about daylight precision bombing, *Victory Through Air Power*. But it also meant a regular cash flow. Money came in all the time, even enough to allow him to produce a couple of minor features for the South American market, *Saludos Amigos* and *The Three Caballeros*.

When the war came to an end, Disney, restless enthusiast that he was, wanted to carry on from where he had left off in 1942. The war had been a necessary interlude in his work. In the five years between 1937 and 1942 he and his studio had been responsible for craftsmanship of the highest class. Films like *Snow White, Pinocchio, Fantasia, Bambi,* even *Dumbo*, had ensured that the name Disney was synonymous with quality.

Disney wanted that five year phase to be no more than 'Act One'. He announced to his brother — and the bank — that he had plans for a new series of features which included *Cinderella, Alice In Wonderland* and *Peter Pan*. It would be a phase two for the organization, an opportunity to build on the pre-war foundations. The next stage of Disney animation would be an improvement on the first. He was sure of that.

The wind was taken right out of his sails, however, when both Roy and the bank insisted that such plans be temporarily shelved. By the end of the first post-war year the studio was again running at a deficit of more than four million dollars. Roy, as always, saw the situation realistically. "After the war was over, we were like a bear coming out of hibernation," he said. "We were skinny and gaunt and we had no fat on our bones. Those were lost years for us."

To make sure that fat was quickly put on those bones, it was decided that as many features as possible would be put into release. It meant producing films which were inexpensive, but which still bore the Disney stamp.

The answer was the package cartoon, a full-length feature made up of eight or ten unconnected segments, linked occasionally by live action sequences. The studio made three such films in as many years, *Make Mine Music, Fun And Fancy Free* and *Melody Time*.

Walt's heart wasn't in them, but he followed the logic of the economic arguments and pressed ahead. He was proud of *Song Of The South*, a film which brilliantly combined live action with animation. The others he regarded as cartoon programmers, serving a function, nothing more. For such an ambitious artist, the crash-programme must have been a bitter pill to swallow.

When, eventually, feature animation began again in 1950 with *Cinderella*, the pre-war brilliance had all but evaporated. Fine draftsmanship, invention and enthusiasm were still in evidence, but one vital ingredient was missing — style. Post-war slickness had replaced the careful craftsmanship of the early 40s.

Cinderella, Alice In Wonderland and *Peter Pan* were not unattractive films. Nor were any of the other delightful cartoons that followed in the 60s and 70s. All had their moments of charm and genuine originality and, in the case of *Cinderella*, a group of engaging animal characters to help the familiar story along. But not one of them — *101 Dalmatians* and *The Aristocats* included — ever quite captured that special artistry and genius that so marked the halcyon days of *Snow White* and *Pinocchio*.

It was once said of Disney: "There were always two Walt Disney's, one the artist with a vivid imagination who produced *Snow White* and *Pinocchio*; the other the insatiable showman, builder of Disneyland, salesman of Mickey Mouse watches, whose genius doomed him to vulgarise his own creations in search of ever-wider audiences."

That Disney should have devoted most of his later years to being an 'insatiable showman' should not count against him. In doing so he brought laughter and enjoyment to millions of children and families and allowed them to escape into a world that was, quite literally, magic. Sometimes it was real-life magic as in the great Amusement Park, sometimes celluloid fantasy when little Volkswagens had minds of their own and goony bears sang 'beat songs' in jungle clearings.

For Disney there were simply not enough mountain peaks to climb. Animation remained his one true passion, but when, in the post-war years, he had to settle for cut-price feature cartoons, his interest slackened a little and he began to cast his eye in other directions.

He wanted to achieve perfection in combining animation with live action and did so with films like *Song Of The South* and *Mary Poppins*. He wanted to enter the live action market and compete on the same level as other major studios. Again he did so, starting in 1950 with *Treasure Island* and continuing with such successful films as *20,000 Leagues Under The Sea, The Shaggy Dog, The Swiss Family Robinson, The Absent Minded Professor* and *The Love Bug*.

He wanted to enter television. In 1954 he did so with astonishing success. A year later he went into the amusement park business. The result, as everyone knows, was Disneyland, one of the greatest tourist attractions in the world. In the last fifteen years of his life Disney was 'showman *extraordinaire*' and at last enjoyed the success that everyone associates with him.

He once told a reporter, "I've always had a nightmare. I've dreamed that one of my pictures has ended up in an art theatre. And I wake up shaking."

It's a neat little anecdote. It sums up Disney's philosophy precisely. Wholesome, warm-hearted and entertaining, best described his films during his lifetime. There are no better words to describe the Disney movies of today.

The Walt Disney studio hasn't changed its image since the death of Walt in 1966 and Roy in 1971. It just carries on. It's an institution, too treacly, naîve and superficial for some but, strangely, now the only Hollywood studio with a recognisable style.

The Disney studio goes on producing its half-a-dozen movies a year. One knows what one is going to get. Adventure, comedy, animals, children, a cartoon reissue and a new animated feature every four years. It's a static formulae, but there's no need to change it. The reason is simple. It works.

Walt Disney, founder of the most magical empire in movies.

The first appearance of Mickey Mouse in the 1928 cartoon *Steamboat Willie*.

Cinderella, Disney's first post-war full-length cartoon.

A scene from Beethoven's Pastoral Symphony from the 1940 Disney classic *Fantasia*.

Mickey's rival and eventual usurper, the belligerent Donald Duck.

Mowgli the man-cub and Baloo the Bear sing 'The Bare Necessities' in *The Jungle Book*.

A nervous *Bambi* plus a merry Thumper enjoy an ice-slide in the first full-length Disney cartoon to feature animals only as characters.

The first animated feature-length movie, *Snow White And The Seven Dwarfs*.

Duchess being wooed by alley cat J. Thomas O'Malley in the 1970 hit, *The Aristocats*.

The perfect combination of live-action and animation. Dick Van Dyke, Julie Andrews plus Disney magic in the record-breaking *Mary Poppins*.

Chronology

1923 The Walt Disney company begins its tentative operations in the rear of a small office occupied by Hollywood-Vermont Realty. The address is 4651 Kingswell Avenue. The rent is thirty-five dollars a month.

On October 16 Walt and his elder brother Roy sign a contract with New York distributor Margaret J. Winkler to make six 'Alice comedy shorts' at 1,500 dollars each and a further six at 1,800.

The Alice comedies stem from *Alice's Wonderland*, an experimental combination of cartoon and live-action produced by Disney the year before in Kansas as part of his Laugh-O-Gram series, a primitive first try at animation which included *Puss In Boots, Cinderella* and *Jack And The Beanstalk.* When the company folded the twenty-one year old Walt took off by train for Hollywood. In his pocket, just forty dollars. Under his arm, *Alice's Wonderland*, the film that began the Disney story.

1924 The first Alice cartoon is *Alice's Day At The Sea.* The brothers, needing to increase their working area, rent a vacant lot on Hollywood Boulevard about three blocks from Kingswell Avenue. The lot is used for outdoor shooting on the Alice films. The brothers, whose outfit now numbers seven, rent a separate garage for seven dollars a month.

A few weeks later they also move to the larger adjoining store at 4649 Kingswell and display in the store window, '*Disney Bros. Studio*'.

The first cartoons, featuring Virginia Davis, the girl star of *Alice's Wonderland,* are disappointing. The distributors protest there's too much live action and not enough cartoon work. They want to cancel. Disney wires boyhood friend and artist Ub Iwerks to come to California to help streamline the cartoons. The move works. More animation *is* included and the series becomes a modest success.

Margie Gay, a flapper-type girl, takes over as Alice and Disney has his foot on the first rung of the ladder.

1925 The Disney team, joined now by Hugh Harman and Rudolph Ising, produce eighteen Alice shorts.

On July 6 they deposit four hundred dollars to secure a lot on 2719 Hyperion Avenue, close to their existing premises. A single storey building is erected. It is the nucleus of the Disney studio which is to grow in size in the next few years. The name of the studio changes. It's now 'The Walt Disney Studio'.

Seven days later Disney marries Idaho girl, Lillian Bounds, one of the two women employed in the studio's inking department.

1926 The Disney studio, at full stretch, produces twenty-six Alice shorts, more than two a month. Among the titles: *Alice At The Carnival, Alice At The Rodeo, Alice In The Alps, Alice The Fire Fighter.*

1927 After sixty comedies, the Alice series fades in popularity. The New York distributors, now Charles Mintz (married to Margaret Winkler) and brother-in-law G. Winkler, suggest a new series, completely animated, featuring a character called Oswald The Lucky Rabbit.

The Disney team, anxious to expand into other areas, agree and start producing Oswald cartoons. The series is a success.

'Oswald The Lucky Rabbit, Created By Walt Disney' say the advertisements, but when Disney travels to New York later in the year to try for a modest increase in terms, he finds that the character *belongs* to Mintz. Lower not higher terms are offered and Mintz threatens to take several Disney animators from the studio if Disney doesn't agree.

Disney refuses point blank and journeys back to Hollywood with his wife, not in a state of dejection, but already trying to think up a new cartoon character. Somewhere between Chicago and Los Angeles the first scenario for Mickey Mouse is conceived. The character owes its origins to a tame field mouse that used to creep into Disney's studio and onto his drawing board in his Kansas days.

1928 Mickey Mouse makes his first appearance in *Steamboat Willie* and causes a sensation when he bows at the Colony

Theatre in New York on November 18, not least because he is a talking mouse. Disney himself voices the character.

The simple story has Mickey as a deck-hand on board a river boat trying to save Minnie Mouse from the clutches of Pegleg Pete. The music in the cartoon includes 'Turkey In The Straw' and 'Steamboat Bill'.

Steamboat Willie is not, in fact, the first Mickey Mouse cartoon to be completed. *Plane Crazy*, inspired by Colonel Lindbergh's headline-making solo flight from New York to Paris, is the first; *Gallopin' Gaucho* with Mickey and Minnie south of the border, the second. But both are silent and held back until 1929 when soundtracks are added.

The independent producer Pat Powers distributes the Mickey Mouse cartoons in the first year of production.

1929 More than a dozen cartoons are produced as Mickey Mouse increases in popularity. During the year he acquires such refinements as gloves and shoes and also a more endearing manner.

In addition to the Mickey Mouse cartoons Disney experiments with animation and music as he produces the first of his Silly Symphony shorts. *The Skeleton Dance*, a cartoon in which some skeletons come alive and dance to music. The music includes part of Edward Grieg's 'The March Of The Dwarfs'.

The Silly Symphonies originate from Carl Stalling who is in charge of the music at the Disney studio. He suggests the basic idea, i.e. finding music that evokes a mood and building a cartoon around the theme. The idea is a simple one at first, devoted solely to inanimate objects coming to life. Later, in the thirties, it broadens to encompass fairy tales and other stories.

1930 Mickey Mouse mania is at its height. Merchandising enters the scene when Disney is offered three hundred dollars to put Mickey's image on a school tablet. Mickey is soon to be known throughout the world, but under different names.

In Italy he is known as Topolino; in Japan as Miki Kuchi; in France as Michel Souris; in Spain as Miguel Ratoncito; in Sweden as Musse Pigg; in Greece as Mikel Mus; in Brazil as Camondongo Mickey; in Argentina as El Raton Mickey; and in Germany as Michael Maus.

Disney, who has now signed with Columbia to distribute his pictures, also begins to introduce other cartoon characters, among them Horace Horsecollar and Clarabelle Cow. Neither catch on. One who does is Pluto, a simple-minded bloodhound who is first glimpsed as one of two dogs chasing Mickey in *The Chain Gang*. Animated by Norman Ferguson, he first appears under the name Pluto in *The Moose Hunt* released in April of the following year.

1931 Mickey Mouse is up for an Oscar for the first time in *Mickey's Orphans* in which he and Minnie host a gala Christmas party for a group of tiny kittens.

The production staff rises to forty. Animators include David Hand, Ben Sharpsteen, Rudy Zamora, Tom Palmer, Jack King, Les Clark and Jack Cutting.

Disney's perpetual drive for improvement in his animation has forced up the cost of a single cartoon to more than 13,000 dollars. Despite the success of Mickey Mouse the studio is barely breaking even.

1932 Disney experiments with three-color Technicolor in the Silly Symphony cartoon *Flowers And Trees*, a fantasy about the romance between two trees. The picture originally starts as a black-and-white film, but the footage is scrapped and the entire movie begun again in colour.

Flowers And Trees premieres at Grauman's Chinese Theatre in July. It supports the MGM movie *Strange Interlude* starring Norma Shearer and Clark Gable and wins an Academy Award, but Technicolor drives the cost of cartoons still higher.

Disney wins another Oscar, a special one for creating Mickey Mouse; changes distributors (United Artists for Columbia); and invents yet another character, Goofy, who appears in a supporting role as Dippy Dawg in *Mickey's Revue*. His first appearance as Goofy is in *Orphans' Benefit* in 1934. Voiced by former circus clown Pinto Colvig, he is animated by Art Babbitt.

1933 Disney produces his most famous Silly Symphony cartoon, *The Three Little Pigs*. Its song, 'Who's Afraid Of The Big Bad Wolf?' becomes a smash hit all over the world.

The Night Before Christmas is another top Silly Symphony short. Mickey Mouse is again honoured with an Oscar nomination for *Building A Building*, but the most ambitious cartoon of the year is *Mickey's Gala Premiere* in which Mickey and Minnie are guests of honour at Grauman's Chinese Theatre and Disney brilliantly caricatures many top Hollywood personalities including Laurel and Hardy, Fredric March, Boris Karloff, Bela Lugosi, Greta Garbo and Charlie Chaplin.

1934 For the first time Disney begins to think seriously about the possibility of a cartoon feature. He alarms both his brother and wife by announcing that he's willing to gamble 500,000 dollars on a full-length animated version of *Snow White And The Seven Dwarfs*.

Just how seriously he's regarding the project is revealed in August when he suggests fifty possible names for the dwarfs. Among them: Gloomy, Crabby, Snappy, Puffy, Weepy, Shifty, Biggy-Wiggy, Biggo-Ego, Hotsy, Hungry, Cranky, Awful, Happy, Sleepy, Sneezy, Bashful and Grumpy. During the initial story-planning the film is referred to as 'The Feature Symphony'.

The Silly Symphonies — *The China Shop, The Grass-Hopper And The Ants* — continually help artists develop their drawing skills and *Goddess Of Spring*, which retells the Greek myth of Persephone, helps them gain experience of the human form.

The most successful Silly Symphony is *The Wise Little Hen* which introduces the irascible Donald Duck to the screen. Said to be a conglomeration of all the people Disney dislikes, he is animated by Dick Lundy and Fred Spencer and voiced by Clarence Nash, a former milk company employee who used to entertain children with animal imitations.

Donald Duck is a short-tempered creature living on a ramshackle houseboat who feigns a stomach ache when asked for assistance. His first words, "Who me? Oh, no! I got a bellyache." Just a few months later he jumps to stardom in *Orphans' Benefit*.

The least successful Silly Symphony is *The Big Bad Wolf*, a sequel to *Three Little Pigs*. Says Disney, "You can't top pigs with pigs!"

1935 Mickey Mouse appears in colour for the first time in *The Band Concert*. He's the conductor of an outdoor band trying desperately to get through the William Tell overture. The desperation creeps in because popcorn hawker Donald Duck is frequently interrupting. Mickey's last black-and-white cartoon is *Mickey's Service Station*.

Preparations on *Snow White* continue. The seven dwarfs are finally named, the last two to be christened being

Sneezy (formerly Jumpy) and the dim-witted Dopey who for some months has been known simply as 'The Seventh'. The line-up now reads: Doc (the leader), pessimistic woman-hater Grumpy, Bashful, Happy, Sleepy, Sneezy and Dopey.

1936 The spring and summer sees production on *Snow White* in full swing. The studio staff now runs into hundreds.

Disney concentrates for much of the time on the songs. He turns down fifteen year old Deanna Durbin for the voice of Snow White. The reason? She sound too mature, between the ages of twenty and thirty. He accepts eighteen year old Adriana Caselotti who has been trained in Italian opera.

Among the shorts: *Mickey's Polo Team, Donald And Pluto, Mickey's Circus, Moving Day, Three Blind Mouseketeers* and the Oscar-winning *Country Cousin.*

1937 *Snow White And The Seven Dwarfs* premieres at the Carthay Circle Theatre in Hollywood on December 21 in front of a star-studded audience. Charlie Chaplin, Marlene Dietrich, Charles Laughton, Mary Pickford, Cary Grant and Ginger Rogers are among those attending.

The movie receives raves from every quarter even though it finishes up costing more than three times Disney's original estimate — 1,750,000 dollars. During 1938 it earns 4.2 million dollars in the United States and Canada alone. It runs for an unprecedented five weeks at the Radio City Music Hall and in Paris runs continuously for thirty-one weeks. It is dubbed into ten languages round the world.

Fred Moore, Bill Tytla, Fred Spencer and Frank Thomas animate the dwarfs; Art Babbitt the queen; Norm Ferguson the witch; three younger animators, Milt Kahl, Eric Larson and Jim Algar are in charge of the animals who befriend Snow White; Ham Luske and Grim Natwick animate Snow White herself; Natwick also draws the prince.

In addition to Caselotti as Snow White, Harry Stockwell voices the prince; Lucille LaVerne the queen, Scotty Mattraw Bashful, Roy Atwell Doc, Pinto Colvig Grumpy *and* Sleepy, Billy Gilbert Sneezy, Otis Harlan Happy, and Moroni Olsen the Magic Mirror.

The movie is Oscar nominated for a best music score, but strangely not one of the famous songs: 'Whistle While

You Work', 'Heigh Ho', or 'Some Day My Prince Will Come' is up for an award.

Says Disney, who has just acquired a new distributor, RKO (a relationship that lasts for more than fifteen years), "We've worked hard and spent a lot of money, and by this time we're also a little tired of it. I've seen so much of *Snow White* that I am conscious only of the places where it could be improved. We've learned such a lot since we started this thing! I wish I could yank it back and do it all over again!"

But there is no need. As Disney speaks, his staff are already at work on two additional animated features, *Pinocchio* and *Bambi*.

1938 On August 31, Disney makes a deposit on a fifty-one acre site in Burbank. New buildings are begun, others are brought from the old studio on Hyperion Avenue. It is the beginning of a buoyant Disney multi-million dream studio.

As work on *Pinocchio* and *Bambi* goes ahead, a third feature, known at first simply as 'The Concert Feature', arrives on the story boards. It evolves because the popularity of Mickey Mouse is at last slipping and Disney attempts to give him a boost in a special double-length music cartoon, *The Sorcerer's Apprentice*. After lengthy discussions, however, the film is shelved for two years and becomes part of a full-length feature which weds serious music and animation — *Fantasia*.

Disney's Oscar is for *Ferdinand The Bull*, a Munro Leaf story about a bull whose only aim in life is to spend his time sniffing flowers; Mickey Mouse tries for a third time to win, unsuccessfully, in *The Brave Little Tailor*; *Mother Goose Goes To Hollywood* is a Silly Symphony caricature of famous movie stars with Katharine Hepburn as Little Bo Peep and Laurel and Hardy as Simple Simon and the Pieman.

Disney also stops calling his shorts 'Mickey Mouse Cartoons' and starts to identify each cartoon by its star character.

1939 The move to Burbank from Hyperion Avenue begins in August and is completed by the spring of 1940; the unlucky Mickey Mouse misses out for a fourth time on Oscar night in *The Pointer*; Disney himself is luckier. On February 23 he gets eight, one big one and seven little ones for *Snow White And The Seven Dwarfs*.

Reads the inscription: 'To Walt Disney for *Snow White And The Seven Dwarfs*, recognised as a significant screen innovation which has charmed millions and pioneered a great new entertainment field for the motion picture cartoon.''

Says little Shirley Temple who presents the award to a somewhat overcome producer, ''Don't be nervous Mr. Disney.''

1940 *Pinocchio*, Carlo Collodi's folk tale about a wooden puppet who is turned into a real boy, is Disney's second full-length animated feature. For many, it's his supreme achievement, visually brilliant and full of invention, but its budget is a phenomenal 2,600,000 dollars and the picture fails to return its cost. The movie wins two musical Oscars — best original music score and best song ('When You Wish Upon A Star') — and is dubbed into seven languages.

Frank Thomas, Milt Kahl and Ollie Johnston draw Pinocchio; Ward Kimball, Wolfgang Reitherman and Don Towsley animate Jiminy Cricket; Bill Tytla Stromboli; Norman Ferguson and John Lounsbery the roguish fox J. Worthington Foulfellow; and Art Babbitt Geppetto.

Dickie Jones (Pinocchio), Christian Rub (Geppetto), Cliff Edwards (Jiminy Cricket), Evelyn Venable (The Blue Fairy), Walter Catlett (Foulfellow), Frankie Darro (Lampwick) and Charles Judels (Stromboli *and* the Coachman) supply the voices.

Fantasia also arrives on the scene. A pictorial interpretation of eight widely differing pieces of classical music ranging from abstract visuals for a Bach fugue to prehistoric visions for Stravinsky's 'The Rite Of Spring', it is another expensive production (2,300,000 dollars) and like *Pinocchio* fails at the box-office just when Disney is in desperate need of revenue for expansion of his new Burbank studios.

Despite the public's indifference there is acclaim among the critics for Disney's courage in tackling the subject at all. Although not a masterpiece *Fantasia* does on occasion reach the heights of animation, heights that Disney is never to reach again.

The eight pieces included in the film (all conducted by Leopold Stokowski and played by the Philadelphia Orchestra) are: 'Toccata and Fugue in D Minor' by Johann Sebastian Bach; 'The Nutcracker Suite' by Tchaikovsky; 'The Sorcerer's Apprentice' by Dukas;

'The Rite Of Spring' by Stravinsky; 'The Pastoral Symphony' by Beethoven; 'Dance Of The Hours' by Ponchielli; 'Night On A Bare Mountain' by Mussorgsky; and Schubert's 'Ave Maria'.

A ninth selection, Debussy's 'Clair de Lune' had been part of the film as late as July 1939.

Among the *Fantasia* animators: Art Babbitt who draws 'The Chinese Dance' from 'The Nutcracker Suite'; John Lounsbery, Howard Swift and Hugh Frazer who are among those responsible for the 'Dance Of The Hours'; Les Clark and Bill Tytla who figure among the top animators on 'The Sorcerer's Apprentice'; and Tytla again who is responsible for the terrifying demon in 'Night On A Bare Mountain'.

During a long series of reissues the picture does, like nearly all Disney cartoons, eventually make a profit. In the 1946 reissue the catch line is the ghastly 'Fantasia will amaze-ya'.

In 1940 Disney says, "*Fantasia* is timeless. It may run ten, twenty, thirty years. It is an idea in itself. I can never build another *Fantasia*. I can improve. I can elaborate. That's all."

Twenty years later he adds, "*Fantasia*? Well, we made it and I don't regret it. But if we had to do it all over again, I don't think we'd do it."

1941 Disney, struggling to overcome the heavy losses incurred by *Pinocchio* and *Fantasia*, again releases two features, but both on a cheaper scale.

The Reluctant Dragon is a patchwork job with Robert Benchley making a tour of the new Disney studio and learning how cartoons are made. It links together three separate cartoons — *Baby Weems, How To Ride A Horse* (with Goofy) and *The Reluctant Dragon.* Costing just 600,000 dollars, it barely breaks even.

Dumbo on the other hand *is* a hit. The story of a baby circus elephant who learns to use his enormous ears to fly, it is produced quickly — 6 months on story work, twelve on animation — and costs just 700,000 dollars. At sixty-four minutes it is one of Disney's shortest ever features, but it does help offset some of the enormous Disney losses. It would almost certainly have been a bigger hit had it not been unlucky enough to be released just a few weeks before the Japanese raid on Pearl Harbour.

The *Dumbo* voices: Timothy Q. Mouse (Edward Brophy),

Ringmaster (Herman Bing), Elephant (Verna Felton), Stork (Sterling Holloway), Jim Crow (Cliff Edwards), Dumbo himself, like that other popular Disney character, Dopey, never speaks.

Frank Churchill and Oliver Wallace win an Oscar for their *Dumbo* music score; one of the film's songs 'Baby Mine' grabs a nomination; and Donald Duck is also a nominee for *Truant Officer Donald*. The year's cartoon winner though is Pluto who stars in '41s best, *Lend A Paw*.

1942 Disney's financial position, despite the success of *Dumbo*, is perilous. The war brings help. The armed forces commission him to make a long series of information films and army and navy training pictures. The commission is a life saver.

Bambi, the picture Disney had been relying on to pull him out of the red is, however, a failure. A sixty-nine minute adaptation of Felix Salten's story about the life of a forest deer from his early days as a baby fawn to the time he reigns supreme as king of the forest, it is another critical hit but an abysmal flop financially. It grosses only 1,300,000 dollars, a million dollars *less* than it costs to produce.

Its enormous cost is due to its five year production schedule, the longest Disney has yet spent on an animated feature. The main reason for the long production is that all the characters in the film are animals. Disney, aiming for perfection, spares no expense.

A cameraman photographs thousands of feet of forests, snowfall, rainstorms, spider webs and changes of light and seasons; two live fawns are provided for the studio and sketched and photographed as they grow; rabbits, ducks, skunks, owls and other species also make their home at the studio; a local naturalist contributes hundreds of photographs of animals in action; and four animators — Frank Thomas, Milt Kahl, Oliver Johnston and Eric Larson — are kept on the picture throughout the entire five years of its production.

Bambi receives two Oscar nominations, but it is the shorts department which again comes up with the winner, *Der Fuehrer's Face* in which Donald Duck at last gets his Academy Award. In the movie he dreams he's having a nightmare working in a German munitions factory. A ripe tomato in the face of a Hitler caricature ends the short and wins the Oscar!

1943 Donald Duck and Goofy star in the forty-three minute *Saludos Amigos*, a part-cartoon, part-travelogue goodwill picture aimed at paving the way for new financial markets in South America, those in Europe having been mostly reduced to rubble.

In the live-action section Disney and his staff visit Chile, the Pampas region and the Carnival in Rio; in the cartoon sequences Goofy features in *El Gaucho Goofy* and Donald is introduced to Rio's Copacabana beach and the samba by a new cartoon character, energetic parrot Joe Carioca.

The propagandist *Victory Through Air Power* is another part live-action, part-animation picture but with a more serious theme — the virtues of wartime strategic bombing. Disney finances the film himself and loses over 400,000 dollars. ''It was a stupid thing to do as a business venture,'' he admits. ''It was just something I believed in and for no other reason than that I did it.''

The Disney cartoon *Reason And Emotion* is Oscar nominated, but the Academy Award goes to the MGM pair Tom and Jerry in *Yankee Doodle Mouse*, a duo who are to provide a great threat to the Disney cartoon characters in the next decade.

1944 It's Goofy's turn to be honoured with an Academy Award nomination in *How To Play Football.*

There are no Disney features this year, just a dozen shorts which include the bad-tempered Donald Duck in *Trombone Trouble, Commando Duck* and *Donald's Day Off.*

1945 In *The Three Caballeros* Disney at last combines live-action and animation in the same scenes, something he has been promising to do for several years. And although the film is not 'The most startling advancement in motion picture technique since the beginning of sound', it is a breakthrough and brings Disney back to somewhere near his best form.

Donald Duck and Joe Carioca star, plus Panchito, a Mexican cartoon rooster with a large sombrero and an itchy trigger finger. Together they go on a riotous tour of South America. Donald has the best time. He falls in love with Aurora Miranda and dances with her in a big production number; he also frolics on the beach with a number of gorgeous bathing beauties.

Despite the overall gaiety and lively animation of the

piece the *New Yorker* finds plenty of things to grumble about:

"A mixture of atrocious taste, bogus mysticism and authentic fantasy. . .a somewhat physical romance between a two-foot duck and a full-sized woman, though one happens to be a cartoon and the other pleasantly rounded and certainly mortal, is one of those things that might disconcert less squeamish authorities than the Hays Office. . .It might even be said that a sequence involving the duck, the young lady, and a long alley of animated cactus plants would probably be considered suggestive in a less innocent medium."

1946 With the war over, the studio is again in desperate financial straits. Disney, not having produced a major cartoon since *Bambi*, wants to regain his touch with another series of major projects such as *Peter Pan* and *Alice In Wonderland*. The most important thing though is to get as many movies into circulation as soon as possible, hence the package cartoon, a feature-length movie made up of eight or ten short pieces, each disconnected.

Make Mine Music, a sort of pop *Fantasia*, is the first of three such films Disney produces in consecutive years. Despite one delightful creation, Willie The Singing Whale (voiced by Nelson Eddy), a whale who wants to sing opera at the Met., and two Benny Goodman pieces, 'All The Cats Join In' and 'After You've Gone', it disappoints a public eager to see Disney return to the form of *Snow White* and *Pinocchio*.

The other Disney film of the year *is* a success however. *Song Of The South* combines live-action with animation even more successfully than *The Three Caballeros*, a stand-out sequence being when Uncle Remus sings the Oscar-winning 'Zip-A-Dee-Doo-Dah' in an animated woodland with birds and butterflies fluttering down upon his shoulders.

James Baskett is the philosophical old Uncle Remus: "You can't run away from trouble — there ain't no such place that far"; Hattie McDaniel sings 'Sooner Or Later' as she feeds him her home-made apple pie; and Bobby Driscoll and Luana Patten are the children who enjoy the animated tales of Brer Rabbit.

1947 *Fun And Fancy Free* is the second of Disney's trio of composite cartoon features. Some live-action with Edgar

Bergen and Luana Patten is also included, but best among the stories is *Mickey And The Beanstalk* in which Mickey Mouse, Donald Duck and Goofy set out to destroy Willie the Giant. This is the only time in a Disney feature that his three cartoon stars appear together.

But the fact that Jiminy Cricket briefly reappears in the film singing the song 'I'm A Happy Go Lucky Fellow', originally written and recorded for *Pinocchio*, indicates what a rag-bag it all is.

Two of Disney's fifteen shorts are up for the best cartoon Oscar, *Pluto's Blue Note* and Donald Duck's new adversaries, chipmunks *Chip an' Dale*. The award however goes to Warners for their canary creation *Tweetie Pie*.

1948 *Melody Time* and *So Dear To My Heart* boost the Disney output to five films in three years.

Melody Time is the last of the package cartoons. The story of American folklore hero Johnny Appleseed is the main segment; The Andrews Sisters sing the story of Mini-tugboat 'Little Toot'; Donald Duck, Joe Carioca and Panchita are reunited in 'Blame It On The Samba'; Roy Rogers tells young Bobby Driscoll and Luana Patten the story of 'Pecos Bill'.

Bobby Driscoll and Luana Patten also feature in *So Dear To My Heart*, a story of a boy and his pet sheep in turn-of-the-century Indiana. It is nearly, but not quite, Disney's first all live action movie. A few animation sequences when Driscoll's scrapbook comes to cartoon life prevent it from becoming the first in the category. Beulah Bondi features as Driscoll's grandmother, Burl Ives ('Lavender Blue') as the singing town blacksmith.

Mickey And The Seal and Donald Duck's *Tea For Two Hundred* are in contention for the cartoon Oscar, but neither win. A Disney short that does is *Seal Island*, a twenty-seven minute colour documentary about the thousands of fur seals that migrate annually to raise their pups on the Pribilof Islands in the Bering Sea. It is the first of a series that is to make Disney famous: 'The True Life Adventures'.

1949 *The Adventures Of Ichabod And Mr. Toad* is Disney's solitary feature, a sixty-eight minute cartoon made up of just two half-hour stories, Washington Irving's 'The Legend Of Sleepy Hollow' and a sequence from Kenneth Grahame's 'The Wind In The Willows'. But it's a good movie. Says *Time* magazine: "This lighthearted, fast-moving romp has inspired some of Disney's most inventive draftsmanship and satire."

Bing Crosby narrates 'Sleepy Hollow', Basil Rathbone 'The Wind In The Willows.' Eric Blore is the voice of Mr. Toad, Pat O'Malley the horse named Cyril, Claud Allister, Rat and Colin Campbell, Mole.

1950 A key Disney year. With the barren years now behind him he starts the new decade with a flourish, making his first full-length cartoon since *Bambi* and achieving another ambition, his first live-action feature.

Cinderella is the cartoon and the first of several fairy stories Disney is to film in the 50s. Not of the standard of *Pinocchio* or *Dumbo*, it nonetheless marks a return to near top form. Numerous secondary animal characters help the familiar tale along: the mice Jacques and Gus, the dog Bruno and the cat Lucifer.

Ilene Woods voices Cinderella, William Phipps Prince Charming, Eleanor Audley the stepmother, Verna Felton the fairy godmother. The six song hits include the Oscar nominated 'Bibbidi Bobbidi Boo'.

In *Treasure Island* Robert Newton becomes immortal as Long John Silver. He rolls his eyes and leers "Ah, Jim Lad," and immediately goes into movie folklore. It's an historic picture but not, surprisingly, an American venture. The film is shot in England with Bobby Driscoll as Jim Hawkins. There's some chastisement from the British critics ('Yo Ho Ho And A Coca Cola') but there's no denying the film's entertainment value and Disney plans more live-action films for England.

Beaver Valley, the second of the 'True Life Adventures' wins Disney his Academy Award but for the first time in ten years there's no Disney cartoon up for an Oscar despite the usual quota from Donald Duck, Goofy, etc.

1951 *Alice In Wonderland* is Disney's second full-length cartoon in consecutive years, but considerably less successful than *Cinderella*. Despite being in production for five years (at a cost of 5,000,000 dollars) the film misses the essence of Lewis Carroll's fable. One Disney animator refers to it as, "a loudmouthed vaudeville show." Disney himself blames its failure on the fact that "Alice lacks heart."

But there are compensations: the songs 'A Very Merry

Un-birthday' and 'I'm Late'; the Mad Hatter's tea party; an opium-smoking Caterpillar and the Cheshire Cat.

Alice is voiced by Kathryn Beaumont, The Mad Hatter by Ed Wynn, The Caterpillar by Richard Haydn, The Cheshire Cat by Sterling Holloway, The March Hare by Jerry Colonna, The Queen Of Hearts by Verna Felton, and The Walrus, Carpenter, Tweedledum and Tweedledee all by Pat O'Malley.

The 'True Life Adventures' are again triumphant. *Nature's Half Acre* brings Disney his third two-reel Academy Award in four years.

1952 Disney remains in England for his next live-action adventure. Taking no chances with his subject material he opts for *The Story Of Robin Hood.* Richard Todd steals from the rich to give to the poor, Joan Rice is Maid Marian, Peter Finch the Sheriff Of Nottingham, James Hayter Friar Tuck, James Robertson Justice Little John.

The usual quota of Disney shorts is released with Donald Duck and Goofy being the two most popular characters; the Academy Award winning *Water Birds* is the fourth 'True Life Adventure'.

1953 Disney is now in full gear and operating on three different levels: the full-length animated feature, the live-action film and, with the arrival of *The Living Desert*, the feature-length documentary.

Peter Pan is Disney's third full-length cartoon in four years. Long in his mind as a possible subject (he first considered it in 1935) it fails to find favour with the critics, but in this case the budget — 4,000,000 dollars — is well spent. The public love it. *Peter Pan* finishes up among the top Disney box-office hits of all time.

Bobby Driscoll is the voice of the ever youthful Peter, Kathryn Beaumont is Wendy, Hans Conried Captain Hook, Bill Thompson Mr. Smee, Heather Angel Mrs. Darling and Paul Collins Mr. Darling.

The Sword And The Rose with Richard Todd and Glynis Johns romancing in the days of Henry VIII continues Disney's British costume adventures, but the surprise hit is the first full-length 'True Life Adventure', *The Living Desert* which draws raves from the critics.

Photographed in different areas of the great American Desert, it reveals, often in fascinating close-up, the innumerable animals and insects that live there. Among the highlights: a mating battle between two male tortoises for a female; the courtship of a tarantula and a battle between a red-tailed hawk and a rattlesnake.

With RKO now almost finished as a studio, Disney ends his distributing arrangements with them and releases *The Living Desert* through his own releasing organization, Buena Vista. All future Disney productions are distributed through Buena Vista.

Disney sweeps the board at Oscar time. *The Living Desert* is named best feature documentary; *The Alaskan Eskimo* (belonging to the 'Peoples And Places' series) best short subject; and *Toot, Whistle, Plunk and Boom* the best cartoon. The latter is the first cartoon to be filmed in CinemaScope.

The studio also releases the first 3-D cartoon, *Melody*, and, sadly, the last to feature the seemingly indestructible Mickey Mouse, *The Simple Things*. It co-stars Mickey and Pluto who try to get away for a relaxing vacation. It is estimated that Mickey has starred or co-starred in some one hundred and twenty cartoons during his twenty-five year screen career.

1954 A giant squid, bigger even than the terrifying DeMille monster in *Reap The Wild Wind* is Disney's big hit of the year. It challenges James Mason and Kirk Douglas for the star spot in Jules Verne's *20,000 Leagues Under The Sea*, Disney's first feature in CinemaScope. The film's a gamble. It pays off, however, with a huge box-office take and Disney is now in the big time as far as live-action is concerned.

The squid weighs two tons, has eight forty foot tentacles and two feelers, each fifty feet long. Twenty-eight men operate the squid with hydraulics, compressed air and electronics.

The submarine Nautilus is built to scale, two hundred feet long, shaped as Verne had described it, as an undersea monster, its headlights appearing as 'eyes' in the dark waters.

Real life drama again brings its rewards, both financially and at Oscar time, in *The Vanishing Prairie*, the second 'True Life Feature' about the wildlife still surviving on the great American prairies. Eleven of Disney's skilled cameramen photograph mountain lions, coyotes, bison, cougars, prairie dogs, etc.

Richard Todd stars in the third and last of his costume

adventures, *Rob Roy, The Highland Rogue* and Disney at last enters into the field of television with his weekly series, *Disneyland.* It is yet another breakthrough. The show, a combination of cartoons, true-life material and old Disney feature films, is a hit from the word go. The series is the beginning of big business for Disney who himself hosts each show.

The Mickey Mouse Club and *The Wonderful World Of Disney* are among the TV shows that follow in the years ahead.

1955 *Lady And The Tramp* is the third feature-length cartoon in five years, but from now on the cartoons are to become increasingly sporadic as Disney turns his attentions more towards live-action features, television, and his new wonder amusement park, Disneyland, which he opens on July 17.

In the first decade of the Park's existence Disney spends millions of dollars over and above his initial investment, but the centre becomes a magnet for tourists all over the world. During the first ten years the number of attractions rises from twenty-two to forty-eight. Says Disney, "I've always wanted something of my very own. I worry about my pictures, but if anything goes wrong in the Park I just tear it down and put it right."

He has little to worry about with *Lady And The Tramp.* The first full-length cartoon in CinemaScope, it is arguably his best since *Bambi.* An adventure of two dogs in a small New England town at the beginning of the century, it features the voice of Peggy Lee and includes the song, 'He's A Tramp'. Three years in production, it costs four million dollars.

Fess Parker makes his first appearance as *Davy Crockett, King Of The Wild Frontier*; *The African Lion* is the year's feature 'True Life Adventure'.

1956 It's the wide open spaces for Disney as he aims at the most traditional form of American movie entertainment, the western.

Fess Parker stars in all three of his live-action movies of '56. He's back in *Davy Crockett And The River Pirates*; a scout who leads a wagon train of settlers in *Westward Ho The Wagons*; and a Union spy who steals a Confederate train from behind enemy lines in *The Great Locomotive Chase.*

Secrets Of Life is the full-length 'True Life Adventure'.

More wide-ranging than most, it looks at plant life, insect life, sea creatures, even volcanoes. The short cartoons are now down to five with Donald Duck the only remaining familiar figure in the CinemaScope *Chips Ahoy*.

1957 Disney goes back even further into American history — the revolutionary war — in *Johnny Tremain*, the first of many Disney films to be directed by Robert Stevenson.

It's *Old Yeller*, however, which provides him with a sure-fire formula for the future. The formula is a simple one. Children plus animals equals eight million dollars. At least it does with *Old Yeller*, a story of the 1860s and the affection of a boy for a stray dog that wanders onto his Texas homestead. Fess Parker and Dorothy McGuire do their best to compete with Kevin Corcoran and 'Spike' but never remotely come close.

The success of the film convinces Disney that live-action movies, i.e. adventure, children plus animals, are now his basic moneymakers and feature-length cartoons a luxury sideline.

Perri, a Felix Salten story about a female pine squirrel is the first 'True Life Fantasy'.

1958 A minor Disney year. James MacArthur is a white boy raised by Delaware Indians in *The Light In The Forest*; Sal Mineo a young Sioux brave in the cavalry western *Tonka*.

White Wilderness, a feature-length 'True Life Adventure' about the animal inhabitants of the Arctic, wins an Academy Award, the third Oscar for the series.

1959 The most expensive cartoon feature of all time, *The Sleeping Beauty* (6,000,000 dollars), opens in a blaze of publicity, but as they say in the trade: 'It lies there and it just dies there.' Produced in Technirama and with music borrowed from Tchaikovsky, it proves to be one of Disney's biggest-ever flops. On its first release — with specially increased prices — it doesn't even recover its production costs.

The story has many of the elements of *Snow White*. But times have changed. It's twenty years on and the fairy-tale cartoon is a thing of the past. It's the end of a Disney era. "I sorta got trapped with it," says Walt. "I had passed the point of no return and I had to go forward with it."

One Disney film that doesn't open with any fanfares

is *The Shaggy Dog*, a story of a teenager who by reciting an ancient spell manages to change himself into a large fluffy white dog. The movie costs a million and makes eight. It's in black-and-white and stars Fred MacMurray as 'the shaggy dog's father,' an actor who is to become a regular on the Disney scene during the 60s.

1960 Despite the success of *The Shaggy Dog*, the Disney studio is suffering another of its financial setbacks – due mainly to *The Sleeping Beauty* disaster.

None of its 1960 films hit the jackpot even though they include an exquisite remake of *Pollyanna* with Hayley Mills, *Kidnapped* with Peter Finch and *Jungle Cat*, the last of the 'True Life Adventure' features.

Only *The Swiss Family Robinson* which stars John Mills, Dorothy McGuire and Hayley Mills and carries Disney's largest ever live-action budget (4,500,000 dollars) stands out as a winner. It is released too late in the year to wipe out the financial loss of 1,300,000.

Disney feels obliged to give one of the talks he's given so often in the past. "We've been through this before," he tells his staff. "We were just one step ahead of foreclosure when we lost our foreign markets before the war. We might have gone under after the war if the bank hadn't agreed to carry us. We'll get out of this slump too."

1961 And they do. Quicker than even Disney expects. The reason? The box-office take of four movies – *The Swiss Family Robinson* (which enjoys its main release in '61), *The Absent Minded Professor, The Parent Trap* with increasingly popular child actress Hayley Mills and the 3,600,000 dollar cartoon, *101 Dalmatians.*

Greyfriars Bobby, the charming story of a Skye terrier who keeps a persistent vigil over his master's grave in mid-nineteenth century Edinburgh, is another modest success.

On April 25 Walt and Roy make a visit to the Bank Of America and pay off all existing loans – loans that have been hanging round their necks since the days of *Snow White*. For the first time in twenty-two years that revenue from all Disney movies goes directly to Walt Disney Productions.

101 Dalmatians is the most inventive cartoon feature of Disney's later period. Based on a book by Dodie Smith, it relates how all the dogs in England come to the rescue of fifteen Dalmatian pups stolen by arch-villainess, Cruella de Ville, who plans to turn them into a fur coat. Rod Taylor voices hero-dog Pongo, Betty Lou Gerson Cruella, and Fred Warlock and J. Pat O'Malley the two inept crooks Horace and Jasper.

The Absent Minded Professor has Fred MacMurray once again turning Disney comedy into a goldmine. He's a college professor who is so forgetful he's missed his own wedding twice. He misses it again when he potters around in his garage and invents a gooey, rubbery substance that floats and bounces and which he calls flubber. When he rigs up his old Model T with the invention he actually gets the car to fly!

For those who believe the substance can actually be made *Time* magazine supplies the special effects department's recipe for flubber:

"To one pound of salt water taffy add one heaping tablespoon polyurethane foam, one cake crumbled yeast. Mix till smooth, allow to rise. Then pour into saucepan over one cup cracked rice mixed with one cup of water. Add topping of molasses. Boil till it lifts lid and says 'Qurlp'."

1962 MacMurray is off form for once in *Bon Voyage*, a comedy misfire about the adventures of a typical American family abroad for the first time in Paris; *Big Red* is another boy-dog story with Walter Pidgeon joining the Disney ranks; *Moon Pilot* with Tom Tryon and Brian Keith takes a mildly satirical swipe at the astronaut programme.

The biggest Disney hit is *In Search Of The Castaways*, a version of Jules Verne's fantasy 'Captain Grant's Children', a South American adventure involving the search for the lost father of two children. Notes in bottles, earthquakes, journeys through ice caverns, are some of the ingredients of a film which is advertised with the words, 'A thousand thrills and Hayley Mills'.

If the picture doesn't exactly live up to the tag line it does prove that young Hayley is the studio's hottest property of the moment. It grosses eight million. Helping out in South America: Maurice Chevalier, George Sanders, Wilfrid Hyde White.

1963 *Son Of Flubber* is the first ever Disney sequel to a feature and is almost as successful as its predecessor *The Absent Minded Professor*. Wacky professor Fred MacMurray again meddles in things which 'man should leave alone'. The result: Dry rain, flubbergas and more flying cars.

Savage Sam is the now traditional boy-dog feature, Hayley Mills co-stars with Dorothy McGuire and Burl Ives in *Summer Magic*; and *The Sword In The Stone* sends the Disney animators to the pages of T. H. White and the legend of King Arthur and Merlin the Magician in fifth century England — without, unfortunately, a great deal of success.

The year's most ingenious movie: *The Incredible Journey*, the story of how three pets, two dogs and a Siamese cat, make a hazardous trek across Canada to their home 250 miles away. The animals — Bodger, a bull terrier, Luath a labrador retriever and Tao the Siamese cat — become three of Disney's best-loved characters.

1964 One word sums up the year: 'Supercalifragilisticexpiali-docious!' It's one of the songs from *Mary Poppins*, the most successful Disney movie of all time. Critics and public alike find that 140 minutes of Julie Andrews as P.L.Travers' magical nanny, complete with umbrella and carpet bag, add up to perfect entertainment.

A brilliant live-action/animation sequence in fantasy land and the performances of artist-sweep Dick Van Dyke, Ed Wynn who floats to the ceiling whenever he laughs, David Tomlinson as a stern father and Matthew Garber and Karen Dotrice as the children in the middle of it all help the film earn a staggering 31 million in the U.S. and Canada alone.

The movie also garners five major Oscars, the first time a Disney film has ever done so. It wins for best actress (Julie Andrews), best song ('Chim Chim Cher-ee'), best original music score, best editing and best visual effects.

The rest of Disney's 64 product looks mild by comparison. Tommy Kirk is a mind-reader in *The Misadventures Of Merlin Jones*; small-town sheriff Brian Keith pursues an escaped circus tiger in *A Tiger Walks*; Karen Dotrice loves her pet cat in *The Three Lives Of Thomasina*; Hayley Mills is in Greece mixed up with jewel thieves in *The Moon-Spinners*.

1965 Hayley Mills, although growing up fast (she's now eighteen) proves she still has box-office appeal. Her feature *That Darn Cat*, a Siamese that does much to uncover the whereabouts of a couple of kidnapping thieves, takes more than twelve million dollars for the Disney studio. Dean Jones as an FBI agent and Neville Brand and Frank Gorshin as the crooks help the gross along but it's Hayley's film, her last for Disney.

Tommy Kirk reappears as Merlin Jones for more college adventures in *The Monkey's Uncle*; Brian Keith, Vera Miles and Brandon de Wilde star in *Those Calloways*, a chronicle of life in a rural New England community.

1966 A lukewarm Disney year with no Hayley Mills to help out at the box-office.

Fred MacMurray, who starts a small-town boy scout troop in *Follow Me, Boys!* and Dick Van Dyke, a navy pilot stranded on an island with lovely Nancy Kwan in *Lt. Robinson Crusoe, USN*, are talented substitutes but their vehicles are poor.

Peter McEnery as *The Fighting Prince Of Donegal* in 16th century Ireland and Dean Jones who in *The Ugly Dachshund* brings home a Great Dane to live with his wife's adored Dachshund puppies, fare little better.

The most charming character of the year is A. A. Milne's Winnie The Pooh whom Disney transfers to the screen in the short *Winnie The Pooh And The Honey Tree*.

The saddest news is the death of Disney himself. He dies just ten days before Christmas from advanced cancer of the lung. He passes away in his room at St. Joseph's Hospital in Burbank directly across the street from his studio. He was sixty-five.

The Jungle Book, the last feature cartoon he was associated with, is not quite finished and his animators are left to complete the film without him.

1967 *The Jungle Book* turns out to be a fitting tribute to Disney's memory. It is released exactly thirty years after the premiere of *Snow White*. Despite a mixed critical reception it catches the imagination of the public and is an enormous financial success. Its take: thirteen million dollars.

Based on Kipling's Mowgli stories, it tells of a small Indian boy abandoned at birth and raised as a wolf cub. Like so many Disney films it owes not a little of its success to its music, the two standout hits being King Louis' 'I Wanna Be Like You' and Baloo's 'The Bare Necessities'.

Phil Harris voices Baloo the Bear, Sebastian Cabot Bagheera the Panther, Louis Prima King Louis of the Apes, George Sanders Shere Khan the Tiger, Sterling Holloway

Kaa the Snake, J. Pat O'Malley Colonel Hathi the Elephant.

The rest of the Disney movies drag their tails. *The Happiest Millionaire* (at 164 minutes Disney's longest ever feature) has Fred MacMurray as an eccentric millionaire sharing his Philadelphia mansion with pet alligators, a boxing Bible class and a bewildered staff; *Monkeys, Go Home* has Dean Jones trying to grow olives on a French farm with the help of four monkeys and local priest Maurice Chevalier; *The Gnome-Mobile* features among other things, Walter Brennan in a dual role as a lumber tycoon and a two foot gnome, a 1930 Rolls Royce and a 1,100 year old gnome king!

1968 Not the best Disney year. Peter Ustinov as *Blackbeard's Ghost*, brought back to Earth when innocent college coach Dean Jones reads an ancient manuscript, creates enjoyable havoc in a small American town. A flamboyant Ustinov more than helps the film take nearly ten million dollars.

Dean Jones also has problems in *The Horse In The Gray Flannel Suit*, both as an advertising executive and the father of a show-jumping daughter; Dick Van Dyke is mistaken for a hired killer and forced by art-loving racketeer Edward G. Robinson to take part in a museum heist in *Never A Dull Moment*; grandpa Walter Brennan heads *The One And Only, Genuine Original Family Band*.

1969 At first sight very much like 1968. Except for one film, *The Love Bug*, which takes everyone by surprise (including those at the Disney studio) by taking twenty-one million dollars and becoming the second biggest live-action grosser in Disney history. The surprise is because the hero is a little Volkswagen named Herbie which has a heart and mind all of its own. Rollicking, fast-moving, zany. Everyone loves it. Dean Jones is the good guy, David Tomlinson a superb villain.

It wouldn't really matter if the studio had no other release for the year. But they have. *Ride A Northbound Horse* is a schoolboy western; *Rascal* is another in the long line of Disney boy-animal movies, the pet this time being a baby racoon; Glenn Ford is western rancher *Smith*.

Three A. A. Milne stories are condensed into twenty-five minutes in the cartoon short *Winnie The Pooh And The Blustery Day*. Sebastian Cabot narrates.

1970 *The Aristocats* is the first full-length cartoon since Disney's death, a feline counterpart to *101 Dalmatians* and smack on target as one of the best examples of the contemporary-style Disney cartoon.

It all happens in Paris in the early 1900's. J. Thomas O'Malley is an enterprising alley cat, Scatcat a jazz lover and Duchess and her three kittens the aristocracy of the cat world. Phil Harris voices O'Malley, Scatman Crothers Scatcat and Eva Gabor Duchess. Top songs: 'Everybody Wants To Be A Cat' and 'The Aristocats'. A big hit financially, the film grosses eleven and a half million dollars.

Kurt Russell finds he has a computer's brain in *The Computer Wore Tennis Shoes*; Earl Holliman stars in the boy-dog story *Smoke*; and a lunatic band of crooks – Phil Silvers, Mickey Shaughnessy and Norman Fell – search desperately for a jewel haul hidden in a food hamper in *The Boatniks*.

1971 The studio again mixes live action with animation in *Bedknobs And Broomsticks*, a musical fantasy of England in World War II. David Tomlinson, owner of a 'College Of Witchcraft', referees a cartoon football match in Naboombu Land; apprentice witch Angela Lansbury travels on a magic bedstead; the Sherman Brothers (*Mary Poppins*) write the score which includes the Oscar nominated song 'The Age Of Not Believing'.

Comedy is the mainstay. A pet duck exposed to radiation starts laying eggs of solid gold in *Million Dollar Duck*; a chimpanzee picks TV programmes that always top the charts in *The Barefoot Executive*; Brian Keith is a white whiskered rancher in *Scandalous John*. Says sheriff Harry Morgan in the latter, "I go unarmed in emulation of the London bobbies."

Five years after the death of Walt, elder brother Roy Disney dies, aged seventy-eight.

1972 A minor year. Accountant Dean Jones tries to run an inherited hotel in the Colorado Rockies in *Snowball Express*; Kurt Russell enjoys the freedom of invisibility in *Now You See Him, Now You Don't*; family togetherness during the Civil War is the basis of *Menace On The Mountain*.

Napoleon And Samantha has the most charm. A boy and a girl (Jodie Foster and Johnny Whittaker) make a trek across the mountains with a pet lion. Mike Douglas and Will Geer co-star.

1973 'The most ambitious cartoon feature ever' trumpet the ads for *Robin Hood*, the first full-length cartoon since *The Aristocats*. Unfortunately it's anything but, despite a 'voice cast' which includes Brian Bedford (Robin), Peter Ustinov (Prince John), Terry-Thomas (Sir Hiss), Roger Miller (Allan-a-Dale), Phil Harris (Little John) and Andy Devine (Friar Tuck).

The highspots of a generally uninspiring feature: the hypnotising snake Sir Hiss and the Johnny Mercer song 'The Phoney King Of England' sung by Phil Harris.

The World's Greatest Athlete has Jan-Michael Vincent being raised Tarzan style in Africa and performing outstanding feats on the athletic field; *One Little Indian* has James Garner on the run with a ten-year-old 'white Indian brave.'

1974 *Herbie Rides Again*, driven with relish all over San Francisco by little Helen Hayes. Up against her, and the car, nasty property developer Keenan Wynn. Net result: over seventeen million dollars.

Adventure is represented by *Island At The Top Of The World* with Donald Sinden and company travelling by airship to the North Pole and discovering a Viking valley undisturbed for a thousand years; sentiment by *The Bears and I* with army veteran Patrick Wayne raising three bear cubs in the wild; and comedy by *The Castaway Cowboy* with James Garner as a shanghaied Texan in Hawaii.

Winnie The Pooh makes another appearance in *Winnie The Pooh And Tigger Too.*

1975 A piece of microfilm smuggled out of China and hidden in a dinosaur in London's Natural History Museum causes all kinds of trouble in the comedy, *One Of Our Dinosaurs Is Missing*. Helen Hayes is a nannie, Peter Ustinov the head of Chinese Intelligence.

Two orphan children with superhuman powers search for their true identity in *Escape To Witch Mountain*; three more orphans, plus gambler Bill Bixby, search for gold in an abandoned mine in *The Apple Dumpling Gang*; Kurt Russell gets superhuman strength from a vitamin-charged breakfast cereal in *The Strongest Man In The World.*

1976 Peter Ustinov stars in another Disney hit, *Treasure Of Matecumbe*, a fast-moving period adventure. He's a quack doctor who searches for buried treasure with two young boys in the Florida Keys. The studio tops it all off with a spectacular hurricane.

It's the year for kids. They figure prominently in *Ride A Wild Pony*, a story of Australia in the 30s; a boy and a girl fake their own kidnapping, much to the chagrin of grandfather David Niven in *No Deposit, No Return*; two more try to save nine Yorkshire pit ponies from the slaughterhouse in *Escape From The Dark*. Based on a novel by Rosemary Anne Sissons, it stars Alastair Sim in his last role as an ageing mine owner.

1977 Two mice set out to rescue an orphan girl trapped by the evil Madame Medusa on a riverboat in the Devil's Bayou. A flying albatross called Orville, two alligator 'guards' and a fabulous buried diamond are other ingredients of the latest cartoon feature, *The Rescuers*. Not the studio's best, but a notch or two up from *Robin Hood*. Bob Newhart and Eva Gabor voice the two mice, Geraldine Page, Medusa.

Thirteen year old Jodie Foster and Mom Barbara Harris swop places in an inventive comedy *Freaky Friday; Herbie Goes To Monte Carlo*; and in *Pete's Dragon* a nine year old boy is adopted by an animated dragon in turn-of-the century America. 'Candle On The Water' sung by Helen Reddy is a best song Oscar nominee.

1978 David Niven looks as though he may do for Disney in the late 70s what MacMurray did for the studio in the 60s. In *Candleshoe* he's seen in four roles — butler, chauffeur, gardener, colonel — as, together with tough tomboy Jodie Foster, he tries to prevent Helen Hayes' picturesque English mansion from falling into the wrong hands. He succeeds and turns the movie into a charming and surprise winner. Leo McKern's blustering English confidence trickster and Ron Goodwin's lively music score are additional plus factors.

Jim Dale is another with a multiple role (he's seen in three parts) as he heads West in *Hot Head And Cold Feet*; Bette Davis and Christopher Lee, whose speciality is turning humans into robots, make their Disney debuts as partners-in-crime in *Return From Witch Mountain*; Harry Morgan and Roddy McDowall feature in the extraterrestrial feline comedy *The Cat From Outer Space*.

COLUMBIA

Columbia

She stands on a pedestal set on a marble dais, holding high, with one hand, a glowing torch and, with the other hand clutching the classical drapery of her Grecian gown. Boldly spreading across the screen behind her are eight huge letters. They spell one word. Columbia.

Today, 'Miss Columbia' looks so regal and dominant that it seems hard to believe she emerged from the shabbiest streets of Hollywood, the area which stretched for a block along Beachwood Drive and around the corner of Sunset Boulevard and became known as Poverty Row.

It was on Poverty Row that the dregs of Hollywood used to hang out. Extras waited hopefully on doorsteps for a day's work; producers and promoters worked feverishly in small offices, backed by single sound stages, to produce quickies that would return a fast profit and, hopefully, enable them to survive another week in the toughest, but most exciting business in the world.

The Columbia Lady, in the silent days no more than a crude drawing, emerged from all this sordid activity. Beautiful and impassive, she never once moved or spoke and no musical soundtrack ever thundered out from behind her. She stood aloof, deliberately designed to give the studio a hint of class and somehow obscure the fact that Columbia lived and operated on Poverty Row.

The man responsible for forging Columbia into an outfit to be reckoned with was Harry Cohn. He ran the Hollywood studio from the earliest days, when it was known as the CBC Company, until his death in 1958. He, his older brother Jack and Joe Brandt (two former Universal employees) formed the company in 1920. Jack and Joe kept a tight hold of the purse strings in New York, Harry operated on the West Coast.

The toughest, most foul-mouthed producer ever to set foot in the movie capital, Harry Cohn wheeled and dealed with enthusiasm on Poverty Row. The third son of orthodox Jewish parents – his father was an immigrant German tailor, his mother Polish – he was raised on New York's Lower East Side and knew all about the 'rules of life'. Very astutely he applied them to the motion picture business.

The result was success; slow at first as the Cohns produced cheap two-reelers and tried to shrug off the fact that their CBC company was known around Hollywood as 'Corned Beef And Cabbage', then fairly rapidly as director Frank Capra joined them in 1927. By 1934 they had already won a best picture Oscar and become a major threat to the larger Hollywood studios.

Capra dubbed Cohn "His Crudeness". No better words could have been found to describe him. Raw power was what the bullying Harry Cohn was all about. There was nothing refined about him. A former song-plugger, trolley bus conductor and vaudeville performer, he called a spade a spade and worse. He once brought success in movies down to the lowest common denominator. "Lemme tell you what this business is about. It's c. . . and horses."

Little wonder that he was in his element on Poverty Row. In those early days he hourly used his wits to survive, operating from a little hired studio on Sunset Boulevard and mixing with people he knew and understood.

Not only were the front men and cheap producers his kind of people, but the film fraternity too — the dinkies and lot hoppers and three-dollar stiffs, the early names for Hollywood extras; the girl extras known as pinkies; the different kind of girl extras, the moths, who did 'favours' in return for jobs; and the wa-wa brigade, the specialists in making incoherent mob noises.

Then there were the drugstore cowboys, a rung or two up from the dinkies and lot-hoppers, but still deep in the manure pile, who used to hang about at 'Gower Gulch', the drugstore at the corner of Sunset Boulevard and Gower Street. Early each morning assistant directors would come by in a truck and select those needed to support the early western stars, Tom Mix, Hoot Gibson and Jack Holt.

For those who weren't picked it meant another day of waiting and making calls to the minor 'studios' on Poverty Row. For those who were selected it meant just a few bucks. It was a heartless existence. No quarter was asked. None given. It was win or lose on Poverty Row. There was no in-between. In the end most of the extras and 'Gower Gulch' cowboys lost. But most of them still thought it worth the risk and preferable to sitting behind an office desk. Whatever they may or may not have had in the way of talent, they certainly weren't lacking in courage.

Courage too was a word that could be applied to Harry Cohn. He never knew when he was beaten and fought tooth and nail to keep first CBC and then Columbia alive. The studio survived often by the most nefarious means. Bills received by Jack Cohn and Joe Brandt in New York would be carefully studied and then mailed by the slowest possible route to California for payment. The same system applied to bills received in California. These were also carefully studied and then sent through to the East.

Luckily for the young company the mail was slow. While demands for the expenses incurred by their most recent two reeler were winging their way back and forth across the States, the money for settling the accounts was being plunged into a new film. By the time that was released there was enough money in the kitty to pay the bills. And, of course, by then yet another two-reeler was on the way to completion. Then another and another.

Eventually, in 1922, CBC had scraped together enough to make its first feature. A schmaltzy six-reel melodrama entitled *More To Be Pitied Than Scorned* it cost twenty thousand dollars. It recouped six times that amount. CBC, shortly to be Columbia, was on its way.

With stars borrowed from other studios, either young hopefuls or has-beens discarded by the majors, Columbia increased its output of features to ten then twenty then thirty a year. ''We get'em on the way up or we get'em on the way down,'' said Cohn about the stars he used. It was a clever way to do business. He knew they were always available. In the mid and late twenties the supply of eager beavers and former stars was never ending. Cohn could literally take his pick.

Cohn, in fact, never had much truck with actors. ''After a while the stars believe in their own publicity,'' he grumbled. ''I've never met a grateful performer in the film business.''

On one occasion he stated categorically, ''We believe here at Columbia that writers are more important than either stars or directors, because the story is the foundation of the film. A weak story with the greatest cast ever assembled cannot produce a great film.''

Not that Cohn's stars were always over-fond of their crude talking boss. Glenn Ford once said of him, ''He could be cruel, kind, giving, taking, despicable, benevolent, compassionate and malevolent all at the same time.''

Cohn's strongest attribute was his regard for writing talent. In the twenties, when he was still finding his feet, he would hand his producers a list of thirty titles and say, ''Find me stories to go with these titles.''

Nothing so basic was adopted in the thirties. By then he had screenwriters like Robert Riskin, Jo Swerling, Sidney Buchman,

Norman Krasna, Charles MacArthur and Ben Hecht on the payroll. ''I kiss the feet of talent,'' he used to say, or, as Hollywood pundits preferred to paraphrase, ''If you've got talent I'll kiss your ass; if you haven't got talent I'll kick it.''

Columbia's writers needed more than talent. They needed a thick skin. A favourite trick of their semi-illiterate boss was to give a newcomer a couple of weeks at the studio and then demand to see what he had written. As the writer nervously forwarded the sixty or seventy completed pages Cohn would rant and rave and decry the work in the most obscene terms.

The writer had two alternatives. He could either agree and say that the work was indeed below par or he could fight back and say, ''What the hell do you mean? This stuff's good, it's some of the best I've written.'' If he adopted the first he was generally on the way out of the studio within a few weeks. If he stuck to the second he was in. Harry Cohn liked a fighter.

Ben Hecht had a favourite name for him, 'White Fang', a name one luckless writer would undoubtedly have agreed with when Cohn called him into his office one day and ranted about a screenplay he had been drafting for an Arabian Nights fantasy.

Cohn stared at the script then looked up at the scriptwriter. ''How far did you get in college?''

''I graduated Mr. Cohn.''

''Uh-huh and when do you figure this movie takes place?''

''1200 A.D.''

Cohn leaned back in his black swivel chair and waited a few seconds. He had him. These educated sons-of-bitches knew next to nothing. What the hell was he paying them thousands of dollars for?

He pointed his finger at the open page. ''If it takes place in 1200 A.D. how come the characters are all saying 'Yes, siree'? It's all through the goddam manuscript.'' He flicked the pages. ''Here, here. . .everywhere in the lousy goddam script. You've got everyone saying 'Yes, siree'.''

A producer, called in with the writer, tentatively asked if he might glance at the script. Cohn, his eyes glowering, shoved it towards him.

''But Harry,'' said the producer softly. ''That's 'Yes, *sire*'!''

Cohn's vulgar, bad-mannered ways did not bother director Frank Capra. Strangely enough they frequently stimulated him. The partnership between the two men in the thirties was one of the strangest in the history of Hollywood — a loud-mouthed, cursing bully and a talented young artist, who quickly proved himself to be one of the most formidable talents in American cinema.

Usually, a partnership between studio power and creative artistry spelt disaster. Not at Columbia. For the most part Cohn and Capra got along famously. Capra brought success and prestige to the studio. Cohn gave him artistic control and never interfered with his work.

Another important factor in the relationship was that Capra's films dealt with subjects that Cohn could readily associate with. Capra's pictures were mostly about the average Joe, the ordinary guy caught up in the horrors of the Depression and Cohn knew all about the hard times from his youth.

Capra caught the mood of the thirties more accurately than any other director. He delved into the heart and mind of the average man and brought a kind of hope with his stories.

A typical Frank Capra-Robert Riskin villain might be an unscrupulous banker, a Wall Street gambler or a corrupt politician, but a Capra-Riskin hero was always the same — honest, idealistic, frequently down, but never out. He might not be sure of where his next meal was coming from, but he never gave up.

Capra's films brought the message that if people believed in each other and joined in a common fight against injustice everything would eventually come right. The honesty of the individual was always stressed.

Time and time again the theme was repeated in his films. In *American Madness* it is the bank directors who are the villains of the piece and bank president Walter Huston who is the hero. He's on the side of right, because he judges people by their characters. It's what is in their hearts that counts not what is in their wallets. On that basis he grants loans much to the disapproval of his board of directors. When, eventually, there's a run on the bank and he's in trouble the people come to his aid.

In *Mr. Deeds Goes To Town* Gary Cooper gives away his inherited twenty million dollar fortune to dispossessed farmers because he finds that the people who have been advising him are a bunch of crooks. Again, in *Mr. Smith Goes To Washington*, James Stewart is the honest young politician who successfully defeats corruption in the senate.

Capra's idealism was put across with such skill and imagination that by the time the thirties came to an end he had won three Academy Awards (*It Happened One Night, Mr. Deeds Goes To Town, You Can't Take It With You*), turned Columbia into a major studio and become one of the most respected names in Hollywood.

Yet, to all intents and purposes, his time had passed. The Depression was his period. He flourished with it. In seven years he made a series of films that only a handful of directors have equalled for quality. But when he left Columbia in 1940 after Jack, not Harry, Cohn had refused to sanction his Technicolor life of Chopin, his great days were over. His postwar *It's A Wonderful Life* (made at RKO) was as good if not better than any of his Columbia efforts but by then the box-office appeal was no longer there. Capra, brilliant as he was, was sadly a man of his time.

Harry Cohn without Capra was like a man without his right arm. Capra had been a permanent fixture at Columbia as the studio basked in glory during the thirties. Now he was gone and Hollywood was beginning to ask, 'Would the studio sink without him?'

Harry Cohn, however, had learned a thing or two during the Capra regime. He had learned for instance that his studio had come to be regarded as one of the leaders in the field of sophisticated comedy and realised that, just because Capra had departed, there was no reason for him to abandon the *genre*. He still had a fine staff of writers. There were other directors. Why not pursue it further? Contemporary comedies were relatively cheap to produce, needed little that was lavish in the way of sets or costumes and, best of all, made money.

Cohn was quick to find new comedy directors. Howard Hawks and George Stevens contributed a classic trio, *His Girl Friday, The Talk Of The Town* and *The More The Merrier*, and stars Rosalind Russell, Cary Grant, Irene Dunne, Jean Arthur and Melvyn Douglas provided the ultimate in sophistication, something one wouldn't have believed possible in a studio run by a man as crude as Harry Cohn.

The Columbia comedies were never remotely vulgar. They were clean, fast, witty. If Cohn saw an offending word in a script he ordered it out. If he heard a word he didn't understand that went too. "If I don't understand it, no-one will," he used to say.

Off-screen, however, his personal morals and behaviour were as questionable as ever. He continued to delight in humiliating his employees; he had sound stages wired so he could listen to private conversations and he frequently used his powerful position to satisfy his formidable sexual appetite by having a secret corridor run from his office to a dressing room specially reserved for selected contract starlets.

At one Christmas party he put a secretary in his swivel chair, whirled her round and invited her to point at anyone in the room. As his Christmas present to her he promised he would fire the person she selected.

His language so infuriated one of his directors, Charles Vidor, that Vidor actually took him to court in an attempt to break his 2,500 dollar a week contract. Vidor charged that Cohn had used vile and obscene language and insulted and humiliated him to such a degree that he became ill and had to consult a doctor.

The judge, who didn't have to work for Cohn, found for Columbia. ''Such language,'' he said, ''was part of Mr. Cohn's speaking vocabulary, used by him as superlative adjectives, and not intended by him as insulting. Mr. Vidor knew the kind of language he and others in the employ of the defendant would have to encounter.''

Charles Vidor had to serve out his contract.

Writer Herman J. Mankiewicz was somewhat luckier. He was in attendance when Cohn informed a group of writers and producers that just the night before he had seen one of the lousiest films of his life. A producer, hesitant at first, took the plunge and stuttered that when he'd seen the picture the audience had simply howled with laughter and had seemed to be enjoying it.

Cohn had seen it alone in his personal viewing theatre. ''Listen,'' he said. ''When I'm alone in a projection room I have a foolproof device for judging whether a picture is good or bad. If my fanny squirms, it's bad. If my fanny doesn't squirm, it's good. It's as simple as that.''

Mankiewicz immediately quipped, ''Imagine — the whole world wired to Harry Cohn's ass.'' Mankiewicz had long wanted to get away from Columbia. After that remark he got his wish.

Comedy remained the strongest part of the Columbia line-up throughout the forties and into the fifties when the gloriously dizzy Judy Holliday and Jack Lemmon and directors George Cukor and Richard Quine carried on the tradition.

But as comedy continued to reap dividends for the studio another entertainment form began to emerge — the musical.

The reason for its emergence can be summed up in two words. Rita Hayworth. Cohn had been so busy filling the comedy gap left by Capra that he had failed to notice the sudden blossoming of one of his contract stars, Rita Hayworth (formerly Rita Cansino), who had been on the Columbia books since 1937.

Columbia had never been a studio of big glamour stars. The women in Columbia pictures had always been attractive, but essentially intelligent actresses, women like Barbara Stanwyck, Jean Arthur, Rosalind Russell. Now that he had a glamour star on his hands Cohn was suddenly nonplussed. He didn't know what to do with her. He could see Rita's potential, but he didn't have any suitable vehicles. While he searched around for scripts he did the only sensible thing. He loaned her to other studios, to Warners for *The Strawberry Blonde* and to Fox for *Blood And Sand*. Critics and public alike sat up and took notice.

If any doubts were still lingering in Harry Cohn's mind about Rita Hayworth they were quickly dispelled when 'Life' magazine had her photographed sprawled on a double bed, wearing only a black lace and satin negligee. Her hair was russet, shoulder length, her legs long, her smile warm and beckoning. The caption underneath the photograph read: 'The Goddess Of Love Of The 20th Century.'

Cohn needed no more convincing and set in motion a series of musicals that were to turn Rita into a star of the first magnitude and one of the most popular pin-ups of World War II. The way she danced was flamboyant, sexual, tantalising. Tossing back her hair with a nonchalant flick of the head she attacked a number with a zeal and exuberance that set the pulse racing.

Cohn astutely cast her with Fred Astaire in her first two musicals, *You'll Never Get Rich* and *You Were Never Lovelier.*

Rita matched the master step for step, especially in the latter movie when they performed 'I'm Old Fashioned' and the zippy 'The Shorty George'. The only thing missing was Technicolor.

That arrived with the next big one, *Cover Girl*, in which she danced with yet another musical genius Gene Kelly, then at the start of his career, and *Tonight And Every Night* in which she co-starred with Janet Blair in a story about an English revue that kept on running throughout the blitz.

Her most famous film, the torrid *Gilda*, was not a musical, but contained the most famous dance Rita ever performed on the screen, 'Put The Blame On Mame Boys'. It caused a sensation. Performed in a South American casino, it was as exciting as a strip-tease, yet there was no way it could be censored for all Rita removed was a glove. Every movement, every gesture caused a sharp intake of breath and raised a vital question among audiences. Would the shimmering black evening gown she was wearing hold up under the strain? It did of course, but it mattered little. For a few minutes in *Gilda* the screen became white hot.

The impact of the film was such that the atomic bomb tested at Bikini atoll after the war was named *Gilda* and had Rita's profile painted on the side. A dubious privilege perhaps, but adequate proof of her explosive qualities.

Rita's personal life was always headlines. Her five marriages included two of the most famous in the history of show business — to Orson Welles in 1943 (they were divorced in 1947) and to Aly Khan in May 1949. The marriage to Welles was nicknamed 'Beauty And The Brain'. When they divorced Rita was quoted as saying, "I just couldn't take his genius anymore."

She settled instead for a prince. "It will be a quiet wedding," Aly had promised. In fact there were eighty guests (plus two hundred guards to keep out intruders) six hundred bottles of champagne, fifty pounds of caviar, forty lobsters, a hundred gallons of eau de cologne to scent the swimming pool in the grounds.

Rita's wedding present? An Alfa Romeo car. Said Rita, "I can hardly think. I'm sort of lost in a dream world."

Just sixteen months later that dream world ended. She left Europe and returned to America. The reason? A divorce.

"An American girl and a man with a European background cannot live happily together," she explained. "I have concluded that a happy and contented home, which I earnestly desire for my children and myself, is unobtainable without a divorce. Various factors, including my husband's extensive social obligations and far-flung interests, unfortunately make it impossible to establish or maintain the sort of home I want, and my children need."

It had always been that way with Rita. Before Welles there had been another marriage. After Aly Khan there were two more, including a two year fling with Dick Haymes.

Unfortunately, the marriage to Aly ruined her career. It came when she was still at the top. In 1949 when she was thirty she was at the peak of her powers. By the time she returned in 1952 the box-office magic had all but disappeared. She was still a major star, but no longer one who exerted a considerable pull over the paying customers.

Harry Cohn put her into new vehicles that were no more than routine — *Affair In Trinidad, Miss Sadie Thompson, Salome*. It wasn't a deliberate policy. The movies weren't cheap. They just turned out that way. Cohn still believed in her right up until a year before his death when he cast her in *Pal Joey*, but even he realised that Rita's great days were over when she shared scenes with Kim Novak, the new Columbia sex symbol of the fifties.

"I never really thought of myself as a sex symbol," said Rita later. "I felt I was more a comedienne who could dance."

"I've always believed that if you want something badly enough you should go all out for it, no matter what the odds. That's the way I've lived. Professionally, I went out for what I wanted and it worked. Personally, I would have played the hand that way over again. I didn't want five husbands, but it happened that way — and that's all there is to it."

More revealing perhaps is a personal statement she once made. "Every man I knew had fallen in love with Gilda and wakened with me."

The fifties proved to be the last decade for Harry Cohn. It was one of the studio's greatest periods. The double line box-office attack through the musical and comedy *genres* continued with films like *Born Yesterday, The Marrying Kind, The Solid Gold Cadillac* (all with Judy Holliday) and *My Sister Eileen, The Eddy Duchin Story* and *Pal Joey*. But this time it was augmented by films of a more serious nature.

The political *All The King's Men* for instance which won the 1949 best picture Oscar; the seamy, all-star war drama *From Here To Eternity*, another Oscar winner; and *On The Waterfront*, a controversial subject about racketeering in the New York docks which director Elia Kazan and writer Budd Schulberg hawked unsuccessfully around every Hollywood studio until Cohn agreed to finance the project. The result? Eight more Oscars to go alongside those won by *From Here To Eternity*.

It really was like old times on Gower Street, now completely swallowed up by the huge Columbia studio. Oscars whichever way you turned. Box-office hits in all directions. Only one thing was missing. Capra. The director's return to the lot would have made things complete for Cohn. But it was not to be. Capra was working only sporadically and his films were having difficulty in finding audiences.

When Cohn died suddenly from a heart attack in 1958 Columbia were on the crest of a wave. David Lean's anti-war *The Bridge On The River Kwai* was cleaning up at the box-office and on the way to becoming the biggest financial hit in the studio's history. It was also on the way to seven Academy Awards, due to be presented in the spring of 1958. It was an Oscar ceremony Harry Cohn never attended. He died in the February and Columbia seemed to sag under the loss.

When the news of his death came through people were stunned. The man had seemed indestructible. Harry Cohn dead! John Ford, who was working on *The Last Hurrah* at the studio, closed his set for the day, something which had never before been done at Columbia. Secretaries wept, executives walked the corridors of the studio in a daze. The famous swivel chair remained still in Cohn's office.

It seemed as though a great and popular star had died, not a ruthless ogre. But suddenly, it seemed, everyone liked Harry Cohn. The tributes poured in from every quarter. Most people — writers, directors, stars — admitted he was a bastard, but then added, a little coyly, that, even allowing for the never-ending obscenities, they had also rather enjoyed his company.

Director Robert Aldrich, who made a Joan Crawford vehicle for Columbia just prior to Cohn's death, was one of many who had bitter rows with the studio head. One day he was waiting in a car outside the Columbia front office when Harry Cohn called down to him from a window. ''Hi, Bob. Come up and have a drink.''

Aldrich who was then not on speaking terms with the Columbia chief ignored him and Cohn withdrew. A week later he was dead.

''It was childish of me,'' says Aldrich. ''All the guy wanted was to make friends. I should have gone. It was not only childish, it was stupid. If I regret one thing in my career it was not going to have a last drink with Harry Cohn.''

Cohn supposedly formed the basis of many screen characters, Willie Stark in *All The King's Men*, the tough junk tycoon in *Born Yesterday* and the movie mogul in Clifford Odet's *The Big Knife* (directed by Aldrich) to name but three. Yet the two former movies were both produced at Columbia and Odets wrote the eulogy for Cohn's funeral.

Two thousand people turned out for the event, crowding onto stages 12 and 14 (no stage 13 exists at Columbia) of the studio. It was all strictly against Cohn's wishes. He had wanted it quiet. No fuss. Red Skelton, when seeing the size of the crowd, quipped, ''Well, it only proves what they always say — give the public what they want to see, and they'll come out for it.''

Bad taste. Yes, unquestionably, but a joke that Harry Cohn himself would have enjoyed.

Since Cohn's death great movies have continued to be made at Columbia. The studio's list of classic films is equal to that of any other company. A random sample proves the point: *Anatomy Of A Murder, Lawrence Of Arabia, Doctor Strangelove, Cat Ballou, A Man For All Seasons, Funny Girl, Oliver!, Guess Who's Coming To Dinner, The Way We Were, Shampoo, Taxi Driver, Close Encounters Of The Third Kind.*

But what of the definitive Columbia film? Is there such a movie and, if so, is it a Capra depression tale, a sophisticated comedy, a Rita Hayworth musical or one of those highly professional, inexpensive melodramas like *Gilda* or Rossen's *Johnny O'Clock* or Fritz Lang's *The Big Heat*?

It is difficult to arrive at a completely satisfactory answer. During Harry Cohn's reign, Columbia was always something of an enigma. It was a studio of comedy, yes, but the Riskin scripts for Frank Capra made audiences think as well as laugh. It was the studio of Rita Hayworth and musicals and yet *Gilda* provided more malevolent undercurrents than a dozen more ambitious melodramas from other studios. Directors Kazan, Zinnemann, Lang, Brooks, all brought craftsmanship, but also they generated controversy and excitement.

It is perhaps appropriate that even the Columbia lady remains an enigma. No-one knows who she is. There have always been rumours, but none has ever been proved.

For some years it was thought she was Evelyn Venable, the attractive wife of cameraman Hal Mohr, but she strongly denied the claim. Other candidates have included a beautiful girl named Lesley Beth Storey, a B movie actress Claudia Dell and an unknown extra who was supposedly photographed as Miss Columbia sometime in 1933.

Helen Hunt, who was in charge of Columbia's hairdressing department for many years, remembers the latter girl quite clearly, but cannot remember her name.

Harry Cohn had Miss Hunt summoned to his office and introduced her to a dress extra, a tall girl with beautiful long auburn hair and a statuesque figure. In dressing the girl's hair Miss Hunt wound a braid around her head to form a crown and added a Grecian wreath of leaves. The current Miss Columbia's hair, however, is not dressed in this fashion.

One Columbia executive remembered that the emblem had been reshot after 1933, but couldn't recall the year or the name of the girl who posed. He did remember that Rita Hayworth posed for it once as a gimmick for use at a sales convention.

More recently, a Chicago woman named Jane Chester claimed the honour. Aged sixteen, she had journeyed from Washington to Hollywood in 1936 hoping to break into movies. She lived in a rooming house for more than a year. Nearby was Columbia Pictures. Like other young hopefuls she made the rounds. When she had almost given up she was asked, along with a group of other girls, to pose as the Statue Of Liberty for what was to be Columbia's screen trademark. "No one really knew if the picture would be used," she said. "We weren't paid but we hoped it would lead to something."

It didn't. Jane moved to Chicago, married and settled down. Two years later she was in a movie theatre and suddenly her picture flashed up on the screen.

True? False? Imagination? Who knows. The mystery of the Columbia lady remains.

Today, she appears only briefly, the camera zooming into her torch and dissolving into a flat, spiked half-circle. If current plans are carried through she will eventually disappear from the screen altogether.

And that will be a pity. She's heralded more "f...... good, goddam son-of-a-bitch movies" than any other lady in movie history!

Director Otto Preminger (right) and James Stewart (centre) discussing a sequence from the courtroom drama *Anatomy Of A Murder*.

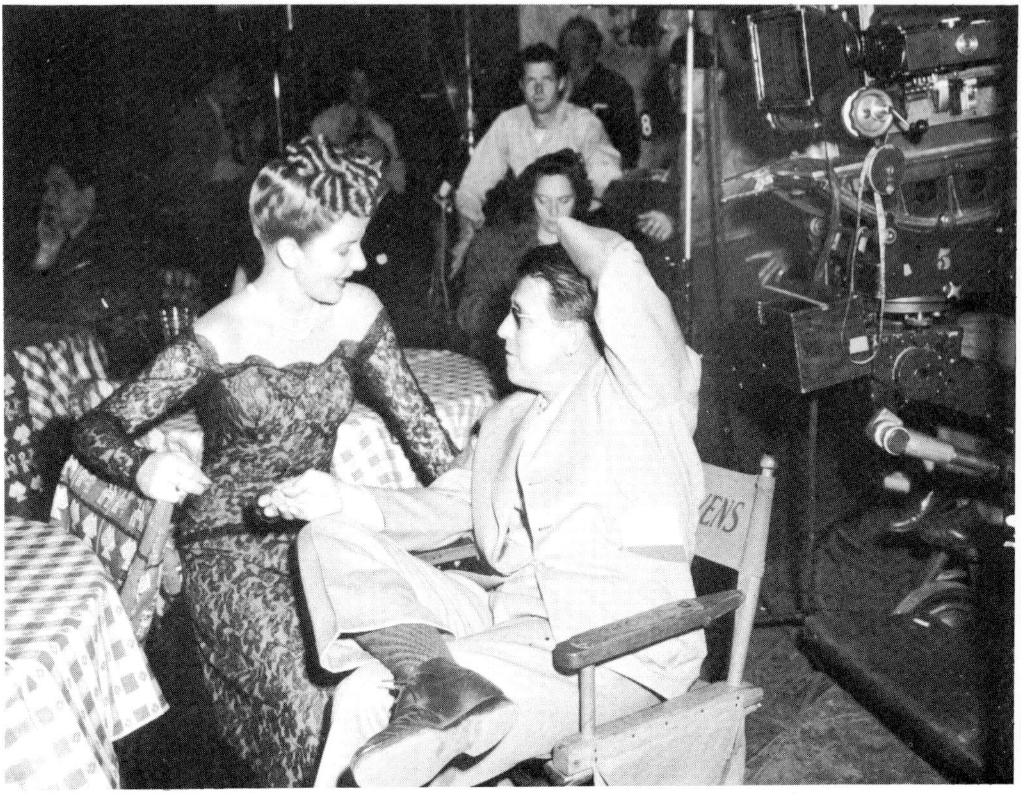

A rare still of director George Stevens caught in an off set moment with his star Jean Arthur during the making of *The More The Merrier*.

Ralph Bellamy, Cary Grant and Rosalind Russell in Howard Hawks' classic newspaper comedy *His Girl Friday*.

Together for the last time. Spencer Tracy and Katharine Hepburn between takes of their final movie together, *Guess Who's Coming To Dinner?*

The most famous beach scene in movie history. Burt Lancaster and Deborah Kerr discover a few home truths in *From Here To Eternity*.

Lee Marvin in his Oscar-winning role of the drunken gunfighter Kid Shelleen in *Cat Ballou*.

Beautiful Elizabeth Taylor, bait for the beach boys in Tennessee Williams' *Suddenly, Last Summer*.

Barbra Streisand, repeating her role as Fanny Brice, in a top production number from *Funny Lady*.

Teenage-hooker Jodie Foster and Robert DeNiro in *Taxi Driver*.

Chronology

1924 Columbia Pictures is officially formed on January 10 after a four year prelude as the CBC Company – run by former song-plugger Harry Cohn, his brother Jack and Joe Brandt, both of whom were Universal employees until the formation of CBC in 1920.

CBC, run on a shoestring with very little capital, is named after the initials of its three founders. It operates on Poverty Row, the poorest quarter of the Hollywood scene, and becomes known throughout the industry as 'Corned Beef And Cabbage'. Its initial productions are two-reelers, among them *Screen Snapshots*, a series of fan magazine shorts dealing with the off-screen lives of film stars and *The Hall Room Boys*, a comedy series based on a comic strip and vaudeville routine.

After two years of steady growth CBC produces its first feature, *More To Be Pitied Than Scorned*, a schmaltzy melodrama starring J. Frank Glendon and Rosemary Theby. A six-reeler, it is produced for 20,000 dollars and brings in 130,000.

By 1924, the company, now Columbia, at last rids itself of its derogatory nickname and releases ten cheap, but respectable pictures.

But Elaine Hammerstein is Columbia's busiest star. In *The Foolish Virgin* she is rescued by Robert Frazer from a forest fire; in *One Glorious Night*, which is just about all she gets, as she is left to suffer in poverty and anguish after marrying the wrong man; and in the railway adventure *The Midnight Express* she's an engineer's daughter.

Columbia's advertising technique for the latter reveals their growing confidence and ability to shrug off the fact that they still operate on Poverty Row.

A 100% Picture
Loudly Proclaimed By The Critics
THE MIDNIGHT EXPRESS
The Story Of A Railroad Man
Who Would Not Be Sidetracked
Featuring
Elaine Hammerstein And An All-Star Cast

1925 A year of consolidation and marking time for Columbia. They're waiting for the big breaks which, through a combination of luck and foresight, are soon to come.

Jack Cohn and Joe Brandt run the business side of things from New York, Harry Cohn operates on the West Coast from a tiny Poverty Row studio (owned by Morris Schlank) between Gower Street and Beachwood Drive.

Adventure, comedy, sex and romance make up the Columbia bill. William Fairbanks, Dorothy Revier, Elaine Hammerstein, William Haines and Cullen Landis are the leading stars; Mal St. Clair, Erle C. Kenton and Reeves Eason the main directors.

The adventure stories spread to the wilds of Canada (*The Lure Of The Wild*) and the arctic (*Justice Of The Far North*); the comedies include an early William Wellman picture, *When Husband's Flirt*, a piece of domestic nonsense starring Dorothy Revier, Forrest Stanley and Tom Ricketts. Said Wellman, "I made the picture for Harry Cohn in three-and-a-half days and nights. We stole long shots from various pictures that he'd made and put our scenes in between them to make the picture look big. It was a wonderful story."

1926 Columbia offers shares to the public on the stock market and purchases its own studio, a small plot on Gower Street which includes two stages and an office building. Although still based on Poverty Row (the studio is to remain there for the rest of its existence, swallowing up offices and property over the years) the company no longer rents studio space. It owns it.

Columbia's few regulars, Elaine Hammerstein (*Ladies Of Leisure*), Dorothy Revier (*The Better Way, When The Wife's Away*) and William Haines (*The Thrill Hunter*) all appear again. New stars to the scene include Dorothy Phillips, a self-sacrificing nurse in love with a blinded war veteran in *Remember*; Betty Compson and Herbert Rawlinson who team in the theatre romance *The Belle Of Broadway*; and Bert Lytell who stars as Louis Joseph Vance's international thief in *The Lone Wolf Returns*.

1927 An historic year, not because any major features are produced but because Frank Capra, a comedy gag man/director working for Mack Sennet joins Harry Cohn's staff. He arrives because his name is at the head of an alphabetical list of unemployed directors. It's how Cohn picks the man who is soon to make the name of Columbia famous throughout Hollywood.

When introduced to Harry Cohn for the first time Capra can't get a word in edgeways. Cohn is on the telephone. Says Cohn to executive Sam Briskin: "For Chrissake Sam, will you get your ass outta here. I'm busy. Put him to work!"

The studio's big breakthrough of the year is *The Blood Ship*, a tough seven-reel sea drama which becomes the first Columbia movie to premiere at the Roxy in New York, the largest movie house in the States. Shot mostly at sea on a rented three-masted schooner, it stars Hobart Bosworth, Jacqueline Logan and Richard Arlen and is directed by George B. Seitz.

Jack Holt appears on the Columbia scene and stars twice with the studio's most popular woman star Dorothy Revier – in the gypsy adventure *The Tigress* in which Miss Revier performs the ritual 'Dance Of Death' and *The Warning* in which both are secret agents tracking down opium smugglers in Shanghai.

Miss Revier is also a trapeze artist in *The Clown*; Bert Lytell returns in *Alias The Lone Wolf*; the regular directors include Walter Lang, George Seitz, Robert Florey and Byron Haskin.

1928 Frank Capra delivers for the studio – seven times!

His first film is the quickie *That Certain Thing* about a young couple who make such a success of a box lunch business that they force the boy's restaurant-owning father to accept their marriage. Written, shot and edited in six weeks, it costs 20,000 dollars and stars Ralph Graves and Viola Dana.

In quick succession follow the comedies *So This Is Love* and *The Matinee Idol*; *The Way Of The Strong* with Mitchell Lewis, Alice Day and Margaret Livingston; *Say It With Sables* with Helen Chadwick and Francis X. Bushman; *The Power Of The Press* in which cub reporter Douglas Fairbanks Jr. covers the murder of a district attorney in the midst of a political campaign; and the action drama *Submarine*.

Capra takes over *Submarine* from Irvin Willat, an expert on sea movies, because Harry Cohn is dissatisfied with the early reels and asks Capra to complete the film. Capra agrees providing he can reshoot the whole picture. Budgeted at 250,000 dollars it proves to be Columbia's biggest moneymaker to date.

Billed as 'A Mighty Drama Of The Sea' it is also Columbia's first picture with sound, Capra showing his immediate mastery of the new process by emphasising the tap tap tapping of those trapped inside a submerged submarine.

Delighted with his protégé, Harry Cohn tears up Capra's one year, 500 dollars a week contract and offers a new one for three years at 1500 a week. Capra accepts.

Jack Holt, as well as making a spectacular rescue dive in *Submarine*, also finds himself up against Betty Compson's outlaw Belle Starr in the Civil War western *Court-Martial*. But it is the women who have most fun. Miss Compson is captured by Arabs in *The Desert Bride*; Estelle Taylor is the society crook *Lady Raffles*; Lois Wilson is involved with the chinese underworld in *Ransom*; and in *Sinner's Parade* Dorothy Revier leads a double life — schoolteacher by day and a cabaret dancer by night.

Says Harry Cohn about the healthy growth of Columbia: "We are growing at Columbia because we haven't put up a false front. We haven't wasted much and are able to progress because we have been able to correct most of our mistakes early in the game and make the kind of pictures our returns prove theatre men want. Just plain common sense, determination and concentration — that's the Columbia motto. . ."

1929 For the next decade Capra's name dominates at Columbia.

In 1929 the director is responsible for three top productions: *The Younger Generation* with Ricardo Cortez as a ruthless, succeed-at-all-costs social climber; *The Donovan Affair*, Columbia's first all-talking picture with Jack Holt as an inspector investigating a murder in a country house; and the first all-talking air drama *Flight*, Columbia's answer to *Wings*. The plot is routine, the stars (Jack Holt, Ralph Graves, Lila Lee) adequate, the flying stunts — shot in the mountains behind San Diego — outstanding.

Barbara Stanwyck, shortly to become a Columbia regular, stars as the scheming *Mexicali Rose*; Bert Lytell returns in *The Lone Wolf's Daughter*; Jack Holt, a wealthy businessman, and Dorothy Revier, a notorious adventuress, are together again in *Father And Son*; Sally O'Neil, Carmel Myers and Jack Egan find themselves in a rare Columbia musical, *Broadway Scandals*.

1930 Capra directs Joe Cook and Louise Fazenda in the Broadway circus musical *Rain Or Shine* (without the music) but his real triumph is turning twenty-three year old Barbara Stanwyck into a major star in *Ladies Of Leisure*. She plays ambitious gold-digger Kay Arnold. The film is dramatic, emotional stuff and well received. Capra is already beginning to glance in the direction of the Oscars — he has success, now he wants status. He is determined to win Hollywood's major award and feels that both he and Stanwyck — and the film — should have been among the year's nominees.

The Columbia of the twenties is still much in evidence as the new decade begins. Jack Holt, in particular, is still very active. In *Hell's Island* he's in the Foreign Legion; in *The Squealer* he's back once more with Dorothy Revier and features as an underworld bootlegger; and in *Vengeance* the two stars are together yet again in the upper reaches of the Congo.

Charles Ruggles is *Charley's Aunt*; Bert Lytell stars in *The Last Of The Lone Wolf*; Richard Cromwell and Noah Beery appear in a remake of Joseph Hergesheimer's piece of Americana *Tol'able David*; the studio start a two-year distribution of Disney's Mickey Mouse cartoons.

1931 The studio gets its first Oscar nomination — for writing achievement. Surprisingly, it's not for a Capra film, but for one directed by Howard Hawks, *The Criminal Code*. The honoured writers are Seton Miller and Fred Niblo Jr. Their story stars Walter Huston as a newly appointed prison warden, a former District Attorney, who is suddenly faced with having to understand his prisoners' way of life, to adapt and learn 'the code of the criminal'.

Capra meanwhile is beginning to find a style. Robert Riskin, the writer with whom he is to be associated in the great days to come, arrives at Columbia and contributes the dialogue to the most memorable Capra film of the year, *Platinum Blonde*. With its story of a newspaper reporter, Robert Williams, who realises that marriage to socialite Jean Harlow and her wealthy family is not worth the loss of his self respect (he settles instead for fellow reporter Loretta Young), the movie is the first Capra picture to explore, albeit tentatively, a social theme within its overall entertainment structure. It's not genuine Capra, but it's getting close.

If nothing else the movie makes a star of Harlow whose

blonde hairstyle catches the imagination of American women. Platinum Blonde Clubs are founded in at least a hundred cities and beauty parlours make sure they stock supplies of bleach. Harlow's dress, make-up and speech are widely copied

Harlow does not remain a Columbia star, however. Within a year she's off to Metro.

Barbara Stanwyck stars as an evangelist in one of Capra's other two movies of the year, *The Miracle Woman*; Jack Holt and Ralph Graves feature in the other, *Dirigible*, an exciting airship adventure which climaxes with a scientific mission to the Arctic.

Capra tries for realism in the Arctic scenes. He persuades the actors to keep dry ice in their mouths so that their breath will show on the screen. The experiment costs ageing actor Hobart Bosworth three teeth and part of his jawbone!

1932 A power struggle within the company results in Harry Cohn assuming the Columbia presidency, Jack becoming vice president and treasurer and Joe Brandt leaving the company altogether. Harry, despite a bid by his brother to remove him from the West Coast, is now the unquestioned boss and remains so until his death.

Meanwhile, throughout all the turmoil, Capra at last reveals what he's all about. In *American Madness* he looks at the Depression in a realistic drama about a bank president (Walter Huston) whose policy of making loans purely on the collateral of good character is severely tested by robbery, scurrilous rumour and a run on the bank. He is saved by the same 'ordinary people' he has trusted, who come to help him in whatever way they can.

It's the Capra theme revealed for the first time. The honesty of the little guy and the goodness of the people versus corruption and authoritarianism in a world staggering under the effects of economic collapse. Believe in and help each other and things will come right in the end.

For many it's all a little too naïve, but it's not a bad philosophy at the time, especially when Roosevelt himself remarks in a famous speech: "The only thing we have to fear is fear itself."

Capra's other '32 contribution is *Forbidden*, a 'Back Street type' soap opera about a spinsterish librarian, Barbara Stanwyck, in love with married Adolphe Menjou.

1933 Capra's *The Bitter Tea Of General Yen* is the first movie to play at the new 6,000 seat Radio City Music Hall, the largest indoor theatre in the world. The Hall's statistics include a 70 ft screen, a stage 144 ft wide and, in the auditorium, an immense proscenium arch, 60 ft in height.

It's a great honour for Columbia, but the film proves to be one of Capra's rare commercial flops, possibly because its Oriental theme – powerful Chinese warlord, Nils Asther, falls in love with American missionary, Barbara Stanwyck – is too much of a departure from *Platinum Blonde* and *American Madness*.

With *Lady For A Day*, however, Capra's on much surer ground. Based on Damon Runyon's story 'Madame La Gimp' it concerns an old apple seller who is helped by good-hearted racketeers to become a society matron in order to impress her daughter (educated in a Spanish convent) and her prospective aristocratic in-laws.

May Robson is Apple Annie and Warren William the leading racketeer Dave The Dude. Capra feels that the Oscar is at last within reach. The picture is nominated for four of the top Academy Awards – best film, direction, actress and writing. It's the first time Columbia's been up for the big awards. Cohn, a gambler, is taking large bets that they'll win.

But, on the night, the batting average is zero. Capra has the humiliation of actually walking towards the rostrum when Will Rogers opens the envelope and cries "Come Up And Get It Frank". The winner is not Capra, but Frank Lloyd for *Cavalcade*. According to Capra the walk back was "the longest, saddest, most shattering walk in my life".

Director Frank Borzage makes a brief visit to Gower Street for *A Man's Castle*, a Depression story about two down-and-outs (Spencer Tracy and Loretta Young) living in a shanty town on the outskirts of New York; Lois Wilson is an impoverished widow in *Obey The Law*; and Nancy Carroll and John Boles star in the Preston Sturges authored comedy *Child Of Manhattan*.

1934 The disappointments of the year before are forgotten as the Capra comedy *It Happened One Night* sweeps the board with all five top Academy Awards – best film, direction, actor, actress, screenplay. No other studio has achieved a clean sweep before. It is a record that stands for more than forty years. For Capra in particular it is a triumph. He has reached his objective and been acknowledged by his peers.

The parting of the ways comes when Capra selects as his next subject *The Life Of Chopin.* He asks to make it in colour. Jack Cohn hits the roof. Harry tries to play the whole thing down, but this time Capra goes and, for the first time since 1928, Columbia is without the greatest director who has ever worked — or will ever work — on its sound stages.

Columbia are just lucky that they have two other top directors working for them in '39, Howard Hawks and Rouben Mamoulian.

Hawks' contribution is *Only Angels Have Wings*, a typically Hawksian tale of a second-rate airline based somewhere near the Andes. A pilot and his companions, one guilt-ridden because of cowardice, the other afraid of failing eyesight, lead dangerous lives complicated by two women, bad weather and death. Cary Grant, Jean Arthur and Richard Barthelmess star, although it is Rita Hayworth, as the wife of shattered pilot Barthelmess, who really catches the eye in her first big feature.

Cary Grant later regrets he never teamed with Rita when she was a big star. "I'd liked to have made one of those big splashy Technicolor musicals. The idea isn't as ridiculous as it sounds. After all, I started out on stage, singing and dancing. Who knows, we might have ended up as the Fred Astaire and Ginger Rogers of Columbia."

Mamoulian's entry is *Golden Boy*, Clifford Odets' drama of a young violinist who finds fame and fortune in a very different walk of life, the boxing ring. The film immediately makes William Holden a star.

Cohn interviews sixty-five actors for the key role in a movie which also features Barbara Stanwyck, Adolphe Menjou and Lee J. Cobb. Holden's interview goes something like this:

Cohn: "Can you act?"
Holden: "I'm not sure."
Cohn: "Can you box?"
Holden: "No."
Cohn: "Can you play the violin?"
Holden: "No."
Cohn: "Then what the hell are you doing here?"
Holden: "I'm here because you sent for me."

1940 Capra may have gone, but Cohn and Columbia keep faith with comedy.

Howard Hawks' *His Girl Friday* is a classic, a reworking

of Milestone's dramatic *The Front Page* about a group of reporters waiting to witness an execution. Hawks transforms it into the fastest comedy on record with dialogue that spits out at machine gun pace. He also changes the leading character into a woman reporter (Rosalind Russell), just divorced from editor Cary Grant and on her way to more blissful matrimony with Ralph Bellamy. Luckily, she never leaves the newsroom.

Wesley Ruggles and Alexander Hall are also no slouches on the comedy scene.

Ruggles films Somerset Maugham's *Too Many Husbands* in which Fred MacMurray (thought dead) and Melvyn Douglas, who loyally marries his widow, finish up sharing Jean Arthur; Hall has brain doctor Ray Milland and bachelor girl Loretta Young mistaken for newlyweds in *The Doctor Takes a Wife*; and Miss Young sheltering on-the-run communist Melvyn Douglas in her Paris apartment in *He Stayed For Breakfast*. "You are always talking about the poor and rich," she complains. "There are only two kinds of people — male and female."

A story of much sharper, often caustic wit, is Ben Hecht's *Angels Over Broadway*. Stylish and highly individual, it takes place in New York between dusk and dawn and revolves around a potential suicide (John Qualen) and his saving at the hands of a drunken playwright (Thomas Mitchell), an unsuccessful dancer (Rita Hayworth) and a crooked gambler (Douglas Fairbanks Jr.).

Nastiest Columbia guy of the year is little Peter Lorre. In *Island Of Doomed Men* he is the sinister master of a Pacific Island and flogs enslaved prisoners while listening to nocturnes by Chopin.

1941 Columbia set their sights on comedy, soap opera, western adventure and the musical. In all fields they succeed.

Top comedy of the year is the fantasy *Here Comes Mr. Jordan* with Robert Montgomery as a boxer who is sent to heaven fifty years ahead of his time because of an error by Messenger 7013 (Edward Everett Horton). Disturbed by the mistake, the celestial powers find him a new body so that he can return to Earth and fight for the championship. Soft-talking Claude Rains is the ever watchful arch-angel Mr. Jordan; writers Harry Segall, Sidney Buchman and Seton Miller win Oscars, the underrated Alexander Hall directs.

Director George Stevens, in the first of three films for Columbia, wins the prize for sentiment. His *Penny Serenade* follows Cary Grant and Irene Dunne as they marry, suffer, adopt and finally lose the child they love. Told in flashback as Miss Dunne listens to old records and remembers their life together, it emerges as an overwhelming wet-eyed experience. It's sentiment with great skill, however. Columbia shows class even in this hackneyed *genre*.

Rita Hayworth, whom Columbia have loaned to Fox for *Blood And Sand*, at last realises her enormous potential and teams her with Fred Astaire in *You'll Never Get Rich*. She proves a more than adequate replacement for Ginger Rogers. Cole Porter's songs include 'So Near And Yet So Far' and 'Dream Dancing'. The only thing missing is Technicolor. The studio still hasn't made a colour movie.

Jean Arthur bakes pies, shoots straight and has big ambitions in the two million dollar western *Arizona*. "I want to own a ranch that'll take two days to cross," she says defiantly. Young William Holden is around to sample the pies and a few other things besides. He's also teamed with Claire Trevor and Glenn Ford in another big Columbia western, *Texas*.

Boston Blackie, a former jewel thief and con-artist turned good guy, debuts in *Meet Boston Blackie*. Chester Morris stars; Peter Lorre is still up to no good. In Robert Florey's *The Face Behind The Mask* he's horribly disfigured in a fire and driven to a life of crime to finance a plastic surgery operation.

1942 For Columbia, comedy and music remain the chief means of escape from World War II.

George Stevens turns to comedy with *The Talk Of The Town*, a picture with more than a hint of Capra in its theme. Cary Grant is a wrongly accused arsonist who hides out in the house of Jean Arthur and tries to convince her tenant, eminent law professor Ronald Colman, that the law should have a human, as well as a legal side.

Full of underlying social and political implications the movie is one of the most intelligent comedies of the 40s. It also has its moments of farce, notably when Miss Arthur slides a fried breakfast egg onto Colman's morning paper in order to hide the face of fugitive Grant.

Alexander Hall is the busiest director on the lot. Fredric March and Loretta Young appear in his *Bedtime Story*,

Joan Crawford and Melvyn Douglas in *They All Kissed The Bride*. His biggest success, however, is the screen version of the Broadway comedy *My Sister Eileen*. Rosalind Russell and Janet Blair star as two sisters from Ohio, one a would-be writer, the other an aspiring stage actress, who have the time of their lives when they get mixed up in the frantic life of Greenwich Village.

Rita Hayworth, now Columbia's major star, dances again with Astaire in *You Were Never Lovelier*. The music is by Jerome Kern, the setting the Argentine, the explosive tantrums by courtesy of Adolphe Menjou.

With her long russet tresses falling seductively over her shoulders Rita proves with this movie that she's as good a dancer as Rogers ever was. The dance duets are breathtaking. 'I'm Old Fashioned' and 'Dearly Beloved' provide the romance, the jive number 'The Shorty George' the verve and snap.

1943 Rita Hayworth marries boy wonder Orson Welles on September 7 in one of the most publicized marriages of the decade. The marriage lasts four years (it ends in November 47) and frequently has its stormy moments.

Rumour has it that on one occasion Rita is awoken at dead of night by her husband and photoflashed by two photographers at her bedside. Orson is quoted as saying that he has done it out of pride — to prove that Rita looks lovely at any hour of the day or night!

Columbia at last opt for Technicolor. Their choice, after waiting eight years since the release of the first three-colour feature, *Becky Sharp*, is nothing more than a routine western. Directed by Charles Vidor, it features Randolph Scott and Glenn Ford as a marshal and reformed renegade who track down an outlaw gang. Its title: *The Desperadoes*.

The war creeps into the studio's line-up. *Destroyer* stars Edward G. Robinson and Glenn Ford; *Sahara* has Humphrey Bogart helping out the allies in the Libyan desert; and *The Commandos Strike At Dawn* features Paul Muni as a Norwegian patriot who leads a resistance movement against the Nazis who have occupied his home town.

The Crime Doctor, a gangster turned psychiatrist who specialises in diseases of the human mind, especially the criminal mind, appears on screen for the first time. Warner Baxter stars in the first two movies of the series, *Crime Doctor* and *Crime Doctor's Strangest Case*.

The top Columbia comedy — and picture — of the

year is George Stevens' *The More The Merrier*. Set against the housing shortage in wartime Washington, it stars Jean Arthur as a government girl who rents half of her four room apartment to retired industrialist Charles Coburn who, in turn, rents half of his half to young aircraft technician Joel McCrea. Chaos inevitably results. Stevens wins the New York Critics director's award, Coburn a supporting Oscar.

1944 Rita Hayworth makes her most famous Columbia musical, *Cover Girl*, directed by Charles Vidor. She's a Brooklyn career girl who rises from obscure singer to cover girl on the Golden Wedding issue of 'Vanity Magazine'. Rita and Gene Kelly provide the on-off romance, wisecracking Eve Arden and Phil Silvers the comedy, Ira Gershwin and Jerome Kern ('Put Me To The Test', 'Long Ago And Far Far Away' and 'Make Way For Tomorrow') the songs. Columbia, convinced at last, provide the Technicolor!

Small town lady mayor Irene Dunne and suave New York artist Charles Boyer come together in the romantic madcap comedy *Together Again* (also directed by Vidor); Ann Miller taps the 'Victory Polka' in *Jam Session*; Edward G. Robinson is a forty-four year old draftee in *Mr. Winkle Goes To War*; Alexander Knox (*None Shall Escape*) and Paul Lukas (*Address Unknown*) are both involved in war-time activities; so too is Pat O'Brien, on an FBI assignment to rout out Nazis in a West Coast shipyard in *Secret Command*.

Attractive Nina Foch sprouts hair and goes around fanging people to death in *Cry Of The Werewolf*, a movie which, somewhere in its sixty-three minutes, includes the line, "What's new at the mortuary?"

1945 "Discontinue that so-called Polonaise jumble you've been playing for days." With a line like that Frank Capra must be pleased he never got round to filming his *Life Of Chopin* for that's where the dialogue comes from. Now entitled *A Song To Remember* it stars Cornel Wilde as Chopin and Merle Oberon (the lady who spits out the offending line) as George Sand.

But with Paul Muni as Chopin's professor, the piano-work of Jose Iturbi and Technicolor — used with startling effect as a dying Chopin coughs blood onto the white keys of his piano — the film is a tremendous hit. Somehow, the music manages to overcome all the banalities.

Technicolor now figures prominently in Columbia movies. Not only does it bathe the romantic goings-on of Rita Hayworth and Janet Blair, two showgirls in a London wartime revue in *Tonight And Every Night*, it also brightens the activities of a musical Aladdin (Cornel Wilde) and his red-headed genie (Evelyn Keyes) in *A Thousand And One Nights*. Comedian Phil Silvers in colour is immaterial, the appearance of ravishing dancing girls is not.

Irene Dunne, Alexander Knox and Charles Coburn star in Ruth Gordon's Broadway comedy *Over 21* (Columbia pay 350,000 for the screen rights); Paul Muni, still at war, is a Russian soldier/interrogator in *Counter Attack*; teenage Shirley Temple bobs up in *Kiss And Tell*; Nina Foch is again in trouble, this time in a classy little B thriller *My Name Is Julia Ross*. She's kidnapped and forced into a new identity by the formidable Dame May Whitty and bow-and-arrow madman George Macready.

1946 A top year for the studio. It produces its biggest ever financial hit, *The Jolson Story* (seven-and-a-half million dollars), and one of the most distinguished 'cult' films of all time, Charles Vidor's *Gilda*.

The Jolson Story follows the life of the great entertainer from boyhood to peak success. Jolson wants to play himself in the movie. The studio insist he's too old. A compromise is reached. Jolson sings the songs, new star Larry Parks acts the role and mimes the tunes. Evelyn Keyes co-stars as his wife.

Oscar nominated Parks becomes a star through his performance, but he's not the first choice for the role. Danny Thomas, a rising young comedian, is first offered the part providing he has an operation to reduce the size of his nose. He refuses!

'There Never Was A Woman Like Gilda' claim the billboards and for once they're right. Rarely has sexuality and malevolence been so brilliantly conveyed on celluloid. The movie is like a ticking time bomb, ready to explode at any minute.

Rita Hayworth stars as torch singer Gilda, Glenn Ford as her ex-lover and George Macready as her new husband, a Buenos Aires casino owner, complete with deadly sword stick, who dreams of world power. Rita's number 'Put The Blame On Mame Boys' rates as one of the sexiest strip-teases in screen history, yet all she takes off is one of her gloves.

Cornel Wilde brings in three million dollars with his performance as the son of Robin Hood in *The Bandit Of Sherwood Forest*; and Glenn Ford is the man who made the first successful American glider flight in Wellman's *Gallant Journey*.

Miss Keyes snaps out one of the studio's best lines of the year in *The Thrill Of Brazil*: "He isn't a man, he's my ex-husband." Even cab-drivers are becoming profound. In the Pat O'Brien-Ruth Warrick mystery *Perilous Holiday*, a Mexican cabbie bemoans: "To die is easy. To live — that is difficult."

1947 That archangel Mr. Jordan makes a return to the screen in *Down To Earth*. This time he's played by Roland Culver and not Claude Rains. Messenger 7013 however is once again played by the fumbling Edward Everett Horton. Their task this time? To send Terpsichore, the Goddess Of Dance', down to earth to help director Larry Parks with his musical play. In view of the fact that Terpsichore is played by Rita Hayworth in glowing Technicolor it's not much of a surprise when she succeeds.

Bogart arrives on the lot to play a World War II veteran trying to solve the murder of his soldier buddy. The movie is *Dead Reckoning*. Slinky Lizabeth Scott is part of the reckoning. She also finishes up dead.

Randolph Scott cleans up a Cinecolored West in Zane Grey's *Gunfighters*; Larry Parks swashbuckles in a Cinecolored Scotland in *The Swordsman*; and *Last Of The Redmen* is a Cinecolor version of James Fenimore Cooper's 'The Last Of The Mohicans'.

What's Cinecolor? A cheap colour process used by Columbia for a few years on their less than notable productions. Its benefits: nil. Its deficiencies: making everyone a glaring bluey-green. It also hurts the eyes.

Neatest Columbia flick of the year: *Johnny O'Clock*, the first directorial venture of former screenwriter Robert Rossen. A small-scale crime melodrama, it stars Dick Powell as a professional gambler. Among those constantly getting in his way: good girl Evelyn Keyes, bad girl Ellen Drew, crooked gambling partner Thomas Gomez and weary cop Lee J. Cobb. Neat, unpretentious, but smartly done.

Grace Moore, star of several operatic Columbia musicals of the thirties dies on January 26 when a Royal Dutch Airplane DC-3 crashes and burns on the runway of Copenhagen's airport. She was forty-five. Her Columbia pictures: *One Night Of Love, Love Me Forever, The King Steps Out, When You're In Love, I'll Take Romance.*

1948 ''Oh my God, what has that bastard done?'' Harry Cohn talking, or more likely roaring, as he discovers that Orson Welles has turned Rita Hayworth into a 'champagne blonde' and cut her trusset hair into a short feather bob. It's for their only film together, *The Lady from Shanghai.*

If the film had been a success it might have been worthwhile. It's not. It's a mess. Welles directs and stars as an Irish sailor who becomes an unsuspecting pawn in a murder plot. Like *Gilda*, though, it becomes a cult film, not least for its bravura climax when *femme fatale* Hayworth and crippled lawyer-husband Everett Sloane shoot each other to bits in a hall of mirrors.

Welles' first line in the film is, ''When I start to make a fool of myself there's very little that can stop me.''

Rita is much more her usual self as Prosper Merimee's Spanish gypsy vamp in *The Loves Of Carmen.* Her Don Jose: *Gilda* co-star Glenn Ford.

Dick Powell is a treasury agent hot on the heels of a gang of international smugglers in *To The Ends Of The Earth*; Johnny Weismuller, having left his Tarzan loincloth at RKO, is now an African white hunter in the first of a new Columbia B series *Jungle Jim*; Robert Young has Barton MacLane, Akim Tamiroff and Mike Mazurki up against him in the Technicolor desert western *Relentless*; Larry Parks swashbuckles in France in *The Gallant Blade.*

The Fuller Brush Man with Red Skelton as a brush salesman who finds himself involved in a murder is Columbia's top box-office hit with a gross of 3.1 million.

1949 Columbia lose their screen goddess Rita Hayworth, not to another studio but to a prince and there's not very much they can do about that. On May 27 Rita marries Prince Aly Khan in France and disappears from the screen for four years.

Compensation comes in the shape of Broderick Crawford, not exactly an ideal replacement for a sex goddess, but the star of the year's Oscar winning film *All The King's Men*, Columbia's first best picture winner for eleven years. Crawford and newcomer Mercedes McCambridge both win awards.

Directed by Robert Rossen from the novel by Robert Penn Warren, it charts the career of an idealistic backwater politician, Willie Stark, who rises swiftly to become governor of his State, but is then corrupted by power and destroyed at the hands of an assassin. Based closely on the real-life career of Huey 'Kingfish' Long, the film emerges as one of the most damning indictments of political corruption ever put on the screen.

If politics take the honours, music makes the money. Columbia bring out a sequel to their '46 Jolson hit entitled *Jolson Sings Again*. The same mixture and stars as before ensure a take of five million dollars. But just a year later, the star who appeared in the first ever talking picture, *The Jazz Singer*, is to die suddenly of a heart attack.

Without a Rita Hayworth movie on show the Columbia machine seems to be operating on three not four cylinders.

The comedy flag is kept flying by Robert Cummings and lady lawyer Rosalind Russell in *Tell It To The Judge*; Lucille Ball, in *Miss Grant Takes Richmond*; and Robert Young and Barbara Hale in *And Baby Makes Three*.

Columbia also distribute the first Mister Magoo cartoon, UPA's *Ragtime Bear*.

Bogart is the airforce veteran *Tokyo Joe* and a lawyer defending a slum kid murderer in *Knock On Any Door*; Lee J. Cobb a psychiatrist probing into the mind of ruthless hood William Holden in *The Dark Past*; and James Mason the suave blackmailer of Joan Bennett in Max Ophuls' *The Reckless Moment*.

Two popular Columbia B series come to an end. Boston Blackie makes his last appearance in *Boston Blackie's Chinese Venture*, his thirteenth film in eight years and The Crime Doctor closes his casebook in *Crime Doctor's Diary*, the tenth case Warner Baxter has investigated since 1943.

1950 "You're just not couth Harry."

"What the hell, I'm as couth as you are!"

Dumb Judy Holliday and big-time junk tycoon Broderick Crawford battling it out in one of their many verbal encounters in Garson Kanin's classic comedy *Born Yesterday*. It's the number one Columbia movie of the year both financially (four million dollars) and Oscar-wise as Miss Holliday snatches the best actress award from such hot favourites as Bette Davis (*All About Eve*) and Gloria Swanson (*Sunset Boulevard*).

William Holden, hired by Crawford to educate his mistress, does what he can with the shrill blonde, but when she comes up with lines like, ''Do me a favour Harry. Drop dead!'' she's best left as she is.

Columbia begin to remake some of their past successes. First on the list is *Craig's Wife*, refilmed as *Harriet Craig* with Joan Crawford taking over as the domineering housewife; Margaret Sullavan makes a rare and very moving appearance as a housewife dying of cancer in *No Sad Songs For Me*; Bogart is still on the lot in *In A Lonely Place*; a many layered film ostensibly about a screenwriter suspected of murder.

The crime list is not unimpressive. Edmond O'Brien tries to outsmart a bookmaking syndicate, and fails, in *711 Ocean Drive*; and prison life is examined in some depth in *Convicted* with Glenn Ford and Broderick Crawford, the story of a prison warden's efforts to help an unjustly accused man.

Arthur Lake and Penny Singleton make their final appearances as Dagwood and Blondie in *Blondie's Hero* and *Beware Of Blondie*. In a twelve year span they have appeared in twenty-eight movies together.

1951 'So Many Women And So Little Time' lament the advertisements for Columbia's romanticized story of *Valentino* starring look-alike Anthony Dexter and Eleanor Parker. Despite the implied sexual urgency the movie's a dud.

For a change it's the dramatic stuff that comes out best. Siodmak's documentary-styled *The Whistle At Eaton Falls* looks at labour unrest in a small town when a plant manager is forced to lay off some workers. In *Sirocco*, Bogart, still with one leg in Burbank and one in Gower Street, is a gun-runner in French occupied Damascus, and in *The Brave Bulls* Robert Rossen delves deeply into the personal and private life of a famous matador.

Broderick Crawford does it right, then does it all wrong. In *The Mob* he cracks a waterfront syndicate; in *Scandal Sheet* he's a newspaper editor who kills his wife and finds that his own reporters are on his trail.

Columbia's quality movies of the year are Joseph Losey's *M* and Laslo Benedek's *Death Of A Salesman*.

Losey's film is a remake of the Fritz Lang classic about a mentally disturbed child-killer who is hunted through the streets by police and criminals alike. The story is transferred from Germany to modern Los Angeles and filmed by Losey in just twenty days. David Wayne is the psychopath, Howard da Silva the chief of police and Luther Adler and Martin Gabel the underworld leaders.

Independent producer Stanley Kramer, much in demand because of his controversial hits *Home Of The Brave* and *Champion*, is responsible for bringing Arthur Miller's *Death Of A Salesman* to the screen. Savage in its indictment of American get rich quick philosophy and worship of success, it follows the last days of a 'failure', a weary travelling salesman who comes home to die with his family after a lifetime of self delusion.

It's harrowing cinema, brilliantly played by Fredric March who earns an Academy Award nomination for his portrayal of Willy Loman. It's a vintage Oscar year, however, and the award goes to Bogart for *The African Queen*. March gets his reward the following spring when he is named best actor at the Cannes film festival.

Kramer signs a $25 million deal to produce thirty films for Columbia on an independent basis. Only ten are made. The films are interesting, offbeat, but failures at the box-office.

1952 Rita Hayworth, after four years away from the screen, but never once failing to make the headlines during her stormy marriage to Aly Khan, makes a comeback in *Affair in Trinidad*. It's a *Gilda*-like story with her old co-star Glenn Ford, but the movie, about a café singer helping the cops nail a gang of international spies, is no more than routine. The comeback turns out to be something of an anti-climax.

The delicious blonde Judy Holliday is much more 'in'. In *The Marrying Kind*, her second movie for Columbia, again directed by George Cukor, she's struggling to save her marriage to Aldo Ray. Asks the women judge sincerely, "What is it that makes you incompatible?" Answer: "Being married to each other."

The film's not all fun and games though. Much of it is uncomfortably realistic as Cukor mixes pathos with humour in telling his story of a failing urban marriage.

Stanley Kramer's deal with the studio produces some of the year's most interesting movies.

Edward Dmytryk directs *The Sniper*, a story of a San Francisco manhunt for a mentally deranged assassin. Arthur Franz is the killer, Adolphe Menjou the hunter; Dmytryk also films *Eight Iron Men* with Lee Marvin and a squad of soldiers under enemy fire in World War II Italy; Millard Mitchell and Gilbert Roland head the cast of a prison comedy *My Six Convicts*; and, on a more sentimental level, Bobby Driscoll comes of age in a French-Canadian household of the 20s in *The Happy Time*. Charles Boyer, Louis Jourdan and Martha Scott add to the mood of gentle nostalgia.

Joseph Walker, Columbia's chief cameraman since the silent days and who has photographed some hundred movies for the studio, retires aged sixty. He photographed all the great Capra successes of the thirties. His final assignments: *Affair In Trinidad* and *The Marrying Kind.*

1953 Harry Cohn films the novel they said could never be filmed, James Jones' *From Here To Eternity* about the seamy day-to-day experiences of a group of soldiers serving in an infantry outfit in Hawaii just before Pearl Harbour. It takes a socko twelve million dollars to become Columbia's biggest ever moneymaker. It also collects eight Oscars, the most ever won by a Columbia movie and the most won by *any* film since *Gone With The Wind.*

Among its awards: best film, best direction (Fred Zinnemann), best supporting actor (Frank Sinatra), best supporting actress (Donna Reed).

Despite the movie's success, Cohn and Zinnemann do not always see eye to eye on the casting. Only Burt Lancaster as Sergeant Warden is a unanimous choice. If Cohn had had his way Aldo Ray would have been Prewitt instead of Montgomery Clift and Joan Crawford Karen Holmes instead of Deborah Kerr. It was a case of compromise. Zinnemann had wanted Eli Wallach for Maggio and got Frank Sinatra. He had wanted Julie Harris for Lorene and got Donna Reed. All in all the compromise works out beautifully.

Fritz Lang is in top form in *The Big Heat*, one of the most ruthless gangster thrillers of the decade. Glenn Ford is an ex-cop who hunts down the racketeers who have murdered his wife.

The advertisements ('A Hard Cop And A Soft Dame') suggest the movie might be dealing with something else, but gangster's moll Gloria Grahame is more down to earth. Says she, "I've had it rich and I've had it poor. Believe me, rich is better." Just how tough the movie is can be determined by the fact that Miss Grahame's hoodlum boyfriend, Lee Marvin, throws boiling coffee in her face in a fit of homicidal temper!

Columbia's series of remakes continues. Jane Wyman and Ray Milland star in *Let's Do It Again*, a reworking of

The Awful Truth; Rita Hayworth tries to re-establish herself by performing 'The Dance Of The Seven Veils' in *Salome* and by rendering a song and dance *Miss Sadie Thompson*, an updating of Somerset Maugham's famous 'Rain'. Jose Ferrer co-stars as the lustful missionary, Mr. Davidson.

Stanley Kramer is again responsible for some of the studio's most unusual films.

The Wild One with Marlon Brando as a leader of a motor cycle gang which invades a small American town; *The Juggler* with one-time circus juggler Kirk Douglas journeying to Israel after suffering in a concentration camp; *The Four Poster*, a delightful series of vignettes covering the married life of Rex Harrison and Lilli Palmer; *The 5,000 Fingers Of Dr. T*, a fantasy about a young boy held prisoner in a castle with the largest piano in the world; and Zinnemann's tender *The Member Of The Wedding*, Carson McCuller's sketch of a young girl (Julie Harris) suffering the growing pains of adolescence in the days prior to her brother's impending marriage.

The studio are quick to seize on the 3-D craze. Its *Man In The Dark*, an Edmond O'Brien thriller is released just a month after United Artists *Bwana Devil*, the first movie in the process. Four Columbia westerns: *Fort Ti* with George Montgomery, *The Stranger Wore A Gun* with Randolph Scott, *Gun Fury* with Rock Hudson and *The Nebraskan* with Phil Carey are all filmed in 3-D during the year.

1954 'It's *Going My Way* with brass knuckles' claims one advertisement for *On The Waterfront*. That's not how most people would describe Elia Kazan's classic film about the corruption and racketeering on New York's waterfront. But it matters little. It's eight more Oscars for Columbia including a second successive best film award and a best actor Oscar for Marlon Brando who, at thirty, becomes the youngest performer ever to win the best actor award for his punch-drunk ex-boxer Terry Malloy.

New blonde star Kim Novak debuts for Columbia after a brief spot in RKO's *The French Line* the year before. She's a gangster's moll who tempts straight cop Fred MacMurray from the straight and narrow in *Pushover*. In view of her charms one can't altogether blame him, but he's come up against this type of thing before in *Double Indemnity* and should know better. He doesn't. End result:

tragedy. The ads sum it all up: 'Hot blooded blonde. . . Cold blooded guy and intrigue! . . .You can have the money and me — just pull the trigger.'

Another new face is that of Jack Lemmon. He debuts as Judy Holliday's boyfriend in *It Should Happen To You.* Anyone who can make an impression when *she's* around is going places, but naturally it's Judy's film. She plays Gladys Glover, an unemployed model who spends her savings by plastering her name across a huge billboard in New York. Chaos follows; Lemmon stars again with Judy Holliday in the unpronouncable *Phffft* — the sound of a dying marriage.

The Caine Mutiny with nearly nine million is Columbia's biggest commercial hit. Bogart stars as Herman Wouk's tormented Captain Queeg; Alec Guinness is *Father Brown*; Vincent Price a three-dimensional *Mad Magician.*

Misfires: *Human Desire* with Fritz Lang off form in a remake of Renoir's *La Bête Humaine*, and *The Black Knight* which has Alan Ladd somehow cast as an English knight in the days of King Arthur!

1955 It's not three best movie Oscars in a row for Columbia, but the studio come close with *Picnic*, a version of William Inge's stage play about a wandering young hobo (William Holden) and his effect on the inhabitants of a small Kansas town during his brief stay there on Labor day.

'From the moment he hit town she knew it was just a matter of time' is the movie's unsubtle tag line. *She* is Kim Novak. Her slow, sultry dance with Holden to the tune of 'Moonglow' raises the temperature of audiences by at least ten degrees. It also raises Columbia's box-office returns by six and a half million dollars.

Columbia at last opt for CinemaScope in the Betty Grable musical *Three For The Show*, a remake of *Too Many Husbands*; *My Sister Eileen* is another remake, again with music, starring Janet Leigh, Betty Garrett and Jack Lemmon; *The Long Gray Line* is John Ford at his most sentimental as he tells the story of a West Point athletic coach and his fifty years at the Academy. Tyrone Power and Maureen O'Hara star.

The West has some brutal moments. James Stewart has a bullet shot through his palm at point blank range in *The Man From Laramie*; the South has Joan Crawford ('So excitingly good when she was so wonderfully bad') as a poisonous socialite in *Queen Bee*; and the East has

Cardinal Alec Guinness, suffering intolerably at the hands of communist interrogator, Jack Hawkins, in *The Prisoner.*

Screenwriter Robert Riskin who worked on many of Frank Capra's most notable films dies aged fifty-eight. Capra/Riskin collaborations at Columbia: *Platinum Blonde, American Madness, Lady For A Day, It Happened One Night, Broadway Bill, Mr. Deeds Goes To Town, Lost Horizon, You Can't Take It With You.*

1956 Music. . .love. . .tragedy. All are combined in just about equal amounts in *The Eddy Duchin Story*, an account of the life of the famous pianist/bandleader of the 30s and 40s. The movie is Columbia's big hit of the year. Tyrone Power is Duchin, Kim Novak his first wife, Victoria Shaw his second. Carmen Cavallaro does the piano work which includes hits like 'Manhattan', 'You're My Everything' and 'Shine On Harvest Moon'.

There's more than a hint of Capra in Judy Holliday's latest offering, *The Solid Gold Cadillac.* Its theme — small stockholder Judy exposes the board of directors of a large company as a bunch of crooks — must evoke fond memories for Harry Cohn and almost suggests that even in the 50s the Capra idealism might still work.

Cohn gets another sharp reminder of Capra with *You Can't Run Away From It.* This time an unpleasant one. The movie is an attempt to modernize and set to music *It Happened One Night.* Jack Lemmon and June Allyson replace Gable and Colbert, but the movie's a dud before it even leaves the floor.

The year also brings shock. Older brother Jack Cohn executive vice president of Columbia for more than thirty years, dies suddenly after surgery for a hernia operation. He was sixty-seven. Harry is now alone to run the company, but his own health is beginning to fail. The pioneer days of Columbia are nearly over.

Humphrey Bogart makes his final screen appearance as a sports writer turned promotor in the boxing drama *The Harder They Fall*; Paul Douglas and Ruth Roman star in 'gangster Shakespeare' *Joe Macbeth*; Joan Crawford is in terrible trouble in *Autumn Leaves* as a middle-aged woman married to young, mentally unstable Cliff Robertson; Bette Davis too has her problems as a stalwart librarian who refuses to remove a controversial book from her shelves in a small American town. The film: *Storm Centre.*

Randolph Scott makes the first of his Budd Boetticher westerns, *Seven Men From Now*; Bill Haley And His Comets bring either unrestrained joy or murder of the eardrums in *Rock Around The Clock*.

1957 It's almost like old times at Columbia. *The Bridge On The River Kwai* wins the studio its third best picture Academy Award in five years.

David Lean's anti-war epic about the construction by British prisoners of a railway bridge in the Siamese jungle and its eventual destruction by a British commando unit garners seven Oscars and brings the total won by *Eternity, Waterfront* and *Kwai* to twenty-three.

Harry Cohn, however, never learns of the film's triumph. The awards are not presented until the spring of '58 and by that time he has passed from the scene. His last public appearance is at the premiere of *Kwai* in New York on December 18.

During his last full Columbia year his stars perform well for him on screen. Judy Holliday is amusingly pregnant in *Full Of Life*; Kim Novak is American stage actress *Jeanne Eagels*; Rita Hayworth has Robert Mitchum and Jack Lemmon for company and sizzles in *Fire Down Below*; and both she and Kim get together for the first and only time in *Pal Joey*.

Joey is Cohn's favourite of his later films. Sinatra's unscrupulous night club climber is toned down from the Broadway original, but the music is still the tops. Rita sings 'Zip' and 'Bewitched', Sinatra deals with 'Small Hotel', 'I Didn't Know What Time It Was' and 'The Lady Is A Tramp'.

Delmer Daves' western *3.10 To Yuma* has farmer Van Heflin risking death at every turn as he escorts outlaw Glenn Ford to the train that will take him to jail; Boetticher's *The Tall T* has Randolph Scott held prisoner at a stagecoach station by Richard Boone, Henry Silva and Skip Homeier.

Bill Haley and his Comets say *Don't Knock The Rock*; director Jacques Tourneur provides the year's sleeper, the British made *Night Of The Demon*. It's a modern version of the M. R. James' story 'Casting The Runes' about the summoning up of devils from outside time and space. If Haley's music doesn't get you, Tourneur's demons will.

1958 Harry Cohn dies on February 27, aged sixty-six, and an era comes to an end. Cohn has ruled Columbia for twenty-six years and seen the studio grow from a minor Gower Street outfit to a major studio. The famous trademark – the mysterious lady with the torch – has come to represent quality, sophistication and craftsmanship. 'His Crudeness' has done quite a job.

Suitably, perhaps, it's a quiet year. Spencer Tracy is an ageing Irish American mayor fighting his last election campaign in Ford's *The Last Hurrah*; tenderfoot Jack Lemmon joins Glenn Ford on a cattle drive in *Cowboy*; Don Siegel stages an exciting car chase in his dope-smuggling thriller *The Lineup*; John Cromwell takes a merciless look at life of a Hollywood sex symbol in *The Goddess*.

Ray Harryhausen's special effects monsters outshine the stars in *The Seventh Voyage Of Sinbad*; Kim Novak, Jack Lemmon and Elsa Lanchester, witches and warlocks the lot of them, bewitch respectable New York publisher James Stewart in *Bell, Book And Candle*. Running them close for scene-stealing is Miss Novak's cat, Piewacket!

1959 Stewart shakes off his spells to deal with a case of Michigan murder (and rape) in Otto Preminger's court-room drama *Anatomy Of A Murder*. Stewart's a defence lawyer, Ben Gazzara, the accused, sexy Lee Remick, his wife. The movie's up for seven Oscars. It finishes with none. Why! It's the year of *Ben-Hur*.

Tennessee Williams' *Suddenly, Last Summer* is another strong Oscar contender, but also misses out. Kate Hepburn and Liz Taylor are both up for the best actress award; the latter for her performance as a young woman on the brink of madness at the memory of her fiancé's death on the beaches of Spain. Little wonder, the magnificent Sebastian is eaten alive in front of her eyes.

The two movies gross twelve million dollars between them, which means that murder, rape and cannibalism are 'in' and sophistication 'out'.

Veteran producer Sam Goldwyn, now seventy-seven, produces his last movie, a screen version of Gershwin's black stage musical *Porgy And Bess*. It's his only film for Columbia. Sadly, it's not one of his best. A great folk opera emerges as a respectable, but uninspired film. Director Otto Preminger and stars Sidney Poitier, Dorothy Dandridge, Pearl Bailey and Sammy Davis Jr. (Sportin'

Life) do their best to inject some vigour into the proceedings, but to no avail.

Charles Vidor, director of some of Columbia's outstanding hits of the forties dies on June 5 whilst filming *Song Without End*. George Cukor takes over the final scenes. Vidor was fifty-eight. Among his films: *The Desperadoes* (the studio's first colour movie), *Cover Girl, Together Again, A Song To Remember, Gilda, The Guilt Of Janet Ames, The Loves Of Carmen*.

Columbia's famous sex symbol of the same period, Rita Hayworth, brings her Columbia career to an end with *They Came To Cordura*. A grinding 'trek' western set in 1916 Mexico, it's not a particularly auspicious end to her Columbia career even though her co-stars include Gary Cooper and Van Heflin. Rita is forty-one and has made thirty-two pictures for the studio.

1960 A less than notable year. Carol Reed's *Our Man In Havana*, with vacuum cleaner salesman Alec Guinness being recruited as a spy by Noel Coward, comes the closest to success. A deft spy satire, it genuinely captures the mood of Graham Greene's novel.

Otherwise, it's strictly routine. *Song Without End* does to Liszt what *A Song To Remember* did to Chopin. Only the personnel have changed, Dirk Bogarde for Cornel Wilde; *Strangers When We Meet* gives happily married Kirk Douglas a chance to commit adultery with Kim Novak in the Los Angeles suburbs; *The Mountain Road* has James Stewart holding together a threadbare story about a demolition team in China in World War II.

1961 An improvement, commercially at least. *The Guns Of Navarone* hits a thirteen million take and that's second only to *The Bridge On The River Kwai* in the Columbia ledgers.

The guns of the film's title are two massive weapons buried deep in the solid rock of a Nazi-occupied Greek island. A six-man sabotage team is sent to destroy them. Heading the unit: world famous mountaineer Gregory Peck, explosives expert David Niven, Greek resistance fighter Anthony Quinn, and knife-man Stanley Baker. Not too surprisingly the team succeeds, but not until 157 minutes of blood, sweat and tears — and explosions — have passed.

Explosions occur too in *The Devil At 4 O'Clock*, the volcanic kind on a steamy French island where priest,

Spencer Tracy, and convict, Frank Sinatra, rescue some children from a leper hospital; Jack Lemmon (*The Wackiest Ship In The Army*) and Glenn Ford (*Cry For Happy*) carry the studio's comedy offerings; sheriff, James Stewart, and cavalry lieutenant, Richard Widmark, ride into Comanche territory to trade for some kidnapped white children in John Ford's western *Two Rode Together*.

Mysterious Island is the surprise hit of the year. Three Union soldiers, a newspaperman and a rebel sergeant escape from a Confederate prison in an air balloon and land on a remote tropical island inhabited by gigantic crabs, bees and prehistoric animals. Michael Craig and Gary Merrill help provide the facial expressions of horror; stop-action animation expert, Ray Harryhausen, the monsters!

1962 David Lean and his crew sweat it out for months in the deserts of Jordan and Morocco to create what one critic describes as 'the first intelligent epic of the screen', *Lawrence Of Arabia*.

Says Lean: "Actors generally had it easy. They sat on camp stools waiting for their scenes, did their business, then went back to the camp stools."

Peter O'Toole (in the part first offered to Albert Finney) is Lawrence; Freddie Young photographs a mirage; Omar Sharif rides through it to make one of the most memorable screen debuts of all time.

Alec Guinness as Prince Feisal, Jack Hawkins as Allenby and Anthony Quinn as sheik Auda Abu Tayi co-star.

The 222 minute film wins seven Academy Awards — best film, direction, colour photography, art direction, editing, music and sound recording.

Kim Novak finishes at Columbia — *The Notorious Landlady*, a comedy mystery, with Jack Lemmon, is her last movie. She has appeared in twelve films for the studio in eight years since her debut in *Pushover*. Her other Columbia movies: *Phffft, Five Against The House, Picnic, The Eddy Duchin Story, Jeanne Eagels, Pal Joey, Bell Book and Candle, Middle Of The Night, Strangers When We Meet, Pepe*.

Chief scene stealer of the year is the black cat which stalks behind the credits to the accompaniment of Elmer Bernstein's music in *Walk On The Wild Side*. Nothing Barbara Stanwyck, Jane Fonda or Laurence Harvey do in the next 114 minutes can top it.

Charles Laughton makes his last screen appearance

as the Southern Senator Seab Cooley in Preminger's *Advise And Consent*; Lee Remick has a vicious heavy-breather to deal with in *Experiment In Terror*; Anthony Quinn proves his acting range as the Biblical thief *Barabbas* and the punch-drunk boxer, Mountain Rivera, in *Requiem For A Heavyweight*.

1963 *Bye Bye Birdie*, a Dick Van Dyke-Janet Leigh-Ann Margret musical, is the most successful Columbia movie; *Jason And The Argonauts* the most inventive, with Ray Harryhausen up to his magical tricks again and creating some of his most famous 'monsters' – Talos, the giant man of Bronze, the seven-headed Hydra and a small army of swordfighting skeletons. Leading man Todd Armstrong does his best, but as always with Harryhausen's films, the actor is running second from the first reel.

Carl Foreman, director as well as producer of the all-star World War II epic *The Victors*, lays on the irony thick and heavy as he executes some soldiers in the snow at Christmas time. A soundtrack Frank Sinatra accompanies the action with 'Have Yourself A Merry Little Christmas'.

Preminger sends Tom Tryon through a long, arduous religious education in *The Cardinal; Gidget Goes To Rome*; Charlton Heston is a bigotted Hawaiian landowner in *Diamond Head*.

Comedy, thin on the ground, is provided by lecherous landlord Jack Lemmon in *Under The Yum Yum Tree* and Danny Kaye in *The Man From The Diners' Club*.

1964 Slim Pickens, whooping with delight on a descending H-bomb and Vera Lynn's subsequent rendering of 'We'll Meet Again' end the decade's blackest comedy *Dr. Strangelove*, the story of an American air force commander who goes berserk and sends his B-52s to H-bomb Russia. Unfortunately, all he succeeds in doing is triggering off the Soviet Union's Doomsday weapon which will destroy all life on Earth for a hundred years.

Stanley Kubrick is the director, Sterling Hayden the offending commander and Peter Sellers appears in three roles – the U.S. President, America's top nuclear scientist and an R.A.F. officer. The five million dollar gross makes it Columbia's biggest box-office hit of the year. No Oscars though. Warners scoop the board with eight for *My Fair Lady*.

By a strange coincidence Columbia tell a similar story

in Sidney Lumet's *Fail Safe* but this time the subject is not played for laughs. Henry Fonda is the harassed President.

Edward Judd and Lionel Jeffries are H. G. Wells' *First Men In The Moon*; Richard Widmark a strange sounding Viking in *The Long Ships*; Jack Lemmon, still a Columbia regular, is *Good Neighbour Sam*; Joan Crawford reduced to cheap budget horror in *Strait-Jacket*.

Two ambitious projects that don't come off. Robert Rossen's *Lilith*, a strange haunting tale of mental illness and Fred Zinnemann's *Behold A Pale Horse*.

1965 The shock death of Judy Holliday from cancer at the early age of forty-one stuns Hollywood. She dies on June 7. She made just six films for Columbia between 1950 and 1957 but all were gems: *Born Yesterday, The Marrying Kind, It Should Happen To You, Phffft, The Solid Gold Cadillac, Full Of Life*. Her sharp, high-pitched tones and dumb innocence made her the most original comedienne since the war.

Several top directors are busy on the lot.

Sam Peckinpah films his first ambitious western, *Major Dundee*; Preminger and Wyler are both submerged in thrillers, *Bunny Lake Is Missing* and *The Collector*; Stanley Kramer tackles Katharine Anne Porter's *Ship Of Fools*, a floating 'Grand Hotel' about a shipful of passengers travelling to Germany from South America in the early thirties. Arthur Penn directs Warren Beatty in *Mickey One*; Bryan Forbes makes his first trip to Hollywood for the prison camp drama *King Rat*, the movie which makes George Segal a star; and Richard Brooks aims for a kind of Lawrence Of The Orient with his version of Joseph Conrad's *Lord Jim*. He has the same star, Peter O'Toole, but the result is somewhat different. A flop instead of a hit.

But when it comes right down to it, an inexpensive western, *Cat Ballou*, is the smash of the year. Not only does it take nearly ten million dollars and become Columbia's biggest financial success, it also wins Lee Marvin an Oscar for his drunken cowboy Kid Shelleen. Jane Fonda adds beauty, Nat King Cole and Stubby Kaye a musical chorus.

1966 Fred Zinnemann's *A Man For All Seasons* is the year's critical and commercial hit. At the box-office it's a thirteen million dollar winner, at the Academy Award ceremonies a six Oscar movie including best picture, best director and best actor – Paul Scofield who repeats his stage performance as Sir Thomas More, the Lord Chancellor of England who, as a matter of conscience, refused to sanction the marriage of Anne Boleyn to Henry VIII.

Composer John Barry also finishes up among the Oscar winners for his music for *Born Free*, the true story of how Joy Adamson raised a wild lion cub to tame maturity in Africa.

Dean Martin, in yet another attempt to find an American equivalent to 007, is Matt Helm in both *The Silencers* and *Murderers' Row*. A carefree agent for ICE (Organization for Intelligence and Counter Espionage) he has Stella Stevens for company in the first, Ann-Margret in the second.

Richard Brooks goes west to Mexico with Burt Lancaster, Lee Marvin and Jack Palance for *The Professionals*; Richard Widmark and William Holden are Civil War adventurers in *Alvarez Kelly*.

Cary Grant features (in the Charles Coburn role) in a remake of George Stevens' *The More The Merrier*. Now called *Walk Don't Run* it's set in a crowded Tokyo at the time of the '64 Olympics. Samantha Eggar and Jim Hutton contribute to the chaos which, although amusing, is not as inspired as that in the Stevens' film.

The picture marks Grant's retirement from the screen at the age of sixty-two. A man of many studios, he has appeared in ten Columbia movies, many of them notable: *When You're In Love, The Awful Truth, Holiday, Only Angels Have Wings, His Girl Friday, The Howards Of Virginia, Penny Serenade, The Talk Of The Town, Once Upon A Time, Walk Don't Run.*

1967 Spencer Tracy makes his last film, *Guess Who's Coming To Dinner*. Appropriately his co-star is Katharine Hepburn. Because of his failing health the insurance companies will not take a risk with him and Spence agrees to take payment after the film is finished. When the last shot is in the can he grins at director Stanley Kramer: "All right you cheap son-of-a-bitch, hand over my money."

Ten days later he dies, aged sixty-seven.

The movie revolves around the reactions of two liberal parents to their only daughter's engagement to black Sidney Poitier.

Katharine Hepburn wins the best actress Oscar for

her performance as the mother. She's filming in Nice on *The Madwoman Of Chaillot* when she learns of the award.

"Did Mr. Tracy win it too?" she asks.

"No madame."

"Well, OK. I'm sure mine is for the two of us!"

Richard Brooks films the Truman Capote book, *In Cold Blood*, an account of the true-life murder of a Kansas family by two young ex-convicts; Richard Burton wrestles with Elizabeth Taylor in Zeffirelli's lavish *The Taming Of The Shrew*; sadistic Nazi Peter O'Toole ruthlessly murders prostitutes in *The Night Of The Generals*; Dick Van Dyke and Debbie Reynolds set about getting a *Divorce, American Style*.

Dean Martin appears again as Matt Helm in *The Ambushers*; *Casino Royale* is a 007 spoof; *The Deadly Affair* is much more serious, a spy thriller set deep in the London suburbs. John Le Carré is the author, Sidney Lumet is the director, James Mason the star.

1968 It's musical year. Carol Reed brings Lionel Bart's *Oliver!* to the screen, complete with songs, and at last wins a long-delayed Academy Award for his direction. The movie takes five awards. Ron Moody is Fagin, Oliver Reed Bill Sykes, Shani Wallis Nancy.

Barbra Streisand debuts on screen as Fanny Brice in William Wyler's version of her Broadway hit *Funny Girl*. She shares an Oscar with Katharine Hepburn (*A Lion In Winter*). She shares the box-office with no-one. The movie's take — twenty-six million plus — is a Columbia record!

The popular spy trend is reflected in *A Dandy In Aspic* and *Assignment K*; Robert Mitchum, Peter Falk and Robert Ryan are at *Anzio*; orchestra conductor Oskar Werner and journalist Barbara Ferris share a bitter-sweet romance in *Interlude*; Burt Lancaster is an executive 'loser' in *The Swimmer*.

One of Columbia's great professional directors, Alexander Hall, dies on July 30 aged seventy-four. Among his Columbia pictures: *There's Always A Woman, I Am The Law, There's That Woman Again, Good Girls Go To Paris, Here Come Mr. Jordan, Bedtime Story, My Sister Eileen, Down To Earth.*

1969 Motorcyclists Dennis Hopper and Peter Fonda make an odyssey across America in *Easy Rider* and for a short time become the cult heroes of the new American cinema.

But despite its massive nineteen million gross the film is hollow material as are the host of imitations that follow in its wake. Jack Nicholson's portrait of an alcoholic Civil Rights lawyer is the film's highspot.

Bob And Carol And Ted And Alice is also 'with it'. Two young couples try for sexual freedom and swap partners. Natalie Wood and Robert Culp, and Elliott Gould and Dyan Cannon co-star, the film (inevitably) cops out. Like *Easy Rider* it's a box-office smash. Nearly fifteen million.

Dean Martin bows out as Matt Helm in *The Wrecking Crew*. Elke Sommer provides a variety of attractions before he quits; major Burt Lancaster defends Belgian art treasures from the Nazis in *Castle Keep*; space controller Greg Peck tries to bring back three stranded spacemen in *Marooned*; he features too in one of the most inept westerns of the decade, *Mackenna's Gold*. Omar Sharif and Telly Savalas are among those who share his misfortune.

Goldie Hawn is the studio's Oscar winner. In *Cactus Flower* she's the lover of middle-aged bachelor dentist Walter Matthau. Secretary Ingrid Bergman eventually gets Matthau. Goldie settles for hopeful young writer Rick Lenz.

1970 Barbra Streisand, as always, proves to be infallible at the box-office. In *The Owl And The Pussycat* (Columbia's comedy hit of the year) she teams with George Segal. He's a normal, sensible bookstore assistant. She's a quick-talking, foul-mouthed call girl. The team sizzles. The dialogue is out of this world.

A sample of Miss Streisand's lines: "Hello, fink! Fink Pansy! You rat! You fruitcake! Rat Fink fruitcake! Creeps like yourself don't have dogs named Wolf. What creeps like you have are little faggy, hairy bitty things with names like Pooky and Doodoo!"

And that's just for openers!

Segal also has problems of the marital kind with Eva Marie Saint in *Loving*; Elliott Gould returns to college to complete his M.A. after a stint in Vietnam in *Getting Straight*; Jack Nicholson is a middle-class American dropout in *Five Easy Pieces*.

Richard Harris is *Cromwell*, one of the studio's most spectacular but least successful movies. Nino Novarese wins an Oscar for costume design, however. William Wyler, for many Hollywood's greatest director, calls it a day. His final film is *The Liberation Of L.B. Jones*, an uncharacteristically violent look at racism in the contemporary South. Lee J. Cobb, Anthony Zerbe and Roscoe Lee Browne star.

1971 Columbia's pictures look back rather than forward.

The expensive and spectacular *Nicholas And Alexandra* recalls the last turbulent years of Tsar Nicholas II (Michael Jayston) and his German-born wife Alexandra (Janet Suzman); *The Last Picture Show*, the studio's box-office hit, has director Peter Bogdanovich remembering life in a small American dust town of the early fifties; and Richard Fleischer prys, in clinical detail, into the odious activities of London mass murderer, John Reginald Christie, in *Ten Rillington Place*.

$, one of the shortest film titles on record has Warren Beatty and Goldie Hawn lifting one and a half million dollars from a bank in Germany. After quite a bit of trouble they make it. In *The Anderson Tapes* Sean Connery doesn't. His plan? To lift the entire contents of a Fifth Avenue apartment house. A series of recording tapes ruin his ambitions.

Rod Steiger and Susannah York star in Mark Robson's version of Kurt Vonnegut's maniacal play *Happy Birthday, Wanda June*; *Doctor's Wives* provides soap opera 'Dr Kildare' style plus murder. Among the several frustrated women: alcoholic divorcee Cara Williams, drug addict Janice Rule, lesbian Rachel Roberts. Among the lines of dialogue, "An orgasm a day keeps the doctor away."

1972 A year of small scale movies.

'Kooky' Goldie Hawn skips around in white undies in *Butterflies Are Free*. Self sufficient, blind songwriter Edward Albert and Oscar winning Eileen Heckhart, as Albert's overly protective ma, co-star.

Cliff Robertson (writer-director-actor) is *J. W. Coop*, star of a small-time rodeo circuit; Kris Kristofferson singer-guitarist *Cisco Pike*; veteran George C. Scott and rookie Stacey Keach a couple of Los Angeles cops in *The New Centurions*.

Keach is at his best in *Fat City*. He's a washed up thirty year old boxer and one of life's losers. The movie, however, is one of John Huston's winners. His best in years. But the old adage is proved yet again. Boxing movies aren't box-office. A shame. The film's a minor classic. Susan Tyrell is Oscar nominated for her alcoholic floosie.

Carl Foreman's expensive *Young Winston* is expected to make money but doesn't. The movie is ten, perhaps twenty years too late. Stars Robert Shaw, Anne Bancroft and Simon Ward and director Richard Attenborough ensure respectability.

The Broadway hit *1776* transfers from stage to screen; Albert Finney stars as an idealistic *Gumshoe* from Liverpool; Susan Hampshire is the new Joy Adamson in *Living Free*, but three lion cubs and the African scenery take the honours.

1973 Barbra Streisand does it again. This time with the help of Robert Redford. They're together in *The Way We Were* which takes twenty-five million, just short of the *Funny Girl* record.

Not only is it a commercial smash it's also a fine movie into the bargain covering the period from the late thirties to the fifties and following the on-off, finally off, romance between college activist Streisand and all-American boy Redford. He eventually sells out to success and Hollywood; she resists and is still battling on street corners at the close. A superb score, a literate Arthur Laurents script, and skilful Sydney Pollack direction.

Godspell, the rock musical of Jesus in modern New York looks less effective on screen than it did on stage although 'Day By Day' still sounds fine; nothing sounds fine in Ross Hunter's musical remake of *Lost Horizon*. The Burt Bacharach-Hal David score is a misfire, the whole film a disaster. Not even Peter Finch for Ronald Colman can save it.

The acting honours of the year? Many and varied. Joanne Woodward and Martin Balsam, as a middle-aged couple trying to rekindle their fading marriage by taking a trip to Europe in *Summer Wishes, Winter Dreams*; Jack Nicholson and Otis Young, two shore patrol sailors escorting prisoner Randy Quail to jail in *The Last Detail*; chauffeur Robert Shaw and Sarah Miles hopelessly enmeshed in the British class system in L. P. Hartley's *The Hireling*.

1974 Without Barbra Streisand the Columbia year would be a mess. Barbra's '74 offering is *For Pete's Sake*, her new partner Michael Sarrazin. Together they tot up 11 million dollars.

The movie's a screwball comedy with Barbra mixed up

with the Mafia, trying her hand as a call girl and even doing a bit of cattle rustling whilst hubby Sarrazin tries to make a meagre living as a cab driver.

Best line: ''It's your word against our computer,'' when Barbra queries her telephone bill.

The Odessa File — spies, intrigue and war criminals living in modern Germany — splutters a bit but dies before it's half over; *The Golden Voyage Of Sinbad* is Harryhausen again; cabbie Carroll O'Connor and chauffeur Ernest Borgnine are a pair of auxiliary cops in the satirical *Law And Disorder*.

1975 A trio of commercial hits.

Shampoo with stud hairdresser Warren Beatty on the Los Angeles circuit hits a socko 22 million. Julie Christie co-stars and looks stunning once Beatty's done her hair.

Funny Lady (19 million) with Streisand repeating her role as Fanny Brice and falling for showman Billy Rose (James Caan) and Ken Russell's extravagant film of the rock opera *Tommy* are the other successes.

Richard Brook's *Bite The Bullet*, about a 700-mile endurance horse race across the West, is one of the year's failures despite the presence of James Coburn, Gene Hackman and Candice Bergman. So too is the knockabout satire of *The Maltese Falcon, The Black Bird* with George Segal as Sam Spade Jr.

Director Bryan Forbes has some success with suggestive horror in *The Stepford Wives*, Ira Levin's chilling story of a mysterious Connecticut organization which turns women into ideal Playboy Playmates; *Hard Times* has Bronson involved in a quality movie for once as a bare knuckle boxer who streetfights his way to a living during the Depression.

Sidney Buchman, a top writer, then producer at Columbia in the thirties and forties dies aged seventy-three. Among his scripts: *The King Steps Out, Theodora Goes Wild, Mr. Smith Goes To Washington, The Howards Of Virginia, Here Comes Mr. Jordan, The Talk Of The Town, A Song To Remember, Jolson Sings Again, Saturday's Hero*.

1976 The experiences of a lonely New York drifter, a former Vietnam marine, in a sordid New York make for Columbia's critical hit of the year. The film is *Taxi Driver*. Robert DeNiro is the drifter, Jodie Foster a twelve-year-old prostitute.

The word 'entertainment' can be better applied to Neil Simon's *Murder By Death*, a freewheeling comedy about an eccentric electronics wizard, Truman Capote, who invites the world's most famous detectives to his mansion for a weekend. Death and laughter are never far away.

Making a complete mess of everything: David Niven and Maggie Smith as the equivalent of an ageing Nick and Nora Charles, Elsa Lanchester as Miss Marble, Peter Falk as a 'Bogart type' Sam Diamond, Peter Sellers as Sidney Wang, (a close relation to Charlie Chan), and blind butler Alec Guinness!

Woody Allen is a restaurant owner who passes himself off as a writer to help blacklisted colleagues in *The Front*; Peter Bogdanovich brings together Burt Reynolds, Ryan and Tatum O'Neal in *Nickelodeon*, an affectionate look at the early days of moviemaking; Richard Lester looks at the Robin Hood legend twenty years on in *Robin And Marian*; and Cliff Robertson and Genevieve Bujold team in Brian De Palma's *Vertigo*-like thriller, *Obsession*.

1977 Columbia doesn't let Fox have things all their own way in the science-fiction field. In *Close Encounters Of The Third Kind* they have a spectacular block-bluster of their own, a two and a quarter hour UFO drama that literally shatters the senses in the last twenty minutes. It zooms into the stratosphere to become the studio's biggest-ever money-maker.

The Deep, Peter (*Jaws*) Benchley's novel about treasure trove, dope and voodoo in sunny Bermuda is another box-office smash. Jacqueline Bisset does a forced slow-motion strip, Robert Shaw and Nick Nolte take on the bad guys. Good Alastair MacLean type stuff. No shark this time. Instead a giant eel which conveniently gobbles up the chief heavy.

Jobless George Segal and wife Jane Fonda turn to crime to keep up their living standards in *Fun With Dick And Jane*; Muhammad Ali plays himself in *The Greatest*; Patrick Wayne heads for the Arctic wastes and unconvincing Harryhausen monsters in *Sinbad And The Eye Of The Tiger*; racing car champion Al Pacino and dying Marthe Keller endure an uneasy love affair in *Bobby Deerfield*.

1978 A varied line-up provides adventure, drama, and comedy with the long-awaited *Guns Of Navarone* sequel, *Force 10 From Navarone*, heading the list. An Alistair Maclean epic, it arrives 17 years after Peck, Niven and co. destroyed those famous guns. The new heroes: Robert Shaw, Harrison Ford, Edward Fox.

Faye Dunaway stars in *Eyes Of Laura Mars*, a stylish New York thriller set in the world of high fashion; George C. Scott finds that his missing daughter is caught up in the underworld of pornography in *Hardcore*; Neil Simon offers *California Suite* with Alan Alda, Michael Caine, Walter Matthau and Jane Fonda and also *The Cheap Detective*, an affectionate parody of *Casablanca, The Maltese Falcon* and *The Big Sleep*. Peter Falk is the shabby private-eye, Ann-Margret, Eileen Brennan, Louise Fletcher, Stockard Channing, Madeline Kahn and Marsha Mason some of the women in the case.

METRO-GOLDWYN-MAYER

Metro-Goldwyn-Mayer

"I wanted warm stories, sentimental entertainment. Sophisticates call that corn. All right, so it's corn. What's wrong with good corn? It is only when rough, crude people put out corn that it becomes corny."

For many, the inference that Metro-Goldwyn-Mayer, the most glamorous star-studded studio in Hollywood history, was built on corn amounts almost to sacrilege. Garbo, Gable, Tracy, Shearer, Harlow, Taylor, Garson and the rest. Built on corn? The very suggestion seems ludicrous. Yet the man who spoke those words knew what he was talking about. He ran the studio for more than a quarter of a century when it was at the height of its powers. His name was Louis B. Mayer and he turned MGM into a glittering wonderland of fabulous Hollywood make-believe.

'Make It Good. . .Make It Big. . .Give It Class' was the studio motto. And it lived up to it. A typical MGM movie, whether comedy or melodrama, *was* good even if it was also often trivial. It *was* big and it *did* have class – quality stars in the leading roles, extravagant sets by Cedric Gibbons, lavish gowns by Adrian, camerawork by Oliver Marsh, William Daniels and Joseph Ruttenberg who photographed all under shimmering white lights.

Yet the inescapable fact remains that for most of its existence MGM was built on schmaltz. Mayer was right. His stories were aimed at the family. No messages. They never probed very deeply into any particular subject. Their sophistication was a facade, a veneer to cover the often paper thin themes that were churned out on the studio assembly line. At Paramount, especially in the 30s, things were different. Sophistication was an integral part of a movie, the very essence of the film. MGM on the other hand was like a shop window, displaying glitter and gold at a fantastic price, but for the most part selling only paste.

Mayer invented the dream factory. He believed in popular entertainment and gave the people what they wanted. He catered for the family going to the movies and produced films accordingly.

The look of disbelief that still crosses the faces of film enthusiasts when the demise of MGM arises in conversation becomes more and more difficult to understand with each successive year. Although in the 30s and 40s it seemed as though MGM would go on forever and remain an American institution, its collapse and loss of eminence, when it did occur, should have come as no surprise. The foundations on which its policy was based were already beginning to crumble by the early fifties. The family, instead of going out to the movies, was staying at home and watching TV. When MGM under new leadership, attempted to change its policy, it foundered.

Only the musicals on which the studio's reputation is justifiably based, remain today as monuments to a great company. *Singin' In The Rain, An American In Paris, The Band Wagon, Meet Me In St. Louis* and a host of others look as good in the 70s as they did when they first appeared on the screen twenty or thirty years ago. The rest of the product, even many of the early works of the much lauded boy genius Irving G. Thalberg, creaks with age. Compared with a Warners thriller or gangster movie, or a Paramount comedy by Lubitsch, an MGM film will generally come a poor third.

All of which infers that Metro was strictly a studio for its time. And so indeed it was.

Russian-born Mayer who had been made studio boss when Metro Pictures, the Goldwyn Company and his own Louis B. Mayer Productions joined forces in 1924, believed in two maxims: that films were first and foremost a business and that the star system was the best way to succeed in that business.

From the outset he began putting his theories into practice. He went after stars, paid them handsome salaries and pushed Metro into the front rank within a year of its formation. With the help of a talented first lieutenant, twenty-four year old Irving Thalberg, who supervised the actual making of the films, he turned MGM into the class company of Hollywood, concentrating on tastefully mounted high life melodramas and society comedies and alternating between the unrealistically classy and idealistically folksy.

Paramount, who until the formation of Metro had held the lead as the most star-studded studio, quickly lost ground in that respect. MGM became the number one studio for stars and went so far as to boast that it had 'more stars than there are in heaven'.

Nicholas Schenck, the president of the company, put MGM's philosophy into one succinct sentence when he commented, "There's nothing wrong with this business that a star worth 10,000 dollars a week can't cure."

The combination of the forty-year old Mayer and almost boyish Thalberg was similar in many ways to the Harry Cohn-Frank Capra combination at Columbia, the only major difference being that Thalberg was a creative producer, still a rarity even today, and Capra a creative director.

Mayer and Cohn were very much alike. Both made it to the top after humble beginnings, the former starting out as a junk dealer, the latter as a Tin Pan Alley song plugger. Both were crude, rough-hewn men who ran their respective studios with ruthless efficiency. Mayer, however, had one big advantage, not only over Cohn but also over every other movie mogul. He ran the largest studio in Hollywood and that meant power, more power than he had ever dreamed of and with it, money. By the mid-thirties he was earning a million dollars a year. The magnificent roaring lion that preceded MGM's films was an ideal trademark. The king of the jungle heralding every movie conjured up by the king of the celluloid jungle.

Yet of all the tycoons, Mayer remains the most enigmatic. Those closest to him swear that he was not the ogre legend paints him out to be. Others, such as a writer who once commented, "I'd rather have T.B. than L.B." loathed and despised him.

Elizabeth Taylor, who began her career at MGM as a child star in family pictures like *Lassie Come Home* and *National Velvet*, was one of the latter. Along with Judy Garland, Mickey Rooney, Virginia O'Brien and others she was part of Mayer's family. On the great man's birthday, on the huge stage 30 at Culver City, they would all get together and sing 'Happy Birthday' whereupon L.B. would call for silence and with emotion in his voice (contrived emotion for he was a brilliant off-stage actor) he would say, "You must think of me as your father. You must come to me, any of you, with any of your problems, no matter how slight they might seem to you, because you are all my children."

When Elizabeth was cast in a singing and dancing role in a picture called *Sally In Her Alley*, her mother took Mayer up on the invitation. If Elizabeth had to make the movie would Mayer allow time for her to have singing and training lessons? It was a reasonable request, but the reception from Big Daddy was not exactly fatherly. He raged at Mrs. Taylor, "You're so goddamned stupid you wouldn't know what day of the week it is. Don't meddle in my affairs. Don't tell me how to make motion pictures. I took you out of the gutter!"

Elizabeth who was also present fired back, "Don't you speak to my mother like that! You and your studio can both go to hell!" And with that she ran from his office vowing never to enter its doors again, a promise she kept. The picture was never made. Liz referred to the MGM chief as a dwarf with a big nose.

Robert Montgomery, a well-known romantic lead at the studio in the thirties, was another who gave as good as he got. Bored with being forever cast as a smooth, debonair leading man he would periodically go to Mayer demanding meatier dramatic parts. After loud and bitter arguments that rebounded off the walls of Mayer's plush office, he usually got them.

On another occasion he went to Mayer asking for a rise in salary, reminding the studio chief that he had been promised a raise as soon as he had established himself as a major star. There had been no contract, just verbal agreement.

''You goddamned liar,'' roared Mayer to a stunned Montgomery. ''Who the hell do you think you are? There was no agreement.'' Instead of turning on his heel and walking from the office Montgomery leaned over Mayer's desk and hissed, ''If you were a younger man Mr. Mayer I'd give you a beating.''

It was a dangerous thing to do. Mayer was a solid, well-built man. He had a low boiling point. One punch and he would have sent Montgomery straight through his office door.

But Montgomery's fighting spirit paid off. Later, in 1934, when it was time for his contract to be renewed, the actor kept the encounter in mind. By that time he had indeed become one of the studio's most valuable properties. He reminded Mayer of the fact and at the same time added 25,000 dollars to his basic salary request. He got it without a murmur.

Mayer, when he was working, was a tough boss, but he had his funny little idiosyncrasies. He was addicted to a special kind of chicken soup so he ordered that it appear every day on the menu of the studio canteen. It was also compulsory for everyone working for him to give him presents on his birthday and at Christmas.

By nature he was a violent, vengeful man. Whereas Harry Cohn would explode into a stream of obscenities when roused, Mayer would lose his self control. He once hurled an ink bottle, full of ink, at a startled agent sitting across from him in his office. On another occasion he literally hurled himself across his desk, grabbed producer Walter Wanger by the lapels and began shaking him vigorously. He also laid out Sam Goldwyn with one punch at a Hollywood party, had a fistfight with Chaplin in a hotel corridor and even tangled with Erich von Stroheim over a remark the great director had passed about all women being whores.

That was like a red rag to a bull as far as Mayer was concerned. Women and motherhood were sacred to him. He worshipped the memory of his mother and anyone saying anything against the female sex was asking for trouble.

Other actors and actresses emerged from his office with entirely different views of the man for he could, when the occasion demanded, turn on the charm. With some it worked. Said Joan Crawford, "I was free to go to him for advice of any kind at any time. He was patient with people, had great judgment and didn't play games. Mr. Mayer always had a magic sense of star material and personality. He knew how to build and protect his properties, and he had a genuine love for them as people."

Robert Taylor also defended him, "Some writers have implied that Mayer was tyrannical and abusive and a male *prima donna* who out-acted his actors. As I knew him, he was kind, fatherly, understanding and protective. I just wish today's young actors had a studio and boss like I had."

When Mayer failed to get his way through threats and violence or charm he turned on the tears. There were those who said that more great performances were given in his office than on the Metro stages. He used to weep for instance when stars (Robert Montgomery excepted) asked for salary increases. He would kneel down and go through the whole gamut of emotions when he demonstrated how Mickey Rooney as Andy Hardy should pray on the screen. He acted out every minute of *Mrs. Miniver* for a reluctant Greer Garson, breaking only for meals, until he had convinced her that the famous mum of war-torn England was the right part for her.

Legend has it that he acted the role for two whole days. By the end of the second day Miss Garson, either through sheer exhaustion or conviction, accepted the role. It made her a household name and won her an Oscar.

Gregory Peck was one who was not so easily convinced although he did witness the tears. "Mayer did actually cry when I refused to sign a contract for MGM," says Peck. "But I think he used to do it every day. Sometimes for two performances. He couldn't bear to be refused anything. He wanted me to sign on a seven year exclusive contract. He wanted to manage my career and be big daddy to me.

"I didn't want to be under contract to any particular studio. So I told him I was flattered and that I'd like to make a picture for him from time to time — which I did — but that I didn't care for an exclusive deal.

"That's when he went into his famous pitch. He was justified in a way because he had made stars out of Gable, Crawford, Rooney, Garland and the rest. And he wanted me to be one of that great list of Louis B. Mayer stars. He did actually cry when

I said no but he enjoyed crying and had a thoroughly good time.''

Gregory Peck was one of the few who got away. When it came to star spotting Mayer had a touch of genius. In the twenties he found a blonde Swedish actress working in a German film studio. ''I think she's got something,'' he said to his companions. ''Yeah, muscles,'' they replied. ''So has Strangler Lewis.'' Mayer ignored their doubts and signed her up. He put her on a diet, gave her English lessons and starred her in films like *Flesh And The Devil* and *Anna Christie*. Later, after films like *Mata Hari, Queen Christina, Anna Karenina* and *Ninotchka*, most people did agree that Greta Garbo had a little 'something'.

Similarly, on a prewar trip to Europe he discovered red-headed Greer Garson, then appearing on the London stage, and the actress who was dubbed 'the most beautiful girl in the world', Hedy Lamarr.

The Austrian born Lamarr had caused quite a sensation by swimming nude in the Czech film *Extase*. When he signed her to a seven-year contract at 500 dollars a week Mayer referred to her nudity, ''You'll never get away with that stuff in Hollywood. A woman's ass is for her husband, not theatregoers. You're lovely but I prefer the family point of view. I don't like what people would think about a girl who flits bare-assed around the screen. We have an obligation to the audience — millions of families. We make clean pictures.''

On another occasion, obviously in a different frame of mind, he said to her, ''You'd be surprised how tits figure in a girl's career.''

Mayer, despite having ''antennae sticking out all over him to tell him what made a good picture'' was never involved in any creative aspect of film-making. That was left to Thalberg and a team of directors headed by Victor Fleming, Jack Conway, Robert Z. Leonard, Clarence Brown, W. S.Van Dyke, Edmund Goulding and George Cukor.

The team was competent, professional and could turn its hand to any form of entertainment. Cukor apart there was no star director such as Capra at Columbia or Lubitsch and DeMille at Paramount. It was because of this absence of star directors, men with artistic vision, that ninety per cent of the MGM output fell into the category of commonplace. Despite all the extravagant trimmings the films were basically without style. More time was spent in dressing the films — sets, costumes, lighting — than in searching for forward thinking script ideas.

Fifty-two pictures a year was the target, by hook or by crook, and if it meant switching Gable with Harlow, Tracy with Crawford, Garbo with Gable, Loy with Tracy, Gable with Tracy and so on *ad infinitum* so be it. Titles like *Reckless, Possessed, Chained, Whipsaw, Riffraff, Bombshell, Mannequin* might all merge together in the mind so that it became difficult to tell them apart, but again that was of no consequence. The films entertained. That was the main thing. And they glittered with two, three and sometimes, in expensive productions (*Grand Hotel, Dinner At Eight*), six or seven stars.

The similarity of MGM's pictures worked well for them commercially, not only at the box-office (moviegoers were eager for stars no matter what they appeared in) but also prior to release. Thalberg would use previews to gauge public reaction. In the thirties audiences generally wanted happy endings. If a film wasn't well received at a preview he would take it back to the cutting rooms and hire a director to shoot replacement scenes.

It mattered little that the director might be different from the one who had worked on the entire picture. Style was non-existent. Any one of six film-makers could have completed a movie by Fleming, Leonard or Conway.

Thalberg lived, ate and slept movies. They were his life twenty-four hours a day.

On one occasion he held a story conference with King Vidor during the funeral of Mabel Normand. The picture under discussion was *Billy The Kid*. Thalberg had no time to waste. As soon as the limousine left for the funeral service he plunged into the pros and cons of the story. During the service itself his mind was still on the film ("Too many murders," he whispered to Vidor about one scene in the movie) and even on the return journey he was still preoccupied and discussing the matter.

On arrival back at MGM he bounded up the steps with an "I'll call you" to Vidor. The story conference was over.

Vidor was luckier than some. Thalberg was one of the most difficult people to see in all Hollywood. The seats in his reception office became known as The Million Dollar Bench because of the hours, sometimes days that highly paid employees spent there waiting for an audience.

Married to beautiful actress Norma Shearer, he was as able a lieutenant as any studio boss ever had. He was the dominant producer in the twenties and thirties and responsible for most of the class films made at MGM during the period, not because of any inspired selection of director, writer or star, but by choice of subject. Invariably he went to literature and the stage for his material, not original stories. It was Thalberg who summoned up Garbo, Crawford, Beery and the two Barrymores for Vicki Baum's *Grand Hotel*. It was Thalberg who teamed Laughton, Shearer and Fredric March in *The Barretts Of Wimpole Street*. And it was

Thalberg who was responsible for *Mutiny On The Bounty, Romeo And Juliet, Camille, The Good Earth.* Artistry, taste and skill were apparent in all his films at all times.

Yet, like Mayer, Thalberg had his ruthless side. It wasn't a vulgar, business ruthlessness like that of his boss, more a consuming passion for getting things on screen his way, and at all costs.

Never a well man, Thalberg suffered from a heart condition and was often so tired he could hardly stand behind his desk when a film conference was about to begin. Yet he never let up. He was acquainted with just about every problem of every movie being shot on the lot. His finger was on the pulse of everything. When directors went to see him about a difficult sequence that was worrying them he would tell them within minutes where there were going wrong.

Clarence Brown once commented, "You would be working with your writer and you would come to this scene in the script. It didn't click. It just didn't jell. The scene was no goddam good. You would make a date with Irving, talk to him for thirty minutes and would come away from his office with the best scene in the picture."

On one occasion, shortly after MGM had been formed, Thalberg had a run-in with Erich von Stroheim, his old enemy from Universal.

Von Stroheim was making a film of *The Merry Widow* and hadn't curbed his extravagance in the least, so Thalberg made sure he had a 'spare' director on the set at all times in case of trouble. Even in the twenties von Stroheim's sexy celluloid was red hot. In one very 'daring' shot he had John Gilbert making love to Mae Murray, his suspenders dangling permanently on the floor.

Thalberg had strictly ordered before filming began, "No dangling suspenders." Von Stroheim ignored it and Thalberg was faced with dangling suspenders in the cutting rooms. Very carefully — at considerable expense — he blotted them out with a trick travelling matte shot. He edited most of the film flat on his back for he was sick in bed at the time. The picture was projected from the floor onto the ceiling above him.

When Thalberg was stricken with a heart attack in December 1932 after a riotous Christmas party at the studio Mayer had to face up to the prospect that his gifted young producer might die a young man. He had known all along that it was a possibility. Now he realised it was a probability and that he would have to find a temporary replacement.

Thalberg, who was forced to take a year's sick leave in Europe was informed of Mayer's decision. He was unhappy about a replacement, but had little option but to agree. David Selznick, Mayer's son-in-law was brought in and for two years provided the studio with pictures that were well up to Thalberg's standards: *Dinner At Eight, David Copperfield, A Tale Of Two Cities*.

When Thalberg returned he found things had changed. Whereas before he had been in charge of fifty pictures a year he was now supervisor of only a select few. Selznick, the in-between man, was embarrassed by the situation and in 1935 embarked on his famous independent career, much against Mayer's advice. "I'm thirty-two," retorted Selznick. "I can afford to fail."

Thalberg too had dreams of independence once his MGM contract had run its course, but he never got the chance to try his arm. Ill-health again struck him down and in September 1936 he died of pneumonia, aged thirty-seven.

By dying young Thalberg became a legend and by dying young he also left Mayer in sole command. On the day of Thalberg's funeral Mayer put on one of his best performances, a tear-stained, numbed performance that had everybody fooled. After the service he waited silently in the car that would take him away from the gloomy scene. His companion was MGM executive Eddie Mannix. As the car pulled clear Mayer looked across to Mannix and smiled, "Isn't God good to me?"

The MGM story changed course after Thalberg's death. There was no replacement. With Mayer in sole command the corn grew taller and taller. The classical approach of Thalberg was out; Andy Hardy, togetherness and patriotism were in.

But the big swing was to the musical. When Arthur Freed was made a producer in 1939 the studio struck oil.

A former lyricist, Freed had been writing songs for Metro musicals for a decade before he turned to producing. Although many of his songs were hits the films in which they were heard were routine putting-on-a-show type musicals, which, at the time, were being more competently produced at Warners.

Nelson Eddy and Jeanette MacDonald were the key figures of the MGM musical scene of the thirties. They represented innocence and romantic fairy tale escapism. Their style was operatic, their films no more than lightweight, fluffy celluloid which relied heavily on composers like Sigmund Romberg. But the war killed their style just as it killed so many other forms of screen entertainment and it was then that Freed came into his own.

Just as *Oklahoma* changed the face of the American stage musical so the films of Arthur Freed altered that of the American film musical, slowly at first with Judy Garland-Mickey Rooney vehicles, *Babes In Arms, Strike Up The Band, Babes On Broadway* (all directed by Busby Berkeley) then with a rush as director Vincente Minnelli came to Hollywood for the all-black *Cabin In The Sky* and *Meet Me In St. Louis.*

A picture postcard of charm, sentiment, taste and style, *Meet Me In St. Louis* proved to be the real turning point in the modern musical. Not that it was modern in theme. It was a family portrait set in turn-of-the-century America. But the style was new, the use of colour imaginative and the musical numbers flowed with the story instead of being simply interludes in the plot.

For the next ten years MGM reigned supreme. Now they really were a studio of glitter and magic and make-believe, but in the right context. They had found their true metier and they made the most of it.

Freed's unit was almost a studio within a studio, comprising of directors Minnelli, Donen, Walters, cameramen Harold Rosson, Harry Stradling and George Folsey, arrangers Roger Edens and Lennie Hayton and actor-performers Gene Kelly, Fred Astaire, Judy Garland, Cyd Charisse, Vera-Ellen, Leslie Caron, Ann Miller, Oscar Levant.

Between them Astaire and Kelly changed partners and sang and danced with a verve and brilliance the like of which had never been seen on screen before.

Imagination and sophistication were the key factors. Nothing was beyond the unit. The artists were so full of creative energy and enthusiasm that nothing, it seemed, was beyond them. If the dance rather than the song was more often in the ascendancy then that was because Kelly and Astaire were the dominant figures, experimenting with dazzling footwork in every conceivable routine, from Astaire dancing on the ceiling in *Royal Wedding* and electrifying an amusement arcade with 'A Shine On Your Shoes' in *The Band Wagon* to Kelly's soft shoe shuffle with a newspaper on bare boards in *Summer Stock* and his famous splash about in *Singin' In The Rain.*

Year after year throughout the forties and into the fifties Freed and other producers on the lot created musical entertainments that even today remain as exciting and rhythmic as when they first appeared: *The Pirate, Easter Parade, On The Town, An American In Paris, Singin' In The Rain, The Band Wagon, Seven Brides For Seven Brothers*, scores of others. It was the happiest of times, the best of times, the most musical of times.

Meanwhile, in the forties, Mayer was in his element. With

the war on everybody's mind it was just the time for the family picture. The situation was made for his philosophy. Young Andy Hardy, the all-American kid, knocked 'em dead at the box-office, noble Robert Taylor went to war, Greer Garson provided tears and sentiment in *Blossoms In The Dust, Mrs. Miniver* and *Random Harvest*, so to did Irene Dunne in *The White Cliffs Of Dover*.

A few films such as the Tracy-Hepburn movies, *Woman Of The Year, Keeper Of The Flame, Without Love*, provided a class content to fit within the class framework, but generally it was the formula as before only this time there was no Thalberg to bring new ideas and steer the studio in new directions. With Thalberg or someone of similar ambition MGM might have moved ahead. Without him they simply marked time.

Things began to go wrong in the late forties. With the war over the scene began to shift towards realism. Over at Twentieth Century-Fox Zanuck was putting into production a series of hard-hitting semi-documentary thrillers that reflected the reality of the post-war world. Similar realism was being expressed at RKO where subjects such as anti semitism, corruption and post war readjustment were being examined, often in some depth and with revolutionary frankness.

Suddenly, the melodramas, comedies and sentimental tear-jerkers, covered with star glitter, began to seem out of place. The stars themselves faltered as their movies proved inadequate and old-fashioned. Gable after the war was never the Gable of the thirties. Robert Taylor was also a pale shadow of his former self. Greer Garson was another who found it difficult to find suitable vehicles.

The success of the musicals and the fact that they were now the studio's main entertainment force hid the decline for a while, but not for long. Mayer who still clung to his old beliefs simply did not move with the times. Writer Dore Schary, formerly with RKO, was brought in as vice president in charge of production to bring something of the new post-war look to the studio. His speciality was the small-scale, topical, thoughtful movie. Mayer was out of his depth. "I wanted to be associated with pictures which showed America in the right light — not as a nation of gangsters and drunkards," he said later.

The clash came in 1951 over the production of John Huston's version of the Civil War classic *The Red Badge Of Courage*. Mayer had opposed it. Schary backed Huston. The film cost a fantastic 1.6 million dollars and ran for just sixty-nine minutes. Mayer appealed to the studio president, Nicholas M. Schenck. Schenck sided with Schary. Mayer was out in the cold. He resigned. MGM would never be the same again.

Schary himself lasted but six years as production boss. Even he couldn't keep the studio on an upward course. The times were changing too fast. TV was now not a threat, but a deadly enemy.

Gable, Tracy, Turner, Garson, Pidgeon, Keel, Grayson and others all left in the first half of the fifties as Schary searched around for new ways to make Metro great again. Unfortunately MGM wasn't MGM anymore without the galaxy of stars. From the very beginning it had been the stars that had made the studio, not the films. When the stars disappeared from the scene there was nothing left.

There was, of course, a cluster of fine films that come out of any studio, even during a bad period — *Bad Day At Black Rock, Julius Caesar, Executive Suite, Blackboard Jungle, Gigi, Ben-Hur* — but when, at the end of the decade the musicals went as well (Astaire and Kelly both made their final films for Metro in 1957) it was all over bar the shouting. The lion's roar which had once guaranteed a glossy escapism that no other Hollywood studio could equal heralded only the commonplace and the mundane.

For most film enthusiasts it was a sad spectacle. The decline from top studio to nothing more than an also ran was all the more tragic because of the enormity of the descent.

In 1973 MGM announced they were withdrawing from world-wide distribution and would, in future, release their product through United Artists in the United States and CIC throughout the world. Many believed that the studio had stopped production entirely. That wasn't and isn't the case, but now only a handful of pictures are being produced a year. Three, four, five films every twelve months is now the norm.

But what was it really like to work at MGM in the golden days when the boast 'More Stars Than There Are In Heaven' didn't even seem like an exaggeration? There are differing views.

Ava Gardner for instance commented, "In a few days I'll be through with Metro. I'm afraid. I never worked for any other company. I never had another job. I hate their guts but for seventeen years they've been there and I just did what they told me to, going from one lousy picture to the other."

Rosalind Russell wasn't quite so bitter although she had her criticisms, "MGM in their heyday was constructed like something that was going to hit the beaches on D-Day. There was a first wave of top stars, then a second wave to replace them in case they got difficult. I was in the second line of defence behind Myrna Loy. I finally got in the first line by loanouts."

And a director's view? Says Fred Zinnemann: "MGM was a

factory geared to putting out fifty-two pictures a year. They were concerned with quantity not quality, with being well-oiled and functioning. That is great for sausages and automobiles, but a director with specific ideas inevitably got into trouble.''

Perhaps Walter Pidgeon catches the real spirit of the old MGM. When he returned to the studio in 1972 to make *Skyjacked* he was grief stricken. It was the first time he had been back to the studio in sixteen years. ''My homecoming was no sentimental affair,'' he said. ''There were not enough of the old gang around. Everybody had gone except for a few old timers on the technical crews. My favourite lot, number 3, had been turned into a housing development. The difference from the old days is both fantastic and sad.

''In the good old days every star had his own suite at the studio. Every day after work he would go to someone's suite — Lionel Barrymore's, Gable's, Fred Astaire's, mine — have a couple of belts and hash over how things had gone. It was like a club.

''Now the suites are gone and they work you so darn hard late you have to go straight home when you finish. In the old days I never worked past six. Now they keep you going eleven hours a day.''

Luckily, Mayer never lived to see the final slip into obscurity. He died in 1957, aged seventy-two, when the studio, through its musicals, was still a household name. Mayer liked the musicals. In a different sort of way they reflected the clean image of American. He understood them.

In the end he was a lonely man. Rich and lonely. Worth a million, but with a minimum of friends. When asked, just two years before his death, what he did with his time he commented, ''Well, I've got a few racehorses and some oil wells. I'm not sure how many.''

He once said that he'd rather be loved than have a million dollars. ''Love and respect, that's what counts. It is best to be loved,'' he said.

But he spent his last days an inconsequential old man, with no power, no driving force, just memories. He had once been the most feared man in all Hollywood as unapproachable to the press as the Grand Lama. In the end he had to hire a press agent to solicit publicity for him, to make sure everyone knew he was still alive.

Fred Astaire, Nanette Fabray and Jack Buchanan in the 'Triplets' number from *The Band Wagon.*

Vincente Minnelli's Oscar-winning musical of turn-of-the-century Paris, *Gigi.*

The first classic MGM musical, *Meet Me In St. Louis* with Judy Garland and Margaret O'Brien.

Frank Sinatra, Jules Munshin and Gene Kelly going *On The Town*.

The most tempestuous romance in screen history. Rhett Butler (Clark Gable) and Scarlett O'Hara (Vivien Leigh) in *Gone With The Wind.*

An ecstatic splash-about. Kelly in the incomparable *Singin' In The Rain.*

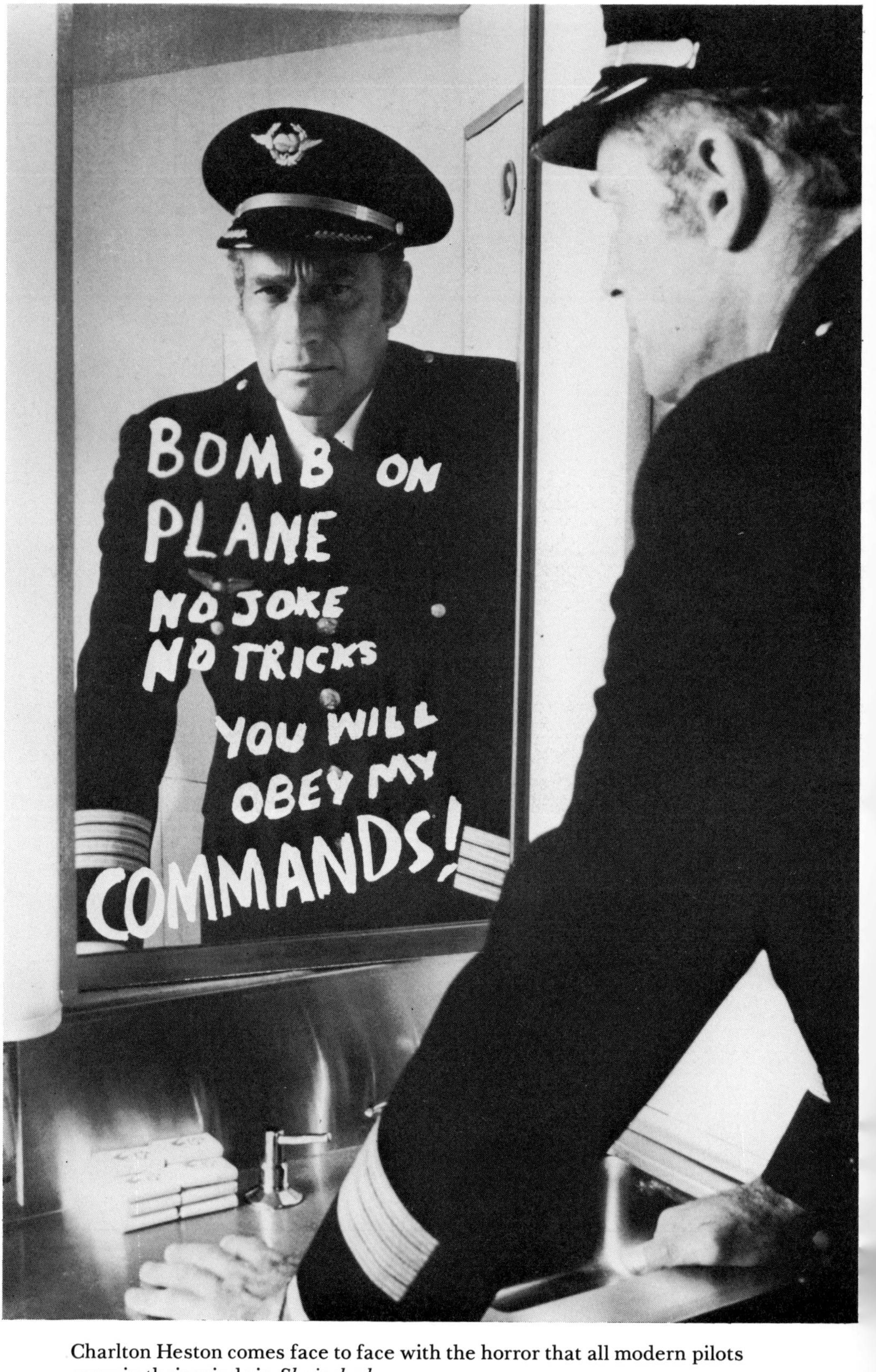

Charlton Heston comes face to face with the horror that all modern pilots carry in their minds in *Skyjacked*.

Chronology

1924 Metro-Goldwyn-Mayer is founded on May 17, 1924 by Marcus Loew of Loews Incorporated. Three companies are merged – Metro Pictures, established in 1915 and acquired in 1920 by Loews Incorporated, a distributing company with a national chain of fifty theatres; Goldwyn Pictures, formed in 1917 by Samuel Goldfish (later Goldwyn), Edgar and Archibald Selwyn; and Louis B. Mayer's small but thriving Louis B. Mayer Productions (1918).

Of the three companies Metro has produced the most famous pictures to date: *The Four Horsemen Of The Apocalypse, The Prisoner Of Zenda* and *Scaramouche*. Goldwyn himself no longer figures in the ownership of the Goldwyn Company having departed in 1922 maintaining a small share of stock.

Nicholas Schenck of Loews is president of the new MGM. Mayer is vice president in charge of production, twenty-four year old Irving G. Thalberg second vice president and supervisor of production. Mayer is so anxious to get started that he doesn't wait for the official announcement and inaugurates his Culver City studio on April 26.

He Who Gets Slapped is the first film to be prepared and produced entirely at MGM. The story of a scientist who starts a new life as a circus clown, it stars John Gilbert, Norma Shearer and Lon Chaney and is directed by Swedish film-maker Victor Seastrom.

Already MGM has an impressive roster of talent at its disposal: Ramon Novarro, Alice Terry, Wallace Beery, Conrad Nagel, Eleanor Boardman, child star Jackie Coogan, Lon Chaney, John Gilbert and Norma Shearer. The top directors: King Vidor, Rex Ingram, Robert Z. Leonard, Fred Niblo.

Among the most popular films of '24: *The Arab* with Bedouin tribesman Ramon Novarro lusting after the white skin of missionary Alice Terry, and two Buster Keaton vehicles, *The Navigator* and *Sherlock Jr.*

Not a commercial success but one of the greatest of all Hollywood films is von Stroheim's *Greed*. Sordid and uncompromising, it traces the slow decline, degradation and death of a San Francisco dentist (Gibson Gowland) and his wife (Zazu Pitts), a woman whose obsession with gold turns her into a crazed miser and her husband into a drunkard and murderer.

Filmed over a period of nine months (originally for the Goldwyn Company), it finishes up at a massive forty-two reels — ten hours of screen time! Von Stroheim himself reduces it to twenty-four reels, MGM director Rex Ingram and June Mathis cut it further, without von Stroheim's permission, to just over two hours.

Von Stroheim shoots the film's climax — when two men die together shackled by the wrist — in the blistering heat of the Mojave desert in Death Valley. He takes some fifty actors and technicians (there is just one woman, a script girl) and works in 142 degrees fahrenheit. Nearly everyone suffers from heat exhaustion. Tempers become so frayed that von Stroheim keeps a pistol by his side day and night.

According to the insurance company covering the expedition the hazards include:

Temperatures of between 120 and 150 degrees
No shade — not a single tree in the Valley
Quicksands
Poisonous reptiles and insects
Air pockets of death dealing gas and poisonous fumes
Waterholes poisoned with arsenic, one drink bringing instant death!

1925 MGM lets everyone know it's going to be a force to be reckoned with by announcing a profit of nearly five million dollars in its first year of production.

Its big release of '25, the Roman spectacular *Ben-Hur*, is a jinxed picture which, like the notorious *Cleopatra* of later years, takes months and months to get off the ground. Begun without success in Italy by director Charles Brabin and with George Walsh as Ben-Hur, it is eventually brought back to Hollywood with a new director Fred Niblo and star, Ramon Novarro.

A new Circus Maximus for the chariot race is erected at Culver city. Twelve chariots, forty-eight horses and ten stunt men take part in the race, plus Novarro and Francis X. Bushman (Messala) who drive their own chariots. It's a time when animals are considered to be expendable in film making. 100 horses and at least one stunt man die during shooting. The picture is a world wide smash, but never regains its four million dollar production cost.

A movie that does make a profit, and a big one, is King Vidor's *The Big Parade*, a memorable anti-war film told from the viewpoint of the ordinary soldier and tracing the experiences of three servicemen in France during the First World War. John Gilbert, Rene Adoree, Karl Dane and Tom O'Brien star.

Swedish actress Greta Garbo arrives on the lot to star opposite Ricardo Cortez in *The Torrent*; John Gilbert in *La Boheme* and Alice Terry in *Mare Nostrum* are also before the cameras.

Norma Shearer gains steadily in popularity; and Lucille LeSueur, having been renamed Joan Crawford in a fan magazine contest, takes the first steps to stardom in *Sally, Irene And Mary*.

Buster Keaton, like so many before him, decides to *Go West* and in *Seven Chances* finds that on his twenty-seventh birthday he must get married by 7 p.m. The reason for the urgency? A prize of seven million dollars.

Lon Chaney, now at the peak of his powers, is driven to madness in *The Tower Of Lies*; a scientist bringing the dead back to life in *The Monster*; and Echo, the Ventriloquist, just one of three circus performers who turn to petty crime and eventually murder in Tod Browning's *The Unholy Three*. Making up the bizarre trio: Victor McLaglen as the strong man, Harry Earles as the midget.

Mae Murray stars in two MGM productions. The first, the enormously successful *The Merry Widow*, the second *The Masked Bride*. Director Erich von Stroheim walks out on the first but later returns; Josef von Sternberg walks out on the second and never comes back.

1926 'Greta Garbo, discovered in stark Sweden, is setting the heart of America aflame!' cry the adds. The mysterious Scandinavian beauty has arrived!

Not that she's nice to know – on screen that is. In *The Temptress* she's a *femme fatale* who drives men to disgrace, murder and suicide; in *Flesh And The Devil* (the first of many films with director Clarence Brown) she's a wealthy married seducer who almost destroys the friendship of two Austrian comrades. In both she gets her come-uppance. Drunkenness, degradation and the gutter in the first, death through an ice floe (which cools some very torrid love scenes with John Gilbert) in the second.

Gilbert also swashbuckles in the Sabatini tale *Bardelys The Magnificent*; Joan Crawford is in the notorious apache quarter of *Paris*; Lionel Barrymore, as a brutal sea captain, begins his twenty-nine year association with the company in Rex Beach's *The Barrier*.

Norma Shearer, very much the girl of today, is a stage struck lass who gets a break on Broadway in *Upstage*. She also invades man's territory, as a criminal lawyer in *The Waning Sex*, much to the disapproval of D.A. Conrad Nagel.

Lon Chaney, down among the darker regions of life, makes two with his favourite director Tod Browning: *The Black Bird* as a Limehouse thief with another identity – the crippled keeper of a rescue mission; and *The Road To Mandalay* as a one-eyed criminal Singapore Joe operating in the underworld of the Far East.

Director Rex Ingram is another who delves into strange, murky goings on in Somerset Maugham's *The Magician*. Alice Terry is the lady who goes through it, being operated on, hypnotised and finally taken to a large tower where her 'virgin blood' is to be extracted for a diabolical experiment. Help arrives in the nick of time. Paul Wegener, the magician of the title, gets 'his' by plunging into a fiery furnace.

1927 Garbo, realising her value to the studio, holds out for more money before embarking on a new movie. She gets her raise. From 600 to 5,000 dollars a week and immediately goes into another picture with John Gilbert (supposedly her lover in real life), appropriately entitled *Love*. It's a version of Tolstoy's 'Anna Karenina'. Garbo is the married Russian aristocrat who deserts her husband and child for the love of another. Once more she fails to get past the last reel. Death in front of a train puts paid to all her suffering and anguish.

'Garbo and Gilbert in *Love*' say the ads which means the film shouldn't miss. And it doesn't.

Lionel Barrymore, Ramon Novarro, Conrad Nagel, Marion Davies, Lillian Gish, Jackie Coogan, Alice Terry and Antonio Moreno are all busy.

So too is ever-rising star Joan Crawford, the assistant of knife thrower Lon Chaney in the circus drama *The*

Unknown and a ten cents a dance girl in love with a gigolo in *The Taxi Dancer*. 'He is convinced of Joslyn's purity when she refuses a cocktail before dinner' reads one of the subtitles.

For Chaney it's a busy year. He's the chinaman *Mr. Wu*; investigating a murder for Scotland Yard in *London After Midnight*; and involved in the Russian Revolution in *Mockery*.

Norma Shearer appears as a cabaret hostess with a heart of gold in *After Midnight*, falls in love with Ruritanian prince Ramon Novarro in *The Student Prince In Old Heidelberg* (a silent musical!) and becomes the first lady of MGM when she marries Irving Thalberg at his home on September 29. Louis B. Mayer is best man.

1928 'Marriage is like a cafeteria. You take the first thing that looks good and pay for it later.' With titles like that, from *Wickedness Preferred* with Aileen Pringle and Lew Cody, who needs sound?

Indeed, of the major studios, MGM is the last to take sound seriously. For most of '28 it clings to the silent film as if things are never going to change. Midway through the year it bows to the inevitable, however, and adds synchronised sound effects and music to *White Shadows In The South Seas* which becomes the first MGM sound film when it is premiered in New York on July 31. The public hear the MGM lion roar for the first time.

White Shadows, directed by W. S. Van Dyke and Robert Flaherty, is a story of a drunken doctor who defends a tribe of South Seas natives from an unscrupulous white trader. It is also the film about which producer Hunt Stromberg exclaims during its production, "Boys, I've a great idea. Let's fill the screen with tits."

Meanwhile, actual talking sequences in MGM films will not occur until 1929 and for the rest of the year the silent cinema reigns supreme.

King Vidor, having looked at the ordinary guy in wartime in *The Big Parade* looks at him at 'peace' in *The Crowd*. The picture, starring James Murray and Eleanor Boardman, reflects the problems and tragedies of an ordinary young clerk and his family as they live out a humdrum existence in a cheap apartment in New York city.

Buster Keaton is *The Cameraman*; Norma Shearer stars as *The Actress*, the film which opens MGM's London showplace, The Empire, and a blackmailer in *A Lady Of Chance* (her last silent); Ramon Novarro is in *Across To Singapore*; Lon Chaney is a clown in love with adopted daughter Loretta Young in *Laugh, Clown, Laugh* and a Limehouse magician paralyzed in both legs in Browning's *West Of Zanzibar*.

Joan Crawford suddenly makes the jump into super-stardom in *Our Dancing Daughters*. She's a vivacious flapper who tries to lure John Mack Brown away from his alcoholic wife. She does. All the girls in the country become Crawford mad.

The quieter, more subtle charms of Garbo continue to fascinate. She's a Sarah Bernhardt type actress in *The Divine Woman*; an exotic Russian spy in *The Mysterious Lady*; and in *A Woman Of Affairs* a reckless heroine who drives her car into a tree when she realises she can't have married John Gilbert. There are compensations. She gets billed above him for the first time.

Footnote from a Hal Roach Laurel and Hardy two-reeler. "What's worse than an aching tooth at three in the morning?" Answer: "Two of them."

1929 William Haines becomes the first MGM star to speak on the screen. In *Alias Jimmy Valentine*, a remake of a 1920 drama about a reformed safecracker, he speaks during the film's climax. Lionel Barrymore and Leila Hyams co-star in the movie which is directed by Jack Conway.

MGM may have been slow in being convinced about talkies, but once they take the plunge they quickly branch out in new directions. They advertise *The Broadway Melody*, the first all-talkie musical, with the words 'All Talking! All Singing! All Dancing!' They also add a 2-colour production number 'The Wedding Of The Painted Doll'. The result? The Anita Page-Bessie Love-Charles King movie wins an Oscar as best film of 1929.

Otherwise, it's a half-and-half year, the end of the silents and the full-scale beginning of the talkies.

Among the last of the silent movies: *The Trail Of '98*, Clarence Brown's spectacular story of the Klondike gold rush (six men die during filming much of which takes place 60 degrees below); *Our Modern Maidens* with Joan Crawford; *Thunder* with Lon Chaney; and Jacques Feyder's *The Kiss*, the last silent film to be made on the Metro lot. The star: Greta Garbo as a married woman on trial for murder.

After *The Broadway Melody* the floodgates open. *The Trial Of Mary Dugan*, a courtroom drama, is the first Norma

Shearer talkie and the studio's first straight all-dialogue picture; Vidor's *Hallelujah* is an all-black drama of religion versus sin in the Deep South; *Untamed* has Joan Crawford as a jazz mad heiress from the South American jungle; and *The Hollywood Revue Of 1929* boasts just about every MGM star on the lot. No story, just seventeen songs. The hit number: 'Singin' In The Rain' sung by Marie Dressler, Bessie Love and Polly Moran. DeMille, in a brief stay at the studio, makes his first sound film, *Dynamite*.

Sound, however, isn't a boon for everybody. Matinee idol John Gilbert, at his peak with 16,000 fan letters a week, reveals a light unromantic voice in his first talkie *His Glorious Night*. Impassioned love scenes draw not sighs, but giggles, and Gilbert is already on the downward path.

1930 'Garbo speaks' trumpet the billboards as the great Swedish actress speaks for the first time in *Anna Christie*. A waterfront postitute, she doesn't appear on screen until thirty minutes have elapsed and then has to wait seven minutes before delivering her historic first line: "Gimme a whisky with a ginger ale on the side. And don't be stingy baby."

It's very much 'women's year' at the studio. Garbo appears again in *Romance*; Norma Shearer wins the plum role of a woman emulating her husband's sexual freedom in *The Divorcee* and gains a best actress Oscar; Joan Crawford, still challenging Shearer for the number one spot shrugs it off with a "Well, she sleeps with the boss" philosophy but gets her big chance when Shearer falls pregnant and can't appear in Sam Wood's *Paid*. The film's about a woman sent to prison for three years for a crime she didn't commit. It's dramatic stuff. Miss Crawford's stock soars.

Sixty-one year old Marie Dressler is another Oscar winner (for the award period 30/31) for her hard-boiled waterfront proprietress in *Min And Bill*. Miss Dressler and co-star Wallace Beery aren't exactly the world's most handsome couple, but they turn the movie into *the* box-office smash of the year.

DeMille comes a cropper with *Madam Satan*, an over-dressed, over spectacular story of marital jealousy; John Mack Brown is King Vidor's *Billy The Kid*; Lon Chaney's first sound movie, a remake of his 1925 success *The Unholy Three*, proves sadly to be his last. He dies shortly after filming has been completed.

The musicals bring more cheer. *The Rogue Song* (based on Franz Lehar's operetta 'Gypsy Love') is the first all

Technicolor (2-color) musical and provides opera star Lawrence Tibbett with his screen debut; Bessie Love stars in a version of the Broadway hit *Good News*. One of the songs is 'The Best Things In Life Are Free'. They have to be. The Depression is about to begin in earnest.

1931 'Mr. Hardy holds that every husband should tell his wife the whole truth'. 'Mr. Laurel is crazy too.' Just the opening title of a Laurel And Hardy short *Come Clean*, but the pair do at least bring smiles instead of tears which is what most of the major MGM stars are doing throughout the year.

In *Inspiration* Garbo is an immoral French artist's model who gives up young diplomat Robert Montgomery for the sake of his career; in *Susan Lennox, Her Fall And Rise* she's immoral again as a farm girl who takes to sleeping around in her pursuit of newcomer Clark Gable; in *Mata Hari* she's even more deadly as the notorious German spy of World War I.

Miss Shearer's in trouble too. She shoots gangster lover Clark Gable in *A Free Soul* and has to stand trial for his murder. Even Joan Crawford's in bad straits with the screen's new he-man. In *Possessed*, an explosive piece about sex and politics, she's slapped round the face by Gable, called a little tramp and told to scram.

The Gable-Crawford combination proves to be box-office dynamite and sets audiences alight; the Gable-Garbo teaming just fizzles.

DeMille films *The Squaw Man* for the third time, with Warner Baxter and Lupe Velez, then heads back to Paramount; W. S. Van Dyke shoots *Trader Horn*, an African jungle adventure filmed during seven months on the dark continent; Robert Montgomery excels in lightweight comedy(*Shipmates, The Man in Possession*)Wallace Beery is a broken down boxer in *The Champ*. He tries for a comeback for the sake of his idolizing son Jackie Cooper — and wins an Oscar, becoming the first star to share (with Fredric March, (*Dr. Jekyll And Mr. Hyde*) a best actor Academy Award.

Grace Moore and Lawrence Tibbett render the music of Sigmund Romberg and Oscar Hammerstein II ('Lover Come Back To Me', 'Softly As A Morning Sunrise') in *New Moon*; Gable, a bit player at the year's start, is a star by the year's end, although he's really had to work for it — nine movies in twelve months; blonde Jean Harlow, seen in a minor role as a gangster's moll in one of those

Gable films, *The Secret Six*, will soon be joining him.

1932 An extraordinary year for MGM which becomes the first studio to win two best picture Oscars. The '32 winner is *Grand Hotel*. It's the most famous portmanteau movie of all time, adapted from Vicki Baum's novel of life in a large luxury hotel. John Barrymore is an impoverished baron, Lionel Barrymore a clerk dying from a fatal disease, Wallace Beery a Prussian business tycoon, Joan Crawford his ambitious stenographer.

Topping them all is Garbo who in the movie actually says those famous words "I want to be alone." The man on the receiving end: John Barrymore. Garbo plays an ageing ballerina named Grusinskaya. In real life she uses several pseudonyms when travelling 'incognito' — Emily Clark, Harriet Brown, Jane Emerson, Gussie Berger, Mary Holmquist, Karin Lund.

Jean Harlow, the wise-cracking blonde MGM have bought from Howard Hughes for $60,000 makes headlines in two ways. She appears with Clark Gable in *Red Dust* ('They Were Born To Co-Star'), a story which becomes white hot when she and Mary Astor fight over Gable in the steamy jungle plantations of Indo China. Miss Astor uses a gun to relieve her repressions, Jean has other means.

The other headlines are less than savoury. Paul Bern, Jean's husband of just two months and a top MGM producer, commits suicide by putting a bullet through his brain. Aged forty-two (twice as old as Harlow) and suspected of being impotent, he is found nude in their bedroom, a .38 calibre revolver in his hand. He leaves the following note to his wife:

"Dearest Dear — Unfortunately, this is the only way
to make good the frightful wrong I have done you and
to wipe out my abject humiliation. I love you, Paul
P.S. You understand that last night was only a comedy"

Apart from Gable and Harlow there are other interesting teamings around. Garbo and von Stroheim upstage each other in *As You Desire Me*; Norma Shearer, all sweetness and light for a change, is with Fredric March and Leslie Howard in *Smilin' Through*; Gable and Shearer make a stab at Eugene O'Neill in *Strange Interlude*; and U.S. swimming champion Johnny Weismuller and Maureen O'Sullivan star in *Tarzan The Ape Man*.

"Me Tarzan You Jane" becomes the catch phrase of the year.

That regular comedy team Laurel and Hardy win their only Oscar for the three-reeler *The Music Box*. It's the one in which the zany pair attempt to deliver a piano to a house at the top of a long flight of stairs.

The most ambitious teaming of all is that of the three Barrymores, John, Ethel and Lionel in *Rasputin And The Empress*, a story of intrigue and seduction in Czarist Russia. Says Ethel, "I thought I was pretty good but what those two boys were up to I'll never know."

1933 Lovable Marie Dressler is still number one at the box-office. Mayer reunites her with Wallace Beery and repeats the *Min And Bill* formula with *Tugboat Annie*. The result is 'socko' at the box-office.

Robert Montgomery (*Made On Broadway, When Ladies Meet*) continues to provide smooth light comedy; Myrna Loy (*The Barbarian*) floats discreetly nude in a sunken bath in her first MGM lead; director W. S. Van Dyke travels to the Arctic by whaling schooner for *Eskimo*; Garbo appears in one of her most famous roles, the tragic 17th century *Queen Christina*. John Gilbert whose last MGM film this is features as her Spanish envoy lover.

Gable is busy with four movies including *Hold Your Man* in which he's a con man and Jean Harlow his moll, and *Dancing Lady* in which he's teamed once more with Joan Crawford. It's one of Crawford's biggest hits as she makes it from shady burlesque shows to Broadway stardom. The movie introduces the song 'Everything I Have Is Yours'; Joan also dances with Fred Astaire (in his screen debut) to 'Heigh Ho, The Gang's All Here'.

If it's anybody's year it's Jean Harlow's. She also appears in Victor Fleming's *Bombshell*, a delicious satire of thirties Hollywood, and *Dinner At Eight*, a production of David O. Selznick, Mayer's son-in-law, whom the studio boss has brought in to strengthen the production team while Thalberg is on sick leave because of overwork.

The movie, an all-star vehicle in the *Grand Hotel* tradition, delves into the private lives of some wealthy guests who attend a dinner party thrown by social climber Billie Burke. John Barrymore, Wallace Beery, Marie Dressler, Lionel Barrymore are among the stars, but it's Harlow's film.

Says she at the picture's close, "I was reading a book the other day. It's about civilization or something. . .

Do you know the guy said machinery is going to take the place of every profession.''

''Oh, my dear,'' says Dressler, pausing to give Harlow the once over. ''That's something you'll never have to worry about.''

1934 MGMs star line-up, already of huge proportions is growing by the year. Gable, Garbo, Shearer, Crawford, Harlow, Montgomery, Beery, Barrymore, now head a glittering roster supported by directors Victor Fleming, George Cukor, Clarence Brown, Jack Conway, Sidney Franklin, Robert Z. Leonard, W. S. Van Dyke, Sam Wood and Edmund Goulding.

A newcomer to the list is handsome Robert Taylor who makes his first MGM appearance in *A Wicked Woman*, eleventh on the cast list.

Spencer Tracy is another new face on the Metro lot. On loan from Fox, he appears opposite Madge Evans in a minor vehicle *The Show-Off*. Within a year he will be a regular MGM player and another of the studio's most valuable properties.

There's also an engaging, sophisticated new sleuthing team, William Powell and Myrna Loy who appear, together with Asta the dog, as Nick and Nora Charles in *The Thin Man*.

Meanwhile, the regulars continue: Joan Crawford is *Sadie McKee* and falls for Argentine rancher Gable in *Chained*; Garbo is in China torn between husband Herbert Marshall and lover George Brent in Maugham's *The Painted Veil*; Johnny Weismuller reappears in *Tarzan And His Mate*, a film co-directed by noted MGM art director Cedric Gibbons.

Norma Shearer, after a year's absence, returns to the lot with husband Irving Thalberg, now recovered but in charge of only a few selected productions. Norma's first *Riptide* has her involved in adultery among the rich. It's not a hit. Her second, *The Barretts Of Wimpole Street*, has her imprisoned by tyrannical pa Charles Laughton and loved by poet Fredric March. It's a smash.

Thalberg brings the Lubitsch-Chevalier-MacDonald team over from Paramount for a glittering remake of *The Merry Widow*, this time with Lehar's music. Lubitsch and Chevalier return to Paramount, but Miss MacDonald stays on at MGM and is yet another star who will shine brightly in the years to come.

Marie Dressler passes tragically from the scene, dying from cancer, aged sixty-five; Wallace Beery, her favourite co-star, continues as Long John Silver in *Treasure Island* and the sadistic Mexican revolutionary Pancho Villa in *Viva Villa!* "You geev Pancho beeg kees, eh?" growls he to Fay Wray. She refuses and gets horsewhipped.

The strangest event of the year: John Dillinger's death on July 22 when he is shot down outside a Chicago theatre by FBI agents. Myrna Loy is supposedly the favourite actress of the notorious Public Enemy. The film he views just prior to his death, *Manhattan Melodrama* starring Clark Gable, William Powell — and Myrna Loy!

1935 Charles Laughton's Captain Bligh sneers down at a thirsty crew member of the Bounty: "I'll give you water. Bos'n, keelhaul this man!" The sadism pays off. *Mutiny On The Bounty* co-starring Clark Gable and Franchot Tone, wins a third best picture Oscar for the studio.

Thalberg brings the Marx Brothers from Paramount for *A Night At The Opera*; Selznick produces *David Copperfield*, the best of all Hollywood adaptations of a Dickens novel; Rosalind Russell is an emerging star in *Rendezvous*; Robert Taylor continues to attract attention.

Garbo and director Clarence Brown remake *Anna Karenina* which they had filmed eight years earlier as *Love*. Fredric March is this time the luring force that makes Greta leave all behind her and fall, once more beneath the train wheels.

There are now so many stars on the Metro lot that it's like musical chairs with the teamings: Tracy and Loy are in *Whipsaw*; Gable, Harlow and Beery in *China Seas*; Joan Crawford, Robert Montgomery and Franchot Tone in *No More Ladies*; Wallace Beery and Lionel Barrymore in Clarence Brown's version of O'Neill's *Ah, Wilderness*.

But the key event of the year is the studio coming to grips for the first time with the musical film.

The Broadway Melody Of 1936, not a sequel to the Oscar winning film of 1929, but the first in a series of movies in a similar vein, brings Broadway tap dancer Eleanor Powell to the sound stages. Robert Taylor and June Knight provide the romance, but it's during the musical numbers 'Sing Before Breakfast', 'You Are My Lucky Star', and 'Broadway Rhythm', that the movie really takes hold.

The musical take-off also sees the first teaming of

soprano Jeanette MacDonald and baritone Nelson Eddy in a 1910 operetta *Naughty Marietta*. 'Ah, Sweet Mystery Of Life' is one of the songs. There's no mystery about their success. Innocence, sentiment, romance, total escapism.

1936 Metro proves its dominance of the early sound years by winning its fourth best picture Academy Award in nine years. No other studio has won more than once. Appropriately enough the winner, *The Great Ziegfeld*, is a lavish semi-musical, a biography of the great Broadway showman. William Powell is Ziegfeld, Luise Rainer (best actress) his first wife Anna Held, Myrna Loy his second, Billie Burke.

Best of the lavish set pieces: The 'A Pretty Girl Is Like A Melody' number, built around a gigantic wedding cake, creamed with pretty girls, immaculate men and ingenious props. The only drawback. No colour. Even so, the movie costs out at two million dollars.

Eleanor Powell's twinkling feet and long legs bring rhythm and movement to a scintillating Cole Porter score ('Easy To Love', 'I've Got You Under My Skin') in *Born To Dance*; Jeanette MacDonald and Nelson Eddy are quickly together again in *Rose Marie* but with songs of a different kind: 'Indian Love Call', 'Rose Marie I Love You'.

Miss MacDonald also appears without Eddy, but with Gable and Tracy in *San Francisco*. Despite a few operatic arias her singing has nothing to do with the film's success. Rather it's the reconstruction of the 1906 earthquake, when buildings crumble, gargoyles crash from rooftops and the earth splits apart at people's feet that brings in the customers. For a few minutes all the stars, even 'King' Gable himself disappear beneath the debris and the special effects man, James Basevi, rules supreme.

It's vintage year all round. Fritz Lang indicts mob violence in *Fury* starring Spencer Tracy; William Powell and Myrna Loy are back in *After The Thin Man*; Johnny Weismuller is in *Tarzan Escapes*; Leslie Howard and Norma Shearer are an elderly, but distinguished *Romeo And Juliet*; Ronald Colman says the "It is a far, far better thing that I do" speech in Selznick's second, almost equally successful, Dickens adaptation *A Tale Of Two Cities*.

In many ways it's a case of other studios 'eat your heart out'. At a time when all Hollywood is searching for new talent Metro is bulging with stars and nonchalantly throws in four of its best, Tracy, Harlow, Powell and Loy in a witty sophisticated comedy *Libelled Lady*.

The one black spot is the death in September from pneumonia of Irving Thalberg. He was thirty-seven. Hollywood is stunned by the loss. Norma Shearer indicates her wish to retire. The Mayer-Thalberg partnership is suddenly over. Mayer is on his own and MGM will slowly take a new course.

1937 Another year of tragedy as the vivacious Jean Harlow dies of uremic poisoning just nine days after collapsing on the set of *Saratoga* with a kidney disorder. Jean's mother, because of her religious beliefs, refuses to let doctors attend her daughter until it is too late. Jean, who dies on June 7, was twenty-six.

Saratoga, a racing story with Clark Gable, is temporarily shelved then completed with a double. Jean made sixteen films for Metro in seven years, six of them with Gable: *The Secret Six, Red Dust, Hold Your Man, China Seas, Wife vs Secretary, Saratoga*. Others: *The Beast Of The City, Red-Headed Woman, Dinner At Eight, Bombshell, The Girl From Missouri, Reckless, Riffraff, Suzy, Libelled Lady, Personal Property*.

Tragedy on screen is portrayed by Greta Garbo, at her brilliant best as Dumas' dying heroine *Camille*. If ever an Oscar is deserved it is for this performance, but the award goes to Luise Rainer for *The Good Earth*.

MGM also captures the best actor award, Spencer Tracy getting the nod for *Captains Courageous*. A Portuguese accent, elementary philosophy, essence of Rudyard Kipling and a gruesome death at sea are the ingredients which help bring home the gold statuette.

Robert Montgomery changes pace as Emlyn Williams' psychotic killer in *Night Must Fall*; Mickey Rooney stars in the first of the *Andy Hardy* pictures, *A Family Affair*;

Walter Pidgeon, around for some years, is emerging as a top Metro star; Joan Crawford is a lady Raffles in *The Last Of Mrs. Cheyney*.

It's a bad year for Gable. Besides being present at the Harlow tragedy he's totally miscast as the Irish patriot *Parnell*. His most famous moment occurs in *The Broadway Melody Of 1938*. He doesn't appear. Only his photograph to which a fifteen-year old girl sings 'You Made Me Love You'. The girl is Judy Garland. She steals the picture and later in the year gets her first top billing opposite Mickey Rooney in *Thoroughbreds Don't Cry*.

Musicals are as big as ever. As well as *The Broadway Melody Of 1938* there's the massive *Rosalie* filmed with twenty-seven cameras and starring 2000 people; the third Jeanette MacDonald/Nelson Eddy operetta *Maytime* with music by Romberg; and *The Firefly* in which Jeanette goes it alone only to have things stolen from her by Alan Jones with 'The Donkey Serenade'.

Groucho continues to be just as rude to Margaret Dumont as he was at Paramount. "Marry me and I'll never look at another horse," he quips in *A Day At The Races*.

1938 *Sweethearts*, a Jeanette MacDonald/Nelson Eddy musical about a temperamental theatrical couple is MGM's first movie in the three-colour Technicolor process. Metro are late on the scene as far as Technicolor is concerned. RKO, Warners, Fox and United Artists have all had colour films on release long before *Sweethearts* appears.

The Andy Hardy series soars into a moneymaking goldmine as Mickey Rooney gets through four movies in the year; Lew Ayres and Lionel Barrymore, now confined to a wheelchair because of arthritis, begin another hit series with *Young Doctor Kildare*.

Meanwhile the big stars continue unabated. Tracy wins another Oscar for his Father Flanagan in *Boys' Town*, co-stars with Joan Crawford in *Mannequin* and Gable in the flying spectacular *Test Pilot*; Robert Taylor appears in a trio of movies, teaming with Franchot Tone and Robert Young in *Three Comrades*, putting on boxing gloves for *The Crowd Roars* and appearing as a cocky American kid brought down to earth with a bump when he attends Oxford university in *A Yank At Oxford*.

Robert Donat is A. J. Cronin's idealistic and ambitious young doctor in *The Citadel*; Reginald Owen is Dickens' miser Scrooge; and Norma Shearer, in her first screen role for two years, *Marie Antoinette*. Her performance is passable, her wedding dress, designed by MGM costume designer Adrian with 500 yards of white satin, superb!

1939 Robert Donat in *Goodbye Mr. Chips*. . .Garbo in *Ninotchka* . . .Mickey Rooney in *The Adventures Of Huckleberry Finn*. . .Judy Garland following the yellow brick road in *The Wizard Of Oz*. In most years that would be more than enough. But 1939 is no ordinary year. It is the year of David Selznick's *Gone With The Wind* and every other movie suffers by comparison.

Gone With The Wind quickly establishes itself as the biggest moneymaker of all time, a record it holds for over a quarter of a century until it is eventually toppled by *The Sound Of Music* in 1965. The casting is perfection: Clark Gable as Rhett Butler; Vivien Leigh as Scarlett O'Hara; Olivia de Havilland as Melanie Hamilton; Leslie Howard as Ashley Wilkes.

Statistics:

Principal photography: January 26 – June 27, 1939
(The burning of Atlanta filmed December 10, 1938)
59 leading and supporting characters
140 days officially recorded on the shooting schedules
(Vivien Leigh worked 125, Gable 71, de Havilland 59 and Howard 32)
2,400 extras
1,100 horses
375 assorted mules, pigs, oxen, cows and dogs
450 wagons, ambulances, gun caissons
3,000 sketches covering all the major scenes in the film
90 sets designed and built by Lyle Wheeler
5,500 separate costume items
Over three hours of music composed by Max Steiner, two hours and 36 minutes being used in the final cut
449,512ft of film shot; 160,000ft printed
First rough cut: five hours
Second rough cut: four hours 27 minutes
Final running time: three hours 42 minutes (20,300 ft)
Negative production cost: $3,957,000
World premiere: Loew's Grand Theatre, Atlanta, December 15, 1939

Note: Ronald Colman, Basil Rathbone, Errol Flynn, Gary Cooper and Fredric March were all considered as possible Rhett Butlers before Gable, the favourite from the start, was signed in August 38; Bette Davis, Katharine Hepburn and Norma Shearer were considered for Scarlett O'Hara. Susan Hayward, Joan Bennett, Lana Turner, Joan Fontaine and Paulette Goddard were among those actually tested for the role; Janet Gaynor was at one time a strong favourite for the role of Melanie.

Several directors worked on the film: Victor Fleming who directed the main story of Rhett and Scarlett, contributed 55%, Sam Wood 15%, George Cukor, who began the movie, 5%, and production designer William Cameron

Menzies 15% including the Atlanta Fire sequences. The rest of the movie comprised of second unit work by Reeves Eason and a galaxy of process shots.

One thing *Gone With The Wind* doesn't have is an all-women cast and that, at least, is where George Cukor's *The Women* scores. There's not a man in sight although it's all about men.

The film also contains some of the most unusual credit titles ever presented on screen, each of its female characters being symbolized by an animal — Norma Shearer is a fawn, Joan Crawford is a lioness, Rosalind Russell a cat, Joan Fontaine a lamb, Paulette Goddard a fox, Marjorie Main a mule, Lucile Watson an owl, Lu Phyllis Povah a cow, Mary Boland a monkey and Virginia Weidler also a fawn.

Of all the snappy, witty lines Roz Russell has perhaps the best: "This scandal will all be forgotten in the morning. Remember what they said about what's her name before she jumped out of that window? See, I can't even remember her name so why worry?"

1940 The modern musical is slowly emerging. Arthur Freed reteams Judy Garland ('La Conga') and Mickey Rooney in Berkeley's campus musical *Strike Up The Band*; Judy goes solo in *Little Nelly Kelly*; Astaire and Eleanor Powell dazzle the eye performing Cole Porter's 'Begin The Beguine' in *The Broadway Melody Of 1940*.

Tracy is busy, ruthlessly wiping out an Indian camp in *Northwest Passage*, inventing the incandescent lamp in *Edison The Man*, and winning and losing oil fortunes with fellow wild-catter Clark Gable in *Boom Town*. Robert Taylor loves Vivien Leigh but to no avail. She sinks from ballerina to prostitute to suicide on *Waterloo Bridge*.

Greer Garson and Laurence Olivier bring style and polish to the high society of Jane Austen in *Pride And Prejudice*; Katharine Hepburn, Cary Grant and James Stewart bring similar attributes to contemporary American society in *The Philadelphia Story*. Hedy Lamarr (*Comrade X*), Joan Crawford (*Strange Cargo*), William Powell (*I Love You Again*) and Norma Shearer (*Escape*) are all prominent, but two new characters arrive on the scene almost unnoticed — Tom and Jerry.

The famous cat and mouse cartoon characters have been developed by William Hanna and Joseph Barbera under producer Fred Quimby in the late thirties. The earliest cartoon in which they are clearly recognisable, but not identifiable by their subsequent names — Tom is known as 'Jasper' and Jerry as 'Dat Mouse' — in *Puss Gets The Boot* (40), an Oscar-nominated short in MGM's 'Cat And Mouse' series.

1941 A great star retires at the peak of her career. Garbo calls it a day at the age of thirty-six. Her last movie is a minor George Cukor comedy *Two Faced Woman.* She has been at MGM for fifteen years and made twenty-five films. Early in her career she commented, "Being in the newspapers is awfully silly to me. It's alright for important people who have something to contribute to talk. I have nothing to contribute."

Among her screen 'contributions': *Flesh And The Devil, The Kiss, Anna Christie, Mata Hari, Grand Hotel, Queen Christina, Anna Karenina, Camille, Ninotchka.*

Joan Crawford suffers in one of her finest roles, as a scarred woman who undergoes plastic surgery in *A Woman's Face*; Spencer Tracy needs no surgery to change his, just a drug in *Dr. Jekyll And Mr. Hyde*; Greer Garson's features on the other hand are full of kindness and sorrow as she plays Edna Gladney, welfare worker for illegitimate children in *Blossoms In The Dust*. The film establishes one of the most popular star teams of the 40s, Garson and Walter Pidgeon.

The musicals are still on course. Jeanette MacDonald (*Smilin' Through*) and Nelson Eddy (*The Chocolate Soldier*) go solo; Garland and Rooney are together again in *Babes On Broadway*; Eleanor Powell hoofs a breathtaking 'Fascinating Rhythm' routine in *Lady Be Good*, a movie which also provides the year's Oscar-winning song 'The Last Time I Saw Paris'.

The ultra-lavish *Ziegfeld Girl* is the big one. Judy Garland sings 'Minnie From Trinidad', Hedy Lamarr provides the glamour, Eve Arden the wisecracks, Lana Turner the ruthless ambition.

1942 The year of *Mrs. Miniver*! Greer Garson and Walter Pidgeon head a 'typically English family' struggling against everything the Nazis can throw at their homeland. Garson (best actress) and William Wyler (best director) win two of the film's six Academy Awards. Walter Pidgeon as Mr. Miniver doesn't figure among the awards, but does get one of the best lines: "She was a good cook as good cooks go and as good cooks go, she went.''

Another top Metro team, Spencer Tracy and Katharine Hepburn, join forces for the first time in George Stevens' *Woman Of The Year*, a comedy about the ups and downs of a marriage between a down-to-earth sports reporter and an intellectual lady journalist.

Rumour has it that when they first meet on set Miss Hepburn comments, ''I'm afraid I'm a little tall for you Mr. Tracy.'' Comes Tracy's retort, ''Don't worry Miss Hepburn, I'll cut you down to size.'' Other sources credit producer Joe Mankiewicz with the remark. One thing is certain. Tracy insists and always receives top billing in all his nine films with Katie.

The pair show they're equally adept at drama in Cukor's *Keeper Of The Flame*. Tracy, again a journalist, probes into widow Hepburn's secrets and discovers that her eminent hero-husband has turned to fascism.

It's exodus time at the studio. Norma Shearer leaves the lot after *Her Cardboard Lover*. She's forty-two and a still beautiful veteran of nearly forty Metro films. Like Garbo she retires at her peak and never returns. Jeanette MacDonald and Nelson Eddy go too after their last film together, *I Married An Angel*. So does Johnny Weismuller who, after the studio dress him in a suit for *Tarzan's New York Adventure*, swings over to RKO in search of his loincloth.

Of those who remain, Hedy Lamarr offers sultry, tropical sex (''I am Tondelayo'') in *White Cargo*; Lana Turner offers herself to gangster Robert Taylor ('T-N-T. . .Turner n' Taylor. . .They're Dynamite Together) in *Johnny Eager*; and Gene Kelly the nimblest pair of dancing feet of the 40s in *For Me And My Gal*.

Gable temporarily leaves the scene when he joins the Army Air Corps in August just a few months after his wife Carole Lombard has been killed in an air crash.

Greer Garson has another smash hit as the year comes to a close. In *Random Harvest* she's back in England once more with World War I amnesiac Ronald Colman. Certain critics aren't that keen. Says James Agee, ''I would like to recommend this film to those who can stay interested in Ronald Colman's amnesia for two hours and who could with pleasure eat a bowl of Yardley's shaving soap for breakfast.''

1943 Another star goes, Joan Crawford after *Above Suspicion* and fifty-five Metro movies. Her next stop. Warners. The old regime of Garbo, Shearer, Russell and Crawford has gone and a new one led by Garson, Turner, Hepburn and Garland has taken its place.

Among the up and comings: swimming star Esther Williams, Van Johnson, Robert Walker, Red Skelton and Donna Reed.

Greer Garson, with the help of husband Walter Pidgeon, discovers radium in *Madame Curie*; Robert Taylor joins the Naval Air Corps after fighting at *Bataan* and for the navy in *Stand By For Action*; Tracy is an angelic ghost guarding over young airman Van Johnson in *A Guy Named Joe*; and two stars make it big in the same film — Lassie and eleven-year-old Elizabeth Taylor in *Lassie Come Home*.

Hedy Lamarr, appropriately enough is *The Heavenly Body*. ''Any girl can be glamorous,'' says she. ''All you have to do is stand still and look stupid.''

The musicals, now on the verge of a breakthrough, include Minnelli's all-black *Cabin In The Sky*; *Girl Crazy* with Judy Garland and Mickey Rooney and songs by George and Ira Gershwin ('I Got Rhythm', 'Embraceable You'); and Joe Pasternak's all-star extravaganza *Thousands Cheer*.

Tom and Jerry *do* make their breakthrough. They win their first Oscar for *Yankee Doodle Mouse*. Jerry is a small time general who battles the enemy, Tom, with fireworks.

C. Aubrey Smith, beloved British character actor of many MGM films, claims the title 'Champion Cricketer of Southern California'. Together with Boris Karloff, he formed the Hollywood Cricket Club and introduced the game to the film colony in the twenties. Basil Rathbone plays occasionally in his side. So does Clive Brook. Other regulars include David Niven, Nigel Bruce and H. B. Warner. According to Karloff, Ronald Colman does not play, but they ''knock him over from time to time for a subscription''.

1944 The first classic MGM musical — *Meet Me In St. Louis*, a nostalgic portrait of a St. Louis family at the turn-of-the-century. It's a valentine to things past, warm-hearted, sentimental, like a picture postcard come to life.

Minnelli directs, Freed produces, Judy Garland, Margaret O'Brien, Lucille Bremer, Mary Astor, Leon Ames and Marjorie Main star. The hit songs: 'The Boy Next

Door', 'The Trolley Song' and 'Have Yourself A Merry Little Christmas'.

Broadway Rhythm ('All The Things You Are') with George Murphy and *Bathing Beauty*, built around swimming star Esther Williams, are other MGM musicals. Miss Williams is one of ten performers, drawn from a list of 155, promoted to official star status. Others include Laraine Day, Kathryn Grayson, Van Johnson, Gene Kelly, George Murphy, Margaret O'Brien.

Tracy is back in the mid-thirties escaping from a Nazi concentration camp in Zinnemann's *The Seventh Cross* and right up to date as Lt. Col. James H. Doolittle, the the man who engineered the bombing raid over Japan in *Thirty Seconds Over Tokyo*; Clarence Brown's *The White Cliffs Of Dover* is another hands across the sea production with Irene Dunne marrying into the English aristocracy just after World War I.

Suave Charles Boyer tries to drive Ingrid Bergman insane in an eerie Thornton Square mansion in *Gaslight*. She gets an Oscar for trembling at the sound of his footsteps on the ceiling; so again do Tom and Jerry in *Mouse Trouble*; Greer Garson this time has to make do with a nomination for *Mrs. Parkington*.

1945 Gene Kelly and Frank Sinatra, two sailors on shore leave, help make *Anchors Aweigh* the top grossing musical of the year. So do the Sinatra numbers 'I Fall In Love Too Easily' and 'The Charm Of You' and two inventive Kelly dance sequences, the first with an enchanting little girl to the music of 'The Mexican Hat Dance', the second with Jerry the cartoon mouse — one of the most successful of the early attempts to combine live action with animation.

It's some year for the little mouse. Together with Tom who actually speaks a few words, and the bulldog (debut) he wins his third Oscar in a row for *Quiet Please*!

Greer Garson is still the first lady. Her period film, *Valley Of Decision*, is top moneymaker with 5.5 million dollars. She's a housemaid who marries the son of a Pittsburgh industrialist. Not a bad choice considering he's played by new young heart-throb Gregory Peck.

She's less well off with Gable in his first post-war film, *Adventure*. 'Gable's back and Garson's got him' cry the ads. He's a sea going bum, she's a shy librarian. Got him or not it's dullsville. She's better off in Pittsburgh.

Judy Garland, in a non-musical role, spends her time

with on-leave soldier Robert Walker in *The Clock*; beautiful youngster Elizabeth Taylor leaves her collie behind and opts for a horse in *National Velvet*. With the help of Judy's former partner, disbarred jockey Mickey Rooney, she wins the Grand National disguised as a boy. The dog, meanwhile, pads off for war heroics in *Son Of Lassie*.

A more serious view of the conflict is taken by Ford's classic *They Were Expendable*, one of the finest films to come out of World War II. Robert Montgomery and John Wayne lead the gallant fight of a squadron of motor torpedo boats in the Philippines during the early days of the war.

The year's most frightening moment: when Hurd Hatfield finally reveals his horrific, decayed portrait — in full bloodcurdling Technicolor — in *The Picture Of Dorian Gray*.

1946 The big commercial hit? *The Yearling*, Clarence Brown's Technicolor version of Marjorie Kinnan Rawlings' prize-winning novel about a farmer's son growing into manhood on a small farm in the wild Florida backwoods. The main star is again Greg Peck. Mayer wants him for a long term contract. A wary Peck says no.

The musical scene comprises of *The Harvey Girls* with Judy Garland; *Till The Clouds Roll By*, a lavish all-star tribute to Jerome Kern; and the ambitious *Ziegfeld Follies*, a no-story musical revue with a top MGM star each doing a speciality. Lean Horne sings 'Love', Esther Williams swims, Judy Garland renders 'A Great Lady Has An Interview', William Powell (as Ziegfeld in heaven) surveys it all with a condescending smile.

The film also includes 'The Babbitt And The Bromide'. It's a George and Ira Gershwin number and until *That's Entertainment II*, marks the only time that Astaire and Kelly dance together on screen. They play two gentleman acquaintances who meet at different periods of their lives and greet each other with the same clichéd routine: "Hello, how are you?" "Howzafolks?" "What's new?"

Tom and Jerry are both in musical mood. Tom gets his big moment as a concert pianist in another Oscar-winning short *The Cat Concerto*.

Seductive Lana Turner (dressed in malevolent white!) and John Garfield dispose of elderly husband Cecil Kellaway in *The Postman Always Rings Twice*; Robert Montgomery is private-eye Philip Marlowe in Chandler's *Lady In The Lake*.

The latter is unusual in that it is photographed with the subjective camera i.e. filmed entirely through the eyes of the central character. Marlowe is seen in the movie only in window reflections, mirrors, etc.

MGM seize on this unique aspect of the film and go to town in their advertising campaign:

'Starring YOU and Robert Montgomery'

'YOU accept an invitation to a blonde's apartment'

'YOU get socked on the jaw by a murder suspect'

'YOU slug the crooked cop who tries to frame you'

'YOU look into the gun of a fear-maddened killer'

What, surprisingly, they fail to mention, is that YOU also kiss Audrey Totter!

1947 A less than successful year. The top male stars — Gable (*The Hucksters, Homecoming*), Tracy (*Sea Of Grass, Cass Timberlane*), Robert Taylor (*High Wall*) are all saddled with inferior vehicles and even the musical temporarily sags.

The brightest musical is Charles Walters' *Good News*, a version of the 20s stage hit with Peter Lawford as a young football hero and June Allyson as his devoted co-ed admirer working her way through college. Top numbers: 'The Varsity Drag', 'The Best Things In Life Are Free', 'The French Lesson'.

Paul Henreid is a gloomy Schumann in *Song Of Love*; Red Skelton *Merton Of The Movies*; Lana Turner in 19th century New Zealand in *Green Dolphin Street* as one of two sisters setting her hat at Richard Hart. Miss Turner, Donna Reed, family conflict, earthquakes and tidal waves help the movie become MGM's top moneymaker with five million.

Some bright spots: Cyd Charisse and Ricardo Montalban dancing together in the otherwise forgettable *Fiesta*; Margaret O'Brien worshipping ballerina Charisse in *The Unfinished Dance*; and a breathtakingly beautiful Elizabeth Taylor triumphing over adolescence in *Cynthia*.

1948 The musical now dominates and will continue to do so until the mid-fifties.

Top box-office hit is *Easter Parade* with Fred Astaire and Judy Garland involved with thirteen Irving Berlin songs including the famous tramp duo 'A Couple Of Swells'. Fred comes out of retirement when Kelly breaks his ankle on the eve of shooting. Eleanor Powell's heir apparent, Ann Miller nearly steals the movie 'Shakin' The Blues Away'.

The Gene Kelly-Vincente Minnelli combination demonstrates brilliant invention in *The Pirate*, a sophisticated period musical with Judy as a young girl living in the Caribbean and Kelly an amorous strolling player. Kelly's 'Mack The Black' dance number sizzles with sex, style and swirling pirate blades.

Words And Music, a biography of Rodgers and Hart (Tom Drake and Mickey Rooney) is in a lower league although Kelly and Vera-Ellen, dancing to the ballet 'Slaughter On Tenth Avenue', lift it for eight magical minutes; Mamoulian films 'Ah Wilderness' as the period family musical *Summer Holiday*; Joe Pasternak contributes two trifles, *On An Island With You* (Esther Williams) and *Luxury Liner* (Jane Powell).

Ten years after producing an all-women movie the studio come up with an all-male cast for *Command Decision*. Clark Gable, Walter Pidgeon, Van Johnson, Brian Donlevy, John Hodiak, Charles Bickford and Edward Arnold grapple with the problems of American bombing missions over Germany in World War II.

Tracy and Hepburn are together again for Capra's *State Of The Union* with Spence as a presidential nominee rebelling against corrupt political backers; Zinnemann films *The Search* and concerns himself with the plight of thousands of refugee children in post-war Europe.

Dore Schary joins the studio as vice-president in charge of production; Jerry Mouse wins another Oscar for saving a baby mouse in *The Little Orphan*; Dame May Whitty, 'grand old lady of the manor' dies on May 29, aged eighty-two. A favourite British character type in Hollywood, she was a regular at MGM in the forties: *Mrs. Miniver, Lassie Come Home, Madame Curie, The White Cliffs Of Dover, Gaslight, Green Dolphin Street.*

1949 The studio's Silver Jubilee Year. They have now eighty stars and featured players under contract and nineteen directors. Among the latter: Clarence Brown, George Cukor, Robert Z. Leonard, Mervyn LeRoy, Vincente Minnelli, George Sidney, Richard Thorpe, Charles Walters, Sam Wood and Fred Zinnemann.

Two great names from the past disappear from the list during the year. Director Victor Fleming (sixty-six) and Wallace Beery who dies from a heart attack on April 15, aged sixty-four.

Fleming's top productions: *Red Dust, Bombshell,*

Treasure Island, Reckless, Captains Courageous, Test Pilot, The Wizard Of Oz, Gone With The Wind, Dr. Jekyll And Mr. Hyde, Tortilla Flat.

Beery's best-known films: *Billy The Kid, Min And Bill, The Champ, Grand Hotel, Dinner At Eight, Tugboat Annie, Viva Villa, Treasure Island, China Seas.*

Several of the year's movies live up to the twenty-five year celebrations. *On The Town* with sailors Kelly, Sinatra and Jules Munshin singing and dancing from the moment they leave ship in New York is the most inventive musical to date; *Take Me Out To The Ball Game*, again with Kelly and Sinatra, plus Esther Williams, intriguingly combines baseball, music and swimming; and *The Barkleys Of Broadway* brings together for the tenth and last time, Fred and Ginger. It's their first in Technicolor. Ten years suddenly drop away as they perform Gershwin's evergreen 'You Can't Take That Away From Me'.

Dore Schary's influence is beginning to be felt. *Intruder In The Dust* casts a jaundiced eye over racial bigotry in the Deep South when an elderly negro is accused of murder; *Battleground* (a personal Schary production) recreates the 1944 defence of Bastogne. Both eschew familiar MGM romanticism and opt for realism.

Tracy and Hepburn scintillate in *Adam's Rib* as married lawyers who carry their differences into the court room when they defend and prosecute in a murder case; Esther Williams and Ricardo Montalban sing the year's Oscar-winning song 'Baby, It's Cold Outside' in *Neptune's Daughter*; new singing sensation Mario Lanza debuts in *That Midnight Kiss*; Gable is below form as a casino gambler in *Any Number Can Play*.

So too is Mervyn LeRoy with his Technicolor remake of *Little Women*. June Allyson, Elizabeth Taylor, Janet Leigh and Margaret O'Brien all try hard, but aren't a patch on the '33 team at RKO.

1950 *Annie Get Your Gun* with Betty Hutton and Howard Keel is the top musical grosser with 4.6 million dollars; *Three Little Words* has Astaire and Skelton as songwriters Bert Kalmar and Harry Ruby; *Summer Stock* is Judy Garland's MGM swan song. It's a 'putting on a barn show musical'. Gene Kelly co-stars. Judy bows out with the zip number 'Get Happy'.

Mario Lanza sings 'Be My Love' in *The Toast Of New Orleans*; Ricardo Montalban and Jane Powell enjoy *Two*

Weeks With Love; Esther Williams and Van Johnson ski, sing and swim in *Duchess Of Idaho*.

British import Stewart Granger immediately proves he's an important asset. His Alan Quartermain, a tribe of 7 ft Watusis and a 25,000 mile safari by camera and crew make *King Solomon's Mines the* MGM hit of the year.

The old guard are now looking tired and jaded. Gable, a racing car driver opposite tough lady journalist Barbara Stanwyck is in *To Please A Lady*; Greer Garson repeats her Oscar winning role in the inept *The Miniver Story*; Lana Turner is an ambitious photographic model in *A Life Of Her Own*; Robert Taylor out West as an Indian in *Devil's Doorway*.

Only Tracy, brilliant as a harrassed father in Vincente Minnelli's domestic comedy *Father Of The Bride* receives quality material.

The Schary touch is evident in Huston's classic heist thriller *The Asphalt Jungle* and Richard Brooks' *Crisis* with Cary Grant as a vacationing surgeon forced to operate on ailing South American dictator Jose Ferrer. Also in the number of controversial small-scale thrillers being turned out by the studio – *The Violent Hour, Mystery Street, Right Cross, The Next Voice You Hear.*

1951 'Metro-Goldwyn-Mayer feel privileged to add something of permanent value to the cultural treasure house of mankind!'

No, not a version of Shakespeare's 'Macbeth' or 'Hamlet', instead the epic *Quo Vadis* with lovely Christian slave Deborah Kerr converting Roman tribune Robert Taylor amid the decadence and debauchery of ancient Rome. Unfortunately for Christianity, debauchery wins hands down in the persons of depraved emperor Nero (Peter Ustinov) and his vixen wife Poppaea (Patricia Laffan), flanked on each side by two cheetahs. The burning of Rome is the spectacular highspot.

Filmed in Italy for seven million dollars, with a cast of thousands and twenty Christian-tasting lions, the movie becomes the studio's biggest ever moneymaker: 12.6 million dollars.

Musically, the studio can do no wrong. *An American In Paris* with Gene Kelly, newcomer Leslie Caron and the music of Gershwin is the best picture Oscar winner; *The Great Caruso* pushes heart-throb Lanza through twenty-seven arias and includes the pop hit 'The Loveliest Night

Of The Year'; *Show Boat* brings Howard Keel, Kathryn Grayson and Ava Gardner to the decks of Captain Andy's famous 'Cotton Blossom'.

The riverboat is one of the most expensive props ever built for a movie, costing more than 125,000 dollars. It measures 171 ft in length, 34 ft across and has a paddle wheel of 19½ ft, powered by two 225 horse-power aircraft engines.

Fred Astaire surpasses himself by dancing on the walls and across the ceiling in *Royal Wedding*. The trick is accomplished by anchoring the camera, cameraman and furniture to the floor and then rotating the set through 360 degrees. Only Astaire remains upright!

Astaire's leading lady is Jane Powell. Together they sing the Alan Jay Lerner/Burton Lane song 'How Could You Believe Me When I Said I Love You When You Know I've Been A Liar All My Life'.

Argentinian Fernando Lamas and singer Vic Damone are new stars on the horizon; Lassie barks for MGM for the last time in *The Painted Hills*; Esther Williams is 'dunked' in *Texas Carnival*; Errol Flynn is the secret agent Mahbub Ali the Red Beard in *Kim*.

Fred Zinnemann provides one of the year's most interesting pictures, *Teresa*, the experiences of an Italian G.I. bride (Pier Angeli) in America after the war; a duelling Tom and Jerry win their sixth Oscar for *The Two Mouseketeers*; Tracy stars in that rarest of rare films, a successful sequel, *Father's Little Dividend*.

The Red Badge Of Courage, Huston's version of the Stephen Crane Civil War classic results in Louis B. Mayer's resignation from the company. Mayer complains bitterly to president Schenck about the film's excessive cost, 1.6 million. Schenck sides with Dore Schary who put the film into production. Mayer is out after twenty-seven years as studio boss. Schary takes over. *The Red Badge Of Courage* never gets its money back.

1952 *Singin' In The Rain*. Just four words but they herald the greatest movie musical of all time. Kelly's ecstatic splash about to the title tune and Donald O'Connor's acrobatic 'Be A Clown' become part of film history. So too does Jean Hagen's squeaky-voiced silent movie queen, Lola Lamont: "If we bring a little joy into your humdrum lives, it makes us feel our work ain't been in vain for nothing."

Lanza, still very much on song, is drafted into screen

army service and blasts *Because You're Mine* into the hit parade; Esther Williams is Australian swimmer Annette Kellermann in *Million Dollar Mermaid*; Astaire and Vera-Ellen are together in *The Belle Of New York*.

The studio also go in for musical remakes. *Lovely To Look At* is the new title for the old RKO hit *Roberta* with Howard Keel, Kathryn Grayson, Ann Miller and company singing the music of Jerome Kern; Lana Turner, teamed with Fernando Lamas, is the third *The Merry Widow*.

Minnelli takes a scathing view of Hollywood in *The Bad And The Beautiful* with Kirk Douglas brilliant as a ruthless movie producer clawing his way to the top and then sinking quickly down to the bottom. The reason? He tries to become a director as well.

Tom and Jerry add yet another Oscar to their mantlepiece with *Johann Mouse*, a comic farce on the life of Strauss, but the king's crown continues to slip as he fights for an independent Texas and a sultry Ava Gardner in *Lone Star*.

Both Taylor and Granger are full of action, the former as Walter Scott's *Ivanhoe* (the studio's biggest grosser with six million), the latter in two swashbucklers – *The Prisoner Of Zenda* in which he duels with sword and dagger with James Mason, and *Scaramouche* in which he crosses rapiers with Mel Ferrer in a crowded 18th century French theatre. The duel, one of the longest in screen history, lasts 6 minutes 30 seconds.

Tracy has his ups and downs. His downs are when he has to transport a group of pious Pilgrim Fathers to the new world in *Plymouth Adventure*. His ups are when he stars again, for the last time at MGM, with Katharine Hepburn. The film is *Pat And Mike*. He's a shady sports promoter, she's a brilliant lady athlete. Says Spence about his protégée: "There ain't much meat on her but what there is, is choice."

1953 The old guard are beginning to move out. *Kiss Me Kate* is Kathryn Grayson's last at the studio; Red Skelton leaves the lot after *The Great Diamond Robbery*; Garson and Pidgeon appear together for the last time in *Scandal at Scourie*.

The end is in sight too for Gable although he does make one last triumphant attack on the box-office in *Mogambo*, a remake of his own *Red Dust* filmed twenty years earlier. It's a rare instance of a star repeating his own role.

Ava Gardner replaces Harlow, ice-cool beauty Grace Kelly, Mary Astor.

Jean Simmons is a regal *Young Bess* and a stage-struck seventeen year old in *The Actress*, George Cukor's version of Ruth Gordon's autobiographical 'Years Ago'; Esther Williams is *Easy To Love*; Joan Crawford, displaying a fine pair of gams as a Broadway musical star, makes a brief return to the studio in *Torch Song*.

Grade A entertainment is provided by the Minnelli musical *The Band Wagon* with Astaire and Jack Buchanan involved in putting on a Broadway musical version of 'Faust'. An Astaire solo in an amusement arcade, 'A Shine On Your Shoes', an idyllic Astaire-Charisse duet, 'Dancing In The Dark' and 'The Girl Hunt Ballet' put the movie in the highest class.

Shakespeare's political thriller *Julius Caesar* is another grade A production. Marlon Brando stars as Marc Antony, Joe Mankiewicz directs. Louis Calhern is the one stabbed to death. James Mason's Brutus plunges in the last knife, Gielgud's Cassius one of the first!

Diverting moments: MGM's first 3-D flick, *Arena*, a rodeo tale with Gig Young and Jean Hagen; Esther Williams swimming with Tom and Jerry in *Dangerous When Wet*; and Ann Miller performing a sizzling 'It's Too Darn Hot' in *Kiss Me Kate*. At her peak this tap dancer *extraordinaire* is officially clocked at doing 500 taps a minute!

1954 *Executive Suite*, Robert Wise's story of the scramble for power by top level executives in a large commercial company, is the critical hit of the year. It's photographed in black and white and projected onto the old style screen.

MGM, however, are more interested in hitting the CinemaScope trail. Just four months after Fox has blazed the way with *The Robe* it releases *Knights Of The Round Table*, a spectacular of King Arthur's Court starring Robert Taylor and Ava Gardner. Made in England by Richard Thorpe, it's the studio's first in the new process. The first American made MGM film in CinemaScope is a remake of *Rose Marie* with Howard Keel and Ann Blyth.

The John Sturges thriller *Bad Day At Black Rock* with Spencer Tracy brilliantly demonstrates the possibilities of the letter box shaped screen; the same quality is achieved when the CinemaScope cameras swing over to the musical backwoods of *Seven Brides For Seven Brothers*, a Howard

Keel-Jane Powell piece about seven Oregon boys who, influenced by the story of the Rape of the Sabine Women, kidnap seven girls from the local township and make them their brides.

The rest of the musicals, *Deep In My Heart* with Jose Ferrer as Sigmund Romberg; *The Student Prince* with a now overweight Lanza dubbing for Edmund Purdom; and *Brigadoon* have a tired look about them. So does Garson's last for the studio, *Her Twelve Men* and *Betrayed*, a World War II espionage story of the Dutch underground. The latter is Gable's Swan song. The 'king' leaves the studio and never returns. An era is over.

The death of Lionel Barrymore, aged seventy-six, on November 15, just rubs it in further.

1955 The exodus continues. Jane Powell goes. So does singing star Howard Keel. And also the girl who's ''only a star when wet'', Esther Williams. Her last is *Jupiter's Darling* in which she's mixed up with Hannibal's crossing of the Alps. No matter. Best to remember her in the water. Experts estimate that in her ten years as a top star she's performed in fifty water routines and swum a total of 1,250 miles. No one argues.

Doris Day and James Cagney, two stars who have never before appeared on the Metro lot, provide one of the year's best movies, *Love Me Or Leave Me*. Miss Day, as singer Ruth Etting, renders 'Ten Cents A Dance', Cagney, as her gangster boy friend, slaps her around.

Plusses: Richard Brooks' *The Blackboard Jungle*, a searing look at teenage violence in New York schools (it also introduces Bill Haley's 'Rock Around The Clock'); *Interrupted Melody* with Eleanor Parker pulling out all the stops as crippled opera singer Marjorie Lawrence; *I'll Cry Tomorrow* with Susan Hayward pulling out all the corks as singing star Lillian Roth who fights and triumphs over alcoholism. The publicity boys get right to the heart of the matter: 'Filmed on location — in a woman's soul'.

Minusses: *The Cobweb* with the patients and doctors of a mental institution wondering who is mad and who is sane; *Moonfleet*, a dismal Fritz Lang attempt at 18th century adventure; *The Glass Slipper*, a mushy musical fairy tale with Leslie Caron; and *The Prodigal* with Lana Turner as an evil High Priestess of the Temple of Love!

The musicals are still on show, but the great inventive

days are past. The '55 musicals are little more than passable, enjoyable entertainment: Goldwyn's *Guys And Dolls*; *Kismet*; *Hit The Deck*; and *It's Always Fair Weather*.

The entertainment prize goes to Frank Sinatra, at his swinging best as a 'got-it-made' New York bachelor in *The Tender Trap*. Spoiling his well ordered sex life, a persistent Debbie Reynolds.

1956 Crosby and Sinatra sing 'Well, did you evah' and create movie history. It's the first time the pair sing together on the screen. The film is *High Society*, a musical remake of George Cukor's 1940 comedy *The Philadelphia Story*. Grace Kelly has the Katharine Hepburn part, Bing Crosby takes over from Cary Grant and Sinatra from James Stewart. The songs: 'Who Wants To Be A Millionaire', 'True Love', 'You're Sensational', and 'Now You Has Jazz' are by Cole Porter.

It's Grace Kelly's last film. The same year she appears in *The Swan* (appropriately enough as a princess) and then skips over to Monaco for a new kind of glitter.

Walter Pidgeon (*The Rack*), Ann Miller (*The Opposite Sex*) and Lana Turner (*Diane*) don't have such luck. It's a quick handshake then through the gates of Culver City for the last time.

Even Schary's six year reign comes to an end at the year's close.

The biggest star of all to leave is Tracy. He walks out of his role as a ruthless cattle baron in *Tribute To A Bad Man* and a twenty-one year contract comes to an end. Cagney takes over but the famous tag 'More Stars Than There Are In Heaven' now looks like a sick joke.

Some highspots: Paul Newman as boxer Rocky Graziano in *Somebody Up There Likes Me*; Brando as the Okinawan interpreter Sakini in *Teahouse Of The August Moon*; Deborah Kerr as a schoolteacher who, in *Tea And Sympathy*, goes to bed with a potentially homosexual student and proves to him that the best things in life are free.

Grisliest death: Robert Taylor being frozen solid in *The Last Hunt*.

1957 Louis B. Mayer dies aged seventy-two. For several years in the thirties and forties he was the highest salaried individual in the United States. First with Thalberg and then on his own he created the classic image of MGM and remained studio boss for more than a quarter of a century until his reluctant resignation in 1951. His funeral is poorly attended.

So are most of Metro's movies. The three-hour romantic Civil War epic *Raintree County* with Elizabeth Taylor and Montgomery Clift takes 5.9 million but costs much much more; Stewart Granger and David Niven, castaway on a desert island with grass-skirted Ava Gardner, don't ring any bells; neither do Gregory Peck or Lauren Bacall in *Designing Woman*, a loose remake of *Woman Of The Year*.

Hoofers Astaire and Kelly both leave the studio. Astaire's farewell is in *Silk Stockings*, a musical version of *Ninotchka* with Cyd Charisse in the Garbo role; Kelly's in *Les Girls* in which he's back in Paris dancing with Kay Kendall, Mitzi Gaynor and Taina Elg.

A slimmed down Mario Lanza however tries for a come-back with *The Seven Hills Of Rome*.

The two movies which do make money: *Jailhouse Rock* with Elvis Presley as an ex-con discovering he has a talent for guitar playing and *Don't Go Near The Water*, a service comedy of the Pacific with Glenn Ford.

1958 The studio returns briefly to musical form with Vincente Minnelli's multi-Oscared *Gigi*.

Just as she was seven years earlier, Leslie Caron is in Paris, this time as a turn-of-the-century schoolgirl being trained by grandmamma Hermione Gingold and aunt Isabel Jeans for the role of grand cocotte. Louis Jourdan provides male charm, Lerner and Loewe the songs (including the bitter-sweet 'I Remember It Well'), Colette the somewhat less than charming story on which it is all based.

The other big one is Richard Brooks' *Cat On A Hot Tin Roof* which has Paul Newman taking to drink and pining for a dead companion in a rambling house in the Deep South.

If it sounds like Tennessee Williams, it is. Venom, greed, sex, mendacity, death are all mixed in together as Maggie The Cat (Elizabeth Taylor) does everything in her power to get Paul Newman between the sheets. Despite looking better than she's ever done she fails. The movie doesn't. It takes nearly ten million at the box-office.

Brooks is less happy in the 19th century Russia of Dostyevsky. Despite an all-star cast headed by Yul Brynner and Claire Bloom *The Brothers Karamazov* fails both with the public and the critics.

Vincente Minnelli, however, demonstrates his versatility by filming William Douglas Home (*The Reluctant Debutante*) and James Jones (*Some Came Running*) with equal skill.

The studio's longest serving star Robert Taylor acts as a mouthpiece for powerful racketeer Lee J. Cobb in *Party Girl* and shoots it out with Richard Widmark in a desert ghost town in *The Law And Jake Wade*.

Glenn Ford, now the studio's most popular box-office attraction, is also out West in *The Sheepman* and in the World War II comedy *Imitation General.*

1959 Metro refilms its silent hit *Ben-Hur* with Christianity once more chipping away at the edges of a pagan Roman society only this time in sound and in front of six cameras. The net result is the same. Ben-Hur (Charlton Heston) defeating Messala (Stephen Boyd) in an eleven minute chariot race. William Wyler directs.

Naturally, it's statistics time again: a six-and-a-half month shooting schedule; 365 speaking parts, over 300 sets, 78 horses and, eventually 11 Oscars. The chariot race, filmed by second unit men Andrew Marton and Yakima Canutt, takes three months to film on an 18 acre set. The most important statistic of all: 36.6 million at the box-office.

Hitchcock visits Culver City for the first and only time for his classic chase thriller *North By Northwest*; Shirley MacLaine fights off New York wolves in *Ask Any Girl*; and Lanza appears in *For The First Time* as an opera star in love with a deaf girl. It's for the last time as well. The popular singing hero of the 50s dies on October 7 of a heart attack. During a ten-year career he has been plagued with illness, weight problems, diets, nervous exhaustion. He was just thirty-eight. His MGM films: *That Midnight Kiss, The Toast Of New Orleans, The Great Caruso, Because You're Mine, The Student Prince, Seven Hills Of Rome, For The First Time.*

1960 Elizabeth Taylor whores her way to an Oscar as John O'Hara's Manhattan prostitute Gloria Wandrous. Simply dial *Butterfield 8* and her services are available. Liz at first rebelled against the script finding it cheap, commercial and in bad taste. But of such roles are Academy Awards made.

David Niven and Doris Day prefer family life, laced with frequent moments of comedy, in *Please Don't Eat The Daisies*; Rod Taylor the future in an imaginative version of H. G. Wells' *The Time Machine*; Glenn Ford the wide open spaces in a remake of *Cimarron*. As for Judy Holliday, well she's trying to come to terms with a telephone operating system in *Bells Are Ringing*. The results are amusing — and disastrous! Director: Vincente Minnelli. Dorothy Malone fights for her life aboard a sinking liner in *The Last Voyage*. Her legs are buried under debris. Panic-stricken husband Robert Stack moves heaven and earth, but not the debris, to save her. The liner sinks a bit further. . .

MGM lose two great figures from the past. Cedric Gibbons, their great art director dies aged sixty-seven and Clark Gable, perhaps the most famous Metro star of them all, goes from a heart attack on November 17, aged fifty-nine.

'The King' appeared in seventy-one films, fifty-two of them at Metro: His key movies: *Possessed, Red Dust, China Seas, Mutiny On The Bounty, San Francisco, Test Pilot, Idiot's Delight, Gone With The Wind, Boom Town, Command Decision, Mogambo.*

Says Lana Turner: "He never took advantage of that marvellous appeal he had. He handled himself very well. I guess that's why men liked him so. He was completely real in every sense of the word. He was just a helluva guy."

The funeral is private. The pallbearers include Spencer Tracy, James Stewart and Robert Taylor.

1961 A wretched year with nearly all the style gone from a once great studio.

Gina Lollobrigida follows Elizabeth Taylor into whoring in *Go Naked In The World*, but no Oscar this time; Susan Hayward is also on the game in *Ada* but reforms and turns to politics no less; Margaret Rutherford opens her account as Agatha Christie's doddery sleuth Miss Marple in *Murder She Said*; racy author Bob Hope romances Lana Turner in *Bachelor In Paradise*.

Nicholas Ray's Life Of Christ, *King Of Kings*, produced by Sam Bronston, is the only real financial success. Jeffrey Hunter is Jesus, Robert Ryan — John The Baptist, Hurd Hatfield — Pontius Pilate, Rita Gam — Herodias, Frank Thring — Herod Antipas.

1962 Metro goes for the big ones, remaking its old Valentino success *The Four Horsemen Of The Apocalypse* but updating the 'cousin against cousin in wartime' theme to World War II. Nevertheless the four horsemen – Conquest, War, Pestilence and Death – still ride. Glenn Ford replaces Valentino.

The three-hour *Mutiny On The Bounty* costs nineteen million and makes ten which is not good business whichever way one looks at it. Brando, who turns Fletcher Christian into a foppish rake, is the main cause, delaying production on innumerable occasions. Director Carol Reed starts but leaves. Lewis Milestone takes over and just about finishes. Trevor Howard is the new Captain Bligh.

Doris Day and a performing elephant *Jumbo* try to keep things on an even keel but most of the MGM films have a dramatic, literary flavour, drawing from William Inge (*All Fall Down*), Tennessee Williams (*Sweet Bird Of Youth, Period Of Adjustment*), Irwin Shaw (*Two Weeks In Another Town*), Nabokov (*Lolita*).

Warren Beatty, Eva Marie Saint, Paul Newman, Kirk Douglas, Geraldine Page, Rossano Brazzi, Jane Fonda are all active; Randolph Scott and Joel McCrea come out of retirement for Sam Peckinpah's western *Ride The High Country*; Ed Begley wins a supporting Oscar for his corrupt Southern patriarch Boss Finley in *Sweet Bird Of Youth.*

Tod Browning, director of many Lon Chaney films of the twenties, dies aged eighty.

1963 *How The West Was Won*, an all-star panorama of sixty years of the Wild West (1839 to 1889) is the first story film in Cinerama. Three directors, thirteen stars, eleven co-stars and a rousing Alfred Newman music score add up to memorable entertainment.

One of the characters, railway engineer Richard Widmark doesn't view the opening up of the West with all that much enthusiasm: "What's a railroad anyway. Two tracks and a whistle."

Margaret Rutherford is another not over-enthusiastic about travel. Says she in *The V.I.P.'s*: "They put you on planes, make you sick and then tell you you're not going at all." Nonetheless she wins an Oscar.

Otherwise, it's a mixed bunch with Robert Wise investigating *The Haunting* and making brilliant use of sound long before Friedkin did similar things in *The Exorcist*;

Nobel prize winning author Paul Newman spying in Stockholm in *The Prize*; Miss Rutherford, in her other hat, investigating in *Murder At The Gallop*; and Glenn Ford trying to raise a six-and-a-half year old son in *The Courtship Of Eddie's Father.*

1964 MGM, no longer the studio of big musicals (all the musical Oscar winners are now coming from Fox, Warners, United Artists) tries for one last big one. *The Unsinkable Molly Brown.* It's about a tomboy orphan girl who sets out to find fame and a rich husband. Debbie Reynolds does her best. So does director Charles Walters, but it's a long, long way from *Singin' In The Rain.* The box-office take: a respectable 8.5 million.

If musicals are out, what's 'in'? As far as Metro is concerned very little. Martin Ritt refilms the Japanese classic *Rashomon* as a Mexican western *The Outrage*; defrocked clergyman Richard Burton is also down Mexico way as a tourist guide in Tennessee William's *The Night Of The Iguana*; Julie Andrews endures *The Americanization Of Emily*; Margaret Rutherford is still sleuthing in *Murder Ahoy.*

Romantic mishaps between sisters, girl friends and airline pilots provide the most diverting entertainment. The film: *Sunday In New York.* Rod Taylor, Cliff Robertson and Robert Culp are all around. Squeezed somewhere in between — Jane Fonda.

1965 Steve McQueen plays the longest game of stud poker in movie history in *The Cincinnati Kid.* He loses everything on a full house to Edward G's straight flush.

Sean Connery escapes from his 007 image but finds himself in a British military stockade in North Africa in *The Hill*; Margaret Rutherford squints at *Murder Most Foul*; beatnik artist Liz Taylor and married minister Richard Burton enjoy illicit Monterey passion in *The Sandpiper*; Rex Harrison, George C. Scott and Ingrid Bergman are the respective owners of *The Yellow Rolls-Royce.*

The top box-office and critical honours go to David Lean's *Doctor Zhivago*, thrillingly photographed by Oscar winner Freddie Young and delicately played by Omar Sharif as the idealistic Russian doctor/poet who finds himself in sympathy with the ideals of the revolution but unable to adjust to the new society. Also in the cast:

Julie Christie, Tom Courtenay, Rod Steiger, Ralph Richardson. Box-office take: 46.5 million.

The Loved One, Tony Richardson's screen version of Evelyn Waugh's satirical novel of Californian cemetery customs is advertised as 'The Motion Picture With Something To Offend Everyone!''

Jeanette MacDonald dies from a heart attack, aged fifty-eight. A singing star of many Metro films she appeared in eight operettas with Nelson Eddy: *Naughty Marietta, Rose Marie, Maytime, The Girl Of The Golden West, Sweethearts, New Moon, Bitter Sweet, I Married An Angel.*

1966 Spy year! Doris Day switches her comedy antics from Universal to Metro in the comedy spy movie *The Glass Bottom Boat*. Director Frank Tashlin and co-star Rod Taylor help the movie earn nearly five million.

Taylor is also John Gardner's best-selling agent Boysie Oakes in *The Liquidator*; Robert Vaughn (Napoleon Solo) and David McCallum (Illya Kuryakin) are in *To Trap A Spy* and *The Spy With My Face*, two spin-offs from the popular TV series 'The Man From Uncle'.

John Ford ends his forty-eight year career with *Seven Women*, a story of a woman doctor who sacrifices herself to save the lives of a group of missionaries held captive by a Chinese warlord. Anne Bancroft, Sue Lyon, Margaret Leighton, Flora Robson, Mildred Dunnock and Betty Field are among those privileged to make a final appearance before Ford's cameras.

The biggest box-office hit is John Frankenheimer's *Grand Prix* (over nine million) which has James Garner, Yves Montand, Brian Bedford and others fighting for the world motor racing championship around the tracks of Europe. Exciting spectacle, flabby story.

1967 Spencer Tracy dies on June 10, aged sixty-seven. One of the greatest of MGM stars (only Gable rivalled him) he once commented on his abilities as an actor. ''I don't like anything about acting. But I've done very well by it. I learned the trade well. It's never been very demanding. It doesn't require much brainwork. Acting is not the noblest profession in the world, but there are things lower than acting — not many mind you — but politicians give you something to look down on from time to time.''

Tracy appeared in over seventy movies, thirty-nine of them for MGM. Among his most famous for the studio:

Fury, San Francisco, Captains Courageous, Test Pilot, Boys Town, Northwest Passage, Edison The Man, Boom Town, Dr. Jekyll And Mr. Hyde, Woman Of The Year, Tortilla Flat, Thirty Seconds Over Tokyo, State Of The Union, Adam's Rib, Father Of The Bride, The Actress, Bad Day At Black Rock.

Jeanette MacDonald's singing partner, Nelson Eddy, dies in March from a stroke aged sixty-five.

The Dirty Dozen, a tough-tough war movie about twelve assorted rapists and murderers who are trained into a commando outfit is a twenty million dollar moneymaker; *Point Blank* is a flashy gangster thriller with Lee Marvin on a vengeance kick; *The Comedians* is an intriguing Graham Greene tale of political turmoil in Haiti.

1968 MGM soar into outer space with the greatest sci-fi epic of all time, *2001: A Space Odyssey*. The fascinating journey to Jupiter (and back?) brings in twenty-four million dollars. Only three Metro movies, *Gone With The Wind, Doctor Zhivago* and *Ben-Hur* have taken more.

Czarist Russia (*The Fixer*), the North Pole (*Ice Station Zebra*) and Hollywood (*The Legend Of Lylah Clare*) provide more down to earth backgrounds to the studio's movies.

Elvis Presley, Raquel Welch, Robert Wagner, George Hamilton, Peter Ustinov, Rock Hudson and Alan Bates are among the stars who appear behind the lion's roar; Robert Z. Leonard (78), director of *The Great Ziegfeld* and scores of other MGM movies and Franchot Tone (63), leading romantic actor of the thirties pass from the scene.

1969 *Where Eagles Dare. . .Mayerling. . .*a musical *Goodbye Mr. Chips* with Peter O'Toole and Petula Clark. . .*The Gypsy Moths. . .*James Garner as *Marlowe*.

All seem commonplace when compared to so many of the movies made by Robert Taylor and Judy Garland, the two former MGM stars who die during the year.

Taylor goes on June 8, aged fifty-seven, from lung cancer. In the thirties he was described as the 'nation's most admired matinee idol since Rudolph Valentino.' He later referred himself in somewhat less ambitious terms: "A punk kid from Nebraska who had an awful lot of the world's good things dumped in my lap."

During his career he played opposite nearly all the MGM beauties in films like *The Gorgeous Hussy, Camille, A Yank At Oxford, Waterloo Bridge, Johnny Eager,*

Undercurrent, The Bribe, Quo Vadis, Ivanhoe, Party Girl. When he finally drove off the Metro lot after twenty-four years of service an executive commented: ''There goes the nicest actor we ever had. In all the years he worked here he never once behaved like an actor.''

Judy Garland goes just 14 days later, in London, from an accidental drug overdose. She was forty-seven and in a word, incomparable. A victim of her own temperament and the relentless pressure of a studio which pushed her through twenty-seven pictures between 1937 and 1950, she was the most loved of all MGM's musical stars.

Her most famous films: *The Wizard Of Oz, Babes In Arms, Strike Up The Band, Little Nelly Kelly, Ziegfeld Girl, Babes on Broadway, For Me And My Gal, Presenting Lily Mars, Meet Me In St. Louis, The Clock, The Harvey Girls, The Pirate, Easter Parade, Summer Stock.*

1970 Again the studio's movies, David Lean's romantic *Ryan's Daughter* apart, take second place to remembrance of things past.

Between May 3 and May 20 MGM hold a public auction of studio props and costumes. The auction is held on stage 27 at the Metro studios. Over 20,000 items are catalogued and the net receipts amount to one-and-a-half million dollars.

Among the items purchased were:

An 1870 locomotive (called Reno) used in 35 movies including *How The West Was Won, Raintree County, Annie Get Your Gun*	$62,500
Judy Garland's ruby red slippers which led her down the yellow brick road to Oz	$15,000
A settee and four armchairs from *Marie Antoinette*	$8,750
A French boule mantle clock used in *Ninotchka*	$6,750
Bert Lahr's cowardly lion outfit from *The Wizard Of Oz*	$2,400
Clark Gable's trench coat	$1,250
Judy Garland's blue and white check gingham dress from *The Wizard Of Oz*	$975
Elizabeth Taylor's wedding dress from *Father Of The Bride*	$625
A Judy Garland dress from *Meet Me In St. Louis*	$600
A clown suit worn by Jimmy Durante in *Jumbo*	$400
Charles Laughton's hat from *Mutiny On The Bounty*	$300
Tarzan's loincloth	$200

A Debbie Reynolds dress from *How The West Was Won*	$200
Elizabeth Taylor's shoes from *Father Of The Bride*	$185
An Esther Williams swimsuit!	$50

1971 The studio's output is small and uninspired. The surprise hit is the all black *Shaft* with Richard Roundtree as a 'cool, hip, black private eye'; the big disappointment, Ken Russell's *The Boy Friend* with Twiggy and Christopher Gable involved in Sandy Wilson's putting on a show musical. Russell tries for large-scale Busby Berkeley effects but the 20s charm of 'I Could Be Happy With You' and 'A Room In Bloomsbury' survives.

A big western, *The Wild Rovers* with William Holden and Ryan O'Neal as a pair of bank robbers bites the dust; Richard Burton is a sadistic thief in *Villain*; George C. Scott a retired getaway driver persuaded to return for one last dangerous job in *The Last Run*.

1972 Charlton Heston pilots a 707 jet liner full of passengers and a mad bomber to the relative safety of Moscow airport. The film is *Skyjacked*. If it sounds far-fetched that's just about right but the tension and a harrowing portrait of a disturbed war veteran by James Brolin give the movie flying power. Its take of nearly seven million is larger than any other MGM movie of the year.

Maggie Smith, in a role originally intended for Katharine Hepburn, is Graham Greene's outrageous aunt Augusta in *Travels With My Aunt*; Raquel Welch has considerably less poise as a professional roller skater in *Kansas City Bomber*; Richard Roundtree is once more the Harlem hard guy in *Shaft's Big Score*.

1973 In October MGM announces its complete withdrawal from distribution. The company's product, such as it is, will be handled by United Artists in the United States and Canada and CIC in the rest of the world.

Westworld with Yul Brynner as a robot gunslinger; Peckinpah's *Pat Garrett And Billy The Kid*; and *Soylent Green*, science-fiction of the not too distant future, are among the company's movies.

Arthur Freed, producer of the greatest musicals in the history of the cinema, dies on April 12, aged seventy-eight. He had seen it all and produced the best: *Meet Me In*

St. Louis, Ziegfeld Follies, The Pirate, Easter Parade, On The Town, Annie Get Your Gun, An American In Paris, Showboat, Singin' In The Rain, The Band Wagon, Silk Stockings, Gigi, Bells Are Ringing.

1974 and after. . .

MGM's films are now down to two or three a year. In January of '74 the company invests its money in the MGM Grand Hotel in Las Vegas. It's the world's largest resort hotel with 2,084 rooms. Its cost: 120 million dollars. The statistics sound as though they have come from an old Metro movie but movies now take second place.

Since '74 MGM has maintained a limited production schedule, *The Sunshine Boys* (75), *The Wind And The Lion* (75), *Logan's Run* (76), *Demon Seed* (77) and *International Velvet* (78) figuring among its handful of productions.

Ironically *That's Entertainment* (74) and *That's Entertainment II* (76), two compilation films of scenes from classic MGM movies, are the biggest financial hits, proving, too late, that there's still a market for old style entertainment.

The MGM story continues, just. . .

R.K.O.

R.K.O.

People used to be rather cruel about RKO Radio Pictures during World War II. "In case of an air raid, go to RKO, they haven't had a hit in years" was a favourite Hollywood quote of the time.

If the wisecrack had a certain amount of truth to it commercially (RKO has a mere eleven films in *Variety's* list of all-time box-office champs), artistically it was well wide of the mark.

For RKO could boast not only of *Citizen Kane* and *The Magnificent Ambersons*, two of the greatest films ever made in America, but also quality in just about every film *genre* – the musical (*Top Hat*), the western (*Cimarron*), comedy (*Bringing Up Baby*), horror (*The Cat People*), soap opera (*Love Affair*), the thriller (*Notorious*), adventure (*Gunga Din*), the private-eye movie (*Farewell My Lovely*).

Why then did the studio last but twenty-five years before crumbling into obscurity in the mid-fifties? Why did films preceeded by the bleep-bleep-bleeping of a radio transmitter bestriding a huge globe of the world fail to make money and in the end, represent nothing but mediocrity?

The answer lies in one basic reason, a reason that made RKO so different from all the other Hollywood studios. They were never once ruled by an iron hand. There was no all-powerful God-like figure to create a firm, far-seeing policy. There was no Zanuck, Warner or Cohn. No Mayer or Zukor. RKO changed its presidents and production heads so quickly that often the eager new men were on their way out again before they had even the time to make a dent in their executive chairs.

David Selznick, who was brought in as production head in the early thirties just three years after the studio's beginnings in 1929, lasted but a year before being lured away to MGM. Merian C. Cooper was another who lasted only a short while. Pandro S. Berman remained in charge of production for just three years and after the war Dore Schary was another short service man. His term of office? Sixteen months.

Only multi-millionaire Howard Hughes who purchased RKO outright in 1948 lasted any length of time and he was the man responsible for the studio's final and rapid decline.

It is little wonder then that it remains difficult to pinpoint a definitive RKO style. The studio was like a yo-yo. Up one year, down the next. Never sure where it was going, never sure where its future lay.

Little wonder too that so many creative directors enjoyed working there. men like George Stevens, John Ford, George Cukor, John Cromwell, Gregory La Cava and Leo McCarey in the thirties, and later, in the forties, William Dieterle, Robert Wise, Jacques Tourneur, Mark Robson.

The lack of an iron hand meant also a lack of tight discipline and a chance of creative freedom not readily available at other studios. To those who worked there RKO became known as the family studio. It had a homely atmosphere. After its demise few directors, writers, actors or technicians were ever heard to complain about the days they worked on the RKO lot.

John Cromwell, director of such RKO films as *Of Human Bondage, Abe Lincoln In Illinois* and *The Enchanted Cottage* recalled: "The studio was rather well-known for its freedom. Each studio in Hollywood had a definite personality. In the thirties there was nothing strict about the regime in charge at RKO. They seemed to have a policy of trying to make everyone happy and contented as the best way to produce a picture. It seemed to be full of free souls who felt that at least they were doing what they wanted to do. In that respect it was very pleasant to be there. I enjoyed every minute of it."

In a studio of such widely changing personnel and no obvious development pattern, RKO's achievements can best be seen by looking at the studio decade by decade – *King Kong*, the Astaire-Rogers musicals and the womens' pictures of the thirties; Orson Welles, Jane Russell and producer Val Lewton (a most unlikely trio) in the forties; and Howard Hughes in the fifties. Linking all three decades, was a constant flow of zany and sophisticated comedies, many of them featuring the studio's most durable and dependable performer, Cary Grant. There were also many minor classics filmed (RKO's total output was some 1500 movies) but it was the aforementioned pictures and personalities on which, basically, the foundations of the studio's reputation were built.

The biggest single RKO hit of the thirties – big in more senses than one – was without a doubt, the giant ape *King Kong*, the most famous and beloved of all screen monsters. A creation of the novelist Edgar Wallace, who died shortly before the film went into production, he was 40 ft of raging and pathetic monster, taken by force from his island domain, hopelessly enraptured by the beauty of Fay Wray and finally machine-gunned by airplanes as he is trapped on top of the Empire State Building.

The film's final line, "It wasn't the airplanes. It was beauty killed the beast" brought out with moving simplicity all the pathos of the tragic story.

Many a Depression audience left a movie theatre with a lump in their throats after witnessing the death of Kong. Many an audience, too, left in a state of wild excitement as it recalled the huge ape roaring defiance from the top of a skyscraper and snatching planes from the air as if they were no more than model toys.

RKO chose New York — Kong's 'City Of Death' — to premiere the picture. They selected not one cinema but two, and the two biggest — the Roxy and the Radio City Music Hall.

King Kong was made at RKO during Selznick's brief reign and,according to the film's producer and co-director Merian C. Cooper, Selznick was the only man, other than brilliant special effects expert Willis O'Brien, the actual creator of Kong, who really believed in the project.

Cooper and Selznick knew that the cost of such an unusual film would be enormous. Their studio, like others during the period, was experiencing money difficulties. Less expensive films such as soap operas were relatively easy to finance. To gamble on an expensive fantasy seemed to be asking for trouble. Just how many of the studio's hierarchy would buy the idea was open to question. After all, as a story outline, *King Kong* was no more than a fairy tale.

"Selznick backed me all the way on the project," said Cooper. "In order to push it through we decided to make a test reel containing the sequence showing Kong shaking the tree trunk to make the sailors fall into the chasm and Kong's subsequent battle with the allosaurus which had been photographed with a combination of Willis O'Brien's unique model animation and other special techniques.

"The footage met with great enthusiasm at the sales meeting and the project was given the go-ahead."

King Kong cost some 650,000 dollars to produce and took a fortune. It comes as no surprise to find that it figures in RKO's 'select' list of all-time moneymakers with a total gross of four million dollars.

Compared with the mighty ape, Fred Astaire and Ginger Rogers were almost doll-like. Miss Rogers standing on the shoulders of the lithe Mr. Astaire wouldn't have reached the monster's kneecaps. Yet when they danced 'The Carioca' in *Flying Down To Rio* their impact was almost as great.

Whereas Kong's feet lumbered along crushing all before them,

Astaire's toes twinkled and flashed and provided a rhythmical magic the like of which had never before been seen on screen.

In Ginger Rogers, Astaire found the ideal partner and in Astaire and Rogers RKO found box-office insurance for an entire decade.

Katharine Hepburn summed up the pair's enduring magic in one crisp sentence. ''He gives her class and she gives him sex.''

Astaire's class wasn't quite so evident to the Paramount executives back in 1928 when Fred first tested for the screen for *Funny Face*. ''Can't act, can't sing, balding. Can dance a little'' was the famous result of those few feet of wasted film.

Even in the early thirties RKO weren't altogether convinced of his box-office potential. When he tested for *Flyng Down To Rio* nearly everyone who saw the test thought he was wrong for films. ''Not good-looking'' and ''No romantic appeal'' were typical comments, but Merian Cooper, who had taken over for a brief spell as production head of the studio, took a chance and the gamble paid off.

If Cooper, a genuine pioneer of the cinema, had been allowed to have his way, *Flying Down To Rio* would have been the very first picture to have been shot in the then new three-colour Technicolor process and Fred and Ginger would have danced together in colour. But RKO turned down the proposal and another two years went by before colour was used in a feature length movie — RKO's *Becky Sharp*.

Fred and Ginger were destined to remain in black and white throughout their entire RKO career (their only film in colour was *The Barkleys Of Broadway* made at MGM after the war), but in essence the lack of colour was of no consequence. The Astaire-Rogers combination would have been a hit even if the pair had been photographed in bilious green.

In their very first film together as stars, *The Gay Divorcee*, the formula was immediately established — boy meets girl, boy rows with girl, boy loses girl, boy wins girl. In between the four acts of the 'plot' Fred and Ginger would go through their dance routines and audiences would be lulled into a simple, make-believe world of musical elegance, filled with the tunes of George Gershwin, Irving Berlin and Jerome Kern.

That same formula was repeated on eight occasions during the thirties. The variations were slight, the story outcome always predictable, but it mattered little. As long as Fred Astaire and Ginger Rogers danced that was all that audiences cared about.

It was magic time. So often and so gracefully did the pair blend together that it seemed the films would never end. When they did it was in 1939 when the opening shots of World War II were beginning to threaten Europe. By then magic time was over and films like *Top Hat, Roberta* and *Swing Time* belonged to the past.

The other *genre* RKO found it could rely upon with some certainty during the thirties was soap opera. Women in distress was a formula that seemed to have limitless opportunities, mainly because women more than men made up the majority of film audiences of the time. Seemingly keen to experience a kind of masochistic desire to see themselves humiliated on the screen, the ladies in the audience saw to it that soap opera flourished for several years at RKO.

RKO were well qualified to promote this particular kind of entertainment for, although all studios had their fallen women, RKO had more than most. Irene Dunne, Constance Bennett, Ann Harding, Kay Francis were just a few who suffered on the studio lot. They were kept as mistresses, dabbled in prostitution and then paid for their sins in a series of soap operas that ranged from the ludicrous to the magnificent.

Those of the latter kind were invariably directed by men like George Stevens and George Cukor both of whom got their first big chance directing 'women's pictures' on the RKO lot.

Stevens, who began his career as a cameraman and later filmed such classics as Paramount's *A Place In The Sun* and *Shane* was thrown in at the deep end while filming a small-scale comedy entitled *The Nitwits*. Someone mentioned to him that RKO was about to film Booth Tarkington's *Alice Adams* and that he was in line for the directing spot.

Quite a daunting prospect for anyone seeking that elusive first break especially when the picture was to star Katharine Hepburn who already, at the ripe old age of twenty-eight, had one Oscar on her mantlepiece.

Even so, Stevens said he was interested. "They said, 'Would you have a visit with Katharine Hepburn?' I said, 'Well, I've got this comedy, and I've got to fix up these gags.' I wanted time to read the book so I said 'Could we wait?' and they said, 'No, because we have to make this decision between you and another young director (William Wyler).' So they said, 'Let's make it this evening,' and I said, 'OK, let's make it at her house after I finish shooting.'

"Well, she was a young but grand lady in the studio and I was shooting this stuff with guys falling into mortar and things. I thought, 'If Katharine Hepburn sees this, she'll want to air the house out, knowing there's this kind of association.'

"Anyway I talked with Kate and I hadn't read *Alice Adams*

which was kind of ridiculous. But I wanted to make it and I knew enough about Tarkington to get by. She told the producer, Pandro Berman, 'I don't know about that guy. He won't talk about the story.' Berman said, 'Well he's a strange fellow, but if he wants to make this picture I think he ought to make it, even if he does have very little to say about the story.' They agreed and we got along just fabulously.''

George Stevens was suddenly in the big time, his years of patience and studying his craft had paid dividends. Luck had played its part, but so too had his long apprenticeship.

One man who made it to the big time without serving any apprenticeship was Orson Welles who arrived in Hollywood in 1939 after scaring the nation half to death with his famous radio broadcast of 'The War Of The Worlds'. Accompanying him was his Mercury Theatre Company which included such players as Joseph Cotten, Everett Sloane, Agnes Moorehead and George Coulouris.

Not surprisingly, he arrived in a blaze of publicity. Curiosity about what the twenty-four year old wonder boy was going to produce was mixed with envy and awe as all eyes turned towards RKO.

Welles had a contract to make a minimum of one film a year on which he could be producer, director, writer, actor or a combination of all four. For a newcomer to films to be offered such terms was unheard of.

Mark Robson, then an editor and later a director at RKO, admitted there was a lot of envy. ''Welles came to RKO with a free-wheeling contract and was given what in those days was a great deal of money to make films. It caused RKO ruptures with several directors who were upset by the freedom given to Orson that they did not have. There were great jealousies around. But Orson's period was not a long one.''

Long it may not have been, but while it lasted it was stormy, exciting and not a little sensational.

In the autumn of '39 Orson announced that his first film would be a version of Joseph Conrad's *Heart Of Darkness*. The budget was set at a million dollars. Orson had not allowed for the outbreak of World War II. As hostilities began, Dito Parlo, an Austrian star whom Orson had contracted to appear with him in the film, was interned in France as an enemy alien and the project was shelved.

Next on the list was *The Smiler With A Knife*, a detective thriller by poet Cecil Day Lewis written under the pseudonym of Nicholas Blake. Carole Lombard was one of those listed for a key role in the film. She wasn't overkeen. ''I can't win working with Welles,'' she said. ''If the film is a hit *he* will get the credit. If it's a flop *I'll* be blamed.''

She wasn't too far off the mark, but she needn't have worried. *The Smiler With A Knife* was another project that never got off the ground.

Welles had admitted in private that he didn't intend to stay in Hollywood for more than a few months and it begun to look as though those months were going to be fruitless. Perhaps, after all, the wonder boy was not going to deliver. RKO's famous transmitter signal almost burped instead of bleeped and the men at head office began to feel decidedly hot under the collar.

Orson Welles, however, had found his subject. It was gelling in his mind, taking gradual shape in script form and by the summer of 1940 was already to go. On July 30, the most famous American film of all time, *Citizen Kane*, went before the cameras. Its story was the life of a powerful newspaper tycoon. Its cast was made up of the players from The Mercury Theatre Company.

When he first walked onto his film set Welles was supposed to have exclaimed, ''This is the biggest electric train set any boy ever had.'' He was lucky. He had as his 'station master', the great cinematographer Gregg Toland. Together, they produced a masterpiece of cinema.

The Mercury players were a little over-awed by the experience of filming. It was entirely new to them. None of them had ever appeared in a movie before. To allay their fears Orson had them visit the set regularly before filming began and 'touch the camera for luck'. He also arranged for them to do something simple on the first day of shooting such as opening and walking through doors or driving a car. If possible no dialogue was to be spoken on that first day. It was 'breaking in' time.

Most of them took it all in their stride. All that is except one, Joseph Cotten, a man who would become, later in the decade, the biggest star of them all. On one particular day early in the schedule, he would have given anything to have been on the train back to New York and the comfort of his Washington Square apartment.

Relaxing one evening during filming and not on call for the following day he received a telephone call informing him that Orson had fallen and broken his ankle. The only immediate scene that could be filmed and in which Welles himself was not appearing was one featuring Cotten made up as an old man and remembering his early days with the young Kane.

It was a long dialogue scene and not due to be filmed for several weeks, but the studio pressed Cotten to do it the next day as a special favour. Orson would direct from a wheelchair.

Cotten had little option but to agree. He sat up all night learning the dialogue. "There were pages and pages of it," he says today, recalling the agony of the moment, "and I had to be in the make-up chair between 4.30 and 5.00 in the morning.

"Well I got there, just. Of course the make-up job took quite a bit of time. I had to age at least forty years. In those days, the rubber-type make-up stuff was brand new and still in the experimental stages. It took a long time to apply. I also had to get some contact lenses because my young eyes were bright and shiny. An optician said he could put some milky liquid behind the lenses and paint some bloodshot red in the corners. Then they needed to fit a wig."

Says Cotten: "Before nine o'clock that day I had mentally resigned from the movies. I was sick because I had drunk too much coffee. The make-up kept cracking and I had to go to an eye doctor on Wilshire Boulevard in bathrobe and pyjamas — my costume for the scene — to get the contact lenses.

"In those days contact lenses were much larger than they are now and damn near covered the whole eye. They had to be made for you. Well there was no time. Mine were kinda off the peg, the kind that *almost* fit. To remove them they used a rubber suction thing that they pressed on to the eye and pulled so that the lenses came out with a kind of loud 'plop'.

"The doctor said to me 'These don't fit too well so I'd better come with you to the studio.' That filled me with even more confidence. Those lenses were the most uncomfortable things. The make-up men painted on them and put some liquid behind them with the result that as well as not really knowing my lines I couldn't see either. Everything was like a vague silhouette.

"Then the rubber make-up and the glue on the wig didn't marry. The make-up guy was going frantic because the two kept coming apart. Everytime I spoke, the wig would pop up off the top of my head and he'd have to start the whole thing again. He got quite angry with me. 'Can't you talk without moving your forehead?' he yelled. I told him I didn't know as I'd never been told to control certain facial muscles when acting.

"But they managed it, at least I thought they did. We shot until lunch with an improvised set. It was meant to be the roof garden of a hospital. All they did was lower a big section of street and put a low wall and a wheelchair in front of it. Nothing more. It was just thrown together in a hurry.

"They came to me after lunch. 'Fine,' said Orson, 'but I think we'll have to go through it again this afternoon. You see, your acting is fine, but everytime you move your head the wig pops up and there's no way to cut away from it on screen. There's no way the audience is *not* going to see it.'

''I was desperate,'' says Cotten. ''Then I had an inspiration. A tennis visor like those worn by Helen Wills Moody in the old days. I rushed out to a tennis shop and bought one. I put it over my head so that it shaded my eyes and it was that and *only* that that kept the wig in place.

''People told me afterwards that it was probably one of the worst days in movies that anyone had ever endured.''

So much for the joys of working on a masterpiece for that's how many of the top critics hailed *Citizen Kane*. ''Brilliant'', ''Outstanding'', ''The Like Of It Has Never Been Seen Before'', were just some of the words filling the columns of enthusiastic reviewers in the spring of 1941.

RKO basked in it all. The gamble had, after all, been worthwhile. The wonder boy had brought it off. If *Kane* didn't exactly set the box-office alight it did at least bring RKO right up there with the greats. If Welles could continue in such form for another four or five years anything might happen.

But Welles couldn't. He had the talent, immense talent, but he didn't have the discipline. To make matters worse, he chose for his second film Booth Tarkington's classic *The Magnificent Ambersons*, a story of the decline of a wealthy Midwestern family at the turn of the century. As a book it was superb. As box-office it had about as much appeal as three lame men taking a walk in an empty field.

For many, it remains almost as fine a film as *Kane*, even in its truncated version of eighty-eight minutes. But in its original form it was remarkable as Mark Robson bears out: ''The original version was simply marvellous. It was truly *The* magnificent *Ambersons*. Theatrically wonderful; photographed superbly by Stanley Cortez. But it was so advanced, so ahead of its time, that people just didn't understand it. Nearly an hour was cut although I can't recall specific sequences. It was a kind of chopped down version of Orson's original conception.''

Welles was away in South America working on the documentary *It's All True* when editing started on the picture. Robson and Robert Wise had the unenviable task of attending all the sneak previews and licking it into some sort of shape. *Ambersons* was re-edited through ten to fifteen previews.

Says Robson: ''When Bob and I took it out to preview I guess that in one fell swoop about a quarter of the theatre audience got up and left. Then about five minutes later, another quarter left and then, finally, the last half of the audience left until there were about two or three people remaining in the theatre and many angry patrons waiting for us outside.''

In the end, in desperation, a happy ending was tacked on to the movie (Robert Wise directed the last two reels) and the film was eventually released. Audiences wouldn't accept it in any form. It failed miserably despite being close to a masterpiece.

Welles' career disintegrated after *Ambersons*. He appeared in and partly directed the Eric Ambler thriller *Journey Into Fear* then strayed over to Fox to appear in *Jane Eyre*, back to RKO for *The Stranger* then on to Columbia for *The Lady From Shanghai*.

With Welles' stay lasting for just about par for the course, RKO slipped back into less sensational ways.

Nevertheless, many of its films of the forties were among the best produced in Hollywood. A random sample reveals such diverse movies as the Ginger Rogers soap opera *Kitty Foyle*, William Dieterle's *All That Money Can Buy*, the comedies *The Devil And Miss Jones* and *Mr. Blandings Builds His Dream House*, the Chandler thriller *Farewell My Lovely*, Hitchcock's *Suspicion* and *Notorious*, Siodmak's terrifying *The Spiral Staircase*.

But apart from Robert Mitchum and Jane Russell who appeared on the scene later in the decade there were no regular stars to speak of. Many top stars *did* appear in RKO movies, but only briefly, for perhaps a year or two, before moving on to a different studio. RKO was almost like a resting place between seven-year-contracts.

One small unit that operated at the studio between 1942 and 1946 did, however, consider RKO very much its home. It was a small unit comprising of producer Val Lewton, directors Jacques Tourneur, Robert Wise and Mark Robson, actors Boris Karloff, Simone Simon, Tom Conway and Kent Smith, and a group of technicians headed by talented cameraman Nicholas Musuraca.

The unit's function was to produce a series of B horror films with titles like *The Cat People, I Walked With A Zombie* and *The Leopard Man*. It brought to these films not gore, sadism, or obvious horror, but class and distinction, and a dark, unnerving menace.

No gruesome horror unveiled itself on the screen in a Lewton film. Audiences were made to scream in other ways — by a long walk through a Caribbean sugar plantation to the throbbing of voodoo drums, by the suggestion of something prowling in the dark, by the sound of a screaming woman trapped behind a locked outside door and by the silence that followed as a slow trickle of blood seeped through under the door and into the house.

The inspiration was Lewton. He hated the titles he was given, but he knew he had to put up with them. If nothing else they were at least saleable and allowed him to hide behind their manufactured triteness and produce small masterpieces of psychological horror. His first film, *The Cat People*, cost just 130,000 dollars. Subsequent pictures in the series were budgeted at similar amounts.

His disciples, Wise, Robson, Tourneur — all of whom owed the start of their directing careers to his generosity — held him in the greatest respect and revered his memory long after his premature death, aged forty-six, in 1951.

Robert Wise, in particular, sums up Lewton's attitude especially well. "His philosophy, in addition to scaring the wits out of people, was that he had a responsibility to the millions who saw our pictures. He aimed at more than mere exploitable spook shows and wanted their impact to result from legitimate psychological conflicts.

"Lewton's pictures were cheaply made, but not cheap. Usually the audience was introduced to a stable, reassuring situation. Then steady pressure was exerted and the people on the screen were thrown off emotional balance, and, we hoped, would take the audience with them. We tried to reveal the inner workings of our characters and to apply the theory that all men can become confused when danger is imminent."

Lewton managed the impossible. He made a silk purse out of a sow's ear and never once lost confidence in what he was doing.

"They may think I'm going to do the usual chiller stuff which will make a quick profit, be laughed at and forgotten," he said, "but I'm going to fool them. They may fight me all along the way, but I'm going to do the kind of suspense movie I like."

He did and he succeeded.

Lewton's period came to an end in 1946. Two years later, after the all too brief regime of Dore Schary — the one man who might have been able to put the studio on a stable and prosperous course — Howard Hughes took over and from then on it was all downhill for RKO. Very slowly downhill at first with hardly a mark of decline as many of Schary's productions reached the screen, but then with ever-increasing swiftness during the fifties.

After Hughes took over, RKO's image became basically kiss-kiss-bang-bang. Crime thrillers and sultry sex were what Mr. Hughes enjoyed and that was what RKO purveyed through an ever increasing number of films. Some of them, thanks mainly to the skill of their directors, were not without a certain style, but the originality of the studio had almost completely disappeared.

Hughes, of course, had, in 1940, already given RKO a certain notoriety when he introduced the magnificently proportioned Jane Russell to the screen in his personal production *The Outlaw*.

The story goes that, after encountering Miss Russell for the first time, he rushed back breathlessly to his office and exclaimed, "Today, I saw the most beautiful pair of knockers I've ever seen in my life."

It probably *was* true. Miss Russell's breasts remained a fixation with Hughes for the rest of his career in movies especially during the shooting of *The Outlaw* when he had Jane's bust photographed from every conceivable angle. No matter whether she was wrestling in a haystack, leaning over a bed in a low-cut blouse, riding a horse or even simply moving around a fire, her breasts were always the highlights of the screen.

Jane Russell was a phenomenon, a movie star before she ever hit the screen. She became known as 'The world's most exciting girl'. The story that Hughes was the first to give her a screen test, however, is untrue. Jane Russell *did* have screen tests before Hughes found her. Fox regarded her as 'unphotogenic' and Warners thought she had 'no energy' and 'no spark'.

When Hughes tested her for the role of Rio in *The Outlaw* (an unlikely tale about Billy The Kid and Doc Holliday) she won out over 700 applicants.

Said Jane, who had been announced by publicist Russell Birdwell as the new Jean Harlow, "Before I even went on location for the film they started giving me the buildup. I christened boats, I judged baby contests, I reclined in haystacks, I sprawled on beaches — always in a low cut blouse."

Jane frequently found herself posing on and off set for cameramen and stills photographers. She spent at least half her day in a forward, leaning position.

"They would tell me to pick up a pail of water or jump up and down in bed in a nightgown while they shot from above and below. I didn't realise what they were doing. I was as green as grass."

Yet so successful was Birdwell's publicity campaign that columnists even began to hint that Hughes had had a special brassiere designed to hold Jane's breasts in place. At one point during the production Hughes was actually heard to mutter, "We're not getting enough production out of Jane's breasts."

The Hays Office was left in no doubt that he had got more than enough when he finally premiered the film in February 1943.

Wrote censor Joseph Breen to his boss Will Hays, "I have never seen anything quite so unacceptable as the shots of the breasts of the character of Rio.. . Throughout half the picture, the girl's breasts which are quite large and prominent, are shockingly uncovered."

'Cut it' ordered the Hays Office. 'No' said Hughes and promptly withdrew the film from circulation.

Hughes finally released *The Outlaw* in 1949 (he allowed it to go on a restricted release without a seal in '46) just a year after he had purchased the RKO studio. By then it seemed like an anti-climax, but it still took big money, five million dollars, and for RKO that made a welcome change.

After starting out as a small-scale production, *The Outlaw* finished up costing some three-and-a-half million dollars and was released nearly a decade after its completion.

Not that such an occurrence was in any way unusual as far as Hughes was concerned. One of his many strange quirks was to withhold completed pictures for years on end. *Vendetta* starring his post-war 'discovery' Faith Domergue was delayed five years, *Montana Belle* with Jane Russell was filmed in 1948 and released in 1952 and *Jet Pilot* starring John Wayne and Janet Leigh had to wait seven years before reaching the screen.

Only a select few saw Hughes. When he bought the studio everyone expected a visit, more or less immediately, from the eccentric millionaire. Fritz Lang was one of the directors working at the studio at the time: "When the news got round that Hughes had bought RKO all the big shot producers who usually turned up for work at 11 o'clock or later were there at 9 a.m. awaiting the new boss who never appeared. This went on for about a fortnight until they said 'Oh the hell with it' and lapsed back into their old ways.

"Then, after several weeks, Howard Hughes finally appeared. I'll never forget it. He had a large entourage and never spoke to *anyone*. He went through the whole studio, looked at every stage, every shop, and after two hours and twenty minutes all he said was 'Paint it'. Then he walked out and was never seen again."

Hughes simply preferred to date beautiful girls, ride around Burbank in his old Chevy or just stay out of sight. Whenever people did catch a glimpse of him he was always wearing his famous tennis shoes and one of his old flight jackets.

Nobody ever quite knew what he would do next as far as the studio was concerned, but there was no doubt that he was in firm control of everything, albeit from a distance.

Director Nicholas Ray was asked by Hughes to take over as production head one Christmas Eve. Ray refused. The same director was also asked to 'save' four pictures that Hughes had made and considered unreleasable — *Macao, The Racket, Androcles And The Lion* and *Jet Pilot*.

One of them, *Macao*, featured Ray's wife Gloria Grahame who was then in the process of getting a divorce from the director.

She considered the film so bad that she told him, "If you cut me out of the film entirely I'll give you a divorce and you won't have to pay any alimony."

When the studio was nearing its final days Hughes hired director John Sturges to direct Jane Russell in her last RKO picture, *Underwater*.

Sturges who had just enjoyed a huge success at MGM directing Spencer Tracy in *Bad Day At Black Rock*, took the assignment because he felt that the story of two guys (Richard Egan and Gilbert Roland) hunting for sunken treasure would make an exciting, straightforward adventure movie.

"I was summoned to the front office and told that Jane Russell was going to be in it," says Sturges. "I said 'But that's insane, there's hardly a girl's part in the film.' Back came the reply. '*She's In It!*' "

"So I called her and said 'I think I ought to tell you Miss Russell that there isn't much of a part for you in the film, it'll never amount to anything and I don't really think you should do it.' She said, 'I've news for you. Maybe it's bad new or maybe it's good news, but have you read the other scripts around?' I said, 'No.' She said, 'Well I have and I have to do a picture and I'm going to do yours'."

Not entirely happy with the situation Sturges went to his agent who looked at him in amazement and said he couldn't really understand Sturges' problem. "You have one of the biggest stars in Hollywood, you have an unlimited budget and a multi-millionaire producer. What exactly is the . . . . . matter?"

Sturges finally agreed to make the movie and went to RKO hopefully to meet Hughes and discuss the picture. When he arrived and reached the main executive office he found a small group of men sitting around chatting to themselves, but all the time glancing over at a telephone in the centre of a large desk. On the telephone a red indicator light was burning. Suddenly the red light turned green.

"It was hilarious," says Sturges. "Everyone jumped up and the nearest man to the phone grabbed it and said immediately '*Howard*, how *are* you?' I just burst out laughing. It was so ridiculous.

"I never actually got to see Hughes although I had met him at a party several years before. But I did speak to him on the telephone several times and I can honestly say he was most helpful. Anything I wanted I got. There was no interference of any kind.

"He was always a recluse, even before he disappeared for good. He used to sneak people into the studio to take some film out so that he could run it in the evening. Then the same people would sneak the film back. We weren't supposed to know. But we used to put little pieces of paper in each can of film, so tiny that the projectionist wouldn't notice when the paper fell out. We knew that if those pieces of paper were missing he'd run the film.

"His favourite movie was *The Frogmen*. It sure doesn't figure on any other people's best-ever list. But he liked it. He loved the gadgetry and reckoned it was the best film ever made. He loved the machinery, the aqua lungs and all that. Extraordinary man."

Underwater had the ultimate in ridiculous premieres — underwater with Jane in a red bathing suit joining the critics several fathoms down. John Sturges did not attend.

When Hughes sold the studio in 1955, William Dozier tried to keep it afloat by casting stars like John Payne, Arlene Dahl, Glenn Ford, Virginia Mayo and Dana Andrews in a series of double-feature melodramas. But it was too late. RKO was finished. The last movie made on the lot was *The Girl Most Likely*, shot by former Paramount ace Mitchell Leison

"When we started shooting there were a couple of other pictures shooting on the RKO lot," said Leison, "but they were eventually finished and we were the only company left on the lot. When the studio decided we no longer needed a certain department, it was shut down and if we needed something after that, we just had to make do ourselves. It was eerie."

The cries of 'Action' from Orson Welles, the sound of Astaire's tapping feet and Kong's mighty roar must have echoed silently round the lot during those final, unhappy days.

Today, more than twenty years after its demise, RKO remains something of an enigma. Moviegoers who first became acquainted with the studio in the fifties must have recollections of a second-rate outfit making crime thrillers and Jane Russell melodramas. Those who came across it a decade earlier and discovered Welles and Lewton must have been thrilled by its potential. Those who remembered it from the very beginning and who followed it right through to the bitter end must have said to themselves, "What a waste. Where did it all go wrong?"

It went wrong because RKO was what it was, a lightweight vessel in a stormy sea with no captain on board and which bravely rode out the storms with a crew that could handle most things, but not a simple matter of policy. When, eventually, a captain did come along, he was the wrong man and, in the end, couldn't have cared less.

Worse, he was too rich to go down with his ship.

John Wayne in one of his most memorable roles, Captain Nathan E. Brittles in Ford's cavalry classic *She Wore A Yellow Ribbon*.

Lex Barker, the replacement Tarzan when Weismuller retired in 1948, seen here in *Tarzan's Savage Fury*.

Howard Hughes discovery Jane Russell in one of her final movies for RKO, the musical *The French Line*.

Ginger Rogers and Fred Astaire sparring together in *Top Hat*, the most famous of their nine RKO musicals of the thirties.

Robert Mitchum in *The Racket* and in trouble, as he usually was in his RKO movies. Not believing a word of his excuses, plain-clothes cop William Conrad in his pre-*Cannon* days.

Chronology

1929 RKO is formed as the Radio Corporation Of America, purchases control of FBO (Film Booking Office Of America), a studio that had begun life as the British company of Robertson-Cole which had made its first film, *Mistress Of Shenstone*, in 1921.

The studio merges FBO with the Keith-Albee-Orpheum vaudeville circuit and broadcasts its hopes to the trade without a hint of modesty. Everything is to be new and forward looking. 'The Radio Titan Opens The Curtains Of The Clouds And A New Greater Year Dawns For The Most Spectacular Show Machine Of All Time!'

Bold words. Not surprisingly, the pictures don't quite live up to the publicity. *Rio Rita*, a version of the Ziegfeld 1927 musical show with Bebe Daniels and John Boles is the one big smash with colour musical sequences and a gross of two million dollars; *Syncopation* with Barbara Bennett and Bobby Watson as a dancing team is another musical comedy; and in *Vagabond Lover* Rudy Vallee and his college friends form themselves into a successful dance band.

The first all-talking picture shot on the lot is *Street Girl*, a Betty Compson romance directed by Wesley Ruggles. On the more dramatic side, Richard Dix, the studio's top male star for several years to come, stars in Earl Derr Bigger's *Seven Keys To Baldpate*.

1930 Musicals again dominate as RKO absorbs another studio, the twenty-six year old Pathe company. *Hit The Deck*, with Jack Oakie and songs by Leo Robin, Clifford Grey and Vincent Youmans ('Sometimes I'm Happy', 'Hallelujah') is the year's big one; *Dixiana* has Bebe Daniels in the New Orleans of the 1840s; and *Lethernecking*, a demusicalized version of the hit Broadway show, is notable for the screen debut of Irene Dunne.

The girls are already beginning to make their mark. Bebe Daniels, much in demand, is 'Gertie The Gun' (jewel thief Ben Lyon is her co-star) in *Alias French Gertie*; Betty Compson is involved with spies in *Inside The Lines*; Mary Astor with gangsters in *The Runaway Bride*; Sally O'Neil is a showgirl stranded in Fiji in *Girl Of The Port*; and Evelyn Brent, out for revenge in *Framed*, is also a notorious dance hall girl in *The Silver Horde*.

The men do get a look in — just. Richard Dix teams romantically with Lois Wilson in *Lovin' The Ladies* and plays an underworld gambler in *Shooting Straight*. Lowell Sherman directs himself as a gang leader in *The Pay Off*.

1931 RKO, in just their third year as a major studio, beat Warners, United Artists and Columbia to a best picture Oscar with *Cimarron*, Edna Ferber's epic tale about the rise of an Oklahoma town from a settlement to a thriving city in the centre of one of the richest oilfields in the world. Costing nearly 1¾ million dollars to produce and grossing 2½ million in return the movie establishes its two stars, Richard Dix and Irene Dunne, as the studio's biggest box office draws.

It also includes the famous real-life Cherokee Strip stampede when pioneers made a frenzied rush in wagons, on horseback and on foot, even on bicycles, for two million acres of free government land. In filming the scene RKO learn the value of statistics. . .Over 1000 vehicles of every description, 3500 horses and mules, 5000 players, 35 cameras in pits, on trucks and in planes. Three days shooting!

But if *Cimarron* aims its sights mainly at the men the studio's other product is aimed primarily at women. It's sin and suffer time for nearly all the major female stars on the lot.

Kay Francis dabbles in an illicit affair with Spaniard Ricardo Cortez in *Transgression*; Ann Harding disguises herself as a cockney governess and goes after estranged barrister Leslie Howard in *Devotion*; and Irene Dunne, as well as helping win the West, marries Pat O'Brien on the rebound in the tearjerker *Consolation Marriage* and finds herself as secretary to woman-chasing Lowell Sherman in *Bachelor Apartment*.

Constance Bennett suffers most however. In the World War I story, *Born To Love*, she is the American nurse who gives birth to the illegitimate child of pilot Joel McCrea. When McCrea is lost in action she marries Paul Cavanagh only to find that Mr. McCrea turns up again at a later date.

McCrea also causes her a lot of trouble in *The Common Law*. This time he's an artist in Paris and she's a kept woman who poses for him in the nude.

The advertisements make the most of the situation: 'Noted for her beauty. . .Notorious for her indiscretion. She didn't care what people said as long as one lone man kept saying 'I love you'. Her beauty made him the world's greatest artist. But in gaining a reputation for him, she lost her own.'

One particular critic isn't as impressed as he should be: "If RKO cannot make better than this, they might just as well shut down ship, saving their investment."

1932 But RKO don't shut down shop. It's the year of David O. Selznick as production head. He is at the studio for just over a year (from November '31 to December '32) before joining MGM. His job is to raise the quality of production and he does just that with the help of directors George Cukor and Gregory La Cava.

RKO also open, on December 27, the largest movie house in the world, the 6,200 seat Radio City Music Hall in New York. The first movie to play there, Columbia's *The Bitter Tea Of General Yen*, opens in January '33.

Meanwhile spunky newcomer Katharine Hepburn catches the eye in her debut picture *A Bill Of Divorcement*, a Clemence Dane story about inherited insanity, directed by George Cukor. Her first co-star? John Barrymore, no less. The story goes that the two 'enjoyed' quite a heated exchange during the making of the picture. "I'll never play another scene with you," snaps Hepburn. "But, my dear, you never have," replies Barrymore.

Cukor also directs *Rockabye* and *What Price Hollywood*? for many the first version of *A Star Is Born* with waitress Constance Bennett being moulded into a top film star by a derelict director (Lowell Sherman) fighting to regain his prestige.

The women still suffer. Ann Harding is the mistress of sensitive young publisher Leslie Howard in *The Animal Kingdom*; the former wife of handsome Laurence Olivier in *Westward Passage*; and Adolphe Menjou's bit of fluff — in Malaya of all places — in *Prestige*.

Irene Dunne goes through it most, however. She's one of thirteen girls victimized by an old school friend in *Thirteen Women* and in Fannie Hurst's soap opera *Symphony Of Six Million* she's a crippled schoolteacher who is cured by the doctor she loves (Ricardo Cortez).

Joel McCrea and Dolores Del Rio are on a volcanic South Seas Island in King Vidor's *Bird Of Paradise*, but when it comes to islands it's the one belonging to the depraved Russian megalomaniac Count Zaroff (Leslie Banks) which holds most menace. Tired of hunting animals Zaroff hunts people instead and keeps in his trophy room human heads floating in jars of liquid. In *The Most Dangerous Game* he pursues McCrea and Fay Wray all over his private island. "Only after the kill does man know the true ecstacy of love," he says to a startled Miss Wary. It isn't the last time in her career that she is to be startled!

1933 She doesn't have long to wait for another opportunity to scream her head off. 1933 is the year in which she lands one of the most famous roles of the decade. Says she: "Merian C. Cooper (the new production head) told me that he had an idea for a film in mind. The only thing he'd tell me was that I was going to have the tallest, darkest leading man in Hollywood. Naturally, I thought of Clark Gable."

She gets *King Kong*!

Kong, a 40 ft ape captured on an unexplored island and brought back to 'civilization' becomes the most famous monster in screen history.

In actuality he is quite small, just 18in high and not one but several models all built of rubber and sponge and covered with shaggy lambskin. Articulated metal frames allow movements of the limbs, mouth and eyes and a 20 ft high bust that includes Kong's head and shoulders is used for close-ups. A mechanical hand and arm, about 8 ft long is used in those close-ups in which Fay Wray is seen in Kong's grasp.

King Kong apart, the year's most significant event takes place in a movie called *Flying Down To Rio*. Dolores Del Rio and Gene Raymond are the film's stars, but it's the supporting team, Fred Astaire and Ginger Rogers, who make the headlines. Together for the first time, they dance 'The Carioca.' Within a year they will be starring in a film of their own.

Kong and *Flying Down To Rio* are two of the studio's financial hits. Another is Cukor's version of Louisa M. Alcott's *Little Women* with Katie Hepburn perfection as the tomboyish Jo and Joan Bennett (Amy), Jean Parker (Beth) and Frances Dee (Meg) not far behind. *Morning Glory* is Hepburn's big triumph however. For her portrayal of a stage-struck girl from Vermont she wins the best actress Oscar in only her third movie.

Try as they might the other RKO actresses are no more than runners-up to Miss Hepburn in '33. But do they try!

Constance Bennett goes philandering in *Our Betters*; works the Mississippi steamboats as a hooker in *Bed Of Roses*; and is even a Russian spy (K-14) in *After Tonight*.

Irene Dunne also has three movies on parade — *No Other Women, Ann Vickers* and *The Silver Cord* in which she stages an effective revolt against her dictatorial mother-in-law, Laura Hope Crews; Ann Harding, after trapping William Powell into marriage in *Double Harness* finds herself unhappily married to Robert Young in *The Right To Romance*.

1934 Fred Astaire and Ginger Rogers, hailed as 'The King And Queen Of Carioca' hit the jackpot in their first starring vehicle *The Gay Divorcee*. Fred is a hoofer on holiday, Ginger the gal about to be divorced and Edward Everett Horton a fussy lawyer. Among the songs: 'Don't Let It Bother You' in which Fred dances for his dinner; the elegant 'Night And Day' and the climactic 17-minute 'The Continental' which becomes the first song to win an Academy Award.

Bette Davis is loaned to RKO from Warners for the role of the sluttish waitress Mildred in Maugham's *Of Human Bondage*. She realises it's the chance of a lifetime. "Mildred is not going to die of a dread disease looking as if a deb had missed her noon nap," she says and insists on doing all her own make-up for the death scenes. It works. *Life* magazine describe her performance as "Probably the best ever recorded on the screen by a U.S. actress."

The rest of the RKO ladies eat their hearts out. Irene Dunne and Ann Harding in particular are still awash in soap opera and melodrama. Miss Dunne has four films on view including John Cromwell's *This Man Is Mine* in which she lures husband Ralph Bellamy away from seductress Constance Cummings, *The Age Of Innocence* in which she's caught up in New York Society of the 1870s and *Stingaree* which teams her once again with 'Australian Robin Hood' Richard Dix.

Ann Harding in *The Fountain* has all manner of emotional problems to contend with. Married to a German (Paul Lukas) who returns home wounded in World War I she also runs across former sweetheart Brian Aherne who complicates things by rekindling old yearnings. What to do or what not to do? Mr. Lukas solves it all by expiring at the right moment.

There are no such worries for director John Ford. There's not a woman in sight in *The Lost Patrol*, just a British platoon lost in the Mesopotamian Desert. Ford has Arabs pick them off one by one until only sergeant Victor McLaglen is left. The movie is shot in typical no-nonsense Ford style — in two weeks in Yuma in a temperature of 110 degrees.

1935 RKO achieve a notable first with *Becky Sharp*, a version of Thackeray's 'Vanity Fair' and the first feature film to be shot in the new three-colour Technicolor process. Other studios, who have been holding back, quickly see the possibilities of colour and follow suit.

Premiered at New York's Radio City Music Hall and Chicago's Palace in June, *Becky Sharp* stars Miriam Hopkins as the unscrupulous gold-digging Becky and is directed by Rouben Mamoulian.

Delighted with the success of *The Gay Divorcee*, RKO serve up not one but two helpings of Astaire and Rogers. In *Roberta* they're joined by Irene Dunne and perform to some beautiful Jerome Kern numbers ('Smoke Gets In Your Eyes', 'Lovely To Look At') and in *Top Hat* their usual plot misunderstandings are accompanied by the music of Irving Berlin. Among the hit numbers: 'Cheek To Cheek', 'The Piccolino' and 'Top Hat, White Tie And Tails', an Astaire solo in which he performs one of his finest routines, shooting down with his cane an army of top-hatted dancers lined up behind him.

Ernest B. Schoedsack, one of the two directors of *King Kong*, blows the top off Vesuvius in *The Last Days Of Pompeii*; Ann Harding is unhappy again as wife of novelist Frank Morgan in *Enchanted April*; and Katharine Hepburn and Cary Grant team in Cukor's *Sylvia Scarlett*.

In fact, it's a year of quality all round. Hepburn is also Booth Tarkington's socially ambitious *Alice Adams* (directed by George Stevens); Barbara Stanwyck is *Annie Oakley*, another Stevens movie; Richard Dix *The Arizonian*; Helen Gahagan Rider Haggard's evil *She*; and Victor McLaglen, who tops them all both physically and artistically, the pathetic Gypo Nolan in *The Informer*, John Ford's version of Liam O'Flaherty's story of betrayal and murder in Dublin during the 20s.

McLaglen wins an Oscar. So do Ford, composer Max Steiner and writer Dudley Nichols. Says Ford: "The picture cost a little over 200,000 dollars — and we made it in under three weeks."

1936 Pandro S. Berman, a producer at RKO for several years, is the new head of production, but that makes no difference to the Astaire-Rogers movies.

Once again, the musical duo have two on parade; *Follow The Fleet* with Fred in the navy and Irving Berlin again providing the music ('Let's Face The Music And Dance', 'Let Yourself Go') and George Stevens' *Swing Time* in which Fred, a gambler seeking his fortune in Manhattan sings the Oscar-winning 'The Way You Look Tonight' and dances one of the most spectacular of all his numbers 'Bojangles Of Harlem.'

Katharine Hepburn walks bravely to her death after spending two hours fighting the cause of *Mary Of Scotland*, John Ford's version of the stage play by Maxwell Anderson; Ford also tackles Sean O'Casey's *The Plough And The Stars*, a story of the Irish rebellion in Easter Week, 1916; and Burgess Meredith sets out to avenge the death of his father, executed twenty years before for a crime he did not commit, in another Maxwell Anderson piece *Winterset*.

William Powell, as an amateur 'Thin Man' type detective, and Jean Arthur as his ex-wife lighten things a little bit by solving some race track murders in *The Ex-Mrs. Bradford*. Ann Harding, too, tries for comedy, but unsuccessfully in *The Lady Consents*.

1937 Gregory La Cava's *Stage Door*, a brilliant version of the Edna Ferber/George S. Kaufman play about the goings-on in the theatrical boarding house 'The Footlights Club' is RKO's quality film of the year. Among the girls bent on show business careers: smug debutante Katharine Hepburn, her acid-tongued but soft-hearted room-mate Ginger Rogers and the tragic, suicidal Andrea Leeds. Taking advantage of them all: Adolphe Menjou as a libertine producer.

The studio release Disney's first full-length feature cartoon, *Snow White And The Seven Dwarfs*, a practice they are to continue into the 50s. They also cast Cary Grant as Jim Fiske in *The Toast Of New York* and feature Katharine Hepburn as a J. M. Barrie heroine in Stevens' *Quality Street*.

Fred Astaire's movie with Ginger Rogers is *Shall We Dance*, a typical lightweight piece of regulated nonsense made to seem sublime by numbers like 'Let's Call The Whole Thing Off' and 'They Can't Take That Away From Me.' Astaire also deserts Ginger for Joan Fontaine in Stevens' *A Damsel In Distress* but the change is only temporary and by 1938 the pair are back together again.

1938 Howard Hawks and George Stevens provide the comedy; Astaire and Rogers, as always, the music.

Best of all is Hawks' classic *Bringing Up Baby* with staid professor Cary Grant and madcap heiress Katharine Hepburn chasing a tame leopard across the Connecticut countryside in search of a missing bone from a reconstructed dinosaur. If it sounds crazy it is. Miss Hepburn loses the back of her dress in a restaurant, Grant confidently wades across a stream only to finish up to his neck in cold water, and Katie actually mouths the incredible lines: "Hey, flatfoot! I'm gonna unbutton my puss and shoot the woiks. An I wouldn' be squealin' if he hadn' a give me the runaround for another twist."

The recipient of this barrage? small town constable Walter Catlett. Said Hawks later: "I think the picture had a great fault. There were no normal people in it. Everybody you met was a screwball!" Right, but what fun!

James Stewart is also a professor in *Vivacious Lady*, Stevens' first film as his own producer. Stewart's cross to bear? Not Katie Hepburn but night club singer Ginger Rogers.

Carefree is the penultimate Astaire-Rogers musical with Fred as a psychiatrist wooing dizzy Ginger through hypnosis. The score is by Irving Berlin. Among the numbers: 'Change Partners', 'The Yam' and 'The Night Is Filled With Music'.

Ginger is also *Having Wonderful Time* with Douglas Fairbanks Jr. at a resort hotel; Irene Dunne,as a 10,000 dollar a week musical comedy star, is another teamed with Fairbanks in *Joy Of Living*; Lucille Ball is mixed up with the Marx Brothers in *Room Service*; and in the 'B' section Louis Hayward appears as Leslie Charteris' amateur sleuth 'The Saint' in *The Saint In New York*, a quite brutal little piece about a committee of businessmen ridding New York of six gangsters.

1939 *Gunga Din* is one of two big RKO movies of the year. The George Stevens films is based on a Rudyard Kipling poem about an Indian water boy (Sam Jaffe) who sacrifices his life to save a British regiment. The poem runs to eighty-five lines. During filming the studio use one thousand extras, one thousand horses, eight camels, four elephants, six hundred rifles, four cannons, two Gatling Guns, fifty thousand cartridges. They also build a British army encampment, a city of tents and a gold-domed temple!

Sergeants Cary Grant, Douglas Fairbanks Jr. and Victor McLaglen thoroughly enjoy themselves. Villain Eduardo Ciannelli on the other hand leaps into a pit of snakes to get away from it all.

Charles Laughton stars in the studio's other big one, *The Hunchback Of Notre Dame*, William Dieterle's often brilliant version of Hugo's novel about Quasimodo, the deformed bell ringer of medieval Paris.

Acting and direction are superb, Laughton's make-up brilliant and grotesque. RKO hire Perc Westmore from Warners (for 10,000 dollars) to do the job. Part of the face is pulled up, part of it pulled down. A bloodshot eye is installed near the corner of Laughton's mouth and a mis-shapen ear on the other side of the face. Special lenses give one eye a milky consistency. The hump strapped to Laughton's back weighs four pounds. The clothes are heavily padded and Laughton's body covered in rubber to suggest immense power.

The other RKO offerings are not without distinction. Garson Kanin's screwball *Bachelor Mother* has ex-salesgirl Ginger Rogers in charge of an abandoned baby; Leo McCarey's *Love Affair* is expert soap opera with jaded man-of-the-world Charles Boyer falling in love with Irene Dunne; *In Name Only* teams Cary Grant with both Carole Lombard and Kay Francis; and *The Story Of Vernon And Irene Castle*, the real-life saga of the king and queen of ballroom dancing, marks the last time that Astaire and Rogers dance together on the RKO lot.

Since 1933 they have appeared in nine films, danced and sung (either solo or together) to over fifty numbers including some of the greatest ever composed by Gershwin, Porter, Berlin and Kern. It is estimated that the total box-office gross of their films runs to well over twenty million dollars.

Down among the 'B's George Sanders takes over from Louis Hayward in *The Saint Strikes Back* and *The Saint In London*; Lupe Velez stars in the first of the Mexican Spitfire comedies, *The Girl From Mexico* and *Mexican*

Spitfire; and Jean Hersholt begins his stint as a small town doctor in *Meet Dr. Christian.*

1940 It's Ginger Rogers' year. Leaving her dancing shoes behind she proves she's a capable dramatic performer by winning the year's best actress Oscar for *Kitty Foyle*, a hardworking salesgirl who falls for a Philadelphia socialite, but eventually has to settle for a man from her own walk of life. The socialite is Dennis Morgan, the luckier guy James Craig.

She's in happier mood in Gregory La Cava's comedy *The Primrose Path* and Lewis Milestone's *Lucky Partners* in which she shares a sweepstake ticket with Ronald Colman and embarks with him on a platonic honeymoon to Niagara Falls.

Irene Dunne also forgets the hearts and flowers bit in Kanin's *My Favourite Wife*, a crazy comedy about a wife, shipwrecked for several years, who returns home to find husband Cary Grant leaving for a honeymoon with new bride Gail Patrick.

John Cromwell guides a superb Raymond Massey through *Abe Lincoln In Illinois*; Dorothy Arzner directs Maureen O'Hara and Lucille Ball in a backstage story of two feuding dancers in *Dance, Girl, Dance*; and Kanin, in more serious vein, films the tragic *They Knew What They Wanted* in which lonely young waitress Carole Lombard marries doting but elderly Italian farmer Charles Laughton.

1941 The best year in the history of the studio. In fact, one of the best years in the history of *any* studio, dominated by the film that many critics regard as the best picture ever made, Orson Welles' *Citizen Kane*, the story of the life of a ruthless newspaper tycoon.

For the record, the film went before the cameras on July 30, 1940 and was completed on October 23. It cost approximately 800,000 dollars to produce. In April 1941 it is premiered in New York and Los Angeles after a long wrangle with the William Randolph Hearst Corporation which maintains that the movie is based on the life of Hearst himself — which it is, despite frequent denials.

At about the time Welles is putting the finishing touches to *Kane* another top RKO personality, somewhat different in build (38-24-36) but nonetheless equally adept at making headlines is filming tests — in the hay — for a Howard

Hughes western. Her name? Jane Russell. She works on the movie for nine months without a break having her torso photographed from every conceivable angle. The film is *The Outlaw* but it will not be seen until 1943 and then only briefly.

Hitchcock ventures through the studio gates to make *Suspicion*, a thriller for which Joan Fontaine wins a best actress Oscar for her terrified heroine. The man she is terrified of is Cary Grant who with irresistible charm does his best to persuade Joan to drink a glass of milk she is convinced is poisoned. In the original screenplay it is, but RKO refuse to give Grant a bad image and Hitch has to opt for a happy ending!

William Dieterle follows his *Hunchback Of Notre Dame* with *All That Money Can Buy*, a version of Stephen Vincent Benet's 'The Devil And Daniel Webster' the story of a young New Hampshire farmer who sells his soul to the Devil for a pot of gold. With Walter Huston as the Devil (Mr. Scratch) he needs little persuading. ''A soul?'' whispers Huston seductively. ''A soul is nothing. Can you sell it? Smell it? Touch it? No. . .''

Comedy is also well to the fore. Working girl Ginger Rogers is dizzily confused by three suitors in *Tom, Dick And Harry*; Ronald Colman enjoys *My Life With Caroline*; and in *The Devil And Miss Jones* department store sales girl Jean Arthur leads a strike against irascible tycoon employer Charles Coburn.

One of the most important events in RKO's history takes place when Sam Goldwyn, fed up with all his wrangles with United Artists, agrees to distribute his future productions through the studio.

It's an arrangement that lasts for more than a decade and begins with two very different movies — Howard Hawks' comedy *Ball Of Fire* with Gary Cooper as a language professor finding that burlesque dancer Barbara Stanwyck offers him more than the inside of a dictionary, and William Wyler's version of *The Little Foxes* in which Bette Davis appears in one of her greatest roles, the scheming Southern vixen Regina Giddens.

It's the one in which she lets husband Herbert Marshall die of a heart attack in front of her eyes. Her pre-heart attack speech does little to help the ailing man's morale.

''I couldn't stand the sight of you,'' she hisses, remembering their earlier life together. ''I couldn't bear to have you touch me. I thought that you were such a soft

weak fool, so kind and understanding, and I didn't want you near me. The lies and excuses I used to make to you — and you believed them. That's when I began to despise you. . .''

On a much more mundane level George Sanders changes personalities. He becomes 'The Falcon' instead of 'The Saint.' But it's been a helluva a year!

1942 Welles again dominates the scene with his near-great version of Booth Tarkington's *The Magnificent Ambersons*, a saga of the slow decline of a wealthy Midwestern family during the early years of the twentieth century. Starring Joseph Cotten, Agnes Moorehead and Tim Holt it might possibly have equalled *Kane* had it not been for extensive cutting which reduces the picture from one hundred and thirty-one to eight-eighty minutes.

Welles also appears with Joseph Cotten in the Eric Ambler spy thriller *Journey Into Fear* but it is fear of a different kind, the psychological variety provided by 'B' film producer Val Lewton that terrifies the most.

In *Cat People*, the first of a series of low budget films, Lewton shows that terror can be registered equally well when it is only suggested and not shown. The picture, a nonsense story about a Balkan-born girl with the ability to change into an outsize homicidal cat, provides some of the scariest moments of the 40s — a young girl being pursued by something unknown through Central Park at night and being trapped in a dark deserted swimming pool where the only sounds are those of lapping water and the breathing of the stalking cat!

The film costs just 130,000 dollars and grosses at least four times that amount for the studio. Lewton's stay at RKO in the 40s is to prove one of the most rewarding producer-studio partnerships of the decade.

Gary Cooper is baseball hero Lou Gehrig in Goldwyn's *Pride Of The Yankees*; crippled night club singer Lucille Ball and star-struck bus boy Henry Fonda struggle to Miami together in a bizarre Damon Runyon tale *The Big Street*; Dieterle pays tribute to the early days of jazz in *Syncopation*; and in Leo McCarey's *Once Upon A Honeymoon* Walter Slezak has one of the best lines of the year. As an Austrian count married to Ginger Rogers he complains: ''She tries reading my mind. If that doesn't work, she reads my mail.''

1943 "It's 'Jane Eyre' in the West Indies", says producer Val Lewton after the premiere of his newest horror opus *I Walked With A Zombie*. With a title like that he has to say something. Or does he? The answer is 'no'. The movie, directed by Jacques Tourneur, is arguably his finest film and is indeed the Bronte story updated to the Caribbean where wealthy planter Tom Conway hired a young nurse to care for his insane wife.

The Leopard Man (a series of nasty murders in Mexico) and *The Seventh Victim* (Devil Worship in Greenwich Village) are Lewton's other horror offerings but for the most part RKO, like the majority of Hollywood studios, reflects the real-life horror of World War II.

Goldwyn's *The North Star*, directed by Lewis Milestone, is a piece of pro-soviet propaganda about Russian villagers defending themselves against the 1941 Nazi invasion; resistance is offered too by meek French schoolteacher Charles Laughton in Jean Renoir's *This Land Is Mine*; the Spanish Civil War is recalled in *The Fallen Sparrow*; Edward Dmytryk's *Hitler's Children* is one of the first movies about life inside Nazi Germany; the same director also investigates the Japanese in *Behind The Rising Sun*, described by one American critic as "Our first all-out atrocity film of World War II, even to wire rammed down a lady's fingernails."

Soap opera too combines with the war in *Tender Comrade* (another Dmytryk movie) about women working in defence plants while their men are away at war. Bob Hope is mixed up with the Gestapo in Goldwyn's *They Got Me Covered* and even Cary Grant gets his draft notice in the comedy *Mr. Lucky*.

In *The Falcon Strikes Back* Tom Conway takes over from brother George Sanders; *The Mexican Spitfire's Blessed Event* is the last in the Lupe Belez series but the studio have a better than average replacement as Johnny Weismuller's Tarzan films (now produced by Sol Lesser) arrive at RKO from MGM. The first two films released by the studio: *Tarzan Triumphs* and *Tarzan's Desert Mystery*.

The year's biggest disappointment? Howard Hughes' *The Outlaw*. It opens in February and is promptly with drawn because of censorship trouble. 'Mean, Moody and Magnificent' roar the ads as Miss Russell stands wide legged before a custom fitted haystack, a pistol in each fist. 'Too much cleavage, too much sex, too much everything' screams the Hays Office. 'Cut, Cut, Cut!' Hughes

won't and Jane Russell becomes one of the most popular pin-ups of the war without ever having been seen in a movie.

1944 ''The joint looked like trouble but that didn't bother me. Nothing bothered me. The two twenties felt nice and snug against my appendix. I tried to picture Malloy in love with somebody but it didn't work.''

With a dialogue like that you can't really go far wrong and RKO don't with Edward Dmytryk's version of Chandler's *Farewell My Lovely*. Dick Powell is private-eye Philip Marlowe, Claire Trevor the bad girl. The picture, a minor classic, costs less than 500,000 dollars and is shot in forty-four days.

If Powell gets knocked about physically then Edward G. Robinson, Warners' tough guy of the 30s, gets an emotional hammering when he falls under the spell of sultry seductress Joan Bennett in Fritz Lang's *The Woman In The Window*. As a meek psychology professor he becomes involved in a nightmare world of murder and blackmail.

Goldwyn introduces a new comedy star, Danny Kaye, who makes his debut as a hypochondriac drafted into the army in *Up In Arms*; John Wayne is *Tall In The Saddle* but Gary Cooper is more domesticated as a schoolteacher who kidnaps his own baby in Sam Wood's comedy *Casanova Brown*.

Lewton's horror movie is *Curse Of The Cat People* which gives Robert Wise his first chance at direction; Ethel Barrymore wins the studio its only Oscar (best supporting actress) for her slum mother of Cary Grant in *None But The Lonely Heart*.

The year's major debut is made by a young Californian in *Days Of Glory*. He's cast as a Russian guerilla holding off Nazi invaders. His name? Gregory Peck.

1945 RKO hit the jackpot with *The Bells Of St. Mary's* which earns more money, eight million dollars, than any RKO picture to date. It's not an altogether surprising statistic. The movie reunites director Leo McCarey with Bing Crosby (again a priest) who a year before had achieved similar success at Paramount in the Oscar-winning *Going My Way*. No Barry Fitzgerald this time. Instead, beautiful nun Ingrid Bergman.

Val Lewton and director Robert Wise contribute one of the best horror films of the 40s, *The Body Snatcher*, a

striking version of Robert Louis Stevenson's tale of body-snatching in 19th century Edinburgh. Karloff is chief robber, Henry Daniell the doctor who pays him for his trouble.

Dick Powell and Edward Dmytryk are together again with *Cornered*, another tough drama, this time with Powell in Buenos Aires tracking down the Nazi murderers of his French wife; director Frank Borzage has an uncharacteristic fling at swashbuckling in *The Spanish Main*. Paul Henreid is out of his depth as the hero, but Maureen O'Hara well at home as a spunky, red-headed heroine; Maria Ouspenskaya is an Amazon Queen in *Tarzan And The Amazons*; Danny Kaye reappears in Goldwyn's *Wonder Man*, this time in a dual role, as a meek librarian haunted by the ghost of his brother; and the ever-eager John Wayne reconquers the Japanese in the South Pacific in *Back To Bataan*.

The war and its effects are best brought home however in John Cromwell's *The Enchanted Cottage*, an updated version of an Arthur Pinero fantasy about the romance between a badly disfigured pilot (Robert Young) and an unattractive girl (Dorothy McGuire) whose deep and mutual love makes them appear beautiful in each other's eyes. A painful theme, delicately handled.

1946 The studio's first full post-war year and Sam Goldwyn makes perhaps the most topical of all topical films in Hollywood history, William Wyler's *The Best Years Of Our Lives*, the story of the adjustment problems facing three returning veterans of World War II. Starring Fredric March, Myrna Loy, Dana Andrews and handless sailor Harold Russell, it wins seven Oscars and grosses over eleven million dollars.

Even so, Hollywood isn't entirely sure how to handle it. Claims one set of ads: "A story of young love. . .sometimes foolish. . .sometimes headstrong. . .but always thrilling, exciting."

Hitchcock is in top form with *Notorious*, a Cary Grant-Ingrid Bergman-Claude Rains thriller set in Rio; so too is Robert Siodmak who provides thrills of a more terrifying kind in *The Spiral Staircase*, a turn-of-the-century story about a psychopath who murders young women with physical deformities. Dorothy McGuire is the one he doesn't get.

Even Orson Welles makes a brief return to the studio in the thriller *genre*. In *The Stranger* he is a Nazi hiding

out in a small American town. War crimes commissioner Edward G. Robinson tracks him down and he meets a nasty demise, speared to death by one of the revolving sword-bearing effigies on the town clock tower.

For Frank Capra, just as it was before the war at Columbia, it is the warmer side of things that matter. James Stewart stars as a small town 'man-of-the-people' hero in *It's A Wonderful Life*. The movie is sincere, sentimental and one of the director's best but, sadly, the time for Capra is past.

Danny Kaye contributes another comedy performance for Goldwyn as a milkman turned boxer in *The Kid From Brooklyn*; Rosalind Russell is *Sister Kenny*, the Australian bush nurse who produces a controversial 'cure' for polio; Howard Hughes tries for a second time to release *The Outlaw* with the same results; schizophrenic Laraine Day drives Robert Mitchum to suicide in *The Locket*; *Till The End Of Time* and *From This Day Forward* both look at post-war problems as does *Tomorrow Is Forever* in which Orson Welles returns from the war with a new face, much to the discomfort of his remarried wife.

Johnny Weismuller's offering is *Tarzan And The Leopard Woman*; Tom Conway appears as The Falcon for the last time in *The Falcon's Alibi* and *The Falcon's Adventure*; and, more sadly, the Val Lewton horror series comes to an end with the gruesome *Bedlam* in which Boris Karloff is walled up alive by the inmates of the notorious mental asylum.

1947 Cary Grant, for years one of the studio's comedy mainstays, proves he's as popular as ever by turning *The Bachelor And The Bobby-Soxer* into RKO's biggest financial smash of the year. Grant is a dashing playboy, Shirley Temple is his teenage admirer, Myrna Loy a lady judge.

John Wayne, however, is not so hot, especially with the critics. In *Tycoon*, a railroad building epic, critic James Agee remarks: "Several tons of dynamite are set off in this picture — none of it under the right people."

The rest of the RKO films (in Dore Schary's first year as production head) fare rather better. *Mourning Becomes Electra*, Eugene O'Neill's tragedy of the disintegration of a New England family following the Civil War contains a remarkable performance by Rosalind Russell as Lavinia; the brutal *Born To Kill*, directed by Robert Wise, features

Lawrence Tierney as a nonchalent killer; John Ford's *The Fugitive* has Henry Fonda as Graham Greene's priest trapped in a South American police state; *Sinbad The Sailor* proves that a post-war Douglas Fairbanks Jr. is as agile as ever; *Tarzan And The Huntress* marks the last appearance of Johnny Sheffield as 'Boy'; and the lightweight comedy *The Farmer's Daughter* provides the year's biggest surprise — an Oscar for Loretta Young for her Swedish maid who wins a seat in the American Congress.

Goldwyn's contributions: Danny Kaye as James Thurber's day-dreaming hero in *The Secret Life Of Walter Mitty* and Cary Grant as an angel who comes to Earth to aid hard-up bishop David Niven in *The Bishop's Wife.*

Two minor classics emerge: Dmytryk's *Crossfire* starring Robert Mitchum, Robert Young and Robert Ryan, a taut melodrama that tackles the subject of anti-semitism (drunken G.I. beats a Jew to death) within the framework of a thriller; and *Build My Gallows High*, a complex and very black thriller with Mitchum as a private-eye, Kirk Douglas as a gang boss and Jane Greer as one of the most deadly *femme fatales* to have emerged since the war. Murder, theft and double-cross are second nature to her.

''She can't be all bad,'' says Virginia Huston to Mitchum. ''No one is.'' Replies Mitchum. ''She comes the closest.''

1948 True to RKO tradition, Schary is out before he has settled in (his reign is just sixteen months). The reason? Clashes with new studio head Howard Hughes who assumes control of RKO on May 11 and remains in charge until its closure in the mid-fifties.

George Stevens, John Ford and Leo McCarey all have films released by the studio as does newcomer Joseph Losey who through his delicate fantasy *The Boy With Green Hair* (Dean Stockwell) illustrates the plight of the still starving war orphans of Europe.

Stevens' movie (his first since the war) is John Van Druten's *I Remember Mama*, a tender tale of a Norwegian family living in San Francisco at the turn-of-the-century; John Ford's is *Fort Apache*, the first of his cavalry trilogy with John Wayne and Henry Fonda as a martinet, Custer-like general; and Leo McCarey's, true to form, is a comedy. *Good Sam* with Gary Cooper so good he's always in trouble.

Johnny Weismuller hangs up his loincloth in his last appearance as the ape-man in *Tarzan And The Mermaids*; audiences and critics hang their heads as the expensive

Joan Of Arc sinks beneath heavyweight dialogue and heavy handed Victor Fleming direction; Danny Kaye fans hang their heads too as the popular comedian finds himself saddled with an inept Goldwyn remake of his own 1941 comedy *Ball Of Fire*. The new picture (again directed by Howard Hawks) is titled *A Song Is Born*. Replacing Barbara Stanwyck? Virginia Mayo.

It is left to Cary Grant and Robert Mitchum to provide the brighter spots, Grant on screen, Mitchum off.

In *Mr. Blandings Builds His Dream House* Cary is an advertising executive persuaded by lovely wife Myrna Loy that family life is much too cramped for comfort in their New York apartment and that a house in the country will be the answer to all their problems. It isn't.

On August 31, Mitchum, now a top RKO star rating a 250,000 dollar-a-year contract, is arrested on a charge of possessing marijuana cigarettes. He is discovered in the cottage of actress Lila Leeds.

The case makes sensational headlines. Freed on bail, the actor offers no defence at his trial, is found guilty as charged and sentenced to sixty days at a Los Angeles County Honor farm — plus two years of probation. Shooting on Mitchum's film *The Big Steal* is temporarily suspended.

Says the judge during sentencing: "I cannot overlook the responsibility that you, Mr. Mitchum, have to hundreds of thousands of young Americans who idolise you. You have worked yourself up to a position of prominence in the motion picture industry. Up to now this has meant nothing but you may have overlooked the responsibility which goes with this prominence."

On his release in March '49 Mitchum is neither bitter nor resentful, "My weeks in jail did much for me. I got what I deserved."

1949 The best pictures are those made by the men coming to the end of their RKO careers. Robert Wise directs a brilliant boxing drama, *The Set Up* in which Robert Ryan as a broken down old pro refuses to throw his last fight, and John Ford films the best of all his cavalry pictures, the classic *She Wore A Yellow Ribbon*.

The Window, a small-scale thriller about a boy who is always 'crying wolf' then sees a murder is the studio's sleeper but *Mighty Joe Young*, another giant ape created by Merian C. Cooper and Ernest Schoedsack fails to create the same stir as his famous predecessor. Once again,

however, beauty — Terry Moore — fascinates the beast especially when she's tinkling the piano and singing 'Beautiful Dreamer!'

Robert Mitchum is romanced by war widow Janet Leigh in *Holiday Affair*; Lex Barker is the new Tarzan in *Tarzan's Magic Fountain*; and a young Farley Granger goes on the run with two hardened criminals in Nicholas Ray's acclaimed *They Live By Night*.

Susan Hayward suffers, via an Oscar nomination, for her wartime romance with pilot Dana Andrews in *My Foolish Heart*; and Bob Mitchum, Jane Greer and William Bendix are described as 'A Man Of Ice', 'A Woman Of Fire', and 'A Guy With A Gun' in Don Siegel's exciting chase thriller *The Big Steal*.

One unusual picture of the year is *The Man On The Eiffel Tower* with Charles Laughton in one of his most forgotten roles, that of Inspector Maigret.

1950 John Ford's leisurely western *Wagonmaster*, the story of a small Mormon wagon train travelling to Utah in the 1870s is the one class film of the year.

Otherwise, everybody seems to be up to no good. Hughes' new discovery Faith Domergue makes her long delayed debut in *Vendetta*, a revenge story of 19th century Corsica; she's also involved with Robert Mitchum in *Where Danger Lives*, a crime melodrama in which she convinces the big guy that he's responsible for the death of husband Claude Rains; Joan Fontaine schemes her way to the top — wealthy socialite Zachary Scott is the prime target — in *Born To Be Bad*; slum youth Farley Granger murders a priest in *Edge Of Doom*; and Claudette Colbert finds herself bordering on the edge of insanity in *The Secret Fury*.

Glenn Ford, Valli, Claude Rains, Cedric Hardwicke, Lloyd Bridges and company also have trouble, climbing *The White Tower*, a vast mountain in the Swiss Alps. So does beautiful young Ann Blyth who in Goldwyn's *Our Very Own*, learns at the age of eighteen that she is an adopted child and sets out to find her real mother.

Only Harold Lloyd seems to be enjoying himself in the long-delayed Preston Sturges comedy *Mad Wednesday* (filmed in 1945/6) in which he continues the adventures of Harold Diddledock, twenty years after his great football triumph in the 1925 film *The Freshman*.

1951 It's a monster from outer space, *The Thing From Another World*, which makes the biggest impression. As it lands, complete with flying saucer, in the snowy wastes of the Arctic it sends a definite chill through audiences all over the world.

'Their Lives Can Be Counted In Seconds As Long As The Thing Is At Large' claim the advertisements about the small group of scientists battling against the unknown.

The life of the studio can now be counted on the fingers of one hand. Despite a not undistinguished output in 1951 and '52 the decline has already begun.

Coincidence decrees that two soap operas, the staple fare of RKO for so long in the thirties, are the most distinguished films of the year — Curtis Bernhardt's *The Blue Veil* with Jane Wyman as a young widow who drifts into the rewarding (and heartbreaking) career of looking after other people's babies, and *Payment On Demand* in which Bette Davis and Barry Sullivan share in flashback the moments that lead up to their impending divorce.

Sam Goldwyn tries to recapture the feeling of *The Best Years Of Our Lives* by having World War II veteran Dana Andrews recalled for the Korean War in *I Want You*. He fails; so does the teaming of Sinatra, Russell and Groucho Marx in *Double Dynamite*.

Bob Mitchum and Jane Russell however are much more in tune. Despite indifferent material the two provide a certain smouldering chemistry in *His Kind Of Woman* in which she plays a nightclub singer and Mitch a gambler down Mexico way.

Mitchum's also a policeman up against gang boss Robert Ryan in John Cromwell's *The Racket* and a Yankee doctor enamoured with 19th century beauty Ava Gardner in *My Forbidden Past*; Claude Rains sides with the Nazis in *Sealed Cargo*; John Wayne and Robert Ryan are *Flying Leathernecks*; Lex Barker faces *Tarzan's Peril*; and Janet Leigh, Ann Miller and Gloria DeHaven are among those after *Two Tickets To Broadway*, a rare RKO musical.

The saddest news of the year is the death of Val Lewton who dies of a heart attack on March 14. The master of the psychological thriller, he was forty-six.

1952 RKO achieve a minor 'first'. Fritz Lang's *Rancho Notorious* becomes the very first western to use a theme song as an integral part of the story. The song is 'The Legend Of

Chuck-A-Luck' by Ken Darby. Most people come to believe that *High Noon* with its famous 'Do Not Forsake Me Oh My Darlin' is the first but *Rancho* precedes it into release by four months.

Hawks' sprawling *The Big Sky* is a more ambitious western and has Kirk Douglas and Dewey Martin travelling with the early fur traders up the Missouri in the 1830s; Nicholas Ray's *The Lusty Men* with Robert Mitchum as a has-been riding ace looks at the modern West and the rough tough life of rodeo riders.

Genteel British rose Jean Simmons plays it rough as a homicidal psychopath in Otto Preminger's *Angel Face* (Robert Mitchum is one of her victims) and another British export, the eye-rolling Robert Newton, is also up to no good as *Blackbeard The Pirate*; Playwright Joan Crawford is another who finds that things aren't going her way when the young actor she has married (Jack Palance) does his best to kill her off. Her suffering pays dividends however. She's up for a best actress Oscar nomination.

Howard Hughes, always one for a pretty face, borrows Marilyn Monroe from Fox for Fritz Lang's seamy sex drama *Clash By Night*, sends Mitchum and Russell to *Macao* and also releases the much delayed *Montana Belle* (made in 1948) with Jane Russell as Belle Starr.

RKO's best picture lasts for no more than seventy minutes. It's Richard Fleischer's *The Narrow Margin*, a tense little train thriller about a gangster's widow making a journey from Chicago to Los Angeles to turn state's evidence against a crime syndicate.

Its biggest financial hit is Sam Goldwyn's *Hans Christian Andersen* with Danny Kaye as the Danish storyteller singing such Frank Loesser songs as 'Wonderful Copenhagen' and 'The Ugly Duckling.' It is the last film that Goldwyn releases through the studio.

1953 The rot has at last set in. Only fifteen pictures are produced on the lot as Hughes loses interest in the studio. Robert Mitchum, Glenn Ford, Jean Simmons and a handful of others appear in films that are now, at best, only double features.

Second Chance stands out because of its climax when Mitchum and Jack Palance fight to the death in a stranded cable car suspended 7000 ft above a valley in the Andes.

Best of the rest: Ida Lupino's *The Hitch-Hiker* about an escaped con who thumbs and kills his way across the country; *Affair With A Stranger* with Victor Mature as a playwright gambler supported by wife Jean Simmons; *Appointment In Honduras* in which Glenn Ford goes adventuring in South America; and Raoul Walsh's smuggling yarn of Napoleonic times *Sea Devils*.

1954 Jane Russell does her best to keep the studio alive in the musical *The French Line*. Her sexy one piece costume, a black satin affair with three big pieces cut out of the midriff, creates censorship problems as she sings a bump-and-grind routine 'Lookin' For Trouble.'

'*That* dance you've heard so much about!' blaze the ads. 'Jane Russell in 3-D. . .It'll knock *both* your eyes out!'

Women, in fact figure mostly on the RKO list. Barbara Stanwyck is *Cattle Queen Of Montana*; Piper Laurie is trailed by gangsters in *Dangerous Mission*; Jean Simmons gives money away in *She Couldn't Say No*; Anne Baxter is a trapeze artist in *Carnival Story*; and Debbie Reynolds is a juvenile delinquent dumped on screenwriter Dick Powell in *Susan Slept Here*.

The last named has its moments but the year is no better than the one before.

1955 *Underwater*, an actioner starring Jane Russell and Richard Egan, has its premiere 'underwater' in Florida. It's Howard Hughes' last ludicrous fling before he sells the studio in July to the General Tire and Rubber Company.

The premiere takes place on January 10 at Silver Springs. Miss Russell, clad in swim suit, aqua lung and flippers, joins those critics brave enough to venture several fathoms down to watch the film unreel. "I've had to do everything else," says Jane. "I might as well do this!"

The rest of the RKO films all sound the same: *The Americano; Escape To Burma; Bengazi; Son Of Sinbad; Tennessee's Partner; Pearl Of The South Pacific.*

Glenn Ford, Barbara Stanwyck, Richard Conte, Dale Robertson, John Payne and Dennis Morgan are among the stars unlucky enough to be associated with them.

1956 William Dozier, a former producer, takes over as production head in a futile attempt to keep the studio going. He is fighting a losing battle. The studio is dead but won't lie down.

Bundle Of Joy a Debbie Reynolds/Eddie Fisher comedy about a baby; *The First Travelling Saleslady*, a Ginger

Rogers embarrassment; a couple of westerns, *Tension At Table Rock* and *Great Day In The Morning*; and two Fritz Lang melodramas, *While The City Sleeps* and *Beyond A Reasonable Doubt* are among those films produced to keep RKO ticking over. All fail.

Strangely, the only film that does succeed is a Howard Hughes leftover, *The Conqueror* in which John Wayne plays Genghis Khan and says: "This Tartar woman is for me — and my blood says 'take her'." The object of his affections? Susan Hayward.

1957 The end for RKO. All films shot on the lot during 1956 are released by Universal — *Escapade In Japan* with Teresa Wright, *The Unholy Wife* with Diana Dors and Rod Steiger, the western *Run Of The Arrow* and Hughes' own five million dollar flying spectacular, *Jet Pilot* with John Wayne and Janet Leigh. The movie was originally completed seven years earlier in 1950.

The last film to be shot on the RKO lot is *The Girl Most Likely*. It stars Jane Powell and is a remake of *Tom, Dick And Harry*. It is eventually released by Universal in 1958. The RKO story is over.

TWENTIETH CENTURY-FOX

Twentieth Century-Fox

Twentieth Century-Fox has always seemed to have had one advantage over other Hollywood studios — its trademark. On screen it lasts for just a few seconds but while it is up there with its drum roll, beaming searchlights and exhilarating fanfare, it reigns supreme. No other trademark, not even Paramount's mountain or Metro's famous lion, can quite match the tingle of excitement it provides. Somehow, it seems to say 'We are the youngest Hollywood studio. We know what you want and we know how to give it to you — in the modern style. So sit back and let us blast you into submission.'

It hasn't always worked of course. Fox, like other studios, has had more than its share of failures and financial crises. It's provided just as many routine and second rate films as any other company, perhaps, in view of its shaky start, considerably more.

But, somehow, that modern futuristic logo has always indicated that Fox is more 'with it' than any other Hollywood studio. Those searchlights and massive letters sprawling across the screen seem to reflect a huge city of the future. They would not have come amiss had they heralded Fritz Lang's famous *Metropolis*. It is certainly appropriate that they precede the industry's biggest ever moneymaker *Star Wars*, a science-fiction film about the future.

Today, Fox means *Star Wars*, *The Omen* and *The French Connection*, but for a long time it meant a long succession of blondes — Alice Faye, Betty Grable, Marilyn Monroe — swinging their hips and heaving their ample chests across a musical Technicolored screen.

It also meant in the 30s, little Shirley Temple; in the 40s courageous, controversial pictures with themes that few other studios dared tackle; and in the 50s, the early CinemaScope films. It meant too a special kind of *sub-genre* that Fox made all its own — the big city movie.

The number of times that Alfred Newman's famous 'Street Scene' music wailed mournfully across the soundtrack (Da, Da, Da, Da Daah, Da Daah) is inestimable as is the number of times a cynical off-screen voice told the audience that times were hard and not likely to get any better.

It was a favourite Fox gambit. It put the audience in the picture straight away; there was no wasting of time. It was literally screen journalism. The first three paragraphs (reels) were cut away and we, the audience, were already zooming in on paragraph four. Such as in *Kiss Of Death* when, to a background of neon, bustle and heavy traffic, Coleen Gray told us just how difficult it was for Victor Mature to get a job.

''Christmas Eve in New York,'' she said wistfully. ''A happy time for some people. The lucky ones. Last minute shopping. Presents for the kids. Hurry home to light the tree and fill the stockings — for the lucky ones. Others aren't so lucky. Nick Bianco hadn't worked for a year. He had a prison record. They say it shouldn't count against him, but when Nick tried to get a job the same thing always happened. Very sorry, no prejudice of course, but no job either. So this is how Nick went Christmas shopping for his kids. . .''

Forty seconds flat! That's all it took and Victor Mature was already on his way up a New York skyscraper to rob a jewellery department store on one of the top floors. He didn't take long to get down to things either. His first words, gun in hand, ''Don't move, put your hands behind you.''

It was typical of Twentieth Century-Fox of the late 40s and early 50s. No time was allowed to ease you gently into the picture. Thrillers were meant to hold the attention, not meander around for twenty minutes wasting two valuable reels of celluloid.

The classic *Laura* of 1944 was equally sharp and to the point. This time it was the measured, precise and cultured tones of Clifton Webb, rising above the ominous ticking of a clock, that told the audience exactly where they were. With David Raksin's beautiful, haunting score fading into the distance, Webb immediately fills the name of Laura with an intriguing mysterious quality all of its own.

''I shall never forget the weekend Laura died. A silver sun burned through the sky like a huge magnifying glass. It was the hottest Sunday in my recollection. I felt as if I was the only human being left in New York. For with Laura's horrible death I was alone. I, Waldo Lydecker was the only one who really knew her and I had just begun to write Laura's story when another of those detectives came to see me. I had him wait.''

Again the introduction is brief, again no time is wasted. The mystery of *Laura* is already beginning to unravel.

The big city movies — *Kiss Of Death, Boomerang, Call Northside 777, Panic In The Streets, Fourteen Hours* — were only a small part of Fox's massive output. Yet they were as much a part of the studio as Grable, Monroe and CinemaScope.

No other studio quite managed to capture the urban atmosphere like Fox. The back streets, the prisons, the squad rooms, the crammed apartments, seemed to be Fox's own backyard, the cameras of Joe MacDonald and Norbert Brodine prying into every nook and cranny of urban life.

That realism should be such a staple diet of Fox's production line-up should have come as no surprise to anyone acquainted with its energetic production head, Darryl F. Zanuck.

The cigar-chomping Zanuck *was* Fox. A human dynamo. In his ten years at Warners he had learned just about everything there was to know about the movie business. In his last four years at that studio he had formulated the policy that survived long after he broke with Jack Warner.

Zanuck's big city movies at Fox were really logical extensions of the gangster movies of Cagney and Robinson at Warners; his controversial films — anti-semitism, colour prejudice, mental illness were all subjects tackled by Fox in the 40s — were cast in the same courageous mould as Warners' history-making *I Am A Fugitive From A Chain Gang*. But if Zanuck's own personality and gut feeling could be detected in his more dramatic pictures, his acute business sense could be found in the films of Shirley Temple, Betty Grable and Marilyn Monroe.

He knew the value of stars. He also knew when he first helped form Twentieth Century-Fox in 1935 (a combination of the newly formed Twentieth Century Pictures and the ailing, once dominant Fox studio of the silent days) that he had precisely two actors on the payroll who could remotely be considered as stars — the homespun all-american comedian Will Rogers and the curly-headed child actress Shirley Temple. The rest, except for the technical staff and director Henry King who was to become one of the Fox stalwarts in subsequent years, were just so much dead wood.

In forming a new company at all during the Depression Zanuck was taking a colossal gamble. The other major studios had all been formed and were making films along their own lines. Every conceivable type of movie was being made on the different Hollywood lots. What could a new studio, the only major new studio to be formed since the beginning of sound, contribute to the scene?

The brash, thirty-three year old Zanuck thought it could contribute quite a lot.

The pundits in the know gave him very little chance of success.

When, shortly after the formation of the studio, Will Rogers was killed in an air crash, they gave him even less. His box-office potential had suddenly been slashed in half and he was left with a seven year old child to carry him through the early, difficult years. And a child could last for just so long as a star — four or five years at most, perhaps even less.

Many men would have baulked at the prospect, but not Zanuck. If anything, he relished the situation. It meant that he personally had to become involved in every aspect of the studio's development. He literally quivered with energy and attacked the job with the zest of three men.

He studied the Fox films in line for production, rejected a dozen as being completely unsuitable, cancelled another six that were already shooting and made economies in all directions, slashing the company's payroll and firing people who did not figure in his future plans. Those he wanted he kept on, otherwise everything was cut to the bone and streamlined.

He was into everything. He was not a Jack Warner or a Louis B. Mayer. He was a film-maker first, an executive second. He knew how to cut a picture, how to read a script, how to gauge public taste. He was a one man show. Without him Twentieth Century-Fox would almost certainly have spluttered and died within a couple of years.

Other than hiring a star occasionally from another studio, he had to make his own and had very little time in which to do it. He also had to produce an immediate hit to get the studio's finances into healthy shape. *Metropolitan*, a Lawrence Tibbetts vehicle and a backstage story of a baritone's coming of age, was his first gamble. It flopped badly.

Bitterly disappointed and realising that he was in no position to afford many more such disasters, he turned to a movie called *Thanks A Million*, a story of a crooner who accidentally runs for governor.

For box-office insurance Zanuck originally considered Paramount's Bing Crosby. In the end he opted for Warners' Dick Powell. It made no difference. The preview was another flop and it looked as though Zanuck had a second successive turkey on his hands.

Zanuck, however, was unwilling to give up on the picture. Seeing something in it that he thought worthwhile, he took it back to the studio and cut more than a reel from its running time. The simple exercise worked. *Thanks A Million* starring Dick Powell, Ann Dvorak and Raymond Walburn turned out to be just the hit Zanuck needed. Today, it doesn't figure too much in the history books, but Zanuck himself maintains that more than anything else it made Twentieth Century-Fox.

For Zanuck, the middle and late 30s was a time of searching and grooming. He found the handsome Tyrone Power; promoted former dance band singer Alice Faye, the first of the studio's blonde musical stars; cast Loretta Young in comedy; signed the smiling Don Ameche; and even gambled on ice-skating champion Sonja Henie.

Yet all the time, as the star nucleus was being formed, he relied heavily on the talents of the young Shirley Temple. So heavily did he rely on her that he insured her for $25,000 with Lloyds of London. So successful was she at the box-office that she topped the Motion Picture Herald Poll four times in a row — in 1935, '36, '37 and '38. Between the ages of five and nine she was unbeatable. The big stars from other studios just couldn't shift her from that number one spot. It was hers and hers alone.

Said Zanuck in 1937 when she was at the peak of her success, "Shirley Temple is endless. There is no-one in the world to compare with that child. I've made eight pictures with her and each time I'm knocked dead. It's just beyond the case of being a freak. The child has rhythm. I always thought when we dropped the curls (removed as she grew older) that this is the end. This mint, this goldmine has gone dry. But now she's good for years."

Of course, she wasn't. The goldmine did run dry — in just three more years — but in the five golden years up until 1940 she could do no wrong.

A Shirley Temple film could fill to the brim a 2000 seat movie house during a Saturday afternoon matinee show and do almost equally as well in the evening, even though there were fewer children in the audience. Her pictures made a million dollars, sometimes a million and a half, during their first runs alone which was some going in the Depression. The figures look even more impressive when one recalls that a child could get into a movie house in the 30s for just fifteen cents.

Said President Roosevelt no less. "During this Depression, when the spirit of the people is lower than at any other time, it is a splendid thing that for just fifteen cents an American can go to a movie and look at the smiling face of a baby and forget his troubles."

The other plus-factor about the Shirley Temple movies was that they were cheap to produce. She didn't need an expensive co-star (not until the final stages of her career, anyway), the stories were simple, brought in on time and had few sets.

Not everybody enjoyed working with her. Irving Cummings, an edgy, temperamental director, often worked himself up into a lather when faced with a Shirley Temple vehicle. The slightest noise on set could turn him into a nervous wreck. "Give me a break, can't you?'' he would say. ''Can't you see what I'm up against. I've got a baby here, I'm working with a kid.''

But other directors like Allan Dwan, even the grumpy, short-tempered John Ford got along well with the child star. And actors who, at first were apprehensive, soon melted under her charm. Victor McLaglen adored her. So, too, did Lionel Barrymore. Gary Cooper called her 'Wigglebritches'.

Her salary was phenomenal. At the beginning of 1936 she was on a revised contract of 4,000 dollars a week for all fifty-two weeks of the year plus a bonus of 20,000 dollars a picture. That kind of money lasted for most of her Fox career.

When, in 1940, *The Bluebird*, an expensive Technicolored version of the Maeterlinck fantasy, flopped, it was the first Shirley Temple movie to do so.

Cruelly, perhaps mercifully, the end was not long in coming. Shirley made just one more picture for Fox then suddenly it was all over. Her mother and father bought up the rest of Shirley's contract from the studio and that was that. Shirley was twelve years old. She reappeared briefly as a teenager at other studios in the 40s, but her time had passed. The Shirley Temple phenomena was over.

Zanuck, by 1940, was established and in full stride. Musicals, comedies, westerns and spectaculars all figured prominently on his production line-up and the stars he had so carefully nurtured in the preceding years had now blossomed into maturity. But even Zanuck with his uncanny instinct and foresight couldn't have conceived the surprise that was in store for him that year.

A very pleasant surprise it was too. A blonde surprise. A young singer-dancer who had been hanging around Hollywood for nearly a decade and been a Goldwyn Girl at the beginning of the thirties. In 1940 she got that traditional 'lucky break'.

Her name was Betty Grable. Her break? The appendicitis of luckless Alice Faye, who was set to appear with Don Ameche in the Technicolored musical *Down Argentine Way*, when illness struck her down. Grable got the lead instead and from that moment on became the studio's biggest star of the decade.

Zanuck couldn't believe his luck. Ever since that first faltering year in 1935 the cards had fallen his way. Shirley Temple had held the studio together as he had searched round for stars. And now, in the forties when Fox had a star line up — Linda Darnell, Gene Tierney and Dana Andrews were others who had joined the studio — one of those stars turned into a goldmine. A goldmine that drove audiences and later, servicemen in particular, wild with delight.

The thought must have crossed Zanuck's mind more than once

that although Metro might have more stars than there were in heaven, Twentieth Century-Fox had Grable's legs and in the war years at least that meant almost as much.

On average, Betty Grable worked her way through two pictures a year. All were trifles. All contained dialogue that often sounded as if it might have been written by a ten-year-old. All were naïve. But all were colourful, zippy and tuneful — and escapist.

Betty Grable happened at just the right time, not only for Fox but for America as a whole. As millions of young G.I.s were being shipped overseas to war, many never to return, she represented something they could identify with, the all-American girl.

She wasn't only a sex symbol. She was also very much the epitomy of the attractive girl next door, the girl who was always the prize date with all the college guys. Her blonde hair, peaches and cream complexion and warm, friendly personality all combined to make her something very special for the American male.

She rarely played the bitch. She was always the good girl, very moral despite her magnificent sex appeal and always being let down by the men in her pictures. Things were never her fault. The trouble invariably lay with a selfish John Payne, a caddish Don Ameche or an immature Dan Dailey. "People write to me as if I were a sister or a friend," she once said. "Maybe it's because of a wholesome quality that I have."

Whatever it was, it didn't work when Zanuck gambled with her in a couple of straight movies, *I Wake Up Screaming* and *A Yank In The R.A.F.* In drama she was out of her depth and she knew it. She had no pretentions. "I will never be the Garbo type," she said. "There's nothing mysterious about me."

But even Zanuck, shrewd genius that he was, refused to learn his lesson about Grable. When he came to film Somerset Maugham's *The Razor's Edge*, his prestige picture for 1946, he wanted her for the key role of the alcoholic Sophie. Betty, never one to kick up a fuss, this time refused point blank.

"My movie lines up until then consisted mainly of 'Hi Joe' in musicals," she said. "Some of my parts required no acting ability. I didn't even study a script. I just worried about my hair and clothes.

"I'm strictly a song-and-dance girl," she added. "I can act enough to get by. But let's face it, that's the limits of my talents. It's not that an acting role scares me. If I have a good enough director he can usually pull me through the tight places. But I feel more secure if they let me do a few numbers.

"I'm no Bette Davis nor am I out to prove anything with histrionics. I just want to make pictures that people will like."

She added with a quip. ''If I play Sophie my fans will expect me to arise from the ocean with seaweed in my hair and sing something.''

Ironically, Anne Baxter, who eventually played Sophie, won an Oscar for her role in *The Razor's Edge*. Betty was never in the running for such awards during her entire career, although one of her regular directors, Henry Koster, once said, ''A girl like Grable who's been carrying the box-office for seven straight years, ought to have some special recognition. Her money-earning musicals have made possible many Oscar earning films. Maybe there should be a small credit line engraved on each Oscar: 'Betty Grable helped pay for this.'

Fox writer-producer Nunnally Johnson summed it up best when he joked, ''I don't know why Betty would ever want an Oscar on her mantlepiece. She has every Tom, Dick and Harry at her feet.''

By the advent of CinemaScope in 1953 Betty's career was near to its close. She had dominated the forties, but now another blonde, arguably *the* star of the post-war era, had arrived on the Fox sound stages, Marilyn Monroe. When Grable took second billing to her in *How To Marry A Millionaire* the writing was on the wall. There were rumours of friction, but Betty denied them. One story goes that when they met for the first time on set Betty smiled at Marilyn and said, ''I've had mine honey, now go get yours.''

Betty said later of Marilyn, ''We were very close. She did an awful lot to boost things up for movies when everything was in a low state. There'll never be anyone like her for looks, for attitude, all of it.''

Betty Grable made her final movies in 1955 and retired from the screen aged thirty-nine.

With the war making the European film market almost non-existent, Hollywood turned to other markets as sources of revenue. South America was an obvious choice. Hence all those nights in Rio and weekends in Havana. Hence, also, Carmen Miranda, the Brazilian Bombshell!

Carmen Miranda was a very different kind of Fox musical star. Her career was short, just five or six years, and for a change she was not a blonde. She was a flamboyant, dark-haired South American spitfire who could sing, dance and do an 'I Yi, Yi, Yi' with more fruit on her head than most families could eat in a month.

Carmen's career might have lasted longer had it not been discovered that during her exotic dance number she refused to wear any knickers beneath her long skirts.

There was nothing disreputable about it. She just preferred it that way. It gave her complete freedom of body movement. Unfortunately for her, a freelance stills photographer happened to have his camera set at a particularly low angle when she danced and whirled to one of her exciting South American sambas. The photographer gasped in astonishment as his innocent camera suddenly revealed all there was to reveal about the lower portions of Miss Miranda's anatomy.

Within days, thousands of photographs were flooding the black market. The storm broke. Womens' pressure groups protested. Fox tried to make light of the whole thing, but they were over a barrel. Carmen Miranda quickly faded into oblivion.

Less than a decade later when Marilyn Monroe's nude calendar became a sensation it didn't affect her career one jot. Carmen Miranda was just unlucky that she went knickerless in the forties.

While Grable and Faye (with knickers) and Miranda (without) were dancing their way through Fox's richly Technicolored musicals, Zanuck was busy running the studio. It was still very much his show. He saw everthing that was shot on the lot. Every evening in his private theatre he viewed rushes and rough cuts with several of his closest colleagues. This was the time that anything could happen and usually did. A finished picture could be cut by a third and the director instructed to reshoot as many scenes again. A new ending could be tacked on, a poor performance cut out cntircly.

Chewing furiously on his cigar, his editor-in-chief Barbara McLean permanently at his side, Zanuck would stare intently as each new reel unfolded before him. Whenever he saw something he didn't like he would give a nudge and McLean would make a mental note.

It could be a harrowing time, especially if you were the director of the film being viewed. When the famous *Three Coins In The Fountain* was first unreeled the initial reaction was so bad that the film's director Jean Negulesco rushed outside and was physically sick.

Another director spent the whole of the viewing of his film in absolute torture simply because he had been told about the nudging process beforehand and was on the lookout for it immediately he took his seat.

Sure enough, within a few minutes, came a nudge. Then another. Then a couple more. The director began to sweat profusely. Things looked bad. Then all of a sudden the nudging stopped. Zanuck didn't move. The director grew more relaxed. By the end of the picture he felt sure he'd got a hit. Just three or four nudges. That must be some kind of Zanuck record. As the lights went up he waited for the words of praise. None were

Elia Kazan who joined Zanuck's outfit in 1945 and was responsible for such films as *Boomerang, Panic In The Streets* and *Viva Zapata!* also admired and respected the producer. "He was always straightforward when I was working with him," says Kazan. "He never went behind my back. Dominant and aggressive, yes, but not dishonest. I really believe he saw every foot of film shot on the lot."

Jean Negulesco, too, thought highly of him. After he had filmed and made a thorough mess of Margery Sharp's novel *Britannia Mews* he took the extreme step of sending a letter to Zanuck apologising for the quality of the film.

"Who the hell do you think you are, playing the hero like that," snapped Zanuck. "I okayed the picture, I bought the book. I okayed the cast. I saw the rushes and approved them. Sure, you made a mistake, but so did we all. Don't try to be a hero. Just don't do it again, that's all."

Producer-director-writer Philip Dunne went as far as to say: "Darryl F. Zanuck is the best working producer in the history of our trade."

Directors found much to their surprise, that their hard but fair-minded taskmaster was not without a sense of humour. His much quoted favourite phrase, "For God's sake, don't say yes until I finish talking" implied a certain tongue-in-cheek sarcasm and he could take as well as play a practical joke along with the best of them. One director who decided to test just how far that humour would stretch was Rouben Mamoulian. The film he was making at the time was the Tyrone Power swashbuckler *The Mark Of Zorro*.

Said Mamoulian: "The last scene in the picture shows Zorro holding up the governor's carriage, taking all the jewels and then, according to his flamboyant manner, inscribing the letter Z on the leather seat with his sword. The governor looks up in panic and says 'Zorro!' I told J. Edward Bromberg, who played the governor, 'Instead of Zorro say Zanuck with a voice full of terror.' He said, 'I can't, I'll be fired.' But I made him do it.

"I did another take with him saying Zorro, but I said, 'Don't print the other one, we'll print that later, just put it in the rushes for Zanuck to see.'

"When Zanuck's entourage at the rushes heard the word Zanuck there was a stony silence and nobody believed their ears. Zanuck buzzed the operator and said, 'Run that last scene again.' They ran it again and 'Boom' it came back. Luckily, he appreciated the joke. After the film was over he gave me a briefcase bearing the legend 'For M to Z from Z'."

Zanuck's own idea of a practical joke was to play on the fear of a writer about to enter his office for a tough story conference. His favourite ploy was to put a trained ape into his executive chair and turn the lights down low so that the poor writer had no idea he was standing, fearful and trembling, in front of nothing more than a monkey.

By the mid-forties Twentieth Century-Fox were firmly established as a major Hollywood studio. In just ten years Zanuck had taken them right to the top. Movies were made that covered the widest range of subjects. Sometimes they were commercial successes, sometimes critical hits, sometimes both.

One disastrous exception was Zanuck's personally produced *Wilson*, a costly Technicolor film about the life and career of President Woodrow Wilson. A dull, dismal flop (it lost two million dollars) it was so painstakingly unimaginative that it bored the pants off nearly everyone who saw it.

Only Zanuck refused to believe that he had a turkey on his hands. He was still smarting three years later when he received the Academy Award for *Gentleman's Agreement*. "Thanks", he said, "But I should have won it for *Wilson*."

The years between 1945 and 1953, before the studio took the plunge with CinemaScope, remain Fox's peak years. Zanuck caught the 'feel' of the post-war period as soon as the war was over, if not before. He realised that 1939, although just seven years away in actual time *seemed* as though it was light years away. People had changed after six years of hell; they had grown up, their tastes had changed. They wanted something different and Zanuck changed his style accordingly.

It was the time of the realistic big city movie, bold courageous films that hit out confidently at every kind of social and moral issue. Anti-semitism, mental illness, colour prejudice, small-town bigotry — all were adapted into quality Fox material by writers and directors of the front rank. Kazan, Mankiewicz; King and Litvak formed the nucleus of the directing team, Richard Murphy, Philip Dunne, Edna and Edward Anhalt, Lesser Samuels and Jay Dratler were the chief writers.

Zanuck did admit to a feeling of apprehension when he agreed to make Anatole Litvak's *The Snake Pit*, a story of a woman writer's breakdown and her admittance into a mental institution. On first hearing of the movie, Zanuck is supposed to have told the director, "You're crazy. Why do you want to do a film about mad people?" However, a quick look at Litvak's treatment did the trick and the movie was soon on the studio's production schedule.

One of Zanuck's proudest boasts during that period was that new legislation covering state mental hospitals was passed in twenty-six States because of *The Snake Pit.*

If he had similar qualms about the Oscar-winning *Gentleman's Agreement* he never mentioned them. Elia Kazan, his director, later remarked: "*Gentleman's Agreement* was really like an illustration for *Cosmopolitan* magazine. Everyone was prettified. It was a series of clichés. But try to put yourself back in films as they were in 1946, when the word 'Jew' had never been mentioned before. For the first time, someone said America is full of anti-semitism, both conscious and unconscious, and among the best and most liberal people.

"It broke new ground. It was saying to the audience 'You are an average American and you are anti-semitic. Anti-semitism is in you.' It would have been much easier to say that a bunch of freaks were anti-semitic. But he didn't and you have to give Zanuck credit for that."

But in the 50s trends were to change again, this time away from realism and controversy.

"Today audiences seem to be shopping for anything that sounds like adventure or escape," said Zanuck in a statement to the press. "They want to get away from the gloomy news of the moment."

It was said almost with regret for it went against what he had stood for during the previous twenty years. He had always been for the topical and hard-hitting. Now it had to be something different. Realist that he was, he could see that clearly.

It was also unfortunate that the themes the studio had built on so successfully in the post-war years should lose their popularity at exactly the time as television began to make serious inroads into movie attendances. In the early 50s the industry's position was, to say the least, perilous.

As every other studio struggled to find an answer to the dilemma — most of them opting for the short lived 3-D as a stop-gap gimmick — Fox gave serious thought to the problem. Something new *had* to be found; something to yank people back out of the soporific comfort of their armchairs.

The answer was CinemaScope, a process with a letter-box shaped screen (ratio 2.55 to 1) that was supposed to give an impression of three dimensions — without the need to use special polaroid glasses — but which simply provided a bigger screen and made good films seem only adequate and bad films abysmal.

It was only a matter of time before Zanuck became restless with the situation. The break came three years after CinemaScope had been introduced. In 1956 he made headlines of his own by resigning as production head of the studio and announcing that he was forming his own production company which would release under the Fox banner.

The theory sounded fine but Zanuck was no longer a young man. He was fifty-four. His marriage had disintegrated and after divorcing his wife he led a much publicised existence in Europe in the company of a number of young women stars including Juliette Greco and Bella Darvi.

It was a bad time for him both personally and professionally. He seemed on a never ending downward path of self destruction. He even seemed to have lost the knack of making good movies. He tried to adapt to the new scene and his courage in choosing controversial film material was still apparent with films like Alec Waugh's *Island In The Sun*, Romain Gary's *The Roots Of Heaven* and Hemingway's *The Sun Also Rises*. But none was particularly successful and it looked as though Zanuck and the film industry might, in the end, part company for good.

Had it not been for one movie, *The Longest Day*, a brilliant account of the Normandy Invasion of World War II, he might have faded into oblivion and never returned. But return he did — luckily for Fox.

Fox had one saving grace during Zanuck's years of disenchantment. She had two shapely legs, an ample bust, an innocent smile and blonde hair. Her measurements were 38-25-37. Her name was Marilyn Monroe, and she shone like a beacon from the mediocrity of the films around her.

Born and raised in Hollywood, she had always wanted to be a movie star. She had no other ambition. Fox signed her to a seven year contract in October 1950 having not renewed, a few years earlier, a former contract hiring her at $125 a week. They made it just in time. MGM had been showing interest but, not wishing to offend Lana Turner, had hesitated for just that moment too long and Fox snapped her up.

"I'm not interested in money," said Marilyn. "I just want to be wonderful."

Well, quite simply, she was. On screen she sang and danced and showed a talent for comedy that combined well with her sexy image. As an actress she remained in league for nearly all her life but when, in *Niagara*, she wiggled across the screen in a clinging red satin dress that was two sizes too small, and someone said, "To wear a dress like that you got to start laying plans at thirteen," it said it all.

At first she dealt with stardom with a flashing smile, a curvaceous pose and a ready wit. What did she have on when posing for the famous nude photo? "The radio." Why did she do it? "Hunger." On being a sex symbol? "I always thought that symbols were things you clashed.'' On whether she wore falsies? ''People who know me better, know better.''

But as the years of stardom wore on so the insecurities grew. Her marriages to Joe DiMaggio and Arthur Miller broke up. Her already chronic insomnia grew worse. So did the state of her nerves. She took drugs to help her cope with stardom, but they did little to alleviate her fears and anxieties. By the late 50s she was regularly late for work, highly temperamental and at times almost impossible to work with.

Fox put up with it all. There was no reason why they shouldn't for they were representative of the system that was slowly breaking Marilyn into little pieces, the same system that had worn out little Judy Garland at MGM.

They put up with it too because her pictures made money, big money. She was certain box-office insurance in an age of uncertainty. But even they eventually had to call 'enough' when her days on set grew fewer and fewer and she found it impossible to remember her lines.

On August 5, 1962, she was found dead, an empty bottle of sleeping pills by her outstretched hand. She had been making the film *Something's Got To Give* and turned up for work on just twelve of the thirty-two days of shooting. George Cukor had only seven and a half minutes of usable film.

A few weeks before her death they fired her. The project was cancelled. It was the end. The title of her last, unfinished film was horribly appropriate. Something did have to give. And it was Marilyn herself.

Said Cukor, ''That film was a terribly sad occasion because she arrived on the set looking absolutely lovely and then found frightful difficulty in concentrating.

''She'd say, 'Oh no, I've lost it' and her inability to concentrate got worse. At the end she couldn't do anything and was quite incapable of sustained mental effort. What the reason for that was I don't know.'' For much of her ten year period as a star many of her fellow actors and directors had similar experiences.

During the filming of *Bus Stop* in 1956 director Josh Logan had to write her lines on a board, so difficult was it for her to concentrate. Billy Wilder summed up working with her with a light-hearted cynicism, ''I have discussed this project with my doctor and my psychiatrist and they tell me I'm too old and too rich to go through the experience again.''

After *Let's Make Love*, producer Jerry Wald said, ''I never ever want to have anything to do with Marilyn Monroe again.'' Writer-director Nunnally Johnson summed her up tartly, ''An arrogant little tail-twitcher who learned to throw sex in your face.''

Tony Curtis, who co-starred with her in Billy Wilder's famous drag movie *Some Like It Hot* (made at United Artists) and who was required to spend extra hours in high heels because Marilyn couldn't remember her lines, said later, "I'd rather kiss Hitler than Marilyn Monroe" to which she came back bravely with, "He only said that because I wore prettier dresses than he did."

Some directors were quick to spring to her defence. Said Jean Negulesco, "She's the girl you'd like to double-cross your wife with. A man, he's got to be dead not to be excited by her. Yet what a terrible problem she has. Conceive for yourself. How can she be a normal human being and do normal acts, like, for instance, eating mashed potatoes, if she knows that 150 million people all over the world want to go to bed with her."

After her death, one of the warmest tributes came from Darryl Zanuck who had known Marilyn during her early years at Fox. "I disagreed and fought with her on many occasions," he said, "but in spite of the fact that I had not seen her for six years, we were always personal friends. Hollywood has suffered a genuine loss as, in spite of her temperament which sometimes flared to conceal her basic shyness, she never let the public down."

Marilyn was thirty-six when she died. It was thought she was worth at least a million dollars. In fact she died broke, owing $917,000 in back taxes. It took until 1969, with re-runs of her pictures, to pay it off.

At the time of Marilyn's death Zanuck was back in harness at Fox, this time as president, but not entirely of his own choosing. If it hadn't been for the catastrophes surrounding the ill-fated *Cleopatra* he would probably have been content to remain in independent production, so pleased was he with the success of his film about D-Day, *The Longest Day*. But Fox was in the deepest trouble and needed Zanuck. So bad was the situation that the net loss for the company in 1962 was over forty-seven million dollars.

Zanuck reacted just as he had done in 1935 when first forming the studio — he cut back on everything. But in 1962 he went a stage further. He actually closed the studio for nine months until the problem of *Cleopatra* was solved and a new line-up could be planned out.

The problems of *Cleopatra*, of course, were never solved. The film, with its final production cost of thirty-seven million dollars, was already past the point of no return, but at least Zanuck saw it through to the bitter end and then went full-steam ahead with the Fox programme of the 60s.

Risking the charge of nepotism, he put his son Richard in

charge of production and, after feeling his way gingerly at first, suddenly found himself with the biggest hit of all time on his hands — the musical *The Sound Of Music*. Elizabeth Taylor had cost the studio a fortune, Julie Andrews made it back twice over. Within five years of becoming president Zanuck had turned a huge deficit into a reasonable profit. Was the old magic still there — even in a man now in his mid-60s?

The answer was 'no'. No sooner had the songs of Rodgers and Hammerstein echoed down into the depths of the Austrian mountains than the Zanucks, father plus son, became slightly drunk with the image of the 'family picture'.

The huge returns of *The Sound Of Music* persuaded them to put their most expensive eggs in one basket. Eighteen million dollars were scheduled for *Doctor Dolittle*, another twenty million for *Star!*, twenty million more for *Hello, Dolly!*

But suddenly it all went wrong. Not one of the three pictures got its money back. Two out of three would have been creditable. One out of three just about bearable. But batting zero to an outlay of nearly sixty million dollars was disaster.

In a panic measure they opted for the sleazy soft porn movie, *Beyond The Valley Of The Dolls* and *Myra Breckenridge*. It was too far beneath them. Said Zanuck with regrets, "They were both tasteless. They went too far in my estimation. *Myra Breckenridge* went wrong all along the line. We thought it was the new trend. So we followed it — to our regret."

Planet Of The Apes, Butch Cassidy And The Sundance Kid, the hit sleeper *M.A.S.H.* went some way to helping offset the heavy losses, but when *Tora! Tora! Tora!* — the story of Pearl Harbour and another costly production job — also fared badly at the box-office Zanuck's days were numbered. His son went at the end of December, 1970, he himself resigned in June of 71. The second reign lasted approximately nine years. It was a long way from being as successful as the first regime which had lasted twenty.

During the 70s Twentieth Century-Fox has remained a major Hollywood studio. Like most companies it's been producing about a dozen movies a year hoping that one of those twelve — one is all that is needed nowadays — will prove to be a blockbuster. *Patton, The French Connection, The Omen, Star Wars* have kept it more than solvent in recent years. The fact that there is to be a series of *Star Wars* pictures is likely to keep things firmly in the black for years to come.

And what of Zanuck, now in his late 70s and firmly in retirement? He must look at the cinema of today and wonder if it has anything remotely to do with the industry he grew up in. The time when a monkey sat in a darkened chair in front of a frightened scriptwriter. . .when technicians sat and smoked and dangled their feet as they watched the clock tick past nine, then ten, then eleven and no Monroe. . .the time when camera units first went out into the streets to capture the real feel of urban America. . .the time when Grable posed for a pin-up that went all over the world.

When asked by a *Variety* reporter how he would like to be remembered Zanuck replied, "I think perhaps the greatest contribution I have made to this industry was the discovery of genuine talent. To have been involved in giving the world personalities like Betty Grable, Gene Tierney, Alice Faye, Linda Darnell, Tyrone Power, Marilyn Monroe and Gregory Peck has given me perhaps my deepest satisfaction."

Perhaps he meant what he said. Perhaps it was a quote for the trade press. But one suspects that Darryl F. Zanuck will be remembered for much more than discovering a line-up of stars.

He will be remembered as the man who created, ran and made a success of a major Hollywood studio. No other man in Hollywood history has successfully combined the three. Zanuck, quite simply, was Twentieth Century-Fox. And Twentieth Century-Fox was Zanuck, the greatest — and last tycoon.

Bette Davis as Margo Channing in the Award-winning *All About Eve*.

Basil Rathbone has the edge but not for long. Tyrone Power eventually triumphs. The famous duelling scene from *The Mark Of Zorro*.

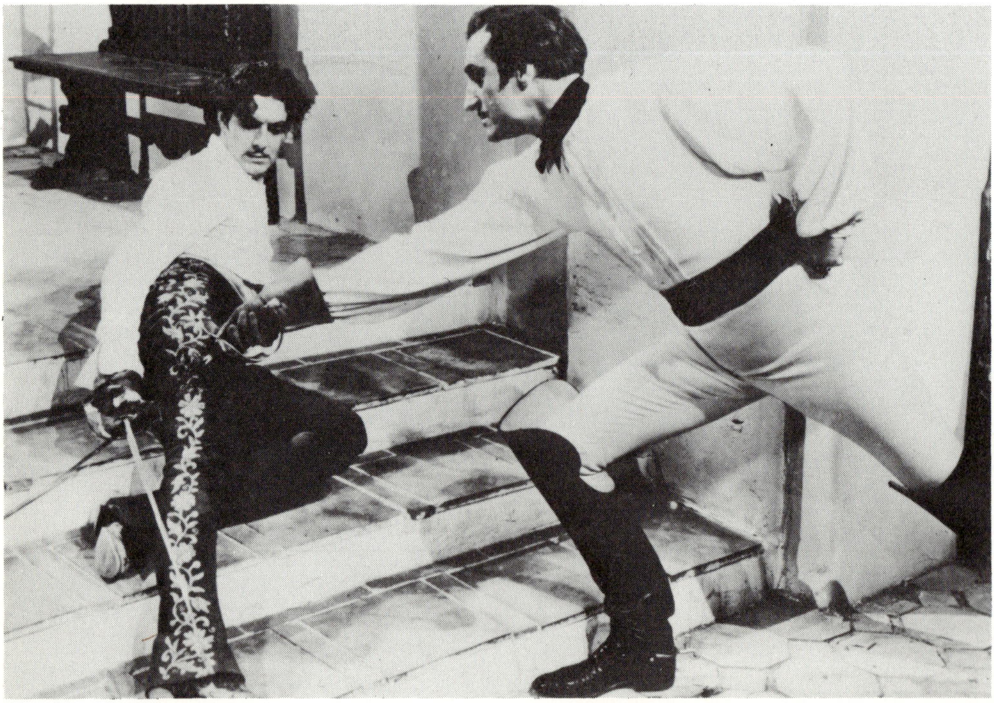

Another famous Fox blonde, Jayne Mansfield, seen here with Tony Randall in *Will Success Spoil Rock Hunter?*

The hills are alive with *The Sound Of Music*. Julie Andrews sings, the children listen, the film becomes a record breaker.

Marilyn Monroe's skirts fly high above the New York subway grating. The most famous scene in Billy Wilder's *The Seven Year Itch*.

Joe Mankiewicz directing Elizabeth Taylor in the ill-fated spectacular *Cleopatra*.

Gregory Peck (left) in one of his finest roles, as martinet airforce commander General Savage in King's *Twelve O'Clock High*.

Raquel Welch emerging from the deep in *Fathom*.

A rare still of master Fox cameraman Leon Shamroy during a break in the filming of *Planet Of The Apes*. Clapping the scene slate: chimpanzee archaeologist Roddy McDowall.

'May The Force Be With You'. Good in the form of Obi Ben Kenobi clashes with evil, Darth Vader, in George Lucas' science-fiction classic *Star Wars*.

Chronology

1935 Twentieth Century-Fox is born. In May, the ailing Fox company, a giant of the silent days (it was formed in 1915 and included among its hits *The Iron Horse, What Price Glory?* and *In Old Arizona*) merges with Joseph Schenck's two year old Twentieth Century Pictures to become the youngest studio in Hollywood.

It is Twentieth Century who are the dominant force. Fox, whose assets total 36 million against the 4 million of Twentieth Century, try for the name of Fox-Twentieth Century but Schenck, chairman of the board and Darryl F. Zanuck, vice president in charge of production of the new company, insist on Twentieth Century-Fox.

The beginnings are hesitant. During the first half-year of the studio's existence Zanuck puts the company's first movies before the cameras. The seven year old Shirley Temple and Will Rogers are the only two star names he has inherited from Fox.

The child star sings 'Animal Crackers In My Soup' in *Curly Top* (in production when the merger takes place) and at Christmas plays at New York's Radio City Music Hall in *The Littlest Rebel*. Her co-star is John Boles and another hit song 'Polly Wolly Doodle' makes her the hottest property on the Fox lot.

Dick Powell runs for governor in the studio's first hit *Thanks A Million*; Warner Oland as Earl Derr Bigger's oriental sleuth Charlie Chan (''When player cannot see man who deals cards, much wiser to stay out of game'') investigates in Paris, Egypt and Shanghai; and Will Rogers becomes involved in an exciting Mississippi steamboat race in John Ford's *Steamboat 'Round The Bend.* Before the year is out, however, Rogers loses his life in an air crash in Alaska and Fox, now with only one star name to their credit, limp hopefully into 1936.

1936 Zanuck, looking for new and different talent, signs up

Sonja Henie, the women's Olympic figure-skating champion of 1928, 32 and 36. Says Miss Henie, "I want to do on skates what Fred Astaire is doing with dancing." Says Zanuck who pays out 75,000 dollars a picture for her services, "I've signed Miss Henie — and her skates. Even if she couldn't skate I'd have signed her but not for so much."

Henie debuts in *One In A Million* but it is still little Shirley Temple upon whom Zanuck mainly relies. She makes four movies, *Captain January, Poor Little Rich Girl, Dimples* and *Stowaway* to earn her salary of 300,000 dollars a year.

Much is made of the fact that she is given only $4.25 a week as an allowance. A typical week's expenses:

candy	25 cents
fruit	40 cents
soda pop	15 cents
box of paints	75 cents
dog collar	95 cents
Sunday school collection	25 cents

New stars are beginning to emerge. Tyrone Power makes it quickly to the top in *Lloyds Of London*, an historical piece about the British banking and insurance company; former dance band singer Alice Faye, the first of the studio's famous blondes, appears in *King Of Burlesque*; and the man with the wide smile, Don Ameche, debuts in *Sins Of Man*.

Ameche is also privileged to appear in the company's first Technicolor movie, *Ramona*, a version of Helen Hunt Jackson's romantic novel of Indian life. Loretta Young co-stars and the picture is directed by Henry King.

Another first, and a strange one, is that Judy Garland (on loan from MGM for *Pigskin Parade*) sings her first song in a full-length feature movie. The song? 'Balboa'.

1937 Shirley Temple stars in a version of Johanna Spyri's *Heidi* and gets together with tough director John Ford in *Wee Willie Winkie*, a Kipling story of India in the 1890s. Surprisingly, the combination works. Shirley's co-star is genial giant Victor McLaglen. "Of all the pictures I've made, including those with adult roles, the one I enjoyed most was when I played soldier as Wee Willie Winkie," says Shirley later.

Handsome Tyrone Power is the busiest Fox star of the year. He makes four movies including three comedies with Loretta Young — *Love Is News, Second Honeymoon,* and *Café Metropole* – and gets Sonja Henie as a bonus in *Thin Ice*.

Alice Faye acquires a sugar daddy in *On The Avenue* and sings for her dinner in *You Can't Have Everything*, the first of her six movies with Don Ameche; Henry King remakes the Parisian love story *Seventh Heaven* with James Stewart and Simone Simon; and Zanuck borrows Wallace Beery and Mickey Rooney from Metro for *Slave Ship*.

Charlie Chan is still busily detecting, this time *At The Olympics* and *On Broadway* although the year also produces a competitor in the form of Mr. Moto, John P. Marquand's bespectacled sleuth from the Far East. Peter Lorre introduces the character in *Think Fast, Mr. Moto*.

1938 Zanuck destroys Chicago just as MGM had destroyed San Francisco with an earthquake two years earlier. This time it's fire that does the damage, and if *In Old Chicago* is not exactly great it's certainly spectacular, especially during the last twenty minutes when a cow accidentally kicks over a lamp in a barn and starts one of the most famous fires in history. The fire costs 1,800,000 dollars to film. No women are allowed on set because it is too dangerous and men, dressed in long skirts and bonnets, double for the female extras. Tyrone Power, Don Ameche, Alice Faye and Oscar-winning Alice Brady star in the family saga; Miss Faye sings 'Carry Me Back To Old Virginny', reveals a handsome pair of legs and wears a pair of jewelled stockings valued at 1,500 dollars.

It's very much Miss Faye's year as she makes the top moneymakers list. She sings 'This Is Where I Came In', in *Sally, Irene And Mary*, and stars again with Power and Ameche in the lavish musical *Alexander's Ragtime Band*. Thirty Irving Berlin songs accompany the trials and tribulations of a mythical dance band of the 20s and 30s.

Shirley Temple is *Rebecca Of Sunnybrook Farm* and *Little Miss Broadway*; Peter Lorre carries on as Mr. Moto; Warner Baxter and Freddie Bartholomew feature in Robert Louis Stevenson's *Kidnapped*; and Sonja Henie, now on 160,000 dollars a picture, skates through *Happy Landing* and *My Lucky Star*.

In *Suez* Tyrone Power stars as Ferdinand de Lesseps, the man who built the Suez Canal. Two loving women and a cyclone complicate the construction.

Charlie Chan At Monte Carlo marks Warner Oland's last appearance as the Chinese sleuth before his death in

August. He has played the role on sixteen occasions between 1931 and '38. Sidney Toler takes over in *Charlie Chan In Honolulu*.

One of the most interesting facts to emerge during the year is that Shirley Temple and not Judy Garland would have been Dorothy in *The Wizard Of Oz* if Metro chief Louis B. Mayer had been allowed to have his way. Mayer offered Gable and Harlow for *In Old Chicago* if Fox would let him have Temple for *Oz*. Harlow's tragic sudden death changed everything, however, and it was Garland who went on the magical road to Oz.

1939 Basil Rathbone and Nigel Bruce get together for the first time as Sherlock Holmes and Dr. Watson in *The Hound Of The Baskervilles*. They appear together a further thirteen times, once more at Fox in '39) (*Adventures Of Sherlock Holmes*) and on a dozen occasions at Universal. The hound of the film's title is played by a dog called Chiet. A 40 lb Great Dane, he got the part after 143 dogs had been tested for the role!

Biographies abound. Henry Fonda is the *Young Mr. Lincoln*; Spencer Tracy and Cedric Hardwicke are *Stanley And Livingstone*; Tyrone Power is *Jesse James* and Henry Fonda his brother Frank; and Don Ameche is composer Stephen Foster in *Swanee River*.

Ameche is also called upon to play the role of the man who invented the telephone, although in the advertisements for *The Story Of Alexander Graham Bell* it seems a miracle he ever got round to it.

''My dearest one,

Ever since I held you in my arms, I've known! My invention must be given up. This is little enough to do if it means that I may call you sweetheart and wife! The telephone will be born some day. . .and I do not care who gets the glory if the world gets the benefit. With all my heart, I am yours. . .Aleck.''

Shirley Temple's contributions to the year are *The Little Princess* (her first film in Technicolor) and *Susannah Of The Mounties* in which she is orphaned in an Indian massacre. It is the last Temple film at Fox to make a profit.

Mr. Moto's screen career comes to an end after three years and nine films; Alice Faye sings 'I'm Just Wild About Harry' in *Rose Of Washington Square*; Linda Darnell debuts in *Hotel For Women*; and Tyrone Power, now the number two money making star, teams again with Sonja Henie in *Second Fiddle*.

Power's most ambitious role, however, is in *The Rains Came*, Louis Bromfield's popular novel about the forbidden romance between an aristocratic Englishwoman (Myrna Loy) and an Indian prince (Power).

The spectacle catches the eye as much as the acting and the Fox publicity department make the most of the statistics during the filming of the earthquakes and floods: 'Ten thousand gallons of rain fell during each shooting minute of the monsoon, forty inches a day' — 'An eighteen acre city was built and then destroyed' — 'fourteen cameras were used to photograph the bursting of the dam and no less than two million gallons of water released as the scene was filmed!'

1940 A bad year for Alice Faye (she gets appendicitis instead of going *Down Argentine Way*) but a good one for Betty Grable who goes instead. Later in the year Miss Faye recovers to co-star with Grable (their only teaming) in *Tin Pan Alley*, but she's lost her spot as the studio's top musical star and Grable rules the lot for more than a decade.

In *Tin Pan Alley*, Faye and Grable perform 'The Sheik Of Araby' number in sheer pantaloons and sequinned bras. The outfit shows for the first time that Betty's legs are something a bit special.

Tyrone Power, in *The Mark Of Zorro*, allows Basil Rathbone a couple of 'Ahas' and a few imperious rapier swings at lighted candles before finally spoiling his immaculate white shirt by piercing him through the heart; Henry Fonda repeats his role of Jesse's brother in *The Return Of Frank James* (a film which also marks the debut of Gene Tierney); Alice Faye is 90's entertainer *Lillian Russell*; Dean Jagger the Mormon leader *Brigham Young*; and Anne Baxter, whom Selznick had tested for *Rebecca*, co-stars with John Barrymore in *The Great Profile*.

The best Fox movie of the year and one of the all-time classics is *The Grapes Of Wrath*, John Steinbeck's story of a family of Oakies who during the Depression are forced to leave their homes in the Oklahoma Dust Bowl and seek new lives in California. Director John Ford and supporting actress Jane Darwell (Ma Joad) both receive Oscars for their work.

Shirley Temple's stardom comes to an end at last. At

the age of twelve, and after the failure of *The Bluebird* and *Young People*, Fox let her go.

1941 The studio wins its first best picture Oscar for *How Green Was My Valley*. John Ford (best director) and Donald Crisp (best supporting actor) both feature among the film's five awards.

In *Blood And Sand* society temptress Rita Hayworth and simple wife Linda Darnell fight for the favours of handsome matador Tyrone Power, but to no avail. It's the bulls that get him.

Sonja Henie's skates are getting blunter although The Glenn Miller Orchestra manages to make *Sun Valley Serenade* a success; Fritz Lang returns to the wide open spaces for *Western Union*, but is more at home with *Man Hunt*, a version of Geoffrey Household's novel 'Rogue Male' with Walter Pidgeon as a big game hunter out to assassinate Hitler. He fails, but does at least dispose of deadly assassin John Carradine, complete with swordstick, in a tunnel in the London underground.

Gene Tierney is Western outlaw *Belle Starr*; Jack Benny *Charley's Aunt*; and Betty Grable one of three gals seeking millionaire husbands in *Moon Over Miami*. Alice Faye makes up for missing her South American trip in *Down Argentine Way* by accompanying Don Ameche for *That Night In Rio* and John Payne for a *Weekend In Havana*. Accompanying all of them: the music and lyrics of Mack Gordon and Harry Warren.

1942 Tyrone Power returns to swashbuckling in *The Black Swan*, piercing this time the heart of red-bearded pirate, George Sanders. The movie wins an Oscar for its Technicolor, but at times is as delightful to the ear as it is to the eye. "Your fulminations, my hosts and gentlemen, are full of bilge and blather," rumbles Laird Cregar as Sir Henry Morgan.

Betty Grable makes the top ten list for the first time. A delighted Fox promise her Technicolor for as long as she's under contract. Victor Mature has to compete with the famous legs in *Song Of The Islands* and *Footlight Serenade* and Cesar Romero in *Springtime In The Rockies*.

Ginger Rogers stars as *Roxie Hart*, a burlesque dancer who is persuaded to use her murder trial for publicity purposes; Glenn Miller and his orchestra are again popular in *Orchestra Wives*; and beautiful Rita Hayworth brightens up the 1890s in the Technicolored *My Gal Sal*.

Charlie Chan's career at Fox comes to an end. The oriental sleuth, with Sidney Toler still in charge, carries on his deductions at Monogram.

1943 Jennifer Jones becomes a star and wins an Academy Award as Bernadette Soubirous, the Maid Of Lourdes in Henry King's *The Song Of Bernadette*. Fox discover there's money in religion. As well as taking four Academy Awards on Oscar night it earns five million dollars at the box-office.

Alice Faye is another lady who helps Fox to an Oscar, not for acting but for singing the melancholy 'You'll Never Know' (best song) from *Hello, Frisco, Hello*. Carmen Miranda has no such pretensions and goes bananas — literally — in 'The Lady In The Tutti-Frutti Hat' sequence from *The Gang's All Here*.

Betty Grable's the gal though. She receives five to ten thousand letters a week, makes it as the industry's number one moneymaker and stays in the top ten list until 1951. In *Coney Island* she sings 'Cuddle Up A Little Closer' and plays a showgirl fought over by rival saloon proprietors George Montgomery and Cesar Romero. There are no such problems in real life. On July 5 she marries jazz trumpeter Harry James in a Las Vegas hotel room. The marriage lasts for twenty-two years.

Most of the male stars are at war. Henry Fonda and Thomas Mitchell are involved in desert warfare in *The Immortal Sergeant*; William Bendix, Preston Foster and Lloyd Nolan join the marines for *Guadalcanal Diary*; and Tyrone Power, an expert on PT boats and submarines, is in action in the North Atlantic in *Crash Dive*. During the year Fonda and Power leave the movies for the real thing, Fonda joining the navy, Power the U.S. marines.

Fox's best movie of the year is *The Ox-Bow Incident*, an uncompromising study of a Western lynch mob who take the law into their own hands, hang three men for cattle rustling only to find, too late, that the men are innocent after all. Henry Fonda, Dana Andrews, Jane Darwell and Anthony Quinn head a brilliant cast. Said Zanuck when director William Wellman first showed him the script, "I don't think it'll ever make a dime, but it's something I want my studio to have. I want to have my name on it."

1944 Betty Grable stars in *Pin Up Girl* which is exactly what she has become to servicemen all over the world. During World War II, two million servicemen request pin-up photographs of the blonde Fox star.

Especially popular is the photo in which, according to one critic, "She is squeezed, perhaps sewn into a white bathing suit and peeks saucily over her shoulder." The studio stock Grable prints in five sizes ranging from the very small 'over-the-heart' size to a huge display print ideal for posting in lockers, barracks and similar semi-private places.

If Grable shows most of what she's got, Joan Fontaine gives nothing away. She stars as *Jane Eyre* and although not exactly enjoying 'A love story every women would die a thousand deaths to live' still has a young and handsome Orsen Welles as a prize for all her patience.

Joel McCrea is a romanticized *Buffalo Bill*; Laird Cregar a magnificently sinister Jack The Ripper in *The Lodger*; Gregory Peck (in his first film for Fox) a priest in *The Keys Of The Kingdom*; and Alexander Knox a very dull and disappointing President *Wilson*. Lovely Jeanne Crain debuts in a warm-hearted piece of Americana, *Home In Indiana*, whilst on the urban scene Clifton Webb is nominated for a supporting Oscar for his murdering columnist Waldo Lydecker in *Laura*.

Otherwise, it's the war that still dominates. Hitchcock casts an assorted group of passengers adrift in *Lifeboat*; five young Americans go down with their ship in the South Pacific in *The Sullivans*; Anne Baxter helps cook a *Sunday Dinner For A Soldier*; Zanuck pays tribute to the Army Air Corps in *Winged Victory*; and Dana Andrews, Richard Conte and Farley Granger bravely endure torture by the Japanese in *The Purple Heart*.

The tragic surprise of the year is the premature death of twenty-eight year old Laird Cregar, Fox's 325 lb answer to Warner's Sydney Greenstreet. During his short career Cregar played primarily villainous roles, among them a psychotic cop in *I Wake Up Screaming*; pirate Sir Henry Morgan in *The Black Swan*; Lucifer in *Heaven Can Wait*; and the afore mentioned Jack The Ripper in *The Lodger*. Twelve of the sixteen films he made between 1940 and '44 were for Fox.

1945 Gene Tierney stars in Fox's biggest moneyspinner of the year, *Leave Her To Heaven*. Miss Tierney plays a psychopath so possessive of her husband that she destroys anyone who as much as breathes on him.

Somehow, Zanuck seems to see some good in her. Says he, "The women in *Leave Her To Heaven* deliberately kills her own unborn child, drowns the crippled brother of her husband and endeavours to send her adopted sister to the electric chair. And yet, despite all this, there are certain things about her that you rather like."

Not all Fox women are bad. Betty Grable co-stars with June Haver and sings 'I Can't Begin To Tell You' in *The Dolly Sisters*; Jeanne Crain reaches stardom in a musical *State Fair* ('It's A Grand Night For Singing', 'It Might As Well Be Spring'); and Alice Faye goes straight in her retirement picture, *Fallen Angel*.

The studio's biggest trendsetter is *The House On 92nd Street*, a true story of how the FBI smashed an American based spy ring trying to gain access to the secrets of the atomic bomb. Inclusion of newsreel footage and an on-the-spot technique make Henry Hathaway's film an influential one for the American cinema, especially Fox cinema, for the rest of the decade.

Lewis Milestone's brilliantly understated war film *A Walk In The Sun* proves to be one of the year's best, Rene Clair's version of Agatha Christie's *And Then There Were None* one of the most bizarre, *Thunderhead, Son Of Flicka* (a horse soap-opera) one of the most beautifully photographed, and *A Tree Grows In Brooklyn* one of the most important in that it brings to Hollywood, for the first time as director, Broadway talent, Elia Kazan.

1946 Zanuck spends his money on a lavish version of Somerset Maugham's *The Razor's Edge*. It pays him back handsomely. It's the studio's biggest moneymaker with Gene Tierney, once again spoiled and rich, setting her sights on Tyrone Power and making sure that poor Anne Baxter keeps well on the road to alcoholism. Drink has its good points, however. Baxter wins an Oscar, Tierney doesn't.

Zanuck tries to make his own *Meet Me In St. Louis* by casting Jeanne Crain and Linda Darnell in *Centennial Summer*. He fails. Even Jerome Kern's music doesn't help. Still, the movie would probably have been even worse had Zanuck been allowed to use his original title: *See You In Philadelphia!*

John Ford, making his first film since the end of the war

heads West and stages the Gunfight At The O.K. Corral in *My Darling Clementine*. Henry Fonda is Wyatt Earp, Victor Mature an unlikely Doc Holliday; Gene Tierney, Walter Huston and Vincent Price play out the melodrama of Anya Seton's *Dragonwyck* (Joe Mankiewicz's first film as director); thin, suave Clifton Webb tips burly William Bendix out of a skyscraper window in *The Dark Corner*; Jeanne Crain loses not her life, just her drawers, in Henry King's charming period piece *Margie*; Irene Dunne and Rex Harrison are *Anna And The King Of Siam*; and Celeste Holm (in her debut) enlivens the musical *Three Little Girls In Blue* with some characteristic racy wit.

1947 *Gentleman's Agreement* wins the best picture Oscar for Fox, its second of the decade. The first in the studio's long line of social protest films of the late 40s, it stars Gregory Peck as a journalist who poses as a Jew to discover first hand that anti-semitism is rife in the upper echelons of contemporary American society. A bold, challenging picture, directed by Kazan, it enhances the reputation of the studio.

Which is more than can be said for *Forever Amber* which makes money, but not many friends. Fox wanted Lana Turner for the lead. They settle for a blonde Linda Darnell. Best moment: George Sanders (as Charles II) to Darnell, "Madam, your mind is like your wardrobe — many changes but no surprises."

Richard Widmark makes a sensational screen debut as a giggling psychopath in the semi-documentary thriller *Kiss Of Death*. James Agee in *Time* sums him up to perfection, "He is rather a frail fellow with maniacal eyes who uses a sinister kind of falsetto baby talk laced with tittering laughs. It is clear that murder is one of the kindest things he is capable of." He's right. Widmark's speciality? Tying an old lady to a wheelchair and pushing her down a long flight of stairs to her death.

It's a good year all round for the tough stuff. Kazan brilliantly recreates the story of a real-life unsolved murder on location in a small town in Connecticut. The film is *Boomerang*. Its stars, Dana Andrews and Lee J. Cobb. George Montgomery is private-eye Philip Marlowe in *The Brasher Doubloon*; and Tyrone Power proves that he can act with the best of them as a bogus fortune teller in the remarkable *Nightmare Alley*.

Power finds himself in more familiar historical surroundings in *Captain From Castile* as he sets off with Cortez across Mexico to the accompaniment of banal dialogue and a rousing Alfred Newman music score.

On the lighter side; Edmund Gwenn, a Macy's Santa Claus in *Miracle On 34th Street*, comes to believe that he really is Father Christmas and wins a supporting Oscar for his thoughts, and Betty Grable joins up with Dan Dailey for the first time in her favourite musical *Mother Wore Tights*.

1948 Fox is now at the height of its semi-documentary thriller period. James Stewart tries to clear a wrongly convicted man in *Call Northside 777*; cop Victor Mature is up against crook Richard Conte in *Cry Of The City*; and Richard Widmark is made to repeat his giggle as a gangleader in *The Street With No Name*.

Among all the realism and violence however the superior wit and snobbery of Clifton Webb shines out. In *Sitting Pretty* he appears for the first time as the self-confessed genius, Mr. Belvedere, and is charged with looking after the less than lovable offspring of Robert Young and Maureen O'Hara. In a memorable scene he turns a bowl of porridge over the head of the youngest; in another he looks aghast at one of the children and utters, "*Don't* call me uncle. By no stretch of the imagination could I be any relation of yours."

Gregory Peck goes West with Widmark and Anne Baxter in *Yellow Sky*; Olivia de Havilland goes insane and suffers terrifying mental tortures in a crowded asylum in *The Snake Pit*. Portraying madness with such realism that cinema audiences were stunned.

No-one notices a movie called *Scudda Hoo! Scudda Hay!* And there's no reason why they should, but it does mark the first screen appearance of Marilyn Monroe in a bit part as a young farm girl. Her single line is cut, however, and it is in another small-scale movie, *Dangerous Years*, that Marilyn is seen on screen for the first time — as a waitress in a juke box joint.

1949 Fox concentrates not on Betty Grable's legs for a change, but on another part of her anatomy. Say the advertisements for *The Beautiful Blonde From Bashful Bend*, "She's got the biggest six-shooters in the West!"

In Joe Mankiewicz's witty *A Letter To Three Wives* Linda Darnell has similar attentions focused on her bust.

Says down-to-earth Thelma Ritter, ''Why don't cha show more of what you got? Wear some beads.'' Replies Linda, ''What I got don't need beads.''

Clifton Webb is back in *Mr. Belvedere Goes To College*; Tyrone Power stars in one of his best swashbucklers *Prince Of Foxes* with Orson Welles as a splendidly malevolent Cesare Borgia; Loretta Young and Celeste Holm don nuns' habits in *Come To The Stable*; and Jeanne Crain proves that she's an actress of some ability by winning an Oscar nomination for *Pinky*, a coloured girl who passes for white.

Gregory Peck is another Fox star among the nominees for his martinet airforce general in *Twelve O'Clock High*, one of the most thoughtful of America's World War II flying dramas. Strangely, but effectively, the movie stays on the ground for all but one sequence made up of actual newsreel footage from the war.

Dean Jagger is Fox's sole Oscar winner in the acting field being named best supporting actor for his ageing adjutant in *Twelve O'Clock High*; Joe Mankiewicz wins for both writing and directing *A Letter To Three Wives*.

The diminutive, always lovable Thelma Ritter has the last word. In *Father Was A Fullback* she gives Fred MacMurray some friendly advice about bringing up his precocious daughter, ''What she needs is a good clip on the chops.''

1950 The studio starts off the 50s in great style. In *All About Eve*, Bette Davis, as fading actress Margo Channing, warns everyone, ''Fasten your seatbelts, it's going to be a bumpy night.''

For audiences it's anything but. Joe Mankiewicz's witty ride through the back corridors of New York's theatre land proves to be one of the most polished movies since Lubitsch was at his peak. A winner of six Oscars (including best picture and two more for Mankiewicz) it still holds the record for the most nominations — fourteen.

Clifton Webb, as the father of twelve children, proves he still has box-office drawing power by helping *Cheaper By The Dozen* become the Fox commercial hit of the year.

But the real meat of the Fox movie scene still lies in the realism of their dramas — Kazan's *Panic In The Streets* with Richard Widmark and Paul Douglas after a plague carrier loose in the streets of New Orleans; *Where The Sidewalk Ends* with Dana Andrews as a tough 'Hit first, talk later' cop; and Mankiewicz's *No Way Out*, the toughest and most convincing of all Hollywood's colour prejudice films with Widmark superb as a pathological negro hater.

Out West Gregory Peck is a tired gunslinger trying to live down his past in King's sombre western *The Gunfighter*, and James Stewart marries a lovely Indian girl in Delmer Daves' pro-Indian *Broken Arrow*, a movie which opens with an unusual and respectful off-screen commentary, "When the Apaches speak they will speak in our language."

Irene Dunne is Queen Victoria in *The Mudlark*; Edmund Gwenn back to his old tricks as the benign counter-feiter *Mr. 880*; and James Stewart the surprise winner of a radio quiz prize in *The Jackpot*.

War is served up hot — Tyrone Power in the Philippines in *I Shall Return*; steamy — Claudette Colbert in a Japanese prison camp in *Three Came Home*; and cold — Montgomery Clift in *The Big Lift*, a story about the Berlin Airlift of 1948.

Yet for all their star quality none of them quite rates the build-up of a star in a strictly minor Fox film of the year. Say the ads, "Just A Little Guy. . .A Punk. . .But On Skates He Was A Flying Demon. He Was A Runt In A Man's Game. . .Crashing To The Top On Screaming Wheels." Who was he? Mickey Rooney as a hot shot roller-skater in *The Fireball*.

1951 The semi-documentary thriller scene is coming to an end. One of the best of them is *Fourteen Hours*, the story of a would-be-suicide (Richard Basehart) who threatens to jump from the ledge of a New York skyscraper. The story is based on a real-life pre-war incident. In real-life the man jumped. In the movie he changes his mind.

The film is brilliantly directed by Henry Hathaway. Another famous director, Howard Hawks, turned it down. The reason? He wanted to make it as a comedy with Cary Grant!

Gregory Peck and Susan Hayward are the biblical *David And Bathsheba*; James Mason is *Rommel — Desert Fox*; Glenn Ford the crippled golfer Ben Hogan in *Follow The Sun*; and Jean Peters pirate Anne Bonney in *Anne Of The Indies*.

Clifton Webb makes it three times in a row as Belvedere in *Mr. Belvedere Rings The Bell*; Cary Grant features as a philosophical doctor in Mankiewicz's unusual *People*

Will Talk; and in *No Highway* James Stewart is a twittery boffin constantly worrying that the tail of the plane in which he is travelling will fall off at any moment.

Lovely Betty Grable is still around, co-starring for the fourth time with Dan Dailey in *Call Me Mister*, but it's the last time she's in the top ten and the career that meant so much to Fox in the forties is slowly ebbing away. The war years in which she flourished are recalled in such movies as *The Frogmen*, the flagwaving *The Halls Of Montezuma* (both with Richard Widmark) and the disturbing *Decision Before Dawn*, Anatole Litvak's study of a group of German P.O.W.'s who are persuaded by their U.S. captors to return and spy on their own country.

The most intriguing character on the Fox screen is Michael Rennie in *The Day The Earth Stood Still*. Together with a huge robot, he descends on Washington in a flying saucer to warn the Earth that unless it stops its war games the rest of the planets in the universe will blow it to smithereens. Not surprisingly, the world takes little notice. The movie's a science-fiction classic just the same.

1952 The last full year before Fox plunges into CinemaScope. Ironically, it's one of their finest ever years with something for everybody — musical biography with Susan Hayward as singer Jane Froman in *With A Song In My Heart*; spy drama with James Mason as the real-life Cicero, nicknamed *Five Fingers* in World War II; superior soap opera with Olivia de Havilland as Daphne du Maurier's enigmatic *My Cousin Rachel*; Hollywood drama with Bette Davis as *The Star*; and even seamy small-town melodrama with Jennifer Jones as *Ruby Gentry* — "A flame who wrecked a whole town. . . step by step. . .sin by sin. . ."

The prestige version of Hemingway's *The Snows Of Kilimanjaro* — with Gregory Peck, Ava Gardner and Susan Hayward — is the studio's biggest moneymaker even though the author dislikes the expansion of his classic story and renames it 'The Snows Of Zanuck'.

Rumour has it that Hemingway oils up his old .577 which he uses to hunt rhino and buffalo and heads for Mount Kilimanjaro where he starts a search for the soul of Zanuck.

Monroe is on the verge of stardom in pictures like *Monkey Business, We're Not Married* and the portmanteau five-story film *O'Henry's Full House*. But it is Marlon Brando who is Fox's star of the year. In Kazan's *Viva*

Zapata! he proves his quality yet again with his brilliant portrait of the Mexican peasant revolutionary Emiliano Zapata.

The explosive actor is hailed for his performance even though at test time Zanuck was reported to have said, "I don't understand a goddam thing the son-of-a-bitch says. Can't you stop him from mumbling. This is just an Illinois boy. What the hell are you trying to make a Mexican out of him for?"

1953 The CinemaScope year! But before the revolutionary new process hits the screen Marilyn Monroe, a star at last in *Niagara*, makes sure the old system goes out with a bang.

Say the advertisements for the picture, "A raging torrent of emotion that even nature can't control." Says Joseph Cotten (Marilyn's husband in the film), "Why was I attracted to her? I guess it was the way she put the beer on the table."

Marilyn is also around in another famous pre-CinemaScope movie, *Gentlemen Prefer Blondes*, in which she duets 'Diamonds Are A Girl's Best Friend' with Jane Russell.

James Mason repeats his role of Rommel in *The Desert Rats* starring Richard Burton; raucous Ethel Merman, Vera-Ellen and Donald O'Connor feature in Irving Berlin's *Call Me Madam*; Richard Widmark picks pockets on the New York subway in *Pickup On South Street*; luckless Clifton Webb is one of those who go down on the *Titanic*; Susan Hayward is the pipe-smoking woman of Andrew Jackson in *The President's Lady*.

Fox prove too that they haven't forgotten how to aim at the lowest common denominator. Their advertisements for the war movie *Destination Gobi* scream, "Listen. . . you griping gobs! You're Uncle Sam's soldiers marooned in the Mongolian Desert. . .NOW FIGHT YOUR WAY OUT!"

But CinemaScope is the big story. It arrives with *The Robe*, an all-star version of Lloyd C. Douglas' biblical novel with Richard Burton as the Roman tribune in charge of the Crucifixion and Jean Simmons as the girl who helps convert him to Christianity. The movie premieres at the Roxy, New York, on September 16, 1953 and quickly becomes the studio's biggest ever grosser with a take of more than 17 million dollars.

Monroe, Grable and Bacall ('Big As Life And A Million

Times More Fun') are the next set of stars to be photographed in wide screen in *How To Marry A Millionaire* — released November — and Robert Wagner and Terry Moore take the process underwater in *Beneath The Twelve Mile Reef*.

After 1953 things are never the same again!

1954 It's now CinemaScope all the year round and in world-wide locations.

Milton Krasner wins an Academy Award for his colour camerawork of Rome in *Three Coins In The Fountain* and Marilyn Monroe travels to the great outdoors to star with Robert Mitchum in *River Of No Return*. Says Marilyn, "A Z cowboy movie in which the acting finishes third to the scenery and CinemaScope."

She has more opportunity in the large-scale musical *There's No Business Like Show Business* (Irving Berlin's sultry 'Heat Wave' is her speciality) and so too do Harry Belafonte and Dorothy Dandridge in the all-black *Carmen Jones*.

MGM's Spencer Tracy is paid 165,000 dollars to play an ageing beef baron in *Broken Lance*; Gary Cooper is in Mexico in *Garden Of Evil* along with cynical gambler Richard Widmark and fiery Susan Hayward; Gregory Peck is in Germany involved in the cold war in *Night People*; Robert Wagner is *Prince Valiant*; Tyrone Power *King Of The Khyber Rifles*; and Jean Simmons *Desiree* opposite Brando's Napoleon.

In a sequel to *The Robe* — *Demetrius And The Gladiators* — slave Victor Mature forgets his Christian vows for a couple of hours and opts instead for the physical pleasures of seductive empress Susan Hayward.

1955 The year of Monroe's *The Seven Year Itch*. It's the one in which she fools around with middle-aged husband Tom Ewell, gets her toe stuck in the bathtap and keeps her undies in the ice-box.

The famous scene in which Marilyn's skirt is blown high above her waist by the air of the New York subway grating is shot by Billy Wilder at 2 a.m. 4,000 people turn up to watch the Monroe legs revealed! Not surprisingly, the movie is Fox's biggest hit of the year — $6 million at the box-office.

Bette Davis returns to satin and silks for her second attempt at Elizabeth I in *The Virgin Queen*; Vivien Leigh tries for suicide over a worthless Kenneth More in *The Deep Blue Sea*; Fred Astaire delivers one of the best of Johnny Mercer's songs, 'Something's Gotta Give' in *Daddy Long Legs*; and Clark Gable has his hands more than full. Jane Russell occupies his mind out West in *The Tall Men* and Susan Hayward out East in Hong Kong in *Soldier Of Fortune*.

Hong Kong is also the setting for one of the most tear-soaked love tragedies of the 50s, *Love Is A Many Splendoured Thing*. Jennifer Jones is a Eurasian doctor, William Holden the married American war correspondent she loves and loses. Composer Alfred Newman drenches everything with sweet strings to win himself an Academy Award.

The exotic Carmen Miranda, '100 lbs of dynamite' and a Fox star of the early 40s suffers a heart attack and dies in Hollywood, aged fifty-one.

1956 The musical dominates. Teenagers go into ecstasies as Elvis Presley makes his screen debut in the post-civil war-western *Love Me Tender*, a natural at the box-office which supposedly recoups its entire production cost in three days. The fans have a bit of a howl too for the rock-and-roll idol is actually killed off in the final reel, the only time this happens to him during his screen career.

A different age group goes into similar ecstasies over Yul Brynner's shaven head in *The King And I*, Rodgers and Hammerstein's musical version of the studio's earlier dramatic hit, *Anna And The King Of Siam*. 'It's A Puzzlement' sings Brynner in one of the songs. Not to the public it isn't who make the movie Fox's biggest box-office success of the year, nor to the Oscar people who name Yul best actor.

Also on the musical scene: Gordon MacRae, Ernest Borgnine and Dan Dailey who play hit songwriters DeSylva, Brown and Henderson in *The Best Things In Life Are Free*; MacRae again, singing 'My Boy Bill' in *Carousel*; and Marilyn Monroe who, as a sleazy entertainer, croaks out 'That Old Black Magic' in Josh Logan's version of *Bus Stop*.

Jayne Mansfield wriggles onto the Fox lot for *The Girl Can't Help It*; Ingrid Bergman makes a comeback and wins a best actress Oscar for *Anastasia*; Robert Taylor and Richard Todd are involved with Dana Wynter — and World War II — in *D-Day, The Sixth Of June*; Clifton Webb, with more cunning, helps fool the Nazis by creating

The Man Who Never Was; and Richard Widmark turns half-breed in Delmer Daves' western *The Last Wagon.*

Fox also dabble briefly with science-fiction in *On The Threshold Of Space*. The movie isn't much, but the advertising is great. Say the billboards, "The most dangerous frontier of them all lies just seventeen miles from your doorstep — straight up!"

The most sensational news from the studio is that Zanuck is resigning as head of production to set up his own production company which will release under the Fox banner.

1957 Small town sex (*Peyton Place*) with thirty-six year old Lana Turner courageously playing the mother of a teenager, and three-way schizophrenia (*The Three Faces Of Eve*) as personified by Joanne Woodward, highlight the Fox year. Both gals are up for awards at Oscar time. Woodward wins, but the Turner movie is the box-office hit, thanks not a little to the best-selling novel by Grace Metalious.

Island In The Sun, Alec Waugh's best-seller about a group of black and whites living out somewhat seamy lives in the West Indies is the first of Zanuck's independent productions. Packed with stars — James Mason, Joan Fontaine, Harry Belafonte, Dorothy Dandridge — it turns out to be a financial but not critical success.

Leo McCarey remakes his pre-war *Love Affair* as *An Affair To Remember* with Cary Grant and Deborah Kerr in the original Charles Boyer and Irene Dunne roles; Tracy and Hepburn get together for the eighth time, but for the first time away from Metro in *The Desk Set*; Deborah Kerr is a nun stranded on a remote island with rugged marine Robert Mitchum in *Heaven Knows, Mr. Allison*; and Alan Ladd and Sophia Loren are in Greece in *Boy On A Dolphin.*

Otherwise, it's primarily American literature that gets a boost from the studio. Tyrone Power is Hemingway's impotent Jake Barnes in Zanuck's version of *The Sun Also Rises*; Rock Hudson and Jennifer Jones the ill-fated lovers in the same author's *A Farewell To Arms* (Selznick's last production); and Dan Dailey, Joan Collins and Jayne Mansfield (as a former bubble dancer) among those aboard John Steinbeck's *The Wayward Bus.*

1958 "Love Had Suddenly Come To Her. . .A White Woman In A Strange Land. . .Love For This Oriental Soldier Who Now Pressed His Earthy Skin Against Her Own." No, not a Marlene Dietrich sex opus, but the story of missionary Gladys Aylward (Ingrid Bergman) in *Inn Of The Sixth Happiness*. Her soldier? Curt Jurgens.

More earthy, but less ambitiously advertised is *The Long Hot Summer* with a torrid Paul Newman — starring for the first time with his new wife Joanne Woodward — as William Faulkner's Mississippi redneck Ben Quick. Gregory Peck features in the revenge western *The Bravados* and Robert Mitchum (*The Enemy Below*) and Marlon Brando (*The Young Lions*) both play war games, the former as the commander of an American destroyer, the latter as a disillusioned officer of the Third Reich.

Zanuck's attempt at transferring Romain Gary's prize-winning *The Roots Of Heaven* to the screen fails, but Mitzi Gaynor cheers everyone up in *South Pacific*, 'Washing That Man Right Out Of Her Hair' — among other things.

The shock news is the death of Tyrone Power, handsome Fox star of nearly forty movies between 1936 and 1957. He dies of a heart attack while filming *Solomon And Sheba* in Spain, collapsing after shooting a sword fight with George Sanders. Ironically, it is with a sword in his hand that his fans best remember him. His dash and verve were never seen to better advantage than in his many swashbucklers: *The Mark Of Zorro, The Black Swan, Son Of Fury, Captain From Castile, Prince Of Foxes, The Black Rose*. He was forty-four.

In the board rooms and offices of Fox the first tiny ripples are beginning about the production of the film that is to bring the studio close to ruin — *Cleopatra*. Producer Walter Wanger interests production chief Buddy Adler, who wants to make the picture with Joan Collins for just over a million dollars, in the idea. Wanger has his heart set on Elizabeth Taylor and wants a budget of at least two million. Negotiations continue as the year draws to a close.

1959 "Here's To The Girls Who Want The Best Of Everything... Here's To Men, Bless Their Clean Cut Faces And Dirty Little Minds." So say the ads for Fox's Madison Avenue melodrama *The Best Of Everything*.

But it's not the best of everything for the studio, not by a long way. Gregory Peck and Deborah Kerr are miscast as Scott Fitzgerald and Sheilah Graham in *Beloved Infidel*; May Britt is a poor substitute for Marlene Dietrich in the remake of *The Blue Angel*; Fabian in *Hound-Dog Man* does little for anybody; and Yul Brynner, plus wig, seems out of his depth in a version of Faulkner's Deep South novel *The Sound And The Fury*.

The most notable Fox movies of the year: *Compulsion* with Orson Welles superb as Clarence Darrow defending Dean Stockwell and Bradford Dillman of callous child murder; *The Diary Of Anne Frank*, George Stevens' long but respectful tribute to the courage of the heroic little Dutch girl; and the Jules Verne fantasy *Journey To The Centre Of The Earth*.

Meanwhile, back at head office, the *Cleopatra* story slowly gains momentum, but it's still wrangle, wrangle all the way as Wanger fights for Liz Taylor. Fox still want Joan Collins as the year begins, but when Wanger lists his ideal cast as Elizabeth Taylor (Cleopatra), Laurence Olivier (Caesar) and Richard Burton (Antony) the studio counter with Elizabeth Taylor (Cleopatra), Cary Grant (Caesar) and Burt Lancaster (Antony).

Among those on the list for Cleopatra is Marilyn Monroe!

Nigel Balchin prepares the first screenplay and by June, the budget, with a shooting schedule of sixty-four days, is up to three million. By the end of the year with the film to be shot in England it's up to five million.

Rouben Mamoulian is signed to direct. Both Elizabeth Taylor and Audrey Hepburn agree to play the role, but Susan Hayward almost steals it when Fox again insist that they must have a contract player for the part. Liz eventually drops her asking price and signs for the film on October 15. Shooting is scheduled to begin in the early months of 1960.

1960 If 1959 was a poor year, 1960 is equally mediocre. Newman and Woodward, together again, star in the year's biggest financial hit *From The Terrace*, but with a take of just five million dollars that's not saying much.

Frank Sinatra and Shirley MacLaine can do little with the limp Cole Porter musical *Can-Can*; Joan Collins livens things up a bit with her shimmy in the Riviera robbery caper *Seven Thieves*; John Wayne and Stewart Granger slug it out in *North To Alaska*; stiff upper lipped Kenneth More, aided by stiff upper lipped Dana Wynter, plans the destruction of a German World War II battleship in *Sink The Bismark*; Peter Sellers is a poor Indian doctor and Sophia Loren spoilt and rich — but lovely — in *The Millionairess*; and at the other end of the scale Elvis Presley is a snarling half-breed in *Flaming Star*.

Best Fox picture of the year is the British-made version

of *Sons And Lovers*. Dean Stockwell is D. H. Lawrence's young Nottingham artist, Mary Ure and Heather Sears the girls who help bring him to maturity. All are outshone by Trevor Howard as Stockwell's drunken coal-miner father.

The most disappointing movie: Marilyn Monroe's last film for Fox, *Let's Make Love*, a musical during the shooting of which she is at her most troublesome. Marilyn sings Cole Porter's 'My Heart Belongs To Daddy'. Yves Montand and Frankie Vaughan are her co-stars.

The *Cleopatra* saga still sizzles, but nothing gets under way until the autumn as delay follows delay.

The budget soars to six million as Lawrence Durrell is brought in for a rewrite. Olivier, much wanted by producer Wanger, is definitely out as Caesar. June 17 is mentioned as a possible starting date, then August 15 which eventually becomes September 30 the date on which the picture finally gets under way — but without Liz Taylor who is laid low with a cold. Peter Finch and Stephen Boyd are the actors finally cast as Caesar and Antony.

Liz's health is up and down like a yo-yo. A virus infection sends her into the London Clinic. So does a meningitis scare. Total disaster ensues — Mamoulian has to shoot round her.

Liz gradually recovers but, by November 18, is still not well enough to start her role. Mamoulian can nolonger shoot without her and filming grinds to a halt. Fox want to cancel the picture and wipe out their losses. Wanger insists they carry on despite the fact that, just a week before, Mamoulian had been filming in thick fog and had difficulty in finding the five hundred extras on set.

As the year ends the insurance companies become involved and everybody is fed up with the name of *Cleopatra*, especially company president Spyros Skouras who keeps insisting that if Susan Hayward or Joanne Woodward had played the role the film would be in the can by now.

January 3 is planned as the new start date.

1961 Fox *Return To Peyton Place*; make a *Voyage To The Bottom Of The Sea*; go West with *The Comancheros* and also make two superior movies — *The Innocents* a version of Henry James' ghost story 'The Turn Of The Screw' with Deborah Kerr as the obsessed governess; and *The Hustler* with pool shark Paul Newman having his thumbs broken on the way to a showdown with pool champ Minnesota Fats (Jackie Gleason).

But the bubbling turmoil that is *Cleopatra* now dominates the Fox scene. What isn't being filmed becomes far more newsworthy than what is.

The January 3 starting date never happens nor does any other London starting date. Disenchanted with working for fifteen months for no result Mamoulian resigns. Writer-director Joe Mankiewicz is hired as his replacement.

The following conversation is supposed to have taken place when they met:

Mankiewicz: "Now you're a director and I'm a director. What do you really think of the picture?"

Mamoulian: "Well, I resigned didn't I?"

Mankiewicz: "Let me rephrase the question. What would you do if you were me?"

Mamoulian: "I'd resign."

Mankiewicz remains, however, but must himself have thought about resignation when Liz Taylor becomes ill again, this time seriously with staphylococcus pneumonia. She is at death's door for nearly five days after undergoing a tracheotomy to help the congestion in her throat. Eleven doctors, including the Queen's physician, attend her.

Any thoughts of continuing with the film in London are cancelled. $600,000 worth of sets, built at Pinewood, are pulled down and the picture rescheduled for Rome in September with a new script and new co-stars for Liz Taylor. Producer Wanger estimates that 10 minutes of usable film have cost Fox some 10 million dollars.

The picture starts at last on September 25. Richard Burton is the new Antony, Rex Harrison the new Caesar. By the year's end three months of shooting are in the can although the movie is still not halfway through its schedule. The total budget for the film is now around 15 million dollars but Wanger is talking enthusiastically about a gross of 100 million!

1962 The worst year in the studio's history. So bad is the position that the company is in danger of going under. After a bitter boardroom battle Zanuck returns to the studio. On July 25 he replaces Skouras as president and is faced with the enormous task of hauling the company back onto its feet. The losses for the year are running at over 40 million. *Cleopatra* is the main cause, but the cancellation of Marilyn

Monroe's *Something's Got To Give* is another important factor. The movie is a two-million dollar write-off.

Just two months after the scrapping of *Something's Got To Give* Marilyn is found dead by her housekeeper, nude on her bed, one hand clutching a sheet to her throat, the other touching a telephone. An empty bottle of sedatives is found by her side. The date is August 5. Marilyn is thirty-six.

She has been in pictures fourteen years and made twenty-nine films, eleven of them as a star and twenty at Fox. Her greatest financial hits: *Some Like It Hot* (UA), *How To Marry A Millionaire, The Seven Year Itch, Gentlemen Prefer Blondes, There's No Business Like Show Business* and *Bus Stop* (all Fox).

'Ironically, producer Jerry Walk, who after *Let's Make Love* vowed he would never work with Marilyn again, dies just a month before.

Zanuck, building up again from the ruins, closes Fox for nine months and puts his son Richard in charge of the production side of the studio. The lot has been reduced from its massive two hundred and eighty two acres to a new seventy-six acre facility (with twenty-one sound stages) after a land sale to the Aluminium Company Of America and Webb & Knapp Inc back in 1958.

The films released are those made before Zanuck's 'second arrival'. His own *The Longest Day* which, with a gross of nearly 18 million dollars, goes some way to recover-in some of the company's losses; the James Stewart comedy *Mr. Hobbs Takes A Vacation*; two inept remakes, *State Fair* and *The Cabinet Of Dr. Caligari*; and a version of Scott Fitzgerald's *Tender Is The Night.*

Meanwhile, Zanuck has to concern himself with the biggest albatros any studio has ever had around its neck, *Cleopatra*. By the time he takes control the film is nine parts complete but, again, has not been without its problems and sensations. Joe Mankiewicz who has practically driven himself into the ground writing by night and directing by day is one of several who suffer from illness and the Taylor-Burton romance makes headlines all over the world.

1963 *Cleopatra* is finished at last. Mankiewicz, after a bitter row with Zanuck as to who has final control over the finished film, is sacked then reinstated and shoots the final battle scenes in Madrid early in the year. The final cost is approximately 37 million dollars. Zanuck states that the film will break even at 62 million. The eventual domestic gross in the U.S. and Canada? A mere 26 million.

When the epic eventually opens in New York on June 19 the critics are lukewarm. Some are unkind, some brutal. There are few raves. The making of the film proves to have been more exciting than the film itself. Out of four hours, Mankiewicz contributes some fine dialogue, especially for Harrison's Caesar, and fashions two exciting moments of grandeur — Cleopatra's triumphant entry into Rome and her journey by Royal Barge to Tarsus. But it is not the picture Walter Wanger had hoped for.

Says Mankiewicz, "The picture was conceived in a state of emergency, shot in confusion and wound up in blind panic. It was the toughest three pictures I ever made."

The Studio reopens on April 23. The first picture to go before the cameras is a James Stewart comedy *Take Her, She's Mine*.

Joanne Woodward stars in *The Stripper*; Horst Buchholz is Ghandi's assassin in *Nine Hours To Rama*; and James Garner and Doris Day add a bit of froth in *Move Over, Darling*, the new title for the ill-fated Monroe picture *Something's Got To Give*.

But really it's a year of picking up the pieces.

1964 Everything is still very tentative.

Fox's biggest hit is the ironically titled *What A Way To Go!* Otherwise things are distinctly mediocre. Airline director Glenn Ford investigates a plane disaster in *Fate Is The Hunter*; Debbie Reynolds is a female reincarnation of a man in Vincente Minnelli's comedy *Goodbye Charlie*; Richard Boone, Stuart Whitman and Tony Franciosa star in the tough western *Rio Conchos*; and Ann-Margret, Carol Lynley and Pamela Tiffin are *The Pleasure Seekers*, a remake of *Three Coins In The Fountain*, but set this time in Madrid.

Critically, the studio regains some dignity by winning Oscars for *Zorba The Greek* (Lila Kedrova is best supporting actress for her fading whore) and plaudits for *Hush. . .Hush, Sweet Charlotte*, Robert Aldrich's follow up to *Whatever Happened To Baby Jane?* with Bette Davis as a demented recluse living in a decaying Louisiana mansion.

Joan Crawford is again scheduled to play opposite Davis but illness prevents her. Rumour has it that she cries for days and days when she doesn't get the part, possibly because one scene demands that Davis be slapped quite heavily round the cheekbones. Replacement Olivia de Havilland manages it quite efficiently, however, in a scene that is reported to have gone to several 'takes'.

1965 The miracle happens. Julie Andrews, a few nuns, beautiful Austrian scenery and a Rodgers and Hammerstein score turn *The Sound Of Music* into the biggest money-maker of all time. The film topples the long reigning champion *Gone With The Wind* which has occupied top spot for more than a quarter of a century.

'The Hills Are Alive With The Sound Of Music' warbles Julie in the film. In real life it's the Beverly Hills around the Fox studio that are alive, not with music, but with tinkling coin as the studio emerges from the doldrums. *The Sound Of Music* wins the best picture Oscar, the studio's first in fifteen years, and nabs four others besides.

It's a pickup year all round. Charlton Heston is Michelangelo and Rex Harrison Pope Julius II in *The Agony And The Ecstasy*; director Robert Aldrich, in *The Flight Of The Pheonix*, strands James Stewart and assorted passengers in the desert with a wrecked plane and says, "Now get out of that!"; Alexander Mackendrick films a delightful version of Richard Hughes' *A High Wind In Jamaica* with Anthony Quinn as the pirate Chavez; Frank Sinatra and Trevor Howard go on a thrilling train ride across Italy in *Von Ryan's Express*; and James Fox, Stuart Whitman, Gert Frobe, Terry-Thomas and Tony Hancock are just some of *Those Magnificent Men In Their Flying Machines*, the story of an early 20th century air race from London to Paris.

Saddest news of the year is the death of former Fox star Linda Darnell who on April 12 is tragically burned to death in a friend's house in Chicago.

Between 1939 and 1952 she made some twenty-eight films for Fox, an average of two pictures a year. Dark haired and often cast as the hard-bitten girl on the make, she made her last film for the studio, *Night Without Sleep* in 1952. Aged forty-three, she left just 10,000 dollars.

1966 Clifton Webb, another Fox stalwart of the 40s and 50s dies of a heart attack at his home in Beverly Hills. He was seventy-four. His caustic wit, sophistication and acid delivery of even the most ordinary lines made him unique in the post-war scene. He made over twenty films for Fox between 1944 and 1962 appearing as Waldo Lydecker in

Laura, three times as Mr. Belvedere and as John Philip Sousa in *Stars And Stripes Forever*.

John Huston (Noah), Richard Harris (Cain), George C. Scott (Abraham) and Stephen Boyd (Nimrod) all contribute to *The Bible*; Steve McQueen is up the Yangtze in a 20s gunboat in *The Sand Pebbles*; Monica Vitti is *Modesty Blaise*; Adam West is *Batman* (with Burt Ward as Robin); and James Coburn *Our Man Flint*, the American equivalent of 007.

Ruthless German fighter pilot George Peppard does everything in his power to win Germany's highest flying award *The Blue Max* (awarded when twenty enemy planes have been shot down) but finishes up very dead when his plane breaks apart in mid-air.

Bing Crosby makes his last movie appearance (as the drunken Doc Boone) in a remake of *Stagecoach*; Audrey Hepburn and Peter O'Toole rob a museum — with a magnet and a boomerang — in *How To Steal A Million*; and Raquel Welch's measurements (37-23-36) are disappointingly reduced to bacteria size in the science-fiction fantasy *Fantastic Voyage*.

1967 Jayne Mansfield (thirty-five), the star who wanted so much to be a success, meets a horrific death — decapitated in a motor accident — on June 29. Little more than a carbon copy of Marilyn Monroe, but king sized (40-21-35), she never really made it to the top although Cary Grant who starred with her in *Kiss Them For Me* said, "She had the potential to become a new Mae West."

Four years before her death, when self-realisation had at last set in, she pitifully enquired, "Once you were a starlet. Then you're a star. Can you be a starlet again?"

Raquel Welch, back to her normal size, shakes it all about quite literally in front of a gulping Dudley Moore in *Bedazzled*; Frank Sinatra is the modern private-eye *Tony Rome*. No dingy Philip Marlowe office for him, instead a Miami houseboat; Jason Robards is Al Capone in *The St. Valentine's Day Massacre*; and James Coburn is back *In Like Flint*.

The critical hits: *Hombre* with Paul Newman in one of his most accomplished roles as a white man raised by Apaches in the 1880's; and *Two For The Road* with Albert Finney and Audrey Hepburn trying to come to terms with their disintegrating marriage as they drive by car across France.

The commercial smash: Mark Robson's version of

Jacqueline Susann's *Valley Of The Dolls*. The take? 20 million dollars.

The commercial flop: the much vaunted family movie *Doctor Dolittle* with Rex Harrison, Samantha Eggar, Anthony Newley and Richard Attenborough all sinking without trace in Hugh Lofting's Puddleby-On-The-Marsh.

1968 Fox discover that Julie Andrews is not a box-office certainty after all. Her *Star!*, the musical biography of Gertrude Lawrence, grosses no more than four million which leaves Fox very much in the red as the film cost 18 million to produce.

It's disasterville, which is a pity because it's a good movie with Julie Andrews giving perhaps her finest performance. The public, however, say, ''No Thank You.''

They do say ''Yes'', though, to the tougher side of things. Frank Sinatra in *The Detecive* and *Lady In Cement*, and Tony Curtis as mass murderer Albert DeSalvo in *The Boston Strangler* go over big. So too does a new kind of animal movie, *Planet Of The Apes*, the story of three astronauts who crashland on a mysterious planet only to find they have broken through the time barrier and landed back on Earth where apes are now dominant.

1969 Paul Newman and Robert Redford prove to be the most popular cowboys in movie history as *Butch Cassidy And The Sundance Kid*. The film chalks up a massive 46 million dollars and snags four awards at Oscar time including one for the year's best song 'Raindrops Keep Falling On My Head'.

The studio's British-made *The Prime Of Miss Jean Brodie* also figures among the awards, Maggie Smith winning best actress for her eccentric fascist schoolmarm.

Elsewhere it's torrid love between Raquel Welch and Jim Brown in *100 Rifles*; gentle love between Dustin Hoffman and Mia Farrow in *John And Mary*; man to man stuff between John Wayne and Rock Hudson in *The Undefeated*; and queen to queen stuff between homosexuals Richard Burton and Rex Harrison in *Staircase*.

Another couple, Omar Sharif and Jack Palance, are miscast as Che Guevara and Fidel Castro in Richard Fleischer's *Che!* So too is Barbra Streisand, too young for Dolly Levi, in the studio's biggest commercial misfire, *Hello, Dolly!*

Sonja Henie, Fox's ice-skating star of the early 40s, dies on an ambulance plane between Paris and Oslo on October 12. She dies from leukaemia, aged fifty-seven.

1970 Worried by the huge losses sustained by *Doctor Dolittle, Star!* and *Hello, Dolly!* the studio probe tentatively into the soft porn market. They get their fingers burned. *Beyond The Valley Of The Dolls* and *Myra Breckenridge* are the first and only trailblazers.

Quote from Mae West who stars with Raquel Welch in the latter movie, ''Forget the six feet, let's talk about the six inches.''

John Huston joins the ranks to make another of his baffling thrillers, *The Kremlin Letter*. Fox realise they have a problem and advertise it thus, ''If you miss the first five minutes, you miss one suicide, two executions, one seduction, and the key to the plot.''

James Earl Jones is a thinly disguised Jack Johnson in the boxing drama *The Great White Hope*; Liz Taylor and Warren Beatty play *The Only Game In Town*; and Charlton Heston reappears briefly in the second of the Ape films, *Beneath The Planet Of The Apes*.

But war occupies the top brass at Fox. *M.A.S.H.*, Robert Altman's sleeper about a medical unit in Korea hauls in a huge 41 million dollars; *Patton* wins a handful of Oscars (including one for best picture and one declined by George C. Scott); even the expensive *Tora! Tora! Tora!* — an account of the events leading up to Pearl Harbour — rakes in a tidy 15 million.

Alfred Newman, leading Fox composer for twenty years and scorer of nearly ninety films for the studio, dies aged sixty-eight. Among his major scores: *The Grapes Of Wrath, The Song Of Bernadette, Captain From Castile, Love Is A Many Splendoured Thing, The Robe, The Diary Of Anne Frank*.

1971 *The French Connection* wins Fox another best picture Oscar and turns Gene Hackman, as a tough cop investigating a multi-million dollar dope smuggling ring, into a star. Hackman wins for best actor. For his reckless car chase beneath an elevated railway he should also have won for best driver.

The studio hold a massive auction of props and costumes used in their movies. The two wheel bicycle ridden by Paul Newman and Katharine Ross in *Butch Cassidy And The Sundance Kid* is bought by friends for Paul's wife,

Joanne Woodward. The cost $3,100, making it the most expensive bicycle in history.

Zanuck resigns in June after nine years as president of the studio.

1972 Hackman again features in the studio's biggest movie, *The Poseidon Adventure*, the first of the popular disaster films of the 70s. The Poseidon of the title is a huge ocean liner, overturned on New Year's Eve by a 90 ft tidal wave. Hackman leads a handful of survivors to the top (bottom) of the ship and freedom. Some make it, some don't. Among those trying to escape: Shelley Winters, Ernest Borgnine, Jack Albertson, Carol Lynley, Stella Stevens, Red Buttons.

Laurence Olivier and Michael Caine (both Oscar nominated) play a murder game in *Sleuth*; Robert Redford and George Segal steal and then lose a diamond in *The Hot Rock*; Cicely Tyson and Paul Winfield head a family of black sharecroppers in the Deep South in Martin Ritt's brilliant, deeply moving *Sounder*; Paul Newman directs his wife Joanne Woodward in *The Effect Of Gamma Rays On Man-In-The-Moon Marigolds*; and Richard Widmark is at his finest as an ageing rodeo rider in *When The Legends Die*.

1973 Cops and robbers (*The Seven Ups, The Laughing Policeman*); young love (*Paper Chase*); more monkey business (*Battle For The Planet Of The Apes*); fights on top of freight trains (Lee Marvin and Ernest Borgnine in *Emperor Of The North Pole*). The pictures mean little in a year in which the industry loses both Betty Grable and John Ford.

Betty Grable dies of lung cancer on July 2, aged fifty-six. Between 1940, when she became a star in *Down Argentine Way*, and 1955 she made twenty-seven movies, nearly two a year. Dan Dailey, John Payne and Victor Mature were her most regular leading men.

She once said, rather jadedly, "Pinning it down to the movies I guess I didn't particularly like any of them." On another brighter occasion she said, "I am what I wanted to be. Just give me the lines that lead into a song-and-dance routine. I'm the girl the truck drivers love."

Seventy-eight year old John Ford dies a few weeks later, also of cancer, at his home in Palm Springs. Generally regarded as being the greatest of all American film directors he belonged to no one particular studio — he worked for them all — but achieved much of his finest work on the Fox lot — *Young Mr. Lincoln, Drums Along The Mohawk, The Grapes Of Wrath, How Green Was My Valley, My Darling Clementine.*

Although poles apart from the world of Miss Grable he remained equally modest about his achievements. "I never thought about what I was doing in terms of art, or 'this is great', or 'world-shaking', or anything like that. To me, it was always a job of work — which I enjoyed immensely — and that's it."

1974 Fox share the cost of *The Towering Inferno* with another studio, Warners, and find that disaster is still box-office. $55 million is the take. Paul Newman, Steve McQueen, William Holden, Robert Vaughn, Richard Chamberlain and Faye Dunaway are among those trying to escape the flames licking upwards on a 138 storey tower block.

Art Carney as an elderly widower travelling across America with his cat, wins a surprise best actor Oscar in *Harry And Tonto*; Gene Wilder is Mel Brooks' *Young Frankenstein*; Michael York is D'Artagnan and Oliver Reed, Richard Chamberlain and Frank Finley *The Three Musketeers* in Richard Lester's semi-spoof version of the Dumas tale.

Veteran cinematographer Leon Shamroy, thirty years at the Fox studio and a master of colour photography, dies aged seventy-two. Among his most notable films: *The Black Swan, Wilson, Leave Her To Heaven, The Snows Of Kilimanjaro, The Robe, Love Is A Many Splendoured Thing, South Pacific, Cleopatra, Planet Of The Apes.*

1975 Boy wonder director Peter Bogdanovich makes a stab at an original screen musical with *At Long Last Love* with disastrous results. Burt Reynolds and Cybill Shepherd are among those who crucify the music of Cole Porter.

Stanley Donen, who should know better, makes a similar mess of the comedy *Lucky Lady*. Burt Reynolds (again), Gene Hackman and Liza Minnelli are the unlucky stars, Fox the unlucky studio.

All told, it's not one of the studio's most accomplished years. Gene Wilder fails with *The Adventure Of Sherlock Holmes' Smarter Brother*; Peter Fonda and Warren Oates have an unpleasant and fatal *Race With The Devil*; and Michael York and company turn up again less effectively in *The Four Musketeers*. Only Gene Hackman enhances his reputation with his recreation of Popeye Doyle in *French Connection II*.

Susan Hayward, popular Fox star of the 50s, dies of a seizure brought on by a brain tumour. She was fifty-five. Unknown to the public she had bravely fought the tumour for several years. Strangely, many of her films dealt with people who were fighters, among them *With A Song In My Heart* in which she played the crippled singer Jane Froman. Tyrone Power (*Rawhide*), Gregory Peck (*The Snows Of Kilimanjaro*), Gary Cooper (*Garden Of Evil*) and Clark Gable (*Soldier Of Fortune*) were among her leading men at Fox.

1976 Gregory Peck dabbles in the occult in *The Omen* and turns the movie into the surprise hit of the year. Lee Remick shares his nightmares over their Devil son Damien as 28 million dollars collect at the box-office.

Otherwise the main diet is comedy and the Old West. Mel Brooks, Marty Feldman and Dom DeLuise silently try to persuade a Hollywood film company to make a *Silent Movie*; ageing Charlton Heston goes after escaped convict James Coburn in the year's most brutal western *The Last Hard Men*; George Segal and Goldie Hawn team in lighter mood, but again out West in *The Duchess And The Dirtwater Fox*; Raquel Welch drives an ambulance in *Mother, Jugs and Speed*; Gene Wilder survives a hazardous train journey in *Silver Streak*.

1977 *Julia*, Fred Zinnemann's film of Lillian Hellman's deep and moving friendship with her childhood friend is the quality movie of the year. Jane Fonda and Vanessa Redgrave co-star, Jason Robards is Dashiell Hammett.

The Other Side Of Midnight is 166 minutes of sexy – and beautifully dressed – soap opera; and *The Turning Point* has Anne Bancroft and Shirley MacLaine at each other's throats, *All About Eve* style, in a bitchy story of the contemporary ballet world.

But it's the fantastic *Star Wars* that takes off into the stratosphere. Boasting no major stars but with plenty of vigour, imagination, music and brilliant special effects it leaves *Jaws* way behind as the all time top moneymaker and revives a *genre* that had seemed all but dead. George Lucas is the director, John Williams the composer.

Gussow, Mel: *Don't Say Yes Until I Finish Talking* (W. H. Allen, 1971)
Halliwell, Leslie: *The Filmgoer's Book Of Quotes* (Hart-Davis, MacGibbon, London, 1973)
Halliwell, Leslie: *Mountain Of Dreams* (Hart-Davis, MacGibbon, London, 1976)
Higham, Charles & Greenberg, Joel: *The Celluloid Muse* (Angus & Robertson, London, 1969)
Huff, Theodore: *Charlie Chaplin* (Henry Schuman, 1951)
Krafsur, Richard P. (executive editor): *The American Film Institute Catalogue, 1961-70* (R. R. Bowker, New York, 1976)
Lambert, Gavin: *The Making Of Gone With The Wind* (Atlantic-Little, Brown, 1973)
Larkin, Rochelle: *Hail Columbia* (Arlington House, New York, 1975)
Martin, Leonard: *The Disney Films* (Crown Publishers, New York, 1973)
Munden, Kenneth W. (executive editor): *The American Film Institute Catalogue, 1921-30* (R. R. Bowker, New York, 1971)
Milne, Tom: *Mamoulian* (Thames & Hudson, 1969)
Nolan, William F: *John Huston: King Rebel* (Sherbourne Press, Los Angeles, 1965)
Parish, James Robert: *The Fox Girls* (Castle Books, 1971)
Parish, James Robert: *The RKO Girls* (Ian Allan, London, 1974)
Parish, James Robert & Bowers, Ronald L: *The MGM Stock Company* (Arlington House, 1973)
Pratt, William: *Scarlett Fever* (MacMillan, New York, 1977)
Scherle, Victor and Levy, William Turner: *The Films Of Frank Capra* (Citadel Press, New York, 1977)
Schickel, Richard: *The Disney Version* (Avon Books, New York, 1968)
Schickel, Richard: *The Men Who Made The Movies* (The Educational Broadcasting Corporation, New York, 1975)
Siegel, Joel E: *Val Lewton, The Reality Of Terror* (Secker & Warburg, 1972) London
Thomas, Bob: *King Cohn* (Barrie & Rockliff, 1967)
Thomas, Bob: *The Walt Disney Biography* (Simon & Schuster, New York, 1977)
Wanger, Walter & Hyams, Joe: *My Life With Cleopatra* (Bantam Books, New York, 1963)
Weinberg, Herman G: *The Lubitsch Touch* (E. P. Dutton & Co., New York, 1968)
Windeler, Robert: *Mary Pickford* (W. H. Allen, 1973)
Windeler, Robert: *Shirley Temple* (W. H. Allen, 1976)

The magazines *Action, Sight & Sound, The Velvet Light Trap, Focus On Film, The Monthly Film Bulletin* of the British Film Institute, *Film Comment* and, especially, *Films In Review* have also proved invaluable.

Finally I would like to thank the following film personalities who, over the years and during lengthy interviews, have helped me in providing much of the atmosphere and background of *The Hollywood Studios*: — James Stewart, Henry Fonda, Gregory Peck, Charlton Heston, Kirk Douglas, Robert Mitchum, Joseph Cotten, Lee Remick, Ann Miller, Ingrid Bergman, Peter Ustinov, Fred Zinnemann, Edward Dmytryk, Lee J. Cobb, Vincente Minnelli, Mervyn LeRoy, Richard Fleischer, John Sturges, Robert Aldrich, Martin Ritt, Samuel Marx, Sam Peckinpah.

* * *

The stills rcproduced in this book first appeared in films distributed by the following companies, to whom thanks are due: Universal, Paramount, United Artists, Warners, Walt Disney, Columbia, MGM, RKO and Twentieth Century-Fox.

Index

Note: All film titles and magazines are italicized. Songs are indicated in single quotes, books, plays and stage musicals in double quotes.

Abbreviations: Producer (prod); Director (dir); Scriptwriter, Novelist or Playwright (writ); Cameraman (cam); Composer (comp); Editor (ed); Costume Designer (ward); Art Director (art dir); Special Effects (spec. eff); Animator (anim); Publicist (pub); Cartoonist (cart).